Also by David Bryant

In the Gap:
What It Means to Be a World Christian

With Concerts of Prayer:
Christians Join for Spiritual Awakening and World Evangelization

The Hope at Hand:
National and World Revival for the 21st Century

Stand in the Gap:
How to Prepare for the Coming World Revival

Messengers of Hope:
Agents of Revival for the 21st Century

Christ Is ALL!
A Joyful Manifesto on the Supremacy of Christ

Christ Is ALL! [revised]
Join in the Joyful Awakening to the Supremacy of God's Son

Christ Is NOW!
7 Groundbreaking Keys to Help You Explore and Experience
the Spectacular Supremacy of God's Son Today

Visit
www.DavidBryantBooks.com

MEET HIM AGAIN
FOR THE FIRST TIME

Christ Is
NOW!

7 Groundbreaking Keys
to Help You Explore and Experience
the Spectacular Supremacy of God's Son Today

NEW
PROVIDENCE
PUBLISHERS

DAVID BRYANT

Published by
New Providence Publishers Inc.
P O Box 770
New Providence, NJ 07974-0770

Design and Layout
Sahlman Art Studio Inc.
20515 Rio Oro Drive
Cornelius, NC 28031

Unless otherwise indicated Scripture taken from:
The New International Reader's Version, Copyright 1996, International Bible Society/Biblica.
Used by permission of The International Bible Society/Biblica.

Library of Congress Catalog Number: 2017914244
International Standard Book Number (ISBN) 978-0-9755038-3-6
Printed in the United States of America

Preface

Meet Him Again for the First Time

The Whole Church (Including You) Wholly Alive
to the Whole Vision of the Whole Christ

Does either of these experiences feel familiar to you?

At a tenth-year class reunion, you get into conversation with an old girlfriend who used to join you at sports and parties. Now as the two of you talk a decade later, you realize she is far more interesting, more personable, more talented, more inspiring than she ever appeared to be back then. In a sense, you meet her again for the first time.

As an avid NBA fan, you end up in the locker room with some of your hometown team heroes after a game, asking them for autographs. As they sign your program, allowing you to interact with them up close and personal, it's apparent they are far warmer, more down-to-earth, and more open-hearted than you had assumed based on how fiercely they battle out on the court. You see them in a new light. In other words, you meet them again for the first time.

Now imagine this: What if similarly striking encounters happened to you practically *every day*? In addition, what if these amazing discoveries were always about *the very same person*?

Most importantly, what if that person happened to be the single most consequential individual in all creation, throughout all history and for all eternity? I'm talking about Jesus, the Son of God.

And what if you started seeing that many previous reports about him were flawed, at best, diminishing him by misguided opinions and misleading claims? What if you found him to be so much greater than his popular reputation—much more alive and active, much more astonishing but also more appealing, much more awesome but also more approachable?

What if you kept on meeting him over and over, day after day, in such unexpectedly fresh and surprising ways that it were almost *as if* with each new encounter you were meeting your Lord and Savior for the first time?

That's How This Book Took Shape

For over forty years I've been caught up in an extraordinary journey with Jesus precisely like this. To be sure, at times it has run hot and cold, fearful then bold, with ups and downs, in the light plus through the night.

Yet for me, this Spirit-guided course has remained a steady trek in the same direction—toward an ever more astonishing wealth of disclosures about who our Lord is today in the fullness of his spectacular supremacy.

And that brings me to *you*.

Finally, after decades of writing parallel books that actually foreshadow this volume, I offer you my *magnum opus* (chief work). *Christ Is NOW!* shares with you my distillation of exciting insights about our Redeemer King — uncovered while I was "meeting him again for the first time" — over and over and over.

In these pages I hand you keys that will unlock doors into the wide-open spaces of a renewed vision of and involvement with God's Son in all of his greatness and goodness and glory. You'll find these insights to be simple but also comprehensive, practical but also radical, breathtaking but also life-giving. Rooted in God's Word, they will *reintroduce* you to the Lord Jesus Christ to help you see him for *all* he is right now.

In its approach lies a way for you to move into deeper intimacy with your Savior, not just in terms of who he was or who he will be, *but in terms of who he is today*. I think you'll find this approach truly is groundbreaking. Long before you finish reading *Christ Is Now!* you will begin undergoing a genuine "Christ Awakening" — which is my great hope not only for you but for the entire Body of Christ.

The Hope at Hand: The Reformation That *Must* Come

Unfolding in answer to decades of concerted prayer globally, a nationwide and worldwide Christ Awakening movement, many believe, is at hand.

This is urgently needed because far too many of this generation of Christians are slumbering concerning the full extent of the supremacy of Christ now. J. I. Packer says most believers only have pieces of him. John Stott calls us pigmy Christians because we worship a pigmy Christ. The late Chuck Colson suggested evangelicals have made him a "product" to meet our needs as consumers. Kendra Creasy Dean's research reports that many Christian youth have lost true passion for Jesus. William Willimon concludes that the reigning Christ is essentially "missing" for us in the thick of all we try to do for him.

We need a grander exaltation of God's Son that is able to breathe new passion into God's people to advance his kingdom purposes at this moment of history; yet we remain asleep. Here's how American theologian Kevin

Vanhoozer puts it (emphasis added): "Present-day Christians need to awaken to the glory of the transfigured, risen Christ in our midst, and we need to *stay awake* so that we, like the disciples, see 'no one but Jesus only' (Matt. 17:8)."

Said another way, we need a "Christological reformation"—one in which God's people wake up to meet God's Son all over again, as if it were for the first time, thus *re-forming* their whole vision of all he is.

On November 1, 1517, citizens of Wittenberg, Germany, found nailed to their church doors an extensive, militant document that spread rapidly throughout Europe due to a recently invented "social media" called the printing press. The Protestant Reformation, which had been brewing for decades, was unleashed!

On the exact date 500 years later, something similar happened: The release of another lengthy treatise was announced on — "nailed" to — current forms of social media: websites, Facebook, Instagram, Twitter. It presented a similarly radical call for a reformation — a magnification — of the Church's vision of who Christ is today.

Like Luther's famous "95 Theses," this contemporary declaration seeks to be revolutionary. It gathers together years of teaching presented around the world regarding the breadth and depth of Christ's spectacular supremacy. A timely volume, it captures the heartbeat of a grassroots insurgency already underway — soon to flourish as a "Christ Awakening movement" in which the whole Church becomes wholly alive to the whole Christ.

You are holding that book. Handle with prayer.

You Absolutely Must Read This First!

How You Can Get the Most Out of a Truly Unconventional Book

 Over Six Hundred Pages Long! *Why?*

History tells us, as I reported in my book *Christ Is ALL!*, that while trying to complete his own work on the supremacy of Christ, the 13th-century Christian leader Thomas Aquinas experienced a literal vision of Jesus, which caused him to exclaim:

> I've just seen the Lord Christ!
> Now I know that all I have written is straw.

The same could be said for everything I've placed inside these two covers. By comparison to who our Lord Jesus is at this very moment, the whole book is nothing but straw — just 600 pages of straw!

So why did I feel compelled to produce it?

Without a doubt, as Paul observes in Ephesians 3, there's far more of the "height, width, length and depth" of the magisterial love of Christ that all of us need to explore and experience because there's so much more of his fullness for all of us to receive!

Yet at the same time, we're pursuing a vision of God's Son, as Ephesians 3 reminds us, that ultimately "surpasses knowledge" — meaning there will never be sufficient words (or pages) to mine the magnitudes of our Master. In the final words of his gospel, the Apostle John attests to this:

> Jesus also did many other things. What if every one of them were written down? *I suppose that even the whole world would not have room for the books that would be written* (John 21, emphasis added).

In other words, never mind six hundred pages. Six *trillion* would never be sufficient!

Still, we must not stop trying to describe him. Doing so honors him. So, I've dared to record here my perspectives on the wonders of Christ and his supremacy, gleaned over decades, to be shared with the Body of Christ.

I confess what you hold here merely skims the surface of who Christ is. Still, despite what little I comprehend even now of the glory of God's Son, I find myself compelled to pass along what I *have* uncovered — which, surprisingly, necessitated these 600 pages.

I do so without apology.

Consider *Christ Is NOW!* a treasure chest jammed with "jewels" of truths about Jesus, each one of which deserves — *he deserves* — our careful reflection. These pages offer readers a matchless opportunity to awaken to Christ in whole new ways — to discover afresh *so much more of who he is today*.

So, take your time. Don't try to unpack it all at once. Enjoy the *expedition* ahead. In many ways it is also your *destination*. That's because for all eternity we'll never come to the end of the adventure of growing to know Christ better.

I suggest you begin the process by reviewing the secrets and suggestions outlined below. Plan on making regular use of them.

Simply plunge into these 600 pages of a truly unconventional book and see what happens to you. I believe you'll find it to be a most fascinating way to enter more fully into the kind of dynamic, life-changing relationship with the Lord Jesus Christ all of us were meant to have — that born-again hearts *long* to have.

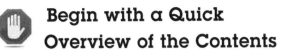

Begin with a Quick Overview of the Contents

To get the most out of this book, start by reading through the annotated "Contents" — just as you would study a map or your GPS mobile app before setting off on a hopeful mission. As you do, you'll be introduced to these major "stopovers" on the road ahead:

Meditations on His Majesty. Here you're given a series of nine brief, wide-ranging reflections on the splendor of Christ. Don't bypass them. They set the stage for the major chapters at the center of the book. Try reading them devotionally, not more than two or three meditations a day perhaps, to prepare yourself *spiritually* to feast on the main meal of the book. Read them with your mind *and* your heart. Let them soak into your spirit and take you to the feet of Jesus before you set out to "meet him again for the first time."

Introducing the Groundbreaking Keys. In this chapter, seven keys — the seven prepositions that unlock a grander vision of Christ's supremacy — are briefly defined. In addition, you'll learn the story behind how, over a period of decades, *Christ Is NOW!* came together. And you'll find out how a comprehensive biblical Christology found itself expressed in these seven simple prepositions. Most of all, this chapter will prepare you for all that awaits you in the ensuing seven.

Seven Chapters on the Seven Keys. The seven major chapters come next — the heart and soul of the book — designed to help you explore and experience the greatness and goodness and glory of God's Son. Each one provides a panoramic view of Christ most followers have never encountered before. To understand some of the creative ways each chapter equips you to engage directly with Christ himself, be sure to read below about the "Snapshots and Starter Thoughts," "Selahs," and "Tributes."

Fervency for His Supremacy. *Christ Is NOW!* is about being changed — changed in how we perceive Jesus and changed in how we pursue Jesus. Therefore, this concluding section provides practical ways to think and act, designed to make what you encounter in the book have a lasting impact on you. First, you're given two essays focused on applications and lifestyles. Then you're introduced to a trove of free online resources to keep you exploring and experiencing the spectacular supremacy of God's Son for years to come.

Enjoy Working Your Way Through the *Snapshots and Starter Thoughts*

Imagine this: Using your smartphone, you share with some friends some pictures from a recent family vacation. As you scroll through your photos, you pause at several to tell the story behind what they see. Of course, each image captures only one moment, but still it triggers a delightful conversation that expands on the person or event portrayed, making the snapshot come alive for everyone around you.

That's the idea behind the sections called "Snapshots and Starter Thoughts." Throughout the seven central chapters that unpack the spectacular supremacy of Christ, you'll come across this special subtitle, followed by a series of bullet points that serve the same purpose as your photos — to present specific dimensions of who Jesus is for further reflection and discussion.

Though the pattern varies from chapter to chapter, wherever this subtitle appears each bullet point that follows provides you with one distinctive insight into God's Son — a "snapshot" of him designed to spark "starter thoughts" about him.

As the "snapshot" insights multiply, they will begin to create for you a whole "photo album" about Jesus, a parade of pictures displaying some of the glory of his sovereignty.

Just like you can enlarge on the details behind any photo to help explain to someone what it's all about, behind each particular truth captured in these "snapshots" of Christ there is much more to uncover — more that could be said and should be said than what's contained in one paragraph.

That is why the title of each of these subsections includes the additional phrase "Starter Thoughts." This suggests that every bullet point is not only designed to give you a distinct nugget of truth about Christ but also to ignite in you fresh ideas about the wonders of Jesus, moving you to ponder wider implications of what is summed up in a few sentences.

In other words, each insight (Snapshot) is meant to launch you or your "Christ Group" (study group) into new ways of thinking and talking (Starter Thoughts) about Christ and his supremacy. Each bullet point is designed to set in motion a joyful exploration and experience of the marvelous riches found in Christ.

Please notice that each bullet point under "Snapshots and Starter Thoughts" opens with a succinct statement in **bold lettering,** usually followed by three or four sentences that amplify that initial statement.

One suggestion: First, read through *all* of the bold statements under a section, one point after another. Doing this gives you an immediate *overview* of the main teachings on that particular facet of Christ's supreme majesty. Then, go back through the section a second time to read and reflect, or as a group to discuss, the entire bullet point. Let that Snapshot serve to inspire Starter Thoughts that lead to meaningful reflection, application, and even prayer.

One other suggestion: Whether alone or with a group you also may find it more meaningful to read each bullet point *out loud*. Try this with the *bold* statements first. Since most of these insights present a "concentrated truth" about Jesus, they often deliver a more lasting impression when they are not only read but also *heard*.

 # Discover the Power of the Prompts

Finally, whenever you or those in your Christ Group decide to focus more thoroughly on a particular bullet point, employ these five prompts to stimulate fruitful interaction with the material. The Holy Spirit will use them to surprise you time after time with wonderful truths about who Jesus is now.

(1) **Explore**: What is the main insight this "snapshot" emphasizes regarding who Christ is today in his spectacular supremacy? How would you describe that insight in your own words?

(2) **Expand**: What are one or two other Scripture verses that would help expand our understanding of this important truth?

(3) **Experience**: Can you name one or two ways this truth about Jesus should directly impact our relationship to him? Or, our ministry for him? Can you give any personal examples of how this would work in your life?

(4) **Express**: In what ways could you pass along this important truth about Jesus to another believer so as to help enrich their vision of him and their passion for him?

(5) **Exalt**: Conclude with a prayer expressing to the Father your praise for what the theme of this insight means to you. Declare your desire to know his Son better and to glorify him more based on what you've learned or what your group has discussed. Finally, pray that many of the believers around you would awaken to Christ in terms of how his spectacular supremacy is revealed through this Snapshot and Starter Thought.

 ## Spend Some Time With the *Selahs!*

"Selah" is a Hebrew word incorporated into a number of the Psalms. Most Bible students translate it to mean: "You've reached a spot in this hymn where you should pause, reflect, worship, and pray before moving on."

For those same reasons, you'll find Selahs showing up at the end of most major sections all through the seven central chapters.

The Selahs encourage you to take a moment to catch your breath after exploring a selection of perspectives on Christ that, most likely, will be grander, more profound, and more challenging than you've encountered before.

But even if some bullet points are simply reminders of what you already know about Jesus, it's important to pause a minute or two to reflect on the insights you've just encountered — to pray over them, to praise the Lord for those particular truths of who he is, or to sit quietly and let them feed you.

Each Selah provides a valuable opportunity to enter into the "experience" dimension of the study by giving you time to engage directly with the Person you are exploring, as you delight in him and in what his supremacy means to you. Don't rush past these breaks. They will prove to be time well spent, helping you become more intimately connected with Jesus.

Additionally, if you're studying the book with a Christ Group, the Selahs offer a logical juncture to pause for further discussion on that section or to engage in group prayer and worship based on what you've uncovered together. The group might also choose to carve out a period of silence for personal reflection before moving to the next section.

 ## Let the *Tributes* Ring Out With Joy!

Each of the seven central chapters, built around the seven prepositions (keys), concludes with a segment titled "A Tribute."

Essentially each Tribute forms a response of praise to the Father about the glory of the Son related to the theme of the chapter it closes. It provides the reader a liturgy of worship, confession, adoration, as well as proclamation — all mingled together.

The Tributes allow you to continue exploring and experiencing more of Christ through a dynamic approach you may have never expressed like this. As the subheading of each one notes, it paraphrases and personalizes a selection of Scriptures that interrelates with each chapter's specific focus on the spectacular supremacy of God's Son.

Note that each Tribute is built on phrases and verses from God's Word with these two objectives:

To Explore. To summarize the major insights gleaned from its chapter, each one weaves a bundle of biblical texts into a liturgy that highlights who Christ is now, in terms of who he is TO us, or FOR us, or BEFORE us, etc. It provides a rich distillation of what you uncovered in the previous pages.

To Experience. But each Tribute also doubles as a prayerful celebration. It allows you to personally declare to the Father what the insights of that chapter have meant to you, how they have increased your vision of and passion for his Son. The words of praise help you express your growing heart of passion for Christ based on your discoveries.

The prophet Hosea said, "Take words with you and return to the Lord" (Hosea 14, NIV). In the same vein, you are encouraged to invest this time at the end of each chapter to take with you the words of the Tribute and pray them — not silently but *out loud*.

If you are by yourself, you might want to recite the Tribute on your knees. In a group setting you might read it responsively — sentence by sentence or paragraph by paragraph — as an act of corporate worship.

 ## Why Not Form a *Christ Group?*

One of the most effective missionary outreaches in the 21st century is planting hundreds of thousands of brand new "Christ Groups," as they call them, across Asia and the Middle East.

But *all* local congregations on planet Earth should be known as CHRIST GROUPS! Our ultimate identity should be defined as a group of people gathered together under the lordship of Christ, for the glory of Christ, to discover more about Christ, and to pursue growth in Christ. We already know for sure we're gathered *around* Christ — even as he promised, he himself is present with even two or three who are meeting in his name (Matthew 18).

Since that's true of every church, it's clearly true of any small group who studies and discusses their way through *Christ Is NOW!*

So if you form such a group to study this book together, you might consider calling yourselves a Christ Group. Then, collectively practice the guidelines outlined under "Snapshot and Starter Thoughts" and "Discover the Power of the Prompts." Also, enjoy implementing the Tributes and Selahs at a group level.

You Are About to Learn a New Language!

Have you ever had to learn a foreign language? As they say, it is difficult to navigate Paris if you don't know French.

In many ways, *Christ Is NOW!* encourages readers to acquire a new language when talking about Jesus. The in-depth, multidimensional portrait of God's Son introduced here, especially as the seven keys unleash a much larger vision of Christ, requires a brand new, refreshingly practical way of thinking and talking about who Jesus is. It helps you develop a much more colorful *vocabulary* for sharing him with others.

Though they may appear unfamiliar or intriguing, or even thrilling, the reconstituted words, terms, phrases, and concepts you're about to meet can help believers chat with one another about the vastness of their ruling Redeemer more confidently, more purposefully, more enthusiastically, more freely, and — best of all — more *frequently*.

What's more, whole congregations can become spiritually revitalized as we reshape how Christians talk together about our matchless King, enthroned and active today. What would happen if, as a way of life, Christians started *hearing* a lot more about Jesus because we were *talking* a lot more about Jesus, the *real* Jesus, with each other?

The secret vitality for every congregation in the world has already been discovered:

> Let the message about Christ, *in all its richness, fill your lives.* Teach and counsel each other with all the wisdom he gives" (Colossians 3, NLT, emphasis added).

To say it differently: Hearing more about Christ requires talking more about Christ. *But talking more about Christ requires expanding our vocabulary about Christ* — so that all Christians will not only know *what* to say about their Savior but also know *how* to say it with clarity and conviction and joy.

It's like learning enough French so you can navigate Paris!

Consider This Modest Thesaurus to Get You Started

Here are a few of the most valuable terms you'll encounter throughout the book. Some may be new to you; familiar ones may be given an unexpected slant; all are deeply relevant to seeing Jesus for who he is today.

These are not dictionary-style definitions for these terms but rather a series of word associations that give color and texture to each. As you work through the book, each of these terms will take on deeper meaning for you, even as additional terms will come into focus!

> **Christ (anointed one)** = Messiah, exalted, authority, royal Son, fulfiller, consummator
>
> **All (Christ is)** = entirety, in totality, comprehensive, undiminished, all inclusive
>
> **Now (Christ is)** = immediate, direct, present, engaged, invasive, decisive, fully alive, today
>
> **Glory (of Christ)** = self-revelation, divine distinctions, grandeur, majesty, victories, renown
>
> **Centrality (of Christ)** = essential, pivotal, necessary, focal point, intermediary
>
> **Supremacy (of Christ)** = primacy, preeminence, sovereignty, dominance, superior, over all
>
> **Spectacular (supremacy)** = breathtaking, stunning, magnificent, unparalleled, unfading
>
> **Ascension (of Christ)** = exaltation, coronation, enthronement, authorization, active reign
>
> **Consummation (in Christ)** = culmination, fulfillment, recapitulation, triumph, apex, climax
>
> **Approximations (of Consummation)** = Spirit-infused, foretastes, miracles, victories, hope
>
> **Christology (study of Christ)** = envision, investigate, contemplate, define, teach, worship
>
> **Crisis (of Christology)** = crossroads, emergency, shortfall, blinding, crippling, defrauding

Awakening (to Christ) = aroused, aware, alert, revived, rising, energized, re-engaged

Reintroduce (to Christ) = recall, re-present, reawaken, reconvert, reconnect, re-engage

Keys = clues, insights, guides, blueprints, approaches, revelations, practical tools

Groundbreaking (keys) = foundational, innovative, trailblazing, revolutionary, exciting

Explore (Christ) = search out, delve into, seek more of, probe, pursue, discover, adventure

Experience (Christ) = encounter, embrace, enjoy, incorporate, apply, intimacy

Fervency (for Christ) = passion, enthusiasm, zeal, consumed with, devoted to, invested in

Messenger (of Hope) = harbinger, pacesetter, herald, change agent, mobilizer, servant

 ## Why the Use of So Many Graphics?

The images embedded throughout the book are not placed there only as a means for embellishing the page to make it more interesting. They do that, but they also serve these two additional purposes:

(1) **To Enrich.** They help you capture the central "feel" for a particular section. They give to the reader a visual experience of the truths explored, often pointing them toward an experience with Christ.

(2) **To Identify.** They provide you "hooks" on which to hang your discoveries. At some later date when you thumb back through the book, the graphics themselves can help you recall some of the most important ways you were able to "meet Jesus again for the first time."

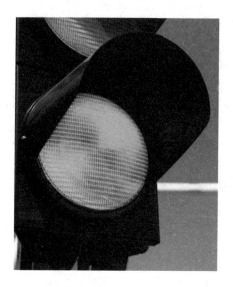

Green Light!
Now You Can Proceed!

Next, your adventure with Christ continues with "Meditations on His Majesty." But before we head off, let me pray over us a prayer based on Jesus' promise in John 16:

> Father, our Lord assured us that after he ascended to the throne, the Spirit of truth would come upon his followers to guide us into wonderful truths about who Jesus is right now. So, as we travel this journey ahead may the Spirit unleash that within each one of us. Reveal more of Jesus to us so as to bring even greater glory to Jesus in us. Your Son is supreme because everything that belongs to you has been given over to him. Therefore, as we navigate these pages, empower us to explore and experience in whole new ways what his spectacular supremacy today is all about. Because he is worthy! Because he is our life! Because he is now! Amen!

Meet Him Again for the First Time
The Whole Church (Including You) Wholly Alive
to the Whole Vision of the Whole Christ

You Absolutely Must Read This First!
How You Can Get the Most
Out of a Truly Unconventional Book

....

Contents
Meditations on His Majesty

Explore and Experience
Who Christ Is FOR Us Today:

3
....

Explore and Experience
Who Christ Is OVER Us Today:

4

....

Explore and Experience

Who Christ Is BEFORE Us Today:

5
....

Explore and Experience
Who Christ Is WITHIN Us Today:

6

....

Explore and Experience

Who Christ Is THROUGH Us Today:

....

A Quick Review

Looking Back at the First Six Keys and Reflecting on Five Personal Questions

7
....

Explore and Experience
Who Christ Is UPON Us Today:

....

Fervency for His Supremacy
Consumed With Christ:
No Holding Back. No Turning Back.

The Seven Joyful Habits of Christians
Who Are Hugely Passionate for Jesus

Appendix I
A Stream of Scripture About His Gory Glory
Page 595

....

Free Online Resources
to Empower Christ Awakenings Everywhere

Visit us at:

www.ChristNow.com
Page 602

www.TheChristInstitutes.com
Page 602

www.DavidBryantBooks.com
Page 603

www.ProclaimHope.org
Page 603

Also follow us at:

facebook.com/christnowonline
twitter.com/christnowonline
instagram.com/christnowonline
Page 604

Acknowledgments
Page 605

Meet David Bryant
Page 607

Meditations
on His Majesty

Meditations on His Majesty
Welcome to Niagara Falls

Niagara Falls. Three cataracts convulsing into one terrifying, titanic torrent. A massive deluge of 750,000 gallons of river descending every second to form the highest flow rate of any waterfall on the planet.

If you've ever visited this natural wonder, commanding a portion of the border between the US and Canada, then like millions of others you too have felt minimized by its magnitude. Mesmerized by its magnificence. Enraptured by its quadraphonic-like cannonade drowning out all conversation.

Niagara Falls. Reverberating. Captivating. Breathtaking.

Believe it or not, there was a moment when a first-century follower of Jesus had a Niagara Falls-type encounter of his own.

Without even being there.

His adventure was an experience meant for all of us.

Mentored by the Master

Come with me into the book of Revelation as we observe the final days of an apostle's astonishing sixty-year mentorship with his Master.

We find John sidelined, now a prisoner in the grip of a self-deified emperor. Confined to a Roman gulag. Elderly and abandoned.

Still he remains resolute, faithful to his "Best Friend Forever" for whom he willingly suffers it all.

Still he goes on waiting, watching for the Judge of all to act on his behalf, even in these dire circumstances.

Still he stands at attention, ready to obey his Lord and Savior to any extent, without conditions.

That's because John remains convinced of one truth above all others: *Jesus is reigning supreme*. Right here and right now.

As he once observed: "The Son of God came to destroy the devil's work" (1 John 3).

But loftier manifestations of the majesty of Jesus wait to be explored — a Niagara Falls-sized connection with Jesus that looms around the corner for John.

John is about to be engulfed in infinity's effusions, swept up into the vastness of the victor he adores. He's about to be overtaken by an explosion of wonders — marvels about the Christ that God intends for *all* of his children to behold — sooner or later.

In some ways, this divine appointment mirrors familiar territory for John. Throughout his ministry for his Lord, he had been regularly reenergized by an array of thrilling episodes springing from his bedrock commitment to Emmanuel.

After all, this devout disciple had taken part in launching the greatest revolution in human history, serving a spiritual insurgency stretching from Jerusalem to Antioch to Rome, and beyond.

It all began for John when he was chosen for a three-year apprenticeship as part of the inner circle of the miracle-working Messiah of God.

But then all hope seemed to end for him one sunless afternoon when he witnessed the inexplicable, sacrificial death of the Lamb of God.

Yet shortly after that the adventure resumed during forty days when, along with fellow disciples, he conferred with the risen Redeemer of God about their continuing mission together.

That extraordinary seminar culminated for John when he witnessed the long-anticipated ascension of the Son of God to sit with universal authority at the right hand of the throne of God.

Subsequent installments of his vocation filled up an additional five decades as the Spirit sent him to serve the people of God in the Holy Land, in Ephesus, and elsewhere.

Then, as a capstone to his ministry, John produced an exquisite, lyrical treatise on Jesus — its final page telling the Church there still was so much more he knew about his Lord that if he wrote it all down, he supposed "that even the whole world would not have room for the books that would be written" (John 21).

Evidently, he considered himself to be more than a little familiar with his Savior!

Until . . . late in life along came this watershed moment on a little Mediterranean island when John intersected one more time with his gracious Lord. But this time it was very different. It was almost *as if* he had never seen his Savior before, *as if* he was meeting him again — for the very first time!

Unexpectedly, this mission-driven martyr ended up, as it were, being *re-introduced* to his Mission-master, who appeared before him in the glory of an unfamiliar guise. Suddenly, John found himself face to face with Jesus as . . .

The Master of Surprises

Surprise! Though wrinkled, weary, and worn, today John is about to enter the crescendo of his ministry, the pinnacle of his extraordinary spiritual walk.

Surprise! Though still a political pawn in a Patmos prison, today John is about to foresee cosmic events destined to consummate all of earth's dominions, subsumed under Jesus as the universal Sovereign.

Surprise! Erroneously perceived as a disenfranchised captive of Caesar, today

John is about to be liberated by "the Ruler of the kings of the earth" (Revelation 1:5), as Jesus invites him to experience "riches in glory" no earthly magistrate could ever claim.

Surprise! Seemingly sidelined in solitary confinement, in reality John is about to be ushered into the control center of the cosmos, surrounded by a festive multitude of saints and angels celebrating the irreversible, redeeming triumphs of the Monarch of mankind.

Surprise! No matter how much he feels temporarily limited by his immediate surroundings, John is soon to discover there's an unlimited grandeur to God's Son beyond all he has yet uncovered — a grandeur that, as John will witness shortly, the entire universe could never design, or define, or refine, or confine.

Surprise! Once and for all, Jesus is determined to decisively display himself to John (and to all of us through John) as heaven's Royal Majesty, robed with irrefutable, irresistible splendor surpassing human conception.

Surprise! John is about to be staggered by the Spirit, inducted into an exhilarating, renovating "Christ Awakening" meant to encapsulate the biblical hope for, and the prototype of, God's promised way to revitalize all of his people throughout all generations.

Get Ready. Get Set. Get Going. Get Down.

Get ready, **John.** Eyes fixed forward. Jesus is approaching you in his spectacular supremacy.

Get set, **John.** Stay poised to dive into the denouement of all divine decrees, based on who Christ is today: Anointed and ascended as this Potentate of time and eternity. Liberator of the nations and the ages. Lord of glory ruling fully and forcefully, not off in far-flung galaxies but right here and right now. Head of the Church who inhabits his people gladly — not just part of him, but all of him, in the fullness of his authority and majesty and sovereignty.

Get going, **John.** Awake! Arise! Your "day of visitation" has come.

Concerning the Christ, who over all these years became your highest passion — well, guess what? There remains much more to him than you ever suspected. A whole lot more!

Shortly you must relay to members of nearby congregations the exceptional, electrifying revelation of Jesus that saturates you. Of course, you'll find yourself grasping for word pictures that you'll know instantly to be totally inadequate for documenting the rapturous vision you behold. Still, don't hold back! To the best of your ability report what you will see, telling your readers:

> I turned around to see the voice that was speaking to me. And when I turned I saw . . . someone like a son of man, dressed in a robe reaching down to his feet and with a golden sash around his chest. The hair on his head was white like wool, as white as snow, and his eyes were like blazing fire. His feet were like bronze glowing in a furnace, and his voice was like the sound of rushing waters . . . his face was like the sun shining in all its brilliance (Revelation 1, NIV).

Don't hesitate, either, to confess to them how you respond instantly, the only way you could:

> When my eyes took in this sight I fell at his feet like a dead man (Revelation 1, PHILLIPS).

Yes, John, for sure, *get down*. Overpowered and spellbound, faint away. Prostrate yourself before God's eternal Son — wordless, breathless, smitten by splendor, stunned by shock and awe!

Like never before, and forever, out of this encounter Christ will become ALL to you, John. He will become NOW to you. You'll be unwilling to settle for anything or *anyone* less — more than that, you'll be *unable* to do so.

Now, dear reader, it is your turn to join John in exploring and experiencing the spectacular supremacy of God's Son in whole new ways, to receive your own radically refreshing reconnection with the Lord Jesus Christ — even though you may have trusted him for many years.

Welcome to the beginning of an unparalleled adventure. Uncontainable! Unsurpassable! Unforgettable!

Welcome to Niagara Falls.

Meditations on His Majesty
Have You Heard the Voice That Roars?

What if during the exquisite manifestation of King Jesus to John recorded in Revelation 1, *you* had been the one standing there instead of John? What if after that extraordinary day on Patmos *you* were the one required to describe for neighboring churches your mind-blowing rendezvous with the Savior, as he saturated you in his spectacular supremacy? How would *you* have handled it?

Before answering, return to the scene. Grasping for descriptive images to express what he had never seen before, John came up with fairly startling word pictures of Jesus:

He was dressed in a long robe with a gold strip of cloth around his chest.
The hair on his head was white like wool, as white as snow.
His eyes were like a blazing fire.
His feet were like bronze metal glowing in a furnace.
His voice sounded like rushing waters . . .
His face was like the sun shining in all its brightness.

If you had seen Jesus like that, what facet of his attributes might have struck you first?

Or struck you down?

Would it have been Jesus' face, lucent like the blazing sun?

Would it have been his eyes, searing with flames of fire?

What about his *voice*?

Yes, his voice. As John notes:

> His voice sounded like rushing waters.

One English version translates the Greek phrase for "rushing waters" as a sound like a powerful "cataract" (MSG); another calls it a voice that "thundered like mighty ocean waves" (NLT).

Personally, I think the Good News Translation expresses the original concept best by suggesting that to John's ears Jesus' words resounded like a *"roaring waterfall."*

Roaring? Jesus' Voice Resembles Roaring?

Are we talking about the Lamb of God, often characterized in children's Sunday school classes as meek and mild?

Are we referring to the Palestinian who dwelt in quiet rural obscurity, incognito his first thirty years?

Is this the same Jesus who humbled himself so fully he refused to debate his detractors? The Jesus about whose trial Isaiah prophesied: "As a sheep before its shearer is dumb, so he opened not his mouth"? The Jesus who surrendered, without protest, to the asphyxiation of crucifixion? Our sacrifice who suffered in silence as he bore the sin of the world?

Does John mean to suggest that now, today, this previously temperate teacher possesses a voice that *thunders*? A voice he's not hesitant to project to John (and to us) at full volume?

It appears so.

Is this vocal delivery like a *lion*, perhaps? In point of fact, Jesus *does* portray himself as a lion in Revelation 5.

But in this case, the image is even more sensational than that. Here, his voice imposes itself on a devoted hearer with rumbling reverberations reminiscent of a colossal waterfall.

It sounds like we're back to Niagara Falls!

I want to suggest to you that this sonic metaphor supplies us with a valuable insight about the depths of the revelation John received during his arresting reintroduction to our Redeemer. John is providing believers everywhere an invaluable, *audible* testimony about the true nature of the monumental personage whom we proclaim as our Savior, the Lord Jesus Christ.

In other words, John's ears enable us to *see* Jesus more clearly by helping us *hear* Jesus more carefully — by focusing us on the *voice* of his Royal Highness, so as not to miss one word he utters.

Considering the Source, Every Word Matters

Jesus' voice speaking Jesus' words — bursting from lips full of virtue and victory to bring vitality to his Church.

Jesus' voice speaking Jesus' words — flooding the nations with abounding hope, amplifying for all earth's peoples the Father's gracious invitation to forsake the dominion of darkness and freely enter into the kingdom of his dear Son.

Jesus' voice speaking Jesus' words — the voice foreshadowed as it was hymned in Psalm 29:

> The **voice** of the Lord is over the waters;
> the God of glory thunders . . .
> The **voice** of the Lord is powerful;
> the **voice** of the Lord is majestic . . .
> The **voice** of the Lord twists the oaks . . .
> And in his temple all cry, "Glory!" . . .
> the Lord is enthroned as King forever
> (NIV, emphasis added).

Jesus' voice speaking Jesus' words — as today it issues forth full-throated to continuously animate and energize all of creation:

> The Son is the radiance of God's glory . . .
> *sustaining all things by his powerful word . . .*
> at the right hand of the Majesty in heaven
> (Hebrews 1, NIV, emphasis added).

Listen to Your Master's Voice

This is the voice that brought Lazarus out of the tomb. Suddenly, as before torrential rivers, death was swept aside. He spoke three simple words:

> "Lazarus, come out!"
> (John 11).

This is the voice that one day will summon all the dead of *all* the ages to stand accountable before him at the final tribunal (Revelation 20), foretold in John 5:

> A time is coming and has now come
> when the dead will hear
> *the voice of the Son of God*
> and those who hear will live
> (NIV, emphasis added).

This is the voice of the good shepherd who invites his redeemed people to rally around him every time he's ready to move out and move forward. As he claims in John 10:

> *My sheep listen to my voice;*
> I know them, and they follow me.
> I give them eternal life,
> and they shall never perish
> (NIV, emphasis added).

This is the voice of the mesmerizing minister of heaven's communications, whose every utterance requires the saints to give him undistracted attention, just as God commanded in Matthew 17:

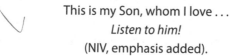

> This is my Son, whom I love . . .
> *Listen to him!*
> (NIV, emphasis added).

Listen to him! The Father's mandate is clear! We must never stop heeding the dictates of the divine Son of whom it can be said, even at this very hour:

> His eyes are a blaze of fire,
> on his head many crowns . . .
> he is *addressed* as *"Word of God."*
> The armies of Heaven . . . follow him . . .
> *A sharp sword comes out of his mouth*
> so he can subdue the nations,
> then rule them with a rod of iron
> (Revelation 19, MSG, emphasis added).

Eyes to the Ground, Ears to the Heavens

Fundamentally, the voice that planted John facedown in the dust of Patmos at Jesus' feet bids *all* believers to draw near in reverent awe — with ears expectant, primed to hear from the Messiah who is anointed to powerfully project God's everlasting promises, proclaimed into our everlasting lives.

The fact is, along with heaven and earth, we are predestined to be captivated throughout coming ages by a wholly holy "thundering waterfall" — unceasingly compelled by our Master's voice.

Have *you* heard the voice that roars? Recently?

That's precisely what Hebrews 12 urges you to do, today and every day:

> You have come to Jesus . . .
> *Be sure that you don't say no to the one who speaks.*
> People did not escape when they said no
> to the one who warned them on earth . . .
> *At that time his voice shook the earth.*
> But now he has promised,
> "Once more I will shake the earth.
> I will also shake the heavens" . . .
> Then what can't be shaken will remain.
> We are receiving a kingdom that can't be shaken.
> So let us be thankful
> (emphasis added).

As the Church we must never cease to tremble at Jesus' voice, because:

> he has a lot to say,
> he has every right to say it,
> and whenever he speaks —
> whenever he *roars* —
> nothing stays the same.

Including inside your heart and mine.

His voice is now.

Meditations on His Majesty
Stupefied With Jesus

Generations of daring explorers have successfully circumvented the precarious hazards of Niagara Falls, daring the full force of its awesome (and audible) frenzy.

Starting as far back as 1846, however, entrepreneurs began marketing a safe way for tourists to experience the sensation of the dynamic power of this natural phenomenon — by boarding the *Maid of the Mist.*

This once-every-hour excursion ferries visitors, protected in yellow rain slickers, to the very base of the Falls. For a few exhilarating minutes they become thoroughly enveloped in its pulsating spell — only to turn around and escape unscathed.

On three separate occasions I've joined the *Maid of the Mist* pilgrims. I can attest that each trip delivers an unforgettably visceral experience.

A Whole Other Kind of Ride
Is Waiting for You

Even so, that thrilling venture only remotely reminds me of the countless times while working on *Christ Is NOW!* that I've become *spiritually* exhilarated by close encounters of a whole other kind. Those moments sprang from bold forays into the amazing person of Jesus as I forged into countless expeditions into more of the immensities of who he is today.

Throughout the process of writing, God's Spirit has regularly shaken me awake as my research took me into uncharted territory (for me) regarding deeper biblical truths about the ascended glory of God's Son — about his spectacular supremacy today.

Mind you, I hold two graduate degrees from esteemed theological institutions! I thought I had the Jesus of the Bible pretty well in hand! So naturally I was startled by the thousands of Bible verses about the greatness of our glorious Savior and King that I had failed to unpack, either in seminary or in all my years of ministry since.

I was staggered by — and I choose this alliteration carefully — the *"profusion of profound perspectives"* on Jesus found not only in Scripture but also in a wealth of insights preserved in reams of writings from scores of renowned Christian thinkers down through the centuries.

To be quite candid, there were moments while working on this book that I could do nothing but simply *sit in silence* — enthralled and engulfed by the presence of Jesus, speechless over newly uncovered truths about God's Son — as the Spirit pulled back the curtain to reveal to me more of the realities of who our Savior truly is at this very moment.

This project turned out to be a Niagara-type "boat ride" for me! However, *this* trip was not into concealing mists; instead it caused mists to be dispelled. The Father used those years of investigation to navigate me into a transaction with Jesus similar to John's, two millennia earlier. Like John, I saw Jesus as I had never seen him before! I felt as though the Father *re-introduced* me to his Son, as if — what shall I say? — as if in some inexplicable way I was meeting Jesus again . . . for the very first time! Sort of like I was being born again . . . *again*!

Have You Been Stupefied With Jesus?

For many readers this story might sound rather peculiar, something reserved for a select (and strange) spiritual elite.

Not at all!

What I've described forms the testimony of countless believers through the ages. Deeper biblical truths about Jesus, freshly revealed by the Spirit, await every disciple today without exception, as a way of life. Our Lord promised us no less:

> I have much more to say to you. It is more than you can handle right now. *But when the Spirit of truth comes, he will guide you into all the truth.* He will not speak on his own. He will speak only what he hears. And he will tell you what is still going to happen. *He will bring me glory.* That's because what he receives from me he will show to you. Everything that belongs to the Father is mine. *That is why I said what the Holy Spirit receives from me he will show to you* (John 16, emphasis added).

Here's how *Christianity Today's* senior editor Mark Galli recounted his deepening encounter with Christ, writing in his book *Jesus Mean and Wild: The Unexpected Love of an Untamable God:*

> The biblical Jesus is a consuming fire, a raging storm, who shocks people into stupefaction or frightens them to run for their lives. He swirls like a tornado touching down, leaving only bits and pieces of our former lives strewn in His path.

Wait a minute. Did you catch that word Galli used? *Stupefaction*? What does that mean?

Stupefaction: The dictionary defines this as the state of a person who is "astonished, bewildered, astounded, flabbergasted [I like that one!], stunned, speechless, totally shocked."

Such as when one sails too close to Niagara Falls, for instance.

Stupefaction provides a good term to describe where I've often ended up while working on *Christ Is NOW!*

Stupefaction helps describe where I hope every reader of *Christ Is NOW!* frequently ends up as he or she navigates page after page, especially the major seven chapters in the middle.

May you become *so* stupefied with Jesus you'll be moved every day to expand the praises you offer to God's Son, reshaping them to celebrate your most recently discovered marvels about his majesty.

May you become *so* stupefied with Jesus you'll be unable to stop talking with other believers about the magnificence of God's Son — not only about his *past* endeavors to secure redemption on our behalf, not only about his *future* victories through apocalyptic intervention on our behalf, but most of all about his *current* exercise of saving power and sovereign sway on our behalf.

Stupefaction: The Destiny for All Creation

Stupefaction is precisely what Paul experienced firsthand as he lay face down on the Damascus Road. He later described his stupefying encounter with Jesus like this in Acts 26 (NIV):

> About noon, King Agrippa, as I was on the road, I saw a light from heaven, brighter than the sun, blazing around me and my companions. We all fell to the ground . . . Then I asked, "Who are you, Lord?"
>
> "I am Jesus, whom you are persecuting," the Lord replied.

Stupefaction is precisely what Revelation 1 tells us John endured firsthand, face down on the island of Patmos. Stupefied with Jesus, he wrote: "When my eyes took in this sight I fell at his feet like a dead man" (PHILLIPS).

Stupefaction is precisely what the Father desires for the Church worldwide — that increasingly believers everywhere might be stupefied with his Son, most of all with his spectacular supremacy today.

For you see, the Bible records that at this very second, myriads of angels along with the redeemed of the ages are also stupefied by the incomparable worthiness of Jesus. They are lifting lofty worship before God's face; regaling Messiah's resounding, relentless, righteous, redeeming rule; celebrating the cosmic champion who is anointed and active, decisive and invasive, unavoidable and unimpeachable, irresistible and irreplaceable.

Everything and everyone, everywhere, is destined to be stupefied with Jesus — exalting him and exulting in him with accolades that cascade forever over all creation — like the thunderous outpouring of Niagara Falls.

> That is why God has now lifted him so high,
> and has given him the name beyond all names,
> so that at the name of Jesus "every knee shall bow,"

whether in Heaven or earth or under the earth.
And that is why, in the end, "every tongue shall confess"
that Jesus Christ is the Lord,
to the glory of God the Father
(Philippians 2, PHILLIPS).

Meditations on His Majesty
The Most Important Thing to Know About You

Karl Barth was one of the 20th century's most influential theologians. Here's a challenge the Swiss professor frequently put before his students:

Show me your Christology and I'll tell you who you are.

Another way to state the good doctor's premise would be to say:

What you think about God's Son is the single most important thing anyone can know about you.

Both statements point to the same truth: In a profound sense, the core identity of any Christian must never be separated from her or his vision of the Christ who is the core identity of Christianity itself — that is, of *Christ*-ianity.

With that in mind, let me be direct:

What DO you think about God's Son?

Before you answer, imagine the following playful scenario.

The Mike Is All Yours. Begin!

You've just been invited to take the microphone during a national radio talk show, with one simple assignment. For the next *three minutes* you are to place before listeners your response to this question:

Who is Jesus Christ *right now*?

Obviously, it's similar to the real-life question with which Jesus probed his disciples as they walked on dusty roads in Caesarea Philippi (recorded in Matthew 16): "Who do you say that I am?"

But let's expand on that by asking:

How would you describe God's Son in terms of all he is at this precise moment?

Mind you, the goal here is not to tell the audience about who Jesus *was* in the past during his earthly ministry; nor is it to tell about who he *will be* one day when he returns in glory (both of which are important topics, for sure).

Rather, your assignment this time is to stay focused on the *present* — to describe vital aspects of who the individual called Jesus Christ is *now* — this very day.

Note further: No one is asking for a testimony about what Jesus has done for you personally since you gave your life to him, as inspiring as your story might be.

You see, this isn't about you. For this project, whether you or I exist is irrelevant.

Instead, you're to talk expressly, exclusively, about the *person* of God's Son. Who is he, in and of himself, exalted at this very instant as Sovereign Lord over heaven and earth?

OK then! Take your seat at the console. Lean into the mike. All ears are tuned to your voice. What an opportunity! Your three minutes begin now. Start talking!

Uhhhhh . . . maybe you find yourself hesitating.

Maybe you're starting to feel inadequately prepared to expand on various qualities of Jesus' nature, or splendors of his character, or breadths of his current activities. Maybe you're not so sure what fascinating features about his ongoing reign you should highlight for others. Maybe you sense you hold an insufficient grasp of the dynamics of his dominion, displayed day after day among his people and throughout the nations.

Maybe you find yourself fumbling for words to help others see him more fully — to see him as the preeminent personality in the universe. Maybe three minutes seem a bit too long to you.

Maybe you need additional coaching before you take on such an assignment!

It's important to admit that, because . . .

> **What you think (and are able to share) about God's Son**
> **is the single most important thing anyone can know about you.**

Who Do You Say I Am?. . . in 3 Minutes

Of course, we tried this role-play just for fun.

But quite honestly, how many Jesus followers do you know who could or would welcome such a three-minute experiment with any degree of confidence?

And out of those who might dare to try, how many do you think would *succeed*?

Frankly, after decades of traveling every stream of the Church, my studied conclusion is that most Christians know far too little about Jesus to competently and comfortably describe him for who he currently is as the Lord of glory.

Far too many believers remain woefully ill-informed about this astonishing personage — the Savior of the world who is alive and active, risen and ruling, moving and ministering, unceasingly adored and served by saints and angels everywhere. It's daunting at times, isn't it?

What if we simplified things and tried this three-minute experiment over coffee with just one close friend — make that a close *Christian* friend? Even then, how many of us would have to scramble to put together twelve whole sentences that boast meaningfully about the wonders and ways of God's Son? What do we have to say that possibly could impress another believer (let alone a Muslim or Hindu!) with why Jesus is the most magnificent figure to ever occupy time or eternity?

Instead, most of us end up straining to converse even halfway coherently with another believer about the excellencies of the one who rightfully claims supremacy in everything (Colossians 1) — whether in a radio studio or a diner.

The failures we experience in such experiments are not inconsequential! They mustn't be ignored! They unmask a spiritual disability that pervades the Church, carrying disturbing implications for renewing the Body of Christ or the reenergizing the mission of Christ.

Most tragically, this insidious blindness is *personal*. It has everything to do with what's true about each of us, with what's going on moment by moment in our relationship with King Jesus, with how fully we grasp that our ultimate identity and destiny are wrapped up in him alone.

This brings us back to our foundational challenge:

**If what you *THINK* about God's Son
is the single most important thing anyone can know about you,**

then

**what you *SAY* about God's Son
is the *second* most important thing anyone can know about you.**

There is an undeniable connection between these two statements. Jesus nailed it in Matthew 12 when he concluded:

For the mouth speaks what the heart is full of (NIV).

For a man's words depend on what fills his heart (PHILLIPS).

For whatever is in your heart determines what you say (NLT).

The Glorious Promise for the Journey Ahead

In the coming chapters, you will be invited over and over to "grow in grace and understanding of our Master and Savior, Jesus Christ. Glory to the Master, now and forever! (2 Peter 3, MSG).

As a result, you will also have many opportunities to discover a whole lot more of who *you* are — living, moving, and having your being in the grasp of Christ's greatness and glory — as you enter more fully into (what I like to call) "intimacy with Christ in his supremacy."

In the end, *that* is the single most important truth anyone could ever know about you:

> Not just what you *think* of Christ;
> not even what you *say* about Christ;
> but ultimately who you *are* in Christ.

Meditations on His Majesty
Put On Your
King Jesus Glasses

Let's talk vision.

The fact is that the time is long overdue for the Church to set itself about the task of recovering a thoroughgoing King Jesus-sized vision.

It's time we get ourselves refitted with the eyewear many of us have misplaced, often inadvertently. Or maybe no one ever gave us the right pair of glasses in the first place.

I'm talking about our very own "King Jesus Glasses" — spiritual spectacles to correct the all too prevalent shortsightedness that keeps many believers from seeing more clearly our Royal Redeemer for who he really is: high and lifted up; seated at the helm of the universe; ruling triumphantly at this very moment from the center of God's throne; Head of the Church; Lord and Master of all who trust in him.

Once you get hold of a pair King Jesus Glasses, however, it changes the way you look at *everything*!

Talking Optics with Chinese Christian Leaders

Let me tell you when and why I started using this optical metaphor to expose the troubling "vision affliction" I uncovered during three decades of interacting with Christians around the world.

In 2004 we published a foundational book titled ***Christ Is ALL! Join the Joyful Awakening to the Spectacular Supremacy of God's Son*** (*CIA*). Sometime later, a request came to print 500,000 copies of *CIA* translated into Mandarin Chinese for use by a major seminary for its extension program inside China where they are currently training tens of thousands of pastors of the nationwide house church movement.

Before signing the contract, however, the Singaporean publishers pressed me with one precondition: that I write a supplementary introduction. They wanted an interpretive essay designed specifically to convince their students of the one goal the faculty deemed essential for pastors and lay leaders to grasp.

That goal? It was that *CIA's* "take" on the greatness and glory of God's Son become the prime lens, the principal filter, through which seminarians would reflect on all their other studies, allowing *CIA's* expansive Christology to inform and infuse every other theological topic and textbook they might tackle.

The governing board was convinced that if during their seminary days students became sufficiently captivated by *CIA's* kind of perspective on Jesus — its unrelenting focus on the extraordinary nature of his person and the decisive dynamics of his life-giving sovereignty — this prerequisite point of view would continue to dominate all other ways they would minister for Christ the rest of their lives.

The school envisioned waves of graduates going forth determined to give the Lord Jesus unmitigated preeminence in everything, infusing the Christians they serve with the very same persuasion.

The truths of Christ's supremacy, they concluded, must become the starting point *and* ending point for how future pastors equip believers to study and apply Scripture, or to practice the discipline of prayer, or to walk out daily obedience to the Master and to share the gospel with neighbors.

Bifocals Guaranteed to Bless

With this desired outcome in mind, I titled my additional introductory chapter "We Need King Jesus Glasses."

In it, I described for church shepherds (whether in China or anywhere else) a unique pair of invisible *bifocals* designed to equip Christ followers to view reality (including ministry) in *two* essential directions at the same time.

First, these sacred lenses serve to provide an uncommonly lofty view of our Lord Jesus himself, helping Christians survey with greater clarity all he embodies as the unparalleled, unrivaled King of kings.

But, I pointed out, concurrently as *bifocals* they are designed to equip us to see *all the rest of life* through the wonders of the lordship of Jesus — interpreting the world around us, and more specifically the entire Christian life, based on how the ascended Son of God is manifesting himself daily as mediatory monarch over every aspect of who we are and what we're about.

By constantly focusing congregations on the all-prevailing sovereignty and sufficiency and saving power of the Christ, I wrote to my readers, pastors would ensure that members increasingly and consistently define everyday existence by Jesus' larger, eternal kingdom agenda.

In *Mere Christianity,* C. S. Lewis describes his bifocal experience this way:

> I believe in Christianity as I believe the sun has risen,
> not just because I see it, but because by it I see everything else.

The rationale for finding and putting on our King Jesus Glasses might then be summed up by paraphrasing Lewis' observation to read like this:

> Christians believe in Jesus Christ
> not only because we see him ascended and active as Lord of all,
> but also because we see everything else in the universe as it really is
> through the lens of his spectacular supremacy.

Dream Along With Me

Are you ready to start enjoying a multitude of blessings that flow from looking *at* Jesus for all he's worth today while simultaneously looking *through* Jesus for all he's about today?

If your bifocals are in position, dream along with me. It's a mental exercise I've encouraged Christian leaders everywhere to try.

How rejuvenated might believers become *if* they were enabled to see *everything* in direct relationship to Christ himself, in view of his spectacular supremacy right now?

In other words, what if *all things* — weekly activities inside our churches; small groups working on growth in discipleship; securing moral victories in daily relationships; pursuing kingdom outreach in the marketplace; missions to plant churches among the nations; efforts at healing the poverty in our cities; mounting redemptive responses to world events like famine; solidifying the battlefront facing the challenges of spiritual warfare — were viewed as directly and continuously engaged with the forever alive, fully active, fiercely advocating, forwardly advancing, fervently adored Son of God? How much more exciting — how much more *fulfilling* — could any walk with Christ become for those who tackle life like this day after day?

Dream with me about just one individual congregation whose members join hands to pursue in every way possible total involvement with God's Son as the sovereign, salvaging, shepherding, sending Savior of heaven and earth. How much more alive would such a fellowship of visionaries become if they had hearts that burned together for Christ and his kingdom?

Biblically speaking, this "dreaming exercise" represents the approach to life God desires for all of his people; it is to define our lifestyle all of the time. As Scripture puts it in Colossians 3:

> If you are then "risen" with Christ, reach out for the highest gifts of Heaven, where your master reigns in power. Give your heart to the heavenly things, not to the passing things of earth. For, as far as this world is concerned, you are already dead, and your true life is a hidden one in Christ (PHILLIPS).

In the Mandarin introduction to *CIA* I noted for my readers that the transformative repercussions of this radically renovating perspective on the exaltedness of Jesus are incalculable — whether for worshiping on Sundays, or building community, or promoting Christian unity among churches, or deepening individual spiritual vitality, or accelerating the witness of the gospel among the unreached.

Of course, this all-inclusive paradigm for life in Christ isn't just for *Chinese* Christians, it belongs to believers of every tongue, of every place, of every generation.

Is It Time For An Eye Exam?

Do you recall Jesus' diagnosis of the well-known Laodicean church in Revelation 3? Remember how his heart broke over this visually impoverished congregation as he appealed to them (and through them to all of us) to let him heal their vision so they might rouse, regain focus, and realize that he was no longer active with them; he had ceased working among them! He put it like this:

> You are poor, blind and naked. So here's my advice . . . buy from me healing lotion to put on your eyes. Then you will be able to see . . . If anyone hears my voice and opens the door, I will come in.

I wonder: How would Jesus diagnose the eyesight of *your* church? How would he critique your members' sharpness of sight for his spectacular supremacy? Would he recommend immediate application of what he offered the Laodiceans — a celestially potent eye salve for restoring to saints a full recognition of their Savior and his readiness to reoccupy them with his ascended glory?

From what I've seen during decades of circulating throughout the Body of Christ, I'm convinced millions of believers today are sick and tired of stumbling along because of their Christological myopia. Millions are eager for Jesus' healing balm to be applied to their desolation of vision.

They're determined to do whatever it takes to locate and permanently put on their King Jesus Glasses.

Are you one of them?

"Heaven's Optometrist," the Holy Spirit, stands able, willing and ready to make this happen.

> God has shown these things to us through his Spirit. The Spirit understands all things. He understands even the deep things of God . . . We have received the Spirit who is from God. The Spirit helps us understand what God has freely given us . . . we have the mind of Christ (1 Corinthians 2).

Appointments are immediately available.

Meditations on His Majesty
More Attention to the Ascension

Here's a question I'll bet no one has ever asked you:

Of the rich spectrum of biblical doctrines underpinning the historic Christian faith, *which truth do you think may be the most widely neglected teaching within the contemporary Church* — particularly among nearly three-quarters of a billion Christians who make up the global evangelical movement?

Could it be the Trinity? The Atonement? The Second Coming? The role of miracles? Moral purity?

Actually, across the Body of Christ, believers are regularly exposed to all of these topics, Sunday after Sunday. But something crucial is missing. What is it?

Here's my answer: It's the doctrine of the *Ascension*. Does that surprise you?

Consider this: Within most congregations how often do you think members *ever* hear someone bring a teaching centered on the ascension of God's Son? When was the last time your church set aside an entire Sunday to highlight the day Jesus was enthroned in heaven in the way same way we celebrate Advent and Easter?

The New Testament, on the other hand, makes it clear that the Ascension loomed large over Jesus' final days with his disciples, and subsequently resurfaced as a prevalent theme in the book of Acts and also in many of the epistles. Should it not, therefore, loom large for us? If there is a general neglect of this doctrine by our generation, should that not give us pause?

Delay Followed by Coronation Day

For a number of weeks following his resurrection, Jesus postponed his foretold departure to the Father. To his followers' amazement, he remained on location, in resurrection glory, to invest an additional forty days equipping them for future ministry. Throughout those weeks, we're told, he unpacked deeper teachings on God's kingdom, which the disciples were now able to grasp in much clearer terms in the light of his sufferings and triumphs (Acts 1, Luke 24, John 20-21).

Foremost, through this unique super-seminar, Jesus was preparing them to follow through on the world-shaking revelation they were about to witness on their "graduation" day, which was also Jesus' Coronation Day — the day when all authority in heaven and on earth was bestowed on him in perpetuity; when he was elevated by the Father to the divine dais, enthroned before saints and angels as sovereign over all.

About that unprecedented moment, Scripture records in Luke 24:

> He told them, "This is what is written. The Messiah will suffer. He will rise from the dead on the third day. His followers will preach in his name. They will tell others to turn away from their sins and be forgiven. People from every nation will hear it . . . Jesus led his disciples out to the area near Bethany. Then he lifted up his hands and blessed them. *While he was blessing them, he left them. He was taken up into heaven. Then they worshiped him.* With great joy, they returned to Jerusalem. Every day they went to the temple, praising God (emphasis added).

Acts 1 expands on the same event:

> . . . he was taken up to heaven. The apostles watched until a cloud hid him from their sight . . . Suddenly two men dressed in white clothing stood beside them. "Men of Galilee, they said, "why do you stand here looking at the sky? Jesus has been taken away from you into heaven. But he will come back in the same way you saw him go."

By that magnificent cosmic shift, the band of Jesus' followers was confronted with dramatic discoveries about the true nature and nobleness of God's exalted Son, insights they would handle and proclaim with unfading wonder the rest of their lives.

Decades later, for example, the apostle John, who had stood on the Mount of Olives years earlier and witnessed that royal processional, required apocalyptic imagery to sum up the profound impact of that great day:

> The Woman gave birth to a Son
> who will shepherd all nations with an iron rod.
> Her Son was seized and placed safely
> before God on his Throne . . .
> Then I heard a strong voice out of Heaven saying,
> "Salvation and power are established!
> Kingdom of our God, authority of his Messiah!"
> (Revelation 12, MSG).

Celebrating the Inaugurating!

Today as God's consecrated, crowned, universal Mediator, His Royal Majesty, the Lord Jesus Christ, continues to actively exercise global jurisdiction. His reign is so extensive we can be assured there's not one square inch of planet earth — including the deepest secrets of every heart — over which he does not assert the claim: "I am King of kings and Lord of lords even there!"

Jesus ascended! All royal enthronements of history *combined* could never excel that one. It is the preeminent imperial investiture of all time.

Jesus ascended! That one historical event, in time and space and history, carried with it eternal consequences that the redeemed will never cease recounting in sheer amazement.

Jesus ascended! That one historical act formed the decisive turning point of the ages, pregnant with the promise of deliverance for all creation, to which our only valid response must be unbridled jubilation.

Jesus ascended! That one unrepeatable hour became the capstone of his ministry, the culmination of every other facet of his redeeming work that is saluted by the Church through liturgy and sacraments and holy days and treasured rituals.

Jesus ascended! That one phenomenal transaction ratified and certified and magnified, once and for all, the man and the mission of the Son of God, and established him over the Church as our everlasting Savior and Supreme Commander.

Jesus ascended! That one infinite initiative within the total enterprise of our eternal salvation confirms to all of us that the scope of his sway will forever dominate us and is irreplaceable, irreducible, irreversible.

Jesus ascended! That one heavenly investiture forms the apex for which our Lord *descended* into our world in the first place. As Scripture recounts:

> . . . he also came down to the lower, earthly places.
> The one who came down is the same one who went up.
> *He went up higher than all the heavens.*
> *He did it in order to fill all creation*
> (Ephesians 4, emphasis added).

Note that phrase: "in order to *fill* all creation."

Right now Jesus is filling the universe with his sovereignty, with his residency, with his activity — with his glory.

One day soon, however, he will fill even the darkest, deadliest corners of the universe with the majesty of his manifested majestic presence, so that *all things* above and below will give their *full* attention to the Ascension — forever. As the Bible clearly states:

> So God lifted him up to the highest place. God gave him the name
> that is above every name. When the name of Jesus is spoken,
> everyone will kneel down to worship him. Everyone in heaven and
> on earth and under the earth will kneel down to worship him.
> Everyone's mouth will say that Jesus Christ is Lord. And God the
> Father will receive the glory (Philippians 2).

That's why, considering how important Jesus' coronation was to his mission, we ought to wonder: **Why is there so little attention to the Ascension throughout the Church today?**

Surely, right now whatever is issuing forth from Jesus as he resides on the throne of heaven should prevail over and pervade throughout everything that matters to believers everywhere — in our churches, in our ministries, in our marriages, in our outreaches, in our daily obedience to him.

How much longer will this history-changing, reality-altering event — with its remarkable revelation of the Son for all he is today — be allowed to remain sidelined in our life together?

As you know, the worldwide Christian family enjoys memorializing *other* key junctures in God's plan of redemption, as we highlight various sacred highpoints in Jesus' ministry. So, why should we not do the same with the Ascension?

We embellish Christmas with candlelight services to honor Jesus' birth. At Lent we fast to focus on his costly defeat of the flesh and the devil. His atoning death on the cross we solemnly recall on Good Friday. His triumphant destruction of death we designate with fanfare on Easter. His empowering of the Church for mission we observe as Pentecost Sunday. Should not a similarly pivotal event — our King's enthronement — at the very least get some form of an annual recital?

Can you imagine how your walk with Christ would suffer if the Church largely ignored the truths behind Advent, Epiphany, Ash Wednesday, Palm Sunday, Maundy Thursday and all the others? What, then, do you think is the negative impact of our long-term amnesia about the event that consummated with Jesus' installment at God's right hand to begin his proactive kingship among us, bringing with it everlasting consequences?

Thankfully, we don't need to start from scratch. The Ascension appears on the religious calendars of some Church bodies (Catholics, Anglicans, Orthodox, Lutherans). Technically, it is designated as a holy day observed seven weeks after Easter. Some traditions also set aside a Sunday later in the liturgical calendar called Christ the King Sunday, to amplify how Jesus is Lord over all.

However, to ignite throughout the Church a wholesale, unified, global retention of the Ascension — giving it the attention it deserves — we need to do more than secure some "official" annual commemoration date.

Rather, an army of God's people need to find a wholehearted passion for restoring this neglected doctrine — the same passion we'd have if a moment ago we ourselves stood on the slopes outside Jerusalem watching Jesus' breathtaking dispatch unfold.

In a sense, for the Father who knows the end from the beginning, *it really did just happen*!

A Call for an "Ascension Reformation"

It's time to pay more attention to the Ascension. We need nothing less than an "Ascension Reformation"!

Of course, we must consistently maintain the centrality of the cross. With Paul we confess, "May I never boast except in the cross of our Lord Jesus Christ" (Galatians 6). However, the cross and the crown are now permanently inseparable, just as Hebrews 1 reminds us:

> *He provided the way for people to be made pure from sin.*
> *Then he sat down at the right hand of the King, the Majesty in heaven.*
> So he became higher than the angels.
> The name he received is more excellent than theirs
> (emphasis added).

When someone is baptized by water into the death, burial, and resurrection of Christ (Romans 6), they also are raised up with Christ to sit with him in the realms of heaven (Ephesians 2). That's throne language. The transaction of baptism, in other words, is ratified by the Ascension. Notice how 1 Peter 3 links baptism *into* Christ with the exaltation *of* Christ:

> The waters of baptism do that for you,
> not by washing away dirt from your skin
> but by presenting you through Jesus' resurrection
> before God with a clear conscience.
> Jesus has the last word
> on everything and everyone, from angels to armies.
> *He's standing right alongside God, and what he says goes*
> (MSG, emphasis added).

Again, my plea: **It's time to pay more attention to the Ascension. We need nothing less than an "Ascension Reformation."**

Weekly Sunday school classes and Sunday morning sermons may expound on practical Christian living, teaching that our character and our actions need to line up with those of Jesus. This has value.

But where is the *other* teaching, the *prior* teaching — the emphasis on *Jesus'* character, and *his* actions, and *his* current reign extending from the throne? We need curricula on discipleship that helps believers respond to who and where our King is at this very hour — how *he* thinks, what *he* is up to, where *he*'s moving, and how *he* is ministering and triumphing. Such a larger vision is essential for effective, victorious Christian living.

The Church must hear a whole lot more about the unbeatable synergy between daily discipleship *to* Christ and the continuing dominion *of* Christ. Consider how Paul interfaces the two in Ephesians 2:

> He took our sin-dead lives and made us alive in Christ . . .
> *Then he picked us up and set us down in highest heaven*
> *in company with Jesus, our Messiah.*
> Now God has us where he wants us,
> with all the time in this world and the next
> *to shower grace and kindness upon us in Christ Jesus . . .*
> *He creates each of us by Christ Jesus*
> *to join him in the work he does,*
> the good work he has gotten ready for us to do,
> work we had better be doing
> (MSG, emphasis added).

Yes, it's time to pay more attention to the Ascension. We need nothing less than an "Ascension Reformation."

Every year denominations and ministry organizations sponsor hundreds of high-level assemblies, seminars, convocations, and conferences. We meet to address pressing topics, such as racial reconciliation, personal evangelism, church growth, end times preparations, leadership principles, kingdom-styled social justice, city/community gospel movements, spiritual gifts and empowerment, challenges in world missions, the need for national revival — as well as to hear experts exchange academic persuasions on the most current theological debates.

All of this is well and good in its proper place.

But what about Jesus our King, installed at the right hand of the Father? Why don't our conversations engage much more with the incomparable, incontrovertible inauguration of God's Messiah, with all of the powerful implications it brings for every other theme we have gathered to address?

If at this moment Jesus on the throne is the single greatest reality defining the fortunes of the universe — *and it is* — should it not comprise the hottest topic in our seminars and our sermons? Not the *only* topic, of course. But at least the *hottest* topic!

Instead, too often we talk around him rather than talk about him.

How About a Convocation on the Coronation?

I wonder what would happen if Christian leaders convened for three days specifically to explore the wider dimensions of Christ's coronation? What if they tried to relate multiple facets of his supremacy to the major doctrines and designs of Christian faith and discipleship with the goal to unpack a biblical perspective on God's Son that incorporates the profound implications of the Apostle's Creed where it says: *"He ascended into heaven and sits on the right hand of God, the Father Almighty, from where he shall come to judge the living and the dead"*?

Such a historic convocation could launch a modern day reformation movement — a spiritual revolution throughout the Church that is fueled by the reclamation of a greater, grander, more glorious Christology — a Christology expanded and deepened by the robust ramifications of his coronation, a Christology that reignites wide-sweeping passion for the reign of Christ and every expression of his kingship today.

An Ascension Reformation. Today. Beginning with a convocation on the Coronation.

Quite honestly, my whole adult life has been devoted to fostering and serving nothing less than such a movement — what I often refer to as a "Christ Awakening movement." *Christ Is NOW!* was written precisely to widen the vision of God's Son among God's people in readiness for an Ascension reformation that we cultivate and nurture together.

This movement can begin here and now with a "reformation" inside our *hearts,* as each of us gives increased attention to the Ascension — and to the Son whose spectacular supremacy blazed two millennia ago on his coronation day.

Meditations on His Majesty
Hear the Royal Decree!

Do you know that every year the entire population of Norway observes Ascension Day?

Surprising as it may be, this official holiday appears annually on their national calendar, a vestigial custom left over from centuries of Lutheran indoctrination.

Unfortunately, the vast majority of Norwegians (mostly unchurched) have little idea what the holiday actually stands for. Nonetheless, every worker happily welcomes it since it provides a mandated paid vacation day! Who wouldn't want that?

However, this 24-hour fringe benefit exists light years from the *true* blessings awaiting God's people because of Jesus' ascension — as we began to explore in the previous meditation.

In fact — and this may shock some readers — the consequences of the coronation of our Savior are so extensive we are compelled to conclude:

> Without the ascension of Jesus
> everything else he did for our salvation
> would be rendered null and void!

Null and void?

Yes. In the final analysis, if Jesus had not gone up on high, everything he did down below would have been rendered incomplete, insufficient, ineffectual — that is, inadmissible.

The entirety of our salvation stands or falls on whether the Father was willing to publicly ratify every facet of Jesus' redemptive mission for us — free to declare unequivocally, without reservation or qualification, his unconditional approval, both *about* his Son as well as *to* his Son.

Think of this divine imprimatur as the Father's *"Royal Decree."*

Decreed to Be "the Christ" Forever

The Father's *decree* brings with it a very special *title* — "the Christ" — reserved for all eternity to be bestowed at just the right moment upon one and only one person.

As you know by now, "Christ" is not Jesus' surname. Someone would never introduce him to an audience as "Mr. Christ." Rather, it's the signature designation that links him directly with his role as Lord of the universe.

Over five hundred times in the New Testament, Jesus is referred to as "the Christ" — which literally means (from the Greek) "the Anointed One" or "the Appointed One." Both the Hebrew Old Testament and the Greek New Testament employ this title to designate the person God finally "sets apart" to assume forever the position of highest honor in his kingdom.

This *title* brings with it a *commission*: The Christ is to assume unrestricted dominion for all time to come, to bring about the culmination of the promises and prophecies and purposes of the Father — including how they are advanced in the 21st century.

As many have suggested, Christians really should respell history as *"His Story."* Seen from the throne room, all events both past and present are being woven together by the triune God around the Son so as to keep everyone and every event, in every place and every age, moving onward and upward — that is, moving *Christ*-ward (even though temporarily most people remain either oblivious of or overtly resistant to this glorious, divine drama).

Best of all, for followers of the Christ, our individual lives also keep moving Christ-ward, as Colossians 3 reminds us:

> Since, then, you have been raised with Christ, set your hearts on things above, where Christ is, seated at the right hand of God. Set your minds on things above, not on earthly things. For you died, and *your life is now hidden with Christ in God* (NIV, emphasis added).

The Royal Decree as Proclaimed by the Early Church

To magnify Jesus *as* the Christ, the early church rallied around one specific biblical text about Jesus — a passage we might designate as God's *official* "Royal Decree" about his Son.

I'm referring to the Old Testament pronouncement quoted or referenced in the New Testament more frequently than any other, and by almost all of its writers. This one edict explains why earthly authorities are dismissed as mere pretenders to the throne.

Remember that after Jesus had departed, the Old Testament provided first-century believers the only source of inspired writings to which they could turn to interpret God's saving activities that were exploding throughout the newly launched Christian movement.

As they did, what passage do you think the early church went back to more often than any other? In the midst of the gospel's advance, of all the thousands of verses of the Hebrew scriptures from which the apostles could have preached in order to explain to God's people the person of God's Son and the priorities of his kingdom, what one text do you think they returned to time and time again?

This is more than a quiz. Nailing the truth of this text is vital. In it resides the singular insight disciples prized most to help them sum up God's plan of salvation through Jesus. Therefore, its truth has become decisive for subsequent generations engaging with the reign of Christ.

The passage?

See His Supremacy: Psalm 110

Surprisingly, Psalm 110 one of the briefest of all the Psalms, comprising only eleven verses. So why did *this* portion of Scripture achieve dominance among New Testament Christians? Could it have something to do with the proactive nature of the vision with which it opens — with its *decree?* We read:

> The LORD says to my lord: "*Sit* at my right hand
> until I *make* your enemies a footstool for your feet."
> The LORD will *extend* your mighty scepter from Zion, saying,
> "*Rule* in the midst of your enemies!"
> (NIV, emphasis added)

One thing was immediately clear to first-century Jesus followers: This ancient hymn foretold the ascension of Jesus. Note how the active verbs — *sit, make, extend, rule* — relate to someone taking a throne. These verses foreshadow Jesus raised on high, actively ruling and prevailing as Lord of all, both for his own people ("Your troops will be willing on your day of battle, arrayed in holy majesty," verse 3) as well as among the peoples of earth ("He will crush kings . . . He will judge nations," verses 5-6).

In the mandate of Psalm 110, the Father ordains the reign of his Son to flourish unabated, forever. As much as any other Scripture, this hymn fulfills — or better yet, it *fills full* — the significance of the royal title reserved for Jesus alone: *"the Christ."* Its poetry reinforces for God's people how the Father is working to coalesce everything under his Messiah, reconstituting even his enemies into a "footstool" destined to complement the throne from which Messiah presides.

During his earthly career, the Master himself recited this Scripture when he confronted swarms of resistive religious leaders, quoting its assertions to confound them because it required them to deal with the biblical basis of his claims to be Messiah and Lord over all — especially over *them* (see Matthew 22).

Following suit, most New Testament writers laced their works with quotes from or references to Psalm 110, prevalent especially in Acts, Ephesians, Colossians, Hebrews, and Revelation.

However, here's what is most intriguing about this prime prophecy that is so foundational to how first-century churches thought about Jesus: It mentions *nothing* about his incarnation, or crucifixion, or resurrection — as utterly essential as all three are to our salvation.

Instead, it focuses exclusively on the unparalleled enthronement of Jesus in heaven — the one paramount event that sovereignly sealed for God's people the full ramifications of his incarnation, crucifixion, and resurrection. His coronation as the Christ unleashed into both Church and cosmos the everlasting benefits of all *other* aspects of Christ's redemptive work. In other words:

> Without the ascension of Jesus
> everything else he did for our salvation
> would be rendered null and void!

Perhaps that's why in Acts 2, as Peter preaches the first recorded sermon of the Christian movement, he drives his message steadily toward the Ascension, making it the core of his climactic appeal (to which 3000 responded in saving faith) by quoting, in conclusion, from Psalm 110:

> Exalted to the right hand of God, he has received from the Father the promised Holy Spirit and has poured out what you now see and hear. For David did not ascend to heaven, and yet he said, "The Lord said to my Lord: Sit at my right hand until I make your enemies a footstool for your feet." Therefore let all Israel be assured of this: God has made this Jesus, whom you crucified, both Lord and Messiah [Christ].

Since that hour, the saints in heaven and on earth continue to rejoice in the declaration of Psalm 110 about God's Messiah, the Lord Jesus Christ — a manifesto never to be revised or rescinded or replaced.

Hear the Royal Decree. . . Expressed in Other Words

Let's close this meditation by expanding on the themes of Psalm 110 and reflecting on their implications as spelled out by a multitude of New Testament teachings.

Picture yourself there with the disciples on that matchless day when, as Luke 24 reports: "He lifted up his hands and blessed them. While he was blessing them, he left them. He was taken up into heaven. Then they worshiped him." Then imagine the Father welcoming our Savior with these words:

Hear the Royal Decree!

**Come up here, my dearly loved Son, and sit beside me
on the throne of heaven.**

You are the one person in the entire cosmos with whom
I am unconditionally pleased.
I'm wholly satisfied with all you have accomplished.
What you have achieved to fulfill our eternal plan, by your
incarnation, crucifixion, and resurrection,
is thoroughly complete and fully sufficient for the salvation of my people.
The perfection of your mission of redemption ensures
the Consummation for all creation.

Hear the Royal Decree!

**Come up here, my dearly loved Son, and sit beside me
on the throne of heaven.**

Put on the royal diadem. Let me anoint you and crown you as
Prince of Peace and Ruler of all.
To you alone belongs the place of preeminence, preserved
for you from the foundation of the world.
You are supreme in all things! You are the end and goal of all things.
One day soon every knee will bow to you, and every tongue will confess
that you are Lord and Christ, which will only serve to focus
all eyes on my glory!

Hear the Royal Decree!

**Come up here, my dearly loved Son, and sit beside me
on the throne of heaven.**

Reign throughout all creation and in every nation.
Reign on behalf of all whom you have redeemed.
Reign until you defeat every enemy, the last enemy being death itself.
Pour out the Spirit of power and revelation as the
primary extension of your ascension.
He will bring your saving victories into every place and
among every tongue and peoples.
Out of the domains of darkness he will transfer a
host of sinners into your kingdom,
called and assembled by your gospel from every corner of the globe;
reconciled by your cleansing blood and filled with your risen life;
folded into your anointed, abounding dominion to thrive in you forever.

**Come up here, my dearly loved Son, and sit beside me
on the throne of heaven!**

Meditations on His Majesty
Seated and Supreme

The 1953 coronation of Queen Elizabeth II, the longest reigning monarch in British history, had to be postponed for a customary year of mourning for the King (her father) before she was allowed to officially replace him. Even then, preparations for the regal festivities took sixteen months, requiring a phalanx of committees and servants to get the job done.

Sadly, despite all the royal embellishments on her day of enthronement, Queen Elizabeth found herself the sovereign of a once mighty empire that was rapidly disintegrating before her eyes. What had been the 19th century's commercial and military behemoth, the United Kingdom was already shrinking to only ten countries out of a former commonwealth upon which the sun never set.

How utterly *unlike* that queen's transition to power was the exaltation of the most magnificent monarch of all times, His Royal Majesty, King Jesus!

For starters, the death that preceded his installment happened to be his *own* — for the sins of the world, no less! Nor was there any delay in the jubilations the day Jesus ascended on high. Heaven's hosts greeted his triumphant return to glory with praises that have never ceased, continuing unabated to this very hour (as we see in Revelation 4-5).

Today, Christ's "Commonwealth" (which means a place rich in blessings shared equally by all who are in it) stretches around the globe and out to the farthest edges of the universe as well — every square inch under the shadow of his saving scepter.

Already his subjects are so vast in number that they cannot be counted, consisting of a full spectrum of humankind, a communion of saints filling earth and heaven — which *continues* to swell by countless thousands every passing day! See Revelation 7:9-17 for more on this.

When all is said and done, one outcome stands sure: Jesus is now and forever **seated and supreme.**

Magisterial Passages on His Prevailing Position of Preeminence

Not only in Psalm 110 (which we reflected on in the previous meditation) but throughout Scripture inspiring testimonies abound that focus on the primacy of Christ today, painting him as nothing less than the "Potentate of Nations" — a position that was firmly authorized by his ascension.

Let's sample a few of them, which like Psalm 110, similarly emphasize Jesus' kingship. Let's start with the passage Jesus himself employed when his claim to be the Messiah, the Son of God, was challenged by the Sanhedrin at his late night trial.

> "You have said so," Jesus replied.
> "But I say to all of you:
> *From now on you will see the Son of Man
> sitting at the right hand of the Mighty One
> and coming on the clouds of heaven"*
> (Matthew 26, NIV, emphasis added).

Scholars agree that by using such graphic imagery, Jesus pointed his accusers to Daniel 7 where Messiah's everlasting reign was foretold with similar words:

> In my vision I saw
> *one who looked like a son of man.
> He was coming with the clouds of heaven.*
> He approached the Eternal God.

He was led right up to him.
And he was given authority, glory and a kingdom.
People of all nations, no matter what language they spoke, worshiped him.
His authority will last forever. It will not pass away.
His kingdom will never be destroyed
(emphasis added).

In other words, Jesus told them he was about to be **seated and supreme**.

Another preview of his forthcoming rule is captured in Psalm 72:

God, give the king the ability to judge fairly.
He is your royal son.
Help him to do what is right.
May he rule your people in the right way . . .
May he save the children of those who are in need.
May he crush those who treat others badly . . .
May he rule for all time to come . . .
May all kings bow down to him.
May all nations serve him
(emphasis added).

Once again, Jesus was destined to be **seated and supreme**.

Centuries after David wrote those words, Zechariah (chapter 9) expanded on the same vision with such specificity that the Gospels confirm his predictions as fulfilled, at least preliminarily, when Jesus offered himself to Israel as their king as he rode into Jerusalem the week before he was crucified:

City of Zion, be full of joy!
People of Jerusalem, shout!
See, your king comes to you.
He always does what is right.
He has won the victory.
He is humble and riding on a donkey.
He is sitting on a donkey's colt . . .
I will break the bows that are used in battle.
Your king will announce peace to the nations.
He will rule from ocean to ocean.

> *His kingdom will reach from the Euphrates River*
> *to the ends of the earth.*
> I will set your prisoners free
> from where their enemies are keeping them.
> I will do it because of the blood
> that put into effect my covenant with you
> (emphasis added).

Bottom line? Jesus' mission would climax with him seated and supreme.

To no one's surprise then, the New Testament writers expand extensively on Jesus' lofty destination, chronicling his crowning from many angles. For instance, brand new believers in Asia Minor were told:

> *God seated [Christ] at his right hand in his heavenly kingdom.*
> There Christ sits far above all who rule and have authority.
> *He also sits far above all powers and kings.*
> He is above every name that is appealed to
> in this world and in the world to come.
> God placed all things under Christ's rule.
> *He appointed him to be ruler over everything for the church*
> (Ephesians 1, emphasis added).

In another robust epistle addressed primarily to Jewish-Christian congregations, the foundational prologue reads:

> He provided the way for people to be made pure from sin.
> *Then he sat down*
> *at the right hand of the King, the Majesty in heaven.*
> So he became higher than the angels.
> The name he received is more excellent than theirs
> (Hebrews 1, emphasis added).

That claim links beautifully with what Paul shared with the tiny church in Colossae:

> For [the Father] has rescued us from the dominion of darkness
> *and brought us into the kingdom of the Son he loves,*
> in whom we have redemption, the forgiveness of sins.

The Son is the image of the invisible God,
the firstborn over all creation . . .
all things have been created through him and for him.
He is before all things,
and in him all things hold together . . .
he is the beginning and the firstborn from among the dead
so that in everything he might have the supremacy
(Colossians 1, NIV, emphasis added).

It comes as no surprise that in full accord with these passages the last book of the Bible declares confidently:

The kingdom of the world has become
the kingdom of our Lord
and of his Christ.
He will rule for ever and ever
(Revelation 11, emphasis added).

Eternally, Jesus will remain seated and regaled as supreme.

Marvelous, as well, are the *personal* implications that result from his active ascendancy, such as:

God himself has given us right standing with himself.
Who then will condemn us?
No one – for Christ Jesus died for us
and was raised to life for us, and
he is sitting in the place of honor
at God's right hand, pleading for us
(Romans 8, NLT, emphasis added).

Scores of scriptural testimonies to the sovereignty of the Son are distilled nicely into this one verse in 1 Corinthians 1:8:

Yet for us there is but one God, the Father,
who is the source of all things, and *we exist* for Him;
and *one Lord, Jesus Christ,*
by whom are all things [that have been created],
and we [believers exist and have life and have been redeemed]
through Him
(AMP, emphasis added).

Behold the "Wow" of Christ Now!

This brief biblical survey provides mere preliminary peeks at the glory of the royalty of our Redeemer. One day soon his glory will be placed on full display universally. Before long his imperial resplendency, which belongs to him alone, will be revealed to all at the hour of his return, when we behold him face to face as triumphant King — which, may I remind you, every one of us *really* will experience!

Doing double duty, however, many passages related to the end times amplify a lot of who our Lord Jesus is to us *right now* — not just who he was, not just who he will be, but rather who he *is* — today.

They testify to the undiminished weightiness of Jesus' reputation and Jesus' occupation in the Kingdom. He possesses the full measure of esteem *currently* that he will maintain ten thousand years from now.

Hundreds of verses exalt the One who, without interruption since his inauguration, takes charge today of all divine activity transpiring *around* the throne as well as all divine works unleashed *from* the throne — just what you'd expect from a King who already has been permanently anointed and installed, already seated and supreme for two thousand years.

And so, it should not seem inappropriate or trivial to refer to the glory of the ascended Lord Jesus, who is vigorously taking charge with all authority in heaven and earth (Matthew 28), as "the *wow* of Christ now!"

"*Wow!*" It's a well-worn word, to be sure, but it provides a contemporary ring, a worshipful cheer that Christians may joyfully shout as we march together in Jesus' royal procession, chanting as we go:

> **Wow**! We celebrate you, Lord Jesus,
> seated and supreme before the Father *right now*!
> **Wow**! We marvel at you, Lord Jesus, sovereign in the
> salvation of your people *right now*!
> **Wow**! We bow down before you, Lord Jesus,
> King forever just as you are King *right now*!

Wow! The very thought of you reigning in our hearts and in our midst,
while at the same time occupying the throne of the universe,
makes us want to throw open our lives to you, for more of you.
We welcome you to conqueror us and fill us afresh
with the fullness of all you are today,
as willing captives in the compass of your coronation.

The "wow" of Christ now! This should be how we revel in Jesus on the annual Ascension Day and every day of the year!

Meditations on His Majesty
Base Camp or Mountaintop? The Choice We All Must Make

Then, calling the crowd to join his disciples, he said,
"If any of you wants to be my follower,
you must give up your own way,
take up your cross, and follow me.
If you try to hang on to your life, you will lose it.
But if you give up your life
for my sake and for the sake of the Good News,
you will save it
(Mark 8, NLT).

The time has come for more than a few of us to pull up stakes and tackle life's most thrilling trek.

The one with Jesus. The one that leads us into *more* of Jesus.

It's the climb that takes us from the base camp to the mountaintop.

It's the adventure meant for every true Jesus follower. It's the journey that transports us above and beyond the bivouac where we enjoy initial spiritual comforts, where too many of us would rather settle down.

It's the challenge of leaving the launch site to scale to the summit, to fully experience the magnificent vistas found in God's Son — to pursue the heart of who Jesus is, where he's headed, what he's doing, and how he gets blessed.

The truth is that every believer began treading up the mountain the moment the Father "rescued us from the dominion of darkness and brought us into the kingdom of the Son he loves" (Colossians 1, NIV). Now our mandate is simply *to keep moving* — to continue climbing up the King's highway as those forever destined to remain "seated with him in the heavenly realms in Christ Jesus" (Ephesians 2, NIV).

Here's how Paul responded to this challenge:

> I have not yet received all these things. I have not yet reached my goal. Christ Jesus took hold of me so that I could reach that goal. So *I keep pushing myself forward to reach it* . . . here is the one thing I do. I forget what is behind me. I push hard toward what is ahead of me. *I push myself forward toward the goal to win the prize.* God has appointed me to win it. *The heavenly prize is Christ Jesus himself* (Philippians 3, emphasis added).

Sustaining such spiritual ambition requires us to clarify the distinction between two terms familiar to most believers. Discerning that difference helps determine how openly and eagerly and boldly we pursue the wonders found in Christ.

One term is the ***centrality* of Christ.** The other is the ***supremacy* of Christ.**

The base camp metaphor depicts what Christians usually mean when we talk about experiencing the "centrality" of Christ. The mountaintop, on the other hand, pictures the role the "supremacy" of Christ ought to play for all of us.

Here's how I sort all of this out.

The Mountaintop of Christ's Supremacy

As observed in the opening pages of this book, *Thesaurus.com* splurges on synonyms for "supremacy." Each one is readily applicable to who the Lord Jesus is right now. In other words, when we declare him to be "supreme" we mean that today he is (here it comes!):

> dominant. . . mighty. . . magisterial. . . flawless. . . commanding. . .
> imperial. . . decisive. . . indomitable. . . superior. . . omnipotent. . .
> preemptive. . . transcendent . . . preeminent. . . paramount. . . irreducible. . .
> unimpeachable . . . unrivaled . . . unsurpassable. . . irreplaceable . . .
> thoroughly sufficient . . . totally in charge. . . master over everything. . .
> exalted above all

Put in current vernacular, "supremacy" affirms how *amazingly awesome* Christ is now!

With these adjectives in mind, consider this working definition of "supremacy" to which we'll return shortly:

The SUPREMACY of Christ expresses
his right to keep me at the center of *his* life —

who *he* is,
where *he* is headed,
what *he* is doing,
and how *he* is blessed.

Scriptures like Colossians 3:1-4 remind us that all we *are* and all that we *have* should be wrapped up in, passionate for, and focused on everything related to Christ enthroned — in other words, lived out at the *center* of our Lord Jesus Christ. "Your life is hidden with Christ in God," Paul wrote.

The full extent of the preeminence and person and purposes of King Jesus comprises our mountaintop destination.

The Base Camp of Christ's Centrality

Contrast this perspective with the other concept regularly used in Christian circles: "the *centrality* of Christ" — as when believers say, "Christ is (or should be) the center of my life."

"Centrality" may sound equivalent to — and is sometimes used interchangeably with — "supremacy" when believers talk about their relationship to the Savior. Applied at the practical day-to-day level, however, the two terms often wind up expressing two very different approaches to that relationship.

Let me clarify by adapting the wording I just used to define supremacy so as to create a definition for how the centrality of Christ is commonly viewed:

The CENTRALITY of Christ defines him
in terms of his role at the center of *my* life —
who *I* am,
where *I* am headed,
what *I* am doing,
and how *I* get blessed.

Without a doubt, Jesus should function as *no less* than the center of every believer's existence. No argument there.

However, new believers must quickly realize that when they come to Christ *they* cease to function as the focal point of their lives. Jesus assumes preeminence in every aspect of their daily walk.

When I hand him the keys to the front door of my life, he is never reticent to get personally involved in my family, my church, my job, my ministry. The moment I roll out the welcome mat, he walks right into my circumstances, my struggles, my heartaches, my fears. Once I issue him my standing invitation, he shows up to take charge of my plans, my ambitions, my dreams, my hopes.

Absolutely, as Lord of all, Jesus does have every *right* to remain at the vortex of every dimension of who I am, where I'm headed, what I'm doing, and how I get blessed.

Let's return to our metaphor. Let's compare the centrality of Christ to the routine of trekkers at a base camp who spend time organizing their gear while being mentored by their Sherpa, as they ready themselves to engage the heights of Mount Everest. In that sense, Jesus' initial ministry at the center of our lives creates a sort of "staging ground" for what lies ahead in our growing relationship with him — that is, for our climb toward the mountaintop.

But note: *The base camp is not where Jesus intends for us to remain*. From the outset he fully expects us to move out of our tents as we scale upwards with him into more — into more *of him*.

The problem arises when we would rather stay put — to settle in and keep warming ourselves around the fire singing "Kum Bah Yah" with fellow believers, opting for the comfort zone of the base camp rather than taking off on an exhilarating trek, reaching for the high places.

A Closer Look at the Two Options

Over time, those who choose to venture no further with Christ than what they've experienced of him at the base camp end up dissatisfied and disappointed, even disillusioned.

Staying behind to snuggle down with fellow campers, they miss the thrill of the breathtaking panorama awaiting all who relocate to the feet of the King sitting on his throne on high. They forfeit the wider, thicker, more exquisite fellowship with him for which reborn hearts yearn — *the joy of intimacy with God's Son in his supremacy.*

To say it another way: When we believers choose to limit the lordship of God's Son to Jesus at the center of "who *I* am, where *I'm* going, what *I'm* doing, and how *I* get blessed," inevitably we divest discipleship of its true significance. That's because, you see, our identity and our destiny are meant to be all about *him,* not about *us!*

We end up depriving ourselves of the fulfillment found only by those who tackle the heights — who press into the center of who *Christ* is, where *he's* headed, what *he's* doing, and how *he* gets blessed.

Far too many of us recast our walk with Jesus so that a constricted view of Christ's centrality becomes the *endpoint* of our quest — which means, ultimately, life becomes primarily about "me."

We conclude (though not daring to say it as blatantly as this):

Jesus came into the world for *me*.
He will always be there for *me*,
constantly available to *me*,
as a ready resource for *me*,
ensuring maximum happiness for *me*,
always ready to respond to *me*,
to protect and deliver *me*,
in order to fulfill all that concerns *me*.

Though we may openly confess a willingness to follow our Savior, deep down we intend to go only as far as we sense we *need* him — that far and no more. If we believers had the guts to get more honest with each other we would soon admit that too often our commitment to Jesus reads along this line (again, we would rarely state it this bluntly):

I'm committed to keeping Jesus at the center of my life *as long as:*
he enables me to become the person I want to be;
he helps me achieve my personal goals
in career, family, location, lifestyle, even ministry;
he empowers what I choose to do with my time
on the job, as a parent, serving church and community;
he keeps me prospering in the cradle of
good health, fruitful circumstances, and helpful relationships;
he functions as my guarantee that after this earthly
chapter is over I'll enter into the joy and peace of everlasting life.

No matter how sincere our intentions may be to prove ourselves as dutiful disciples, if we're stuck with a confining "base camp" view of the role of Jesus in our lives, our attempts to journey into unexplored grandeurs of the splendor of Jesus will sputter and stall. Increasingly, we will find ourselves content to remain housed at the base camp, settling for faint views of the lofty ranges (of the fullness of Christ), scanned from a distance.

Try to imagine this, however:

What if our Sunday morning worship times rose from congregations *already* overflowing with a growing, vibrant vision of the spectacular supremacy of God's Son today — *already* dwelling together with a mountaintop vision of his majesty? What if our hymns of hallelujahs were sung by Christians exploring and experiencing the reign of Christ on a daily basis?

Instead of looking for a blessing for ourselves at church next week, what if our Sunday morning songs and prayers and testimonies would swell from a shared, overriding passion to bless God's Son — as we magnify the Person behind his names; revel in demonstrations of his saving reign; stand in awe at the spreading of his fame among the nations; become thrilled with the fresh gains of his cross; rejoice over how his claims are being ratified in every sphere of society?

How inexpressibly tragic it is when any approach to living the Christian life is traded for a pea-sized replica of the real thing, for a peripheral portrayal of what it means to be fully alive *to* Christ and alive *in* Christ!

To be personal: How grievous it is if I become fixated on how Christ fits into and benefits what *I* want rather than being wholeheartedly surrendered to what *he* wants.

In Mark 8, Christ requires me to deny myself, pick up my cross, and follow him — to lose my life for his name and for the gospel. My entire reason for living is to be for HIM and him alone. He wants me to pour myself out for *his* sake, *his* cause, *his* mission, *his* glory, *his* kingdom. He challenges me to invest my time, talent, and treasure in proclaiming the good news that not only is God's Son redeeming everyone who trusts in him, but beyond that he's renovating the entire cosmos to bring glory to the Father.

He invites me to join him on an upward journey that leads me into more of him. He himself wants to be the direction of my affection, so I invest "my upmost for his highest" (Oswald Chambers).

Standing at Base Camp You Must Choose

What will you do? Will you choose to abandon your tent and press toward the summit?

Will you choose to focus resolutely on Jesus as the Christ, to gain a view of him that is extensive enough and captivating enough to compel you to enter fully into his ascended life and his revolutionary reign?

Will you choose to nurture a growing familiarity with the splendor of his eternal attributes — joining day by day with all of heaven in its singular enterprise of exalting and exulting in the glory of God's Son?

Will you choose the joy of discovering today what pleases him — what fulfills the desires of his heart — and then act on your growing love for him?

Will you choose to give priority to the plans and purposes on his heart, the greater ambitions of his high and holy mission — a mission that's not for your sake alone, but for the sake of spreading the message of his saving power among many, many others, including the nearly two billion souls who at this moment have never heard — not once! — that Jesus Christ is Lord of all?

In *God in the Dock*, C. S. Lewis nails the choice every Christian must make:

> What are we to make of Christ? There is no question of what we can make of Him, it is entirely a question of what He intends to make of us . . . Others say, "This is the truth about the Universe. This is the way you ought to go." But Jesus says, *"I am the Truth, and the Way, and the Life . . .* Try to retain your own life and you will be inevitably ruined. If anything, whatever is keeping you from Me, whatever it is, throw it away. If it is your eye, pull it out. If it is your hand, cut if off. Come to Me. *I am* Re-birth, *I am* Life. Eat Me, drink Me. *I am* your Food. And finally, do not be afraid, I have overcome the whole Universe." *That is the issue* (emphasis added).

Lewis appeals to every one of us to leave behind (as it were) the base camp of Christ's centrality, and to climb the mountaintop of Christ's supremacy — to witness the incredible, unbelievable, incomparable vista found only in the One seated at God's right hand.

In other words, Lewis urges believers to *choose a life lived at the center of Christ's life* — the Messiah of God who resides at the center of the throne, before whom the whole universe bows down.

Delay no longer. Hold back no more.

The mountaintop beckons. The trail ahead is clear.

Awake! Get up! Get packed! Get going!

Explore and
Experience
the
Spectacular
Supremacy of
God's Son Today

Introducing the 7 Groundbreaking Keys:
How to Explore and Experience the Spectacular Supremacy of God's Son Today

One Chapter to Prepare You for the Next Seven

I want them to have complete confidence
that they understand God's mysterious plan,
which is Christ himself.
In him lie hidden all the treasures of wisdom and knowledge
(Colossians 2, NLT, emphasis added).

Christ the Redeemer — internationally recognized as a most remarkable marvel of the modern world.

I'm referring to the seven-hundred-ton *Christ the Redeemer* statue erected on top of Corcovado Mountain, looming imperially over Rio de Janeiro, Brazil. Standing at its base, one can't help being amazed at this extraordinary sculptural achievement and awed by its overpowering image of Jesus.

You may feel the next seven chapters prove similarly overpowering as they lay out for you a wealth of towering truths concerning the vastness of Christ you may not have encountered before.

To be candid, while shaping this book I frequently found myself taken aback by what I was uncovering of the awesome marvels of the *real* Redeemer—the most phenomenal wonder the world has ever beheld — or ever will.

One term often used for this expansive focus on the Lord Jesus Christ is "Christology." What does that involve?

In one sense, Christology could be pictured as the effort of Church scholars to "sculpt" a Trinitarian-grounded testimony to God the Son in order to amaze us with who he is and what he has accomplished.

To say it another way, Christology rises from a scriptural study of Christ in at least four directions: who he is as God's Son; where he is headed in God's purposes; how he is restoring God's universe; and in what ways he exalts God's glory.

Given a contemporary context, we might define Christology as the Bible's perspective on the current reign of Christ, how right now it is impacting individual lives as well as nations and generations, and what this tells us about the person and passions and purposes of our Lord Jesus today.

This book, *Christ Is NOW!,* is all about "Christology." It emerges from over a quarter century of concentrated research, as I focused exclusively on the inexhaustible, foundational biblical doctrine of who Jesus is.

As a result, for me Christology has come down to this: exploring and experiencing multiple dimensions of Christ's spectacular supremacy by making use of seven major categories or "keys" that unlock a great many of the "treasures" hidden in him (Colossians 2).

Soon you too will become quite familiar with these seven keys as the following pages make a most riveting use of them to revolutionize *your* Christology too.

How I Landed on These Seven Groundbreaking Keys

In this chapter, therefore, my first goal is to share with you how my newly gleaned reformulation of my vision of Christ changed my life — because I'm convinced your accrual of the same fresh perspectives will transform in equal measure your *own* relationship with God's Son.

So, here's my story.

For three decades I gave myself to searching out priceless insights on the nature of Jesus' glories as *foreshadowed* and *foretold* in hundreds of Old Testament passages. In the New Testament I found that the revelations of Jesus foreshadowed and foretold in the Old Testament were not only *fulfilled* in him but also *filled full* of him. Without exaggeration, literally thousands of phrases and verses, as well as entire sections of Scripture, laid before me "*boundless* riches" revealed in the Son of God (Ephesians 3, NIV).

Simultaneously, my growing Bible-based view of the King connected with reams of additional insights taken from early church fathers, influential theologians across the centuries, renowned contemporary Christian thinkers, as well as recent volumes and videos inventoried by the Library of Congress.

To give you a taste of this feast, consider this small sampling of volumes whose very titles hint at how they enriched my understanding of (and my walk with) Jesus as Lord of all:

- **Dictionary of Early Christian Beliefs/ "Christology"** (David Bercot, Editor)
- **Christ in Song: Hymns of Immanuel From All Ages** (Philip Schaff, compiler)
- **Pauline Christology: An Exegetical-Theological Study** (Gordon D. Fee)
- **The Glory of Christ** (John Owen)
- **The Glory of Christ** (R. C. Sproul)
- **The Incomparable Christ** (John Stott)
- **Jesus: Son and Savior** (John Paul II)
- **Who Is This King of Glory: Experiencing the Fullness of Christ's Work in Our Lives** (Tony Evans)
- **Knowing Jesus Through the Old Testament** (Christopher J. H. Wright)
- **The Passion of the Lord: African American Reflections** (James Noel, Editor)
- **The Many Faces of Jesus Christ: Intercultural Christology** (Volker Kuster)
- **Christology: An Ecumenical, International and Contextual Perspective** (Veli-Matti Kärkkäinen)
- **Infinity Dwindles to Infancy: History of Catholic and Evangelical Christology** (Edward Oakes)
- **Altogether Lovely: The Glory and Excellency of Jesus Christ** (Jonathan Edwards)
- **Christ Among Other gods: A Defense of Christ in an Age of Tolerance** (Erwin W. Lutzer)
- **The Real Kosher Jesus** (Michael L. Brown)
- **ReJesus: A Wild Messiah for a Missional Church** (Michael Frost, Alan Hirsch)
- **Jesus the King: Understanding the Life and Death of the Son of God** (Tim Keller)
- **Jesus Ascended: The Meaning of Christ's Continuing Incarnation** (Gerrit Scott Dawson)
- **Seeing and Savoring Jesus Christ** (John Piper)
- **The Jesus I Never Knew** (Philip Yancey)
- **Christ: The Spiritual Sum of All Things** (Watchman Nee)
- **The King Jesus Gospel: The Original Good News Revisited** (Scot McKnight)
- **Simply Jesus: A New Vision of Who He Was, What He Did, and Why He Matters** (N. T. Wright)
- **Jesus Mean and Wild: The Unexpected Love of an Untamable God** (Mark Galli)

That's just for starters.

Each treatise (and hundreds more like them) highlighted astounding, life-changing gems about our Savior that far too many faithful followers have overlooked — as I once did — to our great loss.

In addition to all this reading, in the early 1980s I started *listening* a whole lot more when I joined Christian gatherings across the globe in all kinds of settings. What I heard supplemented my research with equally invaluable truths gained simply by paying closer attention to God's people (especially their leaders) as they shared how to think about God's Son based on their own life experiences and traditions.

In more ways than one, growing my Christology also required very *personal* endeavors. Through intimate seasons of heartwarming yet soul-humbling encounters with Jesus, orchestrated by the Holy Spirit, my vision of God's Son was greatly expanded and deepened. During private retreats and in times with fellow believers, through the Word and worship, I forged an unforgettable communion with my Lord that made my Christology grow into something profoundly alive to me and life-giving for others.

You Are the Main Reason I Wrote *Christ Is NOW!*

Throughout this entire process, however, one central concern would not let me go.

Must *all* believers, I wondered, invest years in exhaustive studies on all these various levels if they're to have any hope of finding for themselves a wider, stronger, more enriching, more intimate grasp of who Jesus is today? Does every disciple need to spend countless hours researching biblical passages and scholarly works on Christology to make sense of the magnitude of our Master?

Or instead, might it be possible for me to *distill* and *simplify* the thousands of individual insights acquired by the approaches outlined above in order to gift fellow Christians with an effective approach to unlocking the wonders of Jesus for themselves — a strategy that is less complicated and confusing, more orderly and accessible? If so, how?

Might there be a way to create a resource that helps God's people catch and keep such a wide-ranging vision of Christ's glory that it compels them to embrace and apply the blessings of Christ's spectacular supremacy to everyday life?

Finally, I was able to formulate a plan to do just that.

In the early 1990s I started cataloging my findings on thousands of 3 x 5 index cards. Each contained a specific truth or insight or Scripture or quotation regarding what makes Jesus on the throne so special. Within a few years, the tally packed out more than a dozen shoeboxes!

Next I tried organizing this trove under major headings. After much trial and error, and following extensive field-testing with all kinds of audiences, I landed on an easy-to-recall template to effectively funnel this massive survey of Christ into a manageable, workable, replicable way of describing a host of incomparable qualities found in who Jesus is today as "Ruler of the kings of the earth" (Revelation 1).

I concluded that everything I had uncovered about the glory of Jesus could be summed up in just seven overarching categories. These facets of Christ's supremacy comprise what might be described as the "seven wonders" of God's Son — wonders that reveal who he *was* and who he *will be,* but most importantly, who he *is* at this very moment.

This became my personal "take" on Christology. And what a "take" it has proven to be!

Over the years I've watched these seven fundamental outlooks encourage thousands of Christians to encounter Jesus *as if* (as I often put it) "they were meeting him again for the first time." I don't know another way to say it!

At the same time, I was encouraged to watch how many of these awakened believers started talking a whole lot more with one another about what they were discovering about their Savior. This renewed vision of Christ was spreading!

On top of that, these seven dimensions have furnished Christian leaders with effective teaching tools with which to teach their people about the "whole Christ" and to lead their people to offer themselves more fully to the lordship of Christ, moving them into a God-given awakening to the fullness of Christ.

And now, with this book — especially through what is laid out in the next seven chapters — I get to share many of these rich discoveries with you also! I can hardly wait!

Therefore, I suggest:

Consider this book to be a major *re-introduction* to God's Son, designed to ignite in every reader a new level of decisive devotion toward him.

You Can Be Sure These Keys Are Thoroughly Sufficient

Throughout the years of research I kept crisscrossing the Body of Christ to pass along my new findings, interacting with a variety of audiences. This included open forums with diverse groups during presentations of *The Christ Institutes (TCI)* — a live, 48-hour interactive seminar built around the same seven-fold vision. Responses from the attendees of this multimedia outreach provided me added substantive feedback that sharpened my thinking even more. (Today, *TCI* has evolved into *The Christ Institutes Video Series,* available at *www.ChristNow.com* for free download).

Everywhere I went — including gatherings replete with theological academicians—I openly invited participants to make me aware of any vital characteristics of the person of Christ not captured by one or more of these seven categories.

I have reassuring news to report! To date, no one — *not one individual* — has approached me to suggest these seven dimensions are inadequate for allowing believers to take deep dives into the fullness of God's Son!

Therefore, even though the marvelous realities of the second person of the Trinity remain unfathomable and unsearchable, just as his love for us "surpasses knowledge" (Ephesians 3, NIV), still let me say again:

Consider this book to be a major *re-introduction* to God's Son, designed to ignite in every reader a new level of decisive devotion toward him.

Here Are the 7 Keys, Ready for Your Immediate Use

As a result of my pursuits, I now offer you this most intriguing means for acquiring superb vistas on the wonders of Jesus — insights as robust today as they will be ten thousand years from now. After all, "Jesus Christ is the same yesterday and *today* and forever" (Hebrews 13, emphasis added). Therefore, each key unlocks more of who Jesus is *right now!*

This seven-fold Christology, when applied by the power of the Spirit, can equip any believer to enter into a life purpose and life direction and lifestyle that are *Christ-driven* as never before — which is why I sometimes refer to it as a "*consequential* Christology."

Perhaps surprisingly, this approach to such a crucial and inexhaustible topic is based on seven very simple, ordinary words — tiny prepositions spoken repeatedly in everyday conversations by all of us ever since we were little children.

To be sure, ten million times ten million words could never begin to describe the innumerable glories of our mighty Savior. However, these seven prepositions give Christians a new template to start exploring and experiencing in new ways the *essentials* of who the Lord Jesus is in the majesty of his supremacy.

These are the seven prepositions: Who Christ is **TO** us, **FOR** us, **OVER** us, **BEFORE** us, **WITHIN** us, **THROUGH** us, and **UPON** us.

Think of them as seven sacred keys shaped to open seven sacred doors through which anyone may enter to see, seek, savor, and then share with others more of the truth that *is* Christ.

Let me risk a bold assertion: There is nothing to know about who our Lord Jesus is today beyond what stretches before us on the other side of these seven portals as we work with each of the seven categories. I assert that to explore and experience a fuller measure of who Christ is we need only to discover more of:

who Christ is TO us today
as we take stock of his
divinity, character, names, destiny, supremacy

who Christ is FOR us today
as we investigate his
incarnation, crucifixion, resurrection, and ascension — combined

who Christ is OVER us today
as we unpack his
reign over creation, history, rulers, nations, powers, the Church

who Christ is BEFORE us today
as we follow him
into the future, into the heavens, into the promises, into the world

who Christ is WITHIN us today
as we welcome him
to inhabit his people and rule among us in his fullness

who Christ is THROUGH us today
as we invite him
to open up opportunities to use us in advancing his global cause

who Christ is UPON us today
as we celebrate
his victories promised at the consummation of all things
as well as approximations of that consummation he provides us today

Please, never let the simplicity of this basic outline deceive you. Learning to know Jesus so much better really can be this *profoundly simple.*

Yet at the same time, never be casual about it. Everything you learn about him over the next seven chapters will always be *simply profound!*

Behold then! — the seven-fold exaltation of God's dear Son, designed to foster in you and me fresh fervency for his name.

Behold then! — the seven core characteristics of our King for believers like you and me to ponder and praise and propagate widely.

Behold, then! — the seven-part message about the magnificence of who Christ is today, for the Church to *reclaim* and then *proclaim* to our generation.

A Prayer for the Adventure Ahead

Exploring and experiencing more of the glories of Christ Jesus — it's an adventure unlike any you've taken before!

Over and over in the coming pages you'll be challenged to reevaluate how you view and value your relationship to God's Son. Refuse to turn back. Keep pressing on. With the turn of every page embrace the thrill of growing to know our Savior more fully than ever!

With such prospects in view we close this chapter with a prayer about what's ahead, adapted from the one that closes Ephesians 1. **Pray with me now:**

Father, our destiny rests exclusively in your dear Son and all he is. So, because you are the God and Father of our Lord Jesus Christ, we ask you to grant us through the Holy Spirit a greater measure of supernatural revelation so that we may know your Son more clearly, more thoroughly, and more intimately.

Father, as we *explore* Christ in these next seven chapters, open the eyes of our hearts to a much larger view of him. Especially, give us fresh insight into Jesus' incomparably mighty power that is at work in all who trust in him — that very same power that you exerted when you raised your Son from the dead and seated him at your right hand in the heavenly realms. Dazzle us with how and why his reign today is far above all rule and authority, power and dominion, and every name that is invoked, not only in the present age but also in the one to come.

O dear Father, as a result of these studies we also want to *experience* Christ more deeply. In the most personal sense, may we encounter more of his greatness and goodness and glory — as you fill us with more of the life of the One who at this very moment is filling the entire universe with his presence, his passion, his kingdom activity, and his saving power.

AMEN!

Recommendation to the reader: Take a minute to read back through the section titled "You Absolutely Must Read This First!" found at the opening of this book. Note its practical suggestions on how to get the most out of the unusual layout, creative graphics, and application sections that shape the next seven chapters.

Exploring and Experiencing

Who Christ Is TO Us Today

A roving art show, "Rembrandt and the Face of Jesus," toured the country beginning at the Philadelphia Museum of Art. Critiquing it in *TIME* magazine, Richard Lacayo discussed how the 17th-century artist changed our image of Christ from remote divinity to man on the street. He writes: "You see the great Dutch painter effectively inventing Christ as we tend to picture him now."

Lacayo wondered what caused Rembrandt to shift from turbulent portraits of Jesus in his earlier years, "full of sharp light and emphatic gestures," to more contemplative, subdued portrayals. Was it the loss of three of his four children in infancy and then his wife at age thirty? Was it his growing personal financial crisis? Did these experiences send him on a search for a more gentle, quiet, reflective, intimate Jesus — one who could console him?

So, who is Christ to *you*? How do you see him? How would you paint him?

How would you describe him if you tried to introduce him to someone who knew very little about him? What unique experiences and challenges in your life — even personal setbacks as it was with Rembrandt — have caused you to envision him the way you do?

Who *is* this person to you — the One upon whom your eternal hope is based?

Who is Jesus to you when compared to and contrasted with other gods worshipped among the nations? For instance, how would your vision of him stack up to how multitudes view the Hindu deity Shiva?

Not far from Mumbai, gateway city to India, are the great underground temples dedicated to Shiva, the god of cosmic forces, both creative and destructive, who is sometimes referred to as "The Grand Master." This mirrors the deity proclaimed in the National Anthem of India, which says in part:

> Glory to thee, Master of the thoughts of all men,
> O Thou who directs the destiny of India.
>
> Thy name awakens the hearts of men. Men pray to receive
> Thy benediction and sing Thy praises.
>
> The salvation of all men rests in Thy hand,
> O Thou who directs the destiny of India.

I wonder: How many of us have such a vision of the spectacular supremacy of God's Son that we could declare praises to him with far greater conviction?

If you were asked to write an anthem for Jesus, what kind would you compose? Is he more awesome to you, dearer to you, more immediate and real to you — much more spectacular to you — than the gods of India are to their passionate devotees?

In this chapter, we want to encounter God's Son more fully by exploring a treasure trove of biblical nuggets (both simple and profound) that describe the heights and depths of who Christ is *to* us, today, as the one and only true *"Grand Master."*

Think of this chapter as a "personality profile" of God's Son. Very personal! It is an initial look at what we know (infinitesimal as it may be compared to how much there is to know) about the nature and character of the One enthroned at God's right hand — the One who is the same yesterday, today, and forever (Hebrews 13:8).

The following seven "profiles" focus exclusively on the *personhood* of Jesus the Christ. They will help enlarge and enrich the ways we see all of who Christ is TO us today:

> By the Supremacy of His Deity
>
> By His Intimacy With the Trinity
>
> As the Perfection of Revelation
>
> As the Picture of Scripture
>
> By the Claims of His Names
>
> As Our Identity and Destiny
>
> As the Father's Passion and Ours

Who Christ Is TO Us Today:
By the Supremacy of His Deity

Three of the five Latin phrases that formed a motto for the 16th-century Protestant Reformation are "Sola Fide" (Faith Alone), "Sola Scriptura" (Scripture Alone), and the most important of all, "Solus Christus" (Christ Alone).

What does it mean to proclaim Christ alone? It means that everything he has done and everything he offers is entirely sufficient for our salvation. Why? Above all and first of all, it is because of who he is *to* us as God.

Below are some "Snapshots and Starter Thoughts" (see "You Absolutely Must Read This First!" for an explanation) that can help all of us enlarge our thinking about the deity of Christ so that we live — and pray — with a growing assurance of "Solus Christus!" For now, let's look at four facets of this truth.

 Snapshots and Starter Thoughts

To bow before Christ is to bow before God.

Jesus is Israel's Yahweh in action among us.

Being divine by nature, Jesus must be supreme.

Jesus' intrinsic worth as God is invested in bringing us life.

To Bow Before Christ Is to Bow Before God

- **We have no other choice but to kneel before him.**

  God never said to any of the angels, "You are my Son. Today I have become your Father." Or, "I will be his Father. And he will be my Son." God's first and only Son is over all things. When God brings him into the world, he says, "Let all of God's angels worship him" . . . But here is what he says about the Son. "You are God. Your throne will last for ever and ever. Your kingdom will be ruled by justice . . . your God has placed you above your companions. He has filled you with joy by pouring the sacred oil on your head" (Hebrews 1).

- **The supremacy of Christ is inherent to the *person* of Christ.** That's because he is *God*, up close and personal.

- **There never was a time when he was not God.** In Christ we see God manifested — fully, perfectly, essentially.

- **"In the beginning, the Word was already there.** The Word was with God, and the Word was God" (John 1).

- **"He was with God in the beginning . . . "**

  The Word became a human being. He made his home with us. We have seen his glory. It is the glory of the One and Only, who came from the Father . . . No one has ever seen God. But the One and Only is God and is at the Father's side. *The one at the Father's side has shown us what God is like* (John 1, emphasis added).

- **Christ is not defined by anything outside of himself.** He was "from the beginning." He never came into being. He simply is, always was, and always will be.

- **The Son was not only "with God," but more literally he was "toward God"** (the phrase in the Greek of John 1). In other words, from eternity he shared in an intimate, face-to-face relationship with God — which would be impossible unless he truly is God.

- **The Nicene Creed puts it this way:** "Christ is One Lord, only begotten Son of God; begotten of the Father before all worlds; God of God, Light of Light, very God of very God."

- **"For in Christ lives *all the fullness of God in a human body.*"**

  So you also are complete through your union with Christ, who is the head over every ruler and authority (Colossians 2, NLT, emphasis added).

- **Just as we are *human* by nature, Jesus is *divine* by nature.** However, unlike all of us who have *become* God's children by our union with his Son, Jesus was God's infinite "child" *naturally*.

    Who has gone up to heaven and come down? . . . Who has set in place all the boundaries of the earth? What is his name? What is his son's name? Surely you know! (Proverbs 30).

- **Jesus is utterly distinct from us; we are finite and mortal.** We exist as the *created works* of God. Instead, about Jesus we read:

    No one has seen God at any time; the only begotten God, *who is in the bosom of the Father*, He has explained *Him* (John 1, NASB, emphasis added).

- **Jesus is like "the ray of the sun."**

    For as this Son is undivided and inseparable from the Father, so is he to be reckoned as being in the Father. Suppose the sun were to say, 'I am the sun and there is no other besides me, except my ray.' Would you not have remarked how useless such a statement was, as if the ray were not itself reckoned in the sun? (Tertullian, Church father).

- **Even his enemies caught the implications of his claim.**

    For this reason they tried all the more to kill him; not only was he breaking the Sabbath, but he was even calling God his own Father, making himself equal with God (John 5, NIV).

- **Yes, to bow before Christ is to bow before God — otherwise, Jesus would have been guilty of promoting gross idolatry by accepting worship as God.** It would have constituted cosmic treason against God and his kingdom. Recall the exchanges between Jesus and his disciples during his days of earthly ministry, as well as after the resurrection. For example:

    Then those in the boat worshiped Jesus. They said, "You really are the Son of God!" (Matthew 14:33).

    "Don't be faithless any longer. Believe!" "My Lord and my God!" Thomas exclaimed. Then Jesus told him, "You believe because you have seen me. Blessed are those who believe without seeing me" (John 20, NLT).

- **Now, *finding* God holds no mystery.** For those who want to find God and bow before him, the pathway shines clearly: Simply come to *Jesus* and bow before *him*.

- **Now, *missing* God holds no mystery.** Jesus is so fully God that to walk away from him is to walk away from God, with no other god to turn to.

- **Being God and being Savior go together.** To all for whom Jesus has become their Savior, it logically follows that he also has become their God. In the same way, to all for whom Jesus has become the living God, he encompasses all the Savior they will ever need.

- **We worship Jesus as our God and Savior as we wait for the rest of the world to see what we see.**

  > . . . we look forward with hope to that wonderful day when the glory of our great God and Savior, Jesus Christ, will be revealed. He gave his life to free us from every kind of sin, to cleanse us, and to make us his very own people, totally committed to doing good deeds (Titus 2, NLT).

pause | think | pray

Jesus Is Israel's Yahweh in Action Among Us

- **Through Jesus, Israel's Yahweh speaks in person — not merely through a person or about a person, but *as* a person.** In the Old Testament God is called *Yahweh* (Jehovah) nearly 7000 times. In the New Testament the name most often used of our Redeemer is *Jesus* — about 1000 times. Jesus means "Yahweh saves."

- **It was foretold that Yahweh would come to us in someone like Jesus:**

  > A messenger is calling out, "In the desert prepare the way for the Lord . . . Then the glory of the Lord will appear. And everyone will see it together" . . . Shout the message loudly. Shout it out loud. Don't be afraid. Say to the towns of Judah, "Your God is coming!" The Lord and

King is coming with power . . . He takes care of his flock like a shepherd. He gathers the lambs in his arms (Isaiah 40).

- **Jesus is Yahweh coming to us, reaching across the gulf that separates us from him — seeking us, and summoning us, and saving us.** In Jesus, the God of creation and history and nations — the God of Abraham, Isaac and Jacob — can be seen speaking and acting, saving and healing, loving and reigning, judging and triumphing.

- **Christ said of himself, "He who has seen me has seen the Father"** (John 5). The Father he was speaking of is the one true God proclaimed by Old Testament saints — the God worshiped, prayed to, loved, and obeyed from ancient times. Jesus claimed — and then displayed — the full complement of divine attributes, functions, authority, power, and rights previously reserved by the Old Testament for Yahweh alone.

- **New Testament writers intentionally applied to Jesus the same rights and responsibilities reserved in the Old Testament for Yahweh alone.** They exalted him just like the Old Testament magnified Yahweh.

- **In describing Jesus' person, character, role, and activities, the apostles drew heavily on Old Testament language, originally applied by Scripture exclusively to the one true God.** Boldly, the New Testament writers clothe Jesus with names and claims and honor and adoration that the Old Testament writers originally attributed to the Lord God Jehovah alone. The only conclusion left with their hearers and readers is that Jesus himself must be the everlasting God.

- **In Jesus, Yahweh's long-anticipated kingship takes center stage for the nations.**

    God, give the king the ability to judge fairly. He is your royal son . . . May the king stand up for those who are hurting . . . May his kingdom reach from the Euphrates River to the ends of the earth . . . May all kings bow down to him. May all nations serve him . . . May the king's name be remembered forever. May his fame last as long as the sun shines. Then all nations will be blessed because of him (Psalm 72).

- **Through Jesus, Israel's God now reigns over the world more invasively and personally than ever before.** We see this testimony to God's Son unfold immediately on the Day of Pentecost. Peter and the apostles proclaimed Jesus as Lord and Messiah, ruling at God's right hand, sovereign over all, saying:

> Jesus has been given a place of honor at the right hand of God . . . David did not go up to heaven. But he said, "The Lord said to my Lord, Sit at my right hand. I will put your enemies under your control." So be sure of this, all you people of Israel. You nailed Jesus to the cross. But God has made him both Lord and Christ (Acts 2).

- **Now exalted, Jesus totally displays the glory of Yahweh's name and reign.**

> In the Old Testament God's revelation of his name 'Yahweh' lies at the very center of Israel's existence. They are to be a people who bear and call upon his name. Israel was not to misuse or profane Yahweh's name. The appropriation of the Greek form of the Divine Name (was) bestowed on Christ at his exaltation. So what was formerly done in/by the name of Yahweh is now for Paul done through Christ the Lord (Gordon Fee).

- **The Son embodies the apex of Yahweh's redemptive mission.**

> Going through a long line of prophets, God has been addressing our ancestors in different ways for centuries. Recently he spoke to us directly through his Son. By his Son, God created the world in the beginning, and it will all belong to the Son at the end (Hebrews 1, MSG).

- **The Son assumes for himself Yahweh's throne and kingdom.**

> But he says to the Son, "You're God, and on the throne for good; your rule makes everything right . . . That is why God, your God, poured fragrant oil on your head, marking you out as king, far above your dear companions." And again to the Son, "You, Master, started it all, laid earth's foundations . . . You'll fold them up like a worn-out cloak, and lay them away on the shelf. But you'll stay the same . . . you'll never wear out." And did he ever say anything like this to an angel? "Sit alongside me here on my throne until I make your enemies a stool for your feet" (Hebrews 1, MSG).

Selah

pause | think | pray

Being Divine by Nature, Jesus Must Be Supreme

- **We must conclude, therefore, that it is the *nature* of Christ to be supreme in everything.** This lofty position precedes what he has done for us or is doing for us. It is inherent in his deity — supreme is who he *is*. His deity ratifies his majesty. The validation of his *preeminence* rises from the displays of his *personhood* as the living Son of God.

- **In other words, his *right* to supremacy draws on all his *attributes* as God.** Because he is God, Christ is *inherently* great and above all, higher than rulers of nations, exalted above every created thing, both visible and invisible.

  > For [the Father] has rescued us from the dominion of darkness and brought us into the kingdom of the Son he loves . . . The Son is the image of the invisible God, the firstborn over all creation . . . he is the beginning and the firstborn from among the dead, so that in everything he might have the supremacy. For God was pleased to have all his fullness dwell in him . . . (Colossians 1, NIV).

- **The supremacy of his deity will prevail forever.** When God's full glory is finally revealed at the Consummation of all things — when every tongue confesses that Jesus is Lord (Philippians 2) — we will discover, to his everlasting praise, that the entire time all the wonder and magnificence of the Godhead dwells in Jesus fully (Colossians 2).

- **Because Jesus is *supreme*, sometimes he may seem *petrifying*.** This is how Paul experienced him as he dropped to the dust on the road to Damascus, trembling and pleading:

  > Who are You, Lord? . . . Lord, what do You want me to do? (Acts 9, NKJV).

  This is what John discovered about him when Jesus appeared to him on Patmos. He writes:

  > When I saw Him I fell at His feet like a dead man (Revelation 1, NASB).

- **But, because Jesus also is *Immanuel* (God *with* us) our relationship with God is secure and settled for all eternity — as long as we remain sheltered under Jesus' redeeming reign.** To Paul, shortly after his Damascus shaking, Jesus sent through Ananias gracious words of hope and purpose that changed the direction of his life for the best. To John, Jesus reached out his hand and touched him, reassuring him to "Fear not," then gave him a mission of hope for churches in Asia Minor. As C. S. Lewis writes of Aslan the Lion, the Christ figure in his Narnia series: "'Course he isn't safe. But he's good.'"

- **Only One who is wholly divine could fulfill the Old Testament's expectations of Yahweh's ultimate King, such as those in Psalm 21:**

> Lord, the king is filled with joy because you are strong. How great is his joy because you help him win his battles! You have given him what his heart wished for . . . You placed a crown of pure gold on his head. He asked you for life, and you gave it to him. You promised him days that would never end . . . You have honored him with glory and majesty. You have given him blessings that will never end . . . You, the king, will capture all your enemies. Your right hand will take hold of them. When you appear for battle, you will burn them up like they were in a flaming furnace. . . Lord, may you be honored because you are strong. We will sing and praise your might.

- **So, we submit to Yahweh's royal Son, the one exclusively anointed King of the universe.**

> For the Lord declares, "I have placed my chosen king on the throne in Jerusalem, on my holy mountain." The king proclaims the LORD's decree. "The LORD said to me, 'You are my son. Today I have become your Father. Only ask, and I will give you the nations as your inheritance, the whole earth as your possession. You will break them with an iron rod and smash them like clay pots.'" . . . *Submit to God's royal son* . . . what joy for all who take refuge in him! (Psalm 2, NLT, emphasis added).

Selah

pause | think | pray

Jesus' Intrinsic Worth as God Is Invested in Bringing Us Life

- **Jesus gives us life because he gives us God. And he gives us God because he is God.**

> The Father raises the dead and gives them life. In the same way, the
> Son gives life to anyone he wants to (John 5).

- **As can be true only of the Creator, Christ has life within himself.**
  Therefore, he is the source of life for the entire creation. John summarizes:

  > He was with God in the beginning. All things were made through him.
  > Nothing that has been made was made without him. Life was in him,
  > and that life was the light for all people (John 1).

- **Because he is God, the full guarantee of *our* life is found in him alone.**
  He declared:

  > Do not be afraid. I am the First and the Last. I am the Living One. I was
  > dead. But look! I am alive for ever and ever! And I hold the keys to
  > Death and Hell (Revelation 1).

- **He is not only the source of *created* life, but also the display of
  resurrected life** — "the firstborn from among the dead" (Colossians 1). In
  fact, he so fully embodies "the Resurrection and the Life" that those who
  trust in him will never die (John 11).

- **In Christ, God personally and visibly assumes a singular role in the
  grand, life-giving drama of redemption.** He steps onto the stage to
  carry its plot to culmination, *doing so totally by himself.* Other actors on
  the stage — we sinners — must step back to watch and wait for his
  gracious initiative on our behalf; we must witness and wonder about
  what he suffers and how he triumphs; then, we must welcome and
  worship all he continues to accomplish among his people.

- **Because of Jesus' intrinsic worth as the living God, he saves
  completely those who come to him.** He is the only one throughout all
  the ages to claim sufficient capacity in himself to pay the debt of the sin
  of the world. In Christ's inherent value as God are found inexhaustible
  resources — unsearchable riches (Ephesians 3) — sufficient for our
  salvation and that of people from every tribe and nation, from the
  beginning to the end of time.

- **Jesus will keep on giving us life from the center of God's throne
  forever.**

  > They have washed their robes and made them white in the blood of
  > the Lamb. So they are in front of the throne of God. They serve him
  > day and night in his temple. The one who sits on the throne will be

with them to keep them safe . . . The Lamb, who is at the center of the area around the throne, will be their shepherd. He will lead them to springs of living water. And God will wipe away every tear from their eyes (Revelation 7).

- **Jesus is worth more than all of his redeemed ones *put together.*** Having invested the infinite wealth of his very being in securing new life for us, he deserves everlasting, ever-increasing praise from those who treasure him as the Father's "unspeakable gift" to us (2 Corinthians 9).

Selah

pause | think | pray

The Wrap

C. S. Lewis famously observed in *Mere Christianity*:

> A man who was merely a man and said the sort of things Jesus said would not be a great moral teacher. He would either be a lunatic — on a level with the man who says he is a poached egg — or else he would be the devil of hell. *You must make your choice.* Either this man was, and is, the Son of God, or else a madman or something worse. You can shut him up for a fool, you can spit at him and kill him as a demon, or you can fall at his feet and call him Lord and God.

For those of us who are ready to fall down and worship him as Lord and God, it's time to seek and gain a fuller appreciation of the "Christ-like-ness" of God and the "God-like-ness" of Christ. A strong biblical *theology* (the study of God in Scripture) automatically requires us to pursue a strong biblical *Christology* (a study of what Scripture teaches about the person of God's Son). As popular British theologian N. T. Wright puts it: "I believe the closer we get to the original Jesus the closer we are to recognizing the face of the living God."

In all of this, here's the best news: Because of Christ's divinity, there is nothing God has for us that lies *beyond* who his Son is! Because of who he is TO us (as we're exploring in this chapter), he is also (as we will discover in upcoming chapters) all we need him to be FOR us, OVER us, BEFORE us, WITHIN us, THROUGH us, and UPON us.

But we've only started the adventure of this chapter. There's much more to explore of who Jesus is **to** us. Next we look at his intimacy with the Trinity.

Who Christ Is TO Us Today:
By His Intimacy With the Trinity

The trinitarian dimensions of Jesus' glory can never be emphasized too much. Only by the Father's purpose and the Spirit's power is the Son positioned to bless us as Lord of all.

Consider what the angel showed John in Revelation 5. There we behold a picture of the Trinity at the apex of redemption's plan. Before us, the throne of the Father is set at the core of the universe, surrounded by the worshipping hosts of heaven. However, standing at the very center of that throne we notice a conquering lion, resembling a Lamb once slain, but now victorious. The Lamb inherits the universe as he opens the scrolls to unleash his final victories among the nations. Toward him all the redeemed direct their praise, as they sing:

> You are worthy to take the scroll and break open its seals.
> You are worthy because you were put to death.
> With your blood you bought people for God.
>
> They come from every tribe, language, people and nation . . .
> The Lamb, who was put to death, is worthy!
> He is worthy to receive power and wealth and wisdom and strength!

He is worthy to receive honor and glory and praise! . . .
May praise and honor for ever and ever be given
to the One who sits on the throne and to the Lamb!

Give them glory and power for ever and ever!

But here's what most people miss: *How* is anyone able to actually view this scene in the first place? Where does the lighting come from that allows us to see so clearly the Father's throne with the Lamb seated on it? Answer: The light source comes from seven candlesticks around the throne, which represent, John is told, "the sevenfold Spirit of God that is sent out into every part of the earth" (compare Rev. 4:5 with Rev 5:6, NIV).

Christ's supremacy is confirmed by the Trinity. The Father exalts the Son on his own throne, to reign as the everlasting focus of attention for heaven and earth. Simultaneously, the Spirit makes sure everyone is able to witness what's happening in the throne room — able to see and celebrate the Son the way the Father desires, able to watch the Son as he brings everything to its consummation. Perfect unity. Perfect synergy. Perfect symphony. Everything is focused on the perfect majesty of the Son of God. Let's explore five key biblical teachings on this profound truth about Jesus is *to* us.

Snapshots and Starter Thoughts

Jesus and the Trinity always will remain a mystery.

Jesus lives forever in a "Circle of Love."

We know Christ better by his intimacy with the Trinity.

The ministry of Christ is a trinitarian project.

Jesus brings us into the life of the Trinity.

Jesus and the Trinity Always Will Remain a Mystery

- **"The core of our very faith is the mystery of the Trinity"**
  (Saint Ambrose).

  > You have been chosen in keeping with what God the Father had planned. That happened through the Spirit's work to make you pure and holy. God chose you so that you might obey Jesus Christ. God wanted you to be in a covenant relationship with him. He established this relationship by the blood of Christ (1 Peter 1).

  > May the grace shown by the Lord Jesus Christ be with you all. May the love that God has given us be with you. And may the sharing of life brought about by the Holy Spirit be with you all (2 Corinthians 13).

- **This mystery is beyond our grasp.**

  > God formulated as Trinity confronts us with a largeness, an immensity, a depth that we cannot manage or control or reduce to dealing with on our terms (Eugene Peterson).

- **However, we know that at the heart of this mystery is *relationship*.** The revealed nature of the biblical God (Yahweh) is *triune,* which means that personality, community, and mutual self-giving energizes the pulse beat of eternity.

- **The Son shares everything with the Father and the Spirit.** They hold in common the same will, same desires, same purposes, same love — as well as the same divine essence.

- **The Son is unequivocally at home in the Godhead.** His place is secured not only by his sharing the *nature* of God but also by his sharing in a *relationship* among the "Three-in-One" — as they draw life from one another and give it back to one another.

- **The Father, Son, and Holy Spirit are inseparable, and they operate inseparably.** The church fathers called this dynamic relationship the "divine dance" of the Trinity.

- **Christ is described as coming "from the bosom of the Father"** (John 1, NASB). Before his incarnation, the Son was always the great delight and unbounded joy of the Father.

- **One might say that the Son has always been with the Father in the same way our thoughts are always with us.** Intimate. Inseparable. Existing at the same time and in the same realm.

- **The Son was the "only begotten" of the Father's love before anything existed.** He is the Son of the Father in respect to his nature, which he has shared eternally, unceasingly and coequally with the Father. Recall how Jesus prayed in John 17:

  > So now, Father, give glory to me in heaven where your throne is. Give me the glory I had with you before the world began.

- **There is the Father and there is the Son.** Both identities consist of more than mere metaphors or titles. These two names disclose an inseparable, eternal fellowship within the Godhead — a relationship pictured by, but more intimate than, what is experienced by any earthly fathers and sons.

- **However, the Father did not precede his Son as earthly parents precede their offspring.** The Son was never "brought into existence" from a state of nonexistence. The Father/Son relationship in the Godhead simply has been "there" forever — without beginning, without end.

pause | think | pray

Jesus Lives Forever in the "Circle of Love"

- **For all eternity, love has reigned supreme.** Before anything was made — before there were any *humans* to forgive or restore or reconcile or embrace — still love existed. The Father loved his Son and the Son loved his Father.

- **This mutual loving defines the core of God's nature — "God is love" (1 John 4).** This love is the Son's very breath, and always has been.

- **The Father didn't start loving Jesus only after he came among us in time and space and history.** To the contrary, there never was a moment when love within the Godhead did not exist.

Love never fails [never fades out or becomes obsolete or comes to an end]. (1 Corinthians 13, Amplified Bible).

- **Within the Trinity, love is dynamic, not static; it is relational, not functional.** Even now, the Father and Son never stop showing love to one another. We might say it this way: *The Father* gives everything to the Son; *the Son* offers back all that he has to glorify the Father. The love of each is unleashed, exchanged, and sustained by *the Holy Spirit* who serves them both.

- **Sharing such a life of love means the triune God has remained fully satisfied in his own Being, utterly fulfilled, before and apart from anything he created.** The triune God has never acted out of need. He has acted out of the fullness of perfect love among the Three. That's *how* "God so loved the world" (John 3). Christ brings to us the fullness of triune love — undiluted and unconditional — in bodily form (Colossians 2).

- **The triune nature of God opens up stunning insights into Christ's great love for the world.** Considering the eternal intimacy of the Trinity, we must stand in awe at the unfathomable love Jesus showed us when he left the delights of that "Forever Fellowship" to come into the midst of a world occupied by rebels with hearts hardened against God.

- **Whoever loved us the way Jesus loved us?** Whoever gave up as much as he did when he traded in that unbroken "Circle of Love" to deliver, in God's love, the hope of salvation for his enemies?

  You are familiar with the generosity of our Master, Jesus Christ. Rich as he was, he gave it all away for us — in one stroke he became poor and we became rich (2 Corinthians 8, MSG).

Selah

pause | think | pray

We Grow to Know Christ Better by His Intimacy With the Trinity

- **Seeing the depths of Jesus'** *intimacy* **with the Trinity helps us know him better.** His whole being ultimately is defined by his relationship to his Father.

  > I and the Father are one (John 10).

- **There were predictions in Scripture of Jesus' intimacy with the Trinity, such as:**

  > The Spirit of the LORD will rest on him — the Spirit of wisdom and of understanding, the Spirit of counsel and of might . . . with righteousness he will judge the needy, with justice he will give decisions for the poor of the earth . . . for the earth will be full of the knowledge of the LORD as the waters cover the sea. In that day the Root of Jesse will stand as a banner for the peoples; the nations will rally to him . . . (Isaiah 11, NIV).

  But now he is here. Now we behold in Jesus the richness of Isaiah's words.

- **Christ's communion with the Father was and is the true core of his personality.** Without understanding that, we cannot begin to understand him for all he truly is. Jesus said:

  > My Father has given all things to me. The Father is the only one who knows the Son. And the only ones who know the Father are the Son and those to whom the Son chooses to make him known (Matthew 11).

  Again, Jesus said:

  > Anyone who welcomes me welcomes the one who sent me (Matthew 10).

- **The Trinity works** *together* **to reveal more of Christ's glory to us**. When Peter exclaimed, "You are the Christ, the Son of the living God," Jesus informed him that flesh and blood could not reveal to his disciples (or to us) the true nature of his person and role as God's Messiah, but only the Father in heaven could (Matthew 16, NASB). He explained further how this works in John 16:

  > But when He, the Spirit of truth, comes, He will guide you into all the truth; for He will not speak on His own initiative, but whatever He

hears, He will speak; and He will disclose to you what is to come. He will glorify Me, for He will take of Mine and will disclose it to you. All things that the Father has are Mine; therefore I said that He takes of Mine and will disclose it to you (NASB).

- **At the same time, the Trinity is gradually revealed through the life and ministry of Jesus.** He is the one who introduces us to the mystery of the Godhead. This revelation continues to unfold throughout New Testament teachings about Jesus and his relationship to the Father and the Spirit. In the epistles, the apostles explore God's tripersonal nature, allowing us to gain a radical but exquisite vision of God through the Son of God.

- **This is what makes Jesus so uniquely special.** His "specialness" is not related only to his intimacy and ministry *among us* (as wonderful as that is), but far more, it rises from his intimacy and ministry *within the Trinity*.

- **You can't *see* the Father without the Son.**

  No one has ever seen God, but the one and only Son, who is himself God and is in closest relationship with the Father, has made him known (John 1, NIV).

  Jesus speaks *about* God the Father, doing so authoritatively as God the Son.

- **You can't *know* the Father without the Son.**

  This life has appeared. We have seen him. We give witness about him. And we announce to you this same eternal life. He was already with the Father. He has appeared to us. We announce to you what we have seen and heard. We do it so you can share life together with us. And we share life with the Father and with his Son, Jesus Christ (1 John 1).

- **You can't *have* the Father without the Son.**

  Who is the liar? It is anyone who says that Jesus is not the Christ. The person who says this is the great enemy of Christ. They say no to the Father and the Son. The person who says no to the Son doesn't belong to the Father. But anyone who says yes to the Son belongs to the Father also (1 John 2).

Selah

pause | think | pray

The Saving Mission of Christ
Is a Trinitarian Project

- **One might say the Godhead works as a "team" to further the mission of the Son:**

  > By this [Matthew 28:18-20], Jesus showed that whoever omits any of these three, fails in glorifying God perfectly. For it is through this Trinity that the Father is glorified. For the Father willed, the Son did, and the Spirit manifested (Hippolytus, Church father).

- **Wherever Jesus' reign breaks through, the whole Trinity is on display.** Nothing about Christ robs the Father or the Spirit of equal praise; he only *increases* it. His ministry is from the Father and to the Father, but all of it is by the Spirit.

- **The triune God accomplishes our salvation together, but all of it depends on the blood of Christ.** We have been:

  > . . . chosen according to the foreknowledge of God the Father, through the sanctifying work of the Spirit, to be obedient to Jesus Christ and sprinkled with his blood (1 Peter 1, NIV).

- **Jesus collaborates within the Godhead to bring Heaven's blessings upon us.**

  > Our Lord Jesus Christ and God our Father loved us. By his grace God gave us comfort that will last forever. The hope he gave us is good. May our Lord Jesus Christ and God our Father comfort your hearts. May they make you strong in every good thing you do and say (2 Thessalonians 2).

- **Every saving promise of Scripture is by nature trinitarian: designed by the Father, quickened by the Spirit, focused on the Son**. The Father is the *source* of all our hope, the Son is the *theme* of all our hope, and the Spirit is the *fulfiller* of all our hope. To say it another way: The Father commits to fully redeem, the Son commits to fully obey what redemption requires, and the Spirit commits to fully apply what the Son achieves.

- **Jesus described his mission on earth in trinitarian dynamics**.

  > The One who comes from heaven is above everything. He is a witness to what he has seen and heard. But no one accepts what he says. Anyone who has accepted it has said, "Yes. God is truthful." The One whom God has sent speaks God's words. That's because God gives

the Holy Spirit without limit. The Father loves the Son and has put everything into his hands. Anyone who believes in the Son has eternal life. Anyone who says no to the Son will not have life. God's anger remains on them (John 3).

- **The saving mission of Jesus on our behalf can be accomplished only because of his unique, intrinsic relationship to his Father.**

  The Son can do nothing by himself. He can do only what he sees his Father doing. What the Father does, the Son also does. This is because the Father loves the Son. The Father shows him everything he does. Yes, and the Father will show the Son even greater things than these. And you will be amazed. The Father raises the dead and gives them life. In the same way, the Son gives life to anyone he wants to. Also, the Father does not judge anyone. He has given the Son the task of judging. Then all people will honor the Son just as they honor the Father. Whoever does not honor the Son does not honor the Father, who sent him (John 5).

pause | think | pray

Jesus Brings *Us* Into the Life of the Trinity

- **Trinitarian life — received by us and reflected among us — comes through Jesus Christ alone.**

  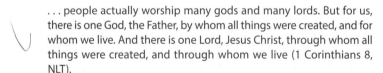 . . . people actually worship many gods and many lords. But for us, there is one God, the Father, by whom all things were created, and for whom we live. And there is one Lord, Jesus Christ, through whom all things were created, and through whom we live (1 Corinthians 8, NLT).

  The Father is indeed above all, and he is the Head of Christ. But the Word is through all things and is himself the Head of the church. While the Spirit is in us all, and he is the living water (Irenaeus, Church father).

- **Because of our total, irreversible identification with Christ, in union with him we may step confidently into the life of the Trinity forever.** Christ brought something new to the Godhead. It didn't exist before he came into the world as one of us! He made possible something the triune

God had not possessed previously — a direct, existential engagement with the tragedy of human suffering and death, as well as the personal exhilaration of human triumph over suffering and death. This "addition" to the eternal God is perhaps the greatest mystery surrounding Christ's intimacy within the Trinity — profound, beyond words to explain.

- **Through Jesus, the whole Trinity becomes intimately involved in the lives of believers.** We read:

  > Anyone who loves me will obey my teaching. My Father will love him. *We will come to him and make our home with him.* Anyone who does not love me will not obey my teaching. The words you hear me say are not my own. They belong to the Father who sent me. I have spoken all these things while I am still with you. But the Father will send the Friend in my name to help you. The Friend is the Holy Spirit. He will teach you all things. He will remind you of everything I have said to you (John 14, emphasis added).

- **Jesus inhabiting his people by his Spirit continually enriches us with the Father's life-giving treasures**.

  > I bow in prayer to the Father because of my work among you. From the Father every family in heaven and on earth gets its name. I pray that he will use his glorious riches to make you strong. May his Holy Spirit give you his power deep down inside you. Then Christ will live in your hearts because you believe in him (Ephesians 3).

- **When new followers of Jesus are baptized, they are baptized (literally in the Greek) "*into* the name of the Father, and of the Son, and of the Holy Spirit" (Matthew 28).** In other words, when we trust in Christ we are initiated into the blessed community of the triune God, which is our nuturing home for the rest of eternity.

- **We do not become "God," but we do share with our Redeemer a great measure of the same fellowship he has known forever as the second person of the Trinity.** Accepted in the "Beloved One" (Ephesians 1), we've become part of the Father's growing family, in heaven and earth, as we're embraced and immersed into his "Circle of Love," to abide there forever (Ephesians 3:14-19).

- **Christ's daily reign in our lives is also trinitarian.** Now we live in a kingdom where his Father *decrees* more and more of his life for us; where the Son *shares* more and more of his life with us; and where the Spirit *increases* more and more of that life within us.

- **Our participation in Trinity-unity overflows — to use the words of the grand invocation that opens the book of Revelation:**

> May grace and peace come to you from God. He is the one who is, and who was, and who will come. May grace and peace come to you from the seven spirits. These spirits are in front of God's throne. May grace and peace come to you from Jesus Christ. He is the faithful witness, so what he has shown can be trusted. He was the first to rise from the dead. He rules over the kings of the earth (Revelation 1).

pause | think | pray

The Wrap

Let's be clear. Nothing about the supremacy of Christ ever robs the Father or the Spirit of equal honor and praise. Recall Jesus' prayer in John 17:

> Father, the time has come. Bring glory to your Son. Then your Son will bring glory to you . . . I have brought you glory on earth. I have finished the work you gave me to do. So now, Father, give glory to me in heaven where your throne is. Give me the glory I had with you before the world began.

At the culmination of all things, Jesus will bring everything back to the Father (1 Corinthians 15). Philippians 2 assures us that at history's grand climax, when all creatures in the universe bow before Jesus to proclaim his everlasting, unopposed, blessing-filled lordship, their grand confession will resound to the greater glory of God the Father who has exalted the Son to the place of absolute supremacy. Simultaneously, the Spirit will ensure that all adoration remains permanently, perfectly focused on the Son for the glory of the Father.

Just as we saw earlier in Revelation 5, even in the Consummation it will remain the mission of the Son to secure before the whole universe the praise of the Godhead, for the sake of the Godhead, doing so in the midst of the Godhead.

Who Christ Is TO Us Today:
As the Perfection of Revelation

Recent polls confirm U.S. church attendance is declining. In 1991, 24 percent of U.S. adults had not been to church for at least six months; today it stands at 37 percent. Disturbing research compiled in *Futurecast* reveals that America is drifting from a clearly defined faith. We are tailoring religious outlooks to fit personal preferences. Many are simply "making up God as they go along," shedding their ties to traditional, biblical beliefs. With a wry hint of exaggeration, one sociologist suggests, "America is headed toward 310 million people with 310 million religions. We are a designer society. We want everything customized to our personal needs — our clothing, our food, our education. *Now it's our religion.*"

Surely there could be no more critical time than now for God's people to re-evaluate how we see God's Son as the "perfection of revelation to us" — as the open disclosure of God's person and promises and purposes. We must rebuild our outlook on all of life through the truth about God manifested in Jesus. As we're about to discover, as the "perfection of revelation" Christ achieves even more validation for his claim of supremacy in all things.

 Snapshots and Starter Thoughts

Christ's whole ministry was and is an act of revelation.

Christ takes the guesswork out of how we grow to know God.

Christ's revelation of God's nature is unique among the nations.

Christ's Whole Ministry Was and Is an Act of Revelation

- **God is known through God alone.** The magnificent "I Am that I Am" (as Yahweh defined himself to Moses in Exodus 3) is totally self-contained. He dwells in light inaccessible and unapproachable. 1 Timothy 6 tells us:

  > God is the blessed and only Ruler. He is the greatest King of all. He is the most powerful Lord of all. God is the only one who can't die. He lives in light that no one can get close to. No one has seen him. No one can see him.

  Therefore, any revelation of the living God totally depends on *him* to take the initiative to come to us and to give of himself to us.

- **Christ is God's self-disclosure.** He is our ultimate picture of God. And he shows this to us in the most visible and understandable way possible — *as a Son.* "The ultimate evidence for the existence of God is Jesus Christ himself" (Tim Keller).

- **What did Christ ultimately bring to the world? He brought us God.** In Jesus, God has opened himself up to us, manifested the deep places of his heart to us, and invited us to know him and love him for who he is.

- **Jesus is like a *"window"* through which we see God.** Through him we can peer into the heart of God. Our understanding of God is forever filtered through the prism of Jesus Christ. Paul wrote about this:

  > How I long for you to grow more certain in your knowledge and more sure in your grasp of God himself. May your spiritual experience become richer as you see more and more fully God's great secret, Christ himself! For it is in him, and in him alone, that men will find all the treasures of wisdom and knowledge . . . it is in him that God gives a full and complete expression of himself (within the physical limits that he set himself in Christ). (Colossians 2, PHILLIPS).

- **Jesus not only *brings* the revelation of God; he *is* the revelation of God.** To see him is to see the Father. To know him is to know the Father. Everything the Father has for us and wants for us is embodied in the person and ministry of Christ. The Christian movement is not just monotheistic; technically, Christians should be called "*Christocentric Monotheists.*" Our view of God cannot be separated from our view of who Jesus is.

- **"The only God we see is the God clothed in the promises of the gospel" (Martin Luther).** As Jonathan Edwards observed, in the good news about Christ and his mission we see the revelation of God's infinite justice intersecting with his inexhaustible grace; we see his hatred of sin simultaneously joined with his mercy toward sinners; we see his incomparable sovereignty coupled with his unparalleled humility.

- **Jesus fully expresses the reality of God, with nothing left out.** God is, in himself, precisely who and what he is toward us in Jesus. Jesus shows us what the very presence of God among us is like, in word, action, and being. This will never be preempted — never.

- **If Christ were not fully human and fully God at the same time, he could not be the ultimate, supreme revelation of God.** Therefore, who Christ is and what he has accomplished challenges us to re-examine, refine, and even at times, reconstitute everything we think we know about the character, designs, and ways of God.

- **Jesus doesn't show us a "part" of God or a "hint" of God but rather the *fullness* of God.** Christ — in his person, his coming, his mission, and his reign — is fully sufficient to help us encounter the fullness of God's attributes and works.

  > Life was in him, and that life was the light for all people. The light shines in the darkness. But the darkness has not overcome the light . . . The true light that gives light to everyone was coming into the world (John 1).

- **Jesus is not merely the vessel through whom the glory of God is communicated; he himself is the very *content* of that glory within the vessel.** He is the focus as well as the fulfillment of all other revelations of God's glory — in creation, in Scripture, in his acts in history.

- **God's revelation of himself to us in Jesus is like a symphony orchestra filling an auditorium with delightful rhapsodies.** All previous revelations were like listening to a single violin or trumpet or oboe playing simple tunes. In Christ, however, now we experience the full-bodied amplification of God's character and ways. His composition is called redemption. It bursts upon us through Jesus' victorious mission — by his incarnation, life and teachings, cross, resurrection, and exaltation — to form one grand cosmic concert, resounding with who God is, what he is doing, and where he is headed.

- **When we look at Jesus in his earthly ministry we get to know God from many angles.** First, Jesus speaks as God. Equally so, God speaks as Jesus. Whenever Jesus taught, God taught. However Jesus healed, God healed. As Jesus wept, God wept. The words and deeds of Jesus are the words and deeds of God. The sufferings of Jesus are God's sufferings. Jesus' joys and triumphs have become the victories of God as well.

- **His whole life among us was an act of revelation.** His story points us toward God's glory. Jesus said:

  > But if it's God's finger I'm pointing that sends the demons on their way, then God's kingdom is here for sure (Luke 11, MSG).

  Christ is like the "finger of God" piercing our world. In him, God has assumed unprecedented proximity to his creation.

- **In him, the long-anticipated Kingdom is at hand.** Through Christ, God has entered actively into history on a much grander scale. Jesus is not only how God reveals himself in his fullness, but also we discover in him how God is acting among, relating to, and ruling over all the nations at this very hour.

pause | think | pray

Christ Takes the Guesswork Out of How We Grow to Know God

- **In God's Son, we find all we will ever need to know about God.** In other words, all of the world's idle speculations about God have now found clarification and resolution in Christ alone.

  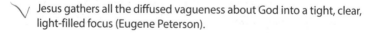 Jesus gathers all the diffused vagueness about God into a tight, clear, light-filled focus (Eugene Peterson).

  The Father imparted himself and his greatness to his Only-Begotten, the First-Born of every creature. He did this so that Christ — being the image of the invisible God — might preserve even in his greatness the image of the Father. For it was not possible that there could exist a well-proportioned, so to speak, and beautiful image of the invisible

God unless the Son also preserved the image of his greatness (Origen, church father).

- **With unmistakable clarity, the good news of Jesus anchors us in God and his saving purposes.**

  > May God receive glory. He is able to strengthen your faith. He does this in keeping with the good news and the message I preach. It is the message about Jesus Christ. This message is in keeping with the mystery hidden for a very long time. The mystery has now been made known through the writings of the prophets. The eternal God commanded that it be made known. God wanted all the Gentiles to obey him by trusting in him. May the only wise God receive glory forever through Jesus Christ (Romans 16).

- **Jesus makes knowing God much simpler for us sinners.** In the face of the unfathomable, massive complexity of God's creation — both the seen and unseen worlds — God has blessed us with a revelation of himself shared in the "simplicity" of knowing Christ alone. Jesus makes the knowledge of God accessible even to little children ("of such is the Kingdom of God").

- **Christ is the "secret" of God revealed to us — openly and without ambiguity.** The more we get to know him as God's Son, the more we get to know what is on God's heart. As Jesus prayed:

  > I praise you, Father. You are Lord of heaven and earth. You have hidden these things from wise and educated people. But you have shown them to little children . . . the only ones who know the Father are the Son and those to whom the Son chooses to make him known (Matthew 11).

- **Christ was the "secret" God kept "hidden" for ages — but not any more.** Paul writes:

  > . . . the message about Jesus Christ . . . is in keeping with the mystery hidden for a very long time. The mystery has now been made known (Romans 16).

  > Then their understanding will be rich and complete. They will know the mystery of God. That mystery is Christ. All the treasures of wisdom and knowledge are hidden in him (Colossians 2).

- **The New Testament frequently refers to Christ as the "image" of the invisible God.** This does not mean he is like a Xerox copy of an original. Rather, like a child is to his dad, Jesus is the likeness of his Father.

The Word became a human being. He made his home with us. We have seen his glory. It is the glory of the One and Only . . . No one has ever seen God. But the One and Only is God and is at the Father's side. The one at the Father's side has shown us what God is like (John 1).

The Son is the exact likeness of God (Colossians 1).

But in these last days, he has spoken to us through his Son . . . The Son is the shining brightness of God's glory. He is the exact likeness of God's being (Hebrews 1).

God said, "Let light shine out of darkness." He made his light shine in our hearts. His light gives us the light to know God's glory. His glory is shown in the face of Christ (2 Corinthians 4).

- **God gave us his Son both to *mediate* the revealing of his glory and to *liberate* us to pursue him to reveal even more.** If we were to see God's grand majesty "straight on," without Jesus to mediate, it would consume us. Moses was told in Exodus 33 that if he saw God's face he would die! But now, through Jesus, we can see Yahweh face to face. God hid Moses in a mountain cleft so that he could see only God's "back" when he passed before him (Exodus 33). Now, however, God has caused all of his glory and goodness to pass in front of us and all creation — to *remain* before us forever — in the person of his dear Son. As Paul explains:

    This veil can be removed only by believing in Christ . . . But whenever someone turns to the Lord, the veil is taken away . . . So all of us who have had that veil removed can see and reflect the glory of the Lord. And the Lord — who is the Spirit — makes us more and more like him as we are changed into his glorious image (2 Corinthians 3, NLT).

- **In Jesus, there are no boundaries to how much of God we may know.** The very person of the reigning Christ is like a bottomless ocean opened up for us to swim in and explore for all ages to come.

- **We may plunge into greater depths in our relationship with God to the degree we continue to enlarge our vision of the person of his dear Son.** Paul prays:

    . . . may you have the power to understand, as all God's people should, how wide, how long, how high, and how deep his love is. May you experience the love of Christ, though it is too great to understand fully. Then you will be made complete with all the fullness of life and power that comes from God (Ephesians 3, NLT).

pause | think | pray

Christ's Revelation of God's Nature Is Unique Among the Religions of the Nations

- **There is no *other* God apart from the God we see revealed in Jesus.**

    > He also is the image of God the Father. And the Son is an imitator of all the Father's works. Therefore, everyone may regard it just as if he saw the Father when they see the Son (Novatian, Church father).

    There's no "hidden" God — no "secret" God lurking behind the façade of what we see in Jesus Christ. He is it! God is none other than who we see him to be in Jesus — and never other than that.

- **Paul reasoned with pagan philosophers that Jesus was God's exclusive revelation of the one true God:**

    > People of Athens . . . I am going to tell you about this 'unknown god' . . . He isn't a statue planned and made by clever people . . . now God commands all people everywhere to turn away from their sins. He has set a day when he will judge the world fairly. He has appointed a man to be its judge. God has proved this to everyone by raising that man from the dead (Acts 17).

- **Wherever and whenever God thinks and expresses himself, there we find Jesus Christ.** The *absoluteness* of Christ is found in the fact that he is the *definitive* revelation of God. He is the standard by which all other claims about God are to be measured.

- **There is nothing God has to show us beyond what he shows us in his Son.** Everything we think we know about God always must be consistent with the truth that already is revealed in Christ. However, if Christ were not at the same time fully *human* as well as fully God, he could not serve as the supreme, definitive revelation of God to us.

- **Some may claim other revelations *from* God among the nations; but Jesus is the singular revelation *of* God.** Jesus is not someone "one step removed" from God. To know him is to know God. God acts like Jesus.

Jesus acts like God. The better we get to know Jesus, the deeper we look into the eyes of God.

- **The most stunning attribute of God, which separates him from all other "gods" of the earth, is the *love* we see exhibited toward the world by and in Jesus.** Nowhere else among the nations is such love revealed. God's love *is* what Jesus *gives*. It is a love that offers up his life for the life of the world. In Christ we discover that God's love actively searches, pursues, connects, salvages, restores, and transforms sinners.

- **Where else among the nations but in Jesus is such knowledge of God to be found?** In the ages to come, we will worship Christ — the slain, risen Lamb of Revelation 5 — as the One who by his cross revealed the suffering heart of God in the only way it truly could ever be known.

- **At the same time, Christ also perfectly reveals to the world that the loving God of the universe is also *holy*.** This is seen in how, faced with our sin, God in his holiness required Jesus to go to the cross. This is seen by how God's Son cleanses us and reconciles us to the holy Judge of all, saving us from God's just wrath toward all that is unholy, at the cost of his own blood.

  > God was pleased to have his whole nature living in Christ. God was pleased to bring all things back to himself. That's because of what Christ has done. These things include everything on earth and in heaven. God made peace through Christ's blood, by his death on the cross (Colossians 1).

  > There is no difference . . . for all have sinned and fall short of the glory of God, and all are justified freely by his grace through the redemption that came by Christ Jesus. God presented Christ as a sacrifice of atonement, through the shedding of his blood — to be received by faith. He did this to demonstrate his righteousness . . . so as to be just and the one who justifies those who have faith in Jesus (Romans 3, NIV).

- **In equal measure, Christ shows the world what the *righteousness* of God involves.** The Law revealed what God's righteousness *requires*. Christ reveals more: what God's righteousness *aspires*. In Jesus, God's righteousness is seen, in part, as God's *faithfulness* to his saving promises on behalf of his sinful people. Above all, the Son's own perfect sacrifice on the cross manifests *how* and *why* the Father makes unrighteous sinners to be righteous before his face. This comes about by our abiding in his righteous Son who died, rose, and then ascended on high for us.

- **Ultimately, Christ reveals the righteous judgments of God upon all that is unrighteous**. No other religion calls its devotees to prepare for such a moment as this one:

> The sky rolled back like a scroll. Every mountain and island was moved out of its place. Everyone hid in caves and among the rocks of the mountains. This included the kings of the earth, the princes and the generals. It included rich people and powerful people. It also included everyone else, both slave and people who were free. They called out to the mountains and rocks, "Fall on us! Hide us from the face of the one who sits on the throne! Hide us from the anger of the Lamb! The great day of their anger has come. Who can live through it?" (Revelation 6).

- **No other religion in the world offers such a refuge in the day of judgment as Christ offers, as we read**:

> After this I looked, and there in front of me was a huge crowd of people. They stood in front of the throne and in front of the Lamb. There were so many that no one could count them. They came from every nation, tribe and people . . . He [one of the elders] said, "They are the ones who have come out of the time of terrible suffering. They have washed their robes and made them white in the blood of the Lamb . . . The Lamb, who is at the center of the area around the throne, will be their shepherd" (Revelation 7).

- **What is a prime difference between Christ and all other religions and their founders and leaders?** Surely it is this: Ultimately, in Christ, God is not simply giving people spiritual insights or religious dogma (whether through meditation, in rituals, or by sacred texts). Rather, in Christ and Christ alone, God is revealing *himself*, doing so by giving us *himself*, and doing so by withholding from us *nothing* of himself.

- **Therefore, we can be confident of this:** Any claims by other religions or their founders — whether teachings, rituals, laws, revelations — that are deemed *inconsistent* with the character and purposes of God as revealed in Jesus Christ and summed up in him *cannot be of God.*

- **By showing us God so perfectly, Jesus connects us to the inescapable realities of who God is and what he's all about.** Therefore, there can be no *legitimate* claims to ultimate Truth from scholars or philosophers or clerics that bypass Jesus because "all the treasures of wisdom and knowledge are hidden in him." (Colossians 2).

Outside of Jesus, God may be vaguely knowable; but a clear vision of God that opens unhindered fellowship with him can come only through knowing and trusting Jesus Christ. Only what God has manifested to us *exclusively* in his Son is sufficient to secure our eternal destiny with him.

- **Because Christ reveals God to us, any other focus of worship finally results in idolatry.**

  We know that we are children of God. We know that the whole world is under the control of the evil one. We also know that the Son of God has come. He has given us understanding. So we can know the God who is true. And we belong to the true God by belonging to his Son, Jesus Christ. He is the true God and eternal life. Dear children, keep away from statues of gods (1 John 5).

pause | think | pray

The Wrap

The revelation of God that Jesus brings us is our starting point for making sense of everything else.

We may not be able to explain how and why the events of our own lives, let alone the dramas of history, unfold the way they do (often leaving us perplexed, even sorrowful). But we *can* know that the God of history, the God of nations, as well as the God of every individual is exactly as we see him in Jesus Christ.

No matter what may transpire in our lives, God's stance toward us remains forever the same as he has revealed himself to be in Jesus. God is who and what he is toward us *in*, and *through*, and *as* the Lord Jesus Christ.

Even in the midst of inexplicable heartaches, sobering setbacks, indiscriminate disasters, or even momentary defeats at the hands of evil powers, peace and confidence remain the portion of those who flee to the God we see in Jesus Christ.

In him, we can find perspectives on God's character and ways that give us new ground from which to engage the darkness around us. That's because all the promises of God are YES! to us — perfectly revealed and sealed for us — *in Christ Jesus* (2 Corinthians 1).

Finally, let's not forget: All current revelations of the wonders of God in Jesus *have only just begun*! Christ will increasingly be the perfect exhibition of God for all time.

When the knowledge of God's glory is displayed, covering the earth like waters cover the sea (as Habakkuk 2 foretells), we will discover that the wonder of it all was marvelously unveiled in the person and work and reign of the Son seated at God's right hand.

The eternal blessing of growing in the knowledge of the glory of God is ours already, *today*. To us belongs the privilege of living in the presence of a Savior who will never cease to enlarge and intensify fresh revelations of the living God for those he has redeemed.

The glad news is that we will continue knowing God more fully and deeply as we continue to unwrap the inexhaustible riches of who God is as seen in his Son (Ephesians 3).

Who Christ Is TO Us Today:
As the Picture of Scripture

When Steve Jobs died in October 2011, one national newspaper headlined his passing with this line: "He Not Only Saw the Future — He Created the Future."

"He created the future" — what does that involve? To explain his approach to life, this creative genius behind iPods, iPhones, and iPads often quoted a famous hockey player's strategy about how he played the game: "You don't skate to where the puck is; you skate to where it's going to be." Jobs' focus stretched beyond the status quo because his focus honed in on the future! It was often said of the founder of Apple Computer Corporation that he did not invent what people *wanted*; instead, he invented what people *needed* even if they had not yet reached the place where they *wanted* it. Then he set out to help them discover why they should *want* it.

In the same way, Scripture compiles historic events, religious rituals, festivals, personalities, poetry, principles, and prophecies with a sharp eye to the future — seeing where God is headed; seeing what is needed before we know we need it or want it; moving God's people toward a vision beyond the status quo. The Bible focuses all of this on the paramount personality of time and eternity, by whom the future is created and shaped: Jesus Christ. From the beginning, he remains the prevailing picture being painted by Scripture — the picture of what we *need* and what multitudes will conclude eventually they truly *want*.

"The picture of Scripture" — this is precisely who he should be *to* us: the One toward whom all Scripture points and in whom all Scripture finds its real meaning. Understanding this dimension adds valuable texture to what we've already explored about who Christ is *to* us.

Snapshots and Starter Thoughts

The Bible is all about Christ.

The Old Testament casts the shadow of Christ.

Precepts, prophets, praises, and promises picture Christ for us.

The calling and chronicles of Israel culminate as a picture of Christ.

The New Testament brings the Old Testament picture of Christ to life!

The Bible Is All About Christ

- **The Scriptures are really one book** and that book is summed up in **Jesus.** This is why the early church fathers liked to say "the Bible *is* Jesus." To be true to the Bible is to be devoted to the Person with whom it is preoccupied. A high view of Scripture is inseparable from a high view of Christ, and vice versa. "The Bible is the cradle in which Christ is laid" (Martin Luther).

- **Every book of the Bible provides further revelations of who God's Son is.** As M. R. DeHaan writes:

    The Bible is filled with word pictures, and all these have as their central figure a Person . . . If we search long enough we shall find upon every page of Scripture, standing somewhere in the shadow, the outline of the central Person of the Book — the Lord Jesus Christ, both the object and end of all Scripture. The last book of the Bible opens with the words, "The Revelation of Jesus Christ," and this is not only the title of the *last* book of the Bible, but it may well be taken as the title of *all* the books in the Bible, for it is truly the "revelation of Jesus Christ."

- **Therefore, all biblical truth must be understood "in Christ."** If not, the truth of any text becomes diminished in one way or another.

- **The Scottish reformer John Knox was always intent on unveiling Christ in every sermon he preached.** It was said of him:

  > Christ is in every verb, in every noun, in every adverb, in every adjective, in every participle — Christ is in every syntactical device in all of Scripture (Ian Hamilton).

- **Charles Spurgeon encouraged fellow pastors like this:**

  > Every text of Scripture provides us a road to take us to Christ. I have not found a text where this is not so. And it is your duty, my brothers and sisters, to find that road and take it.

- **The Biblical narrative from Genesis to Revelation paints the manifold colors of Christ for us.** It is a progressive unfolding of, and expansion on, two overarching themes: the person of Christ and the purposes of his kingdom. Two key questions can help unlock any portion of Scripture: (1) How does this passage show me more of Christ? (2) What more does this passage tell me about his kingdom purposes?

- **The Bible points to Christ from different directions.** The words of the *prophets* point *forward* to the Christ yet to come. The teachings of the *apostles* point *upward* to the Christ who now reigns at God's right hand, even as they point *outward*, calling us to join Christ in the unfolding of God's purposes.

- **Both prophets and apostles serve as *signposts* to direct us to Christ so that through their words our vision of him might increase.** For example, as the last in the centuries-long line of Old Testament prophets, John the Baptizer concluded:

  > The bride belongs to the groom. The friend who helps the groom waits and listens for him. He is full of joy when he hears the groom's voice. That joy is mine, and it is now complete. He must become more important. I must become less important (John 3).

- **Jesus encouraged his disciples to see him pictured in Scripture.**

  > Then Jesus turned to his disciples. He said to them in private, "Blessed are the eyes that see what you see. I tell you, many prophets and kings wanted to see what you see. But they didn't see it. They wanted to hear what you hear. But they didn't hear it" (Luke 10).

- **This makes the Bible more relevant today than ever.** That's because the Person portrayed throughout its pages is alive and reigning right now, as he ushers every passage into glorious fulfillment.

pause | think | pray

The Old Testament Casts the Shadow of Christ

- **Everything Jesus did was foreshadowed in the Hebrew Bible.** Christ was previsioned. His coming was forecast. Then one day he stepped from behind the curtain of the Old Testament, as it were, to come among us in the "fullness of time" (Galatians 4).

- **Christ was concealed (waiting to be revealed) in many facets of the Old Testament.** For example, he was concealed in its myriad of events, personalities, traditions, and rituals. Now, for New Testament saints, he has become the locus of all the principles and promises and prophecies God gave to Israel.

- **Christ did not fail to exhibit what the Old Testament revealed about the character and ways of God.** Instead, he gave God's Word a whole new reality in himself, which only the New Testament can help us appreciate fully.

- **The pages of the Old Testament cast the "shadow" of Christ at every turn.** They provided a *silhouette* of the Savior who was to come, an outline of what he was coming to do. But the Lord Jesus Christ himself becomes the tangible, visible "substance" that was casting the shadow all along. He brings Scriptures to their fulfillment. A shadow always calls attention to the presence of something beyond itself. Even so, Old Testament texts pointed to someone yet to come, who would be far more vivid, delightful, memorable, and compelling than any passage could portray.

- **Here's how Paul contrasts Old Testament shadows with the impact of Christ in the flesh:**

  > He won the battle over them by dying on the cross. So don't let anyone judge you because of what you eat or drink. Don't let anyone judge you about holy days. I'm talking about special feasts and New Moons and Sabbath days. *They are only a shadow of the things to come. But what is real is found in Christ* (Colossians 2, emphasis added).

- **Jesus' mission of redemption fulfilled the Scriptures.** Paul writes:

  > Christ died for our sins, *just as Scripture said he would.* He was buried. He was raised from the dead on the third day, *just as Scripture said he would* (1 Corinthians 15, emphasis added).

- **Jesus emphasized this truth during his inaugural message in the Nazareth synagogue.**

  > He stood up to read. And the scroll of the prophet Isaiah was handed to him. He unrolled it and found the right place. There it is written, "The Spirit of the Lord is on me. He has anointed me to announce the good news to poor people . . . " The eyes of everyone in the synagogue were staring at him. He began by saying to them, "Today this passage of Scripture is coming true as you listen" (Luke 4).

- **To say Jesus "fulfills" the Old Testament is to say, in essence, that he "fills it full" of himself, thus giving it its ultimate meaning.** Every picture painted in the Old Testament of Yahweh and his mighty acts — both his displays of grace and of judgment — must be matched up with the fullness of Jesus as unveiled in the New Testament. There the descriptions find their truest meanings and paramount manifestations.

- **Thus, Christ is *to* us the picture painted for us by Scripture throughout all its pages.** Thinking of Jesus' magnificent manifestation of his inner glory to three disciples by his transfiguration (Matthew 17), Peter who was there that day exclaimed decades later:

  > Because of that experience, we have even greater confidence in the message proclaimed by the prophets (2 Peter 1, NLT).

Selah

pause | think | pray

Precepts, Prophets, Praises, and Promises Picture Christ for Us

- **Christ opens up the Old Testament for us; he makes it come alive.** That's why we should study Christ in light of the Old Testament, while at the same time seek to understand the Old Testament in light of Christ (as the New Testament helps us to do).

- **Often Jesus amplified for his disciples how he was pictured in Scripture.** Consider the experience of the disciples on the Emmaus road on the evening of Resurrection Day, joined by Jesus, incognito:

  > Jesus said to them, "How foolish you are! How long it takes you to believe all that the prophets said! Didn't the Messiah have to suffer these things and then receive his glory?" Jesus explained to them what was said about himself in all the Scriptures. He began with Moses and all the Prophets . . . Their eyes were opened, and they recognized him . . . They said to each other, "He explained to us what the Scriptures meant. Weren't we excited as he talked with us on the road?" (Luke 24).

- **Paul teaches that Christ is the "end of the Law" (Romans 10) — not because he discarded the Law (which he did not) but because the Law was subsumed in him and his redemptive work.** In a sense, he *personalized* the Law as he brought to completion everything it signified, and required, and promoted, and foreshadowed. As Paul observed:

  > I know what enthusiasm they [the people of Israel] have for God, but it is misdirected zeal . . . For Christ has already accomplished the purpose for which the law was given. As a result, all who believe in him are made right with God (Romans 10, NLT).

- **Because he is the fulfillment of the Law, Jesus ushers us into an encounter with God's glory beyond what the Law could ever offer**.

  > The Law was written in letters on stone. Even though it was a way of serving God, it led to death . . . The Law that condemns people to death had glory. How much more glory does the work of the Spirit have! His work makes people right with God. The glory of the old covenant is nothing compared with the far greater glory of the new . . . And this glory comes from the Lord, who is the Holy Spirit (2 Corinthians 3).

- **In the same way, Christ subsumed all of God's *promises* to his people in the Old Testament. He gave all they forecast a grander dimension by anchoring them in himself.** He reconstituted the promises according to how they capture the vastness of his majesty and supremacy. Of the myriad guarantees God gives, Paul claims:

  > The message of Christ has always been "Yes." God has made a great many promises. They are all "Yes" because of what Christ has done. So through Christ we say "Amen." We want God to receive glory (2 Corinthians 1).

- **All biblical *prophecy* intersects at the feet of Jesus.** This is what the angel told John:

  > I'm a servant just like you, and like your brothers and sisters who hold to the witness of Jesus. *The witness of Jesus is the spirit of prophecy* (Revelation 19, MSG, emphasis added).

- **Just as other *prophets* did, Abraham also celebrated Jesus ahead of time.**

  > Jesus replied . . . "Your father Abraham was filled with joy at the thought of seeing my day. He saw it and was glad . . . Before Abraham was born, I am!" (John 8).

- **The *prophets,* who foretold a special Someone coming one day to save God's people, also longed to know his identity.**

  > The prophets searched very hard and with great care to find out about this salvation. They spoke about the grace that was going to come to you. They wanted to find out when and how this salvation would come. The Spirit of Christ in them was telling them about the sufferings of the Messiah. These were his sufferings that were going to come. The Spirit of Christ was also telling them about the glory that would follow. It was made known to the prophets that they were not serving themselves. Instead, they were serving you when they spoke about the things that you have now heard (1 Peter 1).

Selah

pause | think | pray

The Calling and Chronicles of Israel Culminate as a Picture of Christ

- **"The promises were given to Abraham. They were also given to his seed."**

   Scripture does not say, "and to seeds." That means many people. It says, "and to your seed." That means one person. And that one person is Christ . . . You who belong to Christ are Abraham's seed. So you will receive what God has promised (Galatians 3).

- **The story of Jesus is the high point and resolution of Israel's story**.

   The Story of Jesus as Messiah and Lord resolves what is yearning for completion in the Story of Israel . . . The Jesus Story completes Israel's Story. The Plan of Salvation flows out of the Story of Israel and the Story of Jesus (Scot McKnight).

- **Christ embodied the Old Testament calling and mission of Israel, on behalf of Israel.** Christ did not come to found a new religion, but to bring forth the culmination of the redeeming work of Yahweh, the God of Israel, for the sake of Israel and the blessing of all nations through Israel. He took the identity of Israel; then, he took to himself her mission, her moral responsibility before God, her covenant with God. He embodied Israel's calling and secured her destiny to bring hope to the world.

- **Through Isaiah, God actually named the coming Messiah "Israel," meaning he would be the One who would complete Israel's mission to the nations.**

   He made me his straight arrow and hid me in his quiver. He said to me, "You're my dear servant, Israel, through whom I'll shine" . . . He says, "But that's not a big enough job for my servant — just to recover the tribes of Jacob, merely to round up the strays of Israel. I'm setting you up as a light for the *nations* so that my salvation becomes *global*!" (Isaiah 49, MSG).

- **The story of Israel, in a real sense, is *reenacted* in the life, ministry, death, resurrection, and ascension of Jesus Christ.** The various dramas of Israel's calling, her sufferings, her judgments, her restorations, her witness to the nations are all played out, in other forms, in the ministry of Christ — both his earthly ministry and his current reign.

- **At least four major themes formed the restoration of Israel, as promised through the prophets. They have all been summed up in**

Christ alone: the theme of a new king, a new temple, a new priesthood, and a new creation. Jesus embodies all four themes today.

(1) *He is King* even though not acknowledged yet as such by Israel, as well as King over the nations and throughout the universe.

(2) He said his body — crucified and raised from the dead — has become *the final temple,* joined by those united with him through new birth to form a temple that continues to grow.

(3) He ascended on high to become *the great High Priest* over the household of God, and to reconstitute his followers into a holy priesthood serving with him.

(4) In him, all believers already have become *a new creation,* even as we await his return when he will set all creation free from decay to vibrate forever with resurrection life.

- **All things the Hebrew Bible teaches about the three major leadership roles in Scripture — prophet, priest, king — converge in the one who is called "the Christ."** "Christ" means "anointed one." Just as the leaders of Israel were anointed for their roles, so Jesus is now the Christ, the Anointed One, set apart as the "cosmic" Prophet, Priest, and King for all of us, forever. All the blessings we receive from Heaven right now come through how he carries out these three roles on our behalf, day after day.

- **In addition, Jesus is represented as the new Moses.**

  > If you believed Moses, you would believe me, for he wrote about me (John 5, NIV).

  Better than Moses leading his people to fresh drinking water in the desert, Jesus becomes the source of eternal restoration for all who follow him.

  > They were all baptized into Moses in the cloud and in the sea. They all ate the same spiritual food. They all drank the same spiritual water. They drank from the spiritual rock that went with them. That rock was Christ (1 Corinthians 10).

- **What the "promised land" of Palestine represented to Israel is reconstituted a thousandfold in who Jesus is to us.** He has become our home — our place of inclusion, permanence, security, refuge, festival, community, prosperity, and inheritance. In Jesus, we dwell and thrive in

God's presence. In Jesus, we also become God's base of operations to be his witness among the nations.

- **Jesus presented himself to his audiences as the ultimate expression of familiar Old Testament *dramas*. For example:**

  > The Queen of the South . . . came from a distant land to hear the wisdom of Solomon. Now someone greater than Solomon is here . . . The people of Nineveh . . . repented of their sins at the preaching of Jonah. Now someone greater than Jonah is here (Luke 11, NLT).

  > Haven't you read the Law? It tells how every Sabbath day the priests in the temple have to do their work on that day. But they are not considered guilty. I tell you that something more important than the temple is here . . . The Son of Man is Lord of the Sabbath day (Matthew 11).

- **The Old Testament's final "day of the Lord," which promised to restore Israel, has become, in New Testament language, the "day of *Christ*."** Christ is the Father's authorized agent to execute everything God intends whenever Scriptures point to the final hour of redemption and judgment, both for his people and among the nations.

  Even today, living under his reign, we are invited to experience foretastes of the day of Christ. But there's much more to come. The climactic intervention that lies ahead will greatly expand our vision of Jesus as the champion of all of God's redeeming purposes.

- **"We who have been quarried out from the bowels of Christ are the true Israelite race . . ."**

  > Along with Abraham we will inherit the holy land when we receive the inheritance for an endless eternity, being children of Abraham through a similar faith in Christ (Justin Martyr, Church father).

- **"Either Jesus is the Messiah for all, or he is not Messiah at all"** (Lausanne Paper, 2004). If Jesus is not the Messiah promised by the Old Testament for the deliverance of the Jewish people, then he is not the Messiah promised for the salvation of the nations.

pause | think | pray

The New Testament Brings the Old Testament Picture of Christ to Life!

- **As with the Old Testament, every portion of the New Testament is equally rooted in Christ.** The Gospels, Acts, Letters, and Revelation are subject to Christ, concerned about Christ, and can be adequately understood and applied to the Church (and to each believer) only to the degree he remains our primary focus as we do so.

- **Notice how the last book of the Bible paints a portrait of Christ.** It begins:

    > The Revelation of Jesus Christ, which God gave Him to show to His bond-servants . . . (Revelation 1, NASB).

    Toward the end it reminds us:

    > The witness of Jesus is the spirit of prophecy (Revelation 19, MSG).

- **For example, one might call the Beatitudes (Matthew 5) an x-ray of the very heart of Christ.** He became *poor* for us. He showed the servant spirit of the *meek*. He *hungered* for righteousness — not for himself but for his whole creation. He was *pure* in his devotion to the Father and in his commitment to do the Father's will. He *suffered*, both in life and in death, for God's glory and God's purposes. By his death, resurrection, and ascension he became the arch *Peacemaker* for the universe.

- **All New Testament doctrines converge at Jesus' feet — to focus on him, to know him, and to exalt him.** All doctrines — such as God's holiness, reconciliation of sinners, the unity of the Church, the gifts of the Spirit as well as teachings on daily discipleship, spiritual warfare the resurrection, and the end of the world — take us to him.

- **New Testament teachings should never be explored apart from seeing their implications for who Christ is *to* us** — whether texts about worship, or evangelism, or miracles, or dark powers, or suffering, or regeneration, or ministry to the poor. All that was written for the early church is supremely about him and for him. It makes sense to us only because of him. It never ceases to keep enlarging our picture of him.

- **Just as the Old Testament is Yahweh-shaped, the New Testament is Jesus-shaped.** As we've already seen, the early church gave Jesus the honor, titles, and roles of Yahweh, transforming how we get to know the God of the Old Testament as a result.

> We have seen his glory, the glory of the one and only Son, who came from the Father, full of grace and truth (John 1, NIV).

pause | think | pray

The Wrap

One might say the Bible functions a little like a personal *photo album of Jesus*. Or to be more contemporary, call it his very own *Facebook* account! Throughout the Bible's pages we see his face — sometimes shadowed, sometimes shining; sometimes black and white, sometimes painted with a rich palate of colors. Still, it is all his face from one angle or another.

A day is coming, however, when every prospect, projection, and promise in both Old and New Testaments will reach their culmination — when the full scope of biblical hope will be gathered up in one final display of the Son's majesty and supremacy.

That impending cosmic breakthrough of his reign, toward which all Scripture moves, will create the permanent *grand masterpiece portrait of the Grand Master of the universe* — a picture like no other, to dazzle our hearts with him and fuel our worship of him for all that he is *to* us, forever and ever.

Who Christ Is TO Us Today:
By the Claims of His Names

As we've seen more than once in this chapter, many Old Testament names and descriptions for Yahweh have been applied to Jesus, including Holy One, First and Last, Living One, King of kings, Bridegroom, Creator, Redeemer, Lord of heaven's armies.

But the New Testament greatly *expands* his array of titles.

In John 1, for example, Jesus is called "the Word," meaning, among other things, that he has become *to* us God's voice — God speaking, God's language, God's truth, God's final message to the world.

Another example: He designates himself as a foundational "Rock" (Matthew 7); Paul calls him the "One Foundation" (1 Corinthians 3); and Peter says he is the "Living Stone" (1 Peter 2). All these metaphors indicate he's the One upon whom the Father has permanently established his redemptive plan for the ages.

Or again, he called himself the "Light of the World" (John 8). Without him we remain in spiritual darkness, not knowing which way to go. He is "the Way" (John 14). Without him, we will never be able to find a path to forgiveness and fellowship with the living God.

We speak of Christ as "the Righteousness of God" (Romans 1 and 1 Corinthians 1). Many claims for Jesus are implied by this phrase. For starters: His whole life was lived in perfect *obedience* to the Father. Due to his inherent nature as God, he remained *consistently true* to the character of God throughout his life and ministry. He was *loyal* to the purposes of God, extending all the way to the cross. 2 Corinthians 5 concludes: "[God] made Him who knew no sin *to be* sin on our behalf, so that we might become the righteousness of God in Him" (NASB, emphasis added).

In other words, in his sinless perfection Jesus has secured God's forgiveness and eternal blessings for all who are alive in him. He has become *our* righteousness — we are clothed with him — so we might freely live before God's face. Because he is God's perfect righteousness "in bodily form," God will one day judge the world in righteousness through this one Man appointed the *Judge* of all things (Acts 17).

What a claim about the supremacy of Christ lies in this one name alone — "the Righteousness of God"!

Listen to early church fathers as they declared Jesus' names. In A.D. 180, Irenaeus wrote:

> Jesus is Himself in his own right, beyond all men who have ever lived: God, Lord, King Eternal, Incarnate Word, Holy Lord, the Wonderful, the Counselor, the Beautiful in appearance, the Mighty God.

In A.D. 193, Clement of Alexandria penned:

> He is the circle of all powers rolled and united into one unit, called Alpha and Omega.

And in A.D. 248, Origen proclaimed:

> His Son is God the Word, and Wisdom, and Truth, and Righteousness — and everything else that the sacred Scriptures call him when speaking of God.

Jonathan Edwards, the Puritan theologian and revival leader in the 1700s, took the dual names for Christ in Revelation — Lion and Lamb — and reasoned about their claim like this: As a *lion*, Jesus is a devourer. He excels in strength; in appearance and voice he rises up with majesty. Everything is his "prey" to do with as he pleases. As a *Lamb*, however, this same Jesus excels in meekness and patience. He is yielded to the Father's will and to our good — becoming our sacrifice and (like wool) our covering before the Court of Heaven. John's vision of Jesus in the throne room, Edwards correctly deduced, means that in Christ both of the "excellencies" come together in perfect harmony.

Bottom line: The *fame* of his *name* ratifies his *claim* to carry out his *reign*, which is all to his *gain* — and ours.

Snapshots and Starter Thoughts

Hebrews 13 summons us to action: "Through Jesus, therefore, let us continually offer to God a sacrifice of praise — *the fruit of lips that openly profess his name*" (NIV, emphasis added). Or, as expressed in another translation: "Therefore, let us offer through Jesus a continual sacrifice of praise to God, *proclaiming our allegiance to his name*" (NLT, emphasis added).

On the following pages you'll find an explosion of names and titles — a palate of snapshots and starter thoughts, painting the person of Christ. Reflect on what each name represents or implies; on what each title reveals about his attributes, or character, or nature, or roles, or ministries, as the Son of God fulfilling the purposes of God. How would you worship him based on the truths implied by each name on the list? How might declaring (confessing) the meanings behind some of these names for Jesus give you fresh words to use as you praise him, alone or with others, or as you tell a non-Christian what Jesus means to you?

For starters: How might one of these names help you talk more effectively with other believers about his supremacy and majesty to help them see more clearly who Christ is *to* us?

Jesus (Yahweh Saves)
Messiah (The Anointed One)
Immanuel (God With Us)
Radiance of God's Glory (Hebrews 1)
Image of the Invisible God (Colossians 1)
Son From Heaven (1 Thessalonians 1)
Mystery of God (Colossians 2)
Mystery of Godliness (1 Timothy 3)
Son of the Living God (Matthew 16)
Firstborn of All Creation (Colossians 1)
Firstborn From Among the Dead
(Colossians 1)
The Righteousness of God
(1 Corinthians 1)
Alpha and Omega (Revelation 1)
The First and the Last (Revelation 1)

The Beginning and the End
(Revelation 1)
The Beloved One (Ephesians 1)
The Chosen One (Matthew 12)
The Scepter (Numbers 24)
Faithful and True Witness
(Revelation 19)
Savior of the World (John 4)
Israel, My Servant (Isaiah 49)
Great High Priest (Hebrews 4)
Lord of the Dead and the Living
(Romans 14)
King of the Jews (John 19)
Head of the Church (Ephesians 1)
Ruler of the Kings of the Earth
(Revelation 1)
King of Glory (Psalm 24)

Judge of All (2 Corinthians 5)

Commander of the Lord's Army
(Joshua 5)

Redeemer (Isaiah 59)

Lamb of God (John 1)

Son of Man (Matthew 26)

Word of God (Revelation 19)

Messenger of the Covenant (Malachi 3)

Teacher (John 3)

Hope of Glory (Colossians 1)

Our Master (John 13)

Bread of Life (John 6)

Good Shepherd (John 10)

Man of Sorrows (Isaiah 53)

Advocate Before the Father (1 John 2)

The Amen (Revelation 3)

Mighty God (Isaiah 9)

The New and Living Way (Hebrews 10)

The Resurrection and the Life (John 11)

Fragrant Offering to God (Ephesians 5)

Overseer of our Souls (1 Peter 2)

The True Vine (John 15)

Most Excellent of Men (Psalm 45)

Apostle/High Priest of our Faith
(Hebrews 3)

Author/ Finisher of our Faith
(Hebrews 12)

I Am (John 8)

Ancient of Days (Daniel 7)

Root of David (Revelation 5)

Hope of Israel (Acts 28)

Atoning Sacrifice (1 John 2)

Chief Cornerstone (1 Peter 2)

The Foundation (1 Corinthians 3)

Living Stone (1 Peter 2)

The Way, the Truth, the Life (John 14)

One Mediator (1 Timothy 2)

Banner for the Nations (Isaiah 11)

Light for the Nations (Isaiah 49)

The Branch Out of Jesse (Isaiah 11)

Bridegroom (John 1)

Our Brother (Romans 8)

Son of Abraham (Matthew 1)

Heir of All Things (Hebrews 1)

Refiner and Purifier (Malachi 3)

Wonderful Counselor (Isaiah 9)

Wisdom of God (1 Corinthians 1)

Power of God (1 Corinthians 1)

Son of David (Luke 1)

Prince of Peace (Isaiah 9)

Friend of Sinners (Luke 7)

Ransom for Many (1 Timothy 2)

Hidden Treasure (Matthew 13)

God's Indescribable Gift
(2 Corinthians 9)

Bright Morning Star (Revelation 22)

Sun of Righteousness (Malachi 4)

Arm of the Lord (Isaiah 53)

Lamp of the City (Revelation 21)

Light of the World (John 8)

The Good Shepherd (John 10)

Fullness of the Godhead (Colossians 2)

First Fruits (1 Corinthians 15)

The Pearl of Great Price (Matthew 13)

Lion of the Tribe of Judah (Revelation 5)

The King Eternal, Immortal, Invisible,
the Only God (1 Timothy 1)

Name Above Every Name (Philippians 2)

To take another approach: Identify the claims of names we might give him, based on major themes found in each of the 66 books of the Bible. For example:

From Genesis, Jesus is the
Second Adam

From Exodus, Jesus is our Liberator

From Leviticus, Jesus is the
Sacrifice for Sins

From Numbers, Jesus is the
Promised Land

From Deuteronomy, Jesus is our
Master Teacher

From Joshua, Jesus is our
Supreme Commander

From 1 Samuel, Jesus is our
Anointed King

From Ruth, Jesus is our
Kinsman Redeemer

From Psalms, Jesus is our
Worship Leader

From Proverbs, Jesus is our
Life Coach

From Jeremiah, Jesus is our
Weeping Prophet

From Isaiah, Jesus is our
Servant of the Lord

From Haggai, Jesus is our
Glorious Temple

From Malachi, Jesus is our Refiner's Fire

From John, Jesus is Eternal Life

From Acts, Jesus is Savior of All Peoples

From Romans, Jesus is
God's Righteousness

From Ephesians, Jesus is
Head of the Church

From Colossians, Jesus is the
Hope of Glory

From Hebrews, Jesus is our
Great High Priest

From Revelation, Jesus is our
Victorious Champion

That's the idea. Now, why don't you try this approach with other books of the Bible? Pastors and small group leaders: Notice how quickly this gets you started on a full year of weekly topics for sermons and studies on the person of Christ)

The Wrap

Steve Hall, a trainer of Christian leaders in the Pacific Northwest, recently developed a book and online daily audio devotional, *I Want to Know More of Christ* (*http://christnow.com/devotions/*). Each day, he takes one name for Jesus from the Bible, quotes the passage it appears in, and then develops a brief prayer that expands on the claim in that name. He has turned each name or title of Jesus into a combination of adoration and intercession. After Steve created 365 separate meditations he reported that he had discovered sufficient additional names and titles for Jesus to produce a volume two!

Who is Christ **to** us? Steve's prayer for October 14 is one way to answer.

The Radiance of God's Glory

Hebrews 1:1-4
The Son is the Radiance of God's Glory and
the exact representation of his being,
sustaining all things by his powerful word.

Dear Father, I bow before You, the God of glory, and before Your Son, the **Radiance** (splendor, brightness, excellence, perfection, dazzling light) **of God's** (Your) **Glory**. I am deeply grateful that through Christ You fully answered Moses' request in Exodus 33:18, "Now show me more of Christ, the **Radiance of God's Glory**." I rejoice that in the incarnate Son, your magnificent **glory** (the fullness of who you are) is made manifest (radiates out to us), just as John writes in John 1:14: "The Word became flesh and made His dwelling among us. We have seen His **glory,** the **glory** of the One and Only, who came from the Father, full of grace and truth." I want to know all of that **radiance** you will share with me. I pray you will help me grow in my love relationship with Him, experience the depths of his power and **glory**, and speak continually of Him to many, many other believers. I pray you will give me, my family members and all believers in our region an insatiable passion to know all there is to know about Jesus, **the Radiance of God's Glory**, and, thus, to honor and serve and worship you more and more. I join the Doxology in Jude 24-25, "To Him who is able to keep you from falling and to present you before his **glorious** presence without fault and with great joy — to the only God our Savior, be glory, majesty, power, for ever and ever. Amen."

Who Christ Is TO Us Today:
As Our Identity and Destiny

For decades, DC Comics has entertained generations by presenting amazing stories of fictional superheroes such as the Green Lantern, Batman, Spiderman, and Superman. Some of the comics have evolved into global blockbuster movies. Many of these incomparable champions of justice, however, are forced to assume secret identities in order to fulfill their missions.

Take, for example, Superman. Born on the planet Krypton and jettisoned to earth, he was adopted as a baby by a Kansas couple with the surname of Kent. Known from then on as Clark Kent, he grew up incognito. Even as an adult newspaper reporter for the *Daily Planet,* he concealed his blue, red, and yellow Superman uniform underneath the suit of a regular businessman, and further disguised himself by wearing dark-rimmed glasses. His real identity as Superman remained a secret to everyone, even when he disappeared into a phone booth to remove his everyday garments and emerge as Superman, once more ready to fight for "the American way."

In a similar way, *Christians* have a "secret identity." Yes, we are ordinary sinners like everyone around us. Yet, at the same time, we have another identity — an extraordinary one — that only other committed believers can fully appreciate. Our true identity is *Christ himself!* In fact, Christ is the *totality* of our identity before Heaven. That's another facet of who he is *to* us today.

Giving my life to him involved the death of my old self and rebirth of a whole new self; now I'm defined simply as a person who is found *"in Christ."* This means when God looks at me he sees *Christ*, and he sees *me* only in terms of my union with Christ.

Paul writes of this "secret identity" in Colossians 3:

> You died. Now your life is hidden with Christ in God. Christ is your life. When he appears again, you also will appear with him in heaven's glory.

Or as *The Message* paraphrases the passage:

> Your old life is dead. Your new life, which is your *real* life — even though invisible to spectators — is with Christ in God. *He* is your life. When Christ (your real life, remember) shows up again on this earth, you'll show up, too — the real you, the glorious you.

Unfortunately, for many of us Christians this "secret identity" *remains* a secret — not only to our neighbors *but also to ourselves!* Many of us need to reflect much more carefully on how Christ has become *to* us the totality of our own identity. Let's start doing this right now!

 Snapshots and Starter Thoughts

The way God sees his Son is the way God sees us.

Christ has become the riches of Heaven to us.

Christ has become God's righteousness to us.

His story has become our story.

The Way God Sees His Son Is the Way God Sees Us

- **The Father offers us no other identity outside of who we are in his Son.** The Father of our Lord Jesus Christ has become Father to all who belong to him — he "fathers" us *as if* we too were Jesus. The Father's commitment to those who are in Christ is as full and complete as it could ever be. He accepts us exactly the way he accepts and embraces the Son he has always and fully loved from the beginning because we dwell in Jesus (Ephesians 1).

- **God chose us to be his own by uniting us with his Son**.

    All praise to God, the Father of our Lord Jesus Christ, who has blessed us with every spiritual blessing in the heavenly realms because we are united with Christ. Even before he made the world, God loved us and chose us in Christ to be holy and without fault in his eyes . . . So we praise God for the glorious grace he has poured out on us who belong to his dear Son (Ephesians 1, NLT).

- **We are fully accepted because of our total identity with Jesus.** Instead of looking upon our hearts where he sees much that deserves his judgment, the Father sees believers positioned in his Son. He looks upon Jesus' heart — displayed in his life, death, resurrection, and ascension — and treats us *as if* Jesus' heart were our heart. We not only find ourselves to be a new *creation* because we are in Christ but we also have received a new *reputation* before the courts of heaven because we are his.

- **Christ is our peace with God.** Not only does he *offer* us peace with God, but he himself *is* our peace with God.

    At one time you were far away from God. But now you belong to Christ Jesus. He spilled his blood for you. This has brought you near to God. Christ himself is our peace . . . Through Christ we both [Jews and Gentiles] come to the Father by the power of one Holy Spirit (Ephesians 2).

- **Those whom God saves, he saves only "in Christ" — in his person and in his position as the Son of God.** As the Reformers saw it, union with Christ is at the core of every other facet of our salvation.

    And we are in him who is true by being in his Son Jesus Christ. He is the true God and eternal life (1 John 5, NIV).

    . . . the gift of God is eternal life in Christ Jesus our Lord (Romans 6, NIV).

- *Full* **humanity is any humanity in union and communion with God's Son — both**.

    The images of union with Christ, abiding in Christ and participation in Christ present a multifaceted and wide-ranging theology of salvation. No part of human *identity* goes untouched by union with Christ — one's life is found in Christ, by the Spirit, in service to the Father (J. Todd Billings).

- **This is the best of all gifts we receive in Christ.** God gives us more than sins pardoned and a welcome into everlasting life. First, above all else and as the source of all else, he gives us a *new identity* in Jesus. In Jesus, we find the very definition and meaning of our existence.

- **Christ took our identity so we could have his.** As Christ, for our sakes, identified himself with us by becoming one of us, even to the point of dying in our place on the cross, so now we, for *his* sake, are identified with him and exalted in him. As Christ offered himself unconditionally to the Father on the cross, now in the same way we are offered unconditionally to the Father in him because of his cross.

- **He does more than "complete" us; he "repositions" us.** Our coming to Christ is called a "new birth" because we start all over again. Our Savior incorporates us into his own identity so fully that we never again see ourselves as separate from him, and God never sees us outside of him. Jesus "re-places" us — that is, he places us in himself.

- **Without losing our individual uniqueness that was made in God's image, our existence is summed up in who Jesus is — nothing more, nothing less, nothing else.** Christians aren't meant to be defined by who we are *not*, but rather we are people learning every day more of who we have *become* in Christ.

- **Not only have we been redeemed in Christ, we have also been renamed.** "Christian" literally means "of the party of the Christ." We identify with him. We are wrapped up in his kingdom's advance. All we ever will be in God's eyes throughout ages to come is precisely who we are *right now* because we bear his name.

Selah

pause | think | pray

Christ Has Become the Riches of Heaven *to* Us

- **From the beginning, what we sinners lacked above everything else was this: We lacked *Christ*.** Without him, we were eternally impoverished because we lacked all of God's promises that are given only to those who are *in him*. However, united to him who completely encompasses the fullness of the Godhead bodily, we have everything necessary for our eternal salvation (Colossians 2).

- **Jesus defines *our* worth by *his* worth.** He *redeemed* us. Using the vocabulary of business and finance, this means he restored our original value to God. He not only "bought us back" from sin and judgment through the sacrifice of himself, but also, as a result, his infinite value to the Father now guarantees our *own* infinite value to him. God's Son, fully investing his worth in our worth, not only is the totality of our identity but also *our greatest dignity.*

- **We are heirs of Christ because we belong to him** (Romans 8). The Father has decreed that everything Christ is and has — as well as all he has accomplished — is now transferred to those who belong to him.

- **All of God's "riches in glory" are found in Christ alone.** They belong to us only to the extent we belong to him (Philippians 4). In Christ we have everything in heaven and earth we will ever need or want. Paul writes:

  > You know the generous grace of our Lord Jesus Christ. Though he was rich, yet for your sakes he became poor, so that by his poverty he could make you rich (2 Corinthians 8, NLT).

  > As Jerome reminds us: "He is rich enough who is poor *in Christ*" [emphasis added].

- **"Union with Christ does not mean we simply participate in his benefits; rather, we participate in him, in his life, in the fullness of his supremacy,"** writes J. Todd Billings. He continues:

  > In fact, we are so united to him that, as our Mediator, he unites us with the very life of the Godhead. Christ is our identity. We must step into it, live into it and move out from it. This is who we are!

- **Right now, our residence has been relocated permanently to the highest place, into the central courtyard of Jesus' kingdom.**

He has saved us from the kingdom of darkness. He has brought us into the kingdom of the Son he loves. Because of what the Son has done, we have been set free. Because of him, all of our sins have been forgiven (Colossians 1).

Instead, immense in mercy and with an incredible love, he embraced us. He took our sin-dead lives and made us alive in Christ. He did all this on his own, with no help from us! Then he picked us up and set us down in highest heaven in company with Jesus, our Messiah. Now God has us where he wants us, with all the time in this world and the next to shower grace and kindness upon us in Christ Jesus (Ephesians 2, MSG).

- **In Christ, eternal life isn't just something that will happen to us "someday."** It is our "new reality" right now because Christ himself is eternal life *to* us. He is the source, the quality, and the vitality of it — a life available to us every moment because of our union with him.

  And this is the testimony: God has given us eternal life and this life is in his Son. Whoever has the Son has life . . . (1 John 5, NIV).

- **Being "in Christ" is like being a child in a mother's womb.** We draw our existence, our nourishment, our protection, our prospects, and our family status from him   but only so long as we remain in him.

- **We are greatly blessed, not only *by* Jesus but also *with* Jesus because we are *in* Jesus.** We are redefined by the only person in the universe with whom the Father is thoroughly pleased (Luke 3). Therefore, there can be no prospect of lasting blessings for anyone, anywhere, at any time, who remains outside the realm of a relationship with God's dearly loved Son.

Selah

pause | think | pray

Christ Has Become God's Righteousness *to* Us

- **We have peace with God because "the Son gets in his eyes."**

  God is holy, I'm not, and there's no way he can even look at me until I have the covering of Christ's blood. How can a righteous God look at me, a sinner, and see a precious child? Simple: The Son gets in his eyes (Carolyn Arends).

On the other hand, we can't understand how the Father sees us as righteous until the Son gets in *our* eyes too.

- **A marvelous trade has been made!** As the Reformers like Luther taught from Scripture, the Father has brought about a *"happy exchange"*: Christ took upon himself who we are as sinners so that we might take upon ourselves who he is as God's Righteous One.

- **He became our righteousness because he identified with the curse we once bore.**

  Christ redeemed us from that self-defeating, cursed life by absorbing it completely into himself. Do you remember the Scripture that says, "Cursed is everyone who hangs on a tree"? That is what happened when Jesus was nailed to the cross: *He became a curse*, and at the same time dissolved the curse. And now, because of that, the air is cleared . . . We are *all* able to receive God's life, his Spirit, in and with us by believing . . . (Galatians 3, MSG, emphasis added).

- **In Scripture, to be "righteous" means one is standing in a right relationship with God.** Christ's righteousness is the only righteousness that matters before the throne of God. United with Jesus, we share his righteousness; we share *his* right relationship with the Father *as if* it were our own.

- **Christ is our righteousness.** This is not about what we have *done* but about who we *are* in him. He is reckoned by God *to be* **to** us our righteousness (1 Corinthians 1); in fact, we are *made* the righteousness of God in him (2 Corinthians 5). We have received him in place of our transgression, our iniquity, and our treason against Heaven.

- **Christ is our righteousness.** We have no other way to impress God or to escape his tribunal except to hide in, and take as our own, the righteousness of Christ — his eternal righteousness as the Son of God, his earthly righteousness as the Son of Man, his sacrificial righteousness as the Lamb of God, his shared righteousness as the Savior from God.

- **Christ is our righteousness.** Because of *his* righteousness, we have been given a new place before God because we now dwell in his risen Son. All we ever will be in God's eyes throughout all ages to come is precisely who we are to him right now in Jesus.

- **Christ is our righteousness.**

  > I've dumped it all in the trash so that I could embrace Christ and be embraced by him. I didn't want some petty, inferior brand of righteousness that comes from keeping a list of rules when I could get the robust kind that comes from trusting Christ — God's righteousness (Philippians 3, MSG).

- **Christ is our righteousness.**

  > Therefore, if anyone is in Christ, the new creation has come. The old has gone, the new is here! All this is from God, who reconciled us to himself through Christ . . . God made him who had no sin to be sin for us, so that in him we might become the righteousness of God (2 Corinthians 5, NIV).

- **Identified with Jesus' righteousness, the eternal condemnation that would have been ours is rendered in the past tense.** In him, we do not need to fear the slightest hint of accusation, denunciation, or renunciation.

  > So now there is no condemnation for those who belong to Christ Jesus. And because you belong to him, the power of the life-giving Spirit has freed you from the power of sin that leads to death (Romans 8, NLT).

- **For all who are united to Christ, the great judgment day is over**. Just as he will one day gather all things in heaven and on earth to the Father, even so now he has gathered us unto himself so perfectly that God sees us *as if* the day of wrath has come and gone, and we are living with Jesus on the other side in his glorious kingdom. By his Spirit at work in us, we can actually enjoy foretastes of it right now *as if* we were already there.

- **Because his has become our righteousness too, we gladly *boast* in Jesus' righteousness.**

  > God has united you with Christ Jesus. For our benefit God made him to be wisdom itself. Christ made us right with God; he made us pure and holy, and he freed us from sin. Therefore, as the Scriptures say, "If you want to boast, boast only about the LORD" (1 Corinthians 1, NLT).

pause | think | pray

His Story Has Become Our Story

- **What happened to Jesus in his saving ministry to the nations is now reckoned by God to have happened already to us.** The Bible invites believers themselves to reckon these things to be true of us: We were crucified with him (Galatians 2). We were buried with him and then raised again with him (Romans 6). We ascended with him (Ephesians 2). To this moment, our life is hidden with him in God (Colossians 3). His story is now our story.

- **His death was our death.** This has totally rewritten our story and set us off in a new direction.

  > My old self has been crucified with Christ. It is no longer I who live, but Christ lives in me. So I live in this earthly body by trusting in the Son of God, who loved me and gave himself for me (Galatians 2, NLT).

  Here's how *The Message* puts that Galatians 2 passage:

  > I identified myself completely with him. Indeed, I have been crucified with Christ. My ego is no longer central. It is no longer important that I appear righteous before you or have your good opinion, and I am no longer driven to impress God. Christ lives in me. The life you see me living is not "mine," but it is lived by faith in the Son of God, who loved me and gave himself for me. I am not going to go back on that.

- **His resurrection is our resurrection.** His story is our story — our only story — because now he is the only life we have. The whole human race has come under the sentence of death. But, being in union with Christ — the Victor raised from the dead, who is "the firstborn from among the dead" (Colossians 1) — means our new story involves us with him in a new creation, as a new humanity, under a new dominion, all of which will one day encompass the entire universe.

- **Therefore, his *journey* has become our journey, as we walk in union with him In the newness of his resurrected life, from here to eternity.**

As Paul puts it:

> Since we believe that Christ died for all, we also believe that we have all died to our old life. He died for everyone so that those who receive his new life will no longer live for themselves. Instead, they will live for Christ, who died and was raised for them (2 Corinthians 5, NLT).

- **"Let him who would live to God come out of the grave with Christ forever" (Martin Luther).** To be a new person in Christ Jesus means we see ourselves and present ourselves to the Father *as if* we already possessed the freshness and vigor of resurrection victory — *as if* the day of resurrection had already come for us.

- **In Christ, we also enter into the drama of his ongoing intimacy with the Father.** Christ has become *to* us our mouth by which we speak to God. He has become *to* us our eyes by which we see God. He has become *to* us our hands by which we offer service to God.

- **Christian discipleship is a call to live the "ascended life" because of our identity and union with the Ascended One.** Since our story has become part of Christ's story, we are seated with him in heavenly places (Ephesians 2 and Revelation 5) where we reign with him right now.

> ... how much more will those who receive God's abundant provision of grace and of the gift of righteousness reign in life through the one man, Jesus Christ ... so that, just as sin reigned in death, so also grace might reign through righteousness to bring eternal life through Jesus Christ our Lord (Romans 5, NIV).

Abiding in Christ, disciples should live *as if* we already had been to heaven only to be sent back to earth to live for his praises and his purposes in this generation.

- **Even *physically*, his story is our story.** Joined to Christ, our bodies right now are regarded as members of his body even as our spirits are one with his Spirit (1 Corinthians 6). Daily our bodies are presented to him to become instruments for his righteous design as we play our part in the "plot" unfolding in his story (Romans 6).

- **Christ provides himself as the Spirit's armor to cover us as we join the part of the story where he wars against dark spiritual forces.** United to him, we arise encased in his righteousness, truth, salvation, and strength as our protection. Proclaiming the message of who he is **to** us forges for us our mightiest weapon in the battle (Ephesians 6). In fact, we are urged to clothe ourselves with Christ from top to bottom (Romans 13).

- **Forever, *his* story has become *our* story; *his* identity, *our* identity; and *his* destiny *our* destiny.** Every believer's story is wrapped up in and completed by his story. He is the beginning of our new story. He is the climax toward which our story is moving. He is also the *means* to reach the final chapter. The *plot* of our story is all about Christ and his kingdom. We have collapsed our story into the larger drama of *his* story, the one compelling drama that incorporates all of creation into the liberation of those who participate in his story (Romans 8). Our old story has been woven masterfully into his everlasting story, to reappear totally rewritten, incorporated into his grand finale!

The Wrap

We are so engulfed in Jesus that the Father declares us to be dead, buried, alive again, and seated in glory with him forever. Our identity with Christ is so *total* that his present and his future have become our present and our future.

Apart from Jesus, we would be without God and without hope in this world (Ephesians 2). Instead, he has become for us all the hope we have or will ever need. United to him, we get to share in every prospect God decrees for his Son for all ages to come. Reputations we once held dear have perished, to be replaced by God's promises for all of us whose total identity now is found in Christ alone.

It has been said that the eternal past has no other eternal future but Christ alone. The outcome of all things for all creation and for all humankind — and for all believers — is now entirely tied to the outcome of all things for Christ alone.

Only in union with Christ can we become fully engaged in the unfolding of God's kingdom purposes. Our identity and our destiny are defined by who Jesus *is*, right now — who he is **to** us, and consequently who we are in him.

Who Christ Is TO Us Today:
As the Father's Passion and Ours

Augustine is considered by some to be the greatest Christian leader since the apostle Paul. His writings in the 4th century majored on his own devotion to Christ, to which he summoned all believers.

That he was a man of passion should come as no surprise. Augustine moved to Carthage at age 17 to continue his education. Although raised as a Christian, there he deserted the church to pursue a hedonistic lifestyle along with his fellow students. They were consumed with sex — constantly thinking about it, pursuing erotic hookups. During this time, he began an affair with a young lady who became his lover for over thirteen years, with whom he had a son.

Through all these years, Augustine's Christian mother never ceased to pray for his salvation. One day her prayers were answered. On a visit to his childhood home in North Africa, he was caught up in one of the most famous of all recorded Christian conversions. It brought him into a *new* kind of passion — a fire of love for Jesus Christ that never ceased burning from that moment forward. Here's how he described this experience in *Confessions:*

> Lo! I heard from a neighboring house a voice, as of boy or girl, I know not, chanting, and oft repeating, "Take up and read; take up and read." Instantly, my countenance altered . . . I arose; interpreting it to be no other than a command from God to open the book [Bible], and read the first chapter I should find . . . I

seized, opened, and in silence read that section on which my eyes first fell [in Romans 13] "... put on the Lord Jesus Christ, and make no provision for the lusts of the flesh." Instantly at the end of this sentence, by a light as it were of serenity infused into my heart, all the darkness of doubt vanished away.

Years later, reflecting on his conversion and the profound, permanent longing for Christ it had stirred up in him, Augustine wrote:

> You cried, you shouted, you shattered my deafness.
> You sparkled, you burned, you scattered my blindness.
> You shed forth your fragrance and I drew in my breath,
> and now, my soul pants for you alone.

His passion for Jesus was expressed by the human senses of hearing, seeing, smelling, and tasting. Who was Christ *to* him? He was Augustine's *consuming* passion.

And so it should be for all of us! Why? Most of all, because God the Son is the consuming passion of God the Father.

 Snapshots and Starter Thoughts

The Son has always been the one eternal passion of the Father.

Therefore, Jesus must become *our* ever-increasing passion as well.

The Son Has Always Been the One Eternal Passion of the Father

- **Jesus is the Father's magnificent obsession.** Within the Trinity, the Father is so passionate for the Son that he has decreed that in everything the Son is to have the preeminence, the primacy, the supremacy (Colossians 1). Should Jesus be any less to us than the consuming passion of our lives as well?

- **Christ is the one person in the entire universe to whom God has ever said without qualifications, "With you I am well pleased."** We might say, "Jesus is the apple of his father's eye." Peter writes:

  We were there for the preview! We saw it with our own eyes: Jesus resplendent with light from God the Father as the voice of Majestic Glory spoke: "This is my Son, marked by my love, focus of all my delight." We were there on the holy mountain with him. We heard the voice out of heaven with our very own ears. We couldn't be more sure of what we saw and heard — God's glory, God's voice. The prophetic Word was confirmed to us. You'll do well to keep focusing on it (2 Peter 1, MSG).

Taking Peter's exhortation to heart, can we do other than focus on Christ as our overriding delight as well?

- **Christ, the only begotten of the Father, came from "the Father's bosom"** (John 1, NASB). As we've seen, this metaphor suggests deep intimacy and great affection. It means that Jesus is, and always has been, the focus of everything the Father desires, designs, and decrees. Should he not also be that to all believers?

- **Again and again in the New Testament, God wants to be *known* as "the Father of the Lord Jesus Christ."** Just as an earthly father is fully satisfied and honored when an earthly son receives the attention and praise of others, it is the same for God the Father. Have you ever noticed that whenever God speaks audibly in the Gospels it is either to or about his Son? This shows us how attentive a Father he is to his Son.

- **The Father's original passion for his own glory now has assumed its ultimate expression as a passion for the fame and reign of his dear Son.** Yahweh exclaims:

  I am the LORD; that is my name! I will not give my glory to anyone else (Isaiah 42, NLT).

  Yet, he *has* exalted his Son to the highest place — not diminishing the Father's glory but only magnifying it more and more. Jesus prayed in John 17:

  Father, the time has come. Bring glory to your Son. Then your Son will bring glory to you. You gave him authority over all people. He gives eternal life to all those you have given him. And what is eternal life? It is knowing you, the only true God, and Jesus Christ, whom you have sent.

- **In the courts of heaven, the Father places the Son at the center of the throne**:

> One of the Elders said, "Don't weep. Look — the Lion from Tribe Judah, the Root of David's Tree, has conquered" . . . So I looked, and there, surrounded by Throne, Animals, and Elders, was a Lamb, slaughtered but standing tall. Seven horns he had, and seven eyes, the Seven Spirits of God sent into all the earth. He came to the One Seated on the Throne and took the scroll from his right hand. The moment he took the scroll, the Four Animals and Twenty-four Elders fell down and worshiped the Lamb (Revelation 5, MSG).

Do we give him the same honor? In our hearts and in our churches do we give him the same position of supremacy the Father is giving him right now?

- **The Father is so passionate for the triumphs of his Son that he has decreed him to be the heir of all things.** We read:

> . . . but in these last days he has spoken to us by his Son, whom he appointed heir of all things . . . (Hebrews 1, NIV).

In the upper room Jesus declared:

> All that belongs to the Father is mine. That is why I said the Spirit will receive from me what he will make known to you (John 16, NIV).

As we saw earlier, Psalm 2 reports:

> For the Lord declares, "I have placed my chosen king on the throne in Jerusalem, on my holy mountain." The king proclaims the LORD's decree. "The LORD said to me: You are my son. Today I have become your Father. Only ask, and I will give you the nations as your inheritance, the whole earth as your possession" (Psalms 2, NLT).

Is Jesus this precious to us? Do we desire the same inheritance for him that the Father does?

- **The Father's passion for the mission of his Son has never diminished.** He ordained his Son to be the world's redeemer, sent him to fulfill this mission, empowered him at every step, and delivered him from death in order to exalt him to reign over all. Then he poured out his Spirit as testimony to the world about the universal preeminence given his Son. Now through the Son he is reconciling us, and with us he is reconciling the whole universe back to himself. With such purposeful collaboration, we surely must conclude that the Son holds forever the infinite affection of the Father. So the question is: Does Jesus have our undying affection as well?

- **The Father's passion for his Son is the guarantee of our ultimate triumph in every facet of spiritual warfare in the universe.** The greatest threat to Satan's dominion or his power over our lives is the special, unique relationship the Son has to the Father as the Lord of our lives. As we become increasingly passionate for Jesus the way the Father is, we will also experience more of his victory over powers of darkness. Triumphs are secured for the Church by focusing fervently on who Christ is *to* us, not on all the devil throws at us.

- **The Father is zealous to reveal his Son to us as his Messiah; unless we grasp that, he knows we cannot worship the living God for who he really is.** This is what Peter discovered:

  > Simon Peter answered, "You are the Messiah, the Son of the living God." Jesus replied, "Blessed are you, Simon, son of Jonah! No mere man showed this to you. My Father in heaven showed it to you" (Matthew 16).

  Should it not be our fervent prayer that the Father would daily reveal to us more and more of the glory of his Son?

- **The Father is totally wrapped up in the ministry of his Son, committed to securing for him unsurpassed honor among all the redeemed.**

  > What the Father does, the Son also does. This is because the Father loves the Son. The Father shows him everything he does. Yes, and the Father will show the Son even greater works than these. And you will be amazed. The Father raises the dead and gives them life. In the same way, the Son gives life to anyone he wants to. Also, the Father does not judge anyone. He has given the Son the task of judging. Then all people will honor the Son just as they honor the Father. Whoever does not honor the Son does not honor the Father, who sent him (John 5).

What greater destiny do we have than this? As God's people we are invited to bring delight to the Father's heart by delighting in his Son the same way he does.

Therefore, Jesus Must Become *Our* Ever-Increasing Passion as Well

- **Here's how one Christian leader, Paul, spoke of his own preoccupation with Christ:**

  > . . . now, as always, I should honor Christ with the utmost boldness by the way I live, whether that means I am to face death or to go on living. *For living to me means simply "Christ", and if I die I should merely gain more of him* . . . I long to leave this world and live with Christ . . . But whatever happens, make sure that your everyday life is worthy of the Gospel of Christ (Philippians 1, PHILLIPS, emphasis added).

- **Can we ever think too highly of God's Son, or put too much stock in him, or be too infatuated with him, or grow too deeply in love with him?** The Father gave his dearest and his best for us. He sent the One who eternally has captured his very heart to die for us. Then he raised him up "so that in everything Christ might have the supremacy" (Colossians 1). Should Jesus not occupy for us the same kind of attention and affection he receives from the Father? Should we not find Christ to be our highest joy as well, our treasure for whom we would sell everything (Matthew 13)?

- **The Father wants us to hold forever dear *Jesus crucified,* while we celebrate with increasing devotion *Jesus glorified.*** And he is moving toward that great day when *every* being in all creation will join him in the celebration of his Son. Paul writes:

  > He [Jesus] was humble and obeyed God completely. He did this even though it led to his death. Even worse, he died on a cross! So God lifted him up to the highest place. God gave him the name that is above every name. When the name of Jesus is spoken, everyone will kneel down to worship him. Everyone in heaven and on earth and under the earth will kneel down to worship him. Everyone's mouth will say that Jesus Christ is Lord. And God the Father will receive the glory (Philippians 2).

  Why should we not begin the celebration right now? Should we not hold Jesus as precious to us, right now, as we know he is to the Father?

- **The Spirit desires to ignite in us a fire of passion for the Son.** In John 16, we learn the Spirit exhibits the very same passion for the Son that the Father has. In 1 Corinthians 2 we're told the Spirit intends to give us a perspective on the deep things of God as found in Jesus Christ. The Spirit never ceases to seek praises for the Son of God from the people of God

— to cause us to cherish the Son the way the Father cherishes him.

> But when the Spirit of truth comes, he will guide you into all the truth. He will not speak on his own. He will speak only what he hears. And he will tell you what is still going to happen. He will bring me glory. That's because what he receives from me he will show to you. Everything that belongs to the Father is mine. That is why I said what the Holy Spirit receives from me he will show to you (John 16).

- **As the Father looks at creation, or history, or redemption, or the Consummation, *his fondest focal point remains his Son* and who the Son is in the midst of all the rest.** *Should Jesus be any less a focus for us today?* Jesus said about Mary concerning her choice to sit at his feet, caught up entirely with him:

> One thing only is essential, and Mary has chosen it — it's the main course, and won't be taken from her (Luke 10, MSG).

- **To believers everywhere Jesus must remain forever our supreme love.** To the Ephesian church Jesus appealed:

> I see what you've done, your hard, hard work, your refusal to quit. I know you can't stomach evil, that you weed out apostolic pretenders. I know your persistence, your courage in my cause, that you never wear out. But you walked away from your first love — why? What's going on with you, anyway? Do you have any idea how far you've fallen? (Revelation 2, MSG).

The Greek word translated "first" comes from the same root as the word in Colossians 1:18 translated "supremacy." To treat Jesus as our "first love" means we seek to shower on him unsurpassed, unparalleled, undiluted, undistracted love.

- **That means Christ must remain our *only* love too.** Augustine observed that whenever we do love anyone else or anything else, that love must be subsumed into our love for Christ or else our love for Christ is less than what the Father wants it to be. Jesus put it this way:

> Anyone who loves their father or mother more than me is not worthy of me. Anyone who loves their son or daughter more than me is not worthy of me. Whoever does not pick up their cross and follow me is not worthy of me (Matthew 10).

And again:

> If any of you wants to be my follower, you must give up your own way,

take up your cross, and follow me. If you try to hang on to your life, you will lose it. But if you give up your life for my sake and for the sake of the Good News, you will save it (Mark 8, NLT).

- **Paul models for all of us the kind of passion the Father wants every believer to have for his Son.**

Yet every advantage that I had gained I considered lost for Christ's sake. Yes, and I look upon everything as loss compared with the overwhelming gain of knowing Jesus Christ my Lord. For his sake I did in actual fact suffer the loss of everything, but I considered it useless rubbish compared with being able to win Christ. For now my place is in him . . . How changed are my ambitions! Now I long to know Christ and the power shown by his resurrection: Now I long to share his sufferings, even to die as he died . . . But I keep going on, grasping ever more firmly that purpose for which Christ grasped me . . . *All of us who are spiritually adult should set ourselves this sort of ambition . . . Let me be your example here, my brothers: let my example be the standard by which you can tell who are the genuine Christians among those about you* (Philippians 3, PHILLIPS, emphasis added).

The Wrap

The Father's love for his Son is like a fire. It is all-consuming for him — just like *ours* for Christ should be.

Like the flaming bush on Mount Horeb, where Moses fell with his face on holy ground, this passion can never burn itself out. The Spirit keeps it constantly refueled.

Ephesians 6 concludes with this benediction:

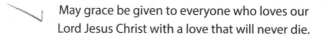

> May grace be given to everyone who loves our Lord Jesus Christ with a love that will never die.

The Greek word refers to a love that's "incorruptible" or "immortal." It is deathless, unwavering — always ablaze.

Forever, Jesus is worthy of the deepest devotion from his people. He must become the preeminent fire of our most passionate affections.

This has always characterized the Father's love for his Son. Now, the Father summons us to settle for nothing less. His passion for Jesus must infuse our own passion for who Jesus is to us today.

Who Christ Is TO Us Today:
A Tribute

Paraphrasing and personalizing a wide selection of Scriptures

Father, we come to you to proclaim the name of your Son together — to spread his fame, embrace his reign, increase his gain, and honor his claim about who he is *to* us. As we do, awake us to him afresh to ALL that he is. May the praise we bring to him in these moments come forth alive in us by your Spirit and rise up as a blessing to you forever. We use your Word to magnify your Son, without whom we are nothing and can do nothing. This tribute is all for Christ alone,⌐ our one and only hope of glory and the hope of all the nations.

**Lord Jesus Christ, this is our tribute to you —
our tribute to who you are TO us.**

There is one God and Father from whom all things come and for whom we exist. There is equally one Lord — you are that one Lord; through you all things come and through you alone we exist. We celebrate you for who you are *to* us. You are the Son the Father loves, with whom he is well pleased — with whom we are well pleased too. All that the Father has is yours. Therefore, the Spirit takes all that is yours and reveals it to us. We receive this revelation with great joy, and we are hungry for more. By the will of God, we are your disciples, focused on you alone and on all you are *to* us, because we have been baptized into the name of the triune One — Father, Son, and Spirit.

Christ Is NOW!

Like John, we stand in awe of your face shining like the sun. We behold your eyes like flames of fire. We hear your voice like the thunder of mighty waters. We are as dead men before you. We declare you to be *to* us Alpha and Omega, Beginning and End, the First and the Last. Before Abraham was, you always were. We have no other past but you; we want no other future but you. This is who you are *to* us, as well as *to* all the nations.

Christ Is NOW!

You were in the beginning with God and you are God. You, the one eternally folded in the bosom of the Father, are the only one who truly knows God, and yet you have declared him to us. You said that those who see you actually do see the Father. Your Word says that those who have you automatically have the Father too. You said that eternal life is to know both you and the Father. John wrote that you, as God's Son, are the true God and eternal life. Truly, you are the holiness of God. You are the perfection of God. You are the righteousness of God. You are the wisdom of God. You are the power of God. You are also the lover of our souls. What wondrous love is this! This is who you are *to* us as well as *to* all the nations.

Christ Is NOW!

Forever you are the radiance of God's glory and the exact representation of his very being. Forever you are the image of the invisible God, the firstborn of creation, the firstborn from the dead. No wonder by you all things were made in heaven and earth, visible and invisible. You are before all things and in you all things are held together, as you alone sustain all things by your powerful word. No wonder you are superior to everything that has ever been created, including even the angels around the throne. No wonder your name is the name above every name, both in this age and in all the ages to come. This is who you are *to* us, as well as *to* all the nations.

Christ Is NOW!

To us you are the one who fulfills the royal praises in Psalm 45, which declares that you are most excellent, anointed with grace, God-blessed forever. In your majesty you ride forth victoriously. Your throne will last forever and ever. You are anointed with joy, with robes fragrant with the glory of God.

You are almighty. Supreme. Majestic. Wonder-filled. Incomparable. We behold you, Lord Jesus, at the center of the Father's throne, with myriads of angels proclaiming you as worthy, worthy, worthy. We behold you magnified by the floodlight from lamps, which represent the seven-fold Spirit. We behold you and rejoice in you as the triumphant Lamb before whom all creation and all the redeemed of all the ages bow down and worship, before whom all of us here and now, bow down and worship. To YOU belong blessing and honor and glory and strength and power forever and ever. All of Scripture, all of creation, all of history, all of the purposes and prophecies and promises of God are summed up *in you alone.*

This tribute expresses only a small part of the inexhaustible riches of who you are TO us and all peoples.

So, Father: Here is how we celebrate your Son, our Lord Jesus Christ, in this hour. We exalt him. We exult in him. We do so because of all he is *to* us — now. Therefore, everything we are and have, every breath we breathe, every step we take, every service we render, every prayer we pray, every praise we bring is possible only by him and him alone. For without him — without all he is *to* us — we are nothing and we can do nothing. More and more, by the revealing work of your Spirit, awaken us to Christ alone — awaken your whole Church to Christ alone — so that increasingly he might become *to* us our all in all.

AMEN!

Exploring and Experiencing

Who Christ Is FOR Us Today

Renowned British scholar Dr. Paul Johnson speaks as a historian and devout Christian: "Ours is an historical religion or it is nothing. It does not deal in myths and states of being. It deals in facts. It presupposes a linear flight of time, through a real universe of concrete events." The consequential nature of this second chapter — looking at who Christ is FOR us today — depends on the validity of Johnson's conclusion. These things really happened.

Many, however, overlook the funda-mental necessity of the historicity of Jesus' earthly ministry. Alain de Botton, for example, argues in *Religion for Atheists* that atheists have a great deal to learn from traditions like Christianity. Claims de Botton:

> One can be left cold by *doctrines* of the Christian trinity ... and yet at the same time be interested in ways in which religions deliver sermons, promote morality, engender a spirit of community, make use of art and architecture, inspire travels, train minds and encourage

> gratitude at the beauty of spring . . . Many aspects of the faiths remain relevant *after their central tenets have been dismissed*" (emphasis added).

Unfortunately, for de Botton and the growing millions around the world who don't believe in God, the "central tenets" of the Christian faith cannot be dismissed. Why? It is because they are thoroughly rooted in actual, historical events (as this chapter explores).

In fact, if God's Son had not literally become incarnate in Mary's womb to later minister among Judean crowds; if he had not literally suffered and died one Friday; if he had not walked bodily from a tomb on a Sunday; if he had not ascended forty days later in that same body to the place of highest honor; then there would be no Church today, no two billion followers of Jesus across the globe.

There are, tragically, other voices *inside* the Church that would dismiss the four great tenets of what Jesus *did for* us — the Incarnation, the Crucifixion, the Resurrection, the Ascension — by trading them in favor of a stronger emphasis on what he *taught* us. *Newsweek* ran a front cover story by respected journalist Andrew Sullivan (who openly claims Catholic affiliation) with his call to "Follow Jesus." The author highlighted, favorably, Thomas Jefferson's snipping of the Gospels to remove all references to the supernatural in order to salvage a record of Jesus' wisdom and good deeds. Sullivan invites his readers to grasp the "core simplicity of Jesus' message of renunciation," proposing that the *message* of Jesus was the deepest miracle.

Sullivan goes on to write: "The cross itself was not the point . . . the point was how he conducted himself through it all — calm, loving, accepting, radical surrendering . . ." In turn, we are urged to follow that example. In this scenario, Jesus could simply be a compelling myth and still serve a useful purpose.

Christian author and editor Trevin Wax wrote a spot-on blog post about the article:

> Sullivan wants to return to the simple message of Jesus as if that message can be divorced from the Man who delivered it . . . His message was about himself, His Kingdom, His identity as king, and the cross that became His throne . . . and a victorious resurrection that launches the new world God promised.

In other words, to echo historian Paul Johnson, either what Scripture reports Jesus *did for us* (not just what he *says to us*, as important as that is) actually did take place in real time, visibly and physically, in space and history, or we are ultimately left with "nothing" at all (per Johnson) regarding our eternal destiny.

In point of fact, Christ's *words* are so closely bound with his miraculous *person* and redeeming *works* that it all stands or falls together. What he did **for** us validates and empowers all he spoke to us. This will become abundantly clear in the following pages, which are filled with "snapshots and starter thoughts" about his historic fourfold action on our behalf.

Jesus' Irreversible Fourfold Revolution

A Christian's great joy is this: "If God is *for us,* who can ever be against us? Since he did not spare even his own Son but gave him up *for us all,* won't he also give us everything else?" (Romans 8: 31-32, NLT, emphasis added).

In the face of our utter destitution, God championed our cause as he descended in order to enter into our despair. He acted **for** our best interests, intervened **for** our brokenness, stood up **for** us in the Judgment, and fought **for** us against evil forces. He did so by providing **for** us One — and there is no other sufficient **for** us but *this* One — who accomplished on our behalf all we needed in order to be rescued from the domain of darkness and transferred into the kingdom of his dear Son (Colossians 1:13-14).

Today's believers live in the full assurance that we have been reconciled back to God by means of four extraordinary and unrepeatable but observable and literal *events*. Because of these four "for us" *facts*, heaven and earth are now entwined forever; our future is permanently defined by a Savior who is alive and "for us" right now.

As amazing as all of this is, there's even more here. Scripture claims all that Christ accomplished **for** us is also intended to happen, at the same time, *with* us — in time, and space, and history. Already believers have been united with him in his "new humanity." Equally, his death and his rising and ascending as one of us, *includes* us. God sees us *as if* we died with him, *as if* we were buried and raised with him, and *as if* we have begun to reign with him (2 Timothy 2:11). Those are additional facts about what Christ has done **for** us.

One vital result of all of this, however, must be kept in mind: Now and always, because he gave himself for *us* we must give ourselves for *him*. Writing in *Christianity Today*, John Koessler cautions:

> Jesus came *for* us, but that does not mean that he came to *please* us. Jesus came *for* us, but he does not answer to us. He will not subject himself to our agenda, no matter how good that agenda might be. Jesus demands that we submit ourselves to his agenda (emphasis added).

Call them Christ's "Irreversible Fourfold Revolution"— these four magnificent events that comprise the work of salvation Christ has accomplished **for** us. They give us every reason to live, unconditionally, *in* him and *for* him. In this chapter we explore and experience this "Irreversible Fourfold Revolution" in this order:

The Invasion of His Incarnation

The Mission of His Crucifixion

The Re-creation of His Resurrection

The Coronation of His Ascension

Who Christ Is FOR Us Today:
By the Invasion of His Incarnation

One of the most popular Christmas hymns, "O Come, All Ye Faithful," contains some interesting phrases in its seven plus verses, such as:

> Behold Him, born the King of angels
>
> God of God . . . he abhors not the Virgin's womb
>
> Word of the Father, now in flesh appearing
>
> Poor and in the manger, we would embrace Thee
>
> O Come, let us adore Him, Christ the Lord

Doesn't that sound like some kind of "invasion" to you?

As this chapter is being written, the Christmas season is bursting out all over the land. A cacophony of carols competes with the clamor, clutter, and confusion confronting frantic shoppers everywhere. Sadly, the holiday — dreaming of white Christmases with all days merry and bright — is about as far from the truth of what happened two thousand years ago as *"inversion"* is from *"invasion."*

What an *invasion* the Incarnation was! Popular theologian and author Michael Horton, in an article titled "The Good God Who Came Down," sees Advent as a rebuke to mankind's preference to climb up to God on our own. "Our hearts are idol factories," he writes, "in bondage to sin and spin. We look for a god we can manage rather than the God who is actually there."

Because of this "inversion," the invasion of the Incarnation has become our only hope. Horton defines the distinctiveness of this invasion this way:

> God has climbed down to us, meeting us not in the "high places" we erect, but in the lowest places: in a barn, suffering our scorn, fellowshipping with sinners . . . the humility of a feeding trough and a cross.

Curiously, this "incarnation invasion" speaks directly to a major contemporary global concern: the challenge the gospel faces in Muslim lands. The debate is not about two religions, Christianity and Islam; nor about two books, the Bible and the Quran; nor about two personalities, Christ and Muhammad. Rather, the tension is between *Christ* and the *Quran*. Why? Because Muslims believe the Quran — every single page with every one of its Arabic words — is an incarnation of Allah himself. In it Christ is portrayed simply as one of the most important, maybe the most unique, of Allah's long line of prophets. But for them the Koran is supreme because it is divine.

The New Testament message, however, is that the living God has come to us *as one of us* — not simply in words on pages, but as a genuine, living, breathing human being. Furthermore, his coming is not passive like a sacred book lying on a coffee table. Rather, Jesus himself is God among us, permanently united to us, taking strategic action **for** us to save us and liberate us. *This* kind of incarnation requires nothing less than a God-orchestrated *invasion*. It's like the game-changing landing of allied troops in Normandy on D-Day during World War II. Only Jesus did it for the "joy set before him" (Hebrews 12) — which was us, redeemed by his blood.

We will survey this invasion of his incarnation around seven themes.

Snapshots and Starter Thoughts

The entirety of the Deity deliberately took on frailty **for** us.

To do what Christ has done **for** us, he had to be united to us.

His incarnation invasion provides **for** our reconciliation.

Becoming one of us, Jesus proves God's *total* commitment to us.

Jesus embodies God's servant heart toward us and **for** us.

In compassion, Christ *personally* engaged our low and lost estate.

Forever as one of us, Christ defines what lies ahead for all of us.

The Entirety of the Deity Deliberately Took on Frailty *for* Us

- **Nearly 317 church fathers, meeting in A.D. 325 at Nicea (in modern Turkey), unanimously defined the Incarnation's mystery in a creed that included**:

  > We believe in one God, the Father Almighty, maker of all things visible and invisible. And in one Lord Jesus Christ, the Son of God, begotten of the Father, Light of Light, very God of very God, begotten, not made, being of one substance with the Father; by whom all things were made; who for us men, and for our salvation, came down and was incarnate and was made man; he suffered, and the third day he rose again, ascended into heaven; from thence he shall come to judge the quick and the dead.

- **It is a mystery how Jesus brings human nature and the Godhead together in a person who will never cease to be one of us and *for* us.**

  > There is no doubt that godliness is a great mystery. *Jesus came as a human being.* The Holy Spirit proved that he was the Son of God. He was seen by angels. He was preached among the nations. People in the world believed in him. He was taken up to heaven in glory (1 Timothy 3, emphasis added).

- **Jesus retains unity with the Trinity and with our humanity, both at the same time.** He embodies two natures, without confusion and without division. He did not change what he was (God); rather he took on what he was not (human). He added to himself our humanity and our frailty without compromising his deity.

- **No other person in the universe has brought human nature and the Divinity together like this.** This is not God *in* a human being; it is God *as* a human being.

  > For in Christ lives all the fullness of God in a human body. So you also are complete through your union with Christ, who is the head over every ruler and authority (Colossians 2, NLT).

- **"The characteristics of humanity become the property of God the Son, while the characteristics of his divine life become the property of his human nature."**

  > In other words, God the Son acquires the qualities of a human being in addition to his divine qualities. He is no longer just a divine person. Now he is a divine person with a human nature. His divinity and humanity are not fused together in some mixture of divine and human characteristics, like many heroes of myth and legend. Rather, his two natures are held together in this one complex person (Oliver D. Crisp).

- **All that makes God *God* took on bodily form in Jesus.** Note how *The Message* expands on this in Colossians 2:

  > Everything of God gets expressed in [Christ], so you can see and hear him clearly. You don't need a telescope, a microscope, or a horoscope to realize the fullness of Christ, and the emptiness of the universe without him. When you come to him, that fullness comes together for you, too. His power extends over everything.

- **In Jesus resides the *entirety* of Deity — not just some portion of it — alive in one single human being.** Jesus did not simply excel in certain endowments of Heaven's gifts and power. He is the true and perfect God with all divine attributes, such as infinite wisdom and goodness, permanently dwelling among us, as one of us, **for** us.

- **No aspect of God's fullness was withheld from us when Jesus came among us.**

  > The Word became a human being. He made his home with us. We have seen his glory. It is the glory of the one and only Son. He came from the Father. And *he was full of grace and truth* (John 1, emphasis added).

  > Don't you know me, Philip? I have been among you such a long time! *Anyone who has seen me has seen the Father.* So how can you say, "Show us the Father"? Don't you believe that I am in the Father? Don't

you believe that the Father is in me? The words I say to you are not just my own. The Father lives in me. He is the One who is doing his work (John 14, emphasis added).

God, who first ordered 'light to shine in darkness', has flooded our hearts with his light. We now can enlighten men only because we can give them knowledge of *the glory of God, as we see it in the face of Jesus Christ* (2 Corinthians 4, PHILLIPS, emphasis added).

- **The annual Advent season especially amplifies this supremely awesome mystery.** Christmas does not mark simply another observance in the liturgical calendar. Rather, it defines a monumental, unparalleled, unrepeatable, inexplicable moment "when eternity entered time, sanctified it and caught it up into eternity" (Thomas Merton); when "infinity dwindled to infancy" (Edward T. Oakes). The all-powerful Son of *God* stepped into frailty — in time and space and history — as the Son of *Man*.

- **Bishop Melito of Sardis, writing late in the second century, captured the mystery beautifully:**

He appeared as one of the sheep, yet He still remained the Shepherd.

He was esteemed a servant, yet He did not renounce his Sonship.

He was carried in the womb of Mary,
yet arrayed in the nature of his Father.

He walked upon the earth, yet He filled heaven.

He appeared as an infant,
yet He did not discard the eternity of his nature.

He needed sustenance inasmuch as He was man;
Yet, He did not cease to feed the entire world inasmuch as He is God.

Selah

pause | think | pray

To Do What Christ Has Done *for* Us, He Had to Be United to Us

- **Christ came *among* us, as one *of* us, to be seen *by* us, forever to be *with* us — all of this *for* us.**

  > Here is what we announce to everyone about the Word of life . . . We have heard him. We have seen him with our eyes. We have looked at him. Our hands have touched him. That life has appeared. We have seen him. We give witness about him . . . He has appeared to us. We announce to you what we have seen and heard. We do it so you can share life together with us. And we share life with the Father and with his Son, Jesus Christ (1 John 1).

- **"Christ became what we are so we could become what he is."** That often quoted observation, written in the fourth century by church father Athanasius of Alexandria, is found in his best-known treatise, *The Incarnation of the Word.* He expanded on it this way:

  > Christ took a human body, born of a pure virgin in whose womb he made human flesh his own, in which to reveal himself, conquer death, and restore life . . . He took pity on our race, and had mercy on our weakness, and lowered himself to our corruption. He could not bear to let death have mastery, to allow these creatures to perish, and his Father's handiwork come to nothing, and so he took on a body, no different from ours . . . Since only death could stop the plague, the Word took a mortal body, so that all who become united with him might receive his immortality.

- **In other words, there was a time when the future reclamation of the universe resided in a helpless baby.**

  > The people who walked in darkness have seen a great light. For those who lived in a land of deep shadows — light! sunbursts of light! . . . For a child has been born — for us! The gift of a son — for us! He'll take over the running of the world (Isaiah 9, MSG).

- **This stunning, divine invasion landed, of all places, in the womb of a teenage Jewish virgin.** The second person of the Trinity chose to reduce himself to a supernaturally fertilized egg, attached to the wall of a womb.

  > Do not be afraid, Mary . . . you will become pregnant and give birth to a son. You must name him Jesus . . . His kingdom will never end . . . The Holy Spirit will come to you. The power of the Most High God will cover you. So the holy one that is born will be called the Son of God . . . Nothing is impossible with God (Luke 1).

- **While still a defenseless infant at his mother's breast, Jesus ignited praise from those who grasped how his advent would make possible their everlasting salvation.** Consider these two witnesses:

  > [Simeon]: Simeon took Jesus in his arms and praised God. He said . . . "My eyes have seen your salvation. You have prepared it in the sight of all nations. It is a light to be given to the Gentiles. It will bring glory to your people Israel . . . This child is going to cause many people in Israel to fall and to rise" (Luke 2).

  > [Anna]: She gave thanks to God. And she spoke about the child to all who were looking forward to the time when Jerusalem would be set free (Luke 2).

- **The invasion of the Incarnation was not improvisation; it had been God's intention from the beginning.**

  > But you, O Bethlehem . . . a ruler of Israel, *whose origins are in the distant past,* will come from you on my behalf. The people of Israel will be abandoned to their enemies until the woman in labor gives birth . . . And he will stand to lead his flock with the LORD's strength, in the majesty of the name of the LORD his God (Micah 5, NLT, emphasis added).

  > . . . you were bought with the priceless blood of Christ . . . He was *chosen before God created the world.* But he came into the world for your sake in these last days (1 Peter 1, emphasis added).

- **Jesus fulfilled a multitude of God's promises that required an actual person to rise from among us, who was like us, to stand up *for* us.** We needed a real person united to us, as one of us, to culminate the promise that Abraham's greater offspring would bring God's blessings to the families of the earth; to seal hundreds of Old Testament Kingdom predictions rooted in David's greater son, physically reigning on his throne forever; and to bring about the reconciliation and restoration of all creation through the "Servant of the Lord" spoken of by Isaiah.

- **His coming among us — as one of us, in order to serve us and save us — was the mightiest of all God's miracles.** Time enfolded eternity. Earth was joined to heaven.

- **Through Jesus, God's irreversible identification with humankind became his grandest intervention of all.** In one divine moment, the Son's "incarnation invasion" became the culmination of the old creation as well as the initiation of the Consummation.

- **Jesus' coming is an act of infinite condescension.**

> He condescends graciously, not only to angels, humbling Himself to behold the things that are done in heaven, but he also condescends to such poor creatures as sinful men; and that not only so as to take notice of prices and great men, but of even to those that are of meanest lowest rank and degree . . . even those who are despised by their fellow human beings — Christ does not despise any. Such as are commonly despised by their fellow creatures, Christ does not despise. He takes notice of beggars, He is gracious to little children, and He dies for sinners in rebellion against Himself (Jonathan Edwards).

- **The passion of Christ on the cross actually began when he emptied himself to become one of us.** The cross was the culmination of a lifetime of condescension that began when he bridged the gulf between God and his creation. Born in a trough, he assumed our sinful flesh (a humanity corrupted by the tragic consequences of sin). Then he lowered himself even more, yielding himself to pain, hunger, mocking, grief, spitting, misery, homelessness, public humiliation, rejection, betrayal, abandonment, agony, and death.

Selah

pause | think | pray

His Incarnation Invasion Provides *for* Our Reconciliation

- **The Incarnation is as crucial to the reconciliation of all things back to the Father as are his death, resurrection, and ascension.** As the "Son of Man," Jesus has become God's climactic, transformational decree about the destruction of the dark powers, the reclamation of the human race, and the reconstitution of his wondrous creation.

> *I saw someone like a son of man coming with the clouds of heaven.* He approached the Ancient One and was led into his presence. He was given authority, honor, and sovereignty over all the nations of the world so that people of every race and nation and language would obey him. His rule is eternal — it will never end. His kingdom will never be destroyed (Daniel 7, NLT, emphasis added).

- **We might say that in order to bring us home God put "skin in the game."** Jesus among us, in a human body, shows us the full scope of the hope — but also the *cost* — of God's superlative saving purposes for the nations. Commissioned with corporal flesh and blood into the arena of human existence, Jesus is God's reconciliation mission in motion — physically, visibly, tangibly, concretely, sacrificially, *permanently* — all of it *for* us.

- **Jesus in the flesh closed the "God-gap" for us.** Without the Incarnation, we would remain at an infinite distance from the Father in terms of our *creatureliness,* as well as in terms of our *fallenness.* When we see how low Christ had to go — how far he had to stoop to reach us and retrieve us from our desperate estate — we get some idea of how far from God we really were and would remain without our Savior.

- **Instead, a *man* has become the singular Mediator between Heaven and earth.** We can pass over to God only because he first passed over to us.

  > There is only one God. And there is only one go-between for God and human beings. *He is the man Christ Jesus.* He gave himself to pay for the sins of everyone. That was a witness given by God at just the right time (1 Timothy 2, emphasis added).

- **There would be no saving faith in God unless Christ put himself in the middle.**

  > All thinking of God, apart from Christ, is a bottomless abyss which utterly swallows up all our senses . . . In Christ, God, so to speak, makes himself little in order to lower himself to our capacity . . . that [we] may dare to intimately approach God (John Calvin).

  > Although God cannot be fully comprehended, yet in Christ he can be fully apprehended (Herman Bavinck).

- **Jesus makes possible God's original intent to dwell with us and walk among us, but in stunningly new ways. Consider these Scriptures:**

  > Then the man and his wife heard the Lord God walking in the garden (Genesis 3).

  > I will live among you. I will not turn away from you. I will walk among you. I will be your God. And you will be my people (Leviticus 26).

  > I will live with them . . . My temple will be among them forever (Ezekiel 37).

And the Word (Christ) became flesh (human, incarnate) and tabernacled (fixed His tent of flesh, lived awhile) among us; and we [actually] saw His glory (John 1, AMP).

The Word became flesh and blood, and moved into the neighborhood. We saw the glory with our own eyes (John 1, MSG).

As they talked and discussed these things, Jesus himself suddenly came and began walking with them . . . Suddenly, their eyes were opened, and they recognized him . . . They said to each other, "Didn't our hearts burn within us as he talked with us on the road and explained the Scriptures to us?" (Luke 24, NLT).

They'll walk with me on parade! . . . Conquerors will march in the victory parade, their names indelible in the Book of Life. I'll lead them up and present them by name to my Father and his Angels (Revelation 3, MSG).

- **Now our eternal prospects before God are fused to a person who is fully human — who was and is exactly like us.** He is called no less than *"Emmanuel,"* which means "God *with* us" (Matthew 1). He is God among us, totally *for* us, forever accessible to us.

- **Jesus invaded our fearful, finite, fallen, futile condition in order to lift us up with him, as one with him, into his very own overflowing fellowship with God.** Such a gift deserves extravagant praise, like that composed by fourth-century church leader, Ambrose:

Come, thou redeemer of the earth and manifest thy virgin birth.
Let every age adoring fall; such birth befits the God of all!
Begotten of no human will, but of the Spirit, Thou art still
The Word of God in flesh arrayed, the promised fruit to man displayed.
O equal to the Father, thou! Gird on thy fleshly mantle now.
The weakness of our mortal state with deathless might invigorate.
Thy cradle here shall glitter bright, and darkness breathe a newer light,
Where endless faith shall shine serene, and twilight never intervene.

Selah

pause | think | pray

Becoming One of Us, Jesus Proves God's *Total* Commitment to Us

- **The Incarnation provides irrefutable evidence that our God is personally and eternally invested in the future of the human race.** We know this because, throughout all the ages to come, a *man* who took on our flesh, came under our judgment, triumphed over our death, and now facilitates Heaven's dominion to our unceasing welfare has secured God's blessings *for* us forever. He reigns on our behalf, true "friend of sinners."

- **By coming among us as one of us, Jesus became the sole advocate for our helpless cause—taking up our defense and prevailing once and for all.** Therefore, no matter how reprobate we humans have become, no matter the extent of our rebellion against God, we can be sure of this: God's Son came to us because he truly *longs* to redeem us. He yearns to reconcile us, re-create us, and restore us to fellowship with the triune God.

- **In other words, Jesus coming among us is evidence that God really *wants* us.** Our God does not desire to remain without us or against us because of our sin. Rather, he wants to involve himself with us and *for* us so that he can have us with him forever. This unprecedented good news resounds with exceeding great joy! The invasion of the Incarnation is the revelation of God's deepest intentions of love toward us.

- **On the other hand, his becoming one of us did not arise out of some *need* God has regarding us.** None of us could ever contribute one mite to the eternal blessedness of the Trinity. The Son is, was, and always will be infinitely perfect, utterly complete, and thoroughly fulfilled in his own nature and in his fellowship with the Father and the Spirit. His coming from glory *for* our sakes, his coming into union with us as one of us, was totally for the purpose of rescuing us and reconstituting us because of *our* need to become all God meant us to be for his unending praise.

- **At the same time, the invasion of the Incarnation demonstrates convincingly that God does not take lightly our sin and our scorning of his glory.** Christ's entry into the human race tells us there's something profoundly intransigent about the nature of evil, and it demonstrates God's utter outrage with sin and his resolute passion to deal with it.

- **For the Son to humble himself to become a man and die *for* us substantiates that there was no *other* way to reverse humankind's spiritual disaster.** Jesus embodies the Father's commitment to abolish all defiance, darkness, demons, and death forever. Jesus, one of us among us, has become *for* us God's everlasting "NO!" to the reign and repercussions of sin and Satan.

- **Jesus' suffering *for* us, as one of us, is proof of God's everlasting commitment to *deliver* us.**

  > In that death, by God's grace, he fully experienced death in every person's place . . . Jesus doesn't hesitate to treat them as family . . . Since the children are made of flesh and blood, it's logical that the Savior took on flesh and blood in order to rescue them by his death . . . he had to enter into every detail of human life. Then, when he came before God as high priest to get rid of the people's sins, he would have already experienced it all himself — all the pain, all the testing — and would be able to help where help was needed (Hebrews 2, MSG).

- **Furthermore, our assurance rests in knowing not only that the Father sent his Son, but also that the Son *himself* willingly took a personal, proactive initiative by coming *for* us.**

  > So when Christ came into the world, he said, "You didn't want sacrifices and offerings. Instead, you prepared a body for me" . . . Then I said, "Here I am. It is written about me in the scroll. God, I have come to do what you want" . . . We have been made holy because Jesus Christ offered his body once and for all time (Hebrews 10).

  > The reason my Father loves me is that I give up my life. But I will take it back again. No one takes it from me. I give it up myself. I have the authority to give it up. And I have the authority to take it back again (John 10).

- **Above all other assurances of God's commitment to us, surely Christ's *cross* remains the prime evidence that God intends nothing but the best *for* us.** The sobering impoverishment of his cradle was required for him to reach the extreme impoverishment of his cross. His hands — once tiny, soft, and tender — were created to be pierced for us.

- **From the womb forward, Jesus submitted himself to our destitute condition to save us from it by sacrificing his physical being at the "Place of the Skull."**

He himself carried our sins in His body on the cross. He did it so that we would die as far as sins are concerned . . . His wounds have made you whole. You were like sheep who were wandering away. But now you have returned to the Shepherd. He is the Leader of your souls (1 Peter 2).

- **Our Savior's sacrificial wounds will remain forever a visible witness to us of who he is *for* us. As John observed:**

  Then, standing in the very centre of the throne and of the four living creatures and of the elders, I saw a Lamb that seemed to have been slaughtered (Revelation 5, Phillips).

- **Considering the extent of God's commitment to us revealed in Christ's incarnation, we might do well to ask: What would God *not* do *for* us now?** The Father's ultimate dedication to our eternal welfare is seen in that he so loved the world he gave his Son *for* us. If, in fact, he did not withhold his *best* from us, is there *any* good thing the Father would keep from us?

  With God on our side like this, how can we lose? If God didn't hesitate to put everything on the line for us, embracing our condition and exposing himself to the worst by sending his own Son, is there anything else he wouldn't gladly and freely do for us? . . . The One who died for us — who was raised to life for us! — is in the presence of God at this very moment sticking up for us. Do you think anyone is going to be able to drive a wedge between us and Christ's love for us? There is no way! (Romans 8, MSG).

Selah

pause | think | pray

Jesus Embodies God's Servant Heart Toward Us and *For* Us

- **Jesus coming in flesh manifested the triune God's resolve and determination to *serve* us.** Christ entered into the world, not like a conquering hero but like a slave — a slave without advantages, or rights, or privileges. He was focused on one thing: ministering to our deepest needs for God's greatest glory.

- **Profoundly, the Incarnation displays a core trait of God's very nature: It shows us the Father's servant heart.**

  Here is my *servant*. I have chosen him. He is the one I love. I am very pleased with him. I will put my Spirit on him. He will announce to the nations that everything will be made right (Matthew 12, emphasis added).

  Even the Son of Man did not come to be served. Instead, he came to *serve* others. He came to give his life as the price for setting many people free (Mark 10, emphasis added).

  The Spirit of the Lord is on me. He has anointed me to announce the good news to poor people. He has sent me to announce freedom for prisoners. He has sent me so that the blind will see again. He wants me to set free those who are treated badly (Luke 4).

- **The *supremacy* of Jesus is significantly revealed in his *humility*.** We cannot understand Christ's *sovereignty* over all things without first understanding the scope of his *submission* for the sake of all things.

  . . . he lived a selfless, obedient life and then died a selfless, obedient death — and the worst kind of death at that — a crucifixion. Because of that obedience, God lifted him high and honored him far beyond anyone or anything, ever, so that all created beings in heaven and on earth — even those long ago dead and buried — will bow in worship before this Jesus Christ (Philippians 2, MSG).

- **Coming down to us, God's Son emptied himself — one even might say he *donated* himself — to become a servant to us, *for* us.** He didn't empty himself of any *thing*. Rather, he emptied *himself*. In this we see unparalleled, unconditional selflessness.

> Do you remember the generosity of Jesus Christ, the Lord of us all? He was rich beyond our telling, yet he became poor for your sakes so that his poverty might make you rich (2 Corinthians 8, PHILLIPS).

- **Jesus served us by living exclusively to satisfy the Father's desires *for* us, constantly at the Father's disposal on our behalf.** He abandoned himself to the Father's will, renouncing any claim to final, personal control over the outcome of his ministry. He yielded to the Father's will because he knew in the end, by the Spirit's power, he would triumph; his Father's desires would prevail. His was a "defenseless superior power" (Hendrikus Berkhof), as he endured *for* us, as one of us, the breadth of sufferings to which the Father called him *for* our sakes.

- **Jesus said: "The Son can do nothing by himself. He can do only what he sees his Father doing."**

> What the Father does, the Son also does. This is because the Father loves the Son. He shows him everything he does . . . I can do nothing by myself. I judge only as I hear. And my judging is fair. I do not try to please myself. I try only to please the One who sent me (John 5).

> Should I pray, "Father, save me from this hour"? But this is the very reason I came! Father, bring glory to your name. Then a voice spoke from heaven, saying, "I have already brought glory to my name, and I will do so again" (John 12).

- **We must us never forget: There would have been no valid sacrifice for our sins apart from Jesus living an earthly life of sustained, unwavering, covenant-keeping, moment-by-moment obedient service to the Father's word and will and ways.** As one of us, he served us by how he flawlessly, perfectly, sinlessly lived out God's uncompromising righteousness, what we sinners — we unrighteous ones — could never produce on our own. In turn, this made his death *for* us totally sufficient because of how he first lived perfectly before God's face on our behalf, in our place, *as if he actually were us.*

> But then the right time came. God sent his Son. A woman gave birth to him. He was born under the authority of the law. He came to set free those who were under the law. He wanted us to be adopted as children with all the rights children have (Galatians 4).

- **"[This is] the way Christ Jesus thought of himself."**

> He had equal status with God but didn't think so much of himself that he had to cling to the advantages of that status no matter what. Not at all. When the time came, he set aside the privileges of deity and took on the status of a slave, became *human*! Having become human, he stayed human. It was an incredibly humbling process. He didn't claim special privileges. Instead, he lived a selfless, obedient life and then died a selfless, obedient death — and the worst kind of death at that — a crucifixion (Philippians 2, MSG).

pause | think | pray

In Compassion, Christ *Personally* Engaged Our Low and Lost Estate

- **For us he lived a life *like* us, unprotected and vulnerable in his humanity.** He shared in our frustrations and futilities and fatigue. He tasted the full spectrum of our helplessness, our burdens, our shame, our fears, our despair.

> So he had to be made like his brothers in every way. Then he could serve God as a kind and faithful high priest. And then he could pay for the sins of the people by dying for them. He himself suffered when he was tempted. Now he is able to help others who are being tempted (Hebrews 2).

Or as Paul puts it in Romans 8, the Son has now become "the firstborn among many brothers."

- **"There was no difference between him and other men — save only this: He was God, and had no sin."**

> But, he ate, drank, slept, walked; he was weary, sorrowful, rejoicing; he wept and he laughed; he knew hunger and thirst and sweat; he talked, he toiled, he prayed. To sum up: He used everything for the need and preservation of this life, he endured good and evil things like anyone else. He worked and suffered like any other man, save that he was without sin (Martin Luther).

- **Christ entered into the tragic consequences of our rebellion toward God.** He plunged right in to encounter firsthand the depths of our spiritual bankruptcy. He did not stand apart; he identified with our experiences of rejection, abuse, loneliness, neediness, and bereavement.

- **Taking on our skin, he directly and actively confronted our sin.** In his public ministry, Jesus began to fulfill the Father's plan to put away sin once and for all. He began by healing, delivering, restoring, and discipling all who received him.

> God has sent his message to the sons of Israel by giving us the good news of peace through Jesus Christ – he is the Lord of us all. You must know the story of Jesus of Nazareth . . . of how God anointed him with the power of the Holy Spirit, of how he went about doing good and healing all who suffered from the devil's power — because God was with him. Now we are eyewitnesses of everything that he did (Acts 10, PHILLIPS).

- **Jesus wept *for* us, but he did so standing among us.**

> Jesus saw her crying. He saw that the Jews who had come along with her were crying also. His spirit became very sad, and he was troubled. "Where have you put him?" he asked. "Come and see, Lord," they replied. Jesus sobbed. Then the Jews said, "See how much he loved him!" (John 11).

> He approached Jerusalem. When he saw the city, he began to sob. He said, "I wish you had known today what would bring you peace!" (Luke 19).

- **Indeed, Jesus has become *for* us a "brother born for adversity."** He understands our plight. Emotionally, relationally, physically — even spiritually — Jesus suffered what we suffer. He knows our destitution as one who himself had nowhere to lay his head. Just like us, he endured the scoffing and rejection of family and friends, finding no welcome but rather disapproval, derision, and unbelief within his hometown.

- ***For* our sakes, he spent one dark, torturous night in prayer when his soul was sorrowful, even unto death.** We read:

> He went a short distance away from them. There he got down on his knees and prayed. He said, "Father, if you are willing, take this cup of suffering away from me" . . . Because he was very sad and troubled, he prayed even harder. His sweat was like drops of blood falling to the ground (Luke 22).

- **He drank of the bitter horror of our "cosmic abandonment" before God.**

> Men looked down on him. They didn't accept him. He knew all about sorrow and suffering . . . He suffered the things we should have suffered. He took on himself the pain that should have been ours . . . the servant was pierced . . . He was crushed . . . His wounds have healed us . . . He was beaten down and made to suffer (Isaiah 53).

> We have a high priest who can feel it when we are weak and hurting. We have a high priest who has been tempted in every way, just as we are. But he did not sin (Hebrews 4).

- **He endured this agony because he knew this sobering truth: No body and no blood meant no blessing for the nations!** Jesus accomplished our deliverance as a *real person*, with his *whole person*. All of him was inextricably engaged with our low and lost estate when he purchased the Church by laying down his life to the last drop of his holy, precious blood.

> . . . [he] said, "Take, eat. This is My body, which is broken for you. Do this to call Me [affectionately] to remembrance . . . This cup is the new covenant [ratified and established] in My blood. Do this, as often as you drink [it], to call Me [affectionately] to remembrance" (1 Corinthians 11, AMP).

Therefore we should:

> . . . shepherd (tend and feed and guide) the church of God which He obtained for Himself [buying it and saving it for Himself] with His own blood (Acts 20, AMP).

- **Jesus knows *exactly* what every single human being has felt and suffered and endured ever since the Fall, because he *became* sin *for* us — he took our sins *into his own body*.** He experienced every bit of sin's ugly consequences and horrible pain — all of it *for* all mankind — *in his own body*, including the eternal pain of separation from God our sin brings, which we who trust in him will never, ever have to experience! Of course, that is an experience he alone can comprehend; for us it is indescribable and unfathomable. There is great comfort for all the saints to know he more than *understands* our pain — he *"became"* our pain!

> God made him who had no sin to be sin for us, so that in him we
> might become the righteousness of God (2 Corinthians 5:21, NIV).

> He Himself bore our sins in His body on the cross, so that we might
> die to sin and live to righteousness; for by His wounds you were
> healed (1 Peter 2:24, NASB).

- **In addition, *for* us, as one of us, he engaged one-on-one with the enemy of our souls.** He took the offense against the "ruler of this dark world." As one of his parables puts it:

> But suppose I drive out demons by the Spirit of God. Then God's
> kingdom has come to you. Or, think about this. How can you enter a
> strong man's house and just take what the man owns? You must first
> tie him up. Then you can rob his house (Matthew 12).

- **During his wilderness testing, not even Satan could assail him in the weakness of his physical flesh.** Satan could not divert Jesus' *power* as Son of Man and Son of God. Satan could not raise doubts about Jesus' *position* as Son of Man and Son of God. Satan could not sabotage Jesus' *mission* as Son of Man and Son of God. Jesus prevailed *for* us. Now he willingly shares his victory *with us*.

> The Father is with me. I've told you all this so that trusting me, you
> will be unshakable and assured, deeply at peace. In this godless world
> you will continue to experience difficulties. But take heart! I've
> conquered the world (John 16, MSG).

> . . . the Son also became flesh and blood. For only as a human being
> could he die, and only by dying could he break the power of the devil,
> who had the power of death . . . Since he himself has gone through
> suffering and testing, he is able to help us when we are being tested
> (Hebrews 2, NLB).

- **He did all of this *for* us to elevate our low estate and transform our lost estate as he absorbed in our place our suffering and death.**

> So God gave us new life because of what Christ has done. He gave us
> life even when we were dead in sin. God's grace has saved you. God
> raised us up with Christ. He has seated us with him in his heavenly
> kingdom because we belong to Christ Jesus. He has done it to show
> the riches of his grace for all time to come (Ephesians 2).

> You have been raised up with Christ. So think about things that are
> in heaven. That is where Christ is. He is sitting at God's right hand . . .

You died. Now your life is hidden with Christ in God. Christ is your life. When he appears again, you also will appear with him in heaven's glory (Colossians 3).

- **To this day he continues urging us to let him bear our burdens *for* us and with us, as one of us!**

  Come to me, all of you who are tired and are carrying heavy loads. I will give you rest. Become my servants and learn from me. I am gentle and free of pride. You will find rest for your souls (Matthew 11).

Or, to say it another way:

  Are you tired? Worn out? Burned out on religion? Come to me. Get away with me and you'll recover your life. I'll show you how to take a real rest. Walk with me and work with me — *watch how I do it.* Learn the unforced rhythms of grace. I won't lay anything heavy or ill-fitting on you. Keep company with me and you'll learn to live freely and lightly (Matthew 11, MSG, emphasis added).

pause | think | pray

Forever as One of Us, Christ Defines What Lies Ahead for All of Us

- **Think of it: Right now Jesus is the most fully alive human personality in the universe!** In him — "the image of the invisible God" (Colossians 1) — we behold what every human should look like, given our inherent capacity to glorify the living God. Jesus encompasses the whole range of what it means for human beings — made in God's image from the beginning (Genesis 1) — to love God with all our affections and words and deeds. In our Savior we see all the goodness, grace, and gifts of which every believer is capable, to the extent that we are living in the power of the Holy Spirit.

- **To see Jesus is to behold what it means to be truly human.** How he lived is the way human life is meant to be lived.

As the man Jesus, he is himself the revealing Word of God; he is the source of our knowledge of the nature of man as created by God (Karl Barth).

God's "Word-in-the-flesh" not only reveals the Father to us but also reveals us to ourselves.

Wherefore also he passed through every stage of life, restoring to all true communion with God . . . (and) recapitulating in himself the ancient formation of man that he might kill sin, deprive death of its power and vivify man (Irenaeus, church father).

- **"Jesus, the revelation of God, is *the* prototype."**

  He is the only one among us who faithfully and perfectly represents what God, the Creator, wished for the human person, created in his image, to be (Veli-Matti Kärkkäinen).

- **Despite his deity, Jesus is the real deal — as fully human as we are meant to be**. Bone of our bone and flesh of our flesh, our Jesus is not fake or fantasy. With him there is no pretense, or playacting, or shadowy slight of hand. The Palestinian multitudes who surrounded him, listened to him, watched him, and walked with him, saw in him how God wants *all* of us to feel, think, act, react, triumph, serve, love, and worship. In Jesus we too come face to face with how God intends all of us who *belong* to his Son to *become* like his Son.

- **More than any other title, Jesus called himself "the Son of Man."** Literally, the phrase could be translated "the Son of *Adam*." God's Genesis design for the first Adam, and for the humanity descended from the first couple, now has been recovered and redesigned in Christ alone. In him, we see not only what we were *meant* to be but also what we *can* be — and what all the saints of all the ages *will* be. Jesus is the *second* Adam. For women and men who trust him, we find that the meaning of our human existence has been reconstituted and made new in him.

- **In addition, calling himself "Son of Man" meant he was willing to identify not only with our humanity but also with our mortality**. He was coming to die *like* us, as well as die *for* us, so that we might one day live *like* him, not just for him.

  > Just as there is an earthly body, there is also a spiritual body. It is written, "The first man Adam became a living person." The last Adam became a spirit that gives life . . . The first man came from the dust of the earth. The second man came from heaven. Those who belong to the earth are like the one who came from the earth. And those who are spiritual are like the one who came from heaven. We are like the earthly man. And we will be like the man from heaven (1 Corinthians 15).

- **Jesus among us has become *for* us the fountainhead of a new breed of people — a fresh beginning for the human race.** As the new Adam — the second Adam — Jesus has restored the "image of God." In him, the failures of the first Adam have been repaid and reversed.

  > Because of Adam, all people die. So because of Christ, all will be made alive (1 Corinthians 15).

  > God's gift is different from Adam's sin. Many people died because of the sin of that one man. But it was even more sure that God's grace would also come through one man. That man is Jesus Christ . . . One man sinned, and death ruled because of his sin. But we are even surer of what will happen because of what the one man, Jesus Christ, has done. Those who receive the rich supply of God's grace will rule with Christ in his kingdom (Romans 5).

  Reflecting on 1 Corinthians 15, third-century church leader Methodius wrote: "He bore flesh for no other reason than to set flesh free and raise it up."

- **Ultimately, all of God's children will be transformed — better yet, *re-formed* — to look like God's incarnate Son.**

  > God knew what he was doing from the very beginning. He decided from the outset to shape the lives of those who love him along the same lines as the life of his Son. The Son stands first in the line of humanity he restored. We see the original and intended shape of our lives there in him. After God made that decision of what his children should be like, he followed it up by calling people by name. After he called them by name, he set them on a solid basis with himself. And then, after getting them established, he stayed with them to the end, gloriously completing what he had begun (Romans 8, MSG).

- **"This is the wonderful exchange which, out of his measureless benevolence, he has made with us . . ."**

  Becoming Son of Man with us, he has made us sons of God with him; that by his descent to earth, he has prepared an ascent to heaven for us; that, by taking on our mortality, he has conferred his immortality upon us; that, accepting our weakness, he has strengthened us by his power; that, receiving our poverty upon himself, he has transferred his wealth to us; that, taking the weight of our iniquity upon himself (which oppressed us), he has clothed us with his righteousness (John Calvin).

- **The moment Christ embraced our humanity he sealed our destiny.** Now our future, and the future of all things, is inseparably linked to the future of the "Lamb on the throne."

  God was pleased to have his whole nature living in Christ. God was pleased to bring all things back to himself because of what Christ has done. That includes all things on earth and in heaven (Colossians 1).

- **Christ's incarnation invasion propels God's people on toward God's new creation.**

  So from now on we don't look at anyone the way the world does. At one time we looked at Christ in that way. But we don't anymore. Anyone who believes in Christ is a new creation. The old is gone! The new has come! It is all from God (2 Corinthians 5).

  As his children, we will receive all that he has for us. We will share what Christ receives . . . Everything God created looks forward to the time when his children will appear in their full and final glory . . . Then he will give us everything he has for us. He will raise our bodies and give glory to them (Romans 8).

  Selah

  pause | think | pray

The Wrap

What should stun us the most in this section? Maybe this: Amazing as it sounds, the incarnation of God's Son is irrevocable and irreversible. Ponder that. Jesus will *never* cease to be one of us, **for** us, inseparable from us, and dwelling among us — never! As he observed for his incredulous disciples the evening of his resurrection:

> "Why are you troubled? Why do you have doubts in your minds? Look at my hands and my feet. It is really I! Touch me and see. A ghost does not have a body or bones. But you can see that I do." After he said that, he showed them his hands and feet . . . They gave him a piece of cooked fish. He took it and ate it in front of them (Luke 24).

Having taken on and redeemed the totality of our humanity, Jesus left none of that humanity behind when he ascended; he took it all with him — *into glory*! Ephesians asks:

> What does "he went up" mean? It can only mean that he also came down to the lower, earthly places. The One who came down is the same as the One who went up higher than all the heavens. He did it in order to fill all of creation.

As a 17th-century Scottish Puritan put it: "The dust of the earth now resides on the Throne of Heaven."

One day, not long from now, we will *see* our Lord Jesus "in the flesh." You will. I will. How might that moment unfold for us? Maybe we'll experience him the way Thomas did:

> The other disciples told [Thomas], "We saw the Master." But he said, "Unless I see the nail holes in his hands, put my finger in the nail holes, and stick my hand in his side, I won't believe it"... Jesus came through the locked doors, stood among them, and said, "Peace to you." Then he focused his attention on Thomas. "Take your finger and examine my hands. Take your hand and stick it in my side. Don't be unbelieving. Believe." Thomas said, "My Master! My God!" (John 20, MSG).

Or maybe that visible encounter with our risen, ascended Lord will unfold for us like it did for apostle John:

> I turned around to see who was speaking to me. When I turned, I saw ... someone who looked "like a son of man." He was dressed in a long robe with a gold strip of cloth around his chest. The hair on his head was white like wool, as white as snow. His eyes were like a blazing fire ... His face was like the sun shining in all of its brightness. When I saw him, I fell at his feet as if I were dead. Then he put his right hand on me and said, "Do not be afraid. I am the First and the Last. I am the Living One. I was dead. But now look! I am alive for ever and ever! And I hold the keys to Death and Hell (Revelation 1).

Whatever the case, we must stay alert. A day *is* coming when we *will* see him — descending in the same way he ascended: bodily, visibly, triumphantly (see Acts 1). John tells us:

> ... stay with Christ. Live deeply in Christ. Then we'll be ready for him when he appears, ready to receive him with open arms (1 John 2, MSG).

> Who knows how we'll end up! What we know is that when Christ is openly revealed, we'll see him — and in seeing him, become like him (1 John 3, MSG).

The experience of those who reject him, of course, will be quite different. The Bible warns that they will also see King Jesus in the flesh:

> ... yes, he's on his way! Riding the clouds, he'll be seen by every eye, those who mocked and killed him will see him. People from all nations and all times will tear their clothes in lament. Oh, Yes. (Revelation 1, MSG).

> Everyone hid in caves and among the rocks of the mountains ... They called out to the mountains and rocks, "Fall on us! Hide us from the face of the One who sits on the throne! Hide us from the anger of the Lamb! The great day of their anger has come. Who can live through it?" (Revelation 6).

In that day he will sum up *everything* under himself as Lord (Ephesians 1). This One, who is bone of our bone and flesh of our flesh, will restore *our* mortal bodies to be like *his* resurrected, incorruptible body. Paul declares:

> But there's far more to life for us. We're citizens of high heaven! We're awaiting the arrival of the Savior, the Master, Jesus Christ, who will transform our earthly bodies into glorious bodies like his own. He'll make us beautiful and whole with the same powerful skill by which he is putting everything as it should be, under and around him (Philippians 3, MSG).

Constantly throughout eternity, we'll keep celebrating *every* facet of Christ's "Irreversible Fourfold Revolution"— his saving work *for* us (the Incarnation, the Crucifixion, the Resurrection, the Ascension). But the *starting place* for our praises — the act without which none of the rest could have happened — is Christ's irreplaceable "*in-flesh-ment*," when he was lowly born in a cave for cattle in order to bring unbounded light and life to our benighted and fallen world.

No wonder at Christmastide the worldwide, worshipping Church heartily sings:

Silent night, holy night!
Son of God, love's pure light.
Radiant beams from thy holy face
With the dawn of redeeming grace,
Jesus, Lord at thy birth.
Jesus, Lord at thy birth.

Who Christ Is FOR Us Today:
By the Mission of His Crucifixion

In Cincinnati, along the banks of the Ohio River, sits one of the most startling museums in America: The National Underground Railroad Freedom Center. Just as with a similar but larger museum on the National Mall, it often leaves visitors shaken to the core.

At the Freedom Center, people are confronted with the stark and startling horror of over three hundred years of African slavery in our nation. By picture walls, videos, artifacts, lectures, recreated life-sized slave markets and slave quarters — through sights, sounds, smells — the gruesome story of the sufferings of millions of men, women, and children at the hands of brutal kidnappers and abusive slave owners is portrayed, relentlessly, from floor to floor.

The story is one of despicable, unconscionable evil. Visitors are faced with a nearly indescribable, incomprehensible level of affliction, adversity, anguish, and agony; but as well we see a remarkable display of the courage, stamina, resilience, and even resistance of those enslaved. The Freedom Center encases an incredible record from America's troubling past of both repulsion and redemption; of both hideousness and hopefulness.

Though unintended, the Freedom Center provides a whole other message for those who have eyes to see. Repeatedly and vividly the themes of the story told there mirror much of what Christ's crucifixion involved for him. Consider this: Like the ancestors of today's African Americans, he too underwent unjust suffering — abusive, horrific, incomprehensible. Yet, just as the African American tragedy has resulted, to a significant degree, in compelling an entire nation to recover issues of human dignity, racial nobility, and civil rights, even so Christ's cross achieved, in a far more profound way, an eternal liberation that is purposeful, redemptive, and transformative — not just for one nation but for the entire creation.

With this next section, we seek to penetrate realms of human and divine afflictions and suffering that none of us really can begin to fathom, not even those who have been in chains. But penetrate we must try because the crucifixion of our Lord Jesus Christ had a *mission* — a mission inseparable from his everlasting *position*, reigning as our Lord and Savior, a mission inseparable from our everlasting *condition* as those redeemed and "washed in the blood of the Lamb."

 Snapshots and Starter Thoughts

Behold the "gory glory" of God's Son, slain **for** the sins of the world!

His earthly agony provides insights into the heart of the Trinity.

At the same time, his crucible gives us insights into the depth of our curse.

The precision of his mission: a closer look at its costs and benefits

How his spectacular supremacy is displayed in his sacred sufferings

Behold the "Gory Glory" of God's Son, Slain *for* the Sins of the World!

- **"O sacred Head, now wounded, with grief and shame weighed down,"**

   Now scornfully surrounded with thorns, Thine only crown.
   O sacred Head, what *glory*, what bliss till now was Thine!
   Yet, though despised and *gory*, I joy to call Thee mine.
   What Thou, my Lord, hast suffered was all for sinners' gain.
   Mine, mine was the transgression, but Thine the deadly pain.
   (Attributed to Bernard of Clairvaux, 12th-century French Catholic reformer priest, emphasis added)

- **"There is a fountain filled with blood drawn from Immanuel's veins."**

   And sinners plunged beneath that flood lose all their guilty stains.
   Ever since by faith I saw the stream thy flowing wounds supply,
   Redeeming love has been my theme and shall be till I die.
   Dear dying Lamb, Thy precious blood shall never lose its power
   Till all the ransomed church of God be saved to sin no more.
   (William Cowper, British hymnist and poet, 1800)

- **God's Son came to suffer with us and *for* us — to substitute himself *for* us.** He chose to assume the full consequences of our sin and anguish, and of our pending mortality and eternal judgment. Jesus chose to be embedded in the convulsive anguish inseparable from our guilty condition in order to set us free on all counts against us.

- **"Gory" is not too repulsive a term to describe the way Christ was slain for the sins of the world.** When Paul writes in Galatians 4 that God sent his Son "in the fullness of times," it must include the fact that at that time in history one primary method of public execution was crucifixion. Historically speaking, no design of capital punishment pictured our fate, apart from God's grace, as vividly as the awful afflictions of the wooden rack called a cross. That kind of death was *excruciating* (which literally means "due to crucifying"). Meant for criminals and rebels, the suffering on the stake was gruesome, painful, shameful — unfathomable. The victim expired through a gradual, ponderous, tormenting combination of blood loss, infection, dehydration, exhaustion, traumatic shock, and ultimately, asphyxiation.

- **No wonder his sacrificial death is referred to as the *passion* of the Christ (which means "to undergo extensive suffering").** Truly, his was a dehumanizing and horrifying passion — an unparalleled and inexplicable passion. It was profoundly *gory*. However, at the same time, it also was splendorous in its *glory*. His were *holy* afflictions — blessed, compassionate, purposeful, and utterly sufficient. They were inexhaustibly redemptive afflictions.

- **The glory of the spectacular *supremacy* of God's Son was magnified by the stunning, staggering, saving *suffering* of God's Son.** Sometimes all we can do is pause, and ponder the cross, and who was on it and why — and then weep. We need to grieve not only over the pain he bore, but also over the fact that he bore it not for himself, but **for** *others* — he endured it **for** *us.*

His Earthly Agony Provides Insights Into the Heart of the Trinity

- **From the start, the heart of the Godhead has enshrined a cross.** The agony of the Son **for** us was, is now, and always will be inseparable from God's very being. Jesus' suffering was not just that of a man, but it was the suffering of God as well.

- **To picture God is to picture the cross, simultaneously. Christ's cross was the self-offering of God, from the very core of his eternal being.**

   For you must realize all the time that you have been "ransomed" . . . not with some money payment of transient value, but by the costly shedding of blood. The price was in fact the life-blood of Christ, the unblemished and unstained lamb of sacrifice. It is true that *God chose him to fulfill this part before the world was founded,* but it was for your benefit that he was revealed in these last days (1 Peter 1, PHILLIPS, emphasis added).

   They are the ones whose names are not written in the Lamb's book of life. The Lamb is the one *whose death was planned before the world was created* (Revelation 13, emphasis added).

   Long ago God planned that Jesus would be handed over to you (Acts 2, emphasis added).

- **In Revelation 4 and 5, a Lamb bearing visible wounds dominates the blazing, breathtaking display of the Trinity.** Forever marked by the nails of crucifixion, Jesus resides at the center of the Father's throne, made visible to the universe by the intense, focused lamplight of the Holy Spirit. Worship arises to the Godhead from a vast multitude because they've been redeemed by Jesus' blood.

   . . . in my vision I saw a throne had been set up in Heaven, and there was *someone seated* upon the throne. His appearance blazed like diamond and topaz . . . Seven lamps are burning before the throne, and they are *the seven Spirits of God* . . . I saw a *Lamb* that seemed to have been slaughtered . . . They sang . . . "you were slain, and have redeemed us to God by your blood out of every tribe and tongue and people and nation . . . Worthy is the Lamb who was slain to receive power and riches and wisdom, and strength and honor and glory and blessing . . . Blessing and honor and glory and power be to him who sits on the throne, and to the Lamb, for ever and ever!" (Revelation 4-5, PHILLIPS, emphasis added).

- **In the cross of Christ, we see God's *omnipotence* manifested most powerfully by *weakness*.** Surprisingly, Jesus' rulership in the universe is most fully displayed not in exercising overwhelming might or by issuing royal edicts and intimidating decrees. Rather, it is seen by his humble submission to our condition, surrendering to the hands of sinners, paying the price *for* our redemption.

> Although he was crucified in weakness, he now lives by the power of God (2 Corinthians 13 NLT).

- **As a result, mercy triumphs over judgment; sin is expiated and expelled permanently; Satan is repelled and routed eternally; and death is swallowed up in victory!** Paul said:

> While Jews clamor for miraculous demonstrations . . . we go right on proclaiming Christ, the Crucified. Jews treat this like an *anti*-miracle . . . But to us who are personally called by God himself — both Jews and Greeks — Christ is God's ultimate miracle . . . Human strength can't begin to compete with God's "weakness" (1 Corinthians 1, MSG).

Paul continued:

> My goal while I was with you was to talk about only one thing. And that was Jesus Christ and his death on the cross. When I came to you, I was weak and very afraid and trembling all over. I didn't preach my message with clever and compelling words. Instead, my preaching showed the Holy Spirit's power (1 Corinthians 2).

- **At the cross of Christ we see God's *wisdom* manifested most impressively by *foolishness*** — the seeming foolishness of Jesus sacrificing himself *for* us. Who ever heard of such a thing? He was afflicted *for* the afflicted to bring them into healing. He died *for* those who were dead to bring them into life. He was penalized *for* criminals to render them not guilty. He reconciled enemies by becoming a curse on their behalf. He sacrificed his dignity to secure our destiny.

- **"The Message that points to Christ on the Cross seems like sheer silliness to those hellbent on destruction, but for those on the way of salvation it makes perfect sense."** Paul goes on to say:

> Since the world in all its fancy wisdom never had a clue when it came to knowing God, God in his wisdom took delight in using what the world considered dumb — *preaching*, of all things! — to bring those

who trust him into the way of salvation . . . Greeks go in for philosophical wisdom, we go right on proclaiming Christ, the Crucified . . . Greeks pass it off as absurd . . . but Christ is God's ultimate miracle and wisdom . . . Human wisdom is so tiny, so impotent, next to the seeming absurdity of God (1 Corinthians 1, MSG).

- **The Son hanging by nails on Golgotha, substituting himself in the place of sinners, displays indisputably the monumental extremes to which the Father is willing to go to extend his abundant, abounding grace toward us.** God's sovereignty and generosity converged in Jesus' agony. God's justice and mercy intersected where Jesus' sacrificial offering was perfected.

- **We see revealed in Jesus a God who is self-sacrificing rather than self-serving, loving rather than exploiting, giving not grasping.**

> Marvelous grace of our loving Lord,
> Grace that exceeds our sin and our guilt!
> Yonder on Calvary's mount outpoured,
> There where the blood of the lamb was spilled.
> Grace, grace, God's grace,
> Grace that will pardon and cleanse within;
> Grace, grace, God's grace,
> Grace that is greater than all our sin
> (Julia H. Johnston).

- **Christ's cross lays bare before us the unrelenting determination of God's heart to save us.** It exposes the magnitude of God's commitment to deal with human guilt, defeat the powers of evil, destroy death, reconcile us back to himself, and restore his whole creation. In the cross we see how totally the living God loves us, how deeply he wants us, how intentionally he seeks us. His *compassion toward* us is a costly *passion **for*** us. Christ on the cross is our guarantee that the tripersonal God will not abandon his creation in its dereliction and death — that the Father, Son, and Holy Spirit are unwavering in their purpose to restore us to their "circle of love."

- **"But God showed his great love *for* us by sending Christ to die *for* us while we were still sinners . . . "**

For since our friendship with God was restored by the death of his Son while we were still his enemies, we will certainly be saved through the life of his Son. So now we can rejoice in our wonderful new relationship with God because our Lord Jesus Christ has made us friends of God (Romans 5, NLT, emphasis added).

- **Nowhere is God more thoroughly *exalted* to us than in Jesus *executed* for us.** Nowhere is God more vividly *glorified* to us than when Christ was *vanquished* **for** us. Nowhere does God's worthiness *shine* more brilliantly to us than when Jesus *suffered* shamefully **for** us. Nowhere is God's *holiness* more wholly displayed to us than when Christ, who knew no sin, was *made sin* **for** us. Nowhere do we see the *righteousness* of God's justice so clearly as when Christ was sentenced to be *judged* **for** us. Nowhere does God appear more *beautiful* to all creation than when his Son was *beaten* and *broken* **for** us.

- **Exalting the glory of the Godhead was the heart cry of Jesus' prayers as he moved toward the cross.** Days before his arrest, Jesus said:

    Now my soul is deeply troubled. Should I pray, "Father, save me from this hour"? But this is the very reason I came! Father, bring glory to your name. Then a voice spoke from heaven, saying, "I have already brought glory to my name, and I will do so again" . . . Then Jesus told them . . . "And when I am lifted up from the earth, I will draw everyone to myself" (John 12, NLT).

    Then on the night of his arrest, we read:

    Then, raising his eyes in prayer, he said: "Father, it's time. Display the bright splendor of your Son so the Son in turn may show your bright splendor . . . I glorified you on earth by completing down to the last detail what you assigned me to do. And now, Father, glorify me with your very own splendor, the very splendor I had in your presence before there was a world" (John 17, MSG).

- **On the other hand, at the cross the grief of the Father was just as poignant as the death of the Son.** What the Son suffered, the Father also suffered with him. Our sin placed on the Son that dark Friday afternoon unleashed an agony of "abandonment" in both directions — for a time the Son became "fatherless" even as the Father became "sonless."

- **Christ on the cross was a *mutual* mission for the Trinity — the self-substitution of God in our place.** The Father loved us and gave his Son **for** us. The Son loved us and gave himself **for** us, as he cooperated with the Father's plan. In Gethsemane he prayed:

> My Father, if there is any way, get me out of this. But please, not what I want. You, what do you want? . . . My Father, if there is no other way than this, drinking this cup to the dregs, I'm ready. Do it your way (Matthew 26, MSG).

- **"The Father did not lay on the Son an ordeal Jesus was reluctant to bear, nor did the Son extract from the Father a salvation he was reluctant to bestow" (John Stott).** The Father gave the cup to drink; the Son chose to drink it. The Father did not delight in the Son's sufferings *for* us, but did delight in the display of triune glory that would come *because* he suffered *for* us.

- **The transaction of the cross was supported, shepherded, sustained, and sealed by the Holy Spirit.** From the beginning, the Spirit shaped and saturated every phase of Christ's mission by: conceiving Jesus in Mary's womb; anointing him at his public baptism; driving him into a wilderness wrestling match with Satan; empowering every facet of his preaching and ministry; unleashing innumerable miracles to confirm the impending nature of Christ's kingdom; and climaxed by his raising of Jesus from the dead (Romans 8). This was no less true with the mission of his crucifixion *for* us:

> . . . think how much more the blood of Christ cleans up our whole lives, inside and out. Through the Spirit, Christ offered himself as an unblemished sacrifice (Hebrews 7, MSG).

Selah

pause | think | pray

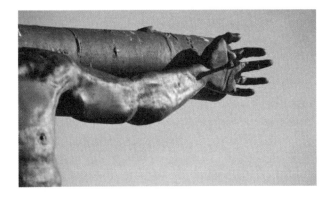

At the Same Time, His Crucible Gives Us Insights Into the Depth of Our Curse

- **First of all, let it be said: The cross is always about Christ before it ever is about us.** Christ died *for* us but not because we *deserved* for him to do so. Rather, he displayed his own supreme worthiness by how he gave himself, despite our lost condition, to rescind and replace our own sobering *un*worthiness so we might proclaim his worth forever.

- **The Son's crucible confirms the magnitude of the curse of sin we sinners bear.** *Who* was dying on the cross helps us grasp the terrible nature of our treason against God. *Who* was hanging between heaven and earth establishes indisputably how utterly and profoundly destructive is the nature and impact of our sin — of *all* sin. If our sin did this to the King of heaven, what must be the power of its plagues on paupers like us?

- **In the *brokenness* of the One who was no less than the foretold "Servant of Yahweh," we see graphically portrayed the depths of our helpless, hopeless destitution before God**. The full measure of his suffering on the cross exposes sin's fierce malignancy that curses *all* things separated from the life of God.

  > We look at it like this: if one died for all men then, in a sense, they all died . . . (2 Corinthians 5, PHILLIPS).

  > He suffered the things we should have suffered. He took on himself the pain that should have been ours . . . the servant was pierced because we had sinned. He was crushed because we had done what

was evil . . .We have wandered away from God. All of us have turned to our own way. And the Lord has placed on his servant the sins of all of us. He was beaten down and made to suffer . . . He was cut off from this life. He was punished for the sins of my people (Isaiah 53).

- **The *greatness* of the righteousness of the One who died *for* us simultaneously unveils the *greatness* of our wretchedness as well as the *greatness* of the remedy we require.** It confirms that our desperate state is far worse than we first dared to imagine. Looking at the *majesty* of the Lamb who was slain, we cannot dismiss nor deny the *magnitude* of our iniquities any longer. There is a curse upon us that must be confronted and crushed by Another. Somehow the wages of sin — which is nothing short of death itself — must itself be put to death by One who is pure, by One who is totally free from all sin.

- **When Jesus voluntarily suffered the full force of our sin and shame, it was as though he himself became morally culpable *for* humankind's wicked ways, from beginning to end.** He took responsibility to accomplish *for* us what we could never do for ourselves — to act in our stead and on our behalf. In doing so, he became our champion, providing in himself alone an unceasing cure of our undeniable curse.

- **In his horrific sacrifice, Jesus shows us that in God's universe sin commands costly, catastrophic consequences.** By the *scope* of what he did *for* us, Jesus confirms that our rebellion against God is no trivial matter. It is no less than the defamation of God's character. It is no less than an attempt at a kind of cosmic insurgency. Clearly, our holy God cannot ignore such a disastrous contamination of his creation. His wrath toward sin cannot not be contained or tamed until his justice prevails. Sending Christ to die *for* us certifies how seriously lost we really are.

- **To remove our condemnation, the only option left was for God himself to *become* the curse of our race by taking our place through and in his dear Son.**

    All who depend on obeying the law are under a curse. It is written, "May everyone who doesn't continue to do everything that is written in the Book of the Law be under God's curse" . . . Christ set us free from the curse of the law. He did it by becoming a curse for us. It is written, "Everyone who is hung on a pole is under God's curse." Christ Jesus set us free . . . so that we might receive the promise of the Holy Spirit by believing in Christ (Galatians 3).

- **Such sacred, sacrificial blood testifies, beyond dispute, before men and angels, that all human efforts to save ourselves from our bankrupt estate remain hopelessly in vain.** Without his sovereign intervention on our behalf, our destiny, starting from the cradle, is fatal. Left to ourselves, without Jesus, we would never be capable of supplying our deepest longings, let alone satisfying God's definitive Law.

  > At just the right time Christ died for *ungodly people*. He died for us when we had *no power* of our own . . . While we were still *sinners*, Christ died for us . . . Once we were God's *enemies*. But we have been brought back to him because his Son has died for us (Romans 5, emphasis added).

- **In his role as God's promised Messiah, Jesus unmasked, by his crucifixion, the awful animosity toward God resident within all hearts.** The very fact and act of his crucible exposed the darkest realms of humankind's rebellious machinations. It peeled back the façade to force into the open the inherent fury of mankind's hostility toward the Trinity — hostility found in all of us. We see this in Acts when we read:

  > You spoke against Jesus when he was in Pilate's court. You spoke against the Holy and Blameless One. You asked for a murderer to be set free instead. You killed the one who gives life (Acts 3).

  > Was there ever a prophet your people didn't try to hurt? They even killed those who told about the coming of the Blameless One. And now you have handed him over to his enemies. You have murdered him (Acts 7).

  Thus, Paul preached in one synagogue:

  > The people and their rulers had no reason at all for sentencing Jesus to death. But they asked Pilate to have him killed. They did everything that had been written about Jesus (Acts 13).

  As Paul concluded later on:

  > The experts of our day haven't a clue about what this eternal plan is. If they had, they wouldn't have killed the Master of the God-designed life on a cross (1 Corinthians 2, MSG).

- **On the cross, Jesus unmasked the evil one for who he really is as the Savior endured the devil's vicious attacks, while at the very same time he effectively exhausted and neutralized Satan's claims to dominion.** In doing so, he thoroughly accomplished *for* us the greatest good we could ever hope for — the everlasting destruction of sin and Satan that opens the door to God's inexhaustible resources *for* us in Christ Jesus.

- **"The cross was the point where evil did all that it could do and God did all that he could do" (N.T. Wright).** That's why we must:

  > . . . proclaim to the Gentiles the incalculable riches of Christ . . . that all the angelic powers should now see the complex wisdom of God's plan being worked out through the Church, in conformity to that timeless purpose which he centered in Jesus, our Lord (Ephesians 3, PHILLIPS).

- **To be supreme in our salvation, our Lord had to effectively engage and then eliminate the basis for the deadly, disastrous estrangement that existed between us and the living God.** Only one like Christ — perfect in both holiness and wholeness — could bring about a thoroughly just and righteous way to remove and replace God's revulsion against our profound spiritual depravity displayed by the world's injustice and cruelty, oppression and exploitation, racism and terrorism, adultery and idolatry.

- **The *majesty* of the perfect One who descended from heaven to die *for* us undercuts every conceivable pretext about our ability to reconcile with God by our own moral achievements.** For if there were any other way to secure eternal life for us, then clearly Christ's agonies were horribly wasted and utterly tragic.

  > The bodily life I now live I live believing in the Son of God, who loved me and sacrificed himself for me . . . For if righteousness were possible under the Law then Christ died for nothing! (Galatians 2, PHILLIPS).

  > Yet God forbid that I should boast about anything or anybody except the cross of our Lord Jesus Christ, which means that the world is a dead thing to me and I am a dead man to the world. But in Christ it is not circumcision or uncircumcision that counts but the power of new birth (Galatians 6, PHILLIPS).

- **A benediction based on the Lamb slain for the sins of the world:**

May God, who puts all things together, makes all things whole,
Who made a lasting mark through the sacrifice of Jesus,
the sacrifice of blood that sealed the eternal covenant,
Who led Jesus, our Great Shepherd, up and alive from the dead,
now put you together, provide you with everything you need
to please him, make us into what gives him most pleasure,
by means of the sacrifice of Jesus, the Messiah.
All glory to Jesus forever and always!
Oh, yes, yes, yes
(Hebrews 13, MSG).

pause | think | pray

The Precision of His Mission: A Closer Look at Its Costs and Benefits

- **"This is how much God loved the world: He gave his Son, his one and only Son."**

And this is why: so that no one need be destroyed; by believing in him, anyone can have a whole and lasting life. God didn't go to all the trouble of sending his Son merely to point an accusing finger, telling the world how bad it was. He came to help, to put the world right again. Anyone who trusts in him is acquitted; anyone who refuses to trust him has long since been under the death sentence without knowing it (John 3, MSG).

- **Sin consists of our choice to substitute ourselves for God; on the cross, God chose to substitute himself *for* us in order to deal with that rebellion.** "The essence of sin is man substituting himself for God. The essence of salvation is God substituting himself for man" (John Stott).

- **We withheld from God the worship and allegiance that is and always will be rightfully his as our Creator; Jesus took responsibility for the fatal consequences of our treason.** As our substitute, he bore our guilt, suffered our punishment, and paid for our transgressions, satisfying the just penalty we were due. Our sin was not simply disregarded; God's Son, in our place, *for* our sakes, perfectly and permanently dealt with it.

- **In Christ, God took action to *absorb* our judgment by *assuming* our sin.** He personally drank the bitter dregs of our spiritual depravity and bankruptcy so we would not have to.

> Bearing shame and scoffing rude,
> In my place condemned He stood;
> Sealed my pardon with His blood.
> Hallelujah! What a Savior!
> (Philip P. Bliss)

- **"For even the Son of Man did not come to be served, but to serve, and to give his life as a *ransom* for many"** (Mark 10, NIV, emphasis added). A *ransom* is money paid to release a prisoner or secure the return of a valuable possession; it is the *means* of redeeming or buying back a person or thing. The way of liberation for sinners was provided when Jesus became God's ransom *for* us.

- **By his cross he paid the perfect price to reclaim us, a cost beyond measure.**

> You must know (and recognize) that you were redeemed (*ransomed*) from the useless (fruitless) way of living inherited by tradition from [your] forefathers, not with corruptible things [such as] silver and gold. *But [you were purchased] with the precious blood of Christ (the Messiah), like that of a [sacrificial] lamb without blemish or spot* (1 Peter 1, AMPC, emphasis added).

Therefore, unto Jesus all creation proclaims:

> Slain! Paying in blood, you bought men and women, bought them back from all over the earth, bought them back for God. Then you made them a Kingdom, Priests for our God, Priest-kings to rule over the earth (Revelation 5, MSG).

- **In the midst of the brutality of the cross, Christ transformed everything *for* us.** Our sin-bearing Sacrifice transferred us from judgment to justification, from condemnation to reconciliation, from death to life, from the power of Satan to the power of God.

> . . . you are privileged to share the lot of those who are living in the light. For we must never forget that he rescued us from the power of darkness, and re-established us in the kingdom of his beloved Son, that is, in the kingdom of light. For it is by his Son alone that we have been redeemed and have had our sins forgiven (Colossians 1, PHILLIPS).

- **His death was sufficient to cleanse us from sin because it was the climax of a life spent in perfect victory over sin.** Christ makes us righteous not only because he died *for* us but also because he was flawlessly righteous when he did.

- **"We see, then, that as one act of sin exposed the whole race of men to God's judgment and condemnation, so one act of perfect righteousness presents to God a multitude freely acquitted in the sight of God."**

> One man's disobedience placed all men under the threat of condemnation, but one man's obedience has the power to present all men righteous before God (Romans 5, PHILLIPS).

- **"Christ didn't have any sin. But God made him become sin *for* us. So we can be made right with God because of what Christ has done *for* us."**

> When anyone lives in Christ, the new creation has come. The old is gone! The new is here! All this is from God. He brought us back to himself through Christ's death on the cross . . . God was bringing the world back to himself through Christ. He did not hold people's sins against them . . . Come back to God! (2 Corinthians 5, emphasis added).

- **On that Good Friday, Jesus scheduled himself to take our "day in court" before the bar of judgment; and there he willingly served the**

sentence *for* our crimes. So now, Scripture teaches that in Christ we are "*justified*" before God. Every believer can say, "It is *just as if I'd* never sinned; *just as if I'd* already passed through the day of judgment to join Christ on the other side in his glorious, unending dominion."

- **What wondrous love is this? We are as fully justified in Jesus *right now* as we will ever be in the ages to come. So today we may *live as if* we were there already!**

> Justification language appears in Paul with reference to both the *inauguration* of the life of faith and also its final *consummation*. It *anticipates* the verdict of the final judgment, declaring *in advance* the verdict of ultimate acquittal. The believer's present justified experience is thus an *anticipation*, an *advance participation* of deliverance from the wrath to come, and an *assurance* in the present of the final eschatological verdict of acquittal (Alister McGrath, Oxford theologian/author, emphasis added).

- **Justified in Jesus, we can rightfully claim liberation from every fear we might harbor toward the Righteous Sovereign of the Universe.** We are released to start life all over again before his face, in his intimate embrace. *Justified in Jesus*, the redeemed can *act as if* there never were reasons for God's holy fury. *Justified in Jesus*, we are as fully vindicated before the throne of God as our Savior was the day the Father raised him from the dead in victory, thus ratifying the indisputable worth of his sacrifice *for* us. *Justified in Jesus,* we remain forever accepted before eternity's Judge because of our unassailable union with the Judge's Son — who he *is **for*** us and with all he has *done **for*** us.

- **"... all are *justified freely* by his grace through the redemption that came by Christ Jesus."**

> God presented Christ as a sacrifice of atonement, through the shedding of his blood — to be received by faith. He did this . . . to demonstrate his righteousness at the present time, so as to be just and the one who *justifies* those who have faith in Jesus (Romans 5, NIV, emphasis added).

> Who will bring any charge against those whom God has chosen? It is God who *justifies*. Who then is the one who condemns? No one. Christ Jesus who died — more than that, who was raised to life — is at the right hand of God and is also interceding for us (Romans 8, NIV, emphasis added).

- **On the cross, *for our sakes,* the Son was *forsaken.*** The Father abandoned his Son as though he were sin; he gave his Son over to sin. Jesus was surrendered (even as he willingly surrendered himself) to the fate of a fallen world as if he were its chief sinner.

- **Hanging between earth and sky, he was relegated to wretchedness from two directions.** Not only did Jesus bear God's wrath against earth; he also endured earth's wrath against Heaven. He was engulfed in the depraved, dark, and demonic defiance of a world without God and without hope. We might say that during those hours God's impenetrable lifetime protection of his Beloved One was sovereignly suspended.

- **Instead, Jesus found himself vulnerable to the barbarity of humankind's immorality and inhumanity, as well as to the diabolical attacks of wicked powers.** At that moment, not only was the Son deserted by the Father, the Father also grieved as one who had lost his only son.

- **The agony of abandonment heard in Jesus' cries of destitution says it all:**

   About three o'clock Jesus cried out in a loud voice. He said, "Eli, Eli, lema sabachthani?" This means "My God, my God, why have you deserted me?" (Matthew 27).

   God, God . . . my God! Why did you dump me miles from nowhere? Doubled up with pain, I call to God all the day long. No answer. Nothing . . . And here I am, a nothing — an earthworm, something to step on, to squash . . . you moved far away and trouble moved in next door . . . If you don't show up soon, I'm done for — gored by the bulls, meat for the lions (Psalms 22, MSG).

- **At the same time, *for* our sakes Jesus willingly entered unfathomable regions of a holy God's just retribution for humankind's sin in order to fulfill that which was mandated by the Father's *justice.*** For the first time in eternity, the Son was excluded from the fellowship of the triune "circle of love" that had been his forever. Yet this was a "trinitarian transaction." His becoming a curse *for* us before the Father also was his act of *love* for the Father, as well as loving cooperation with the leadership of the Holy Spirit. By his selfless substitution under God's judgments toward us, as our perfect representative, Jesus gave to the Court of

Heaven what we could never be able to provide. He satisfied the eternal Law's demands.

- **Christ was supremely sufficient to remove all obstacles to *reconciliation* between God and his people.**

  We have been made right with God because of our faith. Now we have peace with him because of our Lord Jesus Christ. Through faith in Jesus we have received God's grace. In that grace we stand. We are full of joy because we expect to share in God's glory (Romans 5).

- **He achieved this reconciliation not only *for* individual sinners but also *for* the whole universe.**

  It was in [Christ] that the full nature of God chose to live, and through him God planned to reconcile in his own person, as it were, everything on earth and everything in Heaven by virtue of the sacrifice of the cross. And you yourselves, who were strangers to God, and, in fact, through the evil things you had done, his spiritual enemies, he has now reconciled through the death of his body on the cross, so that he might welcome you to his presence clean and pure, without blame or reproach. This reconciliation assumes, of course, that you maintain a firm position in the faith, and do not allow yourselves to be shifted away from the hope of the Gospel, which you have heard, and which, indeed, the whole world is now having an opportunity of hearing (Colossians 1, PHILLIPS).

- **"Once we were God's enemies. But we have been brought back to him because his Son has died for us."**

  Now that God has brought us back, we are even more secure. We know that we will be saved because Christ lives. And that is not all. We are full of joy in God because of our Lord Jesus Christ. Because of him, God has brought us back to himself (Romans 5).

- **Now, Heaven's monumental manifesto is being sent forth to all of earth's peoples, summoning everyone, everywhere, to be reconciled to God through Jesus.**

  The very spring of our actions is the love of Christ. We look at it like this: if one died for all men then, in a sense, they all died, and his purpose in dying for them is that their lives should now be no longer lived for themselves but for him who died and rose again for them . . . All this is God's doing, for he has reconciled us to himself through Jesus Christ; and he has made us agents of the reconciliation . . . (God) has commissioned us with the message of reconciliation. We are now Christ's ambassadors, as though God were appealing direct to you through us. As his personal representatives we say, "Make your peace with God" (2 Corinthians 5, PHILLIPS).

- **"There is only one God. And there is only one go-between for God and human beings. He is the man Christ Jesus."**

> He gave himself to pay for the sins of everyone. That was a witness given by God at just the right time . . . God our Savior . . . wants everyone to be saved. He wants them to come to know the truth . . . I was appointed to be a messenger and an apostle to preach the good news (1 Timothy 2).

- **Jesus is our only hope for reconciliation, from both directions — God with us and us with God.** He reigns as our matchless Mediator — the cosmic Peacemaker.

> After Jesus cried out again in a loud voice, he died. At that moment the temple curtain was torn in two from top to bottom (Matthew 27).
>
> Christ died for sins once and for all time. The One who did what is right died for those who don't do right. He died to bring you to God (1 Peter 3).
>
> Brothers and sisters, we are not afraid to enter the Most Holy Room. We enter boldly because of the blood of Jesus. His way is new because he lives. It has been opened for us through the curtain. I'm talking about his body. We also have a great priest over the house of God. So let us come near to God with an honest and true heart. Let us come near with a faith that is sure and strong (Hebrews 10).

- **The miracle of bringing God and sinners back together as friends is just the beginning. Amazing as it may seem, the same cross that restores our fellowship with the Father also reconciles the redeemed from every tongue and nation *to one another*.** Automatically the saints have become "best friends forever" — and even better than that, we're bonded as brothers and sisters, with God as our Father.

> You were without hope and without God in the world. At one time you were far away from God. But now you belong to Christ Jesus. He spilled his blood for you. That has brought you near to God. Christ himself is our peace . . . He wanted to create one new group of people out of the two. He wanted to make peace between them. He planned to bring both of them as one body back to God because of the cross. Christ put their hatred to death on that cross . . . So you are no longer strangers and outsiders. You are citizens together with God's people. You are members of God's family . . . And because you belong to him, you too are being built together. You are being made into a house

where God lives through his Spirit (Ephesians 2).

And Jesus makes people holy, and the people he makes holy belong to the same family. So Jesus is not ashamed to call them his brothers and sisters (Hebrews 2).

- **The precision of his mission also includes the repercussions of the cross as it disrupts, disarms, dismantles, and defeats the lethal empire fashioned by Satan's forces.** Days before he reached Calvary, Jesus said to a Jerusalem audience:

  Now it is time for the world to be judged. Now the prince of this world will be thrown out. But I am going to be lifted up from the earth. When I am, I will bring all people to myself (John 12).

As one of his hearers summarized decades later:

  But you know that Christ came to take our sins away. And there is no sin in him . . . Those who do what is sinful belong to the devil. They are just like him. He has been sinning from the beginning. But the Son of God came to destroy the devil's work (1 John 3).

- **"He forgave us all of our sins . . . He took away the weapons of the powers and authorities. He made a public show of them. He won the battle over them by dying on the cross" (Colossians 2).**

  So Jesus became human like them in order to die for them. By doing that, he could destroy the one who rules over the kingdom of death. I'm talking about the devil. Jesus could set people free who were afraid of death. All their lives they were held as slaves by that fear (Hebrews 2).

  Then I heard a loud voice in heaven. It said, "Now the salvation and the power and the kingdom of our God have come. The authority of his Christ has come. Satan, who brings charges against our brothers and sisters, has been thrown down . . . They had victory over him by the blood the Lamb spilled for them (Revelation 12).

- **Today, God's grace manifested in Christ's death continues to flow with abounding blessings, far surpassing the crushing consequences of Adam's sin. The cornucopia of redemption in Jesus far outweighs the curse of the Fall.**

  If one man's sin put crowds of people at the dead-end abyss of separation from God, just think what God's gift poured through one man, Jesus Christ, will do! There's no comparison between that death-dealing sin and this generous, life-giving gift . . . can you imagine the breathtaking recovery life makes, sovereign life, in those who grasp with both hands this wildly extravagant life-gift, this grand setting-everything-right, that the one man Jesus Christ provides? . . . All sin can do is threaten us with death, and that's the end of it. Grace, because God is putting everything together again through the Messiah, invites us into life — a life that goes on and on and on, world without end (Romans 5, MSG).

- **The precision of Christ's mission in his crucifixion will forever be his crowning glory. In fact, it secured the very crown he wears right now.** Consider some of the "jewels" in his crown: The curse of sin cannot hold us because Christ has banished it. The Law cannot condemn us because his righteousness and his righteous sacrifice — both — have satisfied God's justice. Death has no claim on us because when Christ died we died with him; when he was buried we were buried with him; when he rose we stepped into a newness of life with him that never ends.

- **Viewed through the lens of the slaughtered Lamb, the boastful, godless illusions of the world have been stripped and exposed.** Now we believers see them for what they really are. Sin may gain temporary inroads into our lives, but its bondage has been broken by his body, which was broken *for* us. Satan was dethroned as ruler over our lives the moment Jesus cried on the tree, "It is finished!"

- **At the cross, God offers each of us a host of remarkable *trades*:** our depravity for Jesus' purity; our mortal death for his immortal life; our despair for a joyous destiny summed up in Christ's inexhaustible riches; our defeat and destruction traded for victory in Jesus; our eternal separation from God replaced by inclusion in God's family, where now our substitutionary Sacrifice has become our Elder Brother.

- **The central miracle of the mission of the Crucifixion will be forever the reconciliation of all things back to the Father by the blood that was shed there (Colossians 1:18-20).** God's long-awaited "grand reversal," the recapitulation of all creation, is now underway. The lost are being found. The sick are being healed. The oppressed, liberated. The shamed, embraced. The guilty, pardoned. The sinned-against, restored. The condemned, swallowed up in forgiveness and grace. The offenders, welcomed home. All of this only *begins* to express the infinite, incomprehensible measure of the potency of Christ's "atoning sacrifice for our sins, and not only for ours but also for the sins of the whole world" (1 John 2, NIV).

pause | think | pray

How His Spectacular Supremacy Is Displayed in His Sacred Sufferings

- **Christ, and him crucified, is the Alpha and Omega of God's grand redemptive mission.** His sacrifice has become *definitive* for all times and all people — bearing judgment; destroying death; undermining unrighteousness; binding Satan's minions; banishing shame and fear; liberating captives; transferring sinners into the empire of the Son.

  > The Son is the gleaming brightness of God's glory ... He provided the way for people to be made pure from sin. Then he sat down at the right hand of the King, the Majesty in heaven. So he became higher than the angels. The name he received is more excellent than theirs (Hebrews 1).

- **The "success" of Christ's sufferings signifies his supremacy because the price he paid was nothing less than an offering up of his very own lifeblood.** This blood (and Scripture says that "the life is in the blood") is the blood of the preeminent Son of God. Inherently, therefore, it boasts unfettered *potential* to cleanse the sins of all people in all the ages. His sacrifice, as Son of man and God, is thoroughly *sufficient* for all who turn to him in faith for salvation "so that in everything he might have the supremacy" (Colossians 1, NIV).

- **What Jesus did *for* us on the cross confirms the vastness of the victory of his sovereign sway.** Because he was God's Son, Jesus' sacrifice potentially offers a matchless, inexhaustible *provision* for the salvation of all people. However, in the final analysis it provides a limited *application,* reserved for those who believe and are saved.

> Jesus gave one sacrifice for the sins of the people. He gave it once and for all time. He did it by offering himself (Hebrews 7).
>
> But now he has appeared once and for all time. He has come at the end of the ages to do away with sin. He has done that by offering himself . . . Christ was offered up once. He took away the sins of many people. He will also come a second time. At that time he will not suffer for sin. Instead, he will come to bring salvation to those who are waiting for him (Hebrews 9).

- **On the cross, Jesus was revealed to be what Pilate's sign over his head declared: "King." Jesus reigned from the tree.** For one day it became his throne — a costly one for sure, but also priceless At that pivotal moment, God's kingdom broke into the world with a finality that one day will be so irrepressibly and unavoidably confirmed that we read:

> Riding the clouds, he'll be seen by every eye, those who mocked and killed him will see him. People from all nations and all times will tear their clothes in lament. Oh, Yes (Revelation 1, MSG).

- **With derision the religious leaders challenged Jesus to come down from the cross to prove he was God's Anointed One; ironically, one day he will "come down"— from heaven itself — publicly vindicating his rightful kingship over the whole earth.**

> Above his head they placed the written charge against him. It read: "This is Jesus, the king of the Jews." . . . They shook their heads and said . . . "Come down from the cross, if you are the Son of God!" . . . "He saved others," they said. "But he can't save himself! He's the King of Israel! Let him come down now from the cross! Then we will believe in him" (Matthew 27).
>
> He will come in blazing fire . . . He will punish those who don't obey the good news about our Lord Jesus . . . On that day his glory will be

seen in his holy people. Everyone who has believed will be amazed when they see him (2 Thessalonians 1).

- **The cross forms the foundation for Jesus' flourishing, forcefully advancing, far-flung dominion.** Because he fully met the claims of God's eternal judgment in the sacrifice of himself *for* us, Jesus is now sovereignly calling out and redeeming by his blood a multitude, "which no one can number" (Revelation 7), drawn from every people, ethnicity, race, language, generation, and social class in every epoch of human history. His sufferings match his reign perfectly: redemptive, victorious, cosmic (see all of Revelation 4-7). His wounds warrant his elevation to be the empathetic, though just, Judge of all in the hour when the course of history and nations converge at his feet for final determination about outcome and destiny.

- **However, we must never forget: It is not the power of the cross that makes Jesus great. It is the greatness of Jesus that makes the cross powerful!**

  > In his sufferings, He stretched forth His hands and measured out the world — so that even then He might show that a great multitude (collected out of all languages and tribes, from the rising of the sun even to its setting) was about to come under His wings (Lactantius, fourth-century church father).

- **Even on the cross, Jesus' reign remained fully in force because at that very moment the impact of his sacrifice ratified the reclamation of God's entire creation under Jesus as Lord.**

  > He [Jesus] told them, "This is what is written. The Messiah will suffer. He will rise from the dead on the third day. His followers will preach in his name. They will tell others to turn away from their sins and be forgiven. People from every nation will hear it" (Luke 24).

  > The reason my Father loves me is that I give up my life. But I will take it back again. No one takes it from me. I give it up myself . . . I have other sheep that do not belong to this sheep pen. I must bring them in too. They also will listen to my voice. Then there will be one flock and one shepherd (John 10).

  > Unless a grain of wheat falls to the ground and dies, it remains only one seed. But if it dies, it produces many seeds . . . But I am going to be lifted up from the earth. When I am, I will bring all people to myself (John 12).

God was pleased to bring all things back to himself because of what Christ has done. That includes all things on earth and in heaven. God made peace through Christ's blood, through his death on the cross (Colossians 1).

There were so many that no one could count them. They came from every nation, tribe, people and language . . . They cried out in a loud voice, "Salvation belongs to our God, who sits on the throne. Salvation also belongs to the Lamb" (Revelation 7).

- **Preeminently, in this age, Christ's kingdom increases wherever God's *love* prevails and conquers — the love most fully exposed at the cross.** Calvary shows how the triune God rules by compassion and sacrifice, rather than by coercion and force. Good Friday exalts Jesus' mercy in his majesty, and his majesty by his mercy.

- **The love that shines from the cross is magnified by the *magnitude* of what it cost Jesus to die there.** But the cost of Jesus' death is magnified by the *magnitude* of the glory he left to die *for* us, and now has received because of what his sacrificial gift accomplished *for* us.

- **One way the supremacy of God's Son is displayed on the cross is this: Every grace the Father has *for* us is unconditionally guaranteed by what Jesus did there *for* us.** The ramifications of his death are so remarkable, its accomplishments are so astonishing, and its consequences are so comprehensive because the promises of God it secures have no horizon and no end.

  With God on our side like this, how can we lose? If God didn't hesitate to put everything on the line for us, embracing our condition and exposing himself to the worst by sending his own Son, is there anything else he wouldn't gladly and freely do for us? (Romans 8, MSG).

- **The blood that saves and keeps us from hour to hour will never lose its power.** It is infinitely valuable because the cross seals forever the new covenant and new life Jesus obtained *for* God's people "until all the ransomed church of God is saved to sin no more" (Cowper).

- **Christ died *for* us so that we might live for him to serve him, and him alone, as supreme Lord of all.**

  He obeyed God completely, even though it led to his death. In fact, he died on a cross. So God lifted him up to the highest place . . . When the name of Jesus is spoken, everyone's knee will bow to worship him . . . Everyone's mouth will say that Jesus Christ is Lord. And God the Father will receive the glory (Philippians 2).

Christ died for everyone. He died so that those who live should not live for themselves anymore. They should live for Christ. He died for them and was raised again (2 Corinthians 5).

Christ died and came back to life. He did this to become the Lord of both the dead and the living (1 Thessalonians 5).

. . . we were buried with Christ into his death. Christ has been raised from the dead by the Father's glory. And like Christ we also can live a new life . . . We died with Christ. So we believe that we will also live with him (Romans 6).

I have been crucified with Christ. I don't live any longer. Christ lives in me. My faith in the Son of God helps me to live my life in my body. He loved me. He gave himself for me (Galatians 2).

- **Even on that great day, when God's promises in Christ reach their climax, the cross will continue to dominate our vision.** It will forever remain the high watermark of any and all exhibitions of Christ's supremacy — unsurpassed throughout endless ages. Since those six hours of unimaginable agony formed the pinnacle of our Lord's earthly mission, should not his holy humiliation inflame every hymn of praise we raise to exalt his reign?

- **Forever, the *Lion* of Judah will be hailed as the *Lamb* of God** (Revelation 5). The feast at Heaven's grand reunion at the end of this age is called the "marriage supper of the *Lamb*" (Revelation 19). It's the *Lamb* who is seen unleashing God's judgments on the wicked of the earth (Revelation 6). It's the *Lamb* who monopolizes as the magnet of majestic worship in the new Jerusalem (Revelation 21). It's the *Lamb* on the throne who releases an endless river of rule and renewal for the saints of God (Revelation 22).

Selah

pause | think | pray

The Wrap

Renowned pastor/theologian John Piper suggests in one of his popular books that Scripture documents fifty reasons why Jesus died. Fifty! Even with all we've covered in this section, we may not have explored every reason on Piper's list, at least not at the level each deserves.

On the other hand, looking back over our journey into the "mission of Christ's crucifixion" it may be that fifty reasons are far too *few*! After all, we "nailed *the Lord of glory* to the cross" (1 Corinthians 2, emphasis added). How can we adequately innumerate "the incalculable riches of Christ" (Ephesians 3, PHILLIPS) made ours because he died *for* us?

At the same time, Christ crucified is also the foundation, the fountainhead, and in many ways, the grand finale of the Consummation that lies before us. Surely a list of 50 or even 500 reasons for the cross is only the beginning!

Vital to our study of the Crucifixion, therefore, is our understanding of this truth: To say "Christ is *now*" is to imply that, though his sacrifice was given "once for all," the cross continues to define the fullness of "him who fills all in all" *right now*.

It's obvious the Crucifixion remained "present tense" for Paul. For example, he firmly declared in Galatians 6, "I never want to brag about anything except the cross of our Lord Jesus Christ." Or again in 1 Corinthians 2 he wrote, "My goal while I was with you was to talk about only one thing. And that was Jesus Christ and his death on the cross."

On a more personal level, Paul's own pursuit of a deepening relationship with Christ included a constant focus on the meaning of the cross for him *right now.* This ambition of his should be ours as well:

> I consider everything to be nothing compared to knowing Christ Jesus my Lord. To know him is the best thing of all . . . I want to know the power that raised him from the dead. I want to share in his sufferings. I want to become like him by sharing in his death (Philippians 3).

The cross was also "now" for the writer of Hebrews. Recall, for example, how he portrays, page after page, the ongoing high priestly work of Christ. Hebrews names Jesus as our *sacrifice* for our sin as well as our *mediator* presenting that sacrifice in Heaven's Sanctuary.

> He entered heaven itself. He did it to stand in front of God for us. He is there right now . . . But Christ did not enter heaven to offer himself again and again . . . He has come at the end of the ages to do away with sin. He has done that by offering himself (Hebrews 9).

Every day, believers inhabit what Paul calls "heavenly realms" (Ephesians 2). This is due to our saving union with God's Son. This means that *every day* we must continue to "come to Jesus, mediator of a new agreement, and to the cleansing of blood, which tells a better story than the age-old sacrifice of Abel" (Hebrews 12, PHILLIPS). That's why Scripture exhorts believers to seize hold of all the privileges the cross opens for us *right now.*

> Brothers and sisters, we are not afraid to enter the Most Holy Room. We enter boldly because of the blood of Jesus. His way is new because he lives. It has been opened for us through the curtain. I'm talking about his body (Hebrews 10).

Finally, every day we walk in fellowship with Christ, let us never cease to celebrate the love God showed us on the cross. Not only did Jesus die **for** us because he *had* to, but also because he was *glad* to. Scot McKnight says it well: "As we face the cross, then, we can say to ourselves both '*I* did it, my sins sent him there' and '*he* did it, his love took him there.' "

On that fateful day, Christ was consumed with *passion* in two directions: a passion to reconcile all creation back to the Father in order to display forever the glory of God, and a passion for each of us to be a part of that spectacular "recapitulation" of all things in Jesus (as the church fathers termed the impending renovation of heaven and earth).

His pain was our gain. His agony reclaimed our destiny.

"He paid no attention to the shame of the cross. He suffered there because of the joy he was looking forward to. Then he sat down at the right hand of the throne of God" (Hebrews 12). And *we*, redeemed by his blood, giving glory to his Father, are and will be forevermore that joy!

It can never be proclaimed too many times: "The Lamb, who was put to death, is worthy! He is worthy to receive power and wealth and wisdom and strength! He is worthy to receive honor and glory and praise!" (Revelation 5).

NOTE: See Appendix I for "A Stream of Scripture on His Gory Glory".

Who Christ Is FOR Us Today:
By the Re-creation of His Resurrection

On December 12, 1931, on a New York City street, Winston Churchill was struck by a car going 30 miles per hour. Said the future Prime Minister: "I do not know why I was not broken like an eggshell or squashed like a gooseberry." What if he had been killed? What might have been the outcome of World War II, not only for Britain but also for the world?

Or what if Abraham Lincoln had survived Booth's assassination attempt and lived to oversee the aftermath of the Civil War? Considering Lincoln's many farsighted gifts of leadership, how might the whole course of reconciliation, healing, and reconstruction transformed the landscape of race relations for future generations?

These are examples of *counterfactuals*. A counterfactual is a way to think about how history might be rewritten if specific events had turned out differently, such as: "If I had known she wasn't coming, then I would not have waited for her."

So, consider *this* counterfactual: What if Jesus had *not* risen from the dead? What if his body had decomposed in a borrowed tomb that later became a shrine to which people would make sacred pilgrimages to honor a moral revolutionary? What then? What would be different about the course of history, or about the shape of Christianity? Would it even have any shape at all? What about you personally: Would that change what you believe, how you live, what you hope? For a Christian, pondering such a counterfactual should make one shutter.

Thankfully, one certain *"factual"* is the one celebrated in a verse of Charles Wesley's popular Easter hymn:

> Christ the Lord is risen today, Alleluia!
> Lives again our glorious King, Alleluia!
> Death in vain forbids Him rise, Alleluia!
> Soar we now where Christ has led, Alleluia!

Or, as we read in the words of 1 Corinthians 15:

> Death came because of what a man did. Rising from the dead also comes because of what a man did. Because of Adam, all people die. So because of Christ, all will be made alive.

Christianity is the only religion in the world that depends on a *miracle* for its raison d'être — its reason to exist. Other faiths may acknowledge miracles, but the Christian movement stands or falls based on the historicity of one grand miracle — which also happens to be one of the greatest miracles ever!

Among spiritual founders, prophets, and leaders of world religions, the resurrection of our Founder and Leader remains unprecedented, lifting Christ beyond all competitors and contenders for the throne of the universe. Resurrection, in the final sense, *has* happened to one person and one only — the One who says to all his followers: "Do not be afraid. I am the First and the Last. I am the Living One. I was dead. But look! I am alive for ever and ever! And I hold the keys to Death and Hell" (Revelation 1).

With this great news comes a parallel fact of similar weight. To paraphrase N. T. Wright: "Other religions take bad men and try to make them better. Christianity takes dead men and makes them alive in Christ." When Paul writes in 1 Corinthians 15 that "as in Adam all die, even so in Christ shall all be made alive," he is only *beginning* to explore how our union with the Savior, who physically and permanently defeated death, causes us not only to regain but also to surpass all that the first Adam forfeited by his deadly rebellion!

Here is one other insight to consider before we take up an overview of what Jesus' resurrection means ***for*** us:

The total number of New Testament passages concerning Christ's resurrection nearly equals the *combined* total of passages that are specifically focused on his incarnation, crucifixion, and ascension. This does not mean his resurrection is more important; all four dimensions of who Christ is **for** us remain forever inseparable. But clearly, in the preaching of Acts and the teachings of the Epistles — even in Jesus' earthly ministry — *the Resurrection forms the dominant theme.* It is pervasive!

Take for example the public preaching in Acts: The cross, as a theological doctrine, appears to be virtually nonexistent. The message of the Resurrection, however, dominates everywhere the apostles go!

Let's begin our exploration with a few summary observations based on Scripture. Then, we'll feast on a thrilling overview of the key, promise-filled passages on Christ's resurrection.

Snapshots and Starter Thoughts

The Resurrection vindicated Christ's person and validated his work.

The nature and triumphs of the Resurrection are truly awesome.

Here are some ways the Gospels reflect on Jesus' resurrection.

This is how the apostles proclaimed Jesus' resurrection.

The early church interpreted Jesus' resurrection in astounding terms.

The Resurrection Vindicated Christ's Person and Validated His Work

- **Christ's resurrection was not a "consolation prize" for his sufferings.** Rather, it was the public declaration of God's total satisfaction with the redemption he accomplished **for** us all. The impact of the sacrifice of God's Son **for** our sins was as immense as God himself, and consequently precious and fully sufficient. By the Resurrection, God openly said so! It was the only proper reward — it was the highest commendation — the Father could give for what the Son provided in his death on our behalf.

- **Since Christ is God, death on a cross could never be the final chapter — he could not remain indefinitely entombed.** Cold stone could not contain the Prince of Life for long. Though Jesus humbled himself as a servant and was obedient unto death on Golgotha, his claim to sonship was manifested when the Spirit's power raised him victorious over the grave (Romans 1; Philippians 2). Freed from the tomb forevermore, Jesus remains and reigns, resoundingly, as God's promised Messiah and Lord.

- **Now, all of Christ's claims and aims have been justified and ratified.** His incarnation, earthly ministry, miracles, teachings, and sacrificial death have been declared permanently praiseworthy for all ages to come. The Lamb, once slain, can now be given all glory, honor, power, and blessing *because*, delivered from death's dirges, he lives evermore to receive unending accolades from heaven and earth.

- **His resurrection was the *turning point* in his ministry to the nations**. He stepped forth from the grave no longer regarded as a Son and Savior of weakness, humility, lowliness, and agony. Today he is the revered Son and Savior of power and sovereignty, of majesty and victory. The servant of all became the greatest of all. Going down, he took our degradation with him; then he rose, bringing all who will ever be redeemed with him.

- **Jesus, raised from the dead, is God's irrevocable "YES!" for us to cheer.** Just as the cross was God's "NO!" to our fallenness, our rebellion, and our unrighteousness, Jesus alive is God's affirmation of his creation, his eternal purposes, his plan of salvation, and everything and everyone that comes out of the grave with the undefeated Redeemer.

- **In Jesus our standing before God has become invincible.** It is sure and unshakeable, just like the One who rules us and fills us by his indestructible life. On the other hand, for those outside of the risen Christ there is nothing left but God's wrath and eternal destruction.

- **Further, Jesus' resurrection prepared the way for his ascension.** It set the stage for his *ultimate* vindication and validation when forty days later he was enthroned at the Father's right hand. His resurrection was the prelude to his coronation — that impending moment when the Lamb who was slain would take his place at the center of the throne (Revelation 5).

- **Because Jesus defeated death decisively, he could rise again to rule over his subjects in a kingdom that will have no end.** This is why the early Christians who served him so passionately also crowned him with a roll call of royal titles previously reserved for Yahweh alone.

- **From the beginning, this glorious outcome was how it always was meant to be.**

  > But it was the LORD's good plan to crush him and cause him grief. Yet when his life is made an offering for sin, he will have many descendants. *He will enjoy a long life, and the LORD's good plan will prosper in his hands.* When he sees all that is accomplished by his anguish, he will be satisfied. And because of his experience, my righteous servant will make it possible for many to be counted righteous, for he will bear all their sins. *I will give him the honors of a victorious soldier, because he exposed himself to death* (Isaiah 53, emphasis added).

Selah

pause | think | pray

The Nature and Triumphs of the Resurrection Are Truly Awesome

- **"The keys of death were hung on the inside of Christ's tomb."**

  > If any were to be raised from the dead, never to die again, Christ would have to die for them, enter the tomb, take the keys, and unlock the door of death from the inside (John Piper).

- **This kind of resurrection life was unknown before Christ's triumph.** Even Lazarus, temporarily brought back from the grave (John 11), finally had to die again. However, Jesus didn't come back to life like that. Rather, he died and three days later entered into a wholly unprecedented expression of life never before witnessed in the universe — a creation to be sure, but also not of this creation. We might call his resurrection a RE-creation — the unveiling of a wholly unprecedented expression of life never before witnessed in the universe, the first installment of the thoroughly renovated heaven and earth promised us in the age to come.

- **Out of a rich man's tomb, a radically fresh kind of existence emerged within time and space and history.** That's because Jesus, in his death-defying supremacy, proved to be sufficient for the reconstituting and replacing of everything perishing under the judgments of the Lord.

- **As the "man from heaven," Jesus has shown the way for all creation to rise together to share in a future filled with the vibrancy of the living God (1 Corinthians 15).** The world is now, and forever shall be, a very different place because its glorious outcome is guaranteed. In fact, it has already *arrived* through the crucial battle won *for* us by the King of glory.

- **Jesus' victory encompasses "the new order of the ages."** The old order of things — corrupted and depraved, filled with evil, sin, suffering and death's doom — has now been replaced by a new creation. It is a brand new beginning able to produce the fruits of health, wholeness, holiness, righteousness, godliness, truth, and unfailing love.

- **Jesus *himself*, alive forever, *is* that re-creation in bodily form.** He embodies the promised new order, the anticipated new beginning. He is the prophesied "inbreaking" of the age to come. We can catch a glimpse of it right now as we grow to know more about our risen Lord.

- **It is clear: God is not willing to relinquish his old creation, leaving it to be dismantled and obliterated because of our sin.** Instead, through our risen Jesus, God is now in the business of *making all things new*.

  > The Resurrection and Ascension cannot be understood in any other way than as the *starting point* for a new world . . . the key to history. He is the one who embodies and accomplishes God's mission for all creation. He is the focal point of the Bible's grand narrative (N. T. Wright, emphasis added).

- **After being mortally wounded, Jesus turned death back on itself.** He defused death — he swallowed it up in life — so we see what immortality in its fullness really looks like when we look at him.

- **In Christ the ashes of our fatal corruption are *replaced* by the boundless incorruption of his liberated body and life-giving spirit (1 Corinthians 15).** In him our mourning and grief are *replaced* by everlasting comfort and gladness because the second Adam makes us part of a new race (Romans 5). In Jesus, unmitigated despair and hopelessness are *replaced* by a place among the saints so we can live out the fulfillment of every promise secured by his victory (see all of Isaiah 61).

- **Death dethroned us; but Christ rose to own us.** Alive in him, we belong to him, exclusively. As our ever-living sovereign, we are bound to him, as it were, the way a wife is bound to her husband in order that through that union we might bring forth lasting fruit for God (Romans 7).

- **Jesus' resurrection triumph vanquished our deadliest foes: sin, evil, Satan, death.** At the same time, he delivered his people from the judgment to come. By overcoming death he showed us how, through himself, we also will ultimately overcome all of the misery, pain, futility, decay, division, disruption, and disaster that poisons this old creation. Thus, all of the deadly desperations of our existence have proven to be far less potent than Christ's unsurpassed victory on our behalf.

- **Tasting death for each of us, Christ bound the "strong man" to spoil him of his prey.** He conquered the Tyrant of hell, releasing us from the dread of the dead. Bruising the serpent's head, Jesus defanged that snake's ability to use the venom of the fear of death to paralyze us. Then Jesus pointed everyone to himself as the "exit door" from the tomb of death into life everlasting.

- **Because of the risen Son of God, futility and despair have been silenced.** The Father proclaims to the ends of the earth one decisive shout of hope: "He is risen!" The good news of re-creation rings throughout the universe.

- **This world does not belong to the prince of darkness. It has become the sole inheritance of our crucified and risen Victor.** Our risen Lord Jesus Christ has permanently absorbed the *sting* of death, dispelled the *fear* of death, renounced the *curse* of death, and disengaged the *clutch* of death.

- **The gospel of Christ assures the world that death may now be regarded as *abnormal*.** Life in Christ, revealed in his resurrection, is now the "new normal" destined to replace the sorrow-filled shroud that presently covers the whole earth. The hope of the gospel is nothing less than the hope of a new creation in Jesus ultimately designed to replace everything currently perishing.

- **Christ is the "firstborn" from among the dead (Colossians 1).** This means as the first to rise again, he has become for all saints the fountainhead of eternal life. It means he is the first installment, the harbinger, pointing toward many others destined to join him in the same victory (Romans 8; Hebrews 2).

- **Jesus is the "firstfruits" of those who will be raised from the dead (1 Corinthians 15).** In him we behold the initial wave of a grand harvest of similarly resurrected followers just waiting to be gathered in. *His* triumph has set in motion everything that assures our own victory.

- **He is the "first installment" of the renovated heaven and earth that lies just ahead.** Jesus alive forevermore is the prototype of what we shall become. On the day we see him we shall be like him when we see him as he is (1 John 3). When he comes he will transform our mortal bodies into copies of his glorious body (Philippians 3).

- **"Make no mistake: If he rose at all, it was as His body; if the cells' dissolution did not reverse, the molecules reknit, the amino acids rekindle, the Church will fail . . ."**

  > Let us not mock God with metaphor, analogy, sidestepping transcendence, make of the event a parable . . . The stone is rolled back, not papier-mache, not a stone in a story, but the vast rock of materiality that in the slow grinding of time will eclipse for each of us the wide light of day (John Updyke).

Selah

pause | think | pray

Here Are Some Ways the Gospels Reflect on Jesus' Resurrection

- **The day of resurrection appeared in a person.**

  Jesus said . . . "I am the resurrection and the life. Anyone who believes in me will live, even if they die. And whoever lives by believing in me will never die. Do you believe this?" (John 11).

- **The Resurrection fulfilled Old Testament promises.**

  Jesus said to them, "This is what I told you while I was still with you. Everything written about me in the Law of Moses, the Prophets and the Psalms must come true." Then he opened their minds so they could understand the Scriptures. He told them, "This is what is written. The Messiah will suffer. He will rise from the dead on the third day . . . You have seen these things with your own eyes" (Luke 24).

- **The Resurrection made Jesus the locus and focus of all worship**.

  Jesus answered them, "When you destroy this temple, I will raise it up again in three days" . . . but the temple Jesus had spoken about was his body . . . after he had been raised from the dead [then] they believed the Scripture. They also believed the words that Jesus had spoken (John 2).

- **The Resurrection restored Jesus to his rightful place in God's purposes.**

  Jesus said to [the chief priests and the Pharisees], "Haven't you ever read what the Scriptures say, 'The stone the builders didn't accept has become the most important stone of all' . . . Anyone who falls on that stone will be broken to pieces. But the stone will crush anyone it falls on" (Matthew 21).

- **The Resurrection confirmed Jesus as the perfect leader for his people.**

  Jesus said, "I give my life for the sheep . . . Then there will be one flock and one shepherd. The reason my Father loves me is that I give up my life. But I will take it back again. No one takes it from me. I give it up myself. I have the authority to give it up. And I have the authority to take it back again. I received this command from my Father" (John 10).

- **Jesus' actual resurrection was preceded by a resurrection-type breakthrough.**

There in front of them his appearance was changed. His face shone like the sun. His clothes became as white as the light . . . A voice from the cloud said, "This is my Son, and I love him. I am very pleased with him. Listen to him!" . . . Jesus told them what to do. "Don't tell anyone what you have seen," he said. "Wait until the Son of Man has been raised from the dead" (Matthew 17).

- **The Resurrection vindicated his claims.**

    [Jesus] answered, "Evil and unfaithful people ask for a sign! But none will be given except the sign of the prophet Jonah. Jonah was in the belly of a huge fish for three days and three nights. Something like that will happen to the Son of Man. He will spend three days and three nights in the grave . . . now one who is more important than Jonah is here" (Matthew 12).

- **The promised and certain results of his resurrection formed his core defense at his trial.**

    Again the high priest asked him, "Are you the Messiah? Are you the Son of the Blessed One?" "I am," said Jesus. "And you will see the Son of Man sitting at the right hand of the Mighty One. You will see the Son of Man coming on the clouds of heaven" (Mark 14).

- **Jesus' victory over death was revealed *vividly* and *concretely* to his disciples.**

    Jesus said to them, "Why are you troubled? Why do you have doubts in your minds? Look at my hands and my feet. It's really me! Touch me and see. A ghost does not have a body or bones. But you can see that I do." After he said that, he showed them his hands and feet. But they still did not believe it. They were amazed and filled with joy. So Jesus asked them, "Do you have anything here to eat?" They gave him a piece of cooked fish. He took it and ate it in front of them . . . He told them, "This is what is written. The Messiah will suffer. He will rise from the dead on the third day" (Luke 24).

- **His victory over death was experienced *intimately* by his disciples.**

    Jesus came in and stood among them. He said, "May peace be with you!" Then he showed them his hands and his side. The disciples were very happy when they saw the Lord . . . Then he said to Thomas, "Put your finger here. See my hands. Reach out your hand and put it into my side. Stop doubting and believe." Thomas said to him, "My Lord and my God!" Then Jesus told him, "Because you have seen me, you have believed. Blessed are those who have not seen me but still have believed" (John 20).

- **His victory over death was explored *intensively* by his disciples.**

  After his suffering and death, he appeared to them. In many ways he proved that he was alive. He appeared to them over a period of 40 days. During that time he spoke about God's kingdom. One day Jesus was eating with them. He gave them a command ... "you will receive power when the Holy Spirit comes on you. Then you will tell people about me ... from one end of the earth to the other" (Acts 1).

- **The Resurrection turned the disciples' shock and sorrow into their greatest joy.**

  They came together in Galilee. Then Jesus said to them, "The Son of Man is going to be handed over to men. They will kill him. On the third day he will rise from the dead." Then the disciples were filled with deep sadness (Matthew 17).

  So [Jesus] said to them ... "Now it's your time to be sad. But I will see you again. Then you will be full of joy. And no one will take your joy away" (John 16).

- **The Resurrection set the disciples' hearts on fire.**

  Jesus said to them, "How foolish you are! How long it takes you to believe all that the prophets said! Didn't the Messiah have to suffer these things and then receive his glory?" ... They said to each other, "He explained to us what the Scriptures meant. Weren't we excited as he talked with us on the road?" (Luke 24).

- **The Raised One proved he was able and ready to raise others too.**

  The Father raises the dead and gives them life. In the same way, the Son gives life to anyone he wants to ... Anyone who hears my word and believes him who sent me has eternal life. They will not be judged. They have crossed over from death to life ... A time is coming for me to give life. In fact, it has already begun. The dead will hear the voice of the Son of God. Those who hear it will live ... A time is coming when all who are in their graves will hear his voice. They will all come out of their graves (John 5).

  My Father wants all who look to the Son and believe in him to have eternal life. I will raise them up on the last day ... No one can come to me unless the Father who sent me brings them. Then I will raise them up on the last day (John 6).

- **The Resurrection is indispensable to the success of his mission.**

  Jesus replied ... "I will build my church. The gates of hell will not be strong enough to destroy it" ... From that time on Jesus began to explain to his disciples what would happen to him . . . [that] he must be killed and on the third day rise to life again (Matthew 16).

- **Jesus told his disciples to spread his victory over death to the nations.**

  When they saw him, they worshiped him. But some still had their doubts. Then Jesus came to them. He said, "All authority in heaven and on earth has been given to me. So you must go and make disciples of all nations. Baptize them in the name of the Father and of the Son and of the Holy Spirit. Teach them to obey everything I have commanded you. And you can be sure that I am always with you, to the very end" (Matthew 28).

- **Bottom line: Jesus is no longer among the dead, just as he said.**

  "Why do you look for the living among the dead? Jesus is not here! He has risen! Remember how he told you he would rise. It was while he was still with you in Galilee. He said, 'The Son of Man must be handed over to sinful people. He must be nailed to a cross. On the third day he will rise from the dead'" (Luke 24).

pause | think | pray

This Is How the Apostles Proclaimed Jesus' Resurrection

- **The Resurrection was a core theme proclaimed at Pentecost.**

  In a loud voice [Peter] spoke to the crowd . . . "You nailed him to the cross. But God raised him from the dead. He set him free from the suffering of death. It wasn't possible for death to keep its hold on Jesus. David spoke about him. He said . . . 'my heart is glad and joy is on my tongue. My whole body will be full of hope. You will not leave me in the place of the dead. You will not let your holy one rot away. You always show me the path that leads to life' . . . David saw what was coming. So he spoke about the Messiah rising from the dead. He said that the Messiah would not be left in the place of the dead. His body wouldn't rot in the ground. God has raised this same Jesus back to life. We are all witnesses of this. Jesus has been given a place of honor at the right hand of God . . . You nailed Jesus to the cross. But God has made him both Lord and Christ" (Acts 2).

- **Peter's defense in the temple made much of the Resurrection.**

    [Peter] said . . . "You killed the one who gives life. But God raised him from the dead. We are witnesses of this . . . The time will come when the Lord will make everything new. He will send the Messiah. Jesus has been appointed as the Messiah for you . . . God raised up Jesus, who serves him. God sent him first to you. He did it to bless you" (Acts 3).

- **Peter and John confronted Jewish religious leaders with it.**

    Peter was filled with the Holy Spirit. He said to them, "You nailed Jesus Christ of Nazareth to the cross. But God raised him from the dead . . . Scripture says that Jesus is 'the stone you builders did not accept. But it has become the most important stone of all.' You can't be saved by believing in anyone else. God has given people no other name under heaven that will save them (Acts 4).

- **The new believers prayed to become God's empowered witnesses to Jesus' resurrection.**

    Then they raised their voices together in prayer to God . . . "Help us to be very bold when we speak your word. Stretch out your hand to heal. Do signs and wonders through the name of your holy servant Jesus" . . . They were all filled with the Holy Spirit. They were bold when they spoke God's word . . . With great power the apostles . . . were telling people that the Lord Jesus had risen from the dead (Acts 4).

- **The message of the Resurrection was God's final offer to his people in Jerusalem.**

    Peter and the other apostles replied, "We must obey God instead of people! You had Jesus killed by nailing him to a cross. But the God of our people raised Jesus from the dead. Now Jesus is Prince and Savior. God has proved this by giving him a place of honor with him . . . We are telling people about these things. And so is the Holy Spirit. God has given the Spirit to those who obey him" (Acts 5).

- **That same offer, which focused on the Resurrection, converted the first Gentiles.**

    Then Peter began to speak . . . "[This is] the good news of peace through Jesus Christ. He is Lord of all . . . You know how God anointed Jesus of Nazareth with the Holy Spirit and with power . . . They killed him by nailing him to a cross. But on the third day God raised him from the dead. God allowed Jesus to be seen. But he wasn't seen by all the people. He was seen only by us. We are witnesses whom God had already chosen. We ate and drank with him after he rose from the dead . . . He told us to tell people that he is the one appointed by God to judge the living and the dead" . . . While Peter was still speaking, the Holy Spirit came on all who heard the message (Acts 10).

- **The Resurrection account formed the heart of Paul's witness to Jewish synagogues.**

  This message of salvation has been sent to us . . . The people and their rulers had no reason at all for sentencing Jesus to death . . . Then they took him down from the cross. They laid him in a tomb. But God raised him from the dead. For many days he was seen by those who had traveled with him from Galilee to Jerusalem. Now they are telling our people about Jesus . . . What God promised our people long ago he has done for us, their children . . . God raised Jesus from the dead. He will never rot in the grave . . . I announce to you that your sins can be forgiven because of what Jesus has done (Acts 13).

- **The truth of the Resurrection shaped Paul's witness to Athenian philosophers**.

  [Philosophers] said, "He seems to be telling us about gods we've never heard of." They said this because Paul was preaching the good news about Jesus. He was telling them that Jesus had risen from the dead . . . Then Paul stood up in the meeting of the Areopagus. He said . . . "Now I am going to tell you about this 'unknown god' [you worship] . . . He has set a day when he will judge the world fairly. He has appointed a man to be its judge. God has proved this to everyone by raising that man from the dead" (Acts 17).

- **Paul ended up on trial precisely for proclaiming the Resurrection as Israel's ultimate hope.**

> I believe everything that is in keeping with what is written in the Prophets. I have the same hope in God that these men themselves have. I believe that both the godly and the ungodly will rise from the dead . . . I believe that people will rise from the dead. That is why I am on trial here today (Acts 24).

> Those bringing charges against [Paul] got up to speak . . . they argued with him about their own beliefs. They didn't agree about a man named Jesus. They said Jesus was dead, but Paul claimed Jesus was alive (Acts 25).

> Today I am on trial because of the hope I have. I believe in what God promised our people long ago. It is the promise that our 12 tribes are hoping to see come true. Because of this hope they serve God with faithful and honest hearts day and night . . . It is also because of this hope that these Jews are bringing charges against me. Why should any of you think it is impossible for God to raise the dead? (Acts 26).

- **In his courtroom defense, Paul turned the Resurrection into the grand appeal of his closing argument.**

> I was on the road. I saw a light coming from heaven. It was brighter than the sun. It was shining around me and my companions. We all fell to the ground. I heard a voice speak to me in the Aramaic language. "Saul! Saul!" it said. "Why are you opposing me? It is hard for you to go against what you know is right." Then I asked, "Who are you, Lord?" "I am Jesus," the Lord replied. "I am the one you are opposing. Now get up. Stand on your feet. I have appeared to you to appoint you to serve me. And you must tell other people about me. You must tell others that you have seen me today" . . . I obeyed the vision that appeared from heaven . . . So I stand here and tell you what is true. I tell it to everyone, both small and great. I have been saying nothing different from what the prophets and Moses said would happen. They said the Messiah would suffer. He would be the first to rise from the dead. He would bring the message of God's light. He would bring it to his own people and to the Gentiles (Acts 26).

Selah

pause | think | pray

The Early Church Interpreted Jesus' Resurrection in Astounding Terms

- **Christ's resurrection vindicates his sonship.**

  > The Good News is about his Son. In his earthly life he was born into King David's family line, and he was shown to be the Son of God when he was raised from the dead by the power of the Holy Spirit. He is Jesus Christ our Lord (Romans 1, NLT).

- **The Resurrection frees the Son to bring his Father praise forever.**

  > We are sure of this because Christ was raised from the dead, and he will never die again. Death no longer has any power over him. When he died, he died once to break the power of sin. But now that he lives, he lives for the glory of God (Romans 6, NLT).

- **True immortality now is manifested by Jesus' triumph over the grave.**

  > . . . that was his plan from before the beginning of time — to show us his grace through Christ Jesus. And now he has made all of this plain to us by the appearing of Christ Jesus, our Savior. He broke the power of death and illuminated the way to life and immortality through the Good News (2 Timothy 1, NLT).

- **Raised from death, the Lord Jesus Christ has become supreme over all.**

  > God rescued us from dead-end alleys and dark dungeons. He's set us up in the kingdom of the Son he loves so much, the Son who got us out of the pit we were in, got rid of the sins we were doomed to keep

repeating . . . He was supreme in the beginning and — leading the resurrection parade — he is supreme in the end. From beginning to end he's there, towering far above everything, everyone (Colossians 1, MSG).

Christ died and rose again for this very purpose — to be Lord both of the living and of the dead (Romans 14, NLT).

- **Raised from the dead, Christ has now been raised on high.**

And you will know his great power. It can't be compared with anything else. His power works for us who believe. It is the same mighty strength God showed when he raised Christ from the dead. God seated him at his right hand in his heavenly kingdom. There Christ sits far above all who rule and have authority (Ephesians 1).

- **Resurrection and exaltation go together for the Risen One.**

He was humble and obeyed God completely. He did this even though it led to his death. Even worse, he died on a cross! So God lifted him up to the highest place. God gave him the name that is above every name (Philippians 2).

- **There is no good news apart from Jesus' victory over the grave.**

Because you believed the good news, you are saved. But you must hold firmly to the message I preached to you . . . it is the most important of all. Here is what it is. Christ died for our sins, just as Scripture said he would. He was buried. He was raised from the dead on the third day, just as Scripture said he would be. He appeared to Peter. Then he appeared to the 12 apostles. After that, he appeared to more than 500 brothers and sisters at the same time . . . He appeared to James. Then he appeared to all the apostles. Last of all, he also appeared to me (1 Corinthians 15).

- **The truth of the Resurrection is decisive for our eternal destiny. If Jesus had not been raised from the dead, life everlasting would not be an option; it would not even exist!**

We have preached that Christ has been raised from the dead . . . if Christ has not been raised, what we preach doesn't mean anything . . . if Christ has not been raised, your faith doesn't mean anything. Your sins have not been forgiven. Those who have died believing in Christ are also lost . . . But Christ really has been raised from the dead. He is the first of all those who will rise. Death came because of what a man did. Rising from the dead also comes because of what a man did. Because of Adam, all people die. So because of Christ, all will be made alive (1 Corinthians 15).

- **Therefore, the Resurrection is the one truth the Church must claim and proclaim for all to hear.**

  If you openly declare that Jesus is Lord and believe in your heart that God raised him from the dead, you will be saved . . . But how can they call on him to save them unless they believe in him? And how can they believe in him if they have never heard about him? And how can they hear about him unless someone tells them? (Romans 10, NLT).

- **Risen again, our Lord Jesus ratifies and applies God's covenant with God's people.**

  Now may the God of peace — who brought up from the dead our Lord Jesus, the great Shepherd of the sheep, and ratified an eternal covenant with his blood — may he equip you with all you need for doing his will . . . through the power of Jesus Christ (Hebrews 13, NLT).

- **Much was accomplished the day Jesus defeated death. For example, rising he justified us freely forever.**

  God will also count us as righteous if we believe in him, the one who raised Jesus our Lord from the dead. He was handed over to die because of our sins, and he was raised to life to make us right with God (Romans 4, NLT).

- **Our Savior rose *for* us to give us a whole new beginning.**

  Because you belong to Christ, you have been made complete. He is the ruler over every power and authority . . . you were buried together with Christ . . . you were raised to life by believing in God's work. God himself raised Jesus from the dead . . . God gave you new life together with Christ. He forgave us all of our sins (Colossians 2).

- **His resurrection has created a whole new world *for* us.**

  Since we believe that Christ died for all, we also believe that we have all died to our old life. He died for everyone so that those who receive his new life will no longer live for themselves. Instead, they will live for Christ, who died and was raised for them . . . This means that anyone who belongs to Christ has become a new person. The old life is gone; a new life has begun! (2 Corinthians 5, NLT).

- **In our union with him in his risen life, Christ makes us truly alive even now.**

  For since our friendship with God was restored by the death of his Son while we were still his enemies, we will certainly be saved through the life of his Son (Romans 5, NLT).

- **He rose again *for* us *then* so that we can triumph *now*.**

  Who then will condemn us? No one — for Christ Jesus died for us and was raised to life for us, and he is sitting in the place of honor at God's right hand, pleading for us . . . overwhelming victory is ours through Christ, who loved us (Romans 8, NLT).

- **Our Lord Jesus Christ defeated death *for* us *then* so that we can prosper *now*.**

  What does not last will be dressed with what lasts forever. What dies will be dressed with what does not die. Then what is written will come true. It says, "Death has been swallowed up. It has lost the battle." Death, where is the victory you thought you had? Death, where is your sting? The sting of death is sin. And the power of sin is the law. But let us give thanks to God! He gives us the victory because of what our Lord Jesus Christ has done . . . Because you belong to the Lord, you know that your work is not worthless (1 Corinthians 15).

- **Jesus alive from the dead removes *for* us the fear of death.**

  But we do see Jesus already given a crown of glory and honor. He was made a lower than the angels for a little while. He suffered death. By the grace of God, he tasted death for everyone. That is why he was given his crown . . . By doing this, he could break the power of the devil. The devil is the one who rules over the kingdom of death. Jesus could set people free who were afraid of death. All their lives they were held as slaves by that fear . . . Then he could serve God as a kind and faithful high priest (Hebrews 2).

- **His indestructible life qualifies him to be our high priest forever.**

  He has become a priest because of his powerful life. His life can never be destroyed . . . Jesus lives forever. So he always holds the office of priest. People now come to God through him. And he is able to save them completely and for all time. Jesus lives forever (Hebrews 7).

- **Victorious over the grave, Christ brings us into a living hope.**

  We have been born again, because God raised Jesus Christ from the dead. Now we live with great expectation . . . Through Christ you have come to trust in God. And you have placed your faith and hope in God because he raised Christ from the dead and gave him great glory (1 Peter 1, NLT).

- **Risen and evermore alive, Jesus unlocks the gates of the grave *for* us.**

> Don't be afraid! I am the First and the Last. I am the living one. I died, but look — I am alive forever and ever! And I hold the keys of death and the grave (Revelation 1).

- **Because we belong to a risen Savior, we can walk with him right out of the tomb.**

> By being baptized, we were buried with Christ into his death. Christ has been raised from the dead by the Father's glory. And like Christ we also can live a new life. By being baptized, we have been joined with him in a death like his. So we will certainly also be joined with him in a resurrection like his . . . We died with Christ. So we believe that we will also live with him . . . When he died, he died once and for all time. He did this to break the power of sin. Now that he lives, he lives in the power of God. In the same way, consider yourselves to be dead as far as sin is concerned. Now you believe in Christ Jesus. So consider yourselves to be alive as far as God is concerned (Romans 6).

- **Right now, Jesus quickens us to serve with him in resurrection glory.**

> God loves us deeply. He is full of mercy. So he gave us new life because of what Christ has done. He gave us life even when we were dead in sin. God's grace has saved you. God raised us up with Christ. He has seated us with him in his heavenly kingdom because we belong to Christ Jesus (Ephesians 2).

- **To know the risen Jesus is to know the *power* of the Resurrection day by day.**

> Even more, I consider everything to be nothing compared to knowing Christ Jesus my Lord . . . I want to be joined to him . . . I want to know the power that raised him from the dead. I want to share in his sufferings. I want to become like him by sharing in his death. Then by God's grace I will rise from the dead (Philippians 3).

- **Risen to begin reigning over everything, Jesus deserves to be the constant focus of the Church's daily existence.**

> So if you're serious about living this new resurrection life with Christ, act like it. Pursue the things over which Christ presides. Don't shuffle along, eyes to the ground, absorbed with the things right in front of you. Look up, and be alert to what is going on around Christ — that's where the action is. See things from his perspective. Your old life is dead. Your new life, which is your real life — even though invisible to spectators — is with Christ in God. He is your life. When Christ (your real life, remember) shows up again on this earth, you'll show up, too — the real you, the glorious you (Colossians 3, MSG).

- **His resurrection impacts our present just as it guarantees our future.**

    We know that God, who raised the Lord Jesus, will also raise us with Jesus and present us to himself together with you . . . That is why we never give up. Though our bodies are dying, our spirits are being renewed every day (2 Corinthians 4, NLT).

- **The Risen One intends no less than to resurrect us with him in order to be like him.**

    We believe that Jesus died and rose again. When he returns, many who believe in him will have died already. We believe that God will bring them back with Jesus . . . The Lord himself will come down from heaven . . . Many who believe in Christ will have died already. They will rise first. After that, we who are still alive and are left will be caught up together with them . . . And we will be with him forever (1 Thessalonians 4).

- **His glorious body forms the prototype of ours to come.**

    He has the power to bring everything under his control. By his power he will change our earthly bodies. They will become like his glorious body (Philippians 3).

- **As the Risen One, he is also the *Returning* One.**

    Grace and peace to you from . . . Jesus Christ . . . the first to rise from the dead, and the ruler of all the kings of the world . . . Look! He comes with the clouds of heaven. And everyone will see him (Revelation 1).

- **One day Christ will resurrect a multitude to share with him in his eternal reign.**

    I saw thrones. Those put in charge of judgment sat on the thrones. I also saw the souls of those beheaded because of their witness to Jesus and the Word of God . . . they lived and reigned with Christ for a thousand years . . . This is the first resurrection — and those involved most blessed, most holy. No second death for them! They're priests of God and Christ; they'll reign with him a thousand years (Revelation 20).

Selah

pause | think | pray

The Wrap

> There's a cemetery plot, somewhere out there, waiting for your corpse. Regardless of who and where you are, you will one day be quite dead. The universe roles around us frenetically, and, in every single case, it eventually kills us.

So warns Russell Moore. But thankfully he doesn't leave us there, adding the reason for Christian hope:

> Jesus doesn't promise us an 'afterlife.' He promises us life — and that everlasting. In his resurrection, Jesus has gone before us as a pioneer of the new creation. Jesus calls us into his life [which is] wild and exhilarating and unpredictable.

Precisely.

In the Resurrection, the RE-creation of the old creation has begun. Just as the Incarnation draws its meaning from the *first* creation, just as the Crucifixion was necessitated by the helpless condition of a *fallen* creation, even so, the Resurrection permanently positions all believers within a *new* creation — at this very moment.

Because Christ arose, we have been born again to a living hope (1 Peter 1), No longer do any of us need to look for the living among the dead (Luke 24). For Christ, death is past; it lies behind him, never to be faced again. Even so, his resurrection encourages anticipation of — even more, direct *participation in* — his indestructible kind of life (Hebrews 9), ordained by God to bring about, in the end, the renewal and recapitulation of the entire universe.

Christian F. Gellert, professor of philosophy at the University of Leipzig in the mid-1700s, struggled with poor health his entire life. Yet, he was held in high esteem by his students and experienced wide popularity due not only to his Christlike character but also to his writings meant to incite spiritual passion.

He is best known in our day for penning this Easter hymn, which in just a few words, captures the marvel of what Christ did **for** us when he rose again — all of it for us, and all of it infusing our walk with him right now as well as ten thousand years from now.

Jesus lives, and so shall I.
Death! thy sting is gone forever!
He who deigned for me to die,
Lives, the bands of death to sever.
He shall raise me from the dust:
Jesus is my Hope and Trust.

Jesus lives, and reigns supreme,
And, his kingdom still remaining,
I shall also be with him,
Ever living, ever reigning.
God has promised, be it must:
Jesus is my Hope and Trust.

Jesus lives, I know full well
Nought from him my heart can sever,
Life nor death nor powers of hell,
Joy nor grief, hence forth forever.
None of all his saints is lost;
Jesus is my Hope and Trust.

Jesus lives, and death is now
But my entrance into glory.
Courage, then, my soul, for thou
Hast a crown of life before thee;
Thou shalt find thy hopes were just;
Jesus is the Christian's Trust.

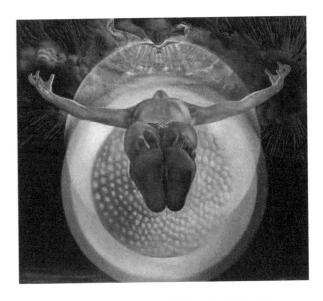

Who Christ Is FOR Us Today:
By the Coronation of His Ascension

The Ascension may be the most neglected truth in the panoply of evangelical doctrines — that's what we proposed in an earlier "Meditation." Consider this: Christmas celebrates Jesus' incarnation. Good Friday remembers his crucifixion. Easter trumpets his resurrection. But how many congregations ever set aside even one Sunday a year, any time in the Church calendar, to proclaim the coronation of God's Son — to celebrate the actual day Jesus was welcomed to God's throne?

And yet, if Jesus had not ascended — if there had not been a day, like today is a day, when the Father invited his Son to sit at his right hand — what would we have left? What if there had not been a moment when, in so many words, the Father announced to his Son an affirmation like this?

All you have accomplished for my people by your incarnation,
your life of righteousness, your teachings and healings,
your atoning sacrifice, and your definitive disabling of death are *totally sufficient*!
You have fulfilled all that's needed for the reclamation of the universe.
So come, my Son, take the crown and the glory;
begin to reign as King of kings and Lord of lords, forever and ever!

Is it not evident that, despite the Resurrection, if there had been no Ascension we still would be lost? If the Father had *not* been fully satisfied with all that his Son did *for* us, would not all that work be rendered null and void? Would we not be forever undone, without help and without hope, if Jesus had not entered heaven on our behalf, celebrated with hymns of victory?

If Christ had *not* ascended *for* us, where else could we go to find the Father's welcoming arms? There would be no High Priest to represent us and intercede *for* us at the throne. We would be stripped of free access into God's presence. There would be no one preparing a home for our eternal dwelling. Our lives, as well as the whole universe, would be without the Mediator to symphonize all things with the will of God.

Pentecost would be permanently postponed because believers would remain forever devoid of the Spirit's indwelling power. The promises meant to be Jesus' inheritance, to be shared with all who belong to him, would be locked up and shelved. Above all, Jesus' very best gift, his saving efforts *for* us, would be stuck in the past, as it were — where he was last seen, visiting with his disciples after exiting the tomb, left at the fringes of history.

But Jesus *has* ascended! Not ascended passively but *actively* — "He went up" (Acts 1). Forty days after he rolled back the stone he sat down on the Divine Throne, the dominant furniture in the universe. He has been exalted above every name in this age and the age to come. Therefore, we are saved! Right now we share in the ascended life of the Ascended One!

Bishop N. T. Wright gives the wonder of the Ascension rich, *historical* perspective by contrasting it with first-century myths about Roman emperors. He writes in *Simply Jesus:*

> Anyone familiar with the world of the early Roman Empire would realize what was happening. After the death of Julius Caesar, people swore they had seen his soul ascending to heaven. Augustus, Caesar's adopted son, promptly declared that Julius was therefore a god; which meant that he, Augustus, was now 'son of god' . . . When Augustus himself died the process was repeated, as it was with many (though not all) of his successors. The parallel is sufficiently close to make any readers in the Roman world realize what is going on. Jesus is radically upstaging Caesar. Actually, if we think of the [Ascension] as the opening frame of the book of Acts, we get the point, because the closing frame is Paul in Rome, under Caesar's nose, announcing

God as king and Jesus as Lord . . . the strange paradox [is] Paul in chains announcing that the Roman world has a new emperor. *[It] sets the tone for all kingdom work in the present time* (emphasis added).

Amazing as it seems, the early disciples took on a mission to proclaim Christ not only as Redeemer but also as Conqueror and the only legitimate Ruler of all, the one whom Wright names as the "Cosmic Caesar."

In point of fact, until the end of the first millennium, many congregations placed graphics portraying the Ascension in the dome of their church buildings. It was their way of reminding members, each time they gathered, that they convened in the presence of the *reigning* Christ.

Therefore, we should not be surprised that the Old Testament passage most frequently quoted or referenced in the New Testament — in Jesus' teachings, in Acts, in the Revelation, and in almost every epistle — is Psalms 110:1-4. Early Christians identified this text as the most helpful in interpreting what was happening before their very eyes, as the gospel spread across the empire. They were convinced that the wonders God was performing all around them in Jesus' name flowed out of and pointed toward his ascension, as fully and as dramatically as predicted in Psalm 110 (NIV).

Of David. A psalm.

The LORD says to my lord:
"Sit at my right hand
until I make your enemies
a footstool for your feet."

The LORD will extend your mighty scepter from Zion, saying,
"Rule in the midst of your enemies!"
Your troops will be willing
on your day of battle.
Arrayed in holy splendor,
your young men will come to you
like dew from the morning's womb.

The LORD has sworn
and will not change his mind:
"You are a priest forever,
in the order of Melchizedek."

David's themes are just as true for us today. Note them: (1) The Messiah sits down at God's right hand; (2) he extends his scepter, making even enemies his subjects; (3) his holy followers volunteer to join him in his kingdom's advance; (4) he reigns on their behalf by assuming the role of God's King-Priest (foreshadowed by Melchizedek's role with Abraham in Genesis 14).

In this section, we want to explore various facets of Jesus' ascension *for* us as the Sovereign of our salvation.

 Snapshots and Starter Thoughts

The Ascension culminated Jesus' earthly ministry *for* us.

The Ascension validated every aspect of his redeeming work *for* us.

The Ascension brought countless honors to God's Son that bless us everyday.

The Ascension unleashed his active, unrelenting reign over us.

Can we expect Jesus to remain supreme as King forever?

The Ascension Culminated Jesus' Earthly Ministry *for* Us

- **Appropriately, Luke's account of Christ's life makes his ascension the capstone.**

Jesus led his disciples out to the area near Bethany. Then he lifted up his hands and blessed them. While he was blessing them, he left them. He was taken up into heaven. Then they worshiped him. With great joy, they returned to Jerusalem. Every day they went to the temple, praising God (Luke 24).

He was taken up to heaven. They watched until a cloud hid him from their sight (Acts 1).

- **Though possibly added by an associate of Mark, the final words of his gospel nevertheless summarize the clear understanding of the early church.**

When the Lord Jesus finished speaking to them, he was taken up into heaven. He sat down at the right hand of God. Then the disciples went out and preached everywhere. The Lord worked with them. And he backed up his word by the signs that went with it (Mark 16).

- **John's gospel does not record the actual ascension itself, but Jesus' words to Mary on the morning of his resurrection anticipated it.**

Do not hold on to me. I have not yet returned to the Father. Instead, go to those who believe in me. Tell them, "I am returning to my Father and your Father, to my God and your God" (John 20).

What's amazing is that "I am returning" is in the *present* tense. Although his ascent was still forty days away, he proclaims it as the very next "chapter" in the redemptive drama. Even in the Resurrection, his coronation filled his vision.

- **In fact, John alone among the gospel writers recounts Jesus' hints about the Ascension at various points throughout his ministry.** At the outset, for example, Nathanael said to him:

Rabbi, you are the Son of God. You are the King of Israel.

Jesus responded by pointing Nathanael and his other disciples to his coming exaltation.

You will see greater things than that . . . You will see heaven open. You will see the angels of God going up and coming down on the Son of Man (John 1).

- **Another example: When many deserted him because he invited them to find eternal life by "consuming" his body and blood, Jesus said to them:**

Does this upset you? What if you see the Son of Man go up to where he was before?

To this, Peter reacted the way all of us should:

Lord, who can we go to? You have the words of eternal life. We believe and know that you are the Holy One of God (John 6).

- **When Jesus washed the disciples' feet at the Last Supper, recorded only in the Gospel of John, he did so with a view to the Ascension.**

  Jesus knew that the time had come for him to leave this world. *It was time for him to go to the Father.* Jesus loved his disciples who were in the world. So he now loved them to the very end . . . Jesus knew that the Father had put everything under his power. He also knew he had come from God and *was returning to God.* So he got up from the meal and took off his outer clothes . . . After that, he poured water into a large bowl. Then he began to wash his disciples' feet . . .

  Many scholars point out that Jesus' final act in this ceremony rehearsed how the Incarnate One shortly would assume his kingly calling by ascending on high.

  When Jesus finished washing their feet, he put on his clothes. *Then he returned to his place* (John 13, emphasis added).

- **It is clear that the Ascension fulfills the Son's exquisite prayer in John 17, voiced 43 days days prior to his crowning.**

  Father, the time has come. Bring glory to your Son. Then your Son will bring glory to you. You gave him authority over all people. He gives eternal life to all those you have given to him . . . I have finished the work you gave me to do. So now, Father, give glory to me in heaven where your throne is. Give me the glory I had with you before the world began . . . *I will not remain in the world any longer . . . I am coming to you now . . .* Father, I want those you have given me to be with me where I am. I want them to see my glory, the glory you have given me. You gave it to me because you loved me before the world was created (emphasis added).

- **Some months earlier, three of the disciples were given a brief peek at Christ's coming coronation in a conversation about Jesus'** "exodus from this world," **which was code for the Ascension.** Luke 9 reports:

  As he was praying, the appearance of his face was transformed, and his clothes became dazzling white. Suddenly, two men, Moses and Elijah, appeared and began talking with Jesus . . . about his exodus from this world, which was about to be fulfilled in Jerusalem . . . Then a voice from the cloud said, "This is my Son, my Chosen One. Listen to him."

- **This mountaintop illumination of Jesus' kingly splendor was a preview of the vision that still awaits all of God's people.** Then, our primary response toward the exalted Son will be precisely what the Father expected of Peter, James, and John on that day: undistracted focus, undivided submission, and undiminished worship.

- **This "transfiguration" drama of Luke 9 corresponds nicely with what took place months later in Jerusalem, often called Jesus' "triumphal entry" into the Holy City.** It provided, as it were, a "dress rehearsal" for his upcoming majestic march into heaven on the day of his ascension. Matthew 21 puts it this way:

    A very large crowd spread their coats on the road. Others cut branches from the trees and spread them on the road. Some of the people went ahead of him, and some followed. They all shouted, "Hosanna [Lord, save us now!] to the Son of David! Blessed is the one who comes in the name of the Lord! Hosanna in the highest heaven!" When Jesus entered Jerusalem, the whole city was stirred up.

Imagine what the infinitely amplified cosmic reprise of this scene was like exactly 47 days later as he made his glorious entry into heaven to be enthroned as King of kings.

- **In fact, the disciples noted how "Palm Sunday" (as it has come to be known) reflected Zechariah's prophetic snapshot of Jesus' ascension.**

    People of Jerusalem, shout! See, your king comes to you. He always does what is right. He has won the victory. He is humble and riding on a donkey . . . I will remove the war horses from Jerusalem. I will break the bows that are used in battle. Your king will announce peace to the nations. He will rule from ocean to ocean . . . Then the Lord will appear over his people . . . The Lord who rules over all will be like a shield to his people . . . The Lord their God will save his people on that day (Zechariah 9).

- **Certainly, the Ascension was implied by Jesus' numerous forecasts regarding his future reign.** That's because Jesus had to be enthroned in heaven first before he could leave heaven to return to earth in power and glory, only to reassume his throne in the joyful splendor of the new heaven and earth. So everything we see of his supremacy manifested in his visible return merely displays more convincingly the authority and power that belong to him *right now*. Think of that as you look at these familiar passages from this whole different angle.

> At that time the sign of the Son of Man will appear in the sky. All the nations on earth will be sad. They will see the Son of Man coming on the clouds of the sky. He will come with power and great glory. He will send his angels with a loud trumpet call. They will gather his chosen people from all four directions. They will bring them from one end of the heavens to the other (Matthew 24).

Or, again:

> The Son of Man will come in all his glory. All the angels will come with him. Then he will sit on his throne in the glory of heaven. All the nations will be gathered in front of him (Matthew 25).

- **This current age might be defined as a season where Jesus reigns unconditionally but also "incognito" — obscured temporarily to the world's eyes.** But his hiddenness will cease the instant he parts the heavens to openly reveal the full extent of his royal majesty! This is precisely what he warned his accusers, the Sanhedrin, while on trial:

> Then the Chief Priest said, "I command you by the authority of the living God to say if you are the Messiah, the Son of God." Jesus was curt: "You yourself said it. And that's not all. Soon you'll see it for yourself: The Son of Man seated at the right hand of the Mighty One, arriving on the clouds of heaven" (Matthew 26, MSG).

- **The decisive impact of the crowning of Jesus is also predicted in Psalms 118.** Portions of this psalm are referred to by Jesus, then repeated in sermons in Acts as well as in the Epistles. For example, when the religious leaders determined to disqualify him outright as God's Messiah, Jesus warned:

> Then what does this Scripture mean? "The stone that the builders rejected has now become the cornerstone." Everyone who stumbles over that stone will be broken to pieces, and it will crush anyone it falls on (Luke 20).

Decades later, reflecting back on the day Jesus referenced Psalms 118, Peter writes:

> You are coming to Christ, who is the living cornerstone of God's temple. He was rejected by people, but he was chosen by God for

great honor. And you are living stones that God is building into his spiritual temple . . . As the Scriptures say, "I am placing a cornerstone in Jerusalem, chosen for great honor, and anyone who trusts in him will never be disgraced" . . . But for those who reject him, "The stone that the builders rejected has now become the cornerstone" (1 Peter 2).

- **Ascended, Jesus guarantees *for* us the completion of the new creation the Father is fashioning right now through the reign of his Son.** His exaltation can be pictured like setting in place the sturdy *foundation stone* on which a massive cathedral is to be built. Or, see him like a *cosmic capstone* inserted at the center of an arch — majestic masonry designed to hold both sides together. Even so, the day of Christ's ascension anchored and locked in everything else he had done *for* us, all that is yet to come.

pause | think | pray

The Ascension Validated Every Aspect of His Redeeming Work *for* Us

- **Christ is our victor!** In the Incarnation, *he showed up* to become victor over the old creation. In the Crucifixion, *he surrendered up* to become victor over the curse of sin. In the Resurrection, *he rose up* to become victor over death and hell. In the Ascension, *he went up* because of the three prior triumphs to become the victor over the new creation.

- **To say it another way: Christ *offered up* himself in two key acts, the second one validating the first.** *On the cross* he offered up himself for our sins. Then, *in heaven,* in triumph, he offered up himself as the all-sufficient sacrifice whose blood continues to cleanse us from all sin (1 John 1).

- **However it is phrased — went up, lifted up, offered up — Christ ascended has become the only hope of salvation *for* all peoples.** Descending, he put himself in the hands of his enemies *for* our sakes.

Ascending, he put himself in the hands of the Father *for* our sakes. In both cases, it would be fair to say he now "draws all people to himself."

> The time for judging this world has come, when Satan, the ruler of this world, will be cast out. And when I am lifted up from the earth, I will draw everyone to myself (John 12).

- **Like most high points during Jesus' earthly life, the validation at his ascension was thoroughly *public*.** Christ was born publicly, witnessed by parents and shepherds. He ministered publicly, constantly pressed by the crowds. He died publicly with scoffers baying at his feet. He rose publicly, seen by as many as five hundred at one time. So it is no surprise that he ascended publicly, before an estimated 120 followers (who afterward banded in prayer), as well as before legions of angels — leaving the promise that his return, to consummate his reign, would be unavoidably *public*, as well. Even so, today we should not be surprised by any public manifestations of his current reign, whether within the Church or among the nations. (We'll discuss more about this in the chapter "Who Christ Is OVER Us").

- **What the Incarnation united (God and flesh) the Ascension ratified and sealed forever.** Who is sitting at God's right hand, enthroned there *for* us? It is none other than Jesus of Nazareth! He carried his humanity with him to heaven, and in that humanity the whole universe will give him unmitigated homage. He is the same Jesus whose voice calmed Lake Galilee even as it encouraged weary disciples. He is the same Jesus whose feet tramped dusty Judean paths only to be nailed to a Roman tree. His glorified body still bears the marks of his sufferings, forever reminding us that our Sovereign remains the only sacrifice *for* our souls.

- **God as *King* enthroned *for* us is simultaneously the *man*, Christ Jesus, who reigns *for* us.** The firmness, tenderness, intentionality, holy anger, sympathies, joys, commitments, convictions, passions, and compassions he exhibited in the years of his humility remain in the heart of King Jesus to this very hour. God intends for his humanity to help shape his hold on everything.

- **Jesus' passion and his coronation are inextricably bound together forever — the cross was corroborated by the crown.** The head once encircled with painful thorns is now anointed amidst pulsating tributes.

The awful agony he once endured has been vindicated by the awesome dominion he now ensures. The sign affixed to the crucible ("This is Jesus of Nazareth, the King of the Jews") is now emblazoned across the galaxies. At his death Jesus cried, "It is finished!" At his Son's coronation the Father cried, "It has begun!" Exaltation was the Father's reward for Jesus' unwavering submission to him *for* us, even to the agony of death on the cross *for* the sin of all mankind.

- **The Ascension also validated the Resurrection.** To be sure, Jesus' *resurrection* verified that it was impossible for our last great enemy, death, to defeat him. But it was the *Ascension* that transformed his victory over death from a one-time act into a *permanent reality* that has become the defining characteristic of all who take shelter under his scepter.

- **By the validation of the Ascension, Jesus' ministry *for* us has come full circle.** He who descended to the lowest point ascended to rule over all. He who moved downward, even into the depths of our sin and disgrace, reversed course and went upward, returning to the place of highest honor. Whatever "distance" was created between Father and Son by Jesus' coming among us, as one of us, was permanently closed when he sat down on high.

- **Consider these utterly breathtaking *contrasts* the angels witnessed the day Christ's exaltation validated his humiliation:** A cradle was replaced by a throne, and a stable by a palace. The reputation of a village carpenter gave way to the only name by which mankind can be saved. Once engaged in a lonely, desert struggle with Satan, now Christ is openly crushing our enemy with a rod of iron. Though he was stripped naked on Golgotha, today all of creation has become his resplendent robe. Once abhorred by religious leaders, he will be adored forever by saints from all ages. Once gasping for enough breath to cry "I thirst," the Lord Jesus Christ declares today with the roar of a lion that "all authority has been given to me in heaven and on earth" (Matthew 28).

- **In Revelation 1, the rejected Servant of Jehovah in Isaiah 53 is now revealed to be thoroughly vindicated and validated by Jehovah himself.** Of Jesus, Isaiah writes:

  > He had no beauty or majesty to attract us to him, nothing in his appearance that we should desire him . . . Like one from whom

people hide their faces he was despised, and we held him in low esteem (Isaiah 53, NIV).

But today, he presides in a regalia of vestments displayed to John:

> ... dressed in a robe reaching down to his feet and with a golden sash around his chest. The hair on his head was white like wool, as white as snow, and his eyes were like blazing fire. His feet were like bronze glowing in a furnace, and his voice was like the sound of rushing waters (Revelation 1, NIV).

- **To the glory of God, Jesus' cosmic crowning re-enforces his uncontested sovereignty over the creation and the Church, across all ages to come.** Of course, inherently Christ always possessed the *power* to govern. What's more, by his redeeming work he could claim the *right* to govern. But once seated at God's right hand, he was given the *active role* of championing the fulfillment of God's eternal plan.

- **Christ did not demand or seize a crown; no, he *received* it.** Just as the rest of his redeeming work required full submission to the Father's will, even so he awaited the Father's initiative to lift him up and give him the name that is above every name. And he was not disappointed! Diadems confirmed Heaven's prior imprimatur upon the Son of God as Lord of all.

- **Christ did not take on himself the glory of becoming the King-Priest. "But God said to him, 'You are my Son; today I have become your Father' " (Hebrews 5).**

> Jesus lives forever. So he always holds the office of priest. People now come to God through him. And he is able to save them completely and for all time. Jesus lives forever. He prays for them. A high priest like that meets our need. He is holy, pure and without blame. He isn't like other people. He does not sin. He is lifted high above the heavens (Hebrews 7).

- **The *extent* of his reign *for* us rests on the *intent* of his redemptive work *for* us.** What he did for us in his earthly ministry reconciles everything back to the Father — things in heaven and things on earth. Therefore, in everything God has made him supreme, holding unqualified preeminence (Colossians 1).

He reigns as Master over everything old that's *passing away*. Simultaneously, Jesus exercises complete dominion over every grand, glowing, good, and glorious promise of God still *coming to pass*.

- **In full view of Christ's majesty, how can we not, like John in Revelation 1, fall at his feet?** How can we not, at times, simply prostrate ourselves in breathless awe, utterly silent before him, "like dead men," offering ourselves to him to be his loyal, loving subjects forever? How can we not wait before him — wanting him, worshipping him, watching him — knowing that in everything the next move is his?

Selah

pause | think | pray

The Ascension Brought Countless Honors to God's Son That Bless Us Everyday

- **Jesus' ascension is not about the distance he has traveled. It is about the magnitude of the honors he has received.** His position in the universe is one of unparalleled dignity and unstoppable supremacy. He is the incomparable Ruler of an empire that will ultimately fill creation with both his power and his piety.

> But in these last days, God has spoken to us through his Son. He is the one whom God appointed to receive all things . . . He uses his powerful word to hold all things together. He provided the way for people to be made pure from sin. Then he sat down at the right hand

of the King, the Majesty in heaven. So he became higher than the angels. The name he received is more excellent than theirs (Hebrews 1).

- **The first honor bestowed upon the risen Jesus took the form of a singular title. Forever he is to be designated the "Christ."** This is the New Testament's code word reserved for the One who would be found sufficient as the sovereign for our salvation. "Christ" means "anointed one." God anointed Jesus as the only person able to fulfill all of Scripture's purposes, promises, and prophecies.

- **He is known as the "Lord Jesus Christ."** "Lord" defines Jesus' rightful role, actively ruling over all. "Jesus" (Jehovah saves) defines his rightful *reputation* as God in the flesh. "Christ" defines Jesus' rightful *rank,* anointed and honored as the focus and fulfillment of all things. Today the role, the reputation, and the rank of this God-man have become so thoroughly merged and so inseparable that the New Testament often addresses him as "the Lord Jesus Christ." *Jesus,* who in his days on earth accomplished our salvation, now through his ascension has become the *Christ,* called to reign over all as *Lord* of heaven and earth.

- **Scripture says Christ sat down at God's "right hand." This means he assumed the loftiest place of recognition, as the One whom Heaven's courts most highly esteems.** It is also the position of greatest power, authority, and initiative. At the same time, sitting at the "right hand" offers him the deepest level of intimacy and nearness to the One on the Throne — where plans are formed, counsel taken, decisions made, judgments rendered, secrets shared. Our Savior is a *part* of all that action. He is the *start* of all that action. He is at the *heart* of all that action.

- **Being "seated" at God's right hand refers to Christ's official *installment* as King.** This was our Savior's irrevocable confirmation, his cosmic inauguration. It was the beginning of a coronation celebration that anticipates the final day when *every* knee will bow to him and *every* tongue confess aloud that Jesus is supreme, to the glory of God the Father (Philippians 2).

- **When Jesus sat down at God's right hand, he became, permanently and unconditionally, the absolute Sovereign of heaven and earth, without restrictions or rivals.** Accordingly, anything that is *incompatible* with his reign will be dethroned and is destined to be destroyed. The rebellion of every human heart against him must be regarded as treason. On the other hand, the submission of every human heart to him will always be received and regaled as worship.

- **In one sense, Jesus' ascension did not bestow on him some measure of glory that was not *already* his to start with.** His coronation was a revelation of the designation that was his, eternally, as the second person of the Trinity. He was not "made" King of kings when he was seated on high. Rather, the Ascension reversed Jesus' humiliation by openly *restoring* to him his age-old right to infinite praise and power.

  > There is no doubt that godliness is a great mystery. Jesus appeared in a body. The Holy Spirit proved that he was the Son of God. He was seen by angels. He was preached among the nations. People in the world believed in him. He was taken up to heaven in glory (1 Timothy 3).

- **And yet, in another sense, when he returned to the throne he brought with him *far more* renown than he had ever known before.** It was the *additional* measure of honor bestowed on him through his incarnation, crucifixion and resurrection — giving him the unprecedented distinction that only a victorious *Redeemer* could claim.

- **When we bow at the name of Jesus and confess him as Lord we magnify his matchless ministry to our race, foretold but not fulfilled until all was accomplished the day he entered the Holy Place with his own blood.** Now we can sing a *new* hymn to Jesus that celebrates his *sacrificial* glory, a psalm that could be raised only after the triumphs of the slaughtered Lamb were displayed at God's right hand.

- **Jesus reclaimed for all humankind our original purpose: the honor of being stewards of the earth on God's behalf.** As the eternal *God*, Christ automatically assumed dominion over creation that always belonged to the Creator. As the perfect *man*, however, Christ inherited forever the dominion over creation once deeded to Adam; now (because of all Jesus has done *for* us) dominion over creation is deeded to Christ. All he rightfully has assumed and inherited he now *shares* with those who belong to him.

- **The dust of earth presides on the throne of heaven.** The same humanity, once fallen, to whom God said, "You are dust and to dust you must return," is the same humanity, now resurrected in righteousness, to which God has said, "Sit at my right hand."

- **Exalted, Jesus is no longer subjected to the sin and brokenness of a fallen world.** Exalted, he has been raised above the weaknesses he once knew, the evil that hounded him, the forces of darkness that badgered and betrayed him.

  > Jesus Christ has saved you by rising from the dead. He has gone into heaven. He is at God's right hand. Angels, authorities and powers are under his control (1 Peter 3).

- **Therefore, we cheer him as our *forerunner*.** Jesus was the first human to ever physically enter heaven. He entered unashamed and unhindered — directly, instantly, in his own name, based on his own fame. Therefore, now he has prepared the way for us to follow in his steps — even to the place where we will one day join him to participate in his vast jurisdiction.

  > I'll give those who overcome the right to sit with me on my throne. In the same way, I overcame. Then I sat down with my Father on his throne (Revelation 3).

- **The explosive nature of Jesus' honors has turned redemption's story upside down**. Mary's little boy has become her blessed Lord. David's greater son has taken over his throne forever. The Servant of Israel has become the Sovereign the saints long to serve. The disciples' Rabbi who washed their feet has become their Ruler at whose feet we fall. The Healer who bent over to lift up the poor and paralyzed has himself been lifted up to heaven to enrich and liberate the universe. The Man stamped by sorrows and rejected by sinners has become the Messenger alive with anthems to be shared with all the redeemed. The Victim has been transformed into the Victor. Bound and executed by Roman soldiers like a convicted felon, Jesus is now and forever acclaimed as the undefeated Warrior who is triumphant over all.

- **The agonies of Mount Calvary have been replaced with the adulations of Mount Zion. As we read in Revelation 14:**

  > I looked, and there in front of me was the Lamb. He was standing on

Mount Zion . . . Then everyone sang a new song in front of the throne . . . They had been set free from the evil of the earth . . . They follow the Lamb wherever he goes. They were purchased from among human beings as a first offering to God and the Lamb.

- **Just as, in God's eyes, we died with Christ, were buried with him, and raised from the dead with him, even so, right now, God sees us as those who have ascended with him to share in his righteous regime. Here is how Paul describes us in Ephesians:**

He has blessed us with every spiritual blessing. Those blessings come from the heavenly world. They belong to us because we belong to Christ . . . It will all come about when history has been completed. God will then bring together all things in heaven and on earth under Christ . . .

You will know God's great power . . . the same mighty strength God showed . . . when he raised Christ from the dead. God seated him at his right hand in his heavenly kingdom. There Christ sits far above all who rule and have authority. He also sits far above all powers and kings. He is above every name that is appealed to in this world and in the world to come. God placed all things under Christ's rule. He appointed him to be ruler over everything for the church. The church is Christ's body and is filled by Christ. He fills everything in every way (Ephesians 1).

So he gave us new life because of what Christ has done . . . He has seated us with him in his heavenly kingdom. That's because we belong to Christ Jesus. He has done it to show the riches of his grace for all time to come (Ephesians 2).

- **Christ should occupy the place of highest honor in our lives right now, just as he already occupies first place in the universe.**

You have been raised up with Christ. So think about things that are in heaven. That is where Christ is. He is sitting at God's right hand. Think about things that are in heaven. Don't think about things that are only on earth. You died. Now your life is hidden with Christ in God. Christ is your life. When he appears again, you also will appear with him in heaven's glory (Colossians 3).

But in your hearts set Christ apart [as holy — acknowledging Him, giving Him first place in your lives] as Lord. Always be ready to give a [logical] defense to anyone who asks you to account for the hope and confident assurance [elicited by faith] that is within you (1 Peter 3, AMP).

pause | think | pray

The Ascension Unleashed His Active, Unrelenting Reign Over Us

- **Right now, Christ is filling the universe with his presence, with his power, and with his proactivity.**

  > When he went up to his place on high, he led a line of prisoners. He gave gifts to people . . . The One who came down is the same as the One who went up higher than all the heavens. He did it in order to fill all of creation (Ephesians 4).

  The ascended Master of the universe is extending his scepter over all. Since being installed as Messiah, Jesus has the work of universal restoration and regeneration clearly underway.

- **Jesus has not been put "on hold" in some heavenly anteroom awaiting an auspicious "re-entrance" at the end of history to claim his awards.** Quite the opposite! Right now, the world turns beneath the feet of the intensely involved Judge of all. As we will see in the next chapter, he is exercising his sovereign sway over the destiny of men and nations.

- **From the mighty arm of the Ascended One, God's eternal purpose streams forth with absolute finality and unstoppable victory.** As he told his disciples in Matthew 28, not only has he received all authority over heaven and earth, but wherever his followers reach out to earth's peoples with his saving offer, he promises to be involved *personally* as the Kingdom advances.

- **The Gospels alert us to how Jesus currently expresses his robust regency in perfect harmony with all facets of his previous earthly ministry.** "Jesus is the same yesterday, today and forever" (Hebrews 13). He rules today by the same mercy and forgiveness he always expressed toward repentant people; by equally valid offers of restoration to those whose lives are broken; by the same willingness to heal the sick and to expel the demons.

- **He is still commissioning disciples to lose their lives for his sake and for the gospel.** He remains relentless in his concern for the poor, the disenfranchised, the sorrowing, the oppressed. He still extends the hope of eternal life to all who receive him. He still expresses deep displeasure with sin, hypocrisy, and heresy. He still receives little children who draw near to him, inviting them to walk with him and learn of him. These, and many other expressions of his earthly dispositions, remain the prevailing priorities of his ongoing dominion.

- **As incredible as it seems, believers are directly engaged with his active reign every time God's people gather to worship.** Reinforced by choirs of angels, the saints on earth join with the saints in heaven to surround the Lamb as we proclaim the worthiness of the Lion of the tribe of Judah. We cast our *lives*, like crowns, before him with an attentive, affectionate intimacy with him in his supremacy, just as they do in Revelation 5:

  > The Lion of the tribe of Judah has won the battle. He is the Root of David . . . Then I saw a Lamb that looked as if he had been put to death. He stood in the center of the area around the throne . . . Then the four living creatures and the 24 elders fell down in front of the Lamb . . . Here is the new song they sang . . . "You are worthy because you were put to death. With your blood you bought people for God. They come from every tribe, language, people and nation . . . You have made them members of a royal family. You have made them priests to serve our God. They will rule on the earth" . . . Then I looked and heard the voice of millions and millions of angels . . . "The Lamb, who was put to death, is worthy!" . . . All creatures in heaven, on earth, under the earth, and on the sea, were speaking.

- **Such intimacy with our Sovereign's royal enterprise is possible in this present age because at Pentecost the Church received from our King the cascading power of his Spirit.** As our Lord's coronation filled all of heaven, his Spirit filled all of his people. One Ascension and one Pentecost — magnificently inseparable manifestations of his one enthronement — have unleashed the Church's forward movement toward the Consummation of all things, a movement that has only swelled from generation to generation. By receiving the Spirit from his Father and then pouring forth the Spirit's fullness upon his people, Jesus *guaranteed* the "universalizing" of his saving reign among the nations.

- **On the day of Pentecost, when Peter addressed a multitude gathered from scores of nations, the theme of his message linked Jesus' active reign with the sending of God's Spirit at that very moment.**

> Here is what the prophet Joel meant. He said, "In the last days, God says, I will pour out my Holy Spirit on all people . . . In those days I will pour out my Spirit even on those who serve me, both men and women. When I do, they will prophesy" . . . God has raised this same Jesus back to life. We are all witnesses of this. Jesus has been given a place of honor at the right hand of God. He has received the Holy Spirit from the Father. This is what God had promised. It is Jesus who has poured out what you now see and hear. David did not go up to heaven. But he said, "The Lord said to my Lord, 'Sit at my right hand. I will put your enemies under your control.'" So be sure of this, all you people of Israel. You nailed Jesus to the cross. But God has made him both Lord and Christ (Acts 2).

[NOTE: The next chapter, "Who Christ Is OVER Us," will explore in greater depth the extent and amazing implications of Christ's active, immediate, unrelenting reign. That chapter will map out how his ascension continually impacts creation, history, world rulers, evil powers, the growth and mission of the Church, and more.]

Selah

pause | think | pray

Can We Expect Jesus to Remain Supreme as King Forever?

- **Today, our crowned Lord summons all nations to full submission to himself to give him the obedience of faith (Romans 1).** Spreading the gospel requires delivering (as it were) a royal decree from earth's Redeemer King. We are announcing that the kingdoms of this world have become his indisputable domain.

- **But will this message ring true throughout all ages? Will Jesus remain King *for* us forever?** What about 1 Corinthians 15:20-28, which describes how, at the end of history, the Son will deliver up the Kingdom to the Father? There we read:

  > When he comes back, those who belong to him will be raised. Then the end will come after Christ destroys all rule, authority and power. Then he will hand over the kingdom to God the Father. Christ must rule until he has put all his enemies under his control. The last enemy that will be destroyed is death. Scripture says that God "has put everything under his control" . . . *When he has done that, the Son also will be under God's rule. God puts everything under the Son. In that way, God will be all in all* (emphasis added).

  To be sure, when the end comes, he will subordinate himself and his kingdom to the Father, as Paul writes. That's what a devoted son would be expected to do. But does that render him any less supreme than he was a moment before? Combining 1 Corinthians 15 with Colossians 1, we might ask: Why would the Father ever rescind the honor of preeminence and supremacy placed on his Son?

- **The first chapter of Colossians verifies that his supremacy impinges on two realities:** (1) who Christ *is* (Son, King, Creator, Redeemer,) and (2) what Christ *did* (reign, create, redeem, reconcile). His bringing everything back to the Father, so that God might be "all in all," rescinds none of this.

- **Furthermore, his supremacy is inherent in his headship of the Church**. Nothing in Scripture suggests the Church will be swallowed up in some kind of eternally "Christless" community.

- **Additionally, the honor of supremacy rises from the emergence of a *new* order made possible exclusively by his blood (Colossians 1:19-20).** Christ is the only explanation for the permanently phenomenal liberation of all creation (Romans 8). Are we to be left with an effect *but no cause?*

- **Would the "Lamb looking as if it had been slaughtered," abiding at the center of the throne right now, someday be airbrushed out of the picture so that even the memory of what he did fades as years roll on?** If the truths of the gospel — the core dimensions of our salvation — continue to echo throughout the universe, how can all of creation ever *stop* worshipping the Savior who made it all possible? As Revelation 5 describes it, everlasting praise rises to "Him who sits on the throne *and* to the Lamb." *Both* are equally worthy to receive honor, glory, wisdom, and power — to *receive* and *retain* all of it forever.

- **Just as early church fathers spoke of the "dance of the Trinity," even so 1 Corinthians 15 suggests — especially when combined with other texts like Philippians 2 or Revelation 11 — that this "dance" will continue into infinity.** Their promenade goes like this: The Father puts everything under the feet of the Son; then, the Son turns around and offers everything back for the glory of the Father. Throughout the "dance" the Spirit brings believing hearts into harmony with the Son to transform us into his "footstool." At the same time, the Spirit inspires the saints to give praise back to the Father for what has been accomplished through the Son reigning at his right hand. This dance continues on and on, assuring that God *is* all — to all, working in all, world without end. Perfection!

- **Throughout ages to come, Jesus will remain as our Mediator who simultaneously prevails as our Monarch, personally weaving all the saints into salvation's unending, ever-expanding saga!** Christ will continue his role as the New Adam of our race. He will remain the Husband to the Bride, who is the "fullness of Christ who fills all in all" (Ephesians 1; 5). Wherever God's inexhaustible grace continues to pour out blessings on the new heaven and new earth, the One who is the "glory of the Father, *full* of grace and truth" (John 1, emphasis added) will remain at the forefront of the action. The Lord Jesus Christ will never cease to be lifted up before the saints, *so as to* bring unceasing tribute to the Father who gave his Son *for* us all (Philippians 2).

The Wrap

Clearly, today, Christ's active supremacy outpaces the machinations of any monarch on earth. The world's magistrates are mortal, to be replaced in every generation; but Christ's immortal monarchy stands eternal, undiminished by time. Presidents and prime ministers may take charge of limited terrain for a limited time; the King of the ages rightfully claims all the earth for all eternity. The nations' leaders deliberate over political spheres; God's Son dominates *every* arena of human existence, even entering enemy camps to turn rebels into disciples.

But *believers* benefit uniquely from the reign of our Savior everyday, because ultimately, he ascended **for** us. Accordingly, by his Spirit the *Ascended One* shares with us the richness of his *ascended life,* which so much of the New Testament explores from every angle. Even though in this age the scepter of Christ is not everywhere *visible,* yet by his Spirit at work among his people, his reign is everywhere *accessible.* As we've referenced a number of times:

> So if you're serious about living this new resurrection life with Christ, act like it. Pursue the things over which Christ presides . . . Your old life is dead. Your new life, which is your real life — even though invisible to spectators — is with Christ in God. He is your life (Colossians 3, MSG).

What we experience living under his reign is only the beginning — just a hint — of all that is yet to come as his kingdom flourishes.

Even though right now Christ is crowned, his fullest exaltation awaits the grand finale at the end of the age. As yet, not all of his enemies are in observable subjection to him. That's why, in one sense, the very next event on God's calendar concerns that great day when the King breaks in upon us to crush exhaustively the forces of darkness and, above all, permanently dissolve death itself (see the chapter "Who Christ Is UPON Us").

Until then, the Church has the joy of living in the midst of *preliminary installments* of his reign. We get to delight in *approximations* of the Consummation. Despite all opposition, we need never waver. We may rest wholly in the sure and certain knowledge that right now the administration of the Lamb's domain constantly and consistently remains *for* us — as much *for* us now as it will be ten thousand years from now.

Revelation 11 reports, "There were loud voices in heaven. They said, 'The kingdom of the world has become the kingdom of our Lord and of his Messiah. He will rule for ever and ever.'" But one might wonder: Is this vision already fulfilled, or is it yet to unfold?

No matter what one answers, we all can agree that *in principle* it transpired the day Christ ascended to God's right hand. *In its fullness*, of course, it is yet to come. But between now and then, in multitudes of ways, throughout the nations and within the Church, God gives us *foretastes* of it — intermediate, yet nonetheless substantial awakenings to more of the breadth and depth of Christ's majesty and supremacy.

Jesus told fisherman along the shores of a lake, the culmination of all things already is "at hand." Already it is hovering over us, ready to break in upon us. Why? Because the coronation of his ascension, which has become a settled, certified fact about who he is *for* us right now, guarantees it.

So we might as well live today *as if* his reign were upon us in all its fullness, because in spirit and in truth *it is!* Already Jesus is crowned as Lord! Therefore, the final, sensational triumph of his kingdom is as good as done — in him, and in his spectacular supremacy.

Who Christ Is FOR Us Today:
A Tribute

Paraphrasing and personalizing a wide selection of Scriptures

Father, we come to you to proclaim the name of your Son together — to spread his fame, embrace his reign, increase his gain and honor his claim about who he is *for* us. As we do, awake us to him afresh for ALL that he is. May the praise we bring to him in these moments come forth alive in us by your Spirit and rise up as a blessing to you forever. We use your Word to magnify your Son, without whom we are nothing and can do nothing. This tribute is all for Christ alone, our one and only hope of glory, and the hope of all the nations.

**Lord Jesus Christ, this is our tribute to you —
our tribute to who you are FOR us.**

You were made flesh and dwelt among us, as one of us, *for* us. You are Emmanuel — God with us — to be *for* us as the Son of Man. You manifested the glory of God in human form, full of grace and truth; and so now, out of the fullness of your incarnation, we will forever receive one blessing after another. You are the One who was from the beginning. You were seen by your disciples' eyes, touched by their hands, heard by their ears, proclaimed by their lips.

You are the mystery of godliness. It is all about you, and we worship you for all you have done *for* us: You appeared in a body; you and your mission of salvation were vindicated by the power of the Spirit; you were seen by angels in resurrection glory, preached among the nations, believed on in the world, taken up to the throne of heaven. You came among us as one of us, yet without sin, so that now we too can have fellowship with you, even as your blood keeps on purifying us from all sin. You did this *for* us! You are ready to do this *for* all the nations!

Christ Is NOW!

In fact, you are the atoning sacrifice not only *for* our sins but *for* the sins of the whole world. You said that you did not come to be served but to serve, and to give your life as a ransom *for* many. Truly, it pleased the Father for all of his fullness to dwell in you, so that through you he might reconcile all things back to himself, making peace by your blood shed on the cross. In you are fulfilled those ancient words that foretold what you would do *for* us: It was you who took up our infirmities; it was you who carried our sorrows; it was you who was pierced *for* our transgressions; it was you who was crushed *for* our iniquities. The punishment that brings us peace with God landed on you. By your wounds we are healed — by yours and yours alone.

Christ Is NOW!

More than that, you are the Resurrection and the Life, both *for* us and *for* the nations — as well as *for* all creation that waits for you to deliver it from its bondage to decay. That's why you said that those who live and believe in you will never die. That's why you also said that whoever hears your word and believes in the Father who sent you has eternal life, and will not be condemned, but has already crossed over from death to life. That's why you said that because you live we shall live also. That's why you said that the time has already come when the dead will hear your voice and those who hear will live because the Father has granted to you, his Son, to have life in yourself — *for* our sakes.

If you had not been raised from the dead, how pitiful would be our condition. But you *are* raised from the dead *for* us! You are firstfruits of our own coming resurrection! In you, all who belong to you will be made everlastingly alive. You have conquered death *for* us. You have brought life and immortality to light and you did it all *for* us. You were dead, but behold you are alive forevermore and you hold the keys to death and Hades — *for* us.

Truly, you *are* the Living One. You were crucified in surrendered weakness, but you now live by the power of God. Even so we are weak as we surrender totally to you; but because of you and you alone, we live by the power of God as we give ourselves to you and to you alone forever.

Christ Is NOW!

But then, before your disciples' eyes, you ascended into the throne room of heaven to take your place *for* us at the right hand of God, the Father almighty. Celestial gates opened wide so that you, the King of glory, the Captain mighty in battle, might enter in with your triumphal procession. Exalted on high, you now have a name that is above every name, both in this age and in the age to come. The kingdom of this world has become the kingdom of our God and of his Christ, and you are now in charge, with no competitors and no successors. Your scepter stretches without limits over creation, over history, over governments, over nations, over demons, and above all, over your Church.

At your coronation, you opened up a new and living way *for* us, bringing your all-sufficient sacrifice into the Holy of Holies on our behalf. Now we too can boldly join you there, by your gracious Spirit, as we draw near to the Father's heart and bow down to worship the Father's Son. Even so, it is here we remain, because all of us, who by faith are united to you, have been seated with you permanently in those heavenly places to reign with you in irreversible victory.

Christ Is NOW!

Therefore, King of the ages, we lift you up as the Lamb of God slain, with wounds still visible above — the One who has become the Lion of Judah, ruling with all authority in heaven and earth. We join the praises of the sacred throngs of heaven as well as the redeemed saints of earth as we say, "You are worthy! You are worthy! You are worthy of all glory, honor, power, and blessing!"

Ascended, anointed, and crowned as supreme in all things, today you are filling the universe with your sovereignty, your majesty, your activity, and your presence. Come, therefore; set up your throne among us, right here and right now. Conquer us. Exercise full sway in our lives, in our churches, in our communities, in our country, in our generation — and above all in our hearts — world without end.

This tribute expresses only a small part of the inexhaustible riches of who you are FOR us and all peoples.

So, Father this is how we celebrate your Son, our Lord Jesus Christ, in this hour. We exalt him. We exult in him. We do so because of all he is *for* us — now. Therefore, everything we are and have, every breath we breathe, every step we take, every service we render, every prayer we pray, every praise we bring, is possible only by him and him alone. For without him — without all he is *for* us — we are nothing and we can do nothing. More and more, by the revealing work of your Spirit, awaken us to Christ alone — awaken your whole Church to Christ alone — so that increasingly he might become *for* us our all in all.

AMEN!

The Spectacular Supremacy of God's Son Today
> Who Christ Is TO Us Today
>
> Who Christ Is FOR Us Today
>
> ■ **Who Christ Is OVER Us Today**
>
> Who Christ Is BEFORE Us Today
>
> Who Christ Is WITHIN Us Today
>
> Who Christ Is THROUGH Us Today
>
> Who Christ Is UPON Us Today

Exploring and Experiencing

Who Christ Is OVER Us Today

Paul told Corinthian believers that, bottom line, stone-cold hearts could confess the truth of Jesus' *lordship* only if the Spirit of God quickened in them the desire to do so. He writes:

> I tell you that no one who is speaking with the help of God's Spirit says, "May Jesus be cursed." *And without the help of the Holy Spirit no one can say, Jesus is Lord* (1 Corinthians 12, emphasis added).

In the late 20th century, on a single day, the Holy Spirit incited confessions of Jesus' lordship *over* us in unprecedented fashion. The supremacy of Christ resounded from a million voices, even in defiance of antagonistic earthly powers. Here's what happened:

Christ Conquers!
Christ Reigns! Christ Governs!

Pope John Paul II, beloved spiritual pastor for Polish Christians, paid his first visit back to his homeland, arriving in Warsaw in June 1979, less than one year after being chosen head of the Catholic Church. On his first day an event transpired, regarded by some historians as a reset of the spiritual and political trajectory of the 20th century, documented in the movie *Nine Days That Changed the World.*

Poland was under the thumb of the officially atheistic Communist Party. Nevertheless, nearly two million people attended a momentous public rally, combining an open-air worship service with a Mass. They gathered on the eve of Pentecost Sunday to mark the day when two thousand years earlier the risen, ascended, reigning Christ poured out the Holy Spirit on a small group of believers in Jerusalem, birthing the Christian movement.

The crowd assembled in Warsaw's Victory Square. Poised before a 50-foot cross erected for the outdoor celebration, they heard John Paul remind them that even though throughout Poland's history many enemies of the gospel had tried to destroy Christianity, Jesus Christ would never cease to prevail as the Lord *over* history and *over* Poland. The enthusiastic multitude responded to the Pope's message by singing in unison a favorite Polish hymn, containing three simple but powerful declarations, repeated over and over: "*Christ conquers! Christ reigns! Christ governs!*"

One wonders what the Communist officials must have been thinking — and fearing — as they listened.

I wonder, however, how many of those who sang so heartily in Victory Square knew the vast array of Scriptures that speak of Christ's conquering, reigning, and governing *over* all of us, not only at the end of history but today as well?

How many realized how their rally pictured the fulfillment of Psalm 2 (referenced so often in the New Testament):

> Why do the nations plan evil together? Why do they make useless the Lord . . . *He says to them, "I have placed my king on my holy mountain of Zion."* I will announce what the Lord has promised. He

said to me, "You are my son. Today I have become your father. *Ask me, and I will give the nations to you.* All nations on earth will belong to you. *You will rule them with an iron rod.* You will break them to pieces like clay pots (emphasis added).

How many assembled that day were familiar with Daniel's vision of the indisputable reign of "one like a son of man" — the title with which Jesus publicly and repeatedly identified?

In my vision *I saw One who looked like a son of man.* He was coming with the clouds of heaven. He approached the Eternal God. He was led right up to him. And he was given authority, glory and a kingdom. People from every nation and language worshiped him. His authority will last forever. It will not pass away. *His kingdom will never be destroyed* (Daniel 7, emphasis added).

His Reign OVER Us Touches Each of Us Where We Live Today

But this vision of who Christ is *over* us is not only about his sovereignty *over* governments or history-making events. It carries very personal and practical applications for each of us as well.

Not long ago, for example, a South Asian Christian was preparing for her final interview at the US Embassy, seeking a Green Card in order to serve Christ in America. Understandably nervous, she needed a reassuring perspective as the appointed day approached. Focusing her on who Christ is *over* us, her spiritual mentor wrote this to her hours before the interview began — words that could apply to a situation you're facing at the moment. (The interview proved to be a superb success, by the way!):

When you finally sit down with your interviewer, "pretend" that Jesus is sitting on the other side of the table. Then, share your responses with *him*, not just with the embassy official.

Jesus is there. Jesus is in charge, delighting in each answer, wanting nothing but the Father's best for you, for his own good purposes.

In point of fact, by the Holy Spirit — living in you, surrounding you, leading you, even at work speaking through you — God's Son is thoroughly engaged with you. He is sovereign over the whole transaction, serving as your "lawyer" at God's right hand. He will be in full control in that hour as surely as he constantly rules over *every* aspect of your life — even as he rules over the course of nations. Not only is the interview because of him, through him, and for him, it actually is taking place, as it were, *in front of him*, the King of kings.

More recently, this same theme — the assurance of who Christ is **over** us — shaped an hour of prayer for three hundred residents of a town in the Pacific Northwest, who had come together in observance of America's National Day of Prayer.

They began their meeting by reciting in unison two familiar verses from Psalm 24:

Open wide, you gates. Open up, you ancient doors. Then the King of glory will come in. Who is the King of glory? The Lord, who is strong and mighty. The Lord, who is mighty in battle.

After reflecting on its fulfillment today in Jesus, the group's prayers invited him to enter as their King of glory to take action regarding various spheres of community concerns. They invited him to conquer, reign and govern among the poor, in city government, **over** schools and businesses, through local social services, in hospitals, among seniors — and especially **over** the life and mission of the Body of Christ in their city.

Every public prayer that day ended with a single, unanimous, audible affirmation all 300 declared over every request: *"Come, Lord Jesus!"*

You can't pray more strategically or more practically than that!

Who's Really in Charge Right Now?

Like a sign reads in the window of a business that recently changed hands, even so at the moment when Jesus ascended on high 40 days after his resurrection, the entire universe and everyone in it came "Under New Management."

Since then, Jesus has provided creation — including all of us as part of it — with a very active, purposeful, unrelenting, and hope-filled administration. In the words of Abraham Kuyper, there is not a square inch of any sphere or dimension of human existence to which Christ does not point and say, "That is mine!!"

Let's be clear: From his enthronement forward, Christ has not been waiting to be *made* King, only to be *recognized* as the King he already is. At this very moment, he is proactively bringing everything to his feet for final determination about its outcome and destiny. Yes, we are under new management; we are under the "Master Manager" of the universe.

The Gospel Is a King's Decree

Early on, the Christian message became identified with the word *gospel* ("good news"), a familiar term across the Roman Empire. Technically, it referred to any royal decree bursting with glad tidings from the Caesar, regarded as supreme ruler of the world. An emperor's gospel might call Roman citizens to celebrate the birth of a male heir to the throne or to announce the winning of a crucial battle. Whatever the news, gospels brought fresh hope for those who heard it.

Similarly, the early church saw the *Christian* message as another kind of "gospel." It was the public decree from the King of heaven that he was ready to redeem, reconcile, and renew all who submit to him, pledging their allegiance to him alone, binding themselves in loyalty to his royalty.

The gospel of Christ served notice: Jesus didn't intend to rule over the shrinking sphere of a privatized religion. Rather, the gospel proclaimed him as salvation's everlasting Sovereign, pressing forward in the spread of his fame, the extension of his reign, and the increase of his gain into every dimension of human existence (as we're about to see in this chapter).

There Are No Enduring Challenges to the Throne

Some, however, looking at the current state of world affairs, might argue that Jesus' reign is, at best, passive and benign. At first blush, facts may seem to support the indictment.

Consider the evidence: rogue states with nuclear weapons; a metastasizing war on terrorism; national and international financial meltdowns; over two billion in poverty, nearly half of those living on the edge of starvation; nearly three billion who have no knowledge of Christ and no one like them, near them to tell them; the fierce persecution of Christians in many lands (the 20th century had more Christian martyrs than the previous 19 centuries combined).

To that add countless hearts broken because of genocide, brutality, sickness, divorce, betrayal, mortality. Where *is* Jesus in all of this? Faced with these tragedies, where do we see convincing evidences of his reign prevailing **over** us despite it all?

As one well-known pundit wrote recently, tongue in cheek: "Jesus has been in office too long and his complacency shows. We still have to deal with death and taxes. Maybe it's time to make Jesus stand for re-election."

These apparent contradictions to Christ's claims to be Lord *over* all are not new. They existed for the first-century Church. Even before being thrown to lions in the Coliseum, many early Christians suffered daily in crowded, chaotic, disease-infested communities, striving for survival in abject poverty. They felt powerless, oppressed, trapped, and enslaved.

However, they persevered because of the scope of their hope in who Christ was reigning *over* them, convinced that his supremacy was:

> as *relevant* as the invasion of his **incarnation**
>
> as *victorious* as the mission of his **crucifixion**
>
> as *radical* as the re-creation of his **resurrection**
>
> as *unlimited* as his rights by virtue of his **ascension**
>
> as *comprehensive* as the **promises** of God he inherits
>
> as *broad* as the **peoples** to be redeemed by his blood
>
> as *thorough* as the extent of the **wounds** he is able to heal
>
> as *universal* as the **consummation** of his purposes for all humankind
>
> as *irresistible* as his consuming **glory** displayed for all ages to come

The Bible's Final Message: The Battle Is the Lord's

On one occasion, to reinforce this faith perspective within struggling New Testament churches, Jesus rejuvenated a company of seven congregations in Asia Minor, by giving them multiple portraits of who he was *over* them in his unwavering kingship.

As you read the following passages, ask yourself: Aren't these truths as fully in force today as they were the day John wrote them down for believers like us to read and heed? Should we not live as they did, fully expecting to see preliminary, even substantial, displays of these realities in our own generation?

- **Revelation 1: Greetings from the Ruler of kings**

    May grace and peace come to you from God. He is the one who is, and who was, and who will come. May grace and peace come to you from the seven spirits. These spirits are in front of God's throne. May grace and peace come to you from Jesus Christ. He is the faithful witness, so what he has shown can be trusted. He was the first to rise from the dead. He rules over the kings of the earth. Glory and power belong to Jesus Christ who loves us! He has set us free from our sins by pouring out his blood for us. He has made us members of his royal family. He has made us priests who serve his God and Father. Glory and power belong to Jesus Christ for ever and ever! Amen.

- **Revelation 5, 6: The Lamb in charge of events**

    Then one of the elders said to me, "Do not cry! The Lion of the tribe of Judah has won the battle. He is the Root of David. He is able to break the seven seals and open the scroll." Then I saw a Lamb that looked as if he had been put to death. He stood at the center of the area around the throne . . . The Lamb went and took the scroll. He took it from the right hand of the one sitting on the throne . . . I watched as the Lamb broke open the first of the seven seals. Then I heard one of the four living creatures say in a voice that sounded like thunder, "Come!"

- **Revelation 6: The judgments of the Lamb prevail**

    Everyone hid in caves and among the rocks of the mountains. This included the kings of the earth, the princes and the generals. It included rich people and powerful people. It also included everyone else, both slaves and people who were free. They called out to the mountains and rocks, "Fall on us! Hide us from the face of the one who sits on the throne! Hide us from the anger of the Lamb! The great day of their anger has come. Who can live through it?"

- **Revelation 11: Only one King and one kingdom**

    The seventh angel blew his trumpet. There were loud voices in heaven. They said, "The kingdom of the world has become the kingdom of our Lord and of his Messiah. He will rule for ever and ever." The 24 elders were sitting on their thrones in front of God. They fell on their faces and worshiped God.

- **Revelation 12: Christ is destined to overcome the dragon**

  She gave birth to a son. He will rule all the nations with an iron scepter. And her child was taken up to God and to his throne . . . The great dragon was thrown down to the earth, and his angels with him. The dragon is that old serpent called the devil, or Satan . . . Then I heard a loud voice in heaven. It said, "Now the salvation and the power and the kingdom of our God have come. The authority of his Messiah has come . . ." They had victory over [Satan] by the blood of the Lamb spilled for them. They had victory over him by speaking the truth about Jesus to others . . . even if it led to death.

- **Revelation 19: The return of the King in final triumph**

  I saw heaven standing open. There in front of me was a white horse. Its rider is called Faithful and True. When he judges or makes war, he is always fair. His eyes are like blazing fire. On his head are many crowns . . . The armies of heaven were following him, riding on white horses . . . Coming out of the rider's mouth is a sharp sword. He will strike down the nations with the sword. Scripture says, "He will rule them with an iron scepter" . . . Here is the name that is written on the rider's robe and on his thigh: "THE GREATEST KING OF ALL AND THE MOST POWERFUL LORD OF ALL."

- **Revelation 22: The Lamb reigns forever, face to face with us**

  Then the angel showed me the river of the water of life. It was as clear as crystal. It flowed from the throne of God and of the Lamb. It flowed down the middle of the city's main street. On each side of the river stood the tree of life, bearing 12 crops of fruit. Its fruit was ripe every month. The leaves of the tree bring healing to the nations. There will no longer be any curse. The throne of God and of the Lamb will be in the city. God's servants will serve him. They will see his face. His name will be on their foreheads.

Similar testimonies to Christ's supremacy have sustained generations of God's people in the midst of all suffering and opposition.

During the dark days of Nazi Germany, for example, a major thorn in Hitler's side was the so-called "Confessing Church," established in opposition to the Furor's newly minted (and totally apostate) "German Church." Leaders like Karl Barth, Dietrich Bonhoeffer, and Martin Niemöller rallied around a high view of Christ's lordship as they opposed the idolatrous nationalism and militarism all around them.

Their protests formalized in the Barmen Declaration, which stated in its very first article: "Jesus Christ as attested to us in Holy Scripture is the one Word of God we must hear and whom we must trust and obey in life and in death."

Ultimately, some of them, like Bonhoeffer, were martyred for this singular conviction. Still, they believed that no matter how the global conflict, full of horrors and holocausts, seemed to contradict any hope of an experience of God's sovereign intervention, one reality remained undiminished for them: "Christ conquers, Christ reigns, Christ governs."

That reality was vindicated, in part, *right before their eyes* by the otherwise inexplicable, total collapse in just one short decade of the Nazi's terrifying continental blitzkrieg — clear evidence to all believers that the Savior's scepter was holding steady its sway **over** the tumult of nations, to rule and to overrule for God's eternal purposes in the end!

Celebrating the Glories of Christ's Reign OVER Us Today

Convinced of Jesus' triumphs and the hope into which he has brought us as a result, Peter assumed that celebrating Christ should automatically mark God's people everywhere, writing: "Though you do not see him now, you believe in him. You are filled with a glorious joy that can't be put into words" (1 Peter 1).

Let's consider a few of the reasons for us to celebrate his reign *over* us. Embrace these declarations about Jesus as your own. Reflect on the truths proclaimed by each chorus. Experience the worship of Jesus by speaking out loud the sentences in bold, then quietly meditating on the rest of the chorus.

 Snapshots and Starter Thoughts

- **SHOUT! In heaven, countless choirs of angelic hosts surround his throne hymning his lordship *over* them.** How their cherubic raptures must have intensified the moment he ascended before their eyes to don the crown of victory. Since then, day after day he is worshipped as the

Captain of heaven's armies, revered by ten thousand times ten thousand angels and archangels who wait to do his bidding and carry out his every decree (Revelation 4-5).

- **CHEER!** **Ever since Christ conquered death and ascended on high, he has been gathering the "spoils of war" — a people of his own, for whose sake he won the victory (Ephesians 4).** They have become his loyal subjects, enriched by the treasury of his triumphs and then scattered among the nations to proclaim his reign everywhere, even as their numbers swell.

- **EXTOL!** **Not only does the Lord Jesus *sit* at the Father's right hand; he *is* the Father's right hand.** He is the One by whom God is establishing, right now, order in the midst of chaos, justice in the midst of oppression, righteousness in the midst of rebellion, healing in the midst of suffering, restoration in the midst of disintegration, peace in the midst of conflict, love in the midst of hate. Day after day. In a million lives. In a million ways. In a million places. As God's mighty right arm (Isaiah 59), Christ has been given all the resources of Heaven so that he might reign forever.

- **REJOICE!** **Christ is *all* — *all over the place*!** Throughout the entire cosmos he has assumed all authority (Matthew 28; Philippians 2). Jesus' reign does not reside in some secluded corner of the universe. Rather, with finality he purposes, upholds, energizes, preserves, and consummates all things in heaven and earth. All of life, whether for individuals or nations or churches, plays itself out under the impending, direct, unstoppable, and inescapable (even if not always recognizable) sovereignty of God's Son. His dominion is as deep and wide and extensive as creation itself. He knows nothing of irreversible defeat. His is the inexhaustible power for the salvation of all who believe, as well as the restoration of all of creation.

- **EXALT!** **The relevancy of Christ's reign is seen by his effectiveness in carrying on the affairs of the universe.** Crowned on high, Jesus in his lordship impacts all dimensions of life in this age: physical, rational, social, existential, structural, as well as spiritual. He fears no rivals, no substitutes, no competition. He stands alone in the solitude of his sovereignty. By the increasing subjugation of all things to himself, Christ is actively restoring creation to match and surpass all the potential inherent in the original creation. The entire cosmos is converging at his feet for his judgments concerning the destiny of all things.

- **REVEL!** **Christ has absolute rights to a dominion that covers the entire world.** His lordship is more than a *legal* right. His access to the throne is a *legitimate* right because it is based on who he already is, both *to* us and *for* us. His incomparably deep *sufferings,* as much as his inherently divine *sovereignty,* provide him the preeminent privilege to rule **over** us forever. In other words, the *passions* of our Christ make the *prevailing* of our Christ irreversible, universal, and eternal.

- **APPLAUD!** **Right now Christ has taken charge and is fully engaged among the nations.** The Lamb on the throne is no "absentee landlord," preoccupied with other concerns. To be sure, much of his authority is mediated, as he uses the peoples and powers of earth, often without their consent, to advance his will in every concern of life. But one way or another, from his position on high, Jesus invades the marketplaces of ideas and events in every generation. With him there are no public or private spheres. Rather, daily he executes his purposes within *every* sphere.

- **PROCLAIM!** **His reign breaks through and transcends every label we Christians might design in order to define him or contain him or control him for our own ends.** Our King is bigger than any one church denomination, or theological system, or Christian cultural expression. We cannot privatize him, claiming him as "our own personal Sovereign." His kingdom is bigger than all of us put together. It is a dominion that knows no end. Under *his* rule, all believers, without exception, are invited daily into the same throne room together — to embrace him, surrender to him, learn from him, obey him, and then follow and proclaim him to the ends of the earth.

- **RAVE!** **His scepter is most often extended to and through the poorest of the poor.** More often than not, the fame of his domain is found not in corporate boardrooms or the halls of government or the arenas of stardom, but rather it is seen among the poorest; the weakest; the most childlike; the most yielded and teachable; the most disenfranchised; the most abused and broken; the most overlooked and despised. He reigns most freely among those who know how much they need him and say so. His reign brings justice to earth's broken peoples, as he defends the defenseless, presses justice for the oppressed, and comforts those who mourn.

- **TRUMPET!** His kingdom is not *from* this world. Rather, it comes **from another place** *into* **this world.** His coronation required no earthly pomp and circumstance, but came by way of the cross. Even so, none of the world's political platforms, past or present, could ever be broad enough to contain what his kingdom's agenda is all about. As he responded in the wilderness when Satan offered him the empires of the world, Jesus still resists every human or demonic blueprint for success — every alternate path to power — choosing, more often than not, to expand his rule through fragile, weak, sinful people like us, who are redeemed by his blood and filled with his Spirit. Unlike worldly regimes, his kingdom for now is mostly *hidden*, in the same way believers' lives also are hidden with Christ in God until his triumphant return (Colossians 3).

- **DECLARE!** Whatever is essential to the final triumphs of his **kingdom, Jesus is quite capable of activating that right now.** Though he won't reveal the full display of his supremacy and glorious reign before the end, even now he is giving his people foretastes, approximations, foreshadowing, precursors, and previews of that great day when we will see the totality of his glory and power in resplendent, wide-open displays of his universal supremacy. At that time we'll discover fully how his reign **over** us *then* is inseparable from who he is as he reigns **over** us *now*.

- **SALUTE!** Jesus' reign is not only *omnipotent* but also *omni-**competent** and **omni-benevolent**. As *omnipotent*, he exercises all power, which originates with him. As *omni-competent,* he is in charge of everything and everyone fully, and keeps all things moving toward the consummation of history and activates all of God's promises. As *omni-benevolent*, he pours out inexhaustible blessings from his throne upon those, and through those, who have found life in him as Lord of all.

- **ANNOUNCE!** His visible rule is seen in this age primarily as a **kingdom of God's grace, which is spreading around the world through the impact of the gospel.**

The Gospel conquers the earth through the Word and the Spirit, rather than through secular powers and cultural labors. Only when Christ returns will he reign in a Kingdom of glory, as the realms of this age are finally made subservient to His will (John Calvin).

- **GLORIFY!** **At the core of Jesus' reign today is the work of reconciliation and re-creation.** As a result of his finished work *for* us — incarnation, crucifixion, resurrection, ascension — every obstacle to new beginnings has been removed from heaven's side. He is the "Mediator Monarch." His primary ongoing activity focuses on *reclaiming* everything for God's purposes, from every corner of creation (Colossians 1). His Royal Majesty intends to reconcile, repair, renovate, and reconstitute all things once plagued by the usurpations of sin and Satan. For all who seek the favor of the King, he gladly asserts his exclusive authority to forgive sins and make us clean before the Father forever.

- **SING!** **Evil and suffering are not ultimate — Christ is!** Even though life so often *seems* random — so frequently painful and disabling — there is One who remains fully in charge, working out all things according to the council of his Father's will. All forces, good or evil, are being summed up under him as Lord (Ephesians 1). Our Royal Master is never caught off guard nor is he ever at a loss for options. Freely and completely he anticipates and outmaneuvers everything the dark schemes of men and demons might dare to throw at him.

- **MARVEL!** **Death and destruction have no place in Christ's kingdom.** The Father's plan is to eliminate *both* at the climax of the age. But even now, Jesus stands opposed to all that brings us despair, affliction, and grief. At every turn, our Lord is there, executing his authority, exalting his name, defending his cause, redeeming his people from their tormenters, and stabilizing them with abounding hope about the final outcome — while he offers to fill them with the same Spirit-infused power that raised him from the dead.

Are we awake to all Christ is **over** us? Have we given him the adoration he so rightly deserves? Do we really see what our King is up to? If so, are we alert and ready to join him in it?

Evidences of King Jesus at work are everywhere.

> Millions around the world claim to have discovered Jesus as a living, challenging, healing presence. Stories abound of changed lives, of physical and emotional healing. New churches have sprung up, full of eager and excited people, often young people. Real help is given to the sick, the poor, the prisoners (N. T. Wright).

Will we dare to boldly point to evidences of his reign and declare to everyone the good news of the lordship of Jesus **over** all?

Scriptural Highlights on Christ's Reign OVER Us Today

Every year millions of Muslim pilgrims from nearly every nation on earth set out for the holiest city in Islam — Mecca, in Saudi Arabia. They go there to perform the "Hajj," one of five major acts of devotion required of the faithful. The pilgrimage brings them to the Kaaba, the most revered object in all of Islam — a black, cube-shaped building, supposedly built by Abraham, and now encompassed by a massive mosque. Muslims worldwide pray five times a day facing the direction of the Kaaba. But once in their lifetime all Muslims seek to fulfill the Quran's requirement to do the Hajj — to come to the Kaaba to join multitudes of worshippers marching around the sacred shrine.

As they do so, voices can be heard crying out in unison with words like, "O Living One, O Self-Subsisting One!" and "Allah is great!" along with the universal Hajj prayer: "Here I am, O Allah, here I am. Here I am. You have no partner, here I am. Verily all praise, grace and sovereignty belong to you. You have no partner." The days-long ceremonies and prayers in Mecca are designed to praise Islam's god (Allah) as the grand, superlative, unrivaled lord of the universe. Their stirring proclamations are based on the 99 names for Allah revealed in the Quran.

Into this vision of divine omnipotence, countering and contrasting the exalted position Muslims give Allah, comes the expansive witness to Jesus' supremacy found in the Hebrew Bible and the New Testament writings. Christians believe that what all of Scripture says about who Christ is reigning **over** us right now, seated at the Father's right hand, supersedes Quranic claims for Allah. What is said about the wonders of God's Son is, in fact, infinitely superior to Islam's definition of Allah's glory.

Let's look at some of the evidence. Though we must be selective at this point, here are a few rather stunning scriptural highlights to inspire our hearts both to worship our Savior and boldly proclaim his kingdom with increasing joy.

Snapshots and Starter Thoughts

Christ's Reign OVER Us Today Is Foreshadowed in Old Testament Passages

These first selections are taken from the Hebrew Bible. In a sense, *every* passage in the Old Testament that describes the sovereignty of Yahweh — *over* creation, nations, rulers, and his covenant people — preeminently should be applied to the Son of God. After all, total authority now resides in Jesus as God in the flesh. Christ expresses matchless displays of the dominion formerly ascribed to Yahweh in the Law, the Psalms, and the Prophets.

In other words, the current reign of Christ was *foreshadowed* through all of the Old Testament descriptions of God's kingdom work, all of which began to be brought to *fulfillment* the moment Jesus came preaching, "The kingdom of God has come near" (Mark 1), adding about himself, "[it] is among you" (Luke 17).

- **There's no ruler like Yahweh – Israel's king, who Christ is now.**

The Lord came from Mount Sinai . . . He came with large numbers of angel . . . All of the Israelites are in your hands. At your feet all of them bow down. And you teach them. They learn the law I gave them . . . The Lord was king over Israel when the leaders of the people came together . . . There is no one like the God of Israel. He rides in the heavens to help you . . . His powerful arms are always there to carry you. He will drive out your enemies to make room for you . . . He keeps you safe. He helps you. He's like a glorious sword to you. Your enemies will bow down to you in fear. You will bring them under your control (Deuteronomy 33).

- **Yahweh is worshipped by his people as their preeminent ruler, like Christ is now.**

    The Lord is the great God. He is the greatest King. He rules over all of the gods. He owns the deepest parts of the earth. The mountain peaks belong to him. The ocean is his, because he made it. He formed the dry land with his hands. Come, let us bow down and worship him. Let us fall on our knees in front of the Lord our Maker. He is our God. We are the sheep belonging to his flock. We are the people he takes good care of (Psalm 95).

- **Yahweh *protects* his people like a king, like Christ does now.**

    People of Zion, sing! Israel, shout loudly! People of Jerusalem, be glad! Let your hearts be full of joy. The Lord has stopped punishing you. He has made your enemies turn away from you. The Lord is the King of Israel. He is with you. You will never again be afraid that others will harm you . . . The Lord your God is with you. He is mighty enough to save you (Zephaniah 3).

- **Yahweh reigns like a *warrior* king, like Christ does now.**

    I am the Lord who rules over all. Human effort is no better than wood that feeds a fire. So the nations wear themselves out for nothing. The oceans are full of water. In the same way, the earth will be filled with the knowledge of my glory . . . But I am in my holy temple. Let the whole earth be silent in front of me . . . When you stood up, the earth shook. When you looked at the nations, they trembled with fear . . . When you were angry, you marched across the earth. Because of your anger you destroyed the nations. You came out to set your people free. You saved your chosen ones . . . God my Savior fills me with joy. The Lord and King gives me strength (Habakkuk 2 and 3).

- **At times Yahweh reigns like a burning fire, like Christ does now.**

    The Lord is honored. He lives in heaven. He will fill Zion's people with what is fair and right. He will be the firm foundation for their entire lives. "Now I will take action," says the Lord. Now I will be honored. Now I will be respected. Assyria, your plans and actions are like straw . . . The nations will be burned to ashes . . . My people who are near, recognize how powerful I am! They say, "Who of us can live through the Lord's destroying fire?" . . . People of Judah, you will see the king in all of his glory and majesty. You will view his kingdom spreading far and wide . . . The Lord is our king. He will save us (Isaiah 33).

- **The everlasting kingdom, which belongs to Yahweh alone, is Christ's now.**

  > Lord, we give you praise. You are the God of our father Israel. We give you praise for ever and ever. Lord, you are great and powerful. Glory, majesty and beauty belong to you. Everything in heaven and on earth belongs to you. Lord, the kingdom belongs to you. You are honored as the One who rules over all. Wealth and honor come from you. You are the ruler of all things. In your hands are strength and power. You can give honor and strength to everyone (1 Chronicles 29).

- **Yahweh reigns as King and Judge *over all* of earth's peoples just as Christ does now.**

  > Say to the nations, "The Lord rules." The world is firmly set in place. It can't be moved. The Lord will judge the people of the world fairly. Let the heavens be full of joy. Let the earth be glad. Let the ocean and everything in it roar. Let the fields and everything in them be glad. Then all of the trees in the forest will sing with joy. They will sing to the Lord, because he is coming to judge the earth. He will judge the people of the world in keeping with what is right and true (Psalm 96).

- **We are called to proclaim the good news that Yahweh reigns, doing so through Christ now.**

  > Zion, you are bringing good news to your people. Go up on a high mountain and announce it. Jerusalem, you are bringing good news to them. Shout the message loudly. Shout it out loud. Don't be afraid. Say to the towns of Judah, "Your God is coming!" The Lord and King is coming with power. His powerful arm will rule for him. He has set his people free. He is bringing them back as his reward. He has won the battle over their enemies . . . To him, all of the nations don't amount to anything. He considers them to be worthless. In fact, they are less than nothing in his sight . . . God sits on his throne high above the earth. Its people look like grasshoppers to him . . . He takes the power of princes away from them. He reduces the rulers of this world to nothing (Isaiah 40).

- **Jehovah's reign *over* his people will be shouldered by Someone coming to us, who is Christ now.**

  > The oceans are full of water. In the same way, the earth will be filled with the knowledge of the Lord. At that time the man who is called the Root from Jesse's family line will be like a banner that brings nations together. They will come to him. And the place where he rules will be glorious. At that time the Lord will reach out his hand to gather

his people a second time . . . The Spirit of the Lord will rest on that Branch. He will help him to be wise and understanding. He will help him make wise plans and carry them out . . . He will not judge things only by the way they look. He won't make decisions based simply on what people say. He will always do what is right when he judges those who are in need. He'll be completely fair when he makes decisions about poor people. When he commands that people be punished, it will happen (Isaiah 11).

- **Yahweh will deliver the nations through his coming appointed, anointed king, who is Christ now.**

  People of Jerusalem, shout! See, your king comes to you. He always does what is right. He has the power to save. He is gentle and riding on a donkey. He is sitting on a donkey's colt. I will take the chariots away from Ephraim. I will remove the war horses from Jerusalem. I will break the bows that are used in battle. Your king will announce peace to the nations. He will rule from ocean to ocean. His kingdom will reach from the Euphrates River to the ends of the earth. I will set your prisoners free from where their enemies are keeping them. I will do it because of the blood that put my covenant with you into effect (Zechariah 9).

- **Yahweh delegates his active reign to a king he calls his Son, who is Christ now.**

  The One who sits on his throne in heaven laughs. The Lord makes fun of those rulers and their plans. When he is angry, he warns them. When his anger blazes out, he terrifies them. He says to them, "I have placed my king on my holy mountain of Zion." I will announce what the Lord has promised. He said to me, "You are my son. Today I have become your father. Ask me, and I will give the nations to you. All nations on earth will belong to you. You will rule them with an iron rod" . . . Rulers of the earth, be warned . . . Obey the son completely . . . Blessed are all those who go to him for safety (Psalm 2).

- **King David himself foreshadows the future ongoing reign of God's Son, who is Christ now.**

  Our king is like a shield that keeps us safe. He belongs to the Lord. He belongs to the Holy One of Israel. You once spoke to your faithful people in a vision. You said, "I have given strength to a soldier. I have raised up a young man from among the people. I have found my servant David. I have poured my sacred oil on his head. My powerful hand will keep him going. My mighty arm will give him strength. No enemies will require him to bring gifts to them. No evil person will beat him down. I will crush the king's enemies. I will completely destroy them. I will love him and be faithful to him. Because of me his power will increase. I will give him a great kingdom" (Psalm 89).

- **Governor Zerubbabel foreshadows the future ongoing reign of God's Son, who is Christ now.**

  The Lord says, "In a little while I will shake the heavens and the earth once more. I will also shake the ocean and the dry land. I will shake all of the nations. Then what they consider to be priceless will come to my temple. And I will fill the temple with glory,' says the Lord who rules over all . . . Speak to Zerubbabel, the governor of Judah. Tell him I will shake the heavens and the earth. I will throw down royal thrones. I will smash the power of other kingdoms ... Zerubbabel, at that time I will pick you," announces the Lord. "You are my servant," announces the Lord. "You will be like a ring that has my royal seal on it. I have chosen you," announces the Lord who rules over all (Haggai 2).

- **Emperor Cyrus foreshadows the future ongoing reign of God's Son, who is Christ now.**

  Cyrus is my anointed king. I take hold of his right hand. I give him the power to bring nations under his control. I help him strip kings of their power to go to war against him. I break city gates open so he can go through them. I say to him, "I will march out ahead of you. I will make the mountains level. I will break down bronze gates. I will cut through their heavy iron bars. I will give you treasures that are hidden away in dark places. I will give you riches that are stored up in secret places. Then you will know that I am the Lord. I am the God of Israel. I am sending for you by name. Cyrus, I am sending for you by name. I am doing it for the good of the family of Jacob" . . . I will stir up Cyrus and help him win his battles. I will make all of his roads straight. He will rebuild Jerusalem. My people have been taken away from their country. But he will set them free (Isaiah 45).

- **Nebuchadnezzar learns about the ongoing reign of God's Son, who is Christ now.**

  While you were watching, a rock was cut out. But human hands didn't do it. It struck the statue on its feet of iron and clay. It smashed them. Then the iron and clay were broken to pieces. So were the bronze, silver and gold. All of them were broken to pieces at the same time. They became like straw on a threshing floor at harvest time. The wind blew them away without leaving a trace. But the rock that struck the statue became a huge mountain. It filled the whole earth . . . In the time of those kings, the God of heaven will set up a kingdom. It will never be destroyed. And no other nation will ever take it over. It will crush all of those other kingdoms. It will bring them to an end. But it will last forever (Daniel 2).

- **The glory of Yahweh's reign is filling the whole earth through Christ now.**

  In the year that King Uzziah died, I saw the Lord. He was seated on his throne. His long robe filled the temple. He was highly honored. Above him were seraphs. Each of them had six wings. With two wings they covered their faces. With two wings they covered their feet. And with two wings they were flying. They were calling out to one another. They were saying, "Holy, holy, holy is the Lord who rules over all. The whole earth is full of his glory" (Isaiah 6).

- **Yahweh's reign will unfold in mighty new ways all over the earth through Christ now.**

  In the last days the mountain where the Lord's temple is located will be famous. It will be the most important mountain of all. It will stand out above the hills. And nations will go to it. People from many nations will go there. They will say, "Come, let us go up to the Lord's mountain. Let's go to the house of Jacob's God. He will teach us how we should live. Then we will live the way he wants us to." The law of the Lord will be taught at Zion. His message will go out from Jerusalem. He will judge between people from many nations . . . Nations will not go to war against one another . . . That's what the Lord who rules over all has promised . . . I will make those who were driven away from their homes a strong nation. I will rule over them on Mount Zion. I will be their King from that time on and forever (Micah 4).

- **Yahweh's reign brings forth his praises throughout the world through Christ now.**

  How wonderful is the Lord Most High! He is the great King over the whole earth. He brought nations under our control . . . God went up to his throne while his people were shouting with joy . . . Sing praises to our King. Sing praises . . . God is the King of the whole earth. Sing a psalm of praise to him. God rules over the nations. He is seated on his holy throne . . . The kings of the earth belong to God. He is greatly honored (Psalm 47).

- **Yahweh intends to be worshipped as King worldwide through Christ now.**

  "After all, I am a great king," says the Lord who rules over all. "The other nations have respect for my name. So why don't you respect it . . . My name will be great among the nations. They will worship me from where the sun rises in the east to where it sets in the west. In every place, incense and pure offerings will be brought to me. That is because my name will be great among the nations" . . . says the Lord who rules over all (Malachi 1).

- **Praises for Israel's earthly rulers ultimately point toward the coming King of rulers, who is Christ now.**

  My heart is full of beautiful words as I say my poem for the king. My tongue is like the pen of a skillful writer. You are the most excellent of men. Your lips have been given the ability to speak gracious words. God has blessed you forever. Mighty one, put your sword at your side. Put on glory and majesty as if they were your clothes. In your majesty ride out with power in honor of what is true and right. Do it in honor of all those who are not proud. Let your right hand do wonderful things. Shoot your sharp arrows into the hearts of your enemies. Let the nations come under your control. Your throne is the very throne of God. Your kingdom will last for ever and ever (Psalm 45).

- **To believers today, like believers of old, the call goes forth: Welcome your victorious Sovereign, the Lord Jesus Christ, into your midst.**

  Open wide, you gates. Open up, you ancient doors. Then the King of glory will come in. Who is the King of glory? The Lord, who is strong and mighty. The Lord, who is mighty in battle. Open wide, you gates. Open wide, you ancient doors. Then the King of glory will come in. Who is he, this King of glory? The Lord who rules over all. He is the King of glory (Psalm 24).

pause | think | pray

Christ's Reign OVER Us Today Is Fulfilled in New Testament Passages

- **As Lord of all, Jesus holds sway *over* the kingdom of light.**

  For we must never forget that he rescued us from the power of darkness, and re-established us in the kingdom of his beloved Son, that is, in the kingdom of light... Through him, and for him, also, were created power and dominion, ownership and authority. In fact, every single thing was created through, and for him... And now he is the head of the body which is composed of all Christian people. Life from nothing began through him, and life from the dead began through him, and he is, therefore, justly called the Lord of all (Colossians 1, PHILLIPS).

- **Jesus rules *over* the activities of heaven.**

  Nathaniel replied, "Rabbi, you are the Son of God. You are the King of Israel." Then he said to the disciples, "What I'm about to tell you is true. You will see heaven open. You will see the angels of God going up and coming down on the Son of Man" (John 1).

- **Jesus will reign up to and beyond the day of judgment.**

  The Son of Man will come in all his glory. All the angels will come with him. Then he will sit on his throne in the glory of heaven. All the nations will be gathered in front of him. He will separate the people into two groups. He will be like a shepherd who separates the sheep from the goats. He will put the sheep to his right and the goats to his left (Matthew 25).

- **Jesus' dominion from heaven is rooted in his earthly ministry.**

  You know the message God sent to the people of Israel. It is the good news of peace through Jesus Christ. He is Lord of all . . . God anointed Jesus of Nazareth with the Holy Spirit and with power. Jesus went around doing good. He healed all who were under the devil's power. God was with him ... God raised him from the dead . . . He told us to give witness that he is the one appointed by God to judge the living and the dead. All the prophets give witness about him. They say that all who believe in him have their sins forgiven through his name (Acts 10).

- **Jesus' reign is extended most powerfully today through the work of the Holy Spirit.**

  God has raised this same Jesus back to life. We are all witnesses of this. Jesus has been given a place of honor at the right hand of God. He has received the Holy Spirit from the Father. This is what God had promised. It is Jesus who has poured out what you now see and hear (Acts 2).

- **Jesus' reign is extended wherever his people minister to others in his name.**

  When the Lord Jesus finished speaking to them, he was taken up into heaven. He sat down at the right hand of God. Then the disciples went out and preached everywhere. The Lord worked with them. And he backed up his word by the signs that went with it (Mark 16).

- **Jesus' reign is extended through works of healing offered in his name.**

  Do you want to know why we were kind to a disabled man? Are you asking how he was healed? Then listen to this, you and all the people of Israel! You nailed Jesus Christ of Nazareth to the cross. But God raised him from the dead. It is through Jesus' name that this man stands healed in front of you . . . You can't be saved by believing in anyone else. God has given us no other name under heaven that will save us (Acts 4).

  You killed the one who gives life. But God raised him from the dead. We are witnesses of this. This man whom you see and know was made strong because of faith in Jesus' name. Faith in Jesus has healed him completely. You can see it with your own eyes (Acts 3).

- **As Lord of all, Jesus actively commissions his servants to proclaim his reign.**

  "I am Jesus," the Lord replied. "I am the one you are opposing. Now get up. Stand on your feet. I have appeared to you to appoint you to serve me and be my witness. You will tell others that you have seen me today. You will also tell them that I will show myself to you again. I will save you from your own people and from those who aren't Jews. I am sending you to them to open their eyes. I want you to turn them from darkness to light. I want you to turn them from Satan's power to God. I want their sins to be forgiven. They will be forgiven when they believe in me. They will have their place among God's people" (Acts 26).

- **Jesus remains sovereignly involved with his servants wherever they may be suffering or imprisoned for his sake.**

  The Lord stood at my side. He gave me the strength to preach the whole message. Then all those who weren't Jews heard it. I was saved from the lion's mouth. Lord will save me from every evil attack. He will bring me safely to his heavenly kingdom (2 Timothy 4).

- **Jesus achieves final victory even when his witnesses are martyred for his sake.**

  But he was full of the Holy Spirit. He looked up to heaven and saw God's glory. He saw Jesus standing at God's right hand. "Look!" he said. "I see heaven open. The Son of Man is standing at God's right hand" . . . They dragged him out of the city. They began to throw stones at him to kill him . . . he prayed. "Lord Jesus, receive my spirit," he said. Then he fell on his knees. He cried out, "Lord! Don't hold this sin against them!" When he had said this, he died (Acts 7).

- **Unconditional grace rules in every life situation where Jesus extends his scepter.**

  But where sin increased, God's grace increased even more. Sin ruled because of death. So also grace rules in the lives of those who are right with God. The grace of God brings eternal life because of what Jesus Christ our Lord has done (Romans 5).

- **Jesus claims the authority to dispense eternal life to peoples everywhere.**

  Father, the time has come. Bring glory to your Son. Then your Son will bring glory to you. You gave him authority over all people. He gives eternal life to all those you have given him (John 17).

  Everyone the Father gives me will come to me. I will never send away anyone who comes to me. I have not come down from heaven to do what I want to do. I have come to do what the One who sent me wants me to do. The One who sent me doesn't want me to lose anyone he has given me. He wants me to raise them up on the last day. My Father wants all who look to the Son and believe in him to have eternal life. I will raise them up on the last day (John 6).

- **Jesus rules today *over* all of those for whom he has become the source of their life.**

  You have been raised up with Christ. So think about things that are in heaven. That is where Christ is. He is sitting at God's right hand. Think about things that are in heaven. Don't think about things that are on earth. You died. Now your life is hidden with Christ in God. Christ is your life. When he appears again, you also will appear with him in heaven's glory (Colossians 3).

- **Salvation is God's gift to those who accept and confess the kingship of Jesus.**

Without the help of the Holy Spirit no one can say, "Jesus is Lord" (1 Corinthians 12).

Say with your mouth, "Jesus is Lord." Believe in your heart that God raised him from the dead. Then you will be saved. With your heart you believe and are made right with God. With your mouth you say that Jesus is Lord. And so you are saved. Scripture says, "The one who trusts in him will never be put to shame" (Romans 10).

- **As Jesus reigns *over* us today, he presses everything and everyone in this world toward his final victory.**

    Christ is the first of those who rise from the dead. When he comes back, those who belong to him will be raised. Then the end will come. Christ will destroy all rule, authority and power. He will hand over the kingdom to God the Father. Christ must rule until he has put all his enemies under his control. The last enemy that will be destroyed is death (1 Corinthians 15).

- **Jesus has full authority *over* both the living and the dead.**

    We don't live for ourselves alone. And we don't die all by ourselves. If we live, we live to honor the Lord. If we die, we die to honor the Lord. So whether we live or die, we belong to the Lord. Christ died and came back to life. He did this to become the Lord of both the dead and the living (Romans 14).

- **This majestic monarchy of God's Son *over* all things is exercised *primarily for the sake of his Church*.**

    [God] showed us the mystery of his plan. It was in keeping with what he wanted to do. It was what he had planned through Christ. It will all come about when history has been completed. God will then bring together all things in heaven and on earth under one ruler. The ruler is Christ . . . Christ sits far above all who rule and have authority. He also sits far above all powers and kings. He is above every title that can be given in this world and in the world to come. God placed all things under Christ's rule. He appointed him to be ruler over everything for the church (Ephesians 1).

- **At times, as Lord of all, Jesus takes charge *over* his people like a commander-in-chief.**

    Like a good soldier of Christ Jesus, share in the hard times with us. A soldier does not take part in things that don't have anything to do with the army. He wants to please his commanding officer (2 Timothy 2).

- **Always, Jesus expresses his kingship *over* us in his role as our high priest.**

    [Christ] uses his powerful word to hold all things together. He provided the way for people to be made pure from sin. Then he sat down at the right hand of the King, the Majesty in heaven. So he became higher than the angels. The name he received is more excellent than theirs (Hebrews 1).

    We have a great high priest. He has gone up into the heavens. He is Jesus the Son of God. So let us hold firmly to what we say we believe (Hebrews 4).

    He has become a priest because of his powerful life. His life can never be destroyed . . . Jesus lives forever. So he always holds the office of priest. People now come to God through him. And he is able to save them completely and for all time. Jesus lives forever. He prays for them. A high priest like that meets our need . . . He is lifted high above the heavens (Hebrews 7).

- **As our gracious Judge, Jesus has every right to expect faithfulness from us as we go forth to fulfill his mission.**

    I give you a command in the sight of God and Christ Jesus. Christ will judge the living and the dead. Because he and his kingdom are coming, here is the command I give you. Preach the word. Be ready to serve God in good times and bad . . . Don't give up when times are hard. Work to spread the good news. Do everything God has given you to do . . . The Lord, who judges fairly, will give [a crown] to me on the day he returns. He will not give it only to me. He will also give it to all those who are longing for him to return (2 Timothy 4).

- **Jesus' supremacy *over* his people is always applied with great patience.**

    Christ Jesus came into the world to save sinners. And I am the worst sinner of all. But for that very reason, God showed me mercy. And I am the worst of sinners. He showed me mercy so that Christ Jesus could show that he is very patient. I was an example for those who would come to believe in him. Then they would receive eternal life. The eternal King will never die. He can't be seen. He is the only God. Give him honor and glory for ever and ever. Amen (1 Timothy 1).

- **The Church needs to seek a clearer vision of the true supremacy of the King reigning *over* us today.**

    I saw seven golden lampstands. In the middle of them was someone who looked like a son of man. He was dressed in a long robe with a gold strip of cloth around his chest. The hair on his head was white like wool, as white as snow. His eyes were like a blazing fire. His feet were like bronze metal glowing in a furnace. His voice sounded like rushing waters. [1] He held seven stars in his right hand. Out of his mouth came a sharp sword that had two edges. His face was like the sun shining in all of its brightness. When I saw him, I fell at his feet as if I were dead. Then he put his right hand on me and said, "Do not be afraid. I am the First and the Last. I am the Living One. I was dead. But look! I am alive for ever and ever! And I hold the keys to Death and Hell" (Revelation 1).

- **Then, as we gain a clear vision, we should increase our celebrations of the wonders of the King who will reign forever and ever.**

  May grace and peace come to you from Jesus Christ. What Jesus gives witness to can always be trusted. He was the first to rise from the dead. He rules over the kings of the earth. Give glory and power to the One who loves us! He has set us free from our sins by pouring out his blood for us. He has made us members of his royal family . . . Look! He is coming with the clouds! Every eye will see Him (Revelation 1).

pause | think | pray

The Wrap

During the Protestant Reformation, a variety of views surfaced regarding the *extent* of the reign of Christ. At that time heated debates were not uncommon.

But on at least three points all agreed. ***First, Jesus is installed and exercising his lordship right now, in at least six arenas.*** He is ruling over the workings of creation, the unfolding of world history, the designs of global leaders, the destiny of earth's peoples, the rebellion of dark powers, and the building of his Church.

On a second point all agreed: ***Finality in all things belongs to Jesus alone.*** There is no middle ground. His rule must either be welcomed or feared. He must be worshipped and obeyed as Redeemer or acknowledged or feared and faced as Supreme Judge.

On one further point all agreed: ***God the Father has given God the Son a "manifest destiny," and there is no turning back.*** In the day of his appearing, his reign will become absolute, unifying, and centralizing for all of life. The Spirit will gather all things in heaven and earth unto the Son, bringing everlasting glory to his Father.

Despite whatever ways you may define the *extent* of Jesus' reign in this hour, based on all the Scriptures we've just surveyed, we can agree that all believers have found refuge with all the saints of all the ages under our Victor's crown. All of us, with one voice, can hail Jesus as King, as we proclaim that in him resides the consummation of God's promises along with the glorious destination of everyone whom he has called and conquered.

In *The Message* paraphrase of Colossians 3:2-3, it says:

> Pursue the things over which Christ presides . . . Look up, and be alert to what is going on around Christ — *that's where the action is.* See things from *his* perspective (emphasis added).

"That's where the action is." So, let's follow the Bible's lead as we focus more specifically on the action going on around God's throne today as we look at:

Six Key Domains of His Reign OVER Us

The Reign of Christ OVER the Workings of Creation

The Reign of Christ OVER the Unfolding of World History

The Reign of Christ OVER the Designs of Global Leaders

The Reign of Christ OVER the Destiny of Earth's Peoples

The Reign of Christ OVER the Rebellion of Dark Powers

The Reign of Christ OVER the Building of His Church

The Reign of Christ OVER
the Workings of Creation

In 2004, the world watched and listened in horror as broadcasters reported that a powerful undersea earthquake in the Indian Ocean had caused a series of tsunamis — waves as high as100 feet that sped across the ocean, devastating the coastal areas of 11 countries. More than 230,000 people died, perhaps a third of them children. Thousands of homes and businesses and even entire villages were obliterated. It was one of the deadliest and most destructive natural disasters in human history.

What *do* such natural disasters imply about the reign of God's Son **over** God's creation? Can we still have confidence in him as Lord of all and **over** all, in spite of — and in the face of — tsunamis or earthquakes or tornadoes or blistering drought?

Where *is* the reign of Christ found in the midst of natural disasters that traumatize multitudes across the globe every year? How do we pair nature's deadly eruptions with Jesus' words to Laodicean Christians:

> Here are the words of Jesus, who is the Amen. What he speaks is faithful and true. *He rules over what God has created* (Revelation 3, emphasis added).

First of all, we know God's Son had direct, sovereign involvement in the design and formation of the universe. Paul writes, for example:

> We look at this Son and see God's original purpose in everything created. For everything, absolutely everything, above and below, visible and invisible, rank after rank after rank of angels — everything got started in him and finds its purpose in him. He was there before any of it came into existence and holds it all together right up to this moment (Colossians 1, MSG).

To which Hebrews 1 adds:

> By his Son, God created the world in the beginning, and it will all belong to the Son at the end . . . He holds everything together by what he says — powerful words (MSG).

Secondly, in that same Colossians 1 passage, Paul hastens to assure us of the lordship of Christ **over** the *reclamation* of a troubled world. He writes:

> Not only that, but all the broken and dislocated pieces of the universe — people and things, animals and atoms — get properly fixed and fit together in vibrant harmonies, all because of his death, his blood that poured down from the cross (MSG).

Clearly, the Bible portrays Christ as sovereign **over** the workings of creation, both at its formation and at its consummation.

Unfortunately, today we find ourselves living *between* the two epochs: creation and reclamation.

In this interim, hurricanes and seaquakes and flash floods keep happening, causing extensive suffering for the peoples of this convulsive sphere. Consequently — speaking candidly — interpreting every facet of the contemporary rule of Christ **over** the workings of creation is not an easy task. Certain questions about what the Lord is up to are beyond human comprehension and must be left unanswered for the present time.

Yet the truth remains, right now Christ reigns, and reigns effectively, **over** this creation, although it has been crippled and corrupted by the Fall, placed under a divine curse from which all "natural disasters" spring.

And that assurance requires us to keep something else in mind: Just as Christ, by the Spirit, currently gives us foretastes of the glories of the Consummation (see more on this in the chapter "Who Christ Is UPON Us"), natural disasters may at times provide a foretaste of something much more threatening. They may act as a way for him to get the attention of earth's peoples and forewarn us all about the judgments to come. In his love, Jesus may permit and even employ them to serve as a "preview" of the final, righteous retributions of God — alerting us that today is the day of salvation (2 Corinthians 6); cautioning us that we may not have tomorrow; reminding us that life is fragile, and that Christ alone is our refuge from the most grievous disaster of all — an eternity separated from God.

Despite the devastations that continue to come upon the earth (predicted throughout Scripture), Jesus' current reign rings with solid hope about the outcome. Paul confirms how creation anticipates a great day of redemption when the King will bring an end to all decay, death, and destruction; he will deliver and renovate the entire universe by the impact of his resurrection victory.

> For the creation waits in eager expectation for the children of God to be revealed. For the creation was subjected to frustration, not by its own choice, but by the will of the one who subjected it, in hope that *the creation itself will be liberated from its bondage to decay* and brought into the freedom and glory of the children of God. *We know that the whole creation has been groaning as in the pains of childbirth right up to the present time* (Romans 8, NIV, emphasis added).

That means, therefore, that every day Christians have every reason to hope in him, even in the midst of nature's setbacks in our own lives. The Savior who multiplied loaves and fishes, calmed storms on the Sea of Galilee, made the crippled to walk, and reversed the putrefying process in Lazarus' corpse remains Lord of the whole creation — including any part of creation that may threaten us — whether we are able to understand what he's up to at any given moment or not.

Happily, there *is* one crucial way we can witness Christ presiding powerfully **over** his creation today: namely, how he does this *through his Church*.

As a recent advertisement placed by the Salvation Army in *TIME* magazine put it (seeking funds for tornado victims): "We combat natural disasters with acts of God" (a word play on people referring to disasters themselves as "acts of God"). Their full-page message proceeded to note that while disasters may remain unpredictable, the compassion of Christ flowing out of his people to those in need remains thoroughly dependable.

The ad reminds us: One undeniable dimension of Christ's reign **over** the workings of creation is how he engages the desperate aftermath of hurricanes or floods or debilitating drought through multitudes of redeemed people around the globe who love him and serve him. Consequently, they spread his love and compassion and resources "serving disaster survivors from the moment of impact until the healing is complete" (as the ad put it).

The "Snapshots and Starter Thoughts" below will move us down the path toward solid — even though always preliminary — praise-inducing perspectives on Jesus' reign **over** nature. Here we will discover how he works in the universe between the first act of creation and the final act of reclamation — even in times when it *seems as if* nature, temporarily has sidestepped his sovereignty.

Snapshots and Starter Thoughts

- **Christ is no tribal deity — *all* of creation owes its origins, its worship, its allegiance, and its destiny to him.** Everything was not only created *by* Christ but also *for* him. Nothing in the universe exists for its own sake, independent of him. As Paul writes:

> But we know that there is only one God, the Father, who created everything, and we live for him. And there is only one Lord, Jesus Christ, through whom God made everything and through whom we have been given life (1 Corinthians 8, NLT).

- **Creation is his to shape, to direct, to employ, to redeem, and ultimately to fill.** Creation finds its true explanation and fulfillment in who Christ is *over* us. It does not exist *alongside of* him but *underneath* him, *looking up to* him — always! — no matter how unhinged things may appear to be at any given moment.

- **Jesus' reign is revealed by his constant preservation of all that exists — just as Psalm 104 puts it:**

> All of those creatures depend on you to give them their food when they need it. When you give it to them, they eat it. When you open your hand, they are satisfied with good things. When you turn your face away from them, they are terrified. When you take away their breath, they die and turn back into dust. When you send your Spirit, you create them. You give new life to the earth.

- **Moment by moment, creation is utterly dependent on the reigning Christ for its continued existence and survival.** On his throne, Christ undergirds and sustains creation so fully that if he were to suddenly withhold his direct, constant involvement with it, everything would come apart, dissipating into nothingness.

- **God is eternal — he alone has life in himself, but through his Son he extends that life to the whole creation.** In the end, "those who have the Son have life" (1 John 5). This was true at the beginning; it is true now and forever. The supremacy of Christ *over* creation is like light from the sun. Although we benefit from the heat and vision sunlight gives us, if the sun would ever shut off, immediately we'd be in terminal cold and unbearable darkness.

- **Jesus' earthly miracles showed his authority and his capacity to bring restoration to the natural order as well as the supernatural order.** Matthew records:

> Jesus now moved about through the whole of Galilee . . . preaching the good news about the kingdom, and healing every disease and disability among the people . . . People brought to him all those who were ill, suffering from all kinds of diseases and pains — including the devil-possessed, the insane and the paralyzed. He healed them, and was followed by enormous crowds (Matthew 5, PHILLIPS).

More than once the disciples witnessed his power *over* creation. For example:

> Suddenly a furious storm came up on the lake, so that the waves swept over the boat . . . Then [Jesus] got up and rebuked the winds and the waves, and it was completely calm. The men were amazed and asked, "What kind of man is this? Even the winds and the waves obey him!" (Matthew 8, NIV).

- **Jesus harmonizes heaven and earth, as the preeminent Mediator who draws all things together in himself.** He does so by the comprehensive *redemption* of creation, "to reconcile to himself all things, whether things on earth or things in heaven, by making peace through his blood, shed on the cross" (Colossians 1, NIV). He also does so by his constant *operation* of creation, as he manages its daily workings, faithfully bringing order out of chaos (just as he did at the beginning — Genesis 1).

- **In a fallen world we must seek refuge in the Lord of creation.** Unpredictable, seemingly unmerciful, natural disasters testify to a deeper, more ominous reality: We live on a cursed planet. Thanks to our stubborn sin and Satan's relentless opposition, there is no safe place on this terrestrial ball. Nature's physical calamities mirror man-made calamities resulting from our rebellion against our Creator. This is displayed by the rampant pollution of creation, by our greedy exploitation of creation, and by the destructive impact of violence and warfare on creation. Only in Christ who rules *over* the workings of creation (and *over* every attempt to diminish his creation) can we find safety for both soul and body, not only now but also in the new heaven and earth to come.

- **From all eternity, God's plans for his creation included his intention for the Son to rule *over* all of it.** The blueprint was already in his mind before anything existed, and then the Son — the Word with God who was God (John 1) — became the master workman to bring it forth in every detail.

  > All creation took place through him, and none took place without him. In him appeared life and this life was the light of mankind . . . He came into the world — the world he had created — and the world failed to recognize him. He came into his own creation, and his own people would not accept him. Yet wherever men did accept him he gave them the power to become sons of God (John 1, PHILLIPS).

- **He is the "*firstborn* of all creation" (Colossians 1; Revelation 1).** This means God's Son was the *cause* of creation. It also means by his incarnation he has become the *crown* of creation. And now he is exalted to rule *over* that creation. As John reported:

  > I heard a company of Angels around the Throne, the Animals, and the Elders — ten thousand times ten thousand their number, thousand after thousand after thousand in full song . . . I heard every creature in Heaven and earth, in underworld and sea, join in, all voices in all places, singing: "To the One on the Throne! To the Lamb! The blessing, the honor, the glory, the strength, for age after age after age" (Revelation 5, MSG).

- **What the psalmist witnessed about creation defines an important dimension of Jesus' reign every day.**

  > The heavens tell about the glory of God. The skies show that his hands created them. Day after day they speak about it. Night after night they make it known . . . their voice goes out into the whole earth. Their words go out from one end of the world to the other (Psalm 19).

- **What Isaiah beheld about creation is greatly magnified in Jesus' reign every day:**

  > I saw the Lord. He was seated on his throne . . . Above him were seraphs. They were calling out to one another. They were saying,

"Holy, holy, holy is the Lord who rules over all. The whole earth is full of his glory" (Isaiah 6).

- **What the prophets predicted about the future of creation, Jesus as King of kings is bringing to fulfillment every day.** To be sure, as Isaiah says, already the earth is full of God's glory. The reign of God's Son, therefore, is focused on filling the earth with the *knowledge* of his glory (Habakkuk 2), all of it embodied "in the face of Jesus Christ" (2 Corinthians 4) as revealed through the gospel.

- **God's royal decree — calling the universe to worship his Son through whom all things were created — resounds throughout the cosmos every day, like this for example:**

  Praise the Lord. Praise the Lord from the heavens. Praise him in the heavens above. Praise him, all his angels. Praise him, all his angels in heaven. Praise him, sun and moon. Praise him, all you shining stars . . . Praise him, you waters above the skies. Let all of them praise the name of the Lord, because he gave a command and they were created . . . Praise him, lightning and hail, snow and clouds. Praise him, you stormy winds that obey him. Praise him, all you mountains and hills . . . Let them praise the name of the Lord. His name alone is honored. His glory is higher than the earth and the heavens (Psalm 148).

- **Christ has full rights to take charge *over* creation because out of his sufferings all of it has become his *inheritance*.**

  God has not put angels in charge of the world that is going to come . . . He said, "What is a human being that you think about him? You placed on him a crown of glory and honor. You have put everything under his control" . . . We do not now see everything under his control. But we do see Jesus already given a crown of glory and honor. He was made a little lower than the angels. He suffered death. By the grace of God, he tasted death for everyone. That is why he was given his crown. God has made everything. He has acted in exactly the right way. He is bringing his many sons and daughters to share in his glory. To do so, he has made the One who saved them perfect because of his sufferings (Hebrews 2).

- **Because Christ is the heir of all things (Hebrews 1), his lordship *over* the workings of creation exists for this one singular, mighty *purpose* — the purpose for which the cosmos was designed—to give God the maximum glory he deserves.** Therefore, the travailing of creation—

because of its bondage to despair, its decay, and its misery — is of great consequence to Jesus. Our Redeemer intends for everything to be renovated, one day soon, as the universe is reconstituted with resurrection power. This will include our own aging bodies because our King does not intend to save us *out of* our bodies but to save us *in* our bodies—bodies that will be like his glorious body (Romans 8; Philippians 3).

• **At the same time, we can say in the midst of this great purpose that Christ is working everything together for one singular, overarching good.** It is for the good of the universe to enter, in its entirety, into "the glorious liberty" of all the saints whom Jesus already has set free (Romans 8).

• **Ultimately, the reign of Christ will prove to be more immense than the farthest stretches of a billion galaxies.** Creation is the *theater* of his kingdom ways, in which the outworking of our redemption takes place inseparably from the wider drama of God's redemption and renovation of all things created, visible and the invisible, on earth and in heaven.

• **One day, who Christ is *over* the workings of creation will be revealed with irrefutable, everlasting evidence — just as we read at the close of the Bible**:

> Then I saw a new Heaven and a new earth . . . I saw the holy city, the new Jerusalem, descending from God out of Heaven . . . Then he who is seated upon the throne said, "See, I am making all things new" . . . I could see no Temple in the city, for the Lord, the Almighty God, and the Lamb are themselves its Temple . . . its radiance is the Lamb. The nations will walk by its light (Revelation 21, PHILLIPS).

pause | think | pray

The Wrap

With just a few words, Bishop N. T. Wright paints for us the magnificence of Christ's reign **over** the workings of creation:

> God will do for the whole cosmos, in the end, what he did for Jesus at Easter . . . the prototype of the new creation. God will do this *through* Jesus himself; the ascended Jesus, remember, is the ruler within the new creation as it bursts in upon the old. And God will do it through the *presence* of the risen and ascended Jesus when he comes to heal, to save and also to judge.

Both then and now, creation serves its Ruler by providing a *showcase* of his supremacy. Creation, then and now, acts as "window dressing" to embellish displays of his kingdom ways. As Creator, Sustainer, Redeemer, and Heir, the Lord Jesus Christ requires all nature to reveal the magnitude of his glory, to amplify the judgments of his enemies, and to rain down (*reign* down!) everlasting blessings upon all he has redeemed by his blood. But even then, *the entire universe will never be big enough to contain him!*

The Reign of Christ OVER
the Unfolding of World History

A while back, the National Geographic Society published a large, 400-page hardback titled *Concise History of the World: An Illustrated Time Line*. It offers a global view of history by placing concurrent events in the world's major regions together in single columns under five major headings of related human culture and experience. Produced by a team of imminent scholars, the authors write:

> [In our] increasingly interconnected and interdependent world, it is essential to understand the networks that link the societies and the forces that can disrupt these networks and set societies at odds . . . [this book] provides a unique framework for comprehending the global past and its impact on the present.

The book even claims it "will help readers make sense of today's headlines and the seemingly chaotic course of current affairs."

What this superb volume does *not* do, however — and really *can't* do — is show us the impact of *God's kingdom* in the midst of all of these reports. More specifically, it does not report history's interconnectedness with the redemptive reign of Jesus for 2000 years. The biblical testimony is clear: the hand of our King has rested on *every* aspect of history — global, national, and personal.

On Mars Hill Paul made a case for the interconnectedness between Christ and history:

[God] himself gives life and breath to all people . . . From one man he made all the people of the world. Now they live all over the earth. He decided exactly when they should live . . . [and] where they should live. God did this so that people would seek him . . . though he is not far from any of us. "In him we live and move and exist" . . . now he commands all people everywhere to turn away from their sins. He has set a day when he will judge the world fairly. He has appointed a man to be its judge. God has proved this to all people by raising that man from the dead (Acts 17).

But even before Paul, in Old Testament times Yahweh made it clear he was involved with developments transpiring among many nations beyond Israel. Look at the prophets, for example. Jonah prophesied to Assyria's capital, Nineveh, and changed the course of their history. Isaiah claimed that God placed Cyrus as ruler of Persia and then gave him the mandate to transform Persian policies so that not only Israel but also numbers of other displaced peoples could repopulate their homelands. Amos declared God's impending judgments on a host of nations besides Israel. In Isaiah 19, Yahweh revealed that he intended to superintend the unfolding histories of Egypt and Assyria so that one day they would share in a three-part harmony with Israel. In fact, if we go all the way back to the Tower of Babel, or even before, the Scriptures leave no doubt that the God of creation is the God of history, involved in how world's events unfold in every part of the earth.

How much more this is true about the reigning Son of God today before whom the Bible says every knee in the universe will bow! History is not random, even among nations or generations in which nothing of Scripture or Christ is known yet.

The History Channel may never produce a documentary on Christ's reign across the ages; but whether they know it or not, every event of history from the beginning of time, both small or large, has transpired directly before the throne of God in response to his righteous purposes in Jesus. Through it all, the Son remains sovereignly proactive — never indifferent or passive or uninvolved — regarding what transpires. To this very hour, fully accurate is the familiar claim: "All of history is *His* Story."

Let's explore other ways of looking at who Christ is over the unfolding of world history.

 ## Snapshots and Starter Thoughts

- **Christ is God's goal for history. There's a plan for a Lamb and there's a Lamb for the plan.** The Father intends to achieve the greatest possible glory for his Son, among an immense host of worshippers, to the fullest extent possible, in a way that magnifies forever the triumphs of Messiah's mercy and majesty.

- **Christ is the undeniable Ruler of history; Christ is what history is all about.** He is not only the *beginning* of human history; he is its *end*. He is the *focus* of the future of all peoples and civilizations; he is also the *force* behind bringing it to fulfillment. In a sense, there is no truly "secular" history because the history of the world remains inherently wedded to the reign of Christ. Mankind's "story" has always been about how God is moving all things toward the greatest of all "goods" — exalting his Son as Redeemer of the nations.

- **Viewed apart from Christ, history often ends up looking to humans like a collection of "confetti."** Eventful movements among the nations can appear unconnected, random, eclectic, purposeless, empty, and meaningless (David Wells). On the other hand, when we look at Jesus on the throne, we see that all history streams from him, flows toward him, and is fulfilled in him. This is what Jesus tried to convey when he answered the disciples' questions about Israel's future this way:

> You should not be concerned about times or dates. The Father has set them by his own authority. But you will receive power when the Holy Spirit comes on you. Then you will be my witnesses in Jerusalem. You will be my witnesses in all Judea and Samaria. And you will be my witnesses from one end of the earth to the other (Acts 1).

- **In a unique sense, Jesus' reign has brought the story of Israel — with all of God's promises to his chosen people about their historical destiny — to its fulfillment in himself.** The promises belong to Jesus and are embodied so fully in him that in Isaiah 49 the promised Messiah actually is *called* "Israel." As Christ binds Gentiles with his Jewish people to form one Body in himself, James describes the unprecedented continuity of this miracle by quoting from Amos 9:

> After this I will return and rebuild David's fallen tent. I will rebuild what was destroyed. I will make it what it used to be. Then everyone else can look to the Lord. This includes all the Gentiles who belong to me (Acts 5).

To this Paul adds the vision of how Israel's history will culminate because of Jesus, quoting from Isaiah 59:

> Part of Israel has refused to obey God. That will continue until the full number of Gentiles has entered God's kingdom. In this way Israel will be saved. It is written, "The God who saves will come from Mount Zion. He will remove sin from Jacob. Here is my covenant with them. I will take away their sins (Romans 11).

- **One might say that in Christ, human history has been unfolding through three "movements":**

  (1) from creation to Christ (the historical *preparations* for his redeeming reign);

  (2) the entire earthly ministry of Christ (the historical *manifestations* of his redeeming reign);

  (3) from the Ascension forward (the historical *progressions* of his redeeming reign toward the Consummation).

- **Through the gospel, the Son at the right hand of the Father has set in motion forces that will determine the outcome of history.** By the

Church's faithfulness to its "Great Commission," these forces will eventually culminate in the new heaven and earth, with its "New Community," where his story will continue to unfold forever and ever.

- **Christ is the superintendent and shepherd of current events, not only in Israel and in the Church, but also worldwide. Countless episodes, both local and global, are destined to converge in the final triumphs of his kingdom.** History is not moving in a vacuum. Rather, it is the aggressive outworking of one increasing mission by God's Son from God's throne to the ends of the earth. Thus, we might say history unfolds not only with political, social, and cultural dimensions, but also, above all, with *theological* as well as *eschatological* dimensions.

  > The kingdom of the world has become the kingdom of our Lord and of his Christ. He will rule for ever and ever . . . Lord God who rules over all, we give thanks to you. You are the One who is and who was. We give you thanks because you have taken your great power and have begun to rule. The nations were angry, and the time for your anger has come . . . There is a reward for all your people, both great and small. It is time to destroy those who destroy the earth (Revelation 11).

- **Imagine how differently the record of the past 2000 years would read if the whole time Jesus had *not* been reigning as Lord of all?** The Ascension was not only a historic event in and of itself, but it was also a history-*making* event that continues to ignite, direct, and encompass millions of other events around the globe. That's because his reign is both proactive and interactive; it is dynamic, not static; it is both personal and purposeful.

- **Throughout history, Christ's ongoing reign has extended itself into the nations by pulsations, like ocean waves washing up onto a beach with the incoming tide.** From time to time it may seem like the waves are receding, but then amazingly new waves come rolling in reaching higher up the sands than the last waves. Despite seeming setbacks, the Kingdom is advancing in crescendos according to divine purposes. "Of the increase of his government and of peace there will be no end," we're told in Isaiah 9 (ESV).

- **No matter what the future holds, we can be certain of this: We are living in the midst of the *increase* of Christ's reign.** Rather than shrivel and shrink, his reign continues to swell and saturate the earth from age to age, pressing toward the consummation of all things in him. Under Christ's scepter every person and every event is "in transition" toward the day when Christ's kingship will become the sole focus of the universe.

- **God has been moving the human race steadily and progressively toward the final resolution when everything is summed up under Jesus as Lord.** Current events reported on the evening news are being woven strategically by the Father into this all-encompassing epic that revolves around his Son, the drama of which Jesus is both the chief character and the central plot. As his followers, we need to watch and learn.

- **Wherever Christ's reign is unveiled, we discover how gloriously creative he can be as he orchestrates the direction and destination of the flow of activities among all of earth's peoples.** His sovereignty is so superb he is able to freely incorporate a vast array of human initiatives — most of all, every person's responses to him as each chooses to either follow him or reject him — as he shapes and culminates a destiny based on what God has decreed from all eternity.

- **From Heaven's perspective the grand narrative of mankind's journey through time reveals how God's kingdom — now subsumed in the reign of his dear Son — has been governing, confronting, adjudicating, and transforming nations and events throughout the ages.** Surely but steadily, God is moving the human race toward the final resolution and ultimate revelation of his purposes in Christ Jesus. Christ's jurisdiction extends to all peoples throughout all history, not just those who are his own by redemption. To call him Lord means we must interpret the entire course of human events on this planet with direct reference to who *he* is, where *he's* headed, what *he's* doing, and how *he* gets blessed.

- **One day, the often invisible reign of Christ that we experience today — Jesus likened it to leaven quietly active in the dough — will one day reach cosmic proportions (the dough, thoroughly leavened, will swell convincingly to its full measure).** The King who acts *within* history in redemption and judgment will soon exercise both, openly and with finality, for all to see and confirm.

- **At the climax of "His Story," Christ will forcefully take charge of the unfolding of decisive events, often portrayed for us in apocalyptic language.** Revelation 5 and 6 (and many other Scriptures) record how Christ intends to assert his supremacy *over* the final chapter of history. We behold that nothing is out of control. Seal after seal is broken to unleash phase after phase of history's preordained outcome when God's judgments are poured out with finality; when the forces of evil are defeated and destroyed; when the sufferings of all martyrs are vindicated; when every form of rebellion and folly is consumed in the wrath of the Lamb; and, above all, when:

  > Everyone in heaven and on earth and under the earth will kneel down to worship him. Everyone's mouth will say that Jesus Christ is Lord. And God the Father will receive the glory (Philippians 2).

- **We see how thoroughly Christ controls the conclusion of history when we read about the Lamb opening a scroll that unleashes history's final episodes leading to the end of this age.**

  > [A mighty angel] said, "Who is worthy to break the seals and open the scroll?" But no one in heaven or on earth or under the earth could open the scroll . . . I cried and cried. That's because no one was found who was worthy to open the scroll or look inside. Then one of the elders said to me, "Do not cry! The Lion of the tribe of Judah has won the battle. He is the Root of David. He is able to break the seven seals and open the scroll." Then I saw a Lamb that looked as if he had been put to death. He stood at the center of the area around the throne . . . I watched as the Lamb broke open the first of the seven seals. Then I heard one of the four living creatures say in a voice that sounded like thunder, "Come!" I looked, and there in front of me was a white horse! Its rider held a bow in his hands. He was given a crown. He rode out like a hero on his way to victory (Revelation 5 and 6).

Selah

pause | think | pray

The Wrap

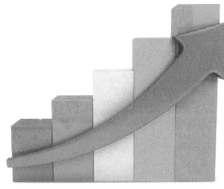

For believers, any theory of historical "progress" must focus primarily on the "progress" of Christ's kingdom.

Of course, apart from the increasing spread of congregations across the earth, there are few other statistics we can use to prove to the world that his kingdom is advancing. At the same time, the validation of its advance can be seen by the quantifiable fruits of its transforming power within people and societies, within cities and nations, within cultures and civilizations.

But the ultimate vindication of the momentum of Jesus' kingship awaits the day of judgment, at the consummation of the age, when the books are opened and the final report is given. From that vantage point, God's people will be able to interpret the full scope and drama of how history served the cause of Christ, and exalt him with the praise that belongs to him alone!

There's one other fact we must not forget. It is highlighted in one of Jesus' parables. He predicts that every stage in the historical unfolding of God's redeeming mission in the world will be matched by increases of spiritual warfare as Satan throws up counterattacks to Jesus' victories. He put it like this:

> The farmer who sows the pure seed is the Son of Man. The field is the world, the pure seeds are subjects of the kingdom, the thistles are subjects of the Devil, and the enemy who sows them is the Devil. The harvest is the end of the age, the curtain of history . . . The Son of Man will send his angels, weed out the thistles from his kingdom . . . At the same time, ripe, holy lives will mature and adorn the kingdom of their Father (Matthew 13, MSG).

For now, much of God's providential activity through his Son within the course of history remains mysterious to us. The road to the Consummation traverses countless zigzags that often make little sense initially.

But at least, as we consider the happenings of the past and the present, we know *where* our Sovereign Redeemer is headed. The goal of history is that the Lord Jesus Christ might have the supremacy in everything (Colossians 1). He is the horizon of history. In him the "riddle" of history is solved. And that should be enough for us to claim for now.

The Reign of Christ OVER
the Designs of Global Leaders

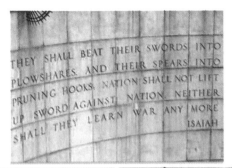

Founded in 1945, the United Nations is the first-ever enduring international organization of its kind. With 193 member states, the UN exists to maintain international peace and security, develop friendly relations among nations and their leaders, and promote social progress, better living standards, and human rights. The UN Security Council has the power to make binding decisions that member governments have agreed to carry out.

But here's a fascinating fact about the organization. Anyone who walks toward the front doors of the UN headquarters in New York City immediately encounters words of Scripture from Isaiah 2:4 emblazoned across a wall! The verse, taken from the King James Version, reads:

> They shall beat their swords into plowshares, and their spears into pruning hooks. Nation shall not lift up sword against nation, neither shall they learn war anymore.

More fascinating still are the verses that come before and after verse 4 in this chapter. They give us insights that explain precisely how Isaiah's vision of international peace will come to pass. Take a look:

> And it shall come to pass in the last days, that the mountain of the Lord's house shall be established in the top of the mountains, and shall be exalted above the hills; and all nations shall flow unto it. And many people shall go and say, Come ye, and let us go up to the mountain of the Lord, to the house of the God of Jacob; and he will teach us of his ways, and we will walk in his paths: for out of Zion shall go forth the law, and the word of the Lord from Jerusalem.
>
> And he shall judge among the nations, and shall rebuke many people: *and they shall beat their swords into plowshares, and their spears into pruning hooks: nation shall not lift up sword against nation, neither shall they learn war any more . . . and the Lord alone shall be exalted in that day* (Isaiah 2, KJV, emphasis added).

In other words, according to Isaiah the success of heads of state who are engaged in peacemaking activities impinges directly on *who* ultimately is in charge. The prophet is clear about who that person must be: Yahweh. Only when God's throne is exalted so that his ways prevail among the peoples, and only when boastful leaders are humbled so fully that Yahweh alone is exalted, can the weapons of war be transformed into instruments of peace.

As Christians we know that Isaiah 2 has found its ultimate fulfillment already in the One who ascended to Yahweh's right hand — the One who is reigning **over** us now while we await the universal display of his sway when he returns bodily at the end of this age.

This means that today, unlike the influence of UN ambassadors or its Security Council members, it is the Lord Jesus Christ who has the final word on the designs of global leaders.

This was precisely Jesus' word to Pilate during his trial. When the Roman magistrate claimed, "Don't you understand? I have the power to set you free or to nail you to a cross," the Master responded, "You were given power from heaven. If you weren't, you would have no power over me" (John 19). Point and counterpoint.

Whether they know it or not, when earthly rulers lay claim to any degree of authority, at best it is only a temporary, delegated authority from King Jesus. Ultimately, Heaven alone determines when kings rise and fall.

When Jesus' mother became pregnant by the Holy Spirit, she lifted up a joyful hymn that included these words:

> My spirit delights in God my Savior . . . The Mighty One has done great things for me . . . He has done mighty things with his arm. He has scattered those who are proud in their deepest thoughts. He has brought down rulers from their thrones. But he has lifted up people who are not important (Luke 2).

Notice that her prenatal praise predicted how Jesus' reign would impact politicians and potentates!

Listen to how Ephesians 1 describes this truth:

> [God] seated him at his right hand in his heavenly kingdom. There Christ sits far above all who rule and have authority. He also sits far above all powers and kings. He is above every title that can be given in this world and in the world to come. God placed all things under Christ's rule.

Or consider John's account. When he was face to face with the One to whom all authority has been given in heaven and on earth (Matthew 28), John issued this benediction:

> May grace and peace come to you from Jesus Christ. What Jesus gives witness to can always be trusted. He was the first to rise from the dead. *He rules over the kings of the earth* (Revelation 1, emphasis added).

Did you catch that? "He rules over the kings of the earth." Present tense. So, let's explore further this third dimension of who Christ is *over* us in his reign *over* the designs of global leaders.

 Snapshots and Starter Thoughts

- **Since the beginning, the Father always intended to bring earth's emperors, presidents, prime ministers, juntas — even dictators — under his Son as Supreme Ruler.**

  > Why do the nations plan evil together . . . The kings of the earth take their stand against the Lord. The rulers of the earth gather together against his anointed king. "Let us break free from their chains," they say. "Let us throw off their ropes" . . . The Lord makes fun of those rulers and their plans . . . He says to them, "I have placed my king on my holy mountain of Zion" . . . He said to me, "You are my son. Today I have become your father. Ask me, and I will give the nations to you. All nations on earth will belong to you. You will rule them with an iron rod" . . . *Kings, be wise! Rulers of the earth, be warned . . . Obey the son completely* (Psalm 2, emphsis added).

- **Not only in Psalm 2 but also in dozens of other passages, what is written generally about Yahweh's sovereign ways among the leaders of nations now applies just as pointedly to our day regarding the Son's decisive interventions.**

  > Hasn't it been told to you from the beginning? Haven't you understood it ever since the earth was made? God sits on his throne high above the earth. Its people look like grasshoppers to him. He spreads the heavens out like a cover. He sets it up like a tent to live in. He takes the power of princes away from them. He reduces the rulers of this world to nothing. They are planted. They are scattered like seeds. They put down roots in the ground. But as soon as that happens, God blows on them and they dry up (Isaiah 40).

- **As the superior Son of David, and who is also King of Israel, Jesus brings with him an everlasting dominion intended to conquer all other realms and those who guide them.** Looking far beyond the historical David to the Lord Jesus Christ, Scripture declares:

  > God, give the king the ability to judge fairly. He is your royal son. Help him to do what is right . . . The king will stand up for those who are hurting . . . He will crush those who beat others down . . . The kings of Tarshish and of places far away will bring him gifts. The kings of Sheba and Seba will give him presents. All kings will bow down to him. All nations will serve him . . . May the king's name be remembered forever. May his fame last as long as the sun shines. All nations will be blessed because of him. May his glory fill the whole earth (Psalm 72).

- **Jesus' impact on the kings of the earth is tied directly to how, before all else, he *suffered* for them and their peoples.**

> Just watch my servant blossom! Exalted, tall, head and shoulders above the crowd! But he didn't begin that way. At first everyone was appalled. He didn't even look human — a ruined face, disfigured past recognition. Nations all over the world will be in awe, taken aback, *kings shocked into silence when they see him* (Isaiah 52, MSG, emphasis added).

> The plan was that he give himself as an offering for sin so that he'd see life come from it — life, life, and more life. And God's plan will deeply prosper through him . . . the best of everything, the highest honors (Isaiah 53, MSG).

- **In the light of Christ's destiny to prevail *over* the designs of global rulers, the early church found boldness to stand against every opposing power, both profane and religious.** For example, hear how the early church anchored their prayers in Psalm 2:

> Long ago you spoke by the Holy Spirit through the mouth of our father David, who served you. You said, "Why are the nations angry? Why do the people make useless plans? The kings of the earth take their stand against the Lord. The rulers of the earth gather together against his Anointed King" . . . They did what your power and purpose had already decided should happen. Now, Lord, consider the bad things they say they are going to do. Help us to be very bold when we speak your word. Stretch out your hand to heal. Do miraculous signs and wonders through the name of your holy servant Jesus (Acts 4).

- **When the early church announced to the world "Jesus is Lord," the clear implication was that Caesar was *not*.** Emperor Nero didn't throw Christians to the lions because they confessed that Jesus merely wanted to be the Lord of people's *hearts*. Rather, through spreading the gospel the early church proclaimed that the One who died, rose again, and ascended on high is Lord *over all* — all Caesars, principalities, monarchs, commanders, overlords, chiefs, maharajahs, potentates, princes, and princesses — and any other ruling power, visible or invisible.

- **Indeed, the claims of Jesus undermine all human authority; they call every ruler into account before the throne of Heaven.** Daniel foresaw this awesome reality:

> As I watched, thrones were set in place. The Eternal God took his seat . . . The court was seated. And the books were opened. The authority of the other animals [representing major empires] had been stripped away from them. But they were allowed to live for a period of time.

> In my vision I saw One who looked like a son of man. He was coming with the clouds of heaven. He approached the Eternal God. He was led right up to him. And he was given authority, glory and a kingdom. People from every nation and language worshiped him. His authority will last forever . . . His kingdom will last forever. Every ruler will worship and obey him (Daniel 7).

- **At every level, Christ commands and orders the ways of the kings and kingdoms of this world.** He does so in a variety of ways: tolerating some; supporting others; limiting some; protecting some; punishing others; deflating some while lifting others so that their administration prospers for generations. Clearly, there is not a single authority related to any facet of society that Jesus cannot providentially use or dismiss to fulfill his kingdom purposes. Therefore, let the Church proclaim how salvation's Champion, the Ruler of the universe, stands *above* politics and retains final say **over** all authorities, both secular and spiritual.

> He breaks the proud spirit of rulers. The kings of the earth have respect for him (Psalm 76).

- **In fact, states and governments of the world are *servants* of Christ, functioning under his realm, as his instruments of restraint among the nations.** At the same time, he is equally prepared to bring down human governors — who are granted their position from him in the first place — if they step too far outside his kingdom's intentions. The fact remains that only King Jesus is primary and absolute. Called to account before him (whether they know it or not), human dignitaries can be replaced at any moment by the One who orders the course of stars that inhabit the heavens and oversees the course of those who inhabit the thrones of the earth.

Notice how Paul links the role of earthly authorities with the grand expectation held by all Christians — that everything, including those who rule, must in the end answer to Christ alone.

> All of you must be willing to obey completely those who rule over you. There are no authorities except the ones God has chosen. Those who now rule have been chosen by God . . . He serves God and will do you good. But if you do wrong, watch out! The ruler doesn't carry a sword for no reason at all. He serves God. And God is carrying out his anger through him. The ruler punishes anyone who does wrong . . . The hour has come for you to wake up from your sleep. Our full salvation is closer now than it was when we first believed in Christ.

The dark night of evil is nearly over. The day of Christ's return is almost here . . . put on the Lord Jesus Christ as your clothing (Romans 13).

- **Similarly, Christ continues to reign *over* evil and often invisible principalities and powers who beguile, and sometimes actually animate, the rulers of the world.** By his assault on the forces of darkness, most decidedly when he stripped them at the Cross (Colossians 2), Jesus maintains final say on *how* and *how much* they influence the designs and decisions of rulers. In the end, consequently, Satan's minions are destined only for destruction on the day of his grand triumph.

- **In the most graphic terms, John paints Christ's assault on the rulers of darkness at the end of the age:**

> Then I saw heaven opened, and a white horse was standing there. Its rider was named Faithful and True, for he judges fairly and wages a righteous war. His eyes were like flames of fire, and on his head were many crowns . . . From his mouth came a sharp sword to strike down the nations . . . On his robe at his thigh was written this title: *King of all kings and Lord of all lords* . . . Then I saw the beast and *the kings of the world and their armies gathered* together to fight against the one sitting on the horse and his army . . . Both the beast and his false prophet were thrown alive into the fiery lake of burning sulfur. Their entire army was killed by the sharp sword that came from the mouth of the one riding the white horse (Revelation 19, emphasis added).

pause | think | pray

The Wrap

Kings and presidents come and go. But Christ remains — the most contemporary ruler there is. From generation to generation and forever, he stands as "ruler of the kings of the earth" (Revelation 1).

Though most in this age do not recognize his throne or his involvement in affairs of state, ultimately within the redemptive purposes of God all authorities remain subservient to him. They would not even exist without his decree.

Thus, all rulers claiming "royal majesty" should know they hold a role that is *relative* — it is defined and determined by the Lord Jesus, unto whom all majesty is gathered. Only the throne of King Jesus is absolute — and absolutely permanent.

Christ will prevail so fully that in the end the nations' leaders and their designs — whether commanders, chieftains, or chief operating officers — will be either purged or purified, and incorporated into the triumphal procession of the King of the whole earth.

Looking forward to Jesus' reign among global rulers, Psalm 47 declares:

> God went up to his throne while his people were shouting with joy ... Sing praises to our King. Sing praises. God is the King of the whole earth ... The nobles of the nations come together. They are now part of the people of the God of Abraham. The kings of the earth belong to God.

John witnessed a vision of the new Jerusalem in Revelation 21 that will be the fulfillment of Psalm 47. He records:

> The city does not need the sun or moon to shine on it. God's glory is its light, and the Lamb is its lamp. The nations will walk by the light of the city. *The kings of the world will bring their glory into it* ... The glory and honor of the nations will be brought into it (emphasis added).

The Reign of Christ OVER
the Destiny of Earth's Peoples

Similar to what the United Nations provides for political leaders, for decades the "Lausanne Movement for World Evangelization" has offered opportunities for united mission outreach for thousands of church leaders from all denominations across the globe.

Founded at the 1974 "Lausanne Congress" in Lausanne, Switzerland — convened by Dr. Billy Graham — this historic coalition of Christian mission strategists has expanded and reassembled many times since.

In Cape Town in 2010, the Lausanne Movement mobilized the most representative gathering of Christian leaders in the last 2000 years of Christian history. Four thousand delegates representing 198 countries convened in South Africa, with several thousand more participating through 650 virtual connections to the Congress in about 90 countries.

The convocation issued a manifesto that declared, in part:

> *We proclaim Christ.* In Christ alone God has fully and finally revealed himself, and through Christ alone God has achieved salvation for the world. We therefore kneel as disciples at the feet of Jesus of Nazareth and say to him with Peter, "You are the Christ, the Son of the Living

> God," and with Thomas, "My Lord and my God" . . . we join Peter and
> John in proclaiming that "there is salvation in no one else, for there is
> no other name under heaven by which we must be saved."

Such a commitment to world evangelization is critically important to the outworking of Christ's redeeming mission. The destiny of billions of people walking the planet today hangs in the balance. That's because, at this moment, billions have no saving knowledge of Christ, and *no one* like them (racially, culturally, linguistically), and *no one* near them (geographically) to tell them (personally) about God's saving grace poured out in Jesus and found only through him. They are lost — without God and without hope in this hour (Ephesians 2).

However, the challenge for spreading the gospel among them is immensely complex. For example, earth's peoples break down into at least 16,000 distinct cultural and linguistic entities, what the Greek New Testament calls "ta ethne" (translated "nations"; also the word from which we get "ethnic"). Christ's reign **over** each of these people groups waits to be embraced by them in ways unique to who they are. Yet nearly half of these groups remain unevangelized, without any established witnessing congregations among them. What Lausanne calls "unreached people groups" are termed by others as the "hidden peoples" — invisible, not to God but to most current Christian mission endeavors.

Great glory still awaits God's Son — and great blessings remain primed to be poured out on many peoples — as his kingdom breaks through to cultures and languages and societies where it has never been manifested before.

The advance of Christ's kingdom must necessarily engage such issues as: the mosaic of world languages; the varieties of religion; nationalities and nations; cultural realms, such as Islamic, Hindu, and Meso-African; the global poor and refugees; the spread and makeup of cities; etc.

All of these categories hold intriguing implications for *how* Jesus can express his rule **over** the destiny of earth's peoples. Clearly, there are multiple dimensions of human experience for our Lord to capture — to redeem and reclaim for himself — as his lordship is made known and owned.

Snapshots and Starter Thoughts

- **The Father's unwavering desire is to display among all of earth's peoples the glory of his Son and the full force of his royal dominion.** He intends for his Son to become the main character in every human narrative, one way or another, either as Redeemer or Judge. Christ's kingdom impacts all realms of human existence — past, present, future.

- **The Father has presented to Jesus the nations as his inheritance, sealing their destiny in the destiny of Jesus' kingdom.** In Psalm 2, the Father promises his Son:

  > For the Lord declares, "I have placed my chosen king on the throne in Jerusalem, on my holy mountain." The king proclaims the LORD's decree: "The LORD said to me, 'You are my son. Today I have become your Father. Only ask, and I will give you the nations as your inheritance, the whole earth as your possession" . . . rejoice with trembling. Submit to God's royal son . . . what joy for all who take refuge in him! (NLT).

- **Christ's reign necessarily places the human race into three categories:** (1) Those who have come under his reign willingly; (2) those who actively oppose it; (3) those for whom, currently, his saving lordship remains unknown. But one day, at Jesus' return, all neutral ground will vanish from planet earth — the destiny of every person and every people group will be sealed once and for all.

- **The ultimate destiny of earth's peoples is tied to how Jesus brings everything, everyone, and every people group to his feet to determine their future.**

> His rule will last forever. His kingdom will never end. He considers all of the nations on earth to be nothing . . . He does what he wants with the nations of the earth. No one can hold his hand back. No one can say to him, "What have you done?" (Daniel 4).

Psalm 113 foreshadowed how this would happen in our own time.

> From the sunrise in the east to the sunset in the west, may the name of the Lord be praised. The Lord is honored over all of the nations. He sits on his throne in heaven. He bends down to look . . . He raises poor people up from the trash pile. He lifts needy people out of the ashes. He lets them sit with princes . . . He gives children to the woman who doesn't have any children. He makes her a happy mother in her own home.

- **To say Jesus reigns *over* all of earth's peoples means we must regard his reign as "supra-cultural."** He is presiding and working within all cultures — none can avoid his divine intervention. He reigns for the sake of all peoples. He intends to have a kingdom made up of citizens of every ethnic and language group (approximately 16,000 distinct groups). However, he refuses to be co-opted or "owned" by any *one* of the world's cultures — including any of the 40,000 separate "tribes" we call "denominations" who currently claim to assemble under his flag!

- **Earth's peoples do not survive in a vacuum in which Christ is remote from them, operating off in celestial clouds.** Instead, he actively rules in the midst of our world's most broken places. He has not abandoned whole people groups to darkness and perdition. This world — all of it, despite all of its squalor, suffering, and sin — remains the arena of active kingdom work.

- **Claiming absolute supremacy in all things, Christ intends one day to give *every* normal and legitimate dimension of human existence a home in God's kingdom.** Just as the Exodus of Israel — when Yahweh took charge by judgments and in redemption — had political, economic, social, and spiritual implications for everyone involved, so does the reign of Christ in our world today.

- **In fact, at this very hour our King engages every domain of human endeavor**: kingdoms of finance and commerce; communications and technology; entertainment and education; industry and labor; arts and sciences; as well as rulers and governments. He shapes and synthesizes the strengths, activities, distinctions, and resources of earth's peoples, as he sways them toward kingdom goals. There is not a square inch of any culture among the billions of earth's people where Jesus does not point and say (paraphrasing Kuyper): "That is destined to serve my kingdom purposes, one way or another."

- **Jesus reigns even *over* numbing human suffering — starvation, slavery, wars, poverty, brutality, disease, war, and barbarity.** His hands are not tied. His clear determined purpose (as he taught us to pray) is that the Father's name would be exalted, his kingdom would be victorious, and his will would be determinative on earth — all three requests applied to the darkest corners of our planet — even as these realities are already secured in heaven.

- **In other words, the work and reign of Christ is not *confined* to just those places where he is *already* acknowledged as Lord of the nations.** Even now within each earthly society, elements of his reign continue to break through in whatever ways they can serve God's eternal plan for the world. Though no state or people group can be equated with Jesus' reign, none is devoid of hints of his involvement.

- **For certain, even now Jesus is restraining human evil across the earth, preventing mankind from destroying itself.** Should he relax on this point at any moment, the human race would be quickly consumed by utter destruction, at our own hands. Hebrews 1 speaks to this point:

  > The Son is the gleaming brightness of God's glory. He is the exact likeness of God's being. He uses his powerful word to hold all things together.

We read in 1 John 3 that:

> Those who do what is sinful belong to the devil. They are just like him. He has been sinning from the beginning. But the Son of God came to destroy the devil's work

- **In fact, we're told in Revelation 5 that the Holy Spirit is "the sevenfold Spirit of God that is sent out into every part of the earth" to carry out Christ's bidding — the same Spirit that Isaiah predicted would fulfill God's purposes through his anointed Servant (Jesus).**

> I will put my Spirit on him. He will make everything right among the nations . . . He will not give up until he makes everything right on the earth. The islands will put their hope in his law. And you will be a light for the other nations. You will open eyes that can't see. You will set prisoners free. Those who sit in darkness will come out of their cells' . . . Now I announce new things to you. Before they even begin to happen, I announce them to you (Isaiah 42).

- **Jesus informed his disciples that the Father had given him authority *over* all mankind so that he might grant eternal life to all who come to him (John 17).** He reinforced this prospect after his resurrection by commissioning his disciples to bring nations ("peoples") under his lordship and into the fellowship of the triune God. Jesus reassured his followers that at every step of the way he personally would be involved, backing all they would do for him (Matthew 28).

- **At the end of this age, therefore, there will be multitudes of redeemed people and people groups whose destinies have been sealed in blood — in the blood of the Lamb.**

> With your blood you bought people for God. They come from every tribe, language, people and nation. You have made them members of a royal family. You have made them priests to serve our God. They will rule on the earth (Revelation 5).

> . . . there in front of me was a huge crowd of people. They stood in front of the throne and in front of the Lamb. There were so many that no one could count them. They came from every nation, tribe, people and language (Revelation 7).

- **Through the gospel, Christ's saving lordship is becoming increasingly visible among the peoples of the world, redemptively shaping their destinies as individuals and societies.** He is saturating the nations with triumphs of his saving grace. God has not abandoned the world, but is at work everywhere in the world to bring all things back to himself through his anointed Son (Colossians 1).

- **Today, God's forgiveness — offered to a sinful world because of who Christ is *for* us — is currently the most powerful extension of the reign of Christ *over* us.** That's because the gospel brings both peace with God and peace with others. Through the witness of the gospel, Jesus calls all peoples back to the Father and, therefore, back to righteousness, justice, human dignity, the end of oppression, the reconciliation of enemies, and — above all and before all — the liberation of hearts and minds to pursue God's kingdom purposes with him.

- **Inexhaustible blessings abound wherever his reign prevails through the spread of the gospel — blessings designed to transform the destiny of many.** So, we sing:

  > No more let sins and sorrows grow, nor thorns infest the ground.
  > He comes to make his blessings flow, far as the curse is found.
  > He rules the world with truth and grace, and makes the nations prove
  > The glories of his righteousness and wonders of his love (Isaac Watts).

- **Here's one current, unprecedented manifestation of Christ's supremacy *over* humanity: For the first time, the world Christian movement has genuinely become a *worldwide* faith — the only "religious faith" to ever claim this.** In other words, currently as the *life* of Christ is ruling within and through millions of his subjects, the *reign* of Christ is entering more and more lives and cultures across the globe. There is greater potential for the message of Christ and his reign to spread among earth's peoples than at any time in history. Like never before, Jesus is filling the nations with the hope of salvation — a hope anchored in the activities proceeding from his throne. One might say there are no *Christ-forsaken* places in the world, only *Church-forsaken* places and peoples where the Christian movement has not yet advanced the work of the gospel as it must.

- **Seated on his throne, Jesus has never ceased directing this 2000-year-old global missionary invasion.** Reaching the ends of the earth with the gospel and reaching the end of this age share a common destiny. The culmination of the missionary invasion will result in the saturation of earth's peoples with the gospel, which in turn will trigger the consummation of the age. Jesus said:

> This good news of the kingdom will be preached in the whole world. It will be a witness to all nations. Then the end will come (Matthew 24).

- **The call of God to his people to serve the mission of his Son is non-negotiable — and it is irrevocable.** He summons all of us to be about the business of bringing to pass "unconditional surrender" among all the peoples of the earth through the spreading of the good news about who Jesus is. Our role is to champion his saving agenda among all nations and languages so that their future hope might be redirected under his lordship toward the new heaven and earth. We must do so among the poor, the young, the spiritually searching, the devotees of other religions, the oppressed as well as the oppressors, the successful, the powerful, and the privileged. But in all cases, the Church must now give *priority* to those people and people groups everywhere currently *beyond* the reach of the gospel — those have no knowledge of the King because they have no one like them, near them, to tell them.

- **As we consider Christ's mission to all the nations, we must not forget that his kingdom holds *unique* implications for the promised destiny of one very special people group — the seed of Abraham, the Hebrew people.** Consider these three passages (and there are many others), each one waiting to be fulfilled for the Jews through their Messiah's reign *over* them:

> The time will come when I will rebuild David's fallen tent [kingship]. I will repair its broken places. I will rebuild what was destroyed. I will make it what it used to be. Then my people will take control of those who are left alive in Edom. They will also possess all of the nations that belong to me (Amos 9).

> The Spirit of the Lord will rest on that Branch . . . He will not judge things only by the way they look . . . He will always do what is right when he judges those who are in need . . . when he makes decisions about poor people. When he commands that people be punished, it will happen . . . At that time the Lord will reach out his hand to gather his people a second time. He will bring back those who are left alive . . . He will lift up a banner. It will show the nations that he is gathering the people of Israel . . . He'll bring them back from all four directions (Isaiah 11).

> Part of Israel has refused to obey God. That will continue until the full number of Gentiles has entered God's kingdom. In this way all Israel will be saved. It is written, "The God who saves will come from Mount Zion. He will remove sin from Jacob's family. Here is my covenant with them. I will take away their sins" (Romans 11).

Selah

pause | think | pray

The Wrap

It was no accident that Pilate decided to designate Jesus as "The King of the Jews" in three different languages — Hebrew, Latin and Greek — written on a sign hanging atop his cross. The proconsul's act foreshadowed how the redeeming work of Christ would determine everywhere the fortunes and futures of thousands of cultures and their citizens.

As we conclude this series of insights about Christ's reign **over** earth's peoples, here are five questions to help us reflect on this dramatic manifestation of his spectacular supremacy:

(1) To what extent do you believe Christ's reign interacts with earth's peoples right now?

(2) To what extent do you believe he is directly involved, right now, in the blessing or the judgment of earth's peoples, in any part of the world?

(3) From now until Christ returns, to what extent do you expect his kingdom to *visibly* advance among the vast array of human cultures and languages?

(4) If it does advance, wherever it advances, how will you know for sure that it actually *is* his reign that's breaking through? What are some evidences that you would know for sure pointed to him?

(5) Bottom line: To the extent you *do* believe Christ's kingdom is the deciding factor in the destiny of earth's peoples, does your own daily sharing of Christ with others show it?

The Reign of Christ OVER
the Rebellion of Dark Powers

If ever the Church felt itself under assault by the very forces of hell, it was from A.D. 303-311 during the "Great Persecution" instigated against Christians throughout the Roman world by emperor Diocletian:

> . . . when Christian buildings and the homes of Christians were torn down, their sacred books destroyed, while Christians were arrested, tortured, mutilated, burned, starved, and condemned to gladiatorial contests to amuse spectators (Wikipedia).

Emperor Constantine the Great brought an end to this crucible, and in 313, with co-emperor Licinius, issued the Edict of Milan legalizing Christian worship. Subsequently, Constantine convened a number of ecumenical councils specifically to sharpen the Church's doctrine of Christology. This resulted in the Nicene Creed, which ever since has sustained and united the global church. Constantine is still revered as a saint in the Eastern Orthodox tradition.

Spiritual warfare was a dominant theme for Constantine throughout his life. At the Battle of Milvian Bridge in 312, contemporary historians claim Constantine looked up to the sun before the battle began and saw a cross of light above it, and with it Greek words that said, "By this sign, conquer!" Although raised by a Christian mother, the emperor claimed that this vision was the moment of his true conversion at the age of 42. Just hours before the fray, Constantine commanded his troops to place on their shields a Christian symbol based on the first two Greek letters in the word "Christos."

When he returned to Rome after his armies were victorious, the newly converted emperor refused to worship in thanksgiving at the altars of any of the Roman deities, as was customary.

In her book *Revelations*, Elaine Pagels, a professor of religion at Princeton University, recounts how Constantine was so taken with John's vision of Christ's victory over the dragon in the book of Revelation that he decided to make that an emblem of his domain. Pagels notes that Constantine emblazoned the image of Christ crushing Satan in the most conspicuous public places, "apparently to show that he, as Roman emperor, far from embodying 'the beast,' was now Christ's agent, who destroys all evil power." The graphic image was placed above the entrance to his palace and atop his throne, declaring to all who entered that as Christ's agent on earth Constantine had the dragon under his feet — but only because, as illustrated by the symbol, the Savior was reigning **over** and through the Emperor.

Whether Constantine himself knew it or not, spiritual warfare has been a major plotline within the biblical narrative as well as throughout the past two millennia of the Christian movement.

Yes, Jesus reigns! *But his dominion encompasses a cosmic battlefield.* The conflict intensifies as steadily, convincingly he confronts and confounds all forms of rebellion by dark principalities and powers. There's no place to hide. Satan and his nefarious accomplices intend to overthrow the government of Messiah.

Therefore, it should come as no surprise that decisive battles are raging all around believers all the time — manifested not only in spiritual realms but often on the global stage as well.

Until the Consummation, the saints of God will find themselves engaged in this spiritual combat in one form or another — deployed by the orders of our heavenly Commander into battles with legions of death, into struggles where the victory for us always remains sure because we serve a Savior who promises us he has *already* "overcome the world" (John 15).

However, Scripture is clear that at times *spiritual* battles can result in temporary *physical* setbacks such as the martyrdom of faithful followers of Christ giving their lives to press the gospel's outward advance — engaging in a resistance so fierce it can almost seem as if Satan is winning. This is illustrated, for example, in Revelation 13 (a passage some believe refers to a Roman emperor, some to a ruler yet to come, but the principle is the same):

> It was also given to him to make war with the saints and to overcome them [temporarily only], and authority over every tribe and people and tongue and nation was given to him. All who dwell on the earth will worship him, *everyone* whose name has not been written from the foundation of the world in the book of life of the Lamb who has been slain (emphasis added).

Yet Scripture also is unequivocal about the promised outcome: Christ's place of supremacy predetermines that one day a thorough "exorcism" of evil from God's creation will be fully and permanently accomplished. Revelation 19 records it this way:

> There in front of me was a white horse. Its rider is called Faithful and True. When he judges or makes war, he is always fair. His eyes are like blazing fire. On his head are many crowns . . . the beast and the false prophet were captured . . . thrown alive into the lake of fire.

As Constantine decreed — and as multiple biblical passages promise — "by this sign, conquer." By Jesus' cross and all that flows from what he secured there — ratified and applied by his resurrection and ascension — all the saints among the nations today are constantly conquering, just as all the saints of all the ages will continue to win in him throughout eternity.

 Snapshots and Starter Thoughts

- **As our Champion and Warrior King, Jesus stands strong as the vanquisher of evil.** It is true: "There is no neutral ground in the universe; every square inch, every split second, is claimed by Christ and counter-claimed by Satan" (C. S. Lewis). The cosmos is rife with anti-forces who are, at their core, anti-Christ. But we have a King who is actively and unceasingly committed to turn back the conspiracies of hell and destroy every conspirator. Jesus is unequivocally the Commander of angel hosts who are ready to obey his every decree.

- **About the *outcome* of Christ's cosmic conflict — the true war to end all wars — there can be no doubt.** All of Satan's domains will be visibly dismantled and destroyed; his lethal forces will be crushed and abolished. The Lamb alone will stand victorious, with his supremacy displayed and vindicated once and for all. Christ's greatness will be celebrated even *more* intensely because of the magnitude of the ruin of the hosts of wickedness by his hands.

- **To say it another way, Jesus reigns at the convergence of two diametrically opposed powers: only one is destined to prevail, but both know "Who" that will be!** This planet is a war zone. Our foe is clearly formidable. The Lord's battle is not a game. Evil is not simply the absence of good — it is adversarial; it is an assault upon everything Christ stands for. Evil is personal and heavily entrenched — but for only a season.

- **However, divine intervention into the enemy's camp — the thrust of Yahweh's mighty right arm (Isaiah 59), *which is Christ himself* — is required.** The glory that awaits God's Son is in direct proportion to the measure of victory he is destined to achieve. The "Lord of Heaven's Armies" is gaining greater praise in the universe with each ensuing victory — praise which will resound throughout all of eternity, specifically because of *how* his reign mastered so magnificently the machinations of the dark powers.

- **Though it may not be physically visible to us, right now Christ is in the process of dethroning all depraved principalities and powers.** Vast domains of evil spirits and angels in revolt remain under his gaze. By the spread of the gospel he is limiting their operations and opposition, rendering them ineffective and unproductive; he is breaking their *strangleholds* on earth's peoples as he tears down their *strongholds* against the truth.

- **The ultimate reversal to Satan's rebellion began with the Incarnation, continued straight through to the Ascension, and since then has increased exponentially with every passing day.** John summarizes it this way:

  > The dragon took his place in front of the woman who was about to give birth to a child, so that as soon as she did so he might devour it. She gave birth to a male child who is to shepherd all the nations "with a rod of iron." Her child was snatched up to God and to his throne . . . The war broke out in Heaven . . . So the huge dragon, the serpent of ancient times, who is called the devil and Satan, the deceiver of the whole world, was hurled down upon the earth, and his angels were hurled down with him. Then I heard a great voice in Heaven cry: "Now the salvation and the power and kingdom of our God, and the authority of his Christ have come . . . they have conquered him through the blood of the Lamb, and through the Word to which they bore witness. They did not cherish life even in the face of death" (Revelation 12, PHILLIPS).

- **Often the reign of Christ is most apparent when displayed "in the *midst* of his enemies," according to Psalms 110:**

  > The LORD says to my lord: "Sit at my right hand until I make your enemies a footstool for your feet." The LORD will extend your mighty scepter from Zion, saying, "Rule in the midst of your enemies!"

  Psalms 110 is the most frequently quoted or referenced Old Testament text by New Testament authors — and for good reason because it describes how Jesus' kingdom comes. Even where demonic opposition rages against the mission of the Church, the gates of hell cannot prevail against it (Matthew 16).

- **Even in the thick of this battle, Christ is subjugating his enemies, forming them into a footstool for his feet.**

  > There arose loud voices in Heaven and they were saying, "The kingship of the world now belongs to our Lord and to his Christ, and he shall be king for timeless ages!" (Revelation 11, PHILLIPS).

- **As Jesus' reign reorients a fallen world toward the coming new creation, he is systematically neutralizing the chaotic, cosmic forces of tyranny.** God made this possible for Jesus when:

  > He raised him from the dead and gave him the place of supreme honor in Heaven — a place that is infinitely superior to any conceivable command, authority, power or control, and which carries

with it a name far beyond any name that could ever be used in this world or the world to come (Ephesians 1, PHILLIPS).

He sat down at the right hand of the King, the Majesty in heaven. So he became higher than the angels. The name he received is more excellent than theirs (Hebrews 1).

- **The impact of Christ's authority *over* the hosts of wickedness shines forth most tangibly wherever the gospel spreads among the nations.** Wherever hope in Christ is heralded and believed, a limit is sovereignly set on the devil's deceptions. By the truths of the gospel the Spirit of God unmasks, names, shames, restrains, contains, exploits, and even routs all the designs of the devil.

- **But what Christ is doing against the forces of darkness right now is only a hint of what is coming.** We can only imagine what will transpire the day he returns in open conquest, when evil hosts flee from his holy presence forever — vanquished and banished throughout all ages by our Warrior King.

- **This entire drama was foreshadowed in the days of Jesus' earthly ministry, as he engaged and dismissed so many of the serpent's minions.** Christ came into the world specifically to *destroy* the works of the devil (1 John 3) — that is, to render Satan impotent, powerless, and pointless; to crush him under his feet as foretold from the beginning (Genesis 3); to undermine his hold on the planet as the "deceiver of the whole world" (Revelation 12); and to set his captives free (Luke 4).

- **In the same way that Jesus rebuked fevers and restored the sick, commanded storms to cease, and drove moneychangers out of the temple — in that same way he dispatched demons and they fled.** Watching the "unclean spirits" obey him without fail, the crowds concluded Jesus was bringing them a vitally fresh message from Yahweh (after four hundred years of God's silence). The demons corroborated that conclusion as they spoke through their victims, causing them to fall down in worship and cry out, "You are the Son of God!"

- **The way Jesus was empowered to cast out demons was reminiscent of how God commissioned ancient Israel to clear the Promised Land of its "occupying forces."** As the Savior put it:

But suppose I drive out demons by the Spirit of God. Then God's kingdom has come to you. Or think about this. How can you enter a strong man's house and just take what the man owns? You must first tie him up. Then you can rob his house. Anyone who is not with me is against me. Anyone who does not gather sheep with me scatters them (Matthew 12).

- **In the wilderness temptation Jesus never recoiled, but compelled by the Holy Spirit he engaged Satan *proactively*, even as he does today.** Jesus did not wait for Satan to come after him; rather like a man on a military campaign he went forth *seeking* his enemy. In the Judean desert, for our sakes, he faced and fought his wicked foe, withstanding every temptation to use his power in the wrong ways and for the wrong reasons. Consequently, because Jesus refused to join Satan's rebellion against God, the Father has handed him all royal prerogatives in heaven and on earth.

- **When the disciples reported how demons submitted to them in Jesus' name, he responded that their experience dramatized how Satan was rapidly descending into his demise, like flashes of lightning falling from sky to earth.** Yet their joy, he cautioned, should center much more on their names being written in heaven, assuring them that they would share forever in the fruits of his eternal victory *over* Satan (Luke 10).

- **Jesus' earthly conflict with demonic opposition unveiled something of what the final battle at the end of the age will look like.** In the same way that during his earthly mission his word was enough to silence all evil beings, so Scripture pictures Christ in the final conflict fighting and defeating the global army raised up by Antichrist with the power of the sword coming out of his mouth — which represents how, by his authoritative commands alone, he will triumph *over* all resistance to his kingdom.

- **Even the night before dying on the cross, Jesus told his disciples that Satan had no hold on him, that what he was about to suffer would ultimately cast Satan out of this world (John 12; 14).** That's precisely what he accomplished when he rose from the dead and sat down in the heavens.

  He died to bring you to God. His body was put to death. But the Holy Spirit brought him back to life . . . Jesus Christ has saved you by rising from the dead. He has gone into heaven. He is at God's right hand. Angels, authorities and powers are under his control (1 Peter 3).

So Jesus became human like them, in order to die for them. By doing that, he could destroy the one who rules over the kingdom of death. I'm talking about the devil. Jesus could set people free who were afraid of death. All their lives they were held as slaves by that fear (Hebrews 2).

- **His cross accomplished a victory** *over* **Satan that shapes how Jesus reigns even now, and how we are invited to reign with him.**

   You received Christ Jesus as Lord. So keep on living in him . . . Because you belong to Christ, you have everything you need. He is the ruler over every power and authority . . . He forgave us all of our sins . . . He took away the weapons of the powers and authorities. He made a public show of them. He won the battle over them by dying on the cross (Colossians 2).

   [Christ] is sitting at God's right hand . . . Now your life is hidden with Christ in God. Christ is your life. When he appears again, you also will appear with him in heaven's glory (Colossians 3).

- **Christ reigns today** *over* **the rebellion of dark powers because of four victories he achieved at the cross,** *four victories* **that continue to serve us to this hour.**

   (1) He reconciled sinners back to God, releasing them from the domain of darkness (Colossians 1).

   (2) Satan, the accuser of God's children (Revelation 12), no longer has any case against us; we are totally forgiven and justified by Jesus' blood.

(3) Christ's death was the death of death, thus Satan can no longer intimidate believers with the fear of death (Hebrews 2).

(4) Christ takes believers captive and incorporates them, as they are converted, into his victory procession (Ephesians 4). In our union with Christ we now are seated *permanently* with him in heavenly realms (Ephesians 2) far beyond Satan's claims on us.

- **Right now, through the gospel, Christ has set in motion** *redemptive* **forces that will eventually overthrow the devices of the devil, displacing the works of wickedness with the fruits of righteousness in every sphere of human experience.** This battle accelerates to the ends of the earth. Solid advances of the Kingdom, which are innumerable and unfolding all around us, cannot be ignored by the enemy. But to the praise of Jesus, multiplied demonic attacks simply provide additional evidence of how fully and relentlessly Christ's saving work proceeds, prevails, penetrates, and prospers "in the midst of his enemies."

- **Wherever Jesus' kingdom breaks through, there the church finds both** *harvest fields* **and** *battlefields*. When fields are sown and harvested by the gospel, counterattackers try to reclaim their lost ground. Predictable, sometimes vicious, struggles ensue, both visible and invisible — at times seemingly intractable, but always only temporary. In the end, the gates of hell can never permanently hold out against the advance of the Church's missionary endeavor (Matthew 16). Wherever believers storm demonic dominions in the power of the Holy Spirit, the ranks of saved "Son worshippers" swell.

- **As we wrestle with spiritual powers, the armor we are called upon to wear is nothing less than the fullness of Christ who fights for us.** According to Ephesians 6, we can stand only by his power within us. We can triumph only because we are fitted with his righteousness to cover our hearts, with his salvation to protect our minds, and with his message to keep us spiritually nimble. Our faith in Christ quenches every attack of our enemy while our proclamation of Christ provides us our essential *offensive* weapon.

> Finally, let the Lord make you strong. Depend on his mighty power. Put on all of God's armor. Then you can stand firm against the devil's evil plans (Ephesians 6).

> The dark night of evil is nearly over. The day of Christ's return is almost here. So let us get rid of the works of darkness. Let us put on the armor of light put on the Lord Jesus Christ as your clothing (Romans 13).
>
> . . . the One who is in you is more powerful than the one who is in the world (1 John 4).

- **Christ on his throne is more than equal to every scheme the enemy might throw against his kingdom.** To Christ belongs the victory that has overcome the world (1 John 5). Therefore, Satan's plethora of hostilities — his counterfeits, beguilements, frauds, subversions, diversions, deceptions, accusations, chaos, confusions, insurgencies, and conflagrations — are countered, exorcised, displaced, and replaced *by and with Christ himself,* in the majesty of his supremacy.

- **Even though we are living in what seems so often like "enemy occupied territory," our King lays siege against every earthly manifestation of celestial insurrections.** This includes calamities of brutal injustice; the dehumanization of poverty and oppression; the diminishment of creation through human greed; the persecution of Christians and destruction of their churches; as well as the retaliations against the gospel by devotees of other gods and saviors. None of these tragic developments ever escapes his active, decisive, concerned involvement.

- **Exalted at God's right hand, Jesus and the themes of his kingship remain dominant and determinative in all of life, especially in every skirmish with the evil one.** There is coming an hour when even the dark powers will finally and publicly *acknowledge* Christ's dominance in everything. The question is not *if* but *when* Satan and his hellish hosts are compelled to concede and lay down their weapons in unconditional, irreversible surrender to King Jesus.

> So, God lifted him up to the highest place. He gave him the name that is above every name. When the name of Jesus is spoken, everyone's knee will bow to worship him. Every knee in heaven and on earth and *under the earth* will bow to worship him. Everyone's mouth will say that Jesus Christ is Lord. And God the Father will receive the glory (Philippians 2, emphasis added).

Selah

pause | think | pray

The Wrap

Abbot Vonier, 18th-century British Benedictine monk and renowned Catholic scholar, in his well-known book *The Victory of Jesus,* poses a most stimulating reflection: "Is there any kind of evil which Christ has left unconquered; or, if he has overcome it once, has the dark power a chance of rising again?"

Vonier continues to answer his own question this way: "If men were *de facto* saved by Christ but were not saved in a supreme and irrevocable fashion from all evil, such salvation would be as nothing compared with the condition of those, many or few, who are delivered from evil [entirely], with no possible or imaginable limitation to their deliverance . . . Christ would have labored in vain had he left one single enemy unchallenged and unconquered."

That's worth pondering. If Christ had defeated every enemy in the universe *but one* — whichever one — what genuine hope would any of us have in him?

But the consistent testimony of Scripture is that *every* force of darkness and *every* evil entity will be destroyed. Forever. Without exception!

To be sure, the battle is not over yet. But in the fog of war Christians can daily run to Jesus to take refuge in him and get clarity on the struggle, doing so with full assurance that as we abide under his extended scepter we remain safe forever.

Strong in this conviction, the disciple John concluded his first epistle this way:

> The Son of God keeps them safe. *The evil one can't harm them.* We know that we are children of God. We know that the whole world is under the control of the evil one. We also know that the Son of God has come . . . we belong to the One who is true. We also belong to his Son, Jesus Christ. He is the true God. He is eternal life (1 John 5, emphasis added).

The Reign of Christ OVER
the Building of His Church

Listen to these three cautionary tales. They are stories about three churches. Three contemporary American evangelical churches. Three of the largest churches in the nation, each with tens of thousands of attendees every Sunday.

Church #1: In response to a question about why he never mentions Jesus in his Sunday sermons, the pastor of this church told a national TV news program that while others are called to preach about Christ, he personally feels he is called to give people more reason to hope.

Church # 2: The pastor of this church was shocked at this conclusion of a professional survey of his congregation: The greatest fear among thousands of his parishioners was the dread of becoming too intimate with Christ.

Church #3: The leadership team of this church, after years of perfecting and marketing ministry programs for every age and every need, published a report to millions of its followers "confessing" a disappointing discovery: Few of their activities and programs actually helped people to *mature* in Christ.

Compare those three accounts with recent reports coming from Asia and Africa about what are termed "Church Planting Movements" (CPM). Those preaching Christ among one remote people group, for example, have planted 200 churches within three years. In another country, 150,000 urban and rural churches have been started over a ten-year span by keeping the ministry focused on Christ alone. In a third nation, tens of thousands of "house churches" are thriving and multiplying as their leaders are being trained to use what they call "King Jesus glasses" — looking at everything in Scripture and in disciple making through the prism of Christ's supremacy ***over*** the life of his people.

These contrasting case studies remind us how critical it is for us to heed the most important organizing principle for every spiritually prospering congregation: *Keep Jesus supreme in every aspect of our life together in him.* Succinctly Paul wrote:

> You are like his building. God has given me the grace to lay a foundation as a master builder. Now someone else is building on it. But each one should build carefully. *No one can lay any other foundation than the one that has already been laid. That foundation is Jesus Christ* (1 Corinthians 3, emphasis added).

The maturity of a congregation should not be measured by how full of people the building is but rather by how full of Christ the people are!

We're talking about the same Christ who visited John on the island of Patmos, clothed in Ascension glory, in order to confirm with breathtaking authority that he was presiding ***over*** and within his people. He was walking among the churches in Asia Minor, grasping their leaders, as it were, in his right hand, and calling each congregation upward and onward with him (Revelation 1).

That day John saw in a new way how the entirety of Christ's sovereignty ***over*** the universe was being brought to bear on the building up of these little flocks. First of all, the Lord presented the groups with reminders of his preeminence. Next, he reviewed with them their strong points ("you have not denied my name") as well as their weak points ("you have deserted me as your primary love"). Then he called believers to overcome every obstacle that would keep them from sharing fully in the work and fruit of his kingdom.

Both then and now, the success of any single congregation — as well as the building of the whole Church — relies on Jesus Christ alone. Whether we're talking about the "Church Triumphant" (the saints in glory), the "Church Militant" (the saints on earth), or the "Church Expectant" (all the saints, both here and there, awaiting the Consummation), God's people are rooted in Christ and built up in him in order to serve him. Their King rules ***over*** them — feeding them, thrilling them, empowering them, comforting them, mentoring them, mobilizing them — in order to *build* them.

This next section investigates the *primary* application of Christ's supremacy in this age: how the reign of the Lord Jesus Christ impacts the shaping and strengthening of his Church.

This section is fairly brief, however, for one major reason: The next four chapters delve into Jesus' incomparable construction project from four perspectives — how he builds his church by going BEFORE us, working WITHIN us, ministering THROUGH us, and coming UPON us.

📷 *Snapshots and Starter Thoughts*

- **The "Master Carpenter" promises us that building his Church is a permanent arrangement:**

  > . . . I will put together my church, a church so expansive with energy that not even the gates of hell will be able to keep it out. And that's not all. You will have complete and free access to God's kingdom, keys to open any and every door: no more barriers between heaven and earth, earth and heaven (Matthew 16, MSG).

  > The person who builds a house has greater honor than the house itself. In the same way, Jesus has been found worthy of greater honor than Moses . . . Christ is faithful as a son over God's house. We are his house if we continue to come boldly to God (Hebrews 3).

- **When we come to Christ, we are incorporated into a dwelling place where the "Cosmic Contractor" simultaneously doubles as the "Chief Cornerstone."**

Christ is the living Stone. People did not accept him. But God chose him. God places the highest value on him. You also are like living stones. As you come to him you are being built into a house for worship. There you will be holy priests. You will offer spiritual sacrifices. God will accept them because of what Jesus Christ has done (1 Peter 2).

You are a building that is built on the apostles and prophets. They are the foundation. Christ Jesus himself is the most important stone in the building. The whole building is held together by him. It rises to become a holy temple because it belongs to the Lord. And because you belong to him, you too are being built together. You are being made into a house where God lives through his Spirit (Ephesians 2).

- **Jesus' reign *over* his Church is symbolized in many ways, such as the metaphor of him as a shepherd.**

    I am the good shepherd. I know my sheep, and my sheep know me . . . I give my life for the sheep. I have other sheep that do not belong to this sheep pen. I must bring them in too. They also will listen to my voice. Then there will be one flock and one shepherd . . . My sheep listen to my voice. I know them, and they follow me. I give them eternal life, and they will never die. No one can steal them out of my hand (John 10).

    To which Peter adds:

    His wounds have made you whole. You were like sheep who were wandering away. But now you have returned to the Shepherd. He is the Leader of your souls (1 Peter 2).

- **Another biblical metaphor that pictures Jesus' building work is marriage; he serves his people the way every husband should serve his wife.** Christ loves the whole world, yes. But his love for his Church is special, intimate, unique, unconditional, and always constructive. It is the love of a perfect spouse. Jesus actively beautifies his people, not just individually but collectively, ministering to his "bride" — all the saints of all the ages gathered together to himself. He frees her, feeds her, favors her, fosters her, fulfills her.

- **Listen to how Paul describes this overarching, all-consuming, attentive love of Christ for his "spouse":**

    The church follows the lead of Christ. In the same way, wives should follow the lead of their husbands in everything. Husbands, love your wives. Love them just as Christ loved the church. He gave himself up for her. He did it to make her holy . . . He wants a church that has no stain or wrinkle or any other flaw. He wants a church that is holy and without blame. In the same way, husbands should love their wives. They should love them as they love their own bodies. Any man who loves his wife loves himself. After all, people have never hated their own bodies. Instead, they feed and care for their bodies. And that is what Christ does for the church (Ephesians 5).

- **No wonder John the Baptist and Paul the Apostle both spoke of themselves as "match-makers" between Christ and his Church.**

John says it this way:

The bride belongs to the groom. The friend who helps the groom waits and listens for him. He is full of joy when he hears the groom's voice. That joy is mine, and it is now complete. He must become more important. I must become less important. The One who comes from above is above everything (John 3).

Paul describes it like this:

My jealousy for you comes from God himself. I promised to give you to only one husband. That husband is Christ. I wanted to be able to give you to him as if you were a pure virgin (2 Corinthians 11).

- **Here is another familiar New Testament metaphor for how Jesus reigns *over* the building of his Church: the role the human head plays for the human body. Jesus is defined as the "Head" for all of God's people who together form his "Body."**

We will grow up into Christ in every way. He is the Head. He makes the whole body grow and build itself up in love. Under the control of Christ, each part of the body does its work. It supports the other parts. In that way, the body is joined and held together (Ephesians 4).

. . . God placed all things under Christ's rule. He appointed him to be ruler over everything for the church. The church is Christ's body. It is filled by Christ. He fills everything in every way (Ephesians 1).

- **As this Head, Jesus serves the Church the way a brain animates a functioning body.** As long as the brain remains alive, alert, and competent, the body remains vitally responsive to everything the person desires, decides, and does. It is the same with Christ and his people.

There is one body. But it has many parts. Even though it has many parts, they make up one body. It is the same with Christ. We were all baptized by one Holy Spirit into one body (1 Corinthians 12).

Now you belong to Christ Jesus . . . He wanted to create one new group of people out of the two. He wanted to make peace between them . . . Through Christ we both come to the Father by the power of one Holy Spirit (Ephesians 2).

- **Being the Head, Jesus also bestows on his people a special *dignity*.** As the King of glory who has joined himself with us (like a head to a body), he honors us as he communicates with us, inspires us, guides us, coordinates us, sustains us, propels us, includes us, sends us, and uses us.

- **To see it from another perspective: He consolidates believers into this one Body so that through the gifts of the Spirit he might perpetuate his ministry through the Church as we serve him together.**

  But each one of us has received a gift of grace, just as Christ wanted us to have it . . . He is the One who gave some the gift to be apostles. He gave some the gift to be prophets. He gave some the gift of preaching the good news. And he gave some the gift to be pastors and teachers. He did it so that they might prepare God's people to serve. If they do, the body of Christ will be built up (Ephesians 4).

  God has joined together all the parts of the body. And he has given more honor to the parts that didn't have any. In that way, the parts of the body will not take sides. All of them will take care of each other. If one part suffers, every part suffers with it. If one part is honored, every part shares in its joy. You are the body of Christ. Each one of you is a part of it (1 Corinthians 12).

- **Actually, Jesus acting as the Head of the Church mirrors his simultaneous rule *over* the entire creation.** The Son has been appointed by the Father to restore all things, causing universal harmony — gathering all things in heaven and earth into one great family by the Spirit, before the Father (Colossians 1; Ephesians 1). In the same way, but much more so, the Son is gathering all of the redeemed to himself. The restoration of their life together as his Body is inseparable from — even more so, it is the apex of — his reconciling mission for the cosmos.

- **The Church is Christ's domain, the *foremost exhibition* of his kingdom today, by which the world can see how God's grace "reigns through life" (Romans 5).** Conquering us does not diminish us; it ennobles us and empowers us. United to Christ, millions of congregations across the planet provide "microcosms" of his active sovereignty *over* the "macrocosm."

  > [The Father] has made you fit to share with all his people. You will all receive a share in the kingdom of light. He has saved us from the kingdom of darkness. He has brought us into the kingdom of the Son he loves (Colossians 1).

- **Yet, Christ's kingdom is *greater* than the Church because his lordship extends *beyond* her borders.** The Church thrives within his kingdom but does not *contain* his kingdom. It does not *replace* his kingdom. The Church is created, defined, and sustained *by* his kingdom. In fact, all the activities of the Kingdom function preeminently for the everlasting welfare of the Church, not the other way around.

  > [The Father] seated him at his right hand in his heavenly kingdom. There Christ sits far above all who rule and have authority. He also sits far above all powers and kings. He is above every title that can be given in this world and in the world to come. God placed all things under Christ's rule. He appointed him to be ruler over everything *for the church* (Ephesians 1, emphasis added).

- **The early Christians did not claim to be the Kingdom, but instead they labored to *proclaim* the Kingdom.** They testified that Jesus was on the throne. Because the churches *already* were experiencing the powers of the coming age — powers that will mark the King's final victory (Hebrews 6) — they provided his kingdom's "bases of operations" from which he daily advanced his reign to the ends of the earth. This is our inheritance today as well. We too should be experiencing and demonstrating displays of the Kingdom's forceful activity that foreshadow the awesome dynamism waiting to create the new heaven and earth under Jesus' final jurisdiction.

- **On the other hand, the Christian movement underscores and reinforces Christ's rightful claim to be the world's supreme monarch.** A monarch without subjects lacks substantial legitimacy; but this is no concern for the Lord Jesus Christ. As citizens of heaven, we confirm his supremacy by the way we give ourselves to him in a life of devotion and service, a life that prefigures the subjection all of creation will exhibit one day.

> The church is Christ's body. He is its Savior. The church follows the lead of Christ (Ephesians 5).

- **To return to the words of Psalm 110, Jesus chooses to extend his scepter "in the midst of his enemies" through *congregations* all across the globe who dwell in the midst of those enemies.** Christian communities everywhere on the map exist to become nothing less than habitations of the King, who by his Spirit sets up his throne in *their* midst for the sake of those in the darkness among whom they dwell.

- **The "Chief Builder" recruits his followers to work *with* him, deploying them from the very throne of Heaven, and calling them to share in a wondrous *collaboration* with his coronation.**

> The One who came down is the same as the One who went up higher than all the heavens. He did it in order to fill all of creation. He is the One who gave some the gift to be apostles. He gave some the gift to be prophets. He gave some the gift of preaching the good news. And he gave some the gift to be pastors and teachers. He did it so that they might prepare God's people to serve. If they do, the body of Christ will be built up. That will continue until we all become one in the faith and in the knowledge of God's Son. Then we . . . will receive everything that Christ has for us (Ephesians 4).

Selah

pause | think | pray

The Wrap

At this hour Christ is ruler over all things, though only his people truly grasp that reality and live in the joy of it. Yet what is true *this* day among God's people, on *another* day will come to fulfillment for a multitude that will be redeemed from among all of earth's peoples. They will form Christ's "coronation procession" as he returns to earth from the royal courts of heaven, to bring everything under his feet as Lord — all of that happening primarily for the sake of his Body, "the fullness of him who fills all in all" (Ephesians 10).

In *that* day, his unsurpassed workmanship will be celebrated universally. At its completion, the "Church Triumphant" will fall down to worship King Jesus — as represented in Revelation 4-5 by 24 elders casting their crowns before a lordly Lamb. There, together, we will describe the wonders of his grand "Architectural Achievement" as we sing:

> . . . you were slaughtered, and your blood has ransomed people for God from every tribe and language and people and nation. And you have caused them to become a Kingdom of priests for our God. And they will reign on the earth . . . Worthy is the Lamb who was slaughtered — to receive power and riches and wisdom and strength and honor and glory and blessing (Revelation 5, emphasis added).

For now, however, walking by faith in the power of the Holy Spirit, we as believers draw daily on the risen life of our King. Doing so, we bear witness before the nations to the promises of his kingdom and invite all who hear us to join us as he places all believers "as living stones" to build a sanctuary of everlasting praise (1 Peter 2).

Who Christ Is OVER Us Today:
A Tribute

Paraphrasing and personalizing a wide selection of Scriptures

Father, we come to you to proclaim the name of your Son together — to spread his fame, embrace his reign, increase his gain, and honor his claim about who he is *over* us. As we do, awake us to him afresh for ALL that he is. May the praise we bring to him in these moments come forth alive in us by your Spirit and rise up as a blessing to you forever. We use your Word to magnify your Son, without whom we are nothing and can do nothing. This tribute is all for Christ alone, our one and only hope of glory, and the hope of all the nations.

Lord Jesus Christ, this is our tribute to you — our tribute to who you are OVER us.

You said that all authority has been given to you already—all authority in heaven and on earth. That's because you have fulfilled the vision of Psalm 110 that speaks of the wondrous day when the Father invited you to sit at his right hand in order to transform your enemies into your footstool. From there you rule in the midst of your Church and among all nations, in this, your appointed season of battle.

Your earliest followers reported that after you had spoken to them you were taken up into heaven in your resurrection brilliance and then sat at the right hand of God. Therefore, as your disciples went out and preached everywhere, you continued to meet them where you sent them, as you ruled *over* them and worked with them to sovereignly confirm their message about you by your signs that accompanied them.

Christ is NOW!

On Pentecost, Peter proclaimed who you are *over* us. He told the multitude that after the Father freed you from the agony of death, he filled you with joy in his presence in the hour when he exalted you to his right hand. Then he gave you the Holy Spirit to pour out upon all flesh, reversing the disgrace of your crucifixion and making you both Lord and Christ ***over*** us. Because you were obedient to death, even death on the cross, we now behold you exalted by God to the highest place, that at your name every knee should bow in heaven and on earth and under the earth, and every tongue confess that you and you alone are Lord ***over*** all of us.

Because you have ascended into the heavens to reign, even angels, authorities, and powers are in submission to you at this very moment. You have crushed Satan under your heel. You alone are the ruler of the kings of the earth — you and no other! You alone are destined to rule all of the nations with a rod of iron, because the kingdoms of the world have become the kingdom of our God and of you, his Christ, and you will reign for ever and ever. In you has come the salvation and the power and the kingdom of our God and the authority of his Christ. Just as the ancient prophet foretold, God's government rests upon your shoulders so that its increase ***over*** us will have no end, as you implement your kingdom ways, establishing them and upholding them among the nations, with justice and righteousness forevermore.

Christ is NOW!

But wonder of wonders, when the Father placed all these things under your feet, appointing you the head ***over*** everything, ultimately he did so for the sake of your subjects, the Church. You are Head ***over*** the redeemed in heaven and earth; we have become your Body. As you rule ***over*** us you continue to saturate us with even more of the fullness of yourself by which you are saturating everything, in every way. When you ascended on high you took your people captive — *to* you and *with* you alone. Therefore, even now as you inhabit the whole universe with your supremacy and your activity, you are also pervading and filling your Body with that same supremacy and activity, bringing us to unity in the faith and in the knowledge of you as the Son of God. Because you are our Head ***over*** us, our destiny together is to attain to the whole measure of your magnificence as the Christ, that we might grow up into you as our Head. This is our hope because of who you are ***over*** us, prevailing with the same incomparable authority by which you are ruling *over* the entire cosmos. No wonder you said that calling you Lord and obeying you as Lord would place our lives on an unshakeable foundation.

This tribute expresses only a small part of the inexhaustible riches of who you are OVER us and all peoples.

So, Father, here is how we celebrate your Son, our Lord Jesus Christ, in this hour. We exalt him. We exult in him. We do so because of all he is *over* us — now. Therefore, everything we are and have, every breath we breathe, every step we take, every service we render, every prayer we pray, every praise we bring, is possible only by him and him alone. For without him — without all he is *over* us — we are nothing and we can do nothing. More and more, by the revealing work of your Spirit, awaken us to Christ alone — awaken your whole Church to Christ alone—so that increasingly he might become *over* us our all in all.

AMEN!

The Spectacular Supremacy of God's Son Today

Exploring and Experiencing

Who Christ Is BEFORE Us Today

The Old Testament prophet Micah encouraged God's people in their time of defeat and despair to expect the arrival of a king who would go **before** them, to lead them into victory. In Micah 2 we read:

> I will surely gather all of you, O Jacob; I will surely bring together the remnant of Israel. I will bring them together like sheep in a pen, like a flock in its pasture; the place will throng with people . . . The One who breaks open the way will go up before them; they will break

through the gate and go out. Their King will pass through before
them, the LORD at their head (NIV).

In John 10, Jesus fulfills Micah's imagery when he tells his disciples:

The shepherd walks right up to the gate. The gatekeeper opens the
gate to him and the sheep recognize his voice. He calls his own sheep
by name and leads them out. When he gets them all out, he leads
them and they follow because they are familiar with his voice (MSG).

Bottom line: Jesus transforms the entire Christian life into one of holy
restlessness, godly anticipation, and passionate pursuit because (referencing
Micah) he is the long-awaited Supreme Shepherd, on the move, forever
going **before** his people.

Consistent with Jesus' out-front leadership, the very first message on
resurrection day focused on how he was still going **before** his followers.
We read in Matthew 28:

The angel said to the women, "Don't be afraid. I know that you are
looking for Jesus, who was crucified. He is not here! He has risen, just
as he said he would! Come and see the place where he was lying. Go
quickly! Tell his disciples, *'He has risen from the dead. He is going ahead
of you into Galilee. There you will see him'"* (emphasis added).

Then, 40 days later, Jesus proceeded to advance even further by ascending
to the Father, going there *ahead of* his followers, as he entered heaven's
throne room on our behalf.

In Ephesians 4, Paul quotes Psalm 68 to describe Jesus triumphantly
preceding us into glory. Recalling the Exodus story of Israel's massive march
out of Egypt many generations earlier, the psalmist declared:

May God rise up and scatter his enemies . . . God, you led your people
out. You marched . . . The ground shook . . . He has entered his holy
place. When he went up to his place on high, he took many prisoners.

The psalmist's portrayal of Jehovah's royal parade, Paul claims, was fulfilled
by Jesus rising from the dead to ascend on high. Jesus went **before** us taking
with him as captives all who finally rally to him for salvation. So it is we read
in Ephesians 4:

When he went up to his place on high, he took many prisoners . . . The
one who came down is the same as the one who went up. He went
up higher than all the heavens. He did it in order to fill all creation
(emphasis added).

No wonder Scripture describes God's children throughout the coming ages as those who will never, ever cease to "follow the Lamb wherever he goes" (Revelation 14).

Let's look at two pictures — two metaphors — to help set the stage for exploring and experiencing the *"BEFORE us"* dimensions of Jesus' spectacular supremacy.

Christ BEFORE Us: Like the Gateway Arch

Completed in 1965, the glittering, stainless steel Gateway Arch in St. Louis allows visitors who ride to its top to view a memorable panorama. The arch commemorates the role the city once played as "the gateway to the West."

Intentionally shaped to resemble a rainbow, it speaks of an era in American history when the lands beyond the Mississippi beckoned daring pioneers with unprecedented promises of bright, new beginnings and fantastic fortunes. The arch commemorates how St. Louis became the departure point for massive migrations (by foot, horse, wagon, railroad, and boat) in keeping with our nation's sense of "Manifest Destiny," transforming the makeup of a whole continent in the process.

Similarly, Jesus Christ, seated at the Father's right hand, serves as "God's Gateway," the entry point into everything the Father has for his children. Think of him as God's eternal "rainbow of hope" for the nations, the one who encompasses Heaven's "manifest destiny" for all believers.

As we'll see in this chapter, Jesus is our launch point, as he precedes us by his Spirit to usher us into four key *destinations* awaiting every Christian: (1) the future; (2) the heavens; (3) the promises; and (4) the world. All four are accessed through Christ alone, and in no other way.

Unlike the founders and teachers of earth's religions who claim to help devotees *find a way* into the meaning of life, Jesus himself *is* the way into the true meaning of life; he himself *is* the road stretching **before** us to take us into God's grand intentions for us and all creation.

One day he will *perfect* our lives. Until then, he *directs* our lives. He does so by how he *precedes* us and *leads* us as Lord of all. Jesus advances his kingdom in ways that are amazing, wonder-filled, and bursting with surprises. His initiatives may prove to be unexpected, unprecedented, and often inexplicable as they unfold. Thus, our only reasonable recourse is to fall in line behind him and follow him in his triumphal procession as "the King who goes **before** us."

Christ BEFORE Us: Like the Story of Moby Dick

Published in 1851, Herman Melville's epic novel *Moby Dick* recounts the adventures of Ahab, captain of a whaling ship harbored in New England, who is consumed with determination to take revenge on a gigantic white sperm whale known as Moby Dick.

Years earlier an encounter with the ferocious sea mammal cost Ahab his leg. Now, driven by hatred, the whaler is determined to kill the monster at all costs. Eventually, he and his crew spot Moby Dick in open waters for the final showdown. In the ensuing battle, the whaler successfully harpoons the beast, but unfortunately the line of his harpoon becomes wrapped around his boat, so that when Moby Dick makes one last desperate plunge into the ocean's depths, in his wake he takes Ahab and the crew with him to their doom.

The fate of Ahab became inextricably wrapped up with the fate of the whale. Wherever Moby Dick decided to go the captain had to follow; the harpoon line bound them together forever.

So it is with believers and Jesus: When we put our faith in God's Son, it is as if we have "harpooned" ourselves to him. We are so united with Jesus that from that point forward, wherever he goes **before** us we are destined to follow. His journey becomes our journey. Surging ahead of us, by the Holy Spirit he draws us after him. He has us so "wrapped up" in himself that our "fate" is defined exclusively by who he is, what he's doing, how he's blessed, and most importantly, *by where he's headed* — into the future, the heavens, the promises, the world.

Jesus is the *goal* of each of these four destinations. He is also the *means* for us to get there. Because he precedes us, he reaches each destination first. Therefore, our lives — similar to Ahab's fate of being irreversibly entwined with Moby Dick — are forever tied up with where he goes **before** us. With us in tow, Jesus plunges into the depths of the everlasting kingdom purposes of our loving God. This represents another expression of his spectacular supremacy.

Christ Goes BEFORE Us Today:
In All Things He Remains Prior

How he goes **before** us depends entirely on the grand implications of the New Testament teaching about our *union* with Christ. Likening Jesus' relationship with us to an arch or a whale makes sense only because, first of all, by the Father's decree and the Spirit's daily initiative all saints *abide in him.*

Paul uses the phrase *"in Christ"* over 150 times, emphasizing how Christians have been enfolded into Christ — we've been *embedded* in him. Our lives have been "hidden with Christ in God" (Colossians 3).

The entire drama of redemption is not only *about* Christ but also *situated in* Christ. Our *identity* in Christ is the basis for our whole journey with him.

The gospel declares that we are freely invited to enter into union with Christ — into a joyful participation in everything that's true about him as well as into everything that belongs to him. Consequently, in every dimension of discipleship *Jesus must remain prior.* Always he must go **before** us into all the Father holds out to us.

 Snapshots and Starter Thoughts

- **Jesus is prior.**

    All things are yours . . . because you are joined to Christ and belong to him. And Christ is joined to God (1 Corinthians 3).

- **Jesus is prior.**

  > You died. Now your life is hidden with Christ in God. Christ is your life. When he appears again, you also will appear with him in heaven's glory (Colossians 3).

- **Jesus is prior**. In Christ we are fully received by the Father. Therefore, all of the inexhaustible riches in Christ (Ephesians 3) have now become ours *unconditionally* because they are ours *positionally* in him.

- **Jesus is prior.** In ourselves we do not possess *anything*. But we do possess Christ, or better yet, we are possessed by him. So we belong to him to whom all things belong. Therefore, for all eternity we can expect to enjoy God's indescribable riches in Christ Jesus, entering into them because already we have entered into *him*.

- **Jesus is prior**. Even so, from the hour of our salvation, the Father has treated each of us *as if* Christ were us and we were Christ. That's why the Father longs to lavish on us every spiritual blessing already poured out on his Son (Ephesians 1).

- **Jesus is prior.** For us to be fruitful, the Father must first graft us into Christ as our Vine so that we become joined to him as we remain in him drawing our life from him (John 15).

- **Jesus is prior.** Our "clothes" already have been laid out for us as we enter each day. We "put on Christ" as our singular identity (Romans 13; Ephesians 6).

- **Jesus is prior.** Therefore, even now we have no life except in Christ alone (Philippians 1).

- **Jesus is prior.** We follow him into his victory. Christ died to sin; now we do too — in him. Christ rose again; now we walk in newness of life — in him. Christ ascended; now, in him, we share in the saving impact of his reign (Romans 6; Ephesians 2).

- **Jesus is prior.** In this union, what Christ inherits, we inherit (Romans 8). We are in full possession of this treasure long before we *experience* all of it.

- **Jesus is prior.** Who he is, right now, is what we are to become! In other words, one day when he returns, our "life hidden with Christ in God" will be gloriously manifested for all it truly is (Colossians 3). We will become fully conformed to his image (Romans 8), with resurrection bodies like the one he enjoys already (Philippians 3).

- **Jesus is prior.** Therefore, to all who are in Christ, Scripture promises we are "predestined" (destined ahead of time) to be presented at the throne "holy and blameless before God in love" (Ephesians 1).

- **Jesus is prior.** Dwelling in him, we have been put on end times' "resurrection ground" because already death has been "swallowed up" in his victory (1 Corinthians 15). I am *justified* before God because in union with his Son I may walk *"just as if I'd"* already been raised from the dead.

- **Jesus is prior.** We should act as if the Consummation is upon us because in Christ it really is! It may not be *chronologically* near, but it is always *Christologically* near. The soon-to-be renovated universe, under Christ's lordship, initially makes itself known wherever new believers become "new creations" in Christ Jesus. In fact, one of Jesus' biblical titles, Son of Man, serves to honor him as the preview of what we all will be like when the Father finally finishes conforming us — body and soul — to the image of Christ.

- **Jesus is prior.** We not only anticipate eternal life after death, but in him, at this very moment, we are nourished with that same eternal life *before* death; right now in him we inhabit eternity as he shares his glorified life with us. The essentials of all that's promised to us in Christ at the *close* of the age, God has made ours in Christ now in the *middle* of the age.

- **Jesus is prior.** We have been sealed in him by the Holy Spirit, marked and kept for all that is yet to come. The Spirit guarantees that nothing of the Father's designs and desires for us in Christ will be missing when it is all said and done.

- **Jesus is prior.** Forever, our existence will be defined by how we flourish in our union with him as the Sovereign of the universe. He will never cease going ***before*** us to take us further and further into all the Father desires for us for all time to come.

- **Jesus is prior.** This is why our union with him creates in us a sense of *restlessness*, an expectant way of looking at life, as we anticipate all that lies ahead of us when his reign reaches its culmination.

  > I do not consider myself to have "arrived", spiritually, nor do I consider myself already perfect. But I keep going on, *grasping ever more firmly that purpose for which Christ grasped me* . . . All of us who are spiritually adult should set ourselves this sort of ambition (Philippians 3, PHILLIPS, emphasis added).

- **Jesus is prior.** As a popular 19th-century hymn put it: "Blessed assurance, Jesus is mine. Oh, what a foretaste of glory divine."

As Jesus Goes BEFORE Us Today: Where Is He Headed?

Like the pace car that leads the way in the opening lap of a NASCAR competition, the Lord Jesus Christ sets the pace for his people. He surges out ahead of his Church in four crucial directions, all at the same time:

He goes before us *into the FUTURE.*

He goes before us *into the HEAVENS.*

He goes before us *into the PROMISES.*

He goes before us *into the WORLD.*

We should have no fears as he advances and we follow. Wherever he goes before us we can safely follow — *onward* (into the future), *upward* (into the heavens), *inward* (into the promises), and *outward* (into the world). Untold blessings await those who follow him every mile of the way because:

He goes before us **onward** into the FUTURE

to bring it back to us.

He goes before us **upward** into the HEAVENS

to bring us into it.

He goes before us **inward** into the PROMISES

to make them ours too.

He goes before us **outward** into the WORLD

to open the way for us to serve.

Let's examine each of these directions, one at a time.

Christ Goes BEFORE Us Today:
Onward Into the Future to Bring It Back to Us

A Nobel Prize winner in 1921, and regarded by many as "the father of modern physics," Albert Einstein is best known for his equation $E=mc^2$.

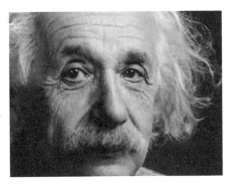

This "general theory of relativity" redefined our understanding of time and space, and even the very structure of the universe. Space and time are relative and flexible rather than absolute concepts. Space and time bend, wave, curve.

The noted scientist concluded that events that seem to be simultaneous may not be. It all depends on the observer's frame of reference. For example, he proved that time passes slightly faster for a hiker at the top of a mountain compared to its speed for those standing at the base. Conceivably, then, someone traveling at the speed of light could find himself in a totally different point of history than another person standing still — years apart, in fact.

The point: Even based on the limited discoveries of Einstein and quantum physicists, it is not a stretch for us to speak of our Lord Jesus going *before* us into the future in order to bring splendid aspects of that future back to us.

Think of it this way: *Geographically*-speaking we know Jesus' reign can be fully but simultaneously present in two cities or two lives on opposite sides of the globe. Even so, *chronologically*-speaking his reign can be fully engaged now and later — in the present and in the future — simultaneously.

It should come as no surprise, therefore, to say that on our behalf he has gone ahead of us into God's future in order to bring vital facets of it — preliminary measures of the fullness of the life that await us — back to us, for us to enjoy *here and now*.

📷 *Snapshots and Starter Thoughts*

- **Who holds the future? Jesus claims *he* does.** He says:

  > I am Alpha and Omega, First and Last, Beginning and End (Revelation 22).

  Not only is he honored as the One who "is and was" but also as the One "who is to come" (Revelation 1). Our Savior has reached the grand climax of history ahead of us. Even now, the future can be seen in him with dramatic specificity.

- **By his resurrection and ascension God's Son precedes us into the future of the universe, thus becoming humankind's one and only hope.**

  > In his great mercy he has given us a new birth and *a hope that is alive.* It is alive because Jesus Christ rose from the dead. He has given us new birth so that we might share in what belongs to him (1 Peter 1, emphasis added).

- **Creation's future will be defined and decided not, first of all, through apocalyptic interventions but through a *Person*.** Not only is Christ leading us to the end, he is waiting for us at the end because he himself *is* the "End." Not only does he call his disciples to follow him to the end, but he also brings back to us foretastes of the end as he reigns among us right now the way he will rule among us then.

- **Christ fulfills in himself our grandest expectations about what eternity holds for us.** All of God's promises are defined by him and consummated in him. Therefore, today those in union with him already are enjoying delights of the life designed eventually to saturate the new heavens and earth. He's been there **before** us. Therefore, he is able to bring his indestructible life back to us, in the present, to share its blessings with us, doing so not superficially but substantively.

- **As the "*firstborn* from the dead" (Colossians 1, emphasis added), he's the vanguard of the day of resurrection.** It has already arrived in him. Furthermore, being designated the *firstborn* means he has become the *source* of and the solitary *heir* of everything and everyone that comes forth from the dead, who thereby gain a share in his death-defying life. Simply put: All that is *alive* in him *belongs* to him, both now and later.

- **Similarly, the ascended Jesus presents himself before the eyes of the universe as the *firstfruits* of the greater harvest yet to come (1 Corinthians 15).** In a profound sense, our own death has already been swallowed up in victory. It happened when the long-anticipated, end-times day of resurrection broke in upon our fallen world that first Easter Sunday. Now, in his continuing incarnation, in his glorified humanity, Jesus is" Exhibit A" of what all of his followers shall become when we are glorified with him in the hour of his radiant reappearing.

- **As the Son of Man, the Son of God portrays for us the destination of God's people *eschatologically*.** In him, as the Son of Man, we see how humankind one day will be reconstituted — humanity as the Creator intended all along. Who Jesus is right now is what the redeemed one day will become when we are fully conformed to his image.

  > God planned that those he had chosen would become like his Son. In that way, Christ will be the first and most honored among many brothers (Romans 8).

- **Because Christ has gone ahead of us into the Consummation, we can look at him and say with the reformer John Calvin:**

  > Although I am weak, there is Jesus — powerful enough to make me stand straight. Although I am feeble, there is Jesus — already living in immortal glory and what he has right now will be given to me, and I will partake of all his benefits.

- **He has gone *before* us into the future to prepare for all saints our dwelling place in his approaching kingdom.** Compare two statements he made in the upper room:

  > There are many rooms in my Father's house . . . I am going there to prepare a place for you. If I go and do that, I will come back. And I will take you to be with me. Then you will also be where I am (John 14).

  Then, a few minutes later he prayed:

  > So now, Father, give glory to me in heaven where your throne . . . Father, I want those you have given me to be with me where I am. I want them to see my glory, the glory you have given me (John 17).

- **Primarily, it is through the Holy Spirit that Jesus brings the future to us.** He promised in the upper room:

  > The Spirit will not speak on his own but will tell you what he has

heard. *He will tell you about the future.* He will bring me glory by telling you whatever he receives from me (John 16, NLT, emphasis added).

Although we may not experience the *quantity* of the future blessings of the Consummation, Christ by the Holy Spirit pours into us the *quality* of the blessings of our coming life with him.

- **Specifically, we have been sealed in Christ by the Holy Spirit as a down payment on all that is waiting for us from our Lord in the coming ages (Ephesians 1).** The Spirit's presence among us as God's people guarantees to us the total fulfillment of the future toward which Christ currently is leading us (2 Corinthians 1).

- **His Spirit abiding within us is, in fact, the very "presence of the future" we will one day share under Christ's reign.** Already through the Spirit's activity among us, we have been allowed to "taste of the powers of the age to come" (Hebrews 6).

- **Now, as we follow Jesus, we are invited to present ourselves to God *as if* we were already raised from the dead, so as to walk in the newness of his risen life.**

  We were therefore buried with him through baptism into death in order that, just as Christ was raised from the dead through the glory of the Father, we too may live a new life (Romans 6, NIV).

- **Outside of Christ, we once were "dead men walking." In union with Christ who has gone *before* us into eternity, today we have become risen men and women reigning.**

  For if, by the trespass of the one man, death reigned through that one man, how much more will those who receive God's abundant provision of grace and of the gift of righteousness reign in life through the one man, Jesus Christ (Romans 5, NIV).

- **Jesus puts us on resurrection ground so that we may present ourselves to the Father as those whom he regards as having passed from death into life through our Savior (Romans 6; John 5).** Participating by faith in Jesus' end-times resurrection, we are treated by God *as if* we currently were standing *on the other side of* judgment day.

- **We have been forged so thoroughly to a destiny inseparable from the destiny of God's Son that we are reckoned by the Father as if we've**

already been *glorified*. He receives us and treasures us as if we are living with Christ at the end in the universal displays of his kingdom. Note how all these verbs are put in the past tense:

> And those he predestined, he also called; those he called, he also justified; those he justified, *he also glorified* (Romans 8, NIV, emphasis added).

- **Therefore, abiding in Jesus we too should follow him daily *as if* the Consummation had arrived because in a very real sense, through our union with the One who has gone *before* us into the future, *it has!***

> We are receiving a kingdom that can't be shaken. So let us be thankful. Then we can worship God in a way that pleases him. We will worship him with deep respect and wonder (Hebrews 12, NIV).

- **In Christ we should live today *as if* already we had stepped into the Holy City that someday soon, at the end, will descend out of heaven (Revelation 21-22).**

> You've come to Mount Zion, the city where the living God resides. The invisible Jerusalem is populated by throngs of festive angels and Christian citizens. It is the city where God is Judge, with judgments that make us just. You've come to Jesus, who presents us with a new covenant, a fresh charter from God. He is the Mediator of this covenant (Hebrews 12, MSG).

- **Around the globe, united to Christ, believers are abiding daily in the coming age through abiding daily in him.** He is for us, here and now, the substance and source of the new creation that one day soon will engulf all things, especially saints from all the ages.

- **So, as we said previously, we might say that even if the end is not yet *chronologically* near, it is always *Christologically* near.** It resides in him, while at the same time he resides among us. What a transaction that is! In Christ the future remains forever "at hand." It is always impending, always imminent because at every moment "the Judge is standing at the door" (James 5).

- **Therefore, we should live in continual anticipation of "*approximations*" of the Consummation.** We should expect to experience such foretastes in very practical ways as Christ brings the future back to us to directly unleash among us preliminary installments of its promises. Specifically, Jesus brings us experiences of the future right now by how he expresses his supremacy *within* us, and *through* us, and *upon* us right now (see the next three chapters which spell out these three manifestations).

pause | think | pray

The Wrap

A homeless army veteran from the Iraq War was seen sitting on a sidewalk outside of Madison Square Garden one cold evening, holding a sign that simply said: *"I have no hope."* Many in our churches might be tempted to replicate his sign if they were to be totally honest about how they feel day to day about their own tough circumstances. Many of us need to discover afresh our hope because Christ has gone **before** us into the future — in order to bring it back to us, to unleash its blessings among us, and in the process to transform us — right now!

The *riches* of the gospel (as Paul terms it) is simply this:

> *Christ is in you! Yes, Christ is in you bringing with him the hope of all the*
> *glorious things to come.* So, naturally, we proclaim Christ! We warn
> everyone we meet, and we teach everyone we can, all that we know
> about him, so that, if possible, we may bring every man up to his full
> maturity in Christ. This is what I am working at all the time, with all
> the strength that God gives me (Colossians 1, PHILLIPS, emphasis
> added).

In contrast to that abandoned vet's experience of hopelessness, another Iraq
War soldier suffering disabilities from the impact of a terrorist's IED, found
out recently there can be extraordinary liberation in Christ that comes with
power straight from the future. Even though permanently confined to a
wheelchair, he testified to his friends: *"I'm beginning to feel like Christ is*
resurrecting me."

In other words, he sensed God's Son infusing him with a substantial
sampling of the future day of resurrection — which is what Romans 8
teaches all believers to expect.

> But your spirit is alive because you have been made right with God.
> The Spirit of the One who raised Jesus from the dead is living in you.
> So the God who raised Christ from the dead will also give life to your
> bodies, which are going to die. He will do this by the power of his
> Spirit, who lives in you (Romans 8, NIV).

Or as the *New Living Translation* puts the passage:

> And Christ lives within you, so even though your body will die
> because of sin, the Spirit gives you life because you have been made
> right with God. The Spirit of God, who raised Jesus from the dead,
> lives in you. And just as God raised Christ Jesus from the dead, he will
> give life to your mortal bodies by this same Spirit living within you
> (Romans 8).

Christ Goes BEFORE Us Today:
Upward Into the Heavens to Bring Us Into It

On July 20, 1969, leading the Apollo 11 mission, Neil Armstrong became the first person to stand on the moon. Millions around the globe watched as he touched the lunar surface, stating on behalf of the entire human race: "One small step for [a] man, one giant leap for mankind."

Apollo 11's official mission patch, which is sewn onto flight suits and other NASA gear used in the mission, portrayed an eagle descending toward the lunar surface with an olive branch, a symbol of peace (the lunar module that landed on the moon was named "Eagle"). In the first draft, the eagle held the olive branch in its beak, but at the end, to avoid any appearance of a warlike image, the branch was placed in its talons. The message conveyed was that Armstrong's mission was one of peace (the landing spot on the moon was named "Sea of Tranquility"), commissioned to bring the nations together around something larger than any of us, and for the sake of all of us.

The Apollo 11 mission provides us a useful metaphor of the second dimension of who Christ is **before** us. He is the One who has entered the heavens to bring us there with him — not later but now. The Son of Man took a "step" that makes it possible for mankind to make the "giant leap" out of sin's domain of doom into the presence of the Father's holy glory because he has gone there ahead of us to prepare the way and make us welcomed.

Jesus' blood shed on the cross effectively reconciles us back to God, making peace where once there was enmity, so that heaven itself now has become for all believers a cosmic "Sea of Tranquility" forever. "Before the Throne it was like a clear crystal sea" (Revelation 4, MSG).

Here's a secret not revealed until years later: As a devout Presbyterian, Buzz Aldrin, the other astronaut in this historic lunar landing, privately celebrated communion on the moon (his chalice is now on display in his local church)—a further reminder of Jesus taking the victory he secured for us on the cross with him as he went **before** us into the heavens.

 Snapshots and Starter Thoughts

- **"Soar we now where Christ has led, following our exalted head,"** wrote Charles Wesley in his popular Easter hymn. He who descended *for* us is the one who now has ascended *with* us.

- **From the moment Jesus entered into the throne room it became the Church's prime focus as well.** Wherever Christ has preceded us we may safely go, even into the presence of the eternal, holy, triune God of the universe.

- **From his place of supremacy Jesus gives us ready access into heaven — unhindered and unlimited — forever.** He gives us permission to enter; he makes our "introductions" for us. Therefore, daily we may *act as if* we have physically entered into the throne room of eternity, invited to walk up freely into direct engagement with the Father the same way the Son is engaged with the Father already.

  > There is One who speaks to the Father in our defense, Jesus Christ, the Righteous One (1 John 2).

- **The Ascension makes the person of the living Lord Jesus our constant, cordial meeting place with our Creator**.

  > Who dares accuse us whom God has chosen for his own? No one — for God himself has given us right standing with himself. Who then will condemn us? No one — for Christ Jesus died for us and was raised to life for us, and he is sitting in the place of honor at God's right hand, pleading for us. Can anything ever separate us from Christ's love? (Romans 8, NLT).

- **We might say our ascended Lord *hosts* us in the Father's presence.**

  > Immense in mercy and with an incredible love, he embraced us. He took our sin-dead lives and made us alive in Christ. He did all this on his own, with no help from us! Then he picked us up and set us down in highest heaven in company with Jesus, our Messiah. Now God has us where he wants us, with all the time in this world and the next to shower grace and kindness upon us in Christ Jesus (Ephesians 2, MSG).

- **He is our "friend in court" because his blood has secured for us a "not guilty" verdict before the Judge of all.**

  > But now in Christ Jesus you who once were far away have been brought near by the blood of Christ . . . He came and preached peace to you who were far away and peace to those who were near. For through him we both have access to the Father by one Spirit. Consequently, you are no longer foreigners and strangers, but fellow citizens with God's people and also members of his household . . . Christ Jesus himself as the chief cornerstone (Ephesians 2, NIV).

- **However, he reigns as a King who is also a Priest, simultaneously.** His person and his priesthood are forever inseparable. Only because he serves in *both* roles are we delivered from spiritual bankruptcy so as to freely pursue all that the heavens hold for those who belong to him.

- **Christ substituted himself for us, living our life for us, in place of us, and then took all of that into heaven ahead of us so we could freely follow.** He did so by incarnation, by a perfect life, by crucifixion, by resurrection, and by a victorious ascension. Then he took his finished work with him, ahead of us, for us, into the Father's house and laid it down, on our behalf, *before* the Father's throne. As our King-Priest he comes before God on our behalf and for our sakes so that we can come *before* the Father offering our passionate prayers of support on behalf of his kingdom agenda and for the sake of his glorious name.

- **We do not go *from* Jesus to the Father. Rather we go *in* Jesus and *with* Jesus to the Father**. In principle, when he ascended and entered the heavens, he took us with him. He is sitting at the right hand of the Father. He does not have to call from afar; he merely needs to "whisper" in the Father's ear (as it were) on our behalf and heaven's treasury is opened to us.

- **By his very presence at God's right hand, Jesus guarantees answers for every prayer we will ever make for the sake of his fame and reign, even before we speak**. Our prayers are powerful and effective, therefore, to the degree that they are shaped by and compatible with his prior agenda and his prior appeals before the Father's face.

  > I will do whatever you ask in my name that the Son may bring glory to the Father (John 14, NIV).

- **Because Jesus has gone *before* us into the heavens, we are now invited into the "Trinity unity" that existed before anything was made.** We are enfolded into the inner life of the triune God because our Redeemer has made a way for us, going ***before*** us. The extraordinary, intimate relationship the Son enjoys with the Father is now opened to us and shared with us. It was his first; now he makes it ours as well. In fact, it is as if when we're speaking to God, Jesus' tongue becomes our tongue; as we behold God's glory, Jesus' eyes become our eyes. It is by the lifting up of his hands that we are lifted to the Father as living sacrifices for him.

- **In Christ we have gained far more than what was lost when Adam rebelled.** Before sin entered the world, Adam walked with God in the cool of the day in a well-defined garden. However, forgiven and reborn in Christ, today we walk into the very heavens to dwell with God in the blaze of his glory. This is a fellowship that has no end and no limits because it is the fellowship that first belonged to the Son, which he now shares with all who are alive in him.

- **Jesus daily demonstrates God's "prevenient grace" toward us.** "Prevenient" describes something that has "preceded" others or "prepared" the way for them. In the same sense, from beginning to end our Savior's saving work is *prevenient*. He precedes us into the heavens to prepare the way for us to enter freely into incomparable riches held out to us in the Father's hands.

Christ BEFORE Us — in the Book of Hebrews

Hebrews, more than any other book of Scripture, abounds with insights on the "BEFORE us" dimensions of Christ's supremacy. It testifies throughout to ways Christ goes ahead of us to open the heavens to us.

- **Hebrews 3: Like an apostle, Jesus pioneers the way for us into the heavens, and now like a high priest he is waiting there to greet us.**

    Therefore, holy brothers and sisters, who share in the heavenly calling, fix your thoughts on Jesus, whom we acknowledge as our apostle and high priest (Hebrews 3, NIV).

- **Hebrews 6: As our *forerunner* into God's presence, Jesus anchors our welcome there.**

    We have this hope as an anchor for the soul, firm and secure. It enters the inner sanctuary behind the curtain, where our forerunner, Jesus, has entered on our behalf. He has become a high priest forever, in the order of Melchizedek (Hebrews 6, NIV).

- **Hebrews 7: Jesus lives to always plead our case in heaven's courtroom so we can abide there without fear.**

    But because Jesus lives forever, he has a permanent priesthood. Therefore he is able to save completely those who come to God through him, because he always lives to intercede for them. Such a high priest truly meets our need – one who is holy, blameless, pure, set apart from sinners, exalted above the heavens (Hebrews 7, NIV).

- **Hebrews 9: Jesus' sacrifice, taken into the Holy Place, gives us free and permanent access there.**

But when Christ came as high priest of the good things that are now already here, he went through the greater and more perfect tabernacle that is not made with human hands, that is to say, is not a part of this creation . . . he entered the Most Holy Place once for all by his own blood, thus obtaining eternal redemption . . . now to appear for us in God's presence . . . he has appeared once for all at the culmination of the ages to do away with sin by the sacrifice of himself (Hebrews 9, NIV).

- **Hebrews 4: As our ascended and reigning High Priest, Jesus invites us to come boldly to join him before God's throne.**

  Therefore, since we have a great high priest who has ascended into heaven, Jesus the Son of God, let us hold firmly to the faith we profess. For we do not have a high priest who is unable to empathize with our weaknesses, but we have one who has been tempted in every way, just as we are – yet he did not sin. Let us then approach God's throne of grace with confidence, so that we may receive mercy and find grace to help us in our time of need (Hebrews 4, NIV).

- **Hebrews 10: Our great High Priest became a way for us into the heavens when there was no way — when we had no hope of finding a way.**

  Therefore, brothers and sisters, since we have confidence to enter the Most Holy Place by the blood of Jesus, by a new and living way opened for us through the curtain, that is, his body, and since we have a great priest over the house of God, let us draw near to God with a sincere heart and with the full assurance that faith brings, having our hearts sprinkled to cleanse us from a guilty conscience and having our bodies washed with pure water. Let us hold unswervingly to the hope we profess, for he who promised is faithful (Hebrews 10, NIV).

Selah

pause | think | pray

The Wrap

The supremacy of Christ serves as our "bridge" to the Father. That's what the Bible means by describing his reign, in part, as *"mediatorial"* in its effects.

He's like the Brooklyn Bridge that provides travelers access into "the Big

Apple" with all the excitements and sights of Times Square. We could say the bridge *"mediates"* a way for us.

Jesus is *our* bridge who "mediates" — who crosses over — the abyss created by sin that separates humankind from God. Furthermore, he is also the *highway on the bridge* by which sinners may access all that God has for us in Christ. Paul declares:

> God our Savior . . . wants all people to be saved and to come to a knowledge of the truth. For there is one God and one mediator between God and mankind, the man Christ Jesus, who gave himself as a ransom for all people (1 Timothy 2, NIV).

As our bridge, Jesus transfers us from the shame of darkness into the reign of light (Colossians 1); he lifts us up to the heavens to share every blessing he has secured. He *dislocates us* from the fallen race of Adam with its tyranny of sin and death, and *relocates us* to share in his triumphs of righteousness and life (Romans 5).

As salvation's bridge, Jesus precedes us into the Holy Father's presence to present us there without fear of condemnation and without limits on the outpouring of the fullness of God's grace. Because he intercedes for us by going **before** us, we can be certain the Father will withhold nothing good from us (Romans 8).

As our bridge, Jesus prepares a "way in the wilderness" (Isaiah 40) so that we can cross over the infinite gulf created by our sin and pursue on the other side eternal treasures filled with the Father's love. All of it belongs to us because the One who has gone **before** us, upward into the heavens, has all authority to invite us to join with him in all the wholeness and holiness that surrounds him.

Christ Goes BEFORE Us Today:
Inward Into the Promises to Make Them Ours Too

Many English literature scholars consider Charles Dickens' *Great Expectations*, though not as long as some of his other novels, to be the height of his literary prowess.

The term "expectations" in 19th-century England referred to one's anticipated inheritance. To have "great expectations" would imply the heirs expected a fairly significant endowment once they came of age.

In the book's title, however, Dickens gave the phrase a double meaning: a promising financial windfall as well as a promising destiny for the main character, Pip.

One of the most dramatic moments in the story occurs when Pip learns that he, though an orphan, has "great expectations" provided by a common criminal named Magwitch, whom Pip tried to rescue from capture years earlier. Deported to Australia for his crimes, Magwitch ended up making a fortune there. He returned to England to repay Pip for his kindness to him those many years ago, determined to see him transformed into a real gentleman. Because of the one who had gone before him, the poor, disillusioned orphan now unexpectedly looked forward to a future filled with "great expectations"—a destiny of unimagined blessings inherited from another who secured it for him years before.

The tale illustrates, in part, what the Lord Jesus Christ has accomplished for us. The world makes many promises that turn out to be fickle, false, and fading. Then, to our utter amazement, from the most unlikely source (from One who was crucified as a common criminal) we are presented with "great expectations" — inexhaustible riches beyond belief, an inheritance that encompasses all of the promises ever made to believers by the triune God, with the entire universe thrown in as well!

Here's how Paul puts it to us:

> You are familiar with the generosity of our Master, Jesus Christ. Rich as he was, he gave it all away for us — in one stroke he became poor and we became rich (2 Corinthians 8, MSG).

Therefore Paul reassures us:

> My God will meet all your needs according to the riches of his glory in Christ Jesus (Philippians 4, NIV).

He adds further:

> The Father has blessed us in the heavenly realms with every spiritual blessing in Christ (Ephesians 1, NIV).

Christ, who has bought and paid for all of God's promises, secured them, first of all, for himself — they are *his alone,* by right and by sacrifice. But now he intends to share them with all of God's people. What a generous Monarch! He endows us with *his* "great expectations"!

 Snapshots and Starter Thoughts

- **All the promises of God's Word to God's people belong to God's Son first of all.** The promises and the "Promise-er" are forged together forever. All of heaven's riches are bound up in our Lord *exclusively* and their ultimate blessings will be culminated in our Lord *conclusively.*

- **The promises were "closed up" into him so that they could be "opened up" unto us with infinite possibilities because he first made them his own.** Only in him do the promises ever become ours. "Christ not only offers us something for nothing. He even offers us *everything* for nothing" (C. S. Lewis).

- **Essentially, Scripture declares God's promises to be *fulfilled in* and *filled full of* his Son.**

For the Son of God, Jesus Christ, who was preached among you by us
... was not "Yes" and "No," but in him it has always been "Yes." For no
matter how many promises God has made, they are "Yes" in Christ.
And so through him the "Amen" is spoken by us to the glory of God
... [He] put his Spirit in our hearts as a deposit, guaranteeing what is
to come (2 Corinthians 1, NIV).

- **There are nearly 7,000 separate promise statements found throughout the Bible (including different ways of announcing similar prospects), and all of them are "Yes" to us *in Christ*.** They *belong* to Jesus to start with. They all are *summed up* in him. They all are *about* him, *embodied* in him, *purchased* by him, *inherited* by him, *enriched* in him, *guaranteed* by him, *fulfilled* in him. Only then does the Father apply them to us — yet even then, this is for the prime purpose of *exalting* Jesus.

- **We have no hope beyond who the *person* of Christ is in his spectacular supremacy.** He gives us access into God's abounding grace, so that we can continually "rejoice in the hope of the glory of God," knowing that in him our hope "will not disappoint us" because God's love for us in Christ is poured into our hearts by the Holy Spirit (Romans 5).

- **Put simply, his *person* and *position* in the universe guarantee to us his promises.** In Christ, the promises have been enhanced, enriched, expanded, and then signed over to those who belong to him.

- **In our Savior, we have become unconditional beneficiaries of the triune God.** Through Jesus we have inherited inexpressible provisions — given by the Father to the Son to be endowed lavishly by the Spirit on all the saints.

- **Our breadth of our "great expectations" in Christ provide additional evidence of his supremacy.** In other words, when the Father's promises are thoroughly implemented in the Son this will make even more obvious and more wonderful — before the Church and the nations — the glorious riches of the reign of Christ.

- **Therefore, we have every reason to be reassured about the prospects of those who rest in Christ.** Life under his scepter may not provide us all the *explanations* we want for what God is up to in our lives, our churches, our nation, our generation. But we have all the *promises* God's people will ever want or need — and that should be enough for now to fill us with confidence and courage in the face of any challenges.

- **Here's what's *new* about the new covenant we celebrate at every Lord's Supper.** As the Father's heir, Jesus has become the guarantee of a *better* covenant with God — a *newly reconstituted* covenant — extending to us far greater promises, according to Hebrews 8.

- **We serve a generous Father who invites us, on the basis of the finished work of his ascended Son, to explore, share in, and benefit from from the "inexhaustible riches in Christ Jesus" (Ephesians 3).** We can be sure, that having given us his Son on the cross, the Father will not withhold any good thing from us, but *with* Christ will freely give us all things (Romans 8).

- **So, we can boldly say that because Christ goes *before* us we have been welcomed into all of heaven's resources.** They are magnificent, undefiled, never fading — laid before us in Christ himself. As a result, he has become our *highest* treasure. Scripture tells us that in him are:

    > . . . hidden all the treasures of wisdom and knowledge (Colossians 2, NIV).

    Even so, in him there is:

    > . . . an inheritance that can never perish, spoil or fade (1 Peter 1, NIV).

    Therefore, with resounding joy we shout:

    > Thanks be to God for his indescribable gift! (2 Corinthians 9, NIV).

- **Furthermore, because Jesus goes *before* us to secure God's promises on behalf of all of God's people, every single believer has received equal rights to all of it.** When an earthly inheritance is distributed, the more heirs there are the less each person receives. Not so with Christ! Every saint participates equally and to the fullest extent in what each promise offers us. Not one single promise is ever diminished for any of us.

- **This is why, in the end, *Christ himself* becomes the final and fullest answer to every *prayer* based on God's promises.** Christ encompasses in his very person everything we long to *receive* from God, as well as everything we long to *become* for God.

- **For example, there's not one of the six requests of "The Lord's Prayer" that does not point us to Christ as the final answer, even if initially**

the Father's response provides only preliminary installments of the promises Christ brings to us. We see:

(1) when Jesus is exalted, the Father's name is exalted

(2) when Jesus reigns, God's kingdom comes

(3) by Jesus' work of redemption and justice, God's eternal purposes are accomplished on earth

(4) Jesus is the source that supplies all the daily needs of his people

(5) Jesus keeps his people bound together in a circle of love and forgiveness

(6) Jesus rescues us to lead us in triumph over all the schemes of the evil one

- **Bottom line, Christ possesses nothing that he does not fully apply to our benefit right now.** As Jesus said:

> And I confer [present tense] on you a kingdom, just as my Father conferred one on me. (Luke 22, NIV).

- **Thus, the scope of this hope should fill us with boundless expectations as long and high and deep and wide as our vision of Christ supreme.** The reality of his lordship over all things in heaven and earth should "explode" with Christ-focused awakenings that renew our churches, our communities, our nation, and beyond with joyful, unshakable confidence about the future and all the good things Christ's kingdom is bringing upon us.

- **Therefore, far more than Abraham who saw Jesus only "at a distance" (John 8), we who know the One who is the final heir of the promises made to Abraham (Galatians 3) should never waver in unbelief.** Abraham is called the "father of all who believe" (Romans 4). How much more should we who have become "fellow heirs with Christ" (Romans 8) replicate Abraham's unwavering certainty of the utter dependability of the Father's promises. Even when fulfillments are delayed, we, like Abraham, should not grow weary in faith, but increase our celebration over all that is to come, "being convinced that he who has promised is able also to perform it" (Romans 4). The whole Church is called to "hold unswervingly" to our hope in Christ, especially as we "see the Day approaching" when the promises are fulfilled dynamically, even at a cosmic level (Hebrews 10, NIV).

- **Christ will continue to go *before* us into the promises throughout eternity as well.**

> God has raised us up with Christ and seated us with Him in the heavenly realms in Christ Jesus, in order that in the coming ages he might show the incomparable riches of his grace, expressed in his kindness to us in Christ Jesus (Ephesians 2, NIV).

Both now and in the Consummation, we can say:

> The Lamb at the center of the throne will be their shepherd . . . He will lead them to springs of living water (Revelation 7, NIV).

- **Because he is in possession of all of God's promises, Christ holds out to us the prospect of plunging ever deeper into God's great love for us, day after day.** Therefore we should pray like Paul:

> And I pray that you, being rooted and established in love, may have power, together with all the Lord's holy people, to grasp how wide and long and high and deep is the love of Christ (Ephesians 3, NIV).

- **What's so amazing is that with Jesus every promise that is fulfilled actually gives birth to even greater reasons to hope!** Every promise that becomes reality encourages us to seek the Father for even more of what he offers us in his Son because the inheritance he has shared with us is never redundant or stagnant, but always bubbling with new beginnings — creative, inventive, full of adventure, and taking us from "glory to glory" (2 Corinthians 3).

> Out of His fullness [the superabundance of His grace and truth] we have all received, grace upon grace [spiritual blessing upon spiritual blessing, favor upon favor, and gift heaped upon gift] (John 1, AMP).

Selah

pause | think | pray

The Wrap

Imagine two hardy ice fishermen, sitting side by side on up-turned buckets in the middle of a frozen lake in Wisconsin, in the clutches of a frigid January afternoon. Both have carved holes in the ice. Both hold poles with their fishing lines dropping through the holes into the water. But look closer. One has carved a hole the size of a bass. The other has spent over an hour sawing out an opening the size of a *whale* (which means, of course, he's fishing for something that makes no sense for Wisconsin!).

Clearly, the first sportsman is thinking only of his next meal; he's hoping to catch something big enough to provide the main course that evening. On the other hand, his companion is focused on catching something big enough to feed himself, and his family and friends, for the next 60 days. What a faith he displays as he fishes! He believes there's something bigger to be caught, somewhere swimming under the icy lake, just waiting for him to come and get it.

Even so, as we follow Jesus, should we not approach each day with a similar perspective? If we believe Christ is supreme, then there's no doubt he has every right and every capacity to go **before** us, inward into God's promises, to secure them and make them his own in order to turn around and share them with us — which is precisely what he has done!

Combined, God's promises are equally "whale-sized"! They are as unbounded in their outcomes as is the Savior himself through whom they have become ours. Ephesians says it well:

> . . . take in with all followers of Jesus the extravagant dimensions of Christ's love. Reach out and experience the breadth! Test its length! Plumb the depths! Rise to the heights! Live full lives, full in the fullness of God. God can do anything, you know — far more than you could ever imagine or guess or request in your wildest dreams! (MSG).

Christ Goes BEFORE Us Today:
Outward Into the World to Open the Way for Us to Serve

For all of us today, King Jesus remains out in front of us, calling us, drawing us, leading us *forward* — even more accurately, leading us *outward,* in all directions — to follow him to the ends of the earth. This fourth iBEFORE us" nitiative "is pictured by a famous statue that dominates the skyline in Madison, Wisconsin.

It doesn't take long for visitors to discover the golden lady atop the dome of the legislative complex in the center of the state's capital city.

There in the heart of the town she stands, elevated so everyone can see her several blocks away, clothed in brilliant gold leaf. The sculpture is actually named "Wisconsin" but is affectionately called "Miss Forward" by many because her right arm is outstretched to symbolize Wisconsin's state motto, which is just one word: "*Forward!*"

It's as if every sunrise she rises again in the midst of the daily bustle below, persistently urging her "subjects" to keep moving *forward* on all fronts — educationally, politically, economically, commercially, socially, culturally.

Similarly, the Head of the Church calls those who dwell under his scepter to think *forward* — to choose to move forward with him as we move *outward* with him — advancing into the world with him to spread his good news and fulfill his kingdom's agenda, especially among the nearly three billion people who have no knowledge of Jesus, and no one like them, near them, to tell them (unless we go to them).

As we've seen so far, wherever Jesus goes **before** us we can safely follow — *onward* (into the future), *upward* (into the heavens), *inward* (into the promises), and now, *outward* (into the world).

Jesus is not only the ultimate *revelation* of God, but because of that he is also the ultimate *revolution* of God. He boldly takes us, his people, into the world to serve him in opportunities that we might not have imagined, often among people quite different from ourselves, and in places where we would have never dared to tread on our own — except for the fact that Jesus already has gone **before** us to open a way for us to serve.

 Snapshots and Starter Thoughts

- **Even in the passage about the Good Shepherd, Jesus indicates clearly that he intends to lead his flock out of familiar pens into wide-open spaces in search of even more sheep to hear his voice and join his fold**. We read in John 10:

  > The shepherd walks right up to the gate . . . He calls his own sheep by name and leads them out . . . they follow because they are familiar with his voice . . . You need to know that I have other sheep in addition to those in this pen. I need to gather and bring them, too. They'll also recognize my voice. Then it will be one flock, one Shepherd (MSG).

- **Jesus plants and tends "crops" and then places workers to harvest them.** According to Matthew 9, the fields are more ready to be harvested than we had imagined. The only thing lacking is enough laborers to be "thrown out" (the literal meaning of the Greek word is even more explosive in its implications) — thrust into the midst of flourishing fields made ready by the One who reigns as Lord over the harvest and prepares the way to send forth the laborers.

- **The second of two parables about a sower (Matthew 13) demonstrates how Jesus makes a way for us to serve.** In the second account, he tells us the "field is the world," the sower "is the Son of Man," and the seeds are "the children of the Kingdom." Observe: The sower flings out his followers into any part of the world he chooses to bring forth fruit. Wherever he sends them, he has prepared the soil. Paul reinforces this truth in Ephesians 2:10 (emphasis added):

> We are God's creation. He created us to belong to Christ Jesus. Now we can do good works. *Long ago God prepared these works for us to do.*

- **Having all authority in heaven and on earth, Jesus promised his newly commissioned disciples that wherever they found themselves as they traversed the nations, he would be with them (Matthew 28).** There is no place his ambassadors go where he does not precede them, set the stage for their arrival, prepare to work through them when they get there, and remain to sustain the impact of his saving reign long after they move on to do it again somewhere else.

- **As a contemporary maxim puts it, "Christ meets us where he sends us."** Every morning when we climb out of bed and prepare to engage with the world again — whether on the job, at school, in the neighborhood, or flying to another country to plant new churches — we rise to serve the One who not only sends us out but who goes ahead of us, is at work before we arrive, waits to greet us when we get there, and then involves us in what he has already initiated in places and people.

- **Our mission to earth's unreached is not a fool's errand, because wherever we go Christ has already gone *before* of us to open the way for us to serve**. Paul reminded Athenian philosophers that in God's presence all of humanity "lives, and moves, and has their being." Therefore, it follows that all people (whether they know it or not at this moment) live and move and have their being under the reign of God's Son — before we ever reach them to tell them of his saving work. Wherever we go, therefore, our job is to help people see, believe, and enter into a kingdom that is already bearing down on top of them.

- **Jesus is the *door opener* for every mission into which he calls his people.** To the church in Philadelphia he declared:

> What he opens no one can shut, and what he shuts no one can open . . . I have placed before you an open door that no one can shut (Revelation 3, NIV).

Since the Father has given his Son the keys to death and Hades (Revelation 1) we can be sure he holds all other keys to unlock every door into cities and nations through which his people may enter to proclaim his name, spread his fame, and increase his gain.

- **Frequently Paul experienced Jesus opening doors *before* him; it became for him a major prayer focus.**

> I hope to spend some time with you, if the Lord permits. But . . . a great door for effective work has opened to me, and there are many who oppose me (2 Corinthians 16, NIV).

> Pray for us that God may open a door for our message so that we may proclaim the mystery of Christ (Colossians 4, NIV).

- **Christ went ahead of Peter and prepared the way for his initial outreach to Gentiles.** We read in Acts 10 that Jesus first prepared the heart of a Roman centurion, Cornelius, so that he was ready to take the gospel seriously. Next, Jesus visited Peter through a vivid vision, which was repeated three times, urging him each time to eat ceremonially unclean animals. This reassured the apostle that going into Gentile territory was thoroughly proper *because* his Lord had gone **before** him to open the way for him to reach them. The results were so amazing that when the church leaders in Jerusalem demanded a full report, Peter responded like this:

> So I ask you: "If God gave the same exact gift to them as to us when we believed in the Master Jesus Christ, how could I object to God?" Hearing it all laid out like that, they quieted down. And then, as it sank in, they started praising God. "It's really happened! God has broken through to the other nations, opened them up to Life" (MSG).

- **Before we're even aware that people are ready to hear and believe the gospel, Christ has gone *before* of us to make them ready; he knows exactly where they are and how we can best reach them.** For example, in Corinth Paul initially found so much resistance that he was ready to move on to the next city. But Jesus opened Paul's eyes to how he had gone **before** him to make Corinth ready for the gospel. We read:

> One night the Lord spoke to Paul in a vision. "Don't be afraid," he said. "Keep on speaking. Don't be silent. I am with you. *No one will attack you and harm you. I have many people in this city.*" So Paul stayed there for a year and a half. He taught them God's word (Acts 18, emphasis added).

Thus, Paul experienced one of his most effective times of ministry ever in Corinth.

- **Often, New Testament witnesses discovered that people's hearts already had been made ready by the Master before they could get to them to give them an invitation to believe in Jesus.** In Psidian Antioch, for example, after being rejected by the local synagogue for three Sabbaths in a row, Paul was delighted that "outsiders" (who also were the least likely to respond) had been prepared beforehand and put their faith in Christ.

  > When the non-Jewish outsiders heard this, they could hardly believe their good fortune. *All who were marked out for real life put their trust in God* – they honored God's Word by receiving that life. And this Message of salvation spread like wildfire all through the region (Acts 13, MSG, emphasis added).

  God gave Paul a vision of a Macedonian man pleading with them to come there. Immediately they obeyed. In just a short time, Jesus brought them to Lydia in Philippi "whose heart the Lord had opened." She became the first convert in Macedonia — the beginning of a tremendous harvest for Christ's kingdom throughout that entire region!

- **Going *before* us into the world, Jesus not only opens doors but also determines the perfect timing for us to go through those doors to serve him.** For example, a few years after not allowing Paul to enter Asia Minor, finally Jesus brought him back to Ephesus. Now, amazingly, many were ready to hear the message, as miracles flowed from the throne! We read:

  > Each day he talked with people in the lecture hall of Tyrannus. This went on for two years. So all the Jews and Greeks who lived in Asia Minor heard the word of the Lord . . . They held the name of the Lord Jesus in high honor. Many who believed now came and openly admitted the evil they had done. [Those who practiced] evil magic brought their scrolls together. They set them on fire out in the open . . . The word of the Lord spread everywhere. It became more and more powerful (Acts 19).

- **Christ marches ahead of us into the nations, leading us in his victory parade.** Borrowing from the familiar scene of Caesar leading captives taken in battle back to Rome in chains — with Caesar riding at the head of the procession of conquered slaves, and all of the city celebrating the victory — so Paul described King Jesus going ***before*** the apostle and his team in similar fashion, opening the way for their mission for him and marching them into it. He wrote:

> In the Messiah, in Christ, God leads us from place to place in one perpetual victory parade. Through us, he brings knowledge of Christ. Everywhere we go, people breathe in the exquisite fragrance . . . This is a terrific responsibility. Is anyone competent to take it on? No . . . We stand in Christ's presence when we speak; God looks us in the face. We get what we say straight from God and say it as honestly as we can (2 Corinthians 2, MSG, emphasis added).

- **Christ promises to lead his followers to and through the gates of Hades itself in order to build his Church (Matthew 16).** He guarantees that no barriers can constrain or prevent his advance. Sometimes he may lead us through very dark valleys to accomplish a mission, but there is no resistance or sacrifice through which he takes us that he has not penetrated himself already, and from which he has not already emerged victorious. It began when he took on our flesh, absorbed our judgment, broke through the tomb, and ascended to the throne with all authority, not only in heaven but also throughout the nations where he sends us.

pause | think | pray

The Wrap

The pastor of the world's largest church told me he often looks to Matthew 11:12 as one explanation for their growth over the past 60 years from fewer than a hundred people to 800,000 members today. It reads:

> Since the days of John the Baptist, the kingdom of heaven has been advancing with force. And forceful people are taking hold of it (Matthew 11, NIV).

His observation? As his people have increasingly recognized Christ's sovereign, saving initiatives on their streets, in their cities, and among the nations, their eagerness to participate with him has increased. As a result, more and more they have become a "people of force" — laying hold of Jesus and where he is headed, and then entering into what he already is doing.

In other words: Recognize the forceful advance of Christ's kingdom. Hear his call to join him. Watch as he makes a way to serve him. Be inspired to lay hold of the forceful advance of his kingdom, no matter what the cost.

The pastor's perspective on Matthew 11:12 and its connection with the tremendous growth of his megachurch reflects the motto of one of the most famous outreaches in Church history — a paraphrase of Jesus' words in Matthew 11:12: *"Our Lamb has conquered. Let us follow him."* Those two sentences formed the marching orders of one of the greatest missionary endeavors ever. Let's take a moment to rehearse the amazing story behind this historic movement.

The Moravian outreach emerged out of what church historians call the "Moravian Pentecost" in August of 1727. As a result of a powerful work of God's Spirit bringing them into a "Christ Awakening," this band of 200 religious refugees, sheltered on the estate of Count Nikolaus Ludwig Von Zinzendorf (located in modern day Czech Republic), moved out on three fronts. First, they began a 24/7 prayer watch (called "The Lord's Watch") that continued for 100 years! As they prayed, they also spawned revival teams that were thrust out into different parts of Europe. Next came hundreds of missionaries who served Christ among unreached people groups across the earth — often at great personal sacrifice, even martyrdom. This spiritual momentum continued for generations!

Why did they pray and go like this? It was because they were convinced of two things: First, Christ is supreme ("The Lamb has conquered!"). Second, since he is Lord of all and advancing his global cause, they could think of no better response than to say, "Let us follow him." They were eager to get behind the One who was going **before** them to open a way for them to serve, even as they called others ("let *us*") to join them in the mission.

Following Eternity's Pathfinder:
Practical Implications

How should we respond to all of this? How do we work with the "BEFORE us" dimensions of Christ's supremacy as they are manifested right now? What does it means to follow Christ as "Eternity's Pathfinder"?

Hebrews 12 answers us in very simple terms. As those running the race that Jesus has already run, we need only to stay faithful to the pathway he has pioneered. It says:

> Such a large crowd of witnesses is all around us! So we must get rid of everything that slows us down, especially the sin that just won't let go. And we must be determined to run the race that is ahead of us. We must keep our eyes on Jesus, who leads us and makes our faith complete (Hebrews 12, CEV).

This passage suggests three things are required of those who follow the Christ who goes **before** us:

(1) Daily Repentance. We are told here to cast away — renounce — *anything* that would hinder our pursuit of him and all he has pioneered for us.

We are to turn from anything that is not *compatible* with who Christ is and where he is headed **before** us. We must leave behind anything not compatible with the future he brings to us, or the heavens he bring us to, or the promises he shares with us, or the mission into the world he has for us.

Repentance isn't just about what we turn *from*; it is also about what we turn *toward*, or rather *Who* we turn toward — the Christ who goes **before** us.

(2) Abounding Hope. We find ourselves running a race *that has already been won*, with our eyes focused ahead to the Victor who waits for us at the finish line. This encourages us to run with our eyes wide open, with the anticipation that there is so much more — to always be watching and waiting and willing. Christians should be anything but complacent or self-satisfied. We're running to win! In Paul's familiar expression:

> But here is the one thing I do. I forget what is behind me. I push hard toward what is ahead of me. I push myself forward toward the goal to win the prize. God has appointed me to win it. The heavenly prize is Christ Jesus himself (Philippians 3).

With such a great King who leads the way, we can be certain there's always *so much more* he deserves, designs, decrees — so much more, therefore, he *desires* for us. Jesus explodes the boundaries of what we have experienced so far of the future, the heavens, the promises, and the mission. The Church is, after all, a band of *receivers* because we are a society of *seekers*. As Paul puts it in 1 Corinthians 2:

> No eye has seen, no ear has heard, and no mind has imagined what God has prepared for those who love him (NLT).

(3) Anticipatory Discipleship. At the 1984 Olympics in Los Angeles, the world witnessed the marvel of what one might call "antici-patory discipline." It so happened that four years earlier the US had boycotted the Games in Russia in 1980 (for political reasons). Therefore, a  number of American athletes had to spend not four but *eight* years getting themselves in shape for an event (like running, pole vaulting, swimming) that would last only a few minutes! All of this determination and sacrifice was inspired by the vision of what lay ahead — a gold medal that might become theirs.

Like those Olympians, training for years in anticipation of an event they intended to win — which offered a medal currently beyond their grasp — even so, followers of God's Son, anticipating so much more as we run the

race he has run **before** us, should retain the view Paul describes in
1 Corinthians 9:

> Don't you realize that in a race everyone runs, but only one person
> gets the prize? So run to win! All athletes are disciplined in their
> training. They do it to win a prize that will fade away, but we do it for
> an eternal prize. So I run with purpose in every step. I am not just
> shadowboxing. I discipline my body like an athlete, training it to do
> what it should (NLT).

In the same way, "anticipatory discipleship" declares:

*Everything I do for Christ today is not only about today, but also about getting
myself prepared for even more of what Christ is getting ready to do with
me tomorrow.*

"Anticipatory discipleship" considers daily:

*What new steps of obedience do I believe Jesus is asking me to take today in
order to be better prepared for additional victories tomorrow?*

Consider the words of Joshua 3:5, as Israel stood ready to advance:

> Purify yourselves, for tomorrow the LORD will do great wonders among
> you (Joshua 3, NLT).

"Anticipatory discipleship" acts on the outlook to which Peter calls us:

> But in your hearts revere [treat as holy — as first place in your lives]
> Christ as Lord. Always be prepared to give an answer to everyone who
> asks you to give the reason for the hope that you have (1 Peter 3, NIV).

How can we respond in any lesser way to the Lord of heaven and earth in
whom we abide, who goes **before** us (as we go with him) into the future,
into the heavens, into the promises —and then into the world.

We never stop proclaiming this one great resolve:

"Our Lamb has conquered. Let us follow him!"

Who Christ Is BEFORE Us Today:
A Tribute

Paraphrasing and personalizing a wide selection of Scriptures

Father, we come to you to proclaim the name of your Son together— to spread his fame, embrace his reign, increase his gain, and honor his claim about who he is *before* us. As we do, awake us to him afresh for ALL that he is. May the praise we bring to him in these moments come forth alive in us by your Spirit and rise up as a blessing to you forever. We use your Word to magnify your Son, without whom we are nothing and can do nothing. This tribute is all for Christ alone, our one and only hope of glory, and the hope of all the nations.

**Lord Jesus Christ, this is our tribute to YOU —
who you are BEFORE us.**

We have set our minds and our affections on things above, where you have gone *before* us into the presence of the Father, making a way for us to follow, as you sat down on his glorious throne. We are dead and our life is hidden now with you. Therefore, we can reckon ourselves to be a part of the same perfect fellowship you have with the Father.

Truly, all things are ours because we belong to the Christ who *precedes* us and *welcomes* us into the presence, promises, and purposes of the triune God. We anticipate the day when, in a similar invitation, you will go *before* us into the climax of the ages so that we might join you and appear with you in glory.

Christ Is NOW!

You said that because your kingdom is forcefully advancing ahead of us, we can lay hold of these *prior* initiatives, follow in the steps of your triumphs, and as a result, become a people of kingdom breakthroughs — all because you go *before* us. In this way you fill up Micah's promise when he foresaw One whose origins are from of old, from ancient times, who would break open the way to go *before* us, that our King will pass through the gate and go ahead of us, leading us at the front lines of God's plan for the nations.

In this way, as you assured us, you are not only the gate of the sheepfold but also the shepherd who calls us by name and leads us, your people, through the gate, as you go on ahead of us to feed us with great expectations by the power of the Holy Spirit. So, lead on, O King Eternal. The day of march has come. We are so ready to follow.

Christ Is NOW!

We celebrate how you died, were buried, and rose again so that we might follow you into death, burial, and resurrection right now. Because you went first, all of us can now reckon ourselves dead to sin but alive to God, passionate for the One who died and rose again ahead of us so we can follow you into the same victory.

Of course, we should declare ourselves new creations! It comes from our union with you, in whom the promised new creation has already begun. As the firstborn from the dead, YOU resound with the recapitulation of the whole universe as you exhibit in yourself an unparalleled transformation that will one day encompass everything, everywhere, including all of us.

You go **before** us! Therefore God, who is rich in mercy, has made us alive with you right now, has raised us with you right now, and has seated us with you right now in heavenly realms. There we can focus entirely on you in order that both now and in the coming ages the Father might pour out on us the incomparable riches that have *already* become yours, now to be shared with your people forever. Yes, your Church has become co-heirs of the living God of the universe because you, God's Son, share with us your inheritance of all things in heaven and earth.

Christ Is NOW!

Furthermore, because you have been raised to life and placed at God's right hand, you intercede for us. You go **before** us by your prayers. You open up to us all the promises of God. You guarantee that those promises will be "YES" to your people, because of who you are and what you have done ahead of time, even while we were still ungodly and reprobate.

Such a high priest meets our every need because you are holy, blameless, pure, set apart from sinners, exalted above the heavens. You have gone *before* us to the throne of grace, making a way for us by the power of your indestructible life. We come with confidence then to enter the Most Holy Place by your blood, Lord Jesus. We now walk the new and living way you have opened for us through the giving of your body for us. With such a great priest over the house of God, we dare now to draw near to the Father without fear and in full assurance of faith.

We bless you, the One who is holy and true, who holds the key of David so that you can go *before* us to open what no one can shut. What wonder is this! Going *before* us, you have become for us an open door into the presence of God, the power of God, the promises of God, the unfolding of the purposes of God, and the everlasting praises of God.

Christ Is NOW!

This tribute expresses only a small part of the inexhaustible riches of who you are BEFORE us and all peoples.

So, Father, here is how we celebrate your Son, our Lord Jesus Christ, in this hour. We exalt him. We exult in him. We do so because of all he is *before* us — now. Therefore, everything we are and have, every breath we breathe, every step we take, every service we render, every prayer we pray, every praise we bring, is possible only by him and him alone. For without him — without all he is *before* us — we are nothing and we can do nothing. More and more, by the revealing work of your Spirit, awaken us to Christ alone — awaken your whole Church to Christ alone — so that increasingly he might become *before* us our all in all.

AMEN!

The Spectacular Supremacy of God's Son Today

Exploring and Experiencing

Who Christ Is
WITHIN Us Today

One Person Within a Team Can Change the Outcome of Its Season

*E*ven as professionals, the New York Knicks, one of the NBA's premiere teams, hit slumps when they can't seem to win for losing. At such moments, regaining a championship reputation can appear illusive at best.

Such was the foreboding outlook as their season collapsed the winter of 2011.

Until Jeremy Lin came along!

Seemingly from out of nowhere, there he was! One night in February a new face showed up on the first-string team, sprinting down the court, exhibiting a positive but fiercely competitive attitude, combined with impressive basketball athleticism. In desperation, his coach had put him into the game because nothing else — and no one else — held out any hope of turning around another embarrassing effort.

In a few minutes, however, Lin's fiery confidence turned the entire game around. As if by magic, *every* player on the team started performing at a higher level of skill and intensity. And to their amazement, they won! But it didn't stop that night.

Over ensuing weeks, the Knicks and their fans were infected with what the local papers coined *"Linsanity."* Overnight, the winning of games seemed not only possible but inevitable. The players rallied, defeating one opponent after another. Largely by his effort and the spark he gave his team, Lin led a turnaround of an 8–15 team that had lost 11 of its last 13 games. The whole city found itself caught up in a drama shaped by the impact of *one person*, Jeremy Lin.

All he had to do was show up each night — not in the press boxes or in the spectator stands but *out on the court*, stepping into the middle of a semi-dysfunctional team, recalibrating it into an NBA phenomenon. It all happened *by his presence*. That alone changed the trajectory of an entire season. "Linsanity!"

This provides a modern-day parable for the Church. It pictures the Bible's promise about what Christ's direct involvement with his people brings to any congregation. The promise of dramatic *spiritual* transformations awaits any group of believers with whom the Lord of glory has chosen to join forces. As he does (to use sports lingo), he "brings his game with him" to share it with us, as he goes to work on the *inside* of — WITHIN — our "team."

Call it *"Him*-sanity"!

There is another intriguing part of the Jeremy Lin story that we should learn from. Jeremy had been available to the Knicks all along. The young star already was thoroughly prepared to step onto the floor that night. Having played four years at Harvard, he'd been around the NBA for some years, working hard, improving his skills; but he had never been put into a pro game for more than a few minutes *until* that fateful night.

Similarly, so often in our churches we lack clear, constant focus on the majesty and supremacy of Jesus. This causes us to leave him on the fringes, like Lin relegated to the bench until a crisis came along. Even though by the Holy Spirit right now Jesus is reigning **within** his Church and its individual congregations, God's transforming plan for the Church becomes temporarily stalled if we fail to give God's Son "full run of the court" in our life together with him.

But once we repent of what we've done to Jesus by "keeping him on the bench" (as it were) and instead invite him to occupy *first place* — to assume his rightful role among us and freely exercise the full scope of his lordship in our midst — everything changes. Capitalizing on our role in his eternal "game plan," he draws his followers around him to restore to them fresh hope, renewed purpose, and unified confidence. Consequently, abundant victories with him are not far off!

Just one person — Christ **within** us — can turn a fellowship of followers into a fervent force for furthering God's kingdom. Whenever that happens, his reign, which is already prevailing in the heavens, presses more forcefully into the midst of his people. This is precisely what Scripture teaches:

> . . . that I might fully declare God's word — that sacred mystery which up to now has been hidden in every age and every generation, but which is now as clear as daylight to those who love God. They are those to whom God has planned to give a vision of the full wonder and splendor of his secret plan for the sons of men. And the secret is simply this: *Christ in you! Yes, Christ in you bringing with him the hope of all glorious things to come* (Colossians 1, PHILLIPS, emphasis added).

In other words, Paul's goal for God's people is that they experience the focus and vigor of *"Him-sanity"*!

Jesus' Reign WITHIN Us Today:
How We Get to Really *Know* Him for All He Is

This fifth dimension of Christ's supremacy could be called "*intimacy* with Christ in his supremacy." The chapter goes beyond just *seeking* him to actually *meeting* him and even *greeting* him for all he is.

That's because he *is* so near to us. He's **within** us. That's why we are able to truly *know* him. That's how we increase our *intimacy* with him, especially in terms of his supremacy.

The Old Testament Hebrew word for "knowing" or "knowledge" is "*yada.*" "Yada" is a fascinating word. It's employed in a variety of ways, even used to describe sexual intercourse. Far beyond academic learning, yada refers to insights gained *experientially,* born out of *personal contact* — not hearing or reading about someone, not observing someone at a distance, but a preoccupation with coming to know and understand someone *face to face.*

Personal contact. Engagement. Rapport. Direct involvement. This is what Scripture calls for when it urges us to "press on to *know* the Lord" (Hosea 5). This was Paul's goal when he counted everything in life as loss for the privilege of "*knowing* Christ Jesus my Lord" (Philippians 3). This was his passion for other Christians too — that they would *know* Christ in the full scope of his love (Ephesians 3).

Gaining this kind of "knowledge" — this deep, intimate knowing — is what churches in every nation should desire and even expect in their ongoing, growing relationship with God's Son. He never stands aloof from us. He walks *among* us. He dwells *in our midst*. Right from the start we're told, "God has called us into fellowship with his Son, our Lord Jesus Christ" (1 Corinthians 1). He is "Christ **within** us."

Personal contact — intimate, uninterrupted, pervasive, powerful personal contact — is how we get to know Jesus. This is why we should remain vigilant for anything more our sovereign Savior may desire to do **within** us, individually or together. Not only do we worship him as the One who reigns *over* us (which is blessing enough) but also we learn to know him — to *cherish* him — as the One who reigns **within** us.

Jesus' Reign WITHIN Us Today:
It's Exceedingly *Proactive*

Think about this: How comfortable would the members of your congregation be if Jesus were directly, persistently, and actively involved with them in the full measure of his supremacy?

Well, in fact, according to the Bible *he already is*!

To be sure, none can encounter and experience God's Son beyond what the Father shares with us. Manifestations of the Monarch within his kingdom must come at his initiative if they are to come at all. In other words, the joys we find in our salvation, without exception, must spring from prior *proactive* revelations of King Jesus among his subjects, as he freely shares with us the riches of his reign.

How many in your church family are genuinely eager to get directly involved with Jesus day after day in the intensity of his activity among us? Once again, the Bible says all who have been transferred into his kingdom *already are!*

The fact is, Jesus refuses to be a passive Savior among his people. Having chosen to save us and indwell us, he fully intends to engage with us — to speak to and inspire us, to guide and teach us, to question and challenge us, even when necessary to rebuke and discipline us. He's committed to rule *within* us in order to refresh and revive us, so as to equip us to follow him into the kingdom purposes of his Father.

In return, our incomparable privilege is to become his enthusiastic "responders." As he introduces more of himself to us, which he is *longing* to do, we too will experience new levels of *longing* for him — longing to know more of him as our Lord and experience more of him as our Leader. With unfettered hope, every congregation should eagerly welcome as much of his revelatory work among us as he's willing to give us — always expecting that it will be above and beyond what we could ask or imagine (Ephesians 3:20).

Snapshots and Starter Thoughts

- **Days before he sat down on the throne of the universe, Jesus promised his disciples he would not abandon them.** He reassured them that as they served him among the nations he would be in constant communion with them as Lord of those nations — always accessible to them, operating *within* them, walking with them, working among them, reaching out to others through them — to the end of this age, and beyond (Matthew 28).

- **This reality carries *practical* implications wherever any church gathers to worship.** Consider Hebrews 2 where Jesus is seen ministering directly *within* any congregation gathered in his name.

  So Jesus is not ashamed to call them his brothers and sisters. He says, "*I will announce your name* to my brothers and sisters. *I will sing your praises* among those who worship you" (emphasis added).

Notice that first of all Jesus joins us in our anthems of praise. He enriches our songs and hymns by actively singing along with us as our High Priest (as our chief worship leader). Not only do we ascend into the worship of heaven through him, but also, just as importantly, *through him the worship of heaven descends to us!* — invading us, inspiring us, and transforming us because of the One who worships among us.

- **In the same way, Hebrews 2 observes that Jesus *preaches* to us whenever God's Word is proclaimed to a congregation.** He strolls among us as his gathered disciples *"announcing"* God's glory to us. Deitrich Bonhoeffer suggested that whenever a preacher speaks, his words go forth as if Jesus himself has stepped down from the pulpit to walk among the people, speaking to each one. To become Jesus' voice, however, a pastor must clearly help people to focus on the majesty of Jesus, and call them to give heed to the Master, not unlike how the first disciples were summoned to sit at his feet.

- **Christ preaches to his people through those he places among them to speak in his name.**

   > The same one who descended is the one who ascended higher than all the heavens, so that he might fill the entire universe with himself. Now these are the gifts Christ gave to the church: the apostles, the prophets, the evangelists, and the pastors and teachers. Their responsibility is to equip God's people . . . until we all come to such unity in our faith and knowledge of God's Son . . . we will speak the truth in love, growing in every way more and more like Christ, who is the head of his body, the church (Ephesians 4, NLT).

   It is as though Christ were beseeching his followers face to face, doing so through those he uniquely empowers to give voice to his passions and priorities.

- **Concerning the churches in Asia Minor, John describes how the proclamations of the ascended Lord walking among them pierced each congregation as if a sword were coming at them right out of his mouth (Revelation 1-3).** This is how *every* church should experience Jesus whenever he proclaims God's message to them through his messengers.

   > The word of God is living and active. It is sharper than any sword that has two edges. It cuts deep enough to separate soul from spirit . . . It

judges the thoughts and purposes of the heart. Nothing God created
is hidden from him (Hebrews 4).

- **The implications of an active Redeemer at work *among* his people
give a whole new purpose for *prayer*.** One might say, "Prayer is opening
the door and inviting Jesus to come in." To pray about anything, first of
all, is to welcome our Lord Jesus, already present, to *manifest* his presence
among us in the full exercise of his supremacy.

- **Drawing on the image of Psalm 24, prayer is an appeal to the Father
to "open the gates" — to remove every obstacle — so our "King of
glory" might enter among us in new ways.**

  > Open wide, you gates. Open up, you ancient doors. Then the King of
  > glory will come in. Who is the King of glory? The LORD, who is strong
  > and mighty. The LORD, who is mighty in battle . . . The LORD who rules
  > over all. He is the King of glory.

- **Paul's priority in praying for God's people was to see them thrive
because of their shared experience of Christ's activity *within* their
midst.** Here's one example of how he prayed for entire congregations:

  > I pray that out of His glorious riches He may strengthen you with
  > power through His Spirit in your inner being, so that Christ may dwell
  > in [in the midst of] your hearts through faith. And I pray that you,
  > being rooted and established in love, may have power, together with
  > all the saints, to grasp how wide and long and high and deep is the
  > love of Christ, and to know this love that surpasses knowledge – that
  > you may be filled to the measure of all the fullness of God
  > (Ephesians 3).

- **Seeking by prayer for more of Christ's kingly work *within* us impacts
the Church on two levels:** (1) We open up ourselves *corporately* to
experience in Jesus more of his extraordinary initiatives, as we welcome
him to accomplish miracles among us as well as among many *others*
beyond us for whom we also pray — all for his glory; (2) at the same time,
we open gates in our lives *individually* to invite fresh displays of Jesus
within each of us as he draws near to take new ground with us.

- **Because Christ chooses to be proactive among his people, we should
regularly anticipate *increased* evidences of his reign.** Every day we
should be looking for how his rule might become more tangible among
us — how he must enrich our routines as he helps us to enter his fullness,

catch his vision, receive his passion, lean on his leadership, respond to his commands, share with those he brings to us, and join him as he advances his global cause.

The Wrap

What does Christ *really* think of your church? To get an answer, imagine this:

What if you contracted with Jesus to become your "church consultant" for the next three months? What would you expect him to report back? What major changes might this bring to your life together, on every level?

In other words, what if he sat in on all of your activities, committee meetings, worship times, potluck suppers, small group studies, evangelistic outreaches, and youth events? What if he also scheduled a meeting with each family in their home, sat at the dinner table and asked how things were going with them?

What recommendations would you expect him to propose at the end of ninety days visiting with, listening to, and consulting with your congregation? What would he *alter*? What would he *eliminate*? What would be allowed to stay? What *new things* would he propose in terms of schedules, organization, plans and priorities, programs, relationship dynamics, Sunday worship, discipleship initiatives, mission outreach? How soon would he want you to get started on the changes?

And most importantly, what would he say about how he himself is regarded among the people of your congregation? How would he describe their relationship to him — that is, what they think about him, the ways they respond to him, the preeminence they give to him, the level of their ambitions for him?

What personal awareness and enjoyment of his life and activities ***within*** your congregation would he find? Would he be able to report that they truly are growing to *know* him for who he really is?

If you fully implemented his recommendations, a year from now do you think you would see any significant changes? Would a member who was gone for a year and then returned recognize your congregation's life together? If so, how different would things be? Specifically, what would be removed? What would be transformed? What would be renewed? What new works of God's kingdom would you be experiencing a year later?

Well, here's the truth: Jesus *is* active among his people, all the time. By his Spirit, whether we acknowledge him or not, he *does* "meet" with all our committees, "share" in all our dinner conversations, and "join" in all our worship services. He does so with full authority as God's grand "Cosmic Consultant," in whom are hidden all the treasures of wisdom and knowledge (Colossians 2). He brings with him all the counsel any church family could ever want or need!

For you see, Jesus never *casually* inhabits our churches. Whenever he decides to make himself known, to manifest himself more tangibly **within** a body of believers, he does so with a definite, even energetic agenda — a strategic plan for each congregation, related to the Kingdom's advance but tailored specifically for each church.

Here's the truth: Jesus is waiting, right now, to share with your people more of his bold blueprint for your church. If you need further proof of his intentions, just review the scope of his "consulting work" (as it were) with the seven churches in Revelation 1-3! There he walked among them, ready to revive them, empower them, and redeploy them in his global cause.

Christ **within** us assures us of his *full provision* whatever our situation or condition. He comes into our midst bringing resurrection victory to supply the *needs* of his people and fulfill the *mission* of his people. Whatever more of him we choose to seek from the Father is already ours to enjoy as we dwell in him at the same time that he dwells **within** us.

As Christ operates among us today by his Spirit, the Lord who already fills the universe with himself (Ephesians 4) is even more eager to fill his Church with himself (Ephesians 1).

As noted before, we may not yet experience the *quantity* of the blessings Christ promises the saints in the Consummation, but right now, every day he unleashes **within** us the *quality* of it. For starters: Having cleansed us from the *guilt* of sin, now he works among us to deliver us, day by day, from the *power* of sin (1 John 2) — until the hour he comes back to forever eliminate among us the *presence* of sin (1 John 3).

Jesus' Reign WITHIN Us Today:
Individual and Corporate Expressions of His Presence

A word search of Google's database of 5.2 million books (at the time) revealed that, between 1960 and 2008, words and phrases that emphasize "individuals" increasingly replaced words and phrases that highlight "community" — terms such as "self"; "I come first"; "personal preferences"; "I can do it myself"; "me"; and "mine.""

In a bestseller, *Going Solo: The Extraordinary Rise and Surprising Appeal of Living Alone,* the author observes that 50% of the American adult population is single. Many lives are marked by fairly tenuous and frequently temporary associations in jobs, in marriages, with political parties, or with neighbors next door — what one sociologist calls a "hook-up culture" (hooking up and quickly unhooking, in all areas of life, not just in sleeping together).

Not surprisingly, researchers conclude the fastest growing religious category in America (now up to 30% and rising rapidly) is "unaffiliated" — sometimes called the "nones." Even among those who say they love God and that their faith is important to them, there's a growing number who make the choice of "going it alone" — to turn from any kind of faith community, including the Church, to go solo.

Often Scripture passages in which the word "you" is *plural* in the original language are nevertheless interpreted by many readers as though "you" is *singular,* applying only to an individual and addressing his or her personal needs and concerns. Our whole culture pushes us in that direction, reinforcing the belief that Scripture's concerns are basically about *me* and *my* life and my walk with the Lord.

What's fascinating about the "spirituality" promoted in the New Testament is that "you" most frequently appears in the *plural* form in the original Greek—for example, in phrases like "Christ in *you,*" meaning "Christ among you believers; Christ in the midst of you when you're gathered together."

Take for example Jesus' teaching on the vine and branches in John 15. Most believers tend to read his metaphor as an encouragement about the fruitfulness of individual branches (each disciple) — which, of course, it is in a secondary sense. But in context, and in the Greek, every single "you" is actually *plural.* What should this tell us?

Picture a vineyard with a thick vine winding its way along supporting trellises. Observe how its branches wrap around the vine, and then entwine around each other forming such a unified embrace that it is nearly impossible to focus on one single branch or one bunch of grapes.

Except for a stray branch disconnected and withered, all the others receive the same life from the same vine, so that the health of the vine is displayed by the combined productiveness of the branches.

The plural "you" in Jesus' upper room discourse highlights the corporate nature of discipleship. Take a closer look:

> *I am the real vine* . . . *You* [pl] must go on growing in me and I will grow in *you* [pl]. As the branch cannot bear any fruit unless it shares the life of the vine, so *you* [pl] can produce nothing unless *you* [pl] go on

growing in me. I am the vine itself, *you* [pl] are the branches . . . the plain fact is that apart from me *you* [pl] can do nothing at all . . . This is how my Father will be glorified – by *you* [pl] becoming fruitful and being my disciples . . . It is I who have chosen *you* [pl]. I have appointed *you* [pl] to go and bear fruit that will be lasting (John 15, PHILLIPS, emphasis added).

Here's a key principle to take from this passage, an insight that's emphasized throughout Scripture and to which we'll return more than once in this chapter:

> **Christ within *me* and Christ within *us* always go together.**
> **But what he accomplishes in *me* is derived primarily**
> **from what he accomplishes, first of all, among *us*.**

Christ at Work WITHIN Each of Us as Individuals

Let me hasten to reaffirm that Scripture never depreciates how essential it is for *every single* "branch" (every *disciple*) grafted into Christ to receive his or her own life-sustaining nourishment from the Vine. Though creating community is his long-range focus, Christ greatly desires to work intimately **within** each one of our lives as well — to minister to us directly, as *individuals*. Let's review a few passages that amplify this truth.

Snapshots and Starter Thoughts

- **Individual concern of Christ**

  See that you don't look down on one of these little ones . . . Suppose a man owns 100 sheep and one of them wanders away. Won't he leave the 99 sheep on the hills? *Won't he go and look for the one that wandered off?* (Matthew 18, emphasis added).

- **Individual revelation from Christ**

  Anyone who has my commands and obeys them loves me. My Father will love the one who loves me. I too will love him. *And I will show myself to him.* Anyone who loves me will obey my teaching. My Father will love him. *We will come to him and make our home with him* (John 14, emphasis added).

- **Individual intimacy with Christ**

  My old self has been crucified with Christ. *It is no longer I who live, but Christ lives in me.* So I live in this earthly body by trusting in the Son of God, who loved me and gave himself for me (Galatians 2, emphasis added).

- **Individual connection to Christ**

  The body is meant for the Lord. And the Lord is meant for the body . . . *Don't you know that your bodies belong to the body of Christ? . . . Anyone who is joined to the Lord becomes one with him in spirit . . .* Don't you know that your bodies are temples of the Holy Spirit? (1 Corinthians 6, emphasis).

- **Individual empowerment by Christ**

  And if anyone does not have the Spirit of Christ, he does not belong to Christ. *But if Christ is in you,* your body is dead because of sin, yet your spirit is alive because of righteousness. And if *the Spirit of Him who raised Jesus from the dead is living in you,* he who raised Christ from the dead will *also give life to your mortal bodies through His Spirit, who lives in you* (Romans 8, emphasis added).

- **Individual triumphs through Christ**

  Through suffering, our [individual] bodies continue to share in the death of Jesus *so that the life of Jesus may also be seen in our* [individual] *bodies.* Yes, we live under constant danger of death because we serve Jesus, so that the life of Jesus will be evident in our [individual] dying bodies. So we live in the face of death, but this has resulted in eternal life for you (2 Corinthians 4, NLT, emphasis added).

Everyone who believes that Jesus is the Christ is born again because of what God has done . . . everyone who is a child of God has won the battle over the world . . . *Who is it that has won the battle over the world? Only the person who believes that Jesus is the Son of God* . . . Those who belong to the Son have life. Those who do not belong to the Son of God do not have life (1 John 5, emphasis added).

- **Individual refreshment from Christ**

  All who drink this water will be thirsty again. But *anyone who drinks the water I give him will never be thirsty*. In fact, the water I give him will become a spring of water in him. It will flow up into eternal life (John 4, emphasis added).

- **Individual restoration by Christ**

  Are you tired? Worn out? Burned out on religion? *Come to me. Get away with me and you'll recover your life*. I'll show you how to take a real rest. Walk with me and work with me – watch how I do it. Learn the unforced rhythms of grace. I won't lay anything heavy or ill-fitting on you. *Keep company with me* and you'll learn to live freely and lightly (Matthew 11, MSG, emphasis added).

- **Individual strengthening in Christ**

  It was a case of Christ's strength moving in on my weakness . . . abuse, accidents, opposition, bad breaks. I just let Christ take over! And so the weaker I get, the stronger I become (2 Corinthians 12, MSG, emphasis added).

  I am content whether I have more than enough or not enough. *I can do everything by the power of Christ.* He gives me strength (Philippians 4, emphasis added).

- **Individual comfort through Christ**

  He comforts us in all our troubles. Now we can comfort others when they are in trouble. We ourselves have received comfort from God. *We share the sufferings of Christ. We also share his comfort. If we are having trouble*, it is so that you will be comforted and renewed. If we are comforted, it is so that you will be comforted (2 Corinthians 1, emphasis added).

- **Individual invitations from Christ**

  Here I am! I stand at the door and knock. *If any of you hears my voice and opens the door, I will come in and eat with you.* And you will eat with me (Revelation 3, emphasis added).

- **Individual obedience to Christ**

    Jesus called the crowd to him along with his disciples. He said, *"If anyone wants to come after me,* he must say no to himself. He must pick up his cross and follow me. If he wants to save his life, he will lose it. But *if he loses his life for me and for the good news, he will save it"* (Mark 8, emphasis added).

- **Individual witness for Christ**

    Stephen was full of God's grace and power. He did great wonders and miraculous signs among the people . . . But he was too wise for them. *They couldn't stand up against the Holy Spirit who spoke through him . . .* All who were sitting in the Sanhedrin looked right at Stephen. They saw that his face was like the face of an angel (Acts 7, emphasis added).

- **Individual surrender to Christ**

    I turned around to see who was speaking to me . . . His face was like the sun shining in all of its brightness. *When I saw him, I fell at his feet as if I were dead.* Then he put his right hand on me and said, "Do not be afraid. I am the First and the Last. I am the Living One" (Revelation 1, emphasis added).

pause | think | pray

The Wrap

Christ's work **within** *individual* Christians is never incidental, never auxiliary. It is part and parcel of our salvation. We should desire it, expect it, receive it, and celebrate it.

This is where the act of *baptism* has played such a significant role in historic Christianity. This nearly universal initiation rite officially incorporates us into the Christian *community* (whatever the specific mode of baptism is used). But without exception it is applied to the *individual*, one by one.

But for sure, by Jesus' design (Matthew 28) the entire company of disciples does the baptizing of members — *no one baptizes himself.*

Furthermore, the very words used at every baptism declare each new believer to be incorporated into nothing less than the eternal fellowship of the triune God from which the fraternity of Jesus' followers derives its existence. Literally, the original reads that we are to baptize new believers *"into* the name of the Father and of the Son and of the Holy Spirit." Scripture also insists that in baptism individuals enter into a sacred, public yet personal transaction with the Godhead through commitment to the Son.

Peter asserts in 1 Peter 3:20-22:

> That water [Noah's flood] is a picture of baptism, which now saves you, not by removing dirt from your body, *but as a response to God* from a clean conscience. It is *effective because of the resurrection of Jesus Christ* (AMP, emphasis added).

The Greek word rendered in this verse as "response," or in other translations as "pledge," comes from the ancient business world. It refers to a verbal promise by one merchant to another, witnessed by associates, to remain loyal to a commercial contract just negotiated.

In other words, the apostle teaches (and what the New Testament generally teaches) that by baptism — with the whole community attesting to the act — individuals are pledged to Christ for the totality of his or her life, from here to eternity.

The rite of baptism corresponds to the prior ministry of the Holy Spirit who *spiritually-speaking* baptizes that person into the corporate body of Christ the moment they first believe (1 Corinthians 12), incorporating each into union with God's people locally and globally (Galatians 3).

In fact, one might go so far as to say that, in reality, *Jesus himself* officiates in the midst of the congregation, serving as the "honorary" baptizer of every person who is joining him and life in his kingdom. As John promised:

> He will baptize you with the Holy Spirit and with fire (Luke 3).

Despite the deeply personal nature of baptism for each individual, in light of the *community* into which one is baptized, we come back to the key principle for this chapter:

> **Christ within *me* and Christ within *us* always go together.**
>
> **But what he accomplishes in *me* is derived primarily**
>
> **from what he accomplishes, first of all, among *us*.**

Next, let's explore the *corporate* aspect of the "us" in "Christ *within* us."

Christ at Work WITHIN the Corporate Life of God's People

Unlike other religions, the Christian pilgrimage ultimately does not lead to a *place* (such as Mecca or Varanasi, or even the Vatican), but to a *Person* who is found in the midst of a *people*. It leads to the company of saints who belong to Christ and are inhabited by him, wherever they gather at any spot on the earth or in heaven!

Spread around the globe, the Church consists of millions of life-giving assemblies ***within*** whom Jesus has set up his throne. Wherever Jesus' followers gather, wherever we join with others to worship him and serve him, that's where Jesus himself chooses to be more fully present — to dwell, to heal, to teach, to equip, to lead.

Therefore, *ecclesiology* (our study of the Church) should never be divorced from *Christology* (our study of the Christ). One might say that the *breadth* of our ecclesiology is defined by, and then refined by, the *depth* of our Christology.

Or to say it another way: Just as there's no such thing as a "Christless church" — without him it ceases to be a church and becomes, at best, just a club — even so there's no such thing as a "churchless Christ." You can't have him without his church. They arrive together inseparable, a complete package — not only because he is *over* the Church to *build* the church, but because he is **within** the Church to *fill* the Church.

In Chapter 3, "Who Christ Is OVER Us Today," we explored how our Lord actively takes charge in shaping his church. Now this chapter emphasizes that he does not do this by remote control. Rather, he does it *directly*, as he pours himself into the thick of the action.

Jesus waits to manifest conspicuous, concrete expressions of his reign **within** any congregation that invites him to take the initiative with them, that allows *him* to draw *them* near to him. Knowing this to be true, Paul appealed to the Corinthian church:

> With promises like this to pull us on, dear friends, let's make a clean break with everything that defiles or distracts us, both within and without. Let's make our entire lives fit and holy temples for the worship of God (2 Corinthians 7, MSG).

As the 19th-century biblical scholar James Bannerman observed in his classic two-volume *The Church of Christ*:

> Christ is both the Church's founder and its administrator – *being the ever-present source of life and influence.* Christ is the Head of the Church, *breathing spiritual breath into the body at the first, and holding it in its being ever since.* If doctrine is taught, it is taught because He has revealed it. If ordinances are administered, they are administered in His name, and because they are His. If government is established and exercised, it is through His appointment and authority. If saving grace is dispensed, it is dispensed through the virtue and power of His Spirit. *If a blessing is communicated, it is because He blesses* (emphasis added).

Here are some other ways to help us dig into the essential *corporate* dimensions of "Christ **within** us."

 Snapshots and Starter Thoughts

- **The ideal in God's redemptive plan is that people come to Christ not in isolation but *"in community."*** The Church is not an ad hoc, freewheeling association of independent, voluntary individualists. Rather it is a sacred corps of committed disciples permanently joined to each other because, simultaneously, like an army they are joined in life-giving obedience to their Supreme Commander.

- **We never stand entirely alone in our relationship to Christ**. We are bound inseparably to the Lord who binds to himself "one holy and apostolic church" (as historic creeds phrase it). That's why, for example, he insists we serve him best by serving one another.

- **Jesus' labor of love *within* us reflects a fundamental reality recorded all through Scripture.** The Bible recounts the determination of our infinite God to quicken, enrich, and transform his people by showing up among them, again and again, to personally, persistently, and passionately dwell among them. The bullet points that follow provide a few examples:

- ***Within* us and among us — this describes how God inhabited his creation**. According to Genesis 3, before Satan and sin entered in God walked with Adam and Eve in Eden "in the cool of the day." God's desire from the beginning was to enjoy fellowship with those made in his image. On the other hand, because of sin Adam and Eve were cast out of Eden; no longer was God willing to be intimate with them, drawing near to them, and interacting unconditionally with them. Placed at the garden's gate, an angel with a flaming sword made the deadly separation feel even more severe for them. *But now,* through Jesus, God has brought about a cosmic reconciliation that allows, once again, for the "dwelling of God to be among men" without reservation (Revelation 21).

- ***Within*** **us and among us — this was how God led his people in the Exodus.** Calling them out of bondage, Jehovah appeared among the Israelites by a pillar of cloud by day and a pillar of fire at night. Similarly, he inhabited the tabernacle they pitched in the center of the Israelite camp. Each of the tribes surrounded his dwelling place when they pitched their tents around it, like numbers circling the hands of a clock. *But now,* in Jesus, that tabernacle has been reconstituted into a Person who is our gathering place, so we surround him forever.

- ***Within*** **us and among us — this was how God preserved Israel during their wilderness journeys.** When the Jewish pilgrims ran out of water, Moses struck a rock (at God's command). Miraculously a refreshing river rushed from the boulder. For the rest of their travels the stream continued to flow in the midst of the camp, providing for everyone's thirst. *But now,* Paul applies that episode to the greater miracle of Christ's soul-quenching ministry within the Church when he writes:

  > They all ate the same spiritual food and drank the same spiritual drink; for they drank from the spiritual rock that accompanied them, and *that rock was Christ* (1 Corinthians 10).

- ***Within*** **us and among us — this was the heart of God's purpose for the temple's Holy of Holies.** When Solomon dedicated the newly built temple, Jehovah visibly invaded it in order to impress the multitude with his immediate, holy, sovereign presence, filling it with himself so tangibly that no one dared enter it. This experience guaranteed that coming generations would be constantly reminded to worship with awe the Holy One who remained among them. *But now,* we freely, joyfully, unhesitatingly worship the Son — the Lamb at the center of the throne — who makes a way for us by coming among us to bring us into God's holy presence without fear.

- ***Within*** **us and among us — this was God's message to Israel through the exceptional ways he revealed his presence to them.** God's fiery habitation of the tabernacle in the wilderness became even more dominant in the temple at the center of Jerusalem, where it became known as his "Shekinah Glory." "Shekinah" is Hebrew, meaning "to dwell." In other words, in the fullness of his power and majesty, coupled with the beauty and purity of his nature — that is, his "glory" — Jehovah was willing to share the wonders of his very nature with his people by dwelling wholeheartedly among his redeemed. *But now,* we see that all of that simply foreshadowed our intimacy with the Son who abides *within* us performing wonders among us no Old Testament believer ever imagined possible.

> *The Son is the gleaming brightness of God's glory. He is the exact likeness of God's being . . .* He provided the way for people to be made pure from sin. Then he sat down at the right hand of the King, the Majesty in heaven (Hebrews 1, emphasis added).

- ***Within* us and among us — such was the vision of God's future involvement with his people promised by so many of the prophets.** Multiple forecasts from ancient seers, over many generations, spoke of Jehovah's permanent dwelling with his holy ones as the ultimate outcome of history. This was graphically portrayed, for example, by the very last Old Testament messenger, Malachi. *But now,* we know Malachi's words pointed toward Christ's coming 400 years later when he would refine and purify God's people by coming among us, never to leave us.

> See, I will send my messenger, who will prepare the way before me. Then suddenly the Lord you are seeking will come to His temple; the messenger of the covenant, whom you desire, will come, says the LORD Almighty. But who can endure the day of His coming? Who can stand when He appears? For He will be like a refiner's fire or a launderer's soap. He will sit as a refiner and purifier of silver; He will purify the Levites and refine them like gold and silver. Then the LORD will have men who will bring offerings in righteousness, and the offerings of Judah and Jerusalem will be acceptable to the LORD, as in days gone by, as in former years (Malachi 3-4).

- ***Within* us and among us — this is who God declared he would become forever upon Immanuel's arrival.** One day Malachi's vision was fulfilled. One day the stunning promise of Isaiah 7 became flesh and blood — the Lord Jesus Christ.

> The Lord himself will give you a miraculous sign. The virgin is going to have a baby. She will give birth to a son. And he will be called *Immanuel* (emphasis added).

So now, referencing Isaiah, Matthew opened his gospel by reminding us that "Immanuel" means "God *with* us" — that is, God's Son has come to where we are, stepping into our space and settling down in our midst (Matthew 1:23).

- *Within* **us and among us — this reality was signaled to the world through the birth name given to God's Son.** It is noteworthy that at the same time, Matthew also reported the angel's command to Joseph to name the baby "Jesus" because he would "save his people from their sins" (Matthew 1:21). The Hebrew form of the Greek word "Jesus" is "Joshua," which means "Jehovah saves." *So now,* the two names put together signify that God's Son has come among his people by inhabiting our race permanently (Immanuel) in order to save us (Joshua). He has arrived among us, to deliver us, as one of us.

- *Within* **us and among us — this was manifested as God's ultimate intention by the *nature* of Christ's incarnation.** In his gospel, the apostle John brings this truth to the forefront of his prologue with two familiar sentences. Here they are in three contemporary translations:

  > *The Word became flesh and made his dwelling among us.* We have seen his glory, the glory of the one and only Son, who came from the Father, full of grace and truth (John 1, NIV, emphasis added).

  > *The Word became flesh and blood, and moved into the neighborhood.* We saw the glory with our own eyes, the one-of-a-kind glory, like Father, like Son, generous inside and out, true from start to finish (John 1, MSG, emphasis added).

  > *And the Word (Christ) became flesh (human, incarnate) and tabernacled (fixed His tent of flesh, lived awhile) among us;* and we [actually] saw His glory (John 1, AMP, emphasis added).

So now, God's Son is *"tabernacling"* (pitching his tent) among us in a way that fulfills all the central themes of the tabernacle in the wilderness (themes that were expressed even more elaborately centuries later by Solomon's towering temple).

- *Within* **us and among us — this was the experience of those who participated in Jesus' dedication day.** Eight days after his birth, Jesus arrived inside the temple when his parents dedicated him to Jehovah. At that moment an elderly saint name Simeon, led by the Spirit, came inside, saw the baby, took him in his arms and prophetically proclaimed:

> My eyes have seen your salvation. You have prepared it in the sight of all nations. It is a light to be given to the Gentiles. It will be the glory of your people Israel . . . This child is going to cause many people in Israel to fall and to rise (Luke 2).

So now, we know Jesus is the true "Shekinah Glory" returned to the temple, concealed in the form of a baby, visible to all who were worshipping there that day, and available to his people today in the glorious reality of Christ *dwelling* ("Shekinah") in the midst of his followers — dwelling **within** his followers.

- *Within* **us and among us — this was the hallmark of Jesus' ministry from its inauguration.** Nearly 30 years after Simeon's prophecy over him, Jesus rose up one Sabbath in the midst of his synagogue in Nazareth and took the scroll of Isaiah. He began his public ministry like this:

> Unrolling the scroll, he found the place where it was written, *"God's Spirit is on me; he's chosen me to preach the Message of good news to the poor,* sent me to announce pardon to prisoners and recovery of sight to the blind, to set the burdened and battered free, to announce, 'This is God's year to act!'". . . He rolled up the scroll, handed it back . . . "You've just heard Scripture make history. *It came true just now in this place"* (Luke 4, MSG, emphasis added).

So now, based on these words, we know the Servant of the Lord openly comforts all of us, just as claimed before his home synagogue. The truth of who he really was among them — the fulfillment of God's redemptive purposes activated for them — is who he remains for the worldwide Church.

- *Within* **us and among us — this theme played out at every moment throughout his ministry.** This became apparent one day when Jesus spoke of the kingdom of God as literally embodied in himself as he stood in the midst of crowds that followed him.

> Once the Pharisees *asked Jesus when God's kingdom would come.* He replied, "The coming of God's kingdom is not something you can see just by watching for it carefully. People will not say, 'Here it is.' Or, 'There it is.' *God's kingdom is among you"* (Luke 17, emphasis added).

So now, this reality prevails in millions of congregations where Jesus abides.

- *Within* us and among us — this theme dominated Jesus' ministry activities over and over. For example, personally he stepped into the boat before rescuing his disciples from a storm at sea. He revealed his glory on a mountaintop standing in the middle of both saints on earth and saints from heaven. Frequently he banqueted with prostitutes and thieves and tax collectors at their tables, to reach them face to face. He visited Bethany to rest in the company of friends he deeply loved. He cleared out commercial establishments in the temple so that every seeker, especially from the Gentile nations, could gather together for worship unhindered, enjoying God's presence. He shared his last supper with those he loved, telling them:

  > I have really looked forward to eating this Passover meal with you. I wanted to do this before I suffer (Luke 22).

  So now, he draws the global Church into even deeper intimacy with him in his supremacy. He lives *within* us!

- *Within* us and among us — this remained God's commitment even while his Son suffered for us on the cross. Stretched out in agony, surrounded by a host of criminals and Pharisees and crowds and followers, Jesus carried out the prediction of Isaiah 53 that says:

  > . . . he poured out his life unto death, and *He was numbered with the transgressors.* For he bore the sin of many, and made intercession for the transgressors (emphasis added).

  So now, he wants to be counted with redeemed transgressors wherever they assemble in his name, week by week.

- *Within* us and among us — this experience was a chief characteristic of Jesus' resurrection appearances. The day of his resurrection proved to be no different. First he was greeted by a band of women; later he walked seven miles with two disciples from Emmaus; then he gathered with his followers in a second floor retreat. Next, he spent 40 days fellowshipping with them, even eating with them. On one day he was surrounded by 500 disciples at the same time and place (1 Corinthians 15). *So now,* taking this pattern to a grander level, this same Jesus has raised us from the dead with him *together*, and has seated us with him in heavenly places *together*, so that we may walk in the newness of his risen life as he lives it out **within** us and among us *together* (Romans 6; Ephesians 2).

- **Within us and among us — this intimate display of Christ's supremacy marked the early church through the Spirit's powerful outpouring at Pentecost.** When he ascended to the throne of Heaven, Jesus promised to send his disciples "another advocate" just like himself to take up residence **within** them and testify to them about the glory of Jesus so fully they would never feel abandoned or "orphaned" by him (John 14). *So now,* since Pentecost, Peter's message to the people explaining what was taking place that day has become our experience as well:

  > *Jesus has been given a place of honor* at the right hand of God. He has received the Holy Spirit from the Father. This is what God had promised. It is *Jesus who has poured out what you now see and hear* (Acts 2, emphasis added).

- **Within us and among us — this experience is how the reign of Christ *below* duplicates his reign *above*.** Ascended to rule over all creation and all ages to come, Jesus is right now by his Spirit filling his people with the richness of himself — calling them, conquering them, communicating with them, collaborating with them, compelling them, completing them. *So now,* as Paul puts it:

  > [God's power] can't be compared with anything else. It is *at work for us who believe. It is like the mighty strength God showed when he raised Christ from the dead.* He seated him at his right hand in his heavenly kingdom. There Christ sits far above all who rule and have authority. He also sits far above all powers and kings. He is above every title that can be given in this world and in the world to come. *God placed all things under Christ's rule. He appointed him to be ruler over everything for the church. The church is Christ's body. It is filled by Christ.* He fills everything in every way (Ephesians 1, emphasis added).

- **Within us and among us — this is the relationship Jesus maintains with us even when he sends us out to reach the nations.** Jesus breathed on the disciples gathered Easter evening (talk about intimacy with him in his supremacy!), inviting them as a group to receive the Holy Spirit. He told them he was doing this because he was sending them out in mission together, just as the Father had sent him out in mission. Later he promised them: "you will receive power . . . and be my witnesses." Note the "you" is plural — the power is *shared* power and the witness is *collaborative.* In Matthew 28, he made it clear that wherever they would go he would be with them, among them, working through them.

> I am *with you always* to the end of the age (emphasis added).

So now, we have witnessed over 20 centuries of his power-filled presence in and among millions of ambassadors of the gospel sent out into all the earth.

- *Within* us and among us — this engagement with his people will define the reign of Christ at the Consummation from that moment onward. "Christ *within* us" finds its boldest expression in the Bible's final book, the Revelation. Here's what the final chapters promise is waiting for all of us:

> I saw the Holy City, the new Jerusalem. It was coming down out of heaven from God. It was prepared like a bride beautifully dressed for her husband. I heard a loud voice from the throne. It said, *"Now God makes his home with people. He will live with them.* They will be his people. And God himself will be with them and be their God. He will wipe away every tear from their eyes"* . . . He who was sitting on the throne said, *"I am making everything new!"* (Revelation 21, emphasis added).

> There will no longer be any curse. The throne of God and of the Lamb will be in the city. God's servants will serve him. *They will see his face. His name will be on their foreheads* (Revelation 22, emphasis added).

So for right now, God's people everywhere get to share in this magnificent drama, but only as a foretaste of all that is to come. Paul summarizes that drama going on among believers today like this:

> God has planned to give a vision of the full wonder and splendor of his secret plan for the sons of men. And the secret is simply this: *Christ is within all of you bringing with him the hope of all glorious things to come.* So, naturally, we proclaim Christ! (Colossians 1, PHILLIPS, emphasis added).

Selah

pause | think | pray

The Wrap

As noted earlier, *ecclesiology* (our study of the Church) should never be divorced from *Christology* (our study of the Christ). The *breadth* of our ecclesiology must be defined by, and continually refined by, the *depth* of our Christology.

These two doctrines are brought together profoundly for the Church through a very special celebration — a most unique meal, vividly portraying the truth of Jesus abiding **within** us and among us.

Different traditions and denominations have coined different terms to speak of the meal. Some call it the *"Lord's Supper"* — a meal to help remember his sacrifice, one that Jesus hosts by his Spirit. Others call it the *"Eucharist"* — a meal by which we focus on and "give thanks" for all Jesus has done for our salvation by his atoning death. *"Communion"* is another term used — a meal where we commune with Jesus and with each other as we eat together, reflecting on his death for us. Still others call this meal a *"Mass"* — a meal viewed as a reenactment of what Christ did for us on Calvary, meant to propel believers out in mission for Christ. "Mass" comes from Latin for "Go!"

Combining all these terms we might say that for every part of the global Church this "dinner" emphasizes one essential, overarching theme: The crucifixion of God's Son — the sacrificing of his body and blood — offered for the forgiveness of our sins, given for all of God's people without qualification, which we receive individually, doing so corporately.

It is to this feast Jesus summons *all* believers. He welcomes us to gather around him and his table as those who share a common life from him. He invites us and unites us to memorialize, to celebrate, to enter into all he has suffered for us. Paul reports about the night when Jesus initiated this supper and defined its significance:

> When he had given thanks, he broke [the bread]. He said, "This is my body. It is given for you. *Every time you eat it, do it in memory of me.*" In the same way, after supper he took the cup. He said, "This cup is the new covenant in my blood. *Every time you drink it, do it in memory of me*" (1 Corinthians 11, emphasis added).

For believers of every tradition and denomination the feast takes place as a *community activity,* where jointly we "declare the Lord's death until he comes" (1 Corinthians 11). The early church understood the *corporate* symbolism of this meal quite readily:

> When we give thanks for the cup at the Lord's Supper, aren't we sharing in the blood of Christ? When we break the bread, aren't we sharing in the body of Christ? *Just as there is one loaf, so we who are many are one body. We all eat from the one loaf* (1 Corinthians 10, emphasis added).

Most importantly, every time we eat this meal together by faith it is Jesus himself among us who provides us himself as the real nourishment. One might say he is the menu, the chef, and the main course, all at the same time. The elements we partake echo his exhortation in John 6:

> What I'm about to tell you is true. *You must eat the Son of Man's body and drink his blood. If you don't, you have no life in you.* Anyone who eats my body and drinks my blood has eternal life. I will raise him up on the last day. My body is real food. My blood is real drink (emphasis added).

This universal *rite* puts Jesus in his *right*-ful place among us, even as it puts us in our proper place before him.

Every time we share the sacred meal together we reaffirm this fifth phenomenon of Christ's supremacy:

Christ within *me* and Christ within *us* always go together.

But what he accomplishes in *me* is derived primarily

from what he accomplishes, first of all, among *us*.

Jesus' Reign WITHIN Us Today:
We Must Give His Supremacy the Priority

Earlier in *Christ Is Now!* we defined what most Christians envision when they talk about Christ's centrality: *"Christ has a right to be at the center of who* **we** *are, where* **we** *are headed, what* **we** *are doing, and how* **we** *get blessed."* Most assuredly, he does have that right! But he is meant to be so much more to us!

The "centrality of Christ" — Christ *within* us — should never be understood apart from what is implied by the "*supremacy* of Christ." The One who inhabits his people is the One who claims, at the same time, his unqualified right *"to keep us at the center of who* **he** *is, where* **he** *is headed, what* **he** *is doing, and how* **he** *gets blessed."* That's the ultimate impact of his supremacy on our lives.

Imagine an empty water bottle cast into the waves of the ocean, swept out to sea, caught up in the currents, taken deeper and further than one could imagine. This pictures believers (individually and corporately) experiencing a life of discipleship that thrills and thrives because we're caught up in and carried forward by the Father's plan to sum up all things under Jesus as Lord. *We're living at the center of who HE is.*

Simultaneously, once lost among the waves that same bottle quickly fills with sea water right to the top and remains that way no matter how far or how deep the currents may take it.

In other words, at the same time we're *in Christ,* he also is *in us.* The ocean (Christ) that submerges the bottle into its depths, representing the reign of Christ (supremacy), is the same ocean that floods the bottle, permeating every bit of it, animating it with the reign of Christ (centrality).

Let's dig into this further.

 Snapshots and Starter Thoughts

- **Jesus is not only *residing* as Lord in our churches (centrality), he also is *presiding* as Lord in our midst (supremacy).** The Father's goal is for the reign of his Son *over* his people to be manifested *to* his people, then replicated **within** his people, in order to be reflected and advanced *through* his people.

- **The One who is near to us, intimate and personal with us (centrality), at the same time is the One transcendent over all of creation, encompassing heaven and earth (supremacy).** He imparts his universal, all-invasive fullness into our localized, day-to-day life together. Scripture puts it simply:

  > *The Church is the fullness of him* who fills all things with Himself (Ephesians 1, emphasis added).

- **With unchallenged dominion, our Jesus comes among us (centrality) to exert his power however he pleases (supremacy).** He does so **within** each separate congregation as well as **within** the Church worldwide — equally with both. He walks among his people, sustaining and empowering us by his risen life (centrality), defining us by where he takes us as he inhabits us (supremacy).

- **He invades us with himself to gather us around himself (centrality) so as to incorporate us into his agenda, his journey, and his triumphs (supremacy).** He indwells us (centrality) in order to draw us daily into the adventure of giving him first place in all things (supremacy).

- **In Colossians 1:26-27, Paul calls "Christ *within* us" a longtime "secret," something God kept "hidden" from mankind but now brings into the open through the gospel for everyone to share in.** As remarkable as it sounds, this new revelation means that, for now and forever, the King of heaven, God's Son, intends to make his home *within* God's people.

At the end of the day the vitality of any congregation is not determined by how many *members* it boasts but by *how much of the fullness of Christ's life its members share in.*

- **Specifically Christ has come among us to be himself our *"hope of glory."*** Hope for Christians rests in a *Person* — a Person who resides among us — a Person who assumes the initiative for all future triumphs of his people, doing so "up close and personal." In other words, his leadership among us today is not about only today (as vital as that is), but also about *tomorrow.* The truth is that "Christ *within* us" should always stir up in us great expectations — anticipations of so much more from him (See Chapter 4, "Who Christ Is BEFORE Us Today").

- **Hope, we might say, is the flag a congregation flies once they wake up to the fact that their King is already in residence.** The more intentionally and consistently Christians unite around their Radiant Redeemer, the more their hope in him comes alive! The more we seek the fulfillment of his reign where we live, the more the blessings of our salvation will explode among us, the more our love for one another will overflow between us, and the more energized our collaborative labors for Jesus' sake will unfold with all of us.

- **None of the mysterious magnificence of Colossians 1:27 is for the sake of believers *only*; it also is for the blessing of many, many *others* too.** See how *The Message* translates verses 26 and 27:

  > This mystery has been kept in the dark for a long time, *but now it's out in the open. God wanted everyone, not just Jews, to know this rich and glorious secret inside and out, regardless of their background, regardless of their religious standing. The mystery in a nutshell is just this: Christ is in you, so therefore you can look forward to sharing in God's glory. It's that simple* (emphasis added).

The good news for earth's peoples, in every nation, is that the Christ of God wants to do for them what he's done for us: reconcile them to the Father and to each other, and then inhabit them without reservation as his forever family.

• *Within* **us is the reigning Son of God — not just a small part of him, or half of him, but** *all* **of him.** He comes not as a sojourner, but as a permanent resident. He has come to abide with us and minister to us — to reign *within* us — for *all* he is.

• **When the "Ascended One" plants in us his "ascended life," he does not do so** *remotely*. Instead, at this hour he has entrenched himself inside the global Church, personally employing the full spectrum of its ethnic, national, and denominational expressions. Clearly, he has no intention of walking away from any whom he has redeemed — not ever! Instead, he is gathering to himself the *totality* of the diversity of his people in order to reproduce in us together his royal, nobler life for the rest of eternity.

> You have begun life as the new man . . . In this new man of God's design there is no distinction between Greek and Hebrew, Jew or Gentile, foreigner or savage, slave or free man. *Christ is all that matters* [supremacy] *for Christ lives in them all* [centrality] (Colossians 3:11, PHILLIPS, emphasis added).

• **And here's the best part: The Son who comes to make his home** *WITHIN* **us individually and corporately also brings with him** *every* **facet of his supremacy we've uncovered in our studies so far.** This means (to review) when he inhabits us he comes to us *undiminished* in terms of who he is *TO* us and *FOR* us; who he is *OVER* us and *BEFORE* us; and (as we'll survey in the next two chapters) who he is *THROUGH* us and *UPON* us. He wants to be ALL and in ALL for ALL of us.

pause | think | pray

The Wrap

What would it look like if the dimensions of "Christ **within** us" were experienced, for instance, by a group of Christians confined for years behind the walls of a maximum security prison? Well, it's happening!

A "Christ Awakening movement" is unfolding in one of America's best known maximum security prisons, where hundreds of inmates are experiencing the impact of the presence and power of the living Christ at work in their midst.

Not long ago, about two hundred inmates memorized a four-line poem written especially to give them a way to testify together to their experience at East Jersey State Prison (EJSP). Since then, when gathered on Sundays for worship, they often lift their voices to recite the verse in unison. It goes like this:

> *Christ is risen in the prison!*
> *He calls among the walls.*
> *He dwells in the cells.*
> *He's the One you see at EJSP!*

But, in point of fact, how can *any* Christian congregation anywhere, no matter what challenges or limitations it faces, embrace any less of a vision than this?

Is not Christ risen in *our* midst too? Does he not also call to us in *our* gatherings? Is he not dwelling in *our* times of worship and fellowship? Does he not also abide **within** every body of believers in order to be magnified through each one for all he is?

Should not the victories in Jesus flowing inside these prison walls become the normal way of life for God's people serving him on the outside?

Jesus' Reign WITHIN Us Today:
The Primary Role of the Holy Spirit

At Pentecost, when the Spirit was poured out on the Church, something extraordinary happened. God's people experienced firsthand *a preliminary phase* of Christ and his kingdom "coming with power," a *foretaste* of Jesus' final revelation at the Consummation of all things.

From that moment forward, the Spirit assumed one major assignment: to make much of the King among his followers; to incite our love for him; to intensify our pursuit of him; to escalate our worship of him; to enlarge our hope in him; and to empower our mission for him.

From Pentecost forward, the Holy Spirit has provided God's people the key to, the reality of, and our experience of, "Christ **within** you, the hope of glory."

In Scripture the third person of the Trinity is known variously as "the Spirit of the Lord," the "Spirit of God's Son," the "Spirit of Christ," and the "Spirit of Jesus Christ." Such titles emphasize how the Spirit's presence in our churches and in our lives is wrapped up in and focused inextricably on the person and reign of Christ himself.

This is true to such a degree that one could say the Spirit **within** us is *equivalent* to Christ himself living among us. Therefore, at all times Christians should live as if Christ is literally present among us — because by his Spirit *he literally is!*

To be sure, "*physically*" speaking, Jesus is exalted and enthroned in heaven. Nonetheless, at the same time *by the Spirit* Jesus occupies us no less tangibly,

right here on earth among us. To say that Jesus lives and works **within** his people testifies to how effectively, and vividly, the *Spirit* serves the Church on Jesus' behalf and as his personal advocate.

The Spirit represents to us — that is, he *re-presents* to us — the very same Jesus who ascended on high (Acts 1), no one else and no one less. Combine Ephesians 4 with Ephesians 1 and Ephesians 3 and you have the whole picture: The Spirit puts Christ **within** us—both at a personal level, and above all, as we come together. Notice:

> The One who came down is the same as the One who went up higher than all the heavens. He did it in order to fill all of creation (Ephesians 4, MSG).

> At the center of all this, Christ rules the church . . . The church is Christ's body, in which he speaks and acts, by which he fills everything with his presence (Ephesians 1, MSG).

> I pray that from his glorious, unlimited resources he will empower you with inner strength through his Spirit. Then Christ will make his home [within] your hearts as you trust in him . . . Then you will be made complete with all the fullness of life and power that comes from God (Ephesians 3, NLT).

 ## Snapshots and Starter Thoughts

- **Without question, where the Spirit abides *all* of Jesus abides, in *all* his fullness.** Above all else, the Spirit brings to us a witness to the Son that makes him so real to God's people that it is *as if* he were bodily spending every moment among us.

- **Thus we can say that because of the Spirit, the Lord Jesus is fully *within* every congregation of believers on planet Earth.** Not just part of him is there, but ALL of him. And wherever Jesus dwells, the triune God is fully involved.

- **Jesus' abiding presence *within* his people by his Spirit brings *the gift of life* to each one of his own.**

> I will ask the Father. And he will give you another Friend to help you and to be with you forever. The Friend is the Spirit of truth . . . you know him. He lives with you, and he will be in you. I will not leave you like children who don't have parents. I will come to you . . . Because I

live, you will live also. On that day you will realize that I am in my Father. You will know that you are in me, and I am in you (John 14).

- **Even though Christ is sitting at the Father's right hand, by the Spirit he can manifest himself** *within* **every gathering of his people, in every part of the earth, in equal measure, all at the same time.** The Spirit keeps the Son "within reach" of the whole Body of Christ at every moment, in every place. By the Spirit, Christ is prepared to pour into every single congregation of believers more of his risen life with all its power, giving himself to them in ways fitted exactly to each group's situation.

- **The Spirit reveals to us everything we require in order to know Christ and enjoy his reign right now.** Moment by moment the Spirit connects the Church directly to Jesus. He is the *invasion* of, *habitation* of, *activation* of, *manifestation* of, and *application* of Jesus' sovereignty among his saved ones. That's why Scripture defines our life in Jesus today primarily as "life in the Spirit."

- **As the Spirit activates the reign of Christ in the midst of the Church, he gives us "interim" experiences of what the lordship of Christ will feel like throughout all ages to come.** In fact, this global invasion of Jesus through the Spirit provides a *preview* of the community life that awaits us when the triune God dwells among us forever in the new Jerusalem "that comes down out of heaven" (Revelation 21) — as we'll explore in depth in the chapter "Who Christ Is UPON Us Today."

- **Accordingly, the Spirit serves as the Father's down payment guaranteeing to us that we will inherit all he has promised about everlasting life in his Son.** That's why the Spirit brings into the community of God's people regular, practical *foretastes* of our anticipated inheritance. Therefore, we should expect to experience in our congregations a "sampling" of the *quality* of life in Christ awaiting us at the climax of all things, when we will taste fully both the quality and the *quantity* of life in Christ. Remember this promise from Jesus:

> But when the Spirit of truth comes, he will guide you into all the truth. He will not speak on his own. He will speak only what he hears. *And he will tell you what is still going to happen.* He will bring me glory (John 15, emphasis added).

- **Christ redeemed us so that this *"life* in the Spirit" might replace the deadly curse of the Law.** The New Testament claims:

  > Now Christ has redeemed us from the curse of the Law's condemnation . . . that the blessing promised to Abraham might reach the Gentiles through Jesus Christ, and the Spirit might become available to us all by faith (Galatians 3, PHILLIPS).

- **In place of the curse, the Spirit brings us into uninterrupted intimacy with Christ in his supremacy, consuming us more and more with the vision of his greatness and glory.** The Holy Spirit *refines* us, *purges* us, *reforms* us, *revives* us, and *empowers* us every time he *opens* us to fresh dimensions of the ministry of Christ *within* us, all of which fulfills in us the righteous ways of the Law.

- **It follows then, that when we are *"filled* with the Spirit" (Ephesians 5), individually or corporately, we find ourselves more fully occupied with Christ alone.** Unavoidably, a person or a congregation will swell with the Spirit's activity as, with one heart, we allow him to carry out his ministry without resistance, as he draws our focus in all things to Christ alone, for his sake alone.

- **The Spirit *fills* us every time he leads us into a *fuller* share of the *fullness* found in Jesus.** He does this by giving us *"accessibility,"* which allows us to freely *come* to Christ, and also by giving us *"capability,"* which enables us to freely *respond* to him as we come to him. In other words, he makes Christ *accessible* to us *as if* literally we were standing before his throne in heaven itself. At the same time, he makes us *capable* of sensing and receiving more of Christ *as if* physically his throne were planted among us here on earth.

- **In John 7, Jesus pictured the Spirit's ministry on his behalf by using the image of rivers flowing into the midst of thirsty disciples — rivers of living water from which they may freely drink.**

  > On the last day, the climax of the festival, Jesus stood and shouted to the crowds, "Anyone who is thirsty may come to me! Anyone who believes in me may come and drink! For the Scriptures declare, "Rivers of living water will flow from his heart."

- **Furthermore, according to John 7, the Spirit's life-giving activity among God's people comes to us in direct relationship to Christ's**

ascension and inauguration on high. The apostle adds for his readers an interpretation of what Jesus said:

> When he said "living water," he was speaking of the Spirit, who would be given to everyone believing in him. *But the Spirit had not yet been given, because Jesus had not yet entered into his glory* (NLT, emphasis added).

- **In John 7, Jesus taught that this river of the Spirit, bringing his fullness to his followers, would flow from out of a *"heart."* But *whose* heart did he mean?** Many scholars believe Jesus was not referring to the heart of disciples (though that might happen as well) but that he was primarily referring to his *own* heart.

When he cites this river as the one forecast by Scripture, the passage most scholars believe he had in mind was the prophetic vision in Ezekiel 47, where we read in part:

> The man brought me back to the entrance to the temple. I saw water flowing east from under a temple gateway . . . He led me through water that was up to my ankles . . . up to my knees . . . up to my waist . . . now the water had risen so high that it was deep enough to swim in . . . Then he led me back to the bank of the river. When I arrived there, I saw a large number of trees. They were on both sides of the river . . . it enters the Dead Sea. When it empties into it, the water there becomes fresh. Large numbers of creatures will live where the river flows . . . So where the river flows everything will live.

The river here represents the Spirit sent from Jesus to God's people. For Jesus, this visionary river flowing out of Ezekiel's Holy of Holies, giving life to creation wherever it runs, is a picture of the Holy Spirit being poured out from him as the King-Priest of the universe, and from his throne, where he reigns supreme. Into the midst of the Church, the Spirit brings to God's people life *from* Jesus, life *in* Jesus — the life that *is* Jesus — not only on the day of Pentecost but throughout this entire age, wherever streams of the Spirit keep flowing across the earth.

- **The Spirit liberates us in order for us to experience a full, face-to-face encounter with the exalted Lord Jesus in our midst, so as to transform us into much more of his likeness.** We read:

> But when anyone turns to the Lord, the veil is taken away. *Now the Lord is the Holy Spirit. And where the Spirit of the Lord is, freedom is also*

> there . . . So we are being *changed to become more like him* so that we
> have more and more glory. And this glory comes *from the Lord, who
> is the Holy Spirit* (2 Corinthians 3, emphasis added).

The principle? We become more like the person with whom we spend the
most time, the one on whom we are focused the most. By the Spirit, Jesus
dwells ***within*** us so we might dwell upon him.

- **Why is the Spirit frequently called "HOLY"?** As we know, in Scripture to
  make something "holy" means "to set it apart" or "to consecrate it for
  sacred purposes." There are at least three ways the word "holy" accurately
  pinpoints who the Spirit *is*, what he *does*, and what this means for putting
  "Christ ***within*** us."

(1) He is God, third person of the Trinity. Therefore, inherently as God
he is set apart as the One who is totally unique in his person and in his
mission. Not only is he unlike every other spirit in the universe, but also
he is the only spirit whose primary assignment is to exalt Christ among
God's people.

**(2) Next, his mission in God's redemptive plan is *"to consecrate"*
Christ—that is, to set apart God's Son before the eyes of God's people.**
He has come to reveal God's Son more fully to God's people; to help us see
Jesus as incomparable, preeminent, and supreme; to honor him as Head
among his people so we continue to celebrate his majesty and serve him
as Lord of all, faithfully giving him his rightful place in our midst. As a
result, the Church will be able to take similar action that glorifies Christ
before the rest of creation (Ephesians 3:9-10).

**(3) Finally, of parallel importance, his mission involves his every effort
"to consecrate" (make holy) *God's people themselves* — to set them
apart for Christ.** The Spirit does this as he draws us more and more into
the fullness of Christ's supremacy, separating us unto Christ so that we live
at the center of all he is, where he is headed, what he is doing, and how
he gets blessed.

- **When the Church is filled with the Spirit and led by the Spirit, the
  evidence of this is how God's people walk in daily *repentance* —
  immediately renouncing anything that *competes* with the glory of
  Christ.** The Spirit helps us to set our hearts on the reign of Christ, to live
  in continual readiness for more of Christ, to eagerly follow him wherever

he wants to take us, and to do so at any cost. In response, we turn away from all that might move us onto a different path that diverts our affections and focus away from Jesus. Every time the Spirit draws us into deeper intimacy with Jesus, it isn't long before we see the contrast of our own imperfections in the light of his holiness. It is also there, in his presence, that we find liberating repentance.

- **Scripture tells us that anything in our lives, individually or corporately, found to be *incompatible* with the person and supremacy of Christ, if not renounced and put away, *"resists"* the Spirit (Acts 7), *"grieves"* the Spirit (Ephesians 4), and *"quenches"* the Spirit (1 Thessalonians 5).** Why is this? It is because any disloyalty or disobedience toward God's Son runs counter to the Spirit's passion to give him his rightful place among God's people. Repentance, on the other hand, keeps us reaffirming and re-embracing the preeminence of Jesus once we realize what our Christ-denying desires, decisions, and actions have done to hurt his heart and his kingdom purposes.

- **The Spirit's mission "to put Christ *within* us" includes the rich biblical teachings about the *gifts* of the Spirit (1 Corinthians 12, 14; Romans 12) and the *fruit* of the Spirit (Galatians 5).** By the *"gifts* of the Spirit"* the Church is equipped to share in the *ministry* of Christ operating among us and through us. By the *"fruit* of the Spirit"* the Church shares in the *character* of Christ lived out among us and in us. Both the gifts and the fruit are evidences of Jesus' interpersonal involvement with his people — manifesting his presence and filling us with himself in the same ways he is filling the entire universe with himself right now (recounted in Ephesians 1 and 4).

The Wrap

From these preliminary insights one thing is clear: The Holy Spirit is not content to postpone until eternity our getting to know God's Son, or our being ignited in passion toward God's Son, or our delighting in communing with fellow Christians gathered around God's Son.

Abiding **within** us, the Holy Spirit is determined to engage us with Jesus, at all costs, in ways that make our devotion to Jesus and to each other grow deeper with every passing day, as we become more fervent in our service to the Savior and to all those he loves.

To our everlasting joy, the Spirit makes tangible and experiential one of the richest treasures offered to believers in the Word: He puts "Christ **within** us." The Spirit unlocks for us the gold mine that comes from knowing God's Son intimately. He does this by making Christ so real and present to us that it is as if the Son is setting up house among us to bless us unconditionally.

By pouring out his Spirit upon us, Jesus' engagement with us "here" remains directly related to who he is and what he's doing "there." The Spirit assures us that Christ's "supremacy" within God's purposes will always be paired with his "intimacy" **within** God's people. The Christ who took on flesh but now dwells with the hosts above, still dwells among those of flesh below — specifically by pouring his Spirit into us *without limits.*

> For the one whom God sent speaks the authentic words of God — and *there can be no measuring of the Spirit given to him!* The Father loves the Son and has put everything into his hand (John 3, PHILLIPS, emphasis added).

Selah

pause | think | pray

Jesus' Reign WITHIN Us Today:
We Become Jesus' Temple, Jesus' Body, Jesus' Bride

The story at the start of this chapter told how the performance of a group of basketball players was radically altered simply by adding one enthusiastic and gifted member to the team. That story is symbolic for what can happen to any community of Christians when Christ resides *within* them and works out his purposes for them in power.

The New Testament describes three metaphors to highlight the significant impact "Christ *within* us" inherently has on the corporate life of God's people: He fashions us into a living *temple*; he forges us into a coordinated *body*; he draws us as his *bride* into a sacred marriage. Let's look at all three.

 Snapshots and Starter Thoughts

- **The first metaphor: Christ fashions us into a living "TEMPLE."** As we've seen, God's Son is the New Testament's answer to the Old Testament temple's "Shekinah Glory." Christ abiding within his churches by his Spirit transforms every congregation from a collection of individuals into a singular, sacred "sanctuary."

    We are built on the foundation of the apostles and prophets, with Christ Jesus himself as the chief cornerstone. In Him *the whole building is joined together and rises to become a holy temple in the Lord.*

And in Him you too are being built together to become a dwelling in which God lives by His Spirit (Ephesians 2, emphasis added).

As you come to Him, the living Stone – rejected by men but chosen by God and precious to Him – *you also, like living stones, are being built into a spiritual house* to be a holy priesthood, offering spiritual sacrifices acceptable to God through Jesus Christ (1 Peter 2, emphasis added).

- **In a sense, Jesus' resurrected body has become the central temple for all of creation from which the secondary temple made up of all the redeemed derives its identity.** During his earthly ministry, Jesus made it clear that when he defeated death, his glorified physical body would be the true, eternal temple, replacing the physical temple in Jerusalem. Now *wherever* he dwells becomes a consummate meeting place between God and his people forever. That time has come.

    "Destroy this temple. I will raise it up again in three days" . . . *The temple Jesus had spoken about was his body.* His disciples later remembered what he had said after he had been *raised from the dead.* Then they believed (John 2, emphasis added).

    I tell you that *one who is more important than the temple is here.* (Matthew 12, emphasis added).

    I saw no temple in the city, for *the Lord God Almighty and the Lamb are its temple* (Revelation 21, emphasis added).

- **In him, we too have become a "Holy House," reconstituting our life together into something sublime and sacred, carrying sobering repercussions:**

    No one can lay any other foundation than the one that has already been laid. *That foundation is Jesus Christ.* A person may build on it . . . Don't you know that you yourselves are God's temple? God's Spirit lives in you. If anyone destroys God's temple, God will destroy him. *God's temple is holy. And you are that temple* (1 Corinthians 3, emphasis added).

- **Jesus is both "cornerstone" and "keystone" of this life-giving structure.** A *cornerstone* is the first stone set in the construction of a building. It determines the position of the building and unites and supports two walls where they come together. In the same way, Jesus, as the cornerstone, is the solid foundation upon which the Church is built so that it might be brought together and kept together in true unity and true direction.

A *keystone* is inserted in the middle at the top of an arch, finishing and joining the two sides of the arch. It is the final stone placed in the arch, which locks all the stones into position, and is held in place by bearing the weight of the supporting columns. Even so, Jesus pulls together in himself the diverse expressions of the Church (originally this meant Jews and Gentiles) to fashion one grand and glorious framework, with him as its firm focal point.

- **The second metaphor: Christ forges us into a coordinated "BODY."** Jesus **within** his people transposes us into an *organism* resembling a fully functioning human body with himself serving as central control — as its *head*. Churches call believers "members" for good reason. It refers not to a static, organizational roster but to colleagues bound in a community, the way hands, feet, legs, and ears compose a "body" — dynamic, vibrant, collaborating.

  > [God] has appointed Him the universal and *supreme Head of the church* [a headship exercised throughout the church], which is *His body, the fullness of Him Who fills all in all* [for in that body lives the full measure of Him Who makes everything complete, and Who fills everything everywhere with Himself] (Ephesians 1, AMPC, emphasis added)

- **To speak of Christ's "headship" over this body (his people) is not simply another way to describe what his lordship involves. Far more, it pictures him as** *actively engaged* **throughout every expression of the Church and within every facet of its life.** As the human brain controls, monitors, and coordinates the limbs, organs, and every system of the human body down to its most infinitesimal component, Jesus is personally concerned for each of us individually and with all of us collectively — supporting, stimulating, sustaining, and synthesizing us as he shapes us into a society of saints in heaven and on earth.

- **As the Head, Jesus takes direct responsibility for every aspect of the "body life" of the Church — from its health, to its growth, to its worship, to its battles with darkness, to its coordinated activities for advancing kingdom purposes.** He determines its identity, its nature, its attributes, its achievements, its future.

  > Speaking the truth in love, we will grow to become in every respect the mature body of him who is the head, that is, Christ. From him the whole body, joined and held together by every supporting ligament,

grows and builds itself up in love, as each part does its work (Ephesians 4).

Just as a body, though one, has many parts, but all its many parts form one body, so it is with Christ. For we were all baptized by one Spirit so as to form one body – whether Jews or Gentiles, slave or free – and we were all given the one Spirit to drink. Even so the body is not made up of one part but of many (1 Corinthians 12).

- **Jesus' identity with his people means the sufferings of members of his body become very personal for him as the Head, as if it were happening *to him* because of his intimacy with us.** One opponent of the early church learned this truth firsthand when the ascended Jesus confronted him with these words:

  "Saul, Saul, why are you persecuting Me [harassing, troubling, and molesting Me]? . . . I am Jesus, Whom you are persecuting. It is dangerous and it will turn out badly for you to keep kicking against the goad" (Acts 9, AMP).

- **The third metaphor: Christ draws us to himself to be his "BRIDE."** Puritan theologian Jonathan Edwards taught that according to the Bible the grand goal of human history is "to provide God's Son with a spouse," made up of the redeemed of all the ages.

- **In John 3, the Baptizer prefigured the New Testament's bride metaphor when he predicted at the outset of Jesus' public ministry:**

  The bride belongs to the groom. The friend who helps the groom waits and listens for him. He is full of joy when he hears the groom's voice. That joy is mine, and it is now complete. He must become more important. I must become less important.

- **The most familiar portrayal of Christ as a husband for his Church is found in Ephesians 5**.

  The church follows the lead of Christ. In the same way, wives should follow the lead of their husbands in everything. Husbands, love your wives. Love them just as Christ loved the church. He gave himself up for her. He did it to make her holy. He made her clean by washing her with water and the word. He did it to bring her to himself as a brightly shining church. He wants a church that has no stain or wrinkle or any other flaw. He wants a church that is holy and without blame.

- **Certainly, marriage is a "mystery" whether on a human level or as an expression of the intimacy of Christ's supremacy among his people.** Just as husband and wife are declared to be "one flesh," so the Church is "one spirit" with Christ (1 Corinthians 6) who nourishes us and cherishes us, laboring among us to purify us, intending one day soon to present the Church before the Father as a glorious "bride" prepared by him to spend eternity by his side — as it was with Eve in Genesis 1, taken *from* Adam's side to be *by* his side as co-regent with her husband.

- **In 2 Corinthians 11, Paul drew on the idea of a woman engaged to become a bride as the metaphor that helped clarify the burden of his ministry to God's people.**

  > My jealousy over you is the right sort of jealousy, for in my eyes you are like a fresh unspoiled girl who I am presenting as fiancé to your true husband, Christ himself. I am afraid that your minds may be seduced from a single-hearted devotion to him (PHILLIPS).

- **Finally, the Bible envisions a bride (the Church) joining her groom (Jesus) in an unprecedented wedding celebration as a way of representing the final outcome for God's people at the consummation of the ages.**

  > Let us give him the glory, *for the wedding-day of the Lamb has come, and his bride has made herself ready* . . . Happy are those who are invited to the wedding-feast of the Lamb! (Revelation 19, PHILLIPS, emphasis added).

Selah

pause | think | pray

Jesus' Reign WITHIN Us Today:
The Basis for the Unity of God's People

In light of all we've covered in this chapter it makes sense for us to take a moment to ponder what Paul asks in 1 Corinthians 1: *"Is Christ divided?"*

Note that the apostle does not ask, "Is the *Church* divided?" The question is about *Christ*: Can *he* be divided. The apostle's choice of words is intentional, suggesting that whatever happens inside the community of Christ followers impinges directly on Christ himself.

Our identity and destiny intertwine with him even as he intertwines with us, dwelling **within** us, walking among us. Therefore, whenever we pull away from each other *it is as if we were dissecting Christ*, carving him up into pieces.

A fundamental question for the worldwide Church as well as for any local church struggling to maintain the unity of the Spirit (Ephesians 4) must be:

If Christ himself cannot be divided up
why do we insist on dividing up among ourselves?

If Christ cannot be compartmentalized — if we can't separate who he is as God's Son from all he is among us — then how can we who call ourselves by Jesus' name justify remaining indefinitely separated from, indifferent toward, suspicious of, competitive with, or worse, in opposition to one another?

On the contrary, the reality is that when any of us accepts Jesus as Lord *automatically we accept all others who have accepted him as their Lord* because in God's sight all believers "abide in him" even as he "abides in us." Therefore, it is incongruous for Christians to choose to love certain "parts" of his Body rather than all of his Body — since it is *his* Body!

Loving one another is inseparable from loving Jesus, who is alive in our midst — they go hand in hand. Out of our solidarity with him we are called to "submit to one another" *specifically* "out of reverence for Christ" to whom we are accountable (Ephesians 5). In fact, if we "sin against a brother" the Father interprets that as actually "sinning against Christ himself" (1 Corinthians 8). What true believer wants to be found guilty of doing that?

On the other hand, the truth in Jesus says this:

> You have been made holy because you belong to Christ Jesus. God has chosen you to be his holy people. *He has done the same for all those everywhere who pray to our Lord Jesus Christ. Jesus is their Lord and ours* (1 Corinthians 1, emphasis added).

Therefore, drawing on the wisdom of Colossians 3, let's weave our life together with a love that "binds all things together," allow the "shalom of Christ to rule" so as to preserve our unity, as we also strengthen our bond by how we allow "the message about Christ to dwell in [us] richly" throughout all we do as his community (Colossians 3).

Positionally (by the nature of who we are in Christ) and *inherently* (by the nature of who Christ is in us) — though not necessarily *organizationally* — we are *one*, locally and globally. In turn, this God-given *relational* unity with Christ should encourage vital demonstrations of *cooperational* unity among us for Jesus' sake.

Snapshots and Starter Thoughts

- **The New Testament word for "church" comes from the Greek "ecclesia," meaning "those called out" or "those assembled," suggesting one facet of what unites believers in Christ.** The issue is not so much about what we have been called out *from* ("transferred from the domain of darkness," Colossians 1) as it is *Who* we have been called forth *to join* ("into the kingdom of God's dear Son," Colossians 1). Into the

Savior's sphere and around the Savior's seat all believers have been assembled.

- **Around A.D. 300, however, another, more popular word came into vogue also translated "church," from the Greek word "kyriakon" meaning "of the Lord."** It indicated how Christian unity is sealed by Christ's ownership of us. "Kyriakon" was used of houses of Christian worship because when believers gathered there for times of adoration and instruction, they submitted to Jesus' rule among them, and thus to each other.

As those who are "of one Lord," we belong to his captive people who stretch out across the earth and across the ages, the "communion of saints" in heaven and earth. The Church is an uncommon fellowship, bound in the Spirit, alive unto and because of one Lord, who works *within* us equally to will and do his good pleasure. Our Master is no "respecter of persons." He invades and invigorates every stream of the Church without discrimination because we all belong to him without exception.

- **Combining "kyriakon" with "ecclesia" helps clarify the "glorious riches" of the gospel, which is "Christ *within* you" (Colossians 1).** Christians are called out of a fallen world to reconvene around Christ as the One to whom we belong, intimately, totally, and exclusively. When believers say, "We're going to church on Sunday," we profess that we're stepping aside from ordinary routines to reconnect with those who belong to Jesus — to meet with our Lord together, joined as one people to celebrate him, to learn from him, to feed on him, and then to be sent out by him.

- **This oneness is God's design for every congregation, of every denomination, from every nation, in every generation.** The fact is, every assembly of God's people is meant to be a microcosm or prototype of what will one day be true in the entire universe when Jesus brings everything to culmination around himself — when all the saved join him to exhibit one fabulous forever family.

- **Thus, in a very real sense, wherever Jesus dwells, *there* the whole church also resides because the whole church already is in union with him just as he already is in union with us and abides in the midst**

of us. The person of Christ indwelling the people of Christ — this is the supreme reality for every stream of the Church, whether Protestant, Evangelical, Catholic, Pentecostal, Anglican, or Orthodox.

- **The One who unites us is so much greater than what often divides us.** He is not only the center but also the *circumference* — the outer boundary — of our life together. There's nothing beyond him to tear us apart. Various traditions and doctrines we may debate; this can be healthy for strengthening our grasp on truth inside the Church. But at the core, we all share in the same Christ, who in his holy love walks and works among us, desiring to become the singular obsession of his people everywhere.

- **Pervasively active among his people, Jesus transforms the Church *as a whole* into a new creation, a new nation, a new ethnicity — a brand new kind of being — one "new man," as Scripture calls us.** Barriers that usually push apart humans in this world — tradition, politics, race, ethnic background, age, nationality, culture, social status — should no longer define how believers view one another. Instead, *Christ alone defines us as one "new man" in him*! Colossians 3 declares:

    > You have finished with the old man and all he did and have begun life as the new man, who is out to learn what he ought to be, according to the plan of God. In *this new man of God's design* there is no distinction between Greek and Hebrew, Jew or Gentile, foreigner or savage, slave or free man. *Christ is all that matters for Christ lives in them all* (PHILLIPS, emphasis added).

- **In other words, instead of being defined by cultural advantages, social influence, theological sophistication, denominational labels, or ministry specialties, our identity rests in *Christ alone*, living and reigning among us.** When we truly accept the fact that right now all of us are seated in heavenly places around our one Lord, Jesus the Messiah (Ephesians 2), much of what we try to use to justify distances among various camps of believers — experiential, racial, ecclesiastical separations — will be seen by us for what they truly are: irrelevant, unhelpful, unhealthy outlooks that are utterly counterproductive to advancing Christ's global cause.

- **The unifying force of King Jesus presiding in our midst means that cooperating with him by cooperating with each other will *empower* the global Church to decisively display his saving majesty to the**

forces of darkness, confounding them in the process (Ephesians 3). As a precursor of Jesus' final victory throughout all of creation, God's people united here and now provides all spiritual powers in heaven and on earth a profound precursor of how God's great redemptive plan will triumph in the end.

- **Demonic dominions are forced to behold — but cannot refute or repel — Jesus demonstrating his role of reconciliation in God's eternal plan by the undeniable unity he sovereignly displays throughout his global Church.**

> But he gave me the grace to preach to the non-Jews about the wonderful riches that Christ gives. God told me to make clear to everyone how the mystery came about . . . He wanted the rulers and authorities in the heavenly world to come to know his great wisdom. The church would make it known to them. That was God's plan from the beginning. He has worked it out through Christ Jesus our Lord (Ephesians 3).

- **In other words, before heaven and earth Jesus is the depository of all the wisdom required to bring about our salvation — all of it embodied in him who is embedded *within* us.**

> I'm also concerned for everyone who has not met me in person. I want their hearts to be made cheerful and strong. I want them to be joined together in love. Then their understanding will be rich and complete. They will know the mystery of God. That mystery is Christ. All the treasures of wisdom and knowledge are hidden in him (Colossians 2).

- **Our unity in Christ requires that we respond to one another *here* in a manner reflective of how we expect to respond to one another *there* — in the day of his appearing when we surround him around his throne, in full view of his face.** We should show our love to God's people everywhere, beginning with those with whom we worship and with whom we serve, because who Jesus will be among us *then* is precisely who he is among us *here and now*, every time we gather or scatter in his name.

Selah

pause | think | pray

The Wrap

Christ inhabiting his people brings about a unity of life and purpose that can come about no other way. Knowing this full well, Jesus prayed:

> I have given them the glory that you gave me,
>   that they may be one as we are one —
>   I in them and you in me j—
>   so that they be brought to complete unity.
>
>   Then the world will know that
>   you sent me
>   and have loved them
>   even as you have loved me . . .
>
>   I have made you known to them,
>   and will continue to make you known
>
>   in order that the love you have for me
>   may be in them
>   and that I myself
>   may be in them
>   (John 17, NIV).

What is Jesus claiming in his prayer? His desire is that his dwelling **within** us remains forever what *unites* us. Why is this? It's because he comes to us to abide with us as the epiphany of God's glory for us.

Jesus *gives* us God's glory because he *is* God's glory "full of grace and truth" (John 1). Jesus reveals this glory to us in a way that is up close and personal, as the Spirit unites us with a singular passion that burns for him alone.

Unlike other world religions, the focus for Christians is not on a place but on a *Person*. Wherever he dwells among his followers, *there* we become his "place" — because he is there.

Any sense we may have of his "absence" is merely an experience of his temporary *bodily* absence. But by his Spirit he is among us fully — more real for us than anything earthly, material, or visible.

In recent wars, some American journalists have been "*embedded*" with troops on the frontlines, right in the thick of battles, able to report to their readers precisely what is taking place. In the same way, our Lord Jesus has embedded himself with his "troops." He is on active duty among us as his kingdom advances among the nations — not as a visiting reporter, but as our Chief Intercessor; not as an observer, but as our Supreme Commander. *There he is!*

This is true for believers worshipping on a Sunday evening in a maximum security prison. This also is true for a Bible study group that gathers in a Masai village in Kenya. This is equally true of a house church meeting secretly in China or Saudi Arabia. *There he is!*

This is no more true if the group is much larger, such as the more than one million men summoned in 1997 to the Mall in Washington, DC, to spend a day in prayer for national revival, or 800,000 worshippers attending the largest church in the world every Sunday. The size of the group is not relevant. The supremacy of the Savior at the vortex of the group is all that matters!

Isn't this what Jesus promised to all of his disciples, no matter where they meet or how many convene? We read in Matthew 18:

> What you lock on earth will be locked in heaven. What you unlock on earth will be unlocked in heaven. Again, here is what I tell you. Suppose two of you on earth agree about anything you ask for. My Father in heaven will do it for you. *Where two or three people meet together in my name, I am there with them* (emphasis added).

If that isn't solid proof of his supremacy, what on earth would be? *There he is!*

Postscript
Jesus' Reign WITHIN Us Today:
It Brings the Fear of the Lord

As we've seen, every time we as believers gather in his name, in every congregation on planet Earth, the Lord Jesus is fully there, *presiding* as King. Not just part of him, but *all* of him. Not passively but *actively* — in all of his *majesty*. Not reigning without us or against us, but rather *near* us and *among* us.

Since this glorious Redeemer has decided to make himself at home **within** his people, one hallmark of our churches must become "the fear of the Lord."

That phrase, "the fear of the Lord," appears frequently throughout Scripture. In its New Testament expression it might be defined best as:

taking God's Son as seriously as God does.

This outlook profoundly marked the early church. Take for example:

> The whole church and all who heard about these things were *filled with fear* (Acts 5, emphasis added).

> The Jews and Greeks living in Ephesus heard about this. *They were all overcome with fear.* They held the name of the Lord Jesus in high honor (Acts 19, emphasis added).

"The fear of the Lord" caused a band of leaders in the Corinthian church to deal decisively with persistent sin in their congregation. One of their members, refusing to renounce sexual relations with his stepmother, had to be expelled. Here's how Paul helped set the stage for the step they needed to take:

> Shouldn't you have put the man who did that out of your church? . . . *When you come together in the name of our Lord Jesus . . . the power of our Lord Jesus will also be with you . . .* hand that man over to Satan. Then his sinful nature will be destroyed. His spirit will be saved on the day the Lord returns . . . Don't you know that just a little yeast works its way through the whole batch of dough? Get rid of that evil person! (1 Corinthians 5, emphasis added).

Clearly, the indwelling "power of the Lord" and the corresponding "fear of the Lord" became for them the primary impetus toward bold, righteous action.

"The fear of the Lord" best describes John's response in Revelation 1 when he beheld the Son in ascended glory walking among seven Asian congregations. The apostle prostrated himself before his Lord in wonder-filled trepidation — and stayed there until Jesus said to him, "Fear not."

This was the the same response Jesus desired from each of the churches he addressed through John, as well. He probed for "awe and reverence," for example, by how he confronted the Laodicean church:

> Since *you are like lukewarm water,* neither hot nor cold, *I will spit you out of my mouth!* You say, "I am rich. I have everything I want. I don't need a thing!" And you don't realize that you are wretched and miserable and poor and blind and naked . . . I correct and discipline everyone I love. So be diligent and turn from your indifference. Look! I stand at the door and knock (Revelation 3, NLT, emphasis added).

In point of fact, Scripture calls churches everywhere today to *intentionally* test the degree of their corporate experience of "the fear of the Lord" — to carefully examine themselves for evidence that they are giving Jesus his rightful place among them as Lord of all.

A chief concern of every congregation should be this:

> **How can we demonstrate undeniable evidence**
> **that we are seriously living out the truth**
> **that the risen, reigning Son of God**
> **is daily moving and ministering *within* our congregation**
> **in order to involve us in his kingdom purposes?**

That's a test worth administering frequently. The stakes are high.

When Paul sensed that a body of believers was moving away from an undiminished focus on the reign of Christ among them, he became intensely concerned, urging them to take this test:

> Christ is speaking through me. He is not weak in dealing with you. *He is powerful among you . . . take a good look at yourselves* to see if you are really believers. *Test yourselves.* Don't you realize that *Christ Jesus is in you? Unless, of course, you fail the test!* (2 Corinthians 13, emphasis added).

Paul carried this same burden for all the churches he served. Often he was distressed by how some were being led away from Christ into the quicksand of legalism and self-righteousness. In his desperate efforts to *reintroduce* them to their Savior's sufficiency and supremacy, Paul portrayed himself as a mother travailing all over again, trying to give birth to a child she *thought* she had already delivered! He writes:

> You can tell for sure that you are now fully adopted as his own children because God sent the Spirit of his Son into our lives crying out, "Papa! Father!" . . . Do you know how I feel right now, and will feel until Christ's life becomes visible in your lives? *Like a mother in the pain of childbirth.* (Galatians 4, MSG, emphasis added).

He took on this degree of spiritual anguish because God's Son, residing in all his fullness in the midst of them, must be taken as seriously as God takes him.

Heartfelt reverence toward Christ must mark all believers, not only when combating apathy or sin, but also when gathering to worship him or joining to collaborate with him. Out of a conscious awareness of the awesomeness of the One **within** us, we will be far more likely to obey him, bringing forth his works "with fear and trembling" because we know he is among us "working in us to will and do his good pleasure" (Philippians 2).

"The fear of the Lord." How can a church settle for less as we surround the throne, occupied by the Lamb who occupies simultaneously our personal walk with him as well as our life together in him?

To take God's Son as seriously as God does requires all of us to give Jesus both the centrality and the the supremacy he deserves — in everything, at all times, and in every way (Colossians 1).

Who Christ Is WITHIN Us Today:
A Tribute

Paraphrasing and personalizing a wide selection of Scriptures

Father, we come to you to proclaim the name of your Son together — to spread his fame, embrace his reign, increase his gain, and honor his claim about who he is *within* us. As we do, awake us to him afresh for ALL that he is. May the praise we bring to him in these moments come forth alive in us by your Spirit and rise up as a blessing to you forever. We use your Word to magnify your Son, without whom we are nothing and can do nothing. This tribute is all for Christ alone, our one and only hope of glory, and the hope of all the nations.

**Lord Jesus Christ, this is our tribute to you—
our tribute to who you are WITHIN us.**

You, the One who sits in the center of heaven's throne, also dwell *within* your people in equal measure. As Revelation portrays you, you walk among your churches, like a priest among lampstands, in the majesty of your ascendancy. To use the words of Zechariah, you are a wall of fire around us, but you also are the glory of God *within* us. Borrowing words from David, we have lifted our gates. Therefore you, the King of glory, may come in. You have invaded our midst to conquer us and to draw us to yourself.

As you inhabit us as your living temple, made up of us as your living stones, even so you have become *within* us the fulfillment of the Shekinah cloud that once blazed in Israel's Holy of Holies. Therefore, we must be silent. We humble ourselves under your mighty hand, that you, at work among us, might lift us at the right time and in the right way, for your sake alone.

Christ Is NOW!

The riches of the mystery of the gospel is this:

YOU, the one anointed to reign over heaven and earth;
YOU, the one anointed to fulfill all the prophecies and promises of God;

YOU, the one anointed to bring all of God's purposes to their consummation;

YOU, the one anointed to have first place in everything;

YOU, the Christ of God;

YOU dwell *within* your people!

You have given us intimacy with you in your supremacy. You do so in order to take us with you into the completion of every hope we have in you. You come among us to remove all veils, so that we might keep gazing on you face to face. Now your Spirit can keep transforming us into your likeness, individually and collectively, with ever-increasing glory.

Christ Is NOW!

Because we each have been crucified with *you,* no longer do any of us really live; it is you living in us! Because you rose again, even when we suffer for you, your life is revealed in us, *within* the weaknesses of our mortal bodies. Inwardly you renew your people day by day.

No wonder, like the Emmaus disciples, our hearts burn *within* us because you are always present within us, sharing yourself with us, magnifying yourself to us by your Spirit and by your Word. Every time we gather together in your name, you are in the midst of us, declaring God's glory to your brothers and sisters.

In fact, you rise up in the presence of the congregation to actually join with us as we sing our praises to the Father. As Zephaniah predicted: You are our mighty Deliverer; you are the One in the midst of us. You take great delight in us. You are here, right now, not only rejoicing with us but rejoicing over us with songs of thanksgiving.

Christ Is NOW!

Every time you draw near to breathe on us we receive greater measures of your power.

By infusions of your Spirit, you dwell *within* every single heart as well as among our hearts united together — both at the same time.

By infusions of your Spirit, we have become one spirit with you.

By infusions of your Spirit, you directly and literally move among us.

By infusions of your Spirit, you draw closer to us than any human being ever could, and you help us draw closer to each other.

By infusions of your Spirit, you bind us together, set us at your feet, and teach us more of who you are so as to unveil to us the mystery of your Person and your purposes, for now and for all ages.

By infusions of your Spirit, you take all that the Father has given to the Son and share it with us, place it *within* us, and unleash it among us. Joel foretold it.

Whenever the Spirit is poured out thoroughly on your people we hear your roar from the bowels of your Church. As we run to you to drink of you, you become *within* us a swelling fountain, flowing out of the very core of our shared existence, so that all peoples might know that the King of heaven dwells among his people.

Christ Is NOW!

Every time we encourage one another with the truth that is in you, Lord Jesus, the message of who you are dwells richly *within* us, soaking us with your glory more and more, because the truth of who you are and of all that you are saturates us with spirit and life.

God's truth is ultimately a Person, not a doctrine. God's ultimate truth for us is *you yourself,* unveiling your marvelous majesty *within* us. Every time we eat the bread and take the cup you become once again our shared feast, the everlasting food and drink for our souls. We consume you into our very beings, individually and corporately, and in turn we are consumed by you.

Christ Is NOW!

When you ascended on high you gave gifts to your Church, gifts of the Spirit, in order that you might work through all of your people to make us the fullness of you who fill all in all. You manifest yourself increasingly to us by how you serve your people, among your people, by your people. Your love is manifested among us in such a way that you vindicate your claims on us as your disciples. As you minister to us by how we love one another, we keep growing up unto you in all things as our Head.

You said you are the vine and we are like branches, abiding in you, wrapped around you, drawing sustenance from you, even as you abide in us, implanting your life *within* us, dwelling among us to produce in us much fruit. You said that without you abiding *within* us, and we in you, we can do nothing.

And so we join you in your passionate prayer of John 17 — for your sake we pray: Place *within* us the glory the Father gave you that we may be one as you and the Father are one — you in us, and the Father in you, that the world may know the Father has sent you. Continue to make the Father known to us in order that the love he has for you may be *within* us so that you yourself may inhabit us and abide *within* us.

Christ Is NOW!

This tribute expresses only a small part of the inexhaustible riches of who you are WITHIN us and all peoples.

So, Father, here is how we celebrate your Son, our Lord Jesus Christ, in this hour. We exalt him. We exult in him. We do so because of all he is *within* us — now. Therefore, everything we are and have, every breath we breathe, every step we take, every service we render, every prayer we pray, every praise we bring, is possible only by him and him alone. For without him — without all he is *within* us — we are nothing and we can do nothing. More and more, by the revealing work of your Spirit, awaken us to Christ alone — awaken your whole Church to Christ alone — so that increasingly he might become *within* us our all in all.

AMEN!

The Spectacular Supremacy of God's Son Today

Who Christ Is TO Us Today

Who Christ Is FOR Us Today

Who Christ Is OVER Us Today

Who Christ Is BEFORE Us Today

Who Christ Is WITHIN Us Today

▪ **Who Christ Is THROUGH Us Today**

Who Christ Is UPON Us Today

Exploring and Experiencing

Who Christ Is
THROUGH Us Today

Congratulations!

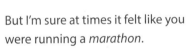

*I*n these previous chapters you've surveyed *thousands* of rich insights providing a robust perspective on who Jesus is today — what we've chosen to call a "consequential Christology."

But I'm sure at times it felt like you were running a *marathon*.

Well, here's good news about marathons:

Marathon runners say they often experience what's called a "second wind" somewhere around mile 21. After such a grueling run, they see the finish line not far off, and hope of victory is renewed. Their energy level rises, propelling them toward the finish line.

Similarly, as we press on in our *Christ Is Now!* marathon, be assured of this: Those who've run it ahead of you have reported an exhilaration as the journey neared culmination because they were convinced the prize of *this* race is worth it all. They found what awaited them at the finish line was a revitalized relationship with God's Son — deepening and flourishing in whole new ways. How could they ask for more?

So, prepare to exhilarate and accelerate! The best is yet to come!

Who Christ Is THROUGH Us Today:
A Reign You Can't Contain!

Our previous chapter explored the "WITHIN us" dimension of Christ's sovereign rule today — how it is displayed within each of us individually as well as within all of us together. However, we must balance this *inward* experience with how he intends to magnify his greatness and glory *outwardly,* by the ways he advances his kingdom **through** his people today.

King Jesus not only *precedes* us by going before us, and *indwells* us when he works within us, but he also *empowers* us as he *sends* us in order to minister **through** us by his Spirit, in this way spreading his salvation to the ends of the earth.

When he broke through the tomb into glorious resurrection life, he announced that from that moment on his reign will never be contained. Not within my life or yours. Not within my congregation or yours. Not even within the worldwide Body of Christ as a whole.

On the contrary, the Church's planet-wide mission provides the most vivid expression in this current age of the massive extent and impact of Jesus' expanding kingdom among the nations. Taken by itself, that two-millennia-long global phenomenon underscores that Christ's reign will never be contained.

Of course, many conclude that the guarantee of this unrestrained expansion of Jesus' dominion over all the nations of the earth is the inexhaustible love of God for *the world.*

But God's love for the world (the "cosmos" in John 3:16, meaning the created universe) pursues an agenda far more comprehensive than many imagine. God so loved the world that he sent Jesus so he could fulfill the Father's ultimate destiny for us — which is to see, seek, and savor the wonder, the splendor, and the renown of the Son of God.

Christ's reign can never be contained because the Father's heart of love is first of all and above all for *his Son* — a love that has existed from eternity.

It is *this* love — the Father's love for the Son — that overflows in his outreach to gather to his Son earth's peoples from every tribe and tongue **through** the mission of God's people.

It is *this* love that desires humankind to become fully involved in exalting and serving the Son who serves and exalts the Father.

John 3 puts it well:

> The Father loves the Son and has put everything into his hands. Anyone who believes in the Son has eternal life. Anyone who does not believe in the Son will not have life. God's anger remains on them.

It is *this* amazing love of the Father toward the Son that draws believers into a relationship with the Son that offers us unending intimacy with him in his supremacy. No wonder it's called "eternal life."

> Father, the time has come. Bring glory to your Son. Then your Son will bring glory to you. You gave him authority over all people. He gives eternal life to all those you have given him. *And what is eternal life? It is knowing you, the only true God, and Jesus Christ, whom you have sent* (John 17, emphasis added).

Christ's reign will never be contained because the love of the Father for the Son has never been and never will be contained. Just as we read in Psalms 2:

> He said to me, *"You are my son. Today I have become your father. Ask me, and I will give the nations to you.* All nations on earth will belong

> to you. You will break them with an iron scepter"... Celebrate his rule
> with trembling. Obey the son completely, or he will be angry. Your
> way of life will lead to your death (emphasis added).

Bottom line: World evangelization is about the Father multiplying
communities across the globe, raised up by the power of the Spirit, marked
by adoration for and wholehearted obedience to the Son, as we hasten
toward the day when all of heaven and earth will be filled forever with
numberless lovers and worshippers of the Lamb on the throne (Revelation
5 and 7).

That's why Christ's reign can never be contained.

From the very outset of his public outreach, Jesus never ceased to emphasize
the expansive nature of his mission.

For example, in Mark 1, Jesus called the first disciples to follow him so that
he might "make" them capable of bringing many others to him, the way
fishermen sail out to sea to bring home a catch.

Uncontained.

In Matthew 16, Jesus predicted the irrepressible, unstoppable, irreversible
nature of his kingdom purposes, unleashed ***through*** his disciples.

> This is the rock on which *I will put together my church, a church so
> expansive with energy that not even the gates of hell will be able to keep
> it out.* And that's not all. You will have complete and free access to
> God's kingdom, keys to open any and every door: no more barriers
> between heaven and earth, earth and heaven. (Matthew 16, MSG,
> emphasis added).

Uncontained.

In John 15, at the close of three years of teaching and training, Jesus reminded his disciples he had chosen them and united them with himself specifically so they would become exceedingly fruitful in ministry for his sake, proving to the world that they enjoyed a life-giving union with the vine (Jesus), which in turn would increasingly glorify the Father.

Uncontained.

Mark 16 (indicating the perspective of early church fathers) states a three-step process: (1) Jesus commands disciples to go into all the world; (2) then he ascends to begin his reign; (3) then as they go out to tell the good news he continues to work *through* them confirming their message in powerful ways.

Uncontained.

Clearly from the beginning, Jesus never expected his reign to be confined to a comfortable cabal of comfortable devotees. Instead, we share in the Father's inextinguishable love for the Son, joining with the Spirit as he spreads this wonderful story so that many others might become part of the story with us — the ageless love story between Father and Son.

This understanding provides us with the core principle to summarize the sixth dimension of his spectacular supremacy. It is potent with promise. It states:

**Because of who Christ is
working *through* us in his spectacular supremacy,
we mean far more to the world than we ever thought possible.**

To pursue more fully all that this core principle implies, let's examine two complementary aspects of this revolutionary "THROUGH us" dimension of Jesus' supremacy — proving that his reign can never be contained. They are:

The *Trajectory* of His Ministry

The *Extension* of His Ascension

Who Christ Is THROUGH Us Today:
The Trajectory of His Ministry

The "WITHIN us" dimension of Christ's supremacy automatically determines the *trajectory* of the "THROUGH us" dimension of his supremacy. This is implied by the insight we highlighted in the last chapter:

> Within every congregation on planet Earth, the Lord Jesus is fully present — not just part of him, but all of him. Furthermore, wherever he dwells, there the triune God is fully involved.

That truth is based on many passages, including Colossians 1:27:

> God has chosen to make known to them [the saints] the glorious riches of that mystery. He has made it known among the Gentiles. And here is what it is. Christ is in you. He is your hope of glory (Colossians 1).

But this verse holds another insight for us. What Christ does *among* us is to be made known *beyond* us. It is to be revealed to the watching eyes of earth's peoples (both Jews and Gentiles). Note the sentence:

He has made it known among the Gentiles (Colossians 1).

Ascended on high to rule as Lord of all (which is why he is called "the Christ"), Jesus continues to dwell intimately *in the midst of* his people by his Spirit so that he might reveal himself and his salvation to the nations — ***through*** his people, individually and corporately.

 Snapshots and Starter Thoughts

- **Therefore, we conclude: Christ's work *within* us must remain forever connected to his work to make the gospel known and available *through* us to all humankind.** The phenomenal future Jesus offers, marked by the triumphant fulfillment of God's redemptive purposes (what Paul calls in Colossians 1:27 our "hope of glory" in Christ), is the same great promise held out ***through*** the Church to all of earth's peoples, as we share him and show him to a world that desperately needs to know him.

- **That being so, we should expect Christ's reign going on in the midst of his people to always keep moving *outward*.** As Lord of all, he continually seeks to minister to the world *through* the people who are indwelt and filled with his risen, ascended life. Right now, residing and presiding among a host of disciples worldwide, the Savior purposes to magnify his majesty by the ways he reaches and redeems neighbors and nations *through* those who belong to him.

- **His intention is to minister *to* the world by extending his reign *across* the world *through* those he previously summoned *out of* the world, only to call them back *into* the world.** This is precisely what he prayed would happen in John 17:

  > I have shown you to the disciples you gave me out of the world. They were yours. You gave them to me . . . *I do not pray that you will take them out of the world.* I pray that you will keep them safe from the evil one . . . *You sent me into the world. In the same way, I have sent them into the world.* . . . Father, I pray they will be one, just as you are in me and I am in you. *I want them also to be in us. Then the world will believe that you have sent me* (John 17, emphasis added).

- **The trajectory of Christ's reign *through* his people can be seen in *how* he sends them into the world, displayed in John 20.** On the night of his resurrection when Jesus materialized in the upper room and stood in the middle of his band of disciples, he drew so close to them he was able to breathe on them. He did so for the express purpose of sending them out, *in the same way* the Father had sent him out. John records:

  > They had locked the doors because they were afraid of the Jewish leaders. Jesus came in and stood among them. He said, "May peace

be with you!" Then he showed them his hands and his side. The disciples were very happy when they saw the Lord. Again Jesus said, "May peace be with you! *The Father has sent me. So now I am sending you.*" He then breathed on them. He said, "Receive the Holy Spirit" (John 20, emphasis added).

In other words, from resurrection day onward, the victorious nature of his risen life dictated the outward nature of our relationship to him as Savior and Lord.

- **In one of his parables about a seed and a sower, Jesus emphasized the priority of the outward trajectory.** According to the story in Matthew 13, the farmer represents the Son of Man (an official Jewish title for the Messiah). The seeds flung from his hand stand for the "the sons of the kingdom" (how Jesus defines his followers). They are flung out by Messiah wherever he chooses across the field — a picture of the entire globe.

  In other words, Jesus teaches us that top priority for him is to deposit every believer in the most strategic place possible to bring forth a kingdom harvest. Jesus positions us where he can work most effectively **through** us to fulfill our part in the Father's plan to extend the Son's redemptive reign into all corners of the earth.

- **But then, look what happens when we match that parable of the sower with the term Jesus uses in Luke 10 to launch his disciples' missionary ventures.** There the "sower" is transformed into a "thrower" because the Greek word used by Luke translated "send out" literally means "to throw out." The disciples are to be thrust vigorously into their mission field, whether that be close at hand or far away. In his sovereignty,

Jesus *hurls* his servants into kingdom work with great force, the way a muscular pitcher unleashes a well-executed fastball across home plate. We read:

> . . . ask the Lord of the harvest *to send out* [to throw out] workers into his harvest field. Go! I am *sending you out* [throwing you out] like lambs among wolves . . . Whoever listens to you, listens to me (Luke 10, emphasis added).

- **Having all authority in heaven and on earth today (Matthew 28), Jesus remains aggressively *proactive* about advancing the gospel outward *through* his own followers.** He claims the right over every believer and every body of believers to execute divinely designed deployments into all kinds of kingdom ministries. That is why as Christians we should joyfully declare:

**Because of who Christ is
working *through* us in his spectacular supremacy,
we mean far more to the world than we ever thought possible.**

Selah

pause | think | pray

Who Christ Is THROUGH Us Today:
The *Extension* of His Ascension

- **Since Pentecost, the Spirit has become for the Church nothing less than *an extension of Jesus' ascension,* both to us and *through* us.** The Holy Spirit's role is to bring Christ's reign *to* his people first, and then bring it *through* his people wherever Jesus sows (throws) them. Fifty days after his resurrection, following his coronation in glory, Jesus dispatched the Spirit from the throne to permanently inhabit, infuse, and inspire the Church with his triumphant life.

- **As a result, God's reigning Son remains free to work anywhere with any group to fulfill his global cause, ministering directly to earth's**

multitudes by his Spirit, who is at work *through* his people. Today he reaches out to the world *through* countless individual believers and even more so *through* millions of congregations, authorizing and equipping one and all to serve him by the Spirit's unparalleled power, the power that raised Jesus from the dead (Ephesians 1).

- **It's no wonder then, that as the disciples preached the gospel in the early days of the Church, not only dozens but literally thousands of people came to Christ, as recorded in the opening chapters of Acts.** The King was exercising his kingship *through* those planted in Jerusalem and Judea who had become his witnesses, and who eventually would be "scattered" (sown/thrown) across the Roman Empire, taking their witness to Jesus everywhere they went. We read in Acts 8:

  > And on that day a great *and* relentless persecution broke out against the church in Jerusalem; and the believers were all scattered throughout the regions of Judea and Samaria . . . those [believers] who had been scattered went from place to place preaching the word [the good news of salvation through Christ] (AMP, emphasis added).

- **Today, as the "extension of the Ascension," the Holy Spirit continues to saturate the Christian movement with the *ruling presence* of Jesus so that in turn we can saturate those around us with the *kingdom proclamation* of Jesus.** In other words, first Jesus infuses his Church with the fullness of his love and life and lordship by the gift of the Holy Spirit. Then the Holy Spirit works *through* us to *extend* the truth of Jesus' love and life and unrivaled lordship to the ends of the earth.

- **This Spirit-saturating, world-changing experience was foretold by Jesus in Acts 1:8. Note that this very familiar verse is often seen as a command, when in fact, it is really a *promise*.** Jesus declares what most assuredly *will* transpire with his followers, in any generation, when they are drenched by the Spirit's ministry.

  > But you *will receive power* when the Holy Spirit *comes on you* [saturates you]. Then you *will tell people* about me in Jerusalem, and in all Judea and Samaria. And you *will even tell other people* about me from one end of the earth to the other (Acts 1, emphasis added).

- **As a result of this extension — this "outpouring" of the Spirit — Jesus *promises* to reach many, many others beyond the company of believers!** The impact will stretch outward toward the very ends of the earth. Our Lord Jesus is focused like a laser on penetrating the peoples of the earth with the Church's united witness to his sovereignty and his salvation — by words and by deeds. Christ's universal reign will proliferate *through* those who are his own to permeate the world with kingdom grace and truth. The Spirit's power *upon* us, infusing us with the fullness of Jesus' ascended life, renders his reign *through* us utterly uncontainable. That is precisely what Habakkuk 2:14 envisioned:

  > The oceans are full of water. In the same way, the earth will be filled with the knowledge of my glory.

- **"With Jesus joining heaven and earth together in his own person, the Holy Spirit, which anointed and equipped Jesus himself for his kingdom work, comes pouring out onto his followers . . ."**

  > Jesus is with them, his life at work in and through them . . . they are the place where the living God, the God who is reclaiming the world for his own, is alive and active and establishing his sovereign rule" (N. T. Wright).

The Wrap

A few years ago Christians around the globe expressed their anticipation of how Jesus would display his kingly glory *through* their outward mission by prayerfully singing:

Shine, Jesus, shine! Fill this land with the Father's glory.
Blaze, Spirit, blaze! Set our hearts on fire.
Flow, river, flow! Flood the nations with grace and mercy.
Send forth your Word, Lord, and let there be light!

Knowing how much the Father desires to answer that prayer for the sake of his Son, we can declare to one another with absolute confidence:

**Because of who Christ is
working *through* us in his spectacular supremacy,
we mean far more to the world than we ever thought possible.**

Who Christ Is THROUGH Us Today:
Our Ministry Grows as We Enlarge Our Vision of Him

Henry Martyn was a promising scholar at Cambridge University in England. He excelled in the sciences, mathematics, and law, assuring him of a distinguished career in the academic world.

Surprisingly, in the early 1800s, Martyn concluded his Savior was calling him to embrace a radically different ambition — to take the gospel to the nations. The Lord thrust him initially into the Hindu world, and later planted him among Muslim populations. During his brief lifetime he translated the New Testament into the Urdu language for the first time ever, then into Persian, and also Judaeo-Persic. At one point he was able to have his completed Persian New Testament placed in the hands of the Shah of Iran.

Martyn intended to travel to Arabia to translate the New Testament into Arabic. Instead, he died of consumption at the age of 31 and was buried in foreign soil. But his decisive devotion to Christ inspired a fresh cohort of young men and women to follow in his path, engaging in Muslim outreach (and more) for a generation.

Obsessed by how his Savior was not being honored among unevangelized peoples, this young volunteer was compelled by his passion for Jesus to increase the knowledge of the glory of Christ among Muslims and Hindus, even if it cost him his life. Henry Martyn explained the *source* of his commitment to Christ's kingdom this way:

> I could not endure existence if Jesus was not glorified. It would be hell to me if he were to be always thus dishonored.

Reflecting on all Christ accomplished through Martyn and so many others like him, Christian statesman John R. W. Stott made this crucial observation (emphasis added):

> **Here lies the supreme missionary motivation:** Not obedience to the Great Commission, not compassion for the lost nor excitement over the Gospel, *but zeal, even jealousy for the honor of Christ's name, longing that Christ be given the honor that is due His name.*

Stott identified where Christ's ministry ***through*** Christians must *begin:* by enlarging our vision of the incomparable nature of the person and preeminence of God's Son, until finally that vision fills us with unabated zeal for his fame and reign. Next we will look at these two aspects of that vision:

We Need a Vision That Makes Us Open, Eager, and Expectant

We Need a Vision That Focuses Us on the WHOLE Christ

 Snapshots and Starter Thoughts

We Need a Vision That Makes Us Open, Eager, and Expectant

- **Seeing the glory of Christ more clearly makes us constantly open to all he wants to accomplish *through* us.** The more thorough and substantial our understanding of Jesus' greatness and glory becomes, the more *open* we'll be to what he wants to accomplish through us for his kingdom purposes. In other words, from our side, Christ's ministry to the world ***through*** us must begin by enlarging our vision of the spectacular supremacy of God's Son.

- **Seeing the glory of Christ more clearly makes us unrelentingly *eager* to be a part of all he wants to accomplish *through* us.** The more our appreciation of the magnitude of his kingship expands, the more *eager* we become for him to carry out his redemptive purposes ***through*** us. In other words from our side Christ's ministry to the world through us must begin by enlarging our vision of the spectacular supremacy of God's Son.

- **Seeing the glory of Christ more clearly makes us unshakably *expectant* about what he actually will accomplish *through* us.** The deeper we plunge into the promises secured for us from his incarnation to his ascension, the more *expectant* we will become about the ministry he intends to accomplish **through** us to bring the blessings of salvation to many others. Once again, from our side, Christ's ministry to the world **through** us must begin by enlarging our vision of the spectacular supremacy of God's Son.

- **An enlarged vision of Christ removes the fear of becoming part of a mission that will overwhelm us.** Christians sometimes pull back, fearing that we already have too many burdens of our own to bear, let alone take on the rest of the world for Christ. But when we have a vision of God's Son that is big enough, it gives us renewed passion and courage to join in his global cause for earth's unreached peoples, and reassures us that he is able to accomplish an awesome impact **through** us, beginning right where we live.

- **This is what kept Paul open, eager, and expectant through a lifetime experience of Christ reaching out to people *through* him.** Standing on trial before King Agrippa, decades after his initial encounter with Christ's spectacular supremacy, Paul was able to claim:

  > So then, King Agrippa, I was not disobedient to the vision from heaven (Acts 26).

His vision of God's Son kept Paul fanatically involved in missionary work for decades. The same can happen to any believer today.

Selah

pause | think | pray

We Need a Vision That Focuses Us on the WHOLE Christ

- **We need to fill in the "holes" in how Christians see the *whole* Christ.** Many popular evangelistic outreaches today define their goal using words similar to these:

> The whole Church
> taking the whole gospel
> to the whole world.

What a difference it would make in our planning, mobilizing, and implementation if we would add the phrase *"focused on the whole Christ,"* so that our mission motto would read instead:

> The whole Church,
> *focused on the whole Christ,*
> taking the whole gospel
> to the whole world.

It takes a more well-rounded, more comprehensive vision of the *whole* Christ to ensure that the *whole* Church gets involved, that the *whole* gospel gets proclaimed, and that the *whole* world remains in view. This is the level of *wholeness* required of us for Christ's global cause to be fulfilled ***through*** us.

- **A shared vision of the *whole* Christ — what better way do we have to bring together today's exceedingly diverse Church to collaborate for the sake of world evangelization?** Only as God's people experience a shared focus on God's Son for *all* he is — celebrating the full extent of the wonders of his greatness, goodness, and glory — can we find a shared basis for fostering a vital, tangible unity that allows the Church to work together in practical ways in serving his global cause. Such a thoroughly Christ-focused unity allows the Spirit to reach out *through* God's people freely and fully.

- **How can we keep the thoroughness, relevancy, and potency of the gospel message itself from becoming significantly diminished or distorted, if we do not continually nurture among ourselves a vision of the *whole* Christ?** Only as God's people grasp a focus on God's Son for *all* he is — as we are grasped by the scope of the hope wrapped up in God's redeeming purposes in him — will we be able to adequately proclaim to the world the saving promises in Christ that can transform people and nations. Such a thoroughly Christ-focused message allows the Spirit to reach out *through* God's people freely and fully.

- **Without a vision of the *whole* Christ — a vision equal to the task — would not our efforts to share the gospel eventually become overwhelmed and paralyzed by the relentless obstacles and challenges the world raises against the mission itself?** Only as God's people are sufficiently convinced of the reality, activity, and victory of the current reign of Christ — that he is filling the nations with his majesty, sovereignty, and saving ministry — will we be able to sustain sufficient passion and courage to labor and sacrifice together in order to penetrate the whole world with the whole gospel about the whole Christ. Only a mission outreach that is thoroughly Christ-focused and Christ-exalting allows the Spirit to reach out *through* God's people freely and fully, despite all odds.

- **Christian leaders committed today to city-reaching and city-transformation agree that many urban churches need to acquire a more robust "urban Christology."** This phrase refers to a vision of Christ that is as big as the challenges and opportunities facing urban mission today. Especially at this hour of history, with the impact of globalization at every level, Christians need to be extra sensitive to what our Lord Jesus wants to do *through* his people to extend his reign into the great cities of the world like Hong Kong, Nairobi, Moscow, Jerusalem, Mumbai, Tehran, New York City.

- **Without seeing the Lord Jesus in the full extent of his supremacy, urban ministries often find themselves gripped by a spirit of hopelessness.** Recently, 300 city-wide consultations involving urban-focused churches and ministries discovered that there are *ten major barriers* for reaching the cities of the world for Christ. However, one barrier is by far the greatest: "the spirit of hopelessness" (their phrase) among God's people, often beginning with their leaders.

In other words, one reason urban churches aren't reaching cities for Christ more aggressively is because urban Christians are paralyzed by the demands of urban mission. Therefore, too often they give up, pull back and in essence take congregations into a defensive "holding pattern," waiting for Jesus to come back. To paraphrase Proverbs 29:

> Where there is no vision of the greatness of God's Son the people perish from lack of hope.

- **We need to break out of boxes of "pea-sized Christologies" that prevent God's people from experiencing the breadth and wonders of Christ's love and power, which he longs to pour out *through* us.** Such pea-sized visions of Christ turn us inward leaving us with few expectations regarding the mighty things Christ is doing already and the kingdom breakthroughs he is prepared to unleash *through* us for the sake of many others.

- **Thankfully, the rich tapestry of biblical truths that introduces us to the wide spectrum of Christ's supremacy has the power to set us free of lingering unbelief about what Christ can do *through* us.** Declaring to one another the kinds of truths explored in *Christ Is Now!* and doing so as a way of life together, can help all of us come alive to him in new ways, ready to be Jesus followers *through* whom he ministers to the world.

In light of what we've already learned about who Jesus is *TO* us and *FOR* us and *OVER* us and *BEFORE* us and *WITHIN* us, every believer should abound in hope about all he is able to accomplish *THROUGH* us, individually and together, to advance salvation's plan to the ends of the earth.

Selah

pause | think | pray

The Wrap

So then, here's what Christ's ministry **through** us requires of us, so that he might use us to demonstrate his sovereign, saving majesty to our generation: We must fill in the "holes" in our vision of God's Son, until we see him wholly for who he is right now, in the glory of his supremacy.

In 2010, a historic gathering of thousands of international Christian leaders from over 200 nations convened in Capetown, South Africa, representing a vast array of mission endeavors in world evangelization.

At the close of their ten days of strategizing and prayer, they issued a document called *The Capetown Commitment,* signed by all of the delegates. It stated the critical need for the Church to embrace the reality of the reign of the Son of God if we're to move forward in his global cause. Here is their declaration (emphasis added):

> **The supremacy and centrality of Christ in our mission**
> **must be more than a confession of faith.**
> *It must govern our strategy, our practice, and our unity.*

Who Christ Is THROUGH Us Today:
There Are No Limits to How Fully Jesus Can Use Us

I'll never forget the day I spent with the universally respected Catholic missionary Mother Teresa (now St. Teresa of Calcutta), observing her outreach to some of the poorest people on our planet.

Clearly, here was someone filled and sent by our Redeemer — someone **through** whom he was manifesting his ascended life. As we conversed in her bare-bones office cubicle, I could not help but be drawn to her passion for the Lord Jesus, and her eagerness to make more of herself available to him.

Her story is well known. As a young schoolteacher in India she sensed Jesus calling her to serve him in a different way. In a literal vision given to her while riding a train toward Darjeeling, the Lord asked her to reside fulltime in the streets of Calcutta. She was to take nothing with her and assume a posture of absolute powerlessness, depending on him alone. Her assignment was to minister in Jesus' name to forsaken inhabitants of a destitute city who were suffering in unfathomable poverty and spiritual darkness.

As the two of us talked, I noticed on the wall behind her desk a large homemade, rough-hewn map of the world on which the local artist had inscribed the motto for the religious order Mother Teresa founded in 1950, the Missionaries of Charity. It declared:

We go into all the world
to preach the Gospel of Christ
to the poorest of the poor.

Over the decades, Jesus multiplied Mother Teresa's mission so extensively that today there are thousands of sisters serving Christ fulltime exactly as she served him, bringing the good news to the poor in nearly every major city around the globe.

How does one explain such Christian servants? What is the source of their phenomenal impact? The answer resides in one of Mother Teresa's most heartfelt claims:

Jesus is my God. Jesus is my spouse.
Jesus is my life. Jesus is my only love.
Jesus is my all. Jesus is my everything.
Because of this, I am never afraid.
I am doing my work *with* Jesus.
I am doing it *for* Jesus.
I am doing it *to* Jesus.
Therefore, the results are *His*, not mine.
(emphasis added)

Her proclamation of passion for Jesus explains why this ninety-pound, five-foot Albanian Christian laid down her life for his sake among the hovels of India's rejected — and why there were no limits to what he accomplished ***through*** her.

Mother Teresa exhibits vividly God's promise to believers everywhere, summed up in the key principle of this chapter:

Because of who Christ is
working *through* us in his spectacular supremacy,
we mean far more to the world than we ever thought possible.

Consistently, Scripture confirms there are no limits to Jesus' outreach ***through*** God's people. Let's look at some examples:

"No Limits" Foreshadowed in the Old Testament

"No Limits" Fulfilled in the New Testament

Snapshots and Starter Thoughts

"No Limits" Foreshadowed in the Old Testament

- **Consider the call and experience of Abraham.** When God summoned Abraham, a nomad with a few camels, he imposed no limits. God said to him in essence (see Genesis 12 and 15): "Get ready. I want to bless you so fully that you will become a blessing not just to your clan but to the families of the whole earth." Can you imagine how stunned the father of our faith was by this proposition?

We are in union with the Redeemer who came to greatly expand Abraham's mission. How much more stunned should we be with God's promises to use us in Christ Jesus? How much more should we anticipate receiving and spreading unlimited blessings in Christ Jesus? How much more of a dynamic force should we expect to be for God's saving purposes in Christ Jesus among the families of the earth?

> *God promised that Abraham would [inherit] the world.* It would not come to him because he obeyed the law. It would come because of his faith, which made him right with God . . . The God that Abraham believed in gives life to the dead. Abraham's God also creates things that did not exist before . . . *He became the father of many nations, exactly as God had promised* . . . But Abraham kept believing in God's promise. He became strong in his faith. He gave glory to God. He was absolutely sure that God had the power to do what he had promised . . . *(this was also) written also for us.* We believe in the God who raised Jesus our Lord from the dead (Romans 4, emphasis added).

- **Or, consider the unbounded, global vision of Israel's mission in Psalm 67.** Here the people of Israel pray with amazing breadth of faith about the impact that Jehovah would have on the nations ***through*** them. How much more should this be true for believers today among whom and ***through*** whom Christ manifests his kingdom initiatives to fulfill what was foreshadowed by Israel?

> May God be merciful and bless us, cause His face to shine on us *so that your ways may be known throughout the earth and your saving people among people everywhere* . . . Yes, God will bless us, and *as a result, people all over the world will fear Him* (Psalm 67, NIV, emphasis added).

- **Then, in Isaiah 66, we read about the international mission God intends to accomplish *through* Israel at the climax of history.** Many New Testament passages, such as Jesus' commission in Matthew 28, pick up on this vision and apply it to the work of Christ going on at this very hour *through* his followers worldwide.

> Heaven is my throne, the earth is my footstool . . . and these are the ones I look on with favor, those who will be humble and contrite in spirit, who will tremble at my word . . . and *I will send some of those who survive to the nations*, to distant lands that have not heard of my fame or seen my glory, and *they will proclaim my glory among the nations* and they will bring all your people from all the nations to my holy mountain in Jerusalem as an offering to the Lord (Isaiah 66, emphasis added).

- **Two words — *centripetal* and *centrifugal* — help sort out the contrast between God's mission before Christ came versus after he came.**

God's mission for Israel was ***centripetal*** (a physics principle defining the force that keeps an object rotating inward, toward a center point). In other words, ***through*** his people (especially his prophets) Jehovah invited the nations to draw near to him, to come into his presence, to make pilgrimages to Jerusalem in order to join the ongoing worship of him in the temple.

As a result of the saving work of Jesus, however, everything got reversed. When Jesus ascended and sat down on God's throne on high, the divine mission became ***centrifugal*** (the physics principle defining the force that rotates everything outward from a center point). Since the coming of the Holy Spirit, the gospel keeps moving outwards, pressed away from any single center point, driving towards all the nations, with no limits except the ends of the earth. Jesus, who remains preeminent in all things, expresses his reign centrifugally, by the advance of his mission in all directions to earth's people, and on all levels ***through*** the worldwide Body of Christ.

Selah

pause | think | pray

"No Limits" Fulfilled in the New Testament

- **When meeting with his disciples just before his ascension to the throne, Jesus foretold the coming of an immense, previously unannounced *expansion* on the mission first given to Abraham and then taken up by the nation of Israel.** Jesus said that after they received an unprecedented empowerment from on high, his disciples would be deployed by him to proclaim his saving reign among all of earth's peoples, taking the revolutionary message to the ends of the earth (as it were) — unfettered, unrestricted, unlimited, undefeated.

> He told them, "This is what is written. The Messiah will suffer. He will rise from the dead on the third day. His followers will preach in his name. They will tell others to turn away from their sins and be forgiven. People from every nation will hear it, beginning at Jerusalem . . . But for now, stay in the city. Stay there until you have received power from heaven" (Luke 24).

- **From the earliest days of the New Testament church, we see this confirmed.** For example, shortly after he had filled them with the Spirit, Jesus deployed Peter and John to minister physical healing. Jesus healed the lame beggar who sat at the temple gate, doing so ***through*** these two faithful followers who were united to him and obedient to him.

Because of how Christ used them to manifest his spectacular supremacy, Peter and John ended up meaning far more to the world for Jesus' sake than they could have ever imagined just a few days earlier. By combining and paraphrasing his statements in Acts 3 and Acts 4, it is clear this was how Peter saw it:

> Well, we don't have any money. What we do have, though, is the power of the living Lord Jesus Christ working through us. So in his name and relying on his reigning authority to graciously break through to you at this moment, we invite you to get up and start walking. For you see, God has brought glory to his servant Jesus by raising him from the dead. We are witnesses of this fact! Therefore, through faith in the power of name of Jesus, you are healed right here and right now. Because Jesus is the supreme God, his is the only name under heaven by which all of us must be saved, physically and spiritually (Acts 3 and 4, paraphrased).

- **Decades later, Paul set the pace for all believers, exemplifying the same "no limits" expectations in his service to Christ.** He writes in

Romans 15:13-30 (paraphrased here to highlight the radical nature of his claims):

> Listen, you know how much Christ already has accomplished through me, from one end of the Roman Empire to the other. And it has all been his work through me, for which I openly give him credit.
>
> But you also know how from the start I've wanted to preach the good news where Christ was not known. I don't want to restrict my labors simply to building on the church planting outreach others have started. You see, I believe God's Word to Old Testament saints that those who have not been told about his Son, wherever they are found, are supposed to understand who he is, and that those who have not heard about Jesus Christ will one day know him.
>
> This is precisely why I plan to visit you in Rome on my way to Spain. Jesus is not yet finished with his mission through me. Yes, I have been on a gospel outreach for almost 25 years, but still it's not completed. So I'm asking you Roman believers to help me press forward to reach the lost people in Spain who have not yet heard about our Redeemer.
>
> For you see, there are no limits to what Christ can carry out through us, especially as we collaborate in him. That's because wherever we go we can anticipate the fullness of Christ's blessings — blessings with no limits as they flow through us to others.

- **This view of Christ's extravagant outreach *through* his people today is the primary explanation as to why everything will culminate in universal jubilation at the consummation of the ages.** Revelation 11 assures us that in that victorious hour all the kingdoms of this world will be found to be subsumed under the kingdom of our God and of his Christ. The Bible ends by describing how redeemed people will congregate to worship the Lamb at the center of the throne, coming from every tongue and people and tribe and culture. Within the renovated City of God, all nations will deposit their treasures at the Savior's feet (Revelation 21). Ultimately, the gospel will reach every facet of the human race because Jesus, by his Spirit, will never cease working ***through*** generations of his followers, advancing his global cause with no limits.

- **However, his reaching out *through* us without limits unfolds in a whole other sense.** His mission for us includes no restrictions or no limits on what Christ's work ***through*** us may *cost* us — the sacrifices we may need to make, the battles we may need to wage, the suffering we may need to endure for the sake of the gospel. That is why Paul writes:

> Now I rejoice in my sufferings on your behalf. *And with my own body I supplement whatever is lacking [on our part] of Christ's afflictions, on behalf of His body, which is the church.* In this church I was made a minister according to the stewardship which God entrusted to me for your sake, so that I might make the word of God fully known [among you] (Colossians 1, AMP, emphasis added).

- **Just as there were no limits on what Jesus would suffer for us, so there should be no limits on what we are willing to suffer for him as we join in his saving purpose.** In John 12 when he said, "The hour has come for the Son of Man to be glorified," primarily he was talking about his crucifixion later that week. But he added for all his disciples, then and now:

> Unless a grain of wheat falls to the ground and dies, it remains only one seed. But if it dies, it produces many seeds. Anyone who loves their life will lose it. But anyone who hates their life in this world will keep it and have eternal life. *Anyone who serves me must follow me. And where I am, my servant will also be. My Father will honor the one who serves me* (John 12, emphasis added).

In serving Jesus, God's people must set no limits on the *cost*, and must be willing, if necessary, to physically die for his sake in order to produce a harvest for his praise. Yet we do so with *expectations* regarding the ultimate outcomes. Our hope in him knows no bounds. Because Jesus is supreme, ready to exercise his reign **through** those who belong to him, with unshakeable confidence Christians should remain open to everything he wants to do **through** them to advance his mission, even if they must lose their lives for his sake and for the gospel (Mark 8).

- **Often the power of Christ working through our witness becomes more tangible to the world *because of* what we suffer for him.** Philippians 1 affirms that what we endure for Jesus' sake serves to "magnify" (enlarge, make far more visible) how the living, reigning Christ is ministering **through** his servants. There are no limits to what Christ can accomplish **through** those who have become *weak* for his sake. Our weakness is precisely the time when we experience the fullness of Christ's power (2 Corinthians 12) and when Christ's message **through** us gains boundless potential (2 Corinthians 13).

- **Jesus' supremacy *through* his church is why Christianity has become today the first truly *universal* religion.** It holds a universal relevance and outreach that is independent of any single global base of operations except for Jesus' throne. Christianity has become the fastest growing, most diverse, most pervasive, most widespread, and the most transforming of lives and cultures of any religion in the world. As a result, one day a multitude without number will unite around the Lamb to adore and serve him forever (Revelation 7).

- **Jesus promised "no limits" to the church in Philadelphia in Revelation 3. It remains true for everyone today *through* whom he is advancing his saving reign.**

> Here are the words of Jesus, who is holy and true. He holds the key of David. No one can shut what he opens. And no one can open what he shuts. He says, "I know what you are doing. Look! I have put an open door in front of you. No one can shut it" (Revelation 3).

The Wrap

The historical record on global missionary movements of the past 200 years documents that many lands have experienced positive social revolutions because of the impact of the gospel, as Christ has extended his reign *through* countless faithful servants.

Ralph Winter, founder of the U. S. Center for World Mission, made this appeal:

> I yearn to see evangelical missions given more direct credible credit to Jesus Christ for the impetus behind the social transformations that they've been doing. There is nothing in the entire mammoth global Islamic movement that compares even remotely to the hundreds of major Christian mission agencies or the thousands of ways in which the Christian movement has reached out with love and tenderness to those who are suffering. *This is the Gospel of Jesus Christ. It is the Gospel of the kingdom, which must extend to the whole world and eventually to all creation* (emphasis added).

"No limits" defines how the love of Christ compels us (2 Corinthians 5) to focus especially on the enslaved and the oppressed, the disenfranchised and the impoverished, the orphan and the widow — many of whom are among the billions who still have no knowledge of Christ and no one like them near them to tell them.

Certainly for the Body of Christ in America, "no limits" must include the surprising opportunities Jesus has given us to express his ministry to many of earth's unreached peoples who live right around us.

Today our King is bringing the nations to the USA. Forty-three million foreign-born people reside here, many from places where the gospel has not yet penetrated. One of every five international migrants worldwide calls the United States their new home. In metro New York City alone, enclaves can be found representing virtually every people group from every part of the globe. They can be found virtually next door, poised for Christ to break through into their lives ***through*** believers who bring them the gospel.

Bottom line: Because Jesus is supreme — because of who he is *TO* us and *FOR* us, *OVER* us, *BEFORE* us, and *WITHIN* us — we can serve with full assurance that if we remain open and ready for him to advance his mission *THROUGH* us, he will do so — without any limits.

Therefore, once again we come back to this:

Because of who Christ is
working *through* us in his spectacular supremacy,
we mean far more to the world than we ever thought possible.

Selah

pause | think | pray

Who Christ Is THROUGH Us Today:
Expressed Individually and Corporately

The Bible emphasizes that in this present age the reign of Jesus is displayed primarily **through** his people.

This moved 20th-century missionary martyr Jim Elliott to pray like this about his life: "Let me not be a milepost on a single road; make me a fork, that men must turn one way or another when facing Christ in me." Jim was heeding exhortations such as 2 Timothy 2:

> Those who cleanse themselves . . . will be instruments for special purposes, made holy, *useful to the Master* and prepared to do any good work (2 Timothy 2, NIV, emphasis added).

In other words, Christ empowers Christians *individually* for his service. Paul provides the preeminent example of this, writing in 1 Corinthians 10:

> Follow my example. I try to please everyone in every way. I'm not looking out for what is good for me. I'm looking out for the interests of others. I do it so that they might be saved.

He continues to make this plea:

> Follow my example, just as I follow the example of Christ (1 Corinthians 11).

However, the New Testament contains many more passages that talk about what Christ wants to accomplish **through** his people *corporately* to further his global cause.

Not only does Christ have a *mission for his church* in the world, but he also has a *church for his mission* in the world.

In other words, Jesus' gospel outreach to the world is displayed primarily **through** a *shared* mission by the Body of Christ. Often this is exhibited as he works **through** all kinds of mission sending structures that emerge out of the community of saints in order to focus on specific places and peoples and needs.

Let's look at both aspects separately:

Biblical Examples: Christ Reigning
THROUGH* Each of Us *Individually

Biblical Examples: Christ Reigning
THROUGH* All of Us *Corporately

 Snapshots and Starter Thoughts

Biblical Examples: Christ Reigning THROUGH Each of Us *Individually*

- **According to Galatians 1**: Right from day one of his Christian journey, Paul shares that when God called him and saved him by grace, the Father was pleased to reveal his Son to him for one express purpose:

  . . . so that I might preach him among the Gentiles (NIV).

  From the outset, Christ was working *in* Paul to reach out to the world **through** Paul.

- **According to Colossians 1**: Paul distills his life-long ministry into three words:

  We preach Christ (NLV).

Then quickly he explains where this effort comes from:

> To this end I strenuously contend with all the energy Christ so powerfully works in me (NIV).

- **According to Romans 15:** This seasoned preacher expected the Roman Christians to support his pioneer mission into Spain as a response of gratitude for how Christ ministered to them by "the full measure of the blessing of Christ" extended to them ***through*** Paul.

- **According to 2 Corinthians 4:** Our preaching of Jesus Christ as Lord can happen only because the power of Christ accomplishes this mission ***through*** us even though we are "broken clay pots," and does so in such a marvelous fashion that everyone knows the results must be his and not our own.

- **According to 2 Corinthians 5:** Christ's love for the world propelled Paul to make this appeal about the gospel to everyone everywhere he went:

> Does what we say make sense? If so, it is because we want to serve you. Christ's love controls us . . . So we are Christ's official messengers. It is *as if God were making his appeal through us*. Here is what Christ wants us to beg you to do. Come back to God! (emphasis added).

- **According to 2 Corinthians 4:** Paul's physical sufferings and setbacks became Jesus' opportunities to minister his saving life to others ***through*** the apostle in more powerful ways.

> For we who are alive are always being given over to death for Jesus' sake *so that his life might be revealed in our mortal bodies.* So then death is at work in us, but life is at work in you (NIV, emphasis added).

- **According to 2 Timothy 4:** When a Roman prison seemed to seriously confine Paul's impact for Christ, he held a far different outlook:

> At my first defense, no one came to my support, but everyone deserted me . . . But the Lord stood at my side and gave me strength, *so that through me the message might be fully proclaimed* and all the Gentiles might hear it. And I was delivered from the lion's mouth (NIV, emphasis added).

- **According to Romans 15:** Looking back over decades of serving Christ, Paul rejoices in what had been accomplished ***through*** him, interpreting it this way:

Therefore I glory in Christ Jesus in my service to God. I will not venture to speak of anything except what Christ has accomplished through me in leading the Gentiles to obey God by what I have said and done — by the power of signs and wonders, through the power of the Spirit of God (NIV, emphasis added).

- **According to 2 Corinthians 2:** The way Jesus sovereignly filled the world with the gospel *through* Paul's outreach caused the apostle to function like an incense burner. When incense spreads its sweet fragrance in a room full of people, immediately one is caught by its distinctive aroma before awareness of anything else in the room. In the same way, Paul describes how the reality and truth about Jesus always should be noticeable by the way Christians "burn" with the fullness of his supremacy.

But thanks be to God, who in Christ always leads us in triumphal procession, and *through us spreads the fragrance of the knowledge of him everywhere.* For we are the aroma of Christ to God among those who are being saved and among those who are perishing, to one a fragrance from death to death, to the other a fragrance from life to life. Who is sufficient for these things? (ESV, emphasis added).

Selah

pause | think | pray

Biblical Examples: Christ Reigning THROUGH All of Us *Corporately*

- **We read in Acts 11: "At Antioch, the believers were called Christians for the first time."** Notice it doesn't say they *called themselves* Christians. Rather, it says they *were called* Christians. Antioch was the third largest city in the Roman Empire, and its cosmopolitan and mostly pagan residents thought they had seen everything. Yet when they saw the dramatic changes that took place in the community of Jesus' followers, they basically said: "We've never witnessed anything like this before. We have no word in our language to define it. We need to coin a new word to give a name to what we see happening."

So, they took the Greek word "Christos," which means "the anointed one" (implying the kingly role of Jesus), and added a shorter word ("ian" in English), which means "belonging to the party of." With this one word, "Christian," the unbelievers were, in effect, saying something like this about the believers in Christ:

> They are people joined together to follow a king they claim has been anointed as Supreme Lord of the universe and Redeemer of all. As his subjects they have become devotees of his party; his agenda is now their agenda; his reign is now what their lives are all about.

- **No wonder that just a short time later the visible, phenomenal explosion of Christ's reign *through* the church in Antioch (the "Christians") ignited a surge of missionary outreach that expanded into every part of the Roman Empire.** We read in Acts 13 that when leaders of the church gathered to fast and pray, Jesus, by the Holy Spirit, commanded the group to set apart Paul and Barnabas for the work he already had prepared them to take on. Eventually, that congregation doubled as a base of operations for Christ's reign to spread abroad, spearheading the Gentile mission that is now two thousand years old and going strong.

Think about it. I'm writing to you in the 21st century about the Son of God because he extended his mighty scepter (Psalm 110) *through* one Christ-focused congregation (in what is now a bustling town of south-central Turkey) so as to launch a work of evangelism that twenty centuries later has penetrated thousands of languages and peoples around the world.

- **As the gospel spread, Paul and his mission team continued to collaborate with entire congregations, so that Christ might minister *through* them *together* for the greatest possible impact.** Here's how Paul saw Christ at work corporately as he co-labored with the church in Philippi:

> I thank my God every time I remember you, and in all my prayers for all of you. I always pray with joy because of [now watch the next phrase] your *partnership* in the Gospel from the first day until now, being confident of this, that *He who began a good work in you will carry it on to completion until the day of Christ* (Philippians 1, NIV, emphasis added).

Frequently, Christians apply that last phrase — "He who began a good work in you will carry it on to completion" — to everything God initiates in their personal lives. However, in the context, the "good work" to be brought to completion was the partnership and collaboration of the Philippian congregation with Paul and his team, working together to fulfill a vital mission to unreached people. In other words, by Jesus extending his kingdom *through* them *together*, he was bringing to completion the outreach the Philippians had embraced with Paul the last time he visited them.

Therefore, Paul concluded this insight asking the Father that these believers be:

> ... *filled* with the fruit of righteousness that comes through Jesus Christ — to the glory and praise of God (Philippians 1, NIV, emphasis added).

- **Nothing demonstrated more dramatically how Christ unleashes his supremacy *through one* local church than what he did in Thessalonica.** Only six months after Paul organized them, he wrote the infant congregation about all that Christ was accomplishing ***through*** them. The gospel was spreading ***through*** them so extensively it must have felt to them as if Jesus was impacting the ends of the earth. Paul put it like this:

> You turned to God from idols to serve the living and true God and to wait for His Son from heaven, whom He raised from the dead, Jesus who rescues us from the coming wrath . . . And so you became a model to all believers in Macedonia and Achaia. *The Lord's message rang out from you* [note he's talking about them corporately] *not only in Macedonia and Achaia, but your faith in God has become known everywhere* (1 Thessalonians 1, NIV, emphasis added).

What about your congregation? What more do you think Christ wants to accomplish ***through*** all of you working together? Anything close to what happened in Thessalonica?

- **Six months after he first wrote to the Thessalonian church, the apostle sent them another letter (2 Thessalonians) with a prayer request that is bursting with promise about how fully Christ wants to work *through any* church, anywhere, anytime.** He writes:

> Finally, brothers, pray for us, that the message of the Lord may spread rapidly and be honored [carefully consider the next phrase] *just as it was with you* (2 Thessalonians 3, NIV, emphasis added).

Paul was convinced that what God had done ***through*** one little body of believers in Thessalonica in just a few months — the powerful, Spirit-filled work of Christ advancing the gospel far and wide ***through*** their faithful corporate efforts — demonstrated what God would be willing to do with any company of believers anywhere. Therefore, you can conclude this must be what Christ wants to do with *your* congregation. He seeks to manifest his reign ***through*** you as convincingly as he did in Thessalonica.

- **In this age, Christ is most fully known where God's people manifest his power working *through* us together to extend his monarchy — as we fulfill his message, his mission, and his ministry to the world.** Our most effective witness to him comes about when we make the outworkings of his invisible reign *visible,* here and now, in our life together as his disciples. That means we should live in such a way that when people look at our congregation they make much of Christ, glorifying him for how he is working ***through*** us to spread God's blessings to the world. As Jesus reassured the church in Philadelphia in Revelation 3:

> Here are the words of Jesus, who is holy and true. He holds the key of David. No one can shut what he opens. And no one can open what he shuts. He says, "I know what you are doing. Look! I have put an open door in front of you. No one can shut it. I know that you don't have much strength. But you have obeyed my word. You have not said no to me. Some people claim they are Jews but are not. They are liars. Their worship comes from Satan. I will make them come and fall down at your feet. I will make them say in public that I have loved you" (Revelation 3).

- **But the Church is not simply a mechanism for delivering the gospel; the Church is the *product* of the gospel, visible *proof* of the supremacy of Christ within its own ranks — which makes our life together inseparable from our message.** We are the embodiment of hope in Christ, the only hope the world has. We are windows through which others may view, right now, how eternal life in Christ will express itself in the ages to come. As Paul told the Corinthians (2 Corinthians 3), working together we provide the world a "letter written by the Spirit of the living God" in which everyone should be able to "read" how Christ transforms a people who love and serve him.

- **Consider the metaphor of a hypodermic needle.** One single congregation is like the pinprick where the needle penetrates the arm. Above the tiny hole and attached to the needle a syringe is positioned, filled with powerful medication for restoring health to the patient. But the remedy can enter the human body only through the tiny opening created by the needle. Often the opening is so small the patient can't locate where the injection entered. Still the pinpoint remains the only way the remedy can penetrate the body.

In a very real sense, every one of the millions of congregations on planet Earth provides an entry point for the reign of Christ to break through — with all the fullness of his saving, healing, and transforming power — among people who do not know him yet, but who are in desperate need of all that his kingdom offers.

Selah

pause | think | pray

The Wrap

Christ at work **through** the Church's *corporate* witness is demonstrated every week in not a few Indian villages (of which there are over 600,000 throughout the nation). Every time believers meet together for open-air Sunday morning worship services, intent on exulting in Christ, the gatherings automatically *double* as evangelistic outreaches to their neighbors.

In contrast with Christians, Hindus regard most of their ancient village gods, who are often temperamental and unpredictable, with fearful groveling rather than with celebration and love. When nonbelievers are confronted with jubilant hope in Jesus expressed so openly by fellow villagers they are forced to ask: "Who is this Lord they sing about with such exuberance? What kind of deity is able to draw followers to himself who are so filled with abounding praise, unfettered joy, and heartfelt devotion? What has Jesus done for them to cause them to trust in him so completely?"

As a result, every Sunday across India, through publicly convened worship communities that are fervent for the saving reign of their Redeemer, the Holy Spirit magnifies the gospel of Christ before the eyes and ears of the Hindu world.

Who Christ Is THROUGH Us Today:
Expressed by Warfare and Martyrdom

Historically, two of the most daunting expressions of Christ's supremacy *through* his people entail significant sacrifices.

One is the intimidating biblical theme of **spiritual warfare** in all its forms, as we encounter the dark powers arrayed against the advancement of the Father's purposes for Christ.

The other is the sobering reality of **martyrdom** for Christ — the call for disciples to lay down their lives, often literally, for Christ's sake in order to and to spread the gospel.

Both are what we might call *extraordinary* manifestations of the triumphant reign of Christ. Often they unfold as two sides of the same coin. Let's take a closer look at each separately.

 Snapshots and Starter Thoughts

- **The first of these exceptional expressions of his kingship involves WARFARE with Satan and his minions — as Jesus defies and defeats the demonic forces of darkness on behalf of, and often *through*, his people.** As God's people enter into more of the fullness of Christ's supremacy and engage in advancing his kingdom throughout the world, we should expect to arouse the "anti-forces" opposed to the saving mission of Christ. The more Jesus fulfills his redeeming purposes among the nations *through* us the more these "principalities and powers of darkness" are pushed into defensive action *against* us.

- **According to Ephesians 6, this requires of us, first of all, a fresh re-engagement with Christ as we put on "the whole armor of God" (breastplate, helmet, shoes, shield, etc.).** Each piece represents different facets of the greatness and glory of our reigning Lord Jesus Christ. Romans 13 restates the Ephesians 6 dress code by appealing to us in plain and simple terms to "put on the Lord Jesus Christ as if he were your clothing." The only hope we have of victory over satanic powers rests in how fully Christ confronts our arch enemy with his liberating lordship, using his Church as his base of operations to attack and rout the oppositional hosts.

- **When Paul talks about preaching the unsearchable riches of Christ to the nations, he puts this effort into the context of spiritual conflagration.** In Ephesians 3, he teaches that *through* the church the manifold wisdom of God — meaning all the Father offers the world out of the saving fullness of his Son   is not being made known only to earth's peoples but also, equally, to rulers and authorities in heavenly realms, thus advancing God's eternal purpose in Christ Jesus on *both* fronts. The more Christ is manifested *through* his people, the further the darkness retreats and the faster malevolent principalities are neutralized.

- **Thankfully, in his reign *through* his disciples, Jesus assures us of ultimate victory, however fierce the battle becomes.** According to Romans 16, he will "crush Satan under your feet." According to Revelation 3, he will cause all who once served Satan's resistance by attacking God's people to "fall down at your feet and acknowledge that I have loved you." According to 2 Timothy 4, even if we find ourselves momentarily neutralized by Satan, we will never be forsaken by Christ, "so that through [us] the message might be fully proclaimed." Paul goes on to say, our King will "rescue [us] from every evil attack and will bring [us] safely to his heavenly kingdom" (NIV).

- **During the Protestant reformation, Martin Luther wrote a hymn that is sung today universally: "A Mighty Fortress is our God." It confirms**

what Luther knew experientially about our warfare. He wrote, in part:

> Did we in our own strength confide, our striving would be losing,
> were not the right man on our side, the man of God's own choosing.
> Dost ask who that may be? Christ Jesus, it is he.
> Lord Sabaoth his name, from age to age the same,
> *and he must win the battle.*
>
> And though this world, with devils filled should threaten to undo us,
> we will not fear for *God hath willed his truth to triumph through us* . . .
> The Spirit and the gifts are ours through him who with us sideth . . .
> The body they may kill; God's truth abideth still;
> his kingdom is forever
> (emphasis added).

- **The second exceptional display of Christ's supremacy *through* us involves an even greater sacrifice — the ultimate sacrifice of MARTYRDOM.** The dictionary defines martyrdom as: "The willingness of a person to endure severe or constant suffering, including death, on behalf of any belief, principle, or cause, rather than renounce his or her convictions." Synonyms include: distress, affliction, torture, anguish, self-sacrifice, mortification.

- **Not surprisingly, as Jesus extends his righteous reign into the world, warfare can lead to martyrdom; frequently the two walk hand in hand.** In Matthew 5, Jesus warned his disciples they would be slandered and persecuted (warfare involving physical suffering) for his sake — to further his kingdom cause. Revelation 12 tells us that when the authority and kingdom of Messiah prevail so thoroughly that Satan is cast down from heaven, the prime explanation will point to the saints who defeated the demonic forces through the blood of the Lamb and their bold word of witness to Jesus. But notice: These Christ proclaimers were so fully in love with him that they were willing to *die* for him. A recent front cover story of a major news magazine called this global phenomenon today *"The War on Christians."*

- **The history of the Church's growth archives incredible stories, reports, and statistics that demonstrate how Christ manifests his supremacy *through* those who suffer martyrdom.** The classic *Fox's Book of Martyrs* records episodes of hundreds of Christians through the ages who have laid down their lives for the gospel, often suffering unspeakable torture and violent retaliations. They embraced this fate in order that Christ might continue to advance his saving work ***through*** them among the nations — not in spite of but because of what they suffered. John Lambert, a martyr for the gospel in England in 1538, while burning at the stake, cried aloud for the whole crowd to hear, "None but Christ! None but Christ!"

- **Historically, the spread of the gospel increases, not inspite of but because of an increase in the number of martyred believers**. Research tells us that in the 20th century more people became believers and more churches were planted than in all the previous centuries of church growth put together. But also during that same century more Christians were martyred for their faith around the world than the previous twenty centuries put together! Again and again, the saving power of Christ becomes most clearly manifested ***through*** those who have laid down their lives for his sake and for the gospel (see Mark 8).

- **In fact, the *willingness* of Christians to pay a personal price because they hope in Christ's sure and certain triumph establishes before the world an irrefutable testimony to his living lordship.** It undergirds the legitimacy of our message about the saving power of our Master, about the pricelessness of his promise about the resurrection and re-creation of his people and the entire universe. Peter urges us:

  > . . . be glad that you are in the very thick of what Christ experienced. This is a spiritual refining process, with glory just around the corner. If you're abused because of Christ, count yourself fortunate. It's the Spirit of God and his glory in you that brought you to the notice of others . . . if it's because you're a Christian, don't give it a second thought. Be proud of the distinguished status reflected in that name! (1 Peter 4, MSG).

- **That's the same outlook Paul had in mind when he reported on his experiences as a Roman prisoner:**

  > I want to report to you, friends, that my imprisonment here has had the opposite of its intended effect. Instead of being squelched, the Message has actually prospered . . . And I'm going to keep that celebration going because I know how it's going to turn out. Through your faithful prayers and the generous response of the Spirit of Jesus Christ, everything he wants to do in and through me will be done . . .

> *everything happening to me in this jail only serves to make Christ more accurately known, regardless of whether I live or die. They didn't shut me up; they gave me a pulpit! Alive, I'm Christ's messenger; dead, I'm his bounty. Life versus even more life! I can't lose* (Philippians 1, MSG, emphasis added).

- **All New Testament leaders counted on Christ's reign to break in *through* their suffering in order to bring the good news of salvation to many others as a result.**

> We always carry around the death of Jesus in our bodies. *In that way, the life of Jesus can be shown in our bodies.* We who are alive are always in danger of death because we are serving Jesus. *This happens so that his life can also be shown in our earthly bodies. Death is at work in us. But life is at work in you* . . . All this is for your benefit. God's grace is reaching more and more people (2 Corinthians 4, emphasis added).

- **For example, look what happened when Stephen was executed, becoming the first martyr of the Christian era.** As stones broke his bones, he looked up to see Jesus standing in the place of all authority, at the right hand of the throne of heaven. Stephen bore witness to the mob:

> "Look!" he exclaimed, "the heavens are opened and I can see the Son of Man standing at God's right hand!" (Acts 7:56, PHILLIPS).

One of the eyewitnesses to Stephen's death was Saul (later named Paul), who soon after was converted to Christ and became the prime proclaimer of Christ in the first century, writing for future generations the richest of the New Testament passages that describe the glory and greatness of God's Son and the full extent of his supremacy.

- **Because we're indwelt by the Spirit of the ascended Lord Jesus, we must be ready to be "given over to death for Jesus' sake so that his life may be revealed in our mortal bodies (2 Corinthians 4, NIV).** The supremacy of Christ can be seen in this: He is able to exalt himself and extend his reign, not in spite of but rather ***through***, the martyrdom of his servants (Philippians 1). Therefore, one day the praises to the Lamb will include the testimony of those who loved him more than life itself and so shared in the victory of his cross, faithfully proclaiming the gospel of his kingdom (Revelation 12).

pause | think | pray

The Wrap

In 1553 in France, four young men ended up in prison, facing execution for publically preaching the gospel. The renowned reformer John Calvin wrote to them words of courage and comfort, summing up the biblical purpose and hope that should reinforce suffering Christians in any age:

> We who are here in Geneva shall do our duty in praying that Christ would glorify Himself more and more by your steadfastness to him.

> By the comfort of His Spirit, may He sweeten and endear all that is bitter to the flesh by absorbing your spirits in Himself.

> May He cause you to contemplate that heavenly crown so that you may be ready without regret to leave all that belongs to this world.

One month later, knowing now that their execution was at hand, John Calvin sent a second letter to the four in which he wrote:

> Since it appears as though Christ would use your blood to seal His truth, there's nothing better for you than to prepare yourselves for that end.

> Beseech Christ to subdue you to His good pleasure in such a way that nothing may hinder you from following Him whithersoever He shall call you.

> And since it pleases Him to employ you to the death in maintaining His witness to the Gospel, He will strengthen your hands in the fight and will not suffer a single drop of your blood to be shed in vain.

Not a single drop of blood would be shed in vain — such was Calvin's conviction about how Christ in his supremacy would prevail through their lives. In every case, individually and corporately, Christ is at work **through** our struggles to bring about triumphs of his grace every time.

In Romans 8, Paul describes how day by day his life as a missionary was like being led to slaughter:

> Because of you [Christ], we face death all day long. *We are considered as sheep to be killed* (Romans 8, emphasis added).

But with the next stroke of the pen his jubilation jumps from the page:

> In all these things we are more than winners! We owe it all to Christ, who has loved us (Romans 8).

Then, in 1 Corinthians 15, the apostle turns around to encourage all of God's people about the everlasting triumph that's ours because Christ is working **through** us to bring forth everlasting results for his kingdom:

> But let us give thanks to God!
> He gives us the victory
> because of what our Lord Jesus Christ has done.
> My dear brothers and sisters, remain strong in the faith.
> Don't let anything move you.
> Always give yourselves completely to the work of the Lord.
> Because you belong to the Lord,
> you know that your work is not worthless.

Selah

pause | think | pray

A Practical Application:
Prayer. Care. Share.

You and I are called to live every day, wherever our Lord Jesus sends us (to a construction job; to a classroom; to an office; to a campus; to next door neighbors), with a spirit of expectation about how he wants to work *through* us in that place and among those people, for his glory and their salvation.

Here are three simple steps that provide a great way for every believer to engage in Christ's global cause right where you are, as you allow him to get more involved in fulfilling his saving ministry to others **through** you.

The three steps are: **Prayer. Care. Share.** Take a look.

- **PRAYER.** Wherever you go throughout your day, you can always be in prayer for those around you — pray for the people on your street; pray for the people where you work; pray for the students and teachers in your school. Let Christ minister to them and extend his reign to them *through* your prayers and the answers that will come. Make this a way of life. As a result you will end up *meaning far more to the world than you ever thought possible.*

- **CARE.** Along with daily intercession, simultaneously show Christ's concern for those for whom you are praying. Be on the lookout for opportunities to minister to them with the love of Christ. In other words, let Jesus himself touch them and serve them *through* you, *making your life count far more for his kingdom than you ever thought possible.*

- **SHARE.** For certain, *through* your praying and caring, Jesus will open up sacred moments when you will be able to explain to them who God's Son is and what a new life in him is all about. But even then, it remains Jesus and only Jesus at work *through* your witness by his Spirit, *influencing more people for eternity than you ever thought possible.*

Who Christ Is THROUGH Us Today:
A Tribute

Paraphrasing and personalizing a wide selection of Scriptures

Father, we come to you to proclaim the name of your Son together — to spread his fame, embrace his reign, increase his gain, and honor his claim about who he is *through* us. As we do, awake us to him afresh for ALL that he is. May the praise we bring to him in these moments come forth alive in us by your Spirit and rise up as a blessing to you forever. We use your Word to magnify your Son, without whom we are nothing and can do nothing. This tribute is all for Christ alone, our one and only hope of glory, and the hope of all the nations.

Lord Jesus Christ, this is our Tribute to
Who you are THROUGH Us.

As Paul says, we will not venture to speak of anything except what you have accomplished *through* us in leading others to obey you. We will boast about only what you have accomplished *through* us by the power of signs and miracles, by the power of the Holy Spirit, so that those who have not heard of your great salvation might come to know you for *all* that you are.

As you did for ancient Abraham, you bless us to make us your blessing to the families of the earth. You infuse us with every blessing in heavenly places as we are united with you in your kingship, so that *through* us those blessings might enrich neighbors and nations.

As Jeremiah envisioned, you come to us to give us a future and a hope in you, so that as we prosper in you, prosperity might come to the cities where we dwell. We celebrate the great promise that *through* your Church you will bring to yourself renown, joy, praise, and honor before all nations on earth that hear of all the good things you have done for us. They will stand in awe of you and tremble at the redeeming work you have unleashed among us.

Like Isaiah envisioned, we want you to shine *through* us with the glory of the Lord so that nations come to your light and kings to the brightness of your dawn. We want you to take us in our barrenness and desolation and produce *through* us so many children that we will spread out to the right and the left, to dispossess nations and resettle desolate cities with your life alone.

As Zechariah envisioned, we want you to take us as prisoners of waterless pits and transform us into prisoners of hope, so that in the battle of the ages you can employ your people like a bow and arrow, and wield us like a warrior's sword.

Christ Is NOW!

As you proclaimed in Nazareth, reading from the sacred scroll, even so, to this very hour, the Spirit of the Lord remains upon you, anointing you. Forever you are Messiah — you are God's *anointed* one. So now, in the same way, clothe us with your anointing so that you might preach good news to the poor *through* us; so that you might bind up the brokenhearted *through* us; so that you might proclaim freedom for the captives and release from darkness for the prisoners through us; so that you might proclaim the year of the Lord's favor *through* us; so that you might comfort all who mourn, rebuild ancient ruins, raise up a people clothed in your garments of salvation, and make righteousness and praise spring up before all nations — all of this *through* us.

Christ Is NOW!

You said that since all authority is yours, we should not hesitate to make disciples for you among all the nations, especially because you would be with us, accomplishing it *through* us, to the end of the age. You said you were sending us the same way the Father had sent you, equipping us with power from on high to thrust us out. So, by the Spirit's filling, bear witness of yourself at all times and in all ways *through* us.

Lead us forth in your triumphal procession, as you journey to ends of the earth. Spread *through* us your truth, in word and deed, as richly and deeply as waters cover the sea. Make us your aroma among those who are being saved and those who are perishing. By how we live in you and by the gospel we proclaim about you, release **through** us the fragrance of the knowledge of all you and you alone are. **Through** us proclaim the invitation to the nations to find life in your life — even as your life works **through** us to bring life to others.

Christ Is NOW!

As Redeemer and Lord you have reconciled us back to the Father. Thank you! But you have also given us the ministry of reconciliation, as though you were making your appeal **through** us. Therefore, as your ambassadors, we implore all those we meet on your behalf to be reconciled to God. We are determined to share, not ourselves but you, Jesus Christ, as the supreme Sovereign you are. We will do this by simply offering ourselves to serve our hearers for your sake alone, so they might encounter you alone the way we have.

In our hearts we set *you* apart as Lord and Christ — we consecrate *you* to your rightful place in our lives and our churches — in order to remain ready and able to give an answer to anyone who asks us for reasons we have such a great hope in you alone.

Lord Jesus, only you can work in us that which is exceedingly pleasing to the Father. Only you can equip us with everything good for doing God's will. Lord Jesus, you are the vine from whom all your branches draw sustaining power to serve you. We did not choose you. You chose us. It was you who ordained that in relationship with you we should go forth and bear much fruit, fruit that endures forever.

Already, all over the world, the good news of who you are is spreading and bearing fruit; so now, may it do so **through** us, for your praise among all peoples. You are building the Church on the foundation of the revelation that you truly are the Christ, the Son of the living God. You have given your people the keys to the Kingdom, to open what heaven has already opened and to shut what heaven has already shut. So, lead us on. **Through** us engage and prevail against the very gates of hell and Hades.

Christ Is NOW!

Now have come the salvation and the power and the kingdom of our God and the authority of you as his Christ. By you, the accuser has been hurled down. Therefore, thoroughly overcome him by your blood, O Lamb of God. Thoroughly overcome him *through* our testimony, spoken to one and all, about who you are, about *all* that you are — even if that means we must lay down our lives for your sake and for the gospel. We are ready to be given over to death for your sake, that your life might be revealed in our mortal bodies. So let death be at work in us, as long as your life is at work in others *through* us. We can do no less. Your love compels us. You deserve for us to lay before you the fruits of the travail of your soul. So exalt yourself *through* us, before the eyes of the world — whether by life or by death — because for us to live and serve is Christ and Christ alone.

Christ Is NOW!

This tribute expresses only a small part of the inexhaustible riches of who you are THROUGH us and all peoples.

So, Father, here is how we celebrate your Son, our Lord Jesus Christ, in this hour. We exalt him. We exult in him. We do so because of all he is *through* us — now. Therefore, everything we are and have, every breath we breathe, every step we take, every service we render, every prayer we pray, every praise we bring, is possible only by him and him alone. For without him — without all he is *through* us — we are nothing and we can do nothing. More and more, by the revealing work of your Spirit, awaken us to Christ alone — awaken your whole Church to Christ alone — so that increasingly he might become *through* us our all in all.

AMEN!

Preparing to Explore and Experience the Seventh Dimension of the Spectacular Supremacy of God's Son

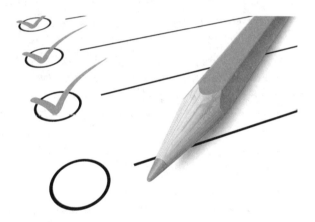

A Quick Review

*D*ue to the breathtaking ramifications of what we're about to uncover in the next chapter concerning who King Jesus is as he comes UPON his people today, it might be wise to review briefly what we've discovered so far about this unparalleled person.

In previous chapters we began to explore and experience six dimensions of Christ's spectacular supremacy.

- **Who Christ Is TO Us Today:** in the supremacy of his deity; in his intimacy with the Trinity; as the summation of God's revelation; by the claims of his names; as the picture of Scripture; as our identity and destiny; and finally, as the Father's passion and ours. These truths comprise the essence of his personhood.

- **Who Christ Is FOR Us Today:** by the invasion of his incarnation; by the mission of his crucifixion; by the re-creation of his resurrection; by the coronation of his ascension. Keeping all four expressions of Christ's redeeming victory inseparably linked, we defined it as his irreversible fourfold revolution.

- **Who Christ Is OVER Us Today**: as he reigns over the workings of all creation; over the unfolding of world history; over the designs of global rulers; over the destiny of earth's peoples; over the rebellion of evil powers; and over the building of his Church. These six expressions of the flow of his kingdom comprise the key manifestations in this present age of his ascension.

- **Who Christ Is BEFORE Us Today**: leading the way into the future in order to bring it back to us; advancing into the heavens in order to bring us there with him; preceding us into the promises of God in order to fulfill them and make them ours as well. Finally, full of majesty he goes out ahead of us into the world in order to open the way for us to follow him and serve him in a variety of kingdom ministries. In all four ways, his building of the Church continues.

- **Who Christ Is WITHIN Us Today:** Where the Spirit abides, King Jesus abides — not just part of him but all of him — in the fullness of his supremacy. Therefore, at all times we should live as if the triumphant, reigning Savior were among us because by his Spirit he truly is. Scripture focuses primarily on the *corporate* dynamics of Christ dwelling among us. What Jesus accomplishes in a single Christian life is dependent more often than not on what his reign is bringing forth within the Christian community to which each person belongs. His building of the Church continues at both levels.

- **Who Christ Is THROUGH Us Today:** Because of who Christ is through us, working through us by his spectacular supremacy, each of us means far more to the world than we ever thought possible. Although his outreach to the world involves both individual and corporate expressions, once again the main biblical emphasis is on how Jesus extends his reign through God's people together, as we collaborate to press the gospel's kingdom agenda locally and globally. There are no limits on how far his mission through us extends among the nations — often by suffering, at times requiring spiritual warfare, sometimes ending in martyrdom. Christ continues to build the Church even by its outreach to the world.

At this point, it might be useful for you to reflect on these five questions:

1 As I've explored these extraordinary wonders magnifying the person of God's Son today, in what ways has this adventure begun to change my *relationship* to him?

2 Am I sensing a reawakening to him and to his spectacular supremacy that in any sense feels like *I'm meeting him again for the first time?*

3 Am I starting to enjoy a deepening *intimacy* with Jesus as I learn more about his majestic qualities and his current activities?

4 How have these studies begun to ignite in me *stronger desires* to know him better, love him more deeply, and exalt him more fully for all he is?

5 As *CIN* has helped me begin to explore and experience Jesus' spectacular supremacy, am I becoming *increasingly determined* to give him wholehearted obedience in my daily walk with him?

Whatever your answers are to these five questions, remember this: Our journey into more of God's Son has only *begun!* As Lord of all, Jesus guarantees for all believers that there is so much more of himself to share with all who are united to him, alive in him, and open to him for more.

The following chapter confirms there's so much more of God's Son that awaits us as he comes UPON us.

To prepare ourselves to receive the riches of this often misunderstood dimension of his supremacy, we would do well to pray — but not just any prayer. Consider praying this radical, even "dangerous" request, which thousands have prayed with me already over the years:

Come Upon Us, Lord Jesus Christ

Come upon us, Lord Jesus Christ!
Ultimately, come in the triumphs
of your victorious return.
But until then, come upon us
with similar transforming power—
right here and right now.

Come upon us, Lord Jesus Christ!
Pour out your Holy Spirit
upon your people gathered before your face.
Pour out remarkable manifestations
of the Father's all-consuming grace and truth in you.

Come upon us, Lord Jesus Christ!
Give us foretastes
of what will fill all of eternity very soon.
Focus us on your unparalleled Person
as the Son of God.
Fill us with your royal resources
as the Regent of God.
Fulfill through us your saving mission
in the purposes of God.

Come upon us, Lord Jesus Christ!
Come upon us to intensify
and deepen, and extend,
and accelerate, and multiply
all you already have become *to* us,
for us, *over* us, *before* us,
within us, and *through* us.

Come upon us, Lord Jesus Christ!
Wake up your followers in every part of the Church.
Empower us to advance the gospel among all peoples.
Invade this place! Conquer us afresh!
Transform us more and more into
a showcase of your glorious reign.
Overtake us as your people!
Unleash your life-changing initiatives
in everything we *are* together
and in everything we *do* together.

Break in and break through upon us without delay!
Answer this cry in ways
that approximate how one day— one grand and glorious day—
your triumphs will be displayed
throughout all heaven and earth,
bringing everlasting praise to our triune God.

With great anticipation we watch
for that crowning hour you come upon us *fully*—
the hour when your glory is revealed *fully;*
the hour when you deliver us and all creation *fully*—
at the consummation of the ages!
Come upon us *that* day!
Come upon us *this day*!

Between this day and that day
never stop coming down upon us!
Come in the fullness of your spectacular supremacy!
Come in the fervor of your magnificent majesty!
Son of the Father,
Focus of the Spirit,
Hymn of the angels,
Ruler of the nations,
Redeemer of the Church!

Our. Lord. Jesus. Christ.
COME!

The Spectacular Supremacy of God's Son Today

Exploring and Experiencing
Who Christ Is
UPON Us Today

Return with me to the metaphor we used in the opening three "Meditations on His Majesty," describing the extraordinary nature of our journey into more of our living Lord Jesus Christ:

Niagara Falls.

Like the daily boat tour that navigates breathless tourists up to the base of Niagara's deafening cascades, we've been transported into awesome sightings of the "high-ness" and the "nigh-ness" of Christ. We've witnessed how God's Son, alive and ascended, occupies the throne of the universe, with a reign that surges outward and onward unrelentingly like Niagara's river.

That dynamic metaphor perfectly portrays one of *CIN's* foundational Scriptures: Colossians 1:18-19. In these verses, God's Word asserts that in everything and forever God's Son retains unconditional, unbounded dominion. As we've seen, this is true for two major reasons: The first is because in Jesus the full nature of God abides; the second is because through him we have every reason to expect heaven and earth will be redeemed and reconciled back to God.

Therefore, the Church must jubilantly proclaim that Christ is *now!*
All he will be Lord of at the end he is Lord of *now!*
All of the glory he will display ultimately belongs to him *now!*
All of the promises he will fulfill one day he has already inherited *now!*

Let me be more specific as relates to this seventh "key": Just as he will come **upon** the *universe* at his glorious, visible return, causing it to rise fully alive to him, even so he desires to come **upon** his people right here and *now*, causing *us* to rise more fully alive in him.

Like dwelling every day at the unrelenting confluence of multiple cataracts, Christians reside permanently at the footstool of the Lion of Judah who is ready to pour **upon** us even *more* of his presence — to descend **upon** us with so much more of his power — and then do so even *more*.

Of course, *chronologically speaking* the full displays of his transforming kingdom still lie ahead of us, reserved for the day of the Lord, the day of his visible return.

But *Christologically speaking* every facet of his *end* times reign is operative in significant measures around us, within us, and through us during *these* times.

In this chapter we want to welcome God's Son to come — to come **upon** us — and to do so today in ways that thoroughly *saturate* us with himself. Like tourists who decide they don't simply want to *look at* the falls, who instead choose to go *straight under* the falls, we want to open ourselves up to a much fuller permeation of our lives with Christ and his spectacular supremacy.

Beyond such an encounter with the Son of God, there is nothing more the Father has for us.

Who Christ Is UPON Us Today:
The Prevailing Promise of Scripture

Take a look at another prayer agenda, similar to our "Prayer of Invitation," once spoken by an ancient Hebrew prophet:

> *I wish you would open up your heavens and come down to us . . . come down and make yourself known . . .* cause the nations to shake with fear when they see your power . . . No one's ears have ever heard of a God like you. No one's eyes have ever seen a God who is greater than you. No God but you acts for the good of those who trust in him (Isaiah 64, emphasis added).

Paul claims in 1 Corinthians 2 that Isaiah's forecast of divinely disruptive interventions found its fullest expression in God's equally startling, stunning actions toward us when the Son of God himself came down ***upon*** the earth to shake the nations by becoming our one and only Savior:

> But before time began, God planned that his wisdom would bring us heavenly glory. None of the rulers of this world understood God's wisdom. If they had, they would not have nailed the Lord of glory to the cross. It is written that "no eye has seen, no ear has heard, and no human mind has known" (Isaiah 64:4). God has prepared these things for those who love him. God has shown these things to us through his Spirit . . . we have the mind of Christ.

Heaven opened and Jesus came down. By his incarnation, crucifixion, resurrection, and ascension he overtook the world — making himself known to humankind in no uncertain terms.

But 1 Corinthians 2 promises us an additional fulfillment of Isaiah 64. This happens as the Holy Spirit comes *upon* all who belong to Christ today to pour into us the "deep things of God," giving us "the mind of Christ" — that is, the ability to see everything as it relates to Christ.

It should not come as a surprise then, that the last prayer of the Bible expands on the passionate appeal of Isaiah 64: **"Amen. Come, Lord Jesus!"** (Revelation 22, emphasis added).

In fact, in hundreds of other texts the Bible summons God's people to tackle life with the same spirit of *expectancy* because our King has a whole lot more of himself to share with us — but not only at some future apocalyptic visitation. He wants to come *upon* us in much deeper ways *today*!

Any time Christ comes *upon* his followers — any time he "opens up the heavens and comes down" — whether on this day or the final day, he comes with one grand intention: to permeate our lives with the one abounding blessing Paul describes so forcefully. He wrote:

> God said, "Let light shine out of darkness." (Genesis 1:3) He made his light shine in our hearts. His light gives us the light to know God's glory. His glory is shown in the face of Christ (2 Corinthians 4).

Therefore, we should encourage one another along these lines:

- **Heads up!** Right now something awesome from Jesus is on its way. He draws near. He is at the door. A fresh inbreaking from our Lord is at hand, promising us more manifestations of his kingdom *upon* us than we've known before.

- **Be prepared!** This "UPON us" dimension may prove to be the most unsettling expression of his supremacy we've explored so far. The transformative possibilities it holds for both our present and future walk with Jesus supersede our dreams and are most certainly out of our control.

- **Get ready!** There's a climatic hour not long from now when Christ will return triumphantly, coming *upon* all the saints in resurrection power while simultaneously coming *upon* the whole creation in redemption and judgment, to forever take charge, visibly and unchallenged, at the consummation of all things. Each one of us will be there! Each one of us will witness this glorious culmination with our own eyes.

- **Stay alert!** The impending nature of this cosmic cataclysm should reshape our walk with the Lord of glory right now because as personally and purposefully as he will bring all things under his dominion at the end, even so Jesus wants to come **upon** disciples walking planet Earth today to bring about life-giving changes around us and in us and through us.

- **Watch out!** Both then and now, our Savior intends to come **upon** his own in order to bring us into *more* of himself — in order to intensify and deepen and extend and multiply and accelerate whatever experiences of his spectacular supremacy we currently enjoy.

- **Be advised!** Whenever Christ floods any believer or any church with more of himself — with greater displays of his presence and power — anticipate nothing less than marvelous *approximations* of the Consummation, as the Spirit of God comes **upon** the people of God to provide us substantial foretastes of the coming kingdom of God.

Selah

pause | think | pray

Who Christ Is UPON Us Today:
The Greatest Longing of Our Hearts

For decades Christian leaders and their churches have gathered in hundreds of prayer rallies dedicated to seeking God for church renewal and gospel advance. Convened in communities across America and beyond, sometimes they congregate in stadiums and arenas, weaving together Christians from every expression of the Body of Christ. Frequently these rallies are referred to as "Concerts of Prayer."

It's a term initially coined by the renowned Puritan pastor and scholar Jonathan Edwards. He gave leadership to what church historians identify as America's first spiritual firestorm, called the First Great Awakening, which emerged during the early to mid-1700s.

This extensive, Bible-based revival was preceded by Christians praying together in concerts of prayer, fostered on both sides of the Atlantic. It not only transformed Edwards' parish, the second largest church in New England, but also swept through many of the colonies. For multitudes of believers it provided fresh encounters with Christ — what we would describe today as Christ Awakenings.

Unfortunately, by 1745 the hottest coals of this mighty work of the Holy Spirit began to cool. As was true in Reverend Edwards' congregation, many Christians fell back into the level of spiritual lethargy and moral indifference that had marked them before the awakening began.

Eventually, this burdened pastor determined that the decline occurred because too many New England believers falsely concluded that the opening phase of their renewal in Christ was the *only* phase God intended for them; that for the moment nothing else remained of God's kingdom promises for them to experience; that they had encountered all of the fullness of Christ they should expect to enjoy for now.

Contrary to that tragic assumption, Edwards' study of Scripture convinced him that the revitalization that the churches of New England recently had experienced was only the *beginning* of all God wanted to share with them through his Son. Far too many were willing to stop far short of the long-lasting, all-pervasive awakening to Jesus the Father desired for them.

Taking the matter in hand, in 1747 this prolific author (already a shelf full of books bore his name) penned his next volume. In it he appealed for a renewed effort in corporate prayer, urging believers to join in offering bold prayers that refused to settle for less than God's best for the glory of God's Son.

In his treatise, Edwards alerted Christians to how there was so much more of the reign of Christ that the Holy Spirit wanted to unleash in their lives if only they increasingly pursued it, if only they would unite in sustained, heartfelt intercession until God granted it.

His hundred-page book bears a rather lengthy title, typical of authors in those days who worded titles as a way to summarize the book's contents. This one read:

An Humble Attempt
to Promote Explicit Agreement and Visible Union
of God's People in Extraordinary Prayer
for the Revival of Religion
and the Advancement of Christ's Kingdom on Earth,
Pursuant to Scripture-Promises and Prophecies
Concerning the Last Time.

Recently a major Christian publisher in Great Britain decided to reissue the work. They invited me to write an introductory interpretive essay to provide 21st-century readers an overview of its main theses. (Thankfully the new edition carries a briefer title: *A Call to United Extraordinary Prayer*).

Reviewing Edwards' arguments, I rediscovered that his emphasis was not about the doctrine of prayer per se, or about united prayer or about how to pray correctly.

Rather, it was a study on the greatness of Christ and the outworking of his kingship now and later. Here's how he approached it: He highlighted many marvels that lie ahead for the saints at the consummation of all things. Then he reasoned that because of Jesus' ascension many of those future blessings could be entered into here and now, which led him to what many consider to be the scholar's most profound insight:

If Christians are not uniting regularly in "extraordinary prayer" — that is, prayer for the revival of the Church and the global advance of Christ's saving reign — it is not because they lack sufficient sermons on the topic of prayer. *It is because they lack a clear focus on the triumphs and dominion of Christ right now* — a focus centered on (as I would say it) who he is, where he's headed, what he's doing, and how he gets blessed.

Only as the Church grasps more fully the extent of the awesome authority inherent in the person seated at the Father's right hand, and concludes that therefore much more of Christ's fullness awaits those who are eager to move deeper into him at this very moment, will we be motivated to pray — to pray aggressively the *way* we should, and for *what* we should.

More specifically, using words from the title of his book, Edwards appealed for united prayer *"pursuant to the Scripture-promises and prophecies concerning the last times."*

In other words, let our agenda in prayer begin with what Scripture teaches about the end of the age when Jesus comes **upon** us to bring to climax everything God has purposed. That is, first we should shape our requests based on what we expect to behold when God's plan for the universe is consummated in Christ. Mark how the kingdom will prevail once the King of glory visibly reappears to renovate and rule over a new heaven and earth. *Then*, walk that vision back to the current generation and ask this one basic question:

How much of what God's Word has promised us in Christ at the inauguration of the *age to come* is God's Spirit willing to unleash **upon** God's people in this *current age* through fresh kingdom initiatives by God's Son taking place here and now?

We should also ask: How many of the dynamics to be displayed when all prophecies and promises are fulfilled in the last times — when Jesus "comes down" in finality — are available for us to experience today, at least in preliminary fashions, if he would come **upon** his Church right now by the power of the Holy Spirit?

Edwards concluded that every expectation we hold of increased applications of God's promises today should stir the Church to pray with greater clarity, stronger convictions, unshakeable hope, and unwavering perseverance — to pray prayers that will not relent until the Father blesses his people with more of the favor and fullness found in his risen, reigning Son.

The Puritan writers in Edwards' day referred to this effort as praying for (this was their specific phrase) *"the manifest presence of Christ,"* which meant to pray for Christ to come **upon** his followers in ways that provide us *substantial furetastes* of how ultimately he will reveal himself when he comes **upon** the whole creation.

To put it in a simple phrase we're about to unpack: We need to pray for *approximations of the Consummation.*

Who Christ Is UPON Us Today:
Impending, Like Thunderclouds Hovering

Chapter 1 of Mark's gospel (NLT) reports that Jesus opened up his public campaign by preaching a four-part message:

(1) The time promised by God has come at last.

(2) The kingdom of God is near!

(3) Repent of your sins.

(4) Believe the good news!

In the original language, the phrase "is near" can be translated "is *at hand*" — or more literally "the kingdom *is bearing down on top of you.*"

Christ bearing down on top of us? Many find the thought of that rather unsettling. Here is one way to explain what's going on:

Picture yourself picnicking with friends on a humid summer afternoon. Taking a bite of your sandwich, you scan the horizon. In the distance you notice thunderclouds rapidly forming. First they come *toward* you. Then they come *at* you. Soon they are directly *on top* of you, casting foreboding shadows over your little band. You feel the electricity in the air. You know a downpour threatens — soon!

True, the storm hasn't let loose yet; but clearly it's "at hand." It's impending, hovering — primed to release a suffusion of showers **upon** you, requiring a rapid change of plans!

In a similar sense, whenever our Redeemer comes **upon** his Church, sovereignly he intrudes like a portending downpour, intending to permeate, even saturate, his people — individually and corporately — with fresh revelations of his glory and greatness, challenging our plans and priorities. You could say he *invades* his followers, bringing normal routines to a halt in order to take us with him where we've never gone before.

This brings us to a central question of this chapter: How open are we — how open are *you* — for Jesus to come **upon** us in ways far more intensive and decisive than the most potent thunderstorm?

In other words, how willing are we for him to disrupt our routines and overturn our plans? To reconstitute every facet of our relationship with him? To reengage us with himself in a way that increases, accelerates, intensifies, enlarges, and deepens all he already has begun to accomplish in us and through us in our walk with him?

Samuel Rutherford, a devout Scottish reformer of the 1600s, was so deeply committed to Christ he willingly endured multiple imprisonments for preaching the gospel. So how do we explain the extraordinary confession he placed in his journal when he wrote:

> After I've committed to him everything and after I have given him my heart, I still must pray, every day: "*Lord Jesus, come and conquer me*" (emphasis added).

Quite simply, Rutherford was expressing an unquenchable desire for Christ to come **upon** him — to *recapture* him in whole new ways that would immerse him into even greater depths of ministry for his Savior.

Moment by moment, Christ hovers over *every* disciple for this very same purpose — to "rend the heavens and come down" **upon** us, in order to conquer us afresh for his sake.

To unpack more of this seventh "key" to a fuller vision of his supremacy, let's break the remainder of the chapter into three major segments:

Who Christ Is UPON Us Today:

At the Consummation of All Things

Through Approximations of the Consummation

As We Embrace a Lifestyle of Anticipation

First, we'll begin with the end, the *Consummation* itself, exploring what will transpire at a *cosmic* level when Christ comes **upon** the Church, **upon** all of earth's peoples, as well as **upon** the whole created universe — the culminating revelation of his greatness and goodness and glory at the climax of God's plan for the ages.

Then we'll take up *current* expressions of Christ **upon** us, appropriately termed "*approximations of the Consummation*" because they draw on themes of the Consummation. Such transactions take place every time Jesus reasserts his kingship among his people to carry out transformative initiatives within us and through us that are totally separate from, but clearly reflective of, what will happen in fullest measure in the age to come.

Finally, we'll take stock of how this great truth — Christ **upon** us — should impact daily discipleship and create a lifestyle of *anticipation* for every follower of Jesus, so that:

> . . . by the power of the Holy Spirit you will abound in hope *and* overflow with confidence in His promises (Romans 15, AMP).

Who Christ Is Upon Us Today:
At the Consummation of All Things

As revealed in Scripture, the ascended Christ shows himself to be someone fully engaged, clearly decisive, always proactive, and resolutely goal-oriented. The one "who is, and who was, and who is to come" (Revelation 1, NIV) is driving toward the Consummation; the future glory resides in his very nature. In fact, one might say that for him his ascension and coronation meant the "inauguration" of the Consummation.

That may be why the book of Revelation speaks of Christ's return as coming "soon" and "suddenly" and "unexpectedly." He's that *eager* to bring everything to its climax — when it's the right time.

The verb "consummate" means to fully achieve, to bring to completion; to finish; to perfect; to raise to the highest point or degree. Accordingly, Bible scholars define *the* Consummation as both *the ultimate goal itself* and *the completion of that goal*.

Using the analogy of American football, the Consummation is a combination of the celebration of victory at the end of the game *plus* the success of running plays that get you across the goal line so that you have something to celebrate.

Looking at it another way, Scripture marks the Consummation as the *arrival* of both some*thing* and some*one*. It is the tangible and total dominance of God's purposes over human affairs when Jesus returns, ratifying once and for all that the kingdom of this world truly has been subsumed into the reign of our God and of his Christ forever (Revelation 11:15).

With those definitions in mind, let's dig deeper.

 ## *Snapshots and Starter Thoughts*

- **We are promised that Christ will come *upon* the whole world in Acts 17:**

   But now he commands all people everywhere to turn away from their sins. He has set a day when he will judge the world fairly. He has appointed a man to be its judge. God has proved this to everyone by raising that man from the dead.

- **We are promised it in Philippians 2 (NLT):**

   Therefore, God elevated him to the place of highest honor and gave him a name above all other names that at the name of Jesus every knee should bow in heaven and on earth and under the earth, and every tongue confess that Jesus Christ is Lord to the glory of God the Father.

- **We are promised it in Titus 2 (NLT):**

   For the grace of God has been revealed, bringing salvation to all people . . . but we look forward with hope to that wonderful day when the glory of our great God and our Savior, Jesus Christ, will be revealed.

- **We are promised it in Philippians 3:**

   But we are citizens of heaven. And we can hardly wait for a Savior from there. He is the Lord Jesus Christ. He has the power to bring everything under his control. By his power he will change our earthly bodies. They will become like his glorious body.

- **We are promised it in 2 Thessalonians 1:**

   All these things will happen when the Lord Jesus appears from heaven. He will come in blazing fire. He will come with his powerful angels. He will punish those who don't know God. He will punish those who don't obey the good news about our Lord Jesus . . . On that day his glory will be seen in his holy people. Everyone who has believed will be amazed when they see him. This includes you, because you believed the witness we gave you.

- **We are promised it in Revelation 21 and 22:**

  > I didn't see a temple in the city. That's because the Lamb and the Lord God who rules over all are its temple. The city does not need the sun or moon to shine on it. God's glory is its light, and the Lamb is its lamp. The nations will walk by the light of the city. The kings of the world will bring their glory into it (Revelation 21).

  > There will no longer be any curse. The throne of God and of the Lamb will be in the city. God's servants will serve him. They will see his face. His name will be on their foreheads. There will be no more night. They will not need the light of a lamp or the light of the sun. The Lord God will give them light. They will rule for ever and ever (Revelation 22).

- **In its profoundest sense, ultimately the Consummation is all about revelation.** Because the Bible ends with Jesus returning to earth, the Consummation becomes the *culmination* of the glorious revelation of God's Son — previously displayed by creation, in Scripture, during his mission for our redemption, with the coming of his Spirit, and throughout the myriad advances of the gospel across the history of the Church.

- **In other words, our questions about the future are not about when or what, but about *who*. In the climax everything will be engulfed with Christ alone.** The universe will become permanently enthralled with Christ alone. The responsibility of all beings will be to Christ alone. The outcome of all decisions will be determined by Christ alone. The worship of all creation will be directed by Christ alone. Despite the magnitude of all that transpires at the Consummation, and despite the massive heavenly bounty we as believers will inherit, the focus and desire of all the saints remain forever on Christ alone.

Before that day appears, therefore, each of us should ask himself: "Could I remain satisfied with the colossal promises fulfilled in the Consummation IF I discovered when the time came that Jesus — the true source and substance *of*, and the reason *for* all those benefits — was nowhere to be found once I got there?" In other words, could I enjoy the blessings minus the Bless-er? That deserves some honest reflection.

To put it another way: Can the Consummation even commence until, first of all, Christ comes **upon** the redeemed in heaven and earth to consume us (that is, to "consummate" us) with himself and his kingdom agenda exclusively?

The truth is that how we view what the singular role and renown of Jesus will be *then* determines in no small measure how we choose to love him and live for him *now*.

- **A day is coming when the conflict of the ages will cease — when the grandest expression of the preeminence of Christ's kingdom will prevail.** Its strategies will be perfected, its claims vindicated, its promises implemented, its judgments activated, its enemies eliminated, its dominion renovated, its moral order instituted, its citizens resurrected, and its King universally celebrated. Thus, to study the breadth and depth of all that will unfold in the Consummation is to know what Christ's kingdom purposes are all about *today*.

- **In the Consummation the supremacy of Christ will become irresistibly spectacular.** That's why every knee will bow (even in hell), confessing the truth of his primacy as Lord (Philippians 2). Our Redeemer will be acknowledged as supreme enough to complete God's plan in every detail — supreme enough to seal the destiny of the people of God with the glory of God in the presence of God; supreme enough to bring all heaven and earth into subjection to himself (Philippians 3); supreme enough to saturate everything, visible and invisible, with the fullness of life that flows from his innermost being (Ephesians 1).

- **The whole creation looks forward to its day of regeneration, when the Son of Man returns to sit on his glorious throne (Matthew 25; Romans 8).** The cosmos will be rescued from oblivion and transferred into the beauty and blessedness of "Paradise Regained." Death itself will die, the grave will be no more, mortality will be swallowed up in victory (1 Corinthians 15) — all of this is not only guaranteed to the saints but also to the whole universe. Church father Irenaeus called it the "recapitulation" of all things in Christ.

- **Jesus' return will bring about the convergence of every biblical truth related to the end.** These include the day of the Lord; the resurrection of the dead; reunion with all of God's people; the final judgment of all evil, sin, sickness, and death; the re-creation of a new heaven and earth; the love and peace and justice of Christ saturating the nations.

- **When Christ comes down at the close of history, he will do so visibly, tangibly, unmistakably.** In the same way that every Old Testament prophecy about Jesus' first coming to earth was *literally* and *publically* fulfilled, likewise his second coming will achieve in an equally concrete fashion every outcome promised in Scripture.

- **There's a great day just ahead when Christ will be *confrontational* like never before.** One way or another, the entire universe will be forced to engage directly with Christ himself — immediately, unavoidably, radically, and permanently. Everything will be summed up in our Lord forever when he comes ***upon*** everything and everyone, either by *final judgment* or by *final redemption*. Paul describes it this way:

   > He thought of everything, provided for everything we could possibly need, letting us in on the plans he took such delight in making. He set it all out before us in Christ, a long-range plan in which everything would be brought together and summed up in him, everything in deepest heaven, everything on planet earth. It's in Christ that we find out who we are and what we are living for (Ephesians 1, MSG).

By Final Judgment

- **Here's what we know about King Jesus' descent in *judgment* at the Consummation:** All evil and sin will be exposed, defeated, and purged once and for all. Despite generations who have long rejected his claims, he will be vindicated. He will sweep away all opposition and all competition. He will humble all the proud powers of this world so as to fill the earth with the knowledge of his glory. The nature of evil is such that the end can come no other way. The intervention of Christ to shut down age-old conflicts with sin and Satan is required. This is our only hope for bringing the wicked to total destruction and the righteous (in Christ) to total deliverance and wholeness.

- **As the indisputable judge of all peoples of all generations, he will come *upon* the earth to bring each and every person to account before him**. Every heart will be revealed. The Consummation will settle the ultimate destiny of all. Scripture teaches that Christ's judgment of the secrets of every heart is part of the Good News we preach to the nations (Romans 2)! How so? When everything is brought into the light, then the *full* extent of Jesus' saving reign will be revealed, to his increasing and unceasing praise, and to our everlasting joy.

- **At the end of this age, every person who has ever lived either will be consumed *with* Christ or consumed *by* Christ**. Consumed *with* him means caught up with all the saints Into everlasting adoration of him and loving service to him. Consumed *by* him means brought into accountability and judgment before him — banished forever by him from his presence and the love and life of God found in him. Our eternal destiny comes down to the one outcome or the other. This is utterly unavoidable. No one will be exempt.

- **Through Jesus, God's will and God's kingdom will come *upon* the earth just as it already prevails throughout the heavens.** The Lamb on the throne will overwhelm the nations with himself so as to put all things right. He will bring an end to all injustice and deception, all brutality and violence.

- **The hosts of darkness will be obliterated**. Due to the nature of evil, their full and final defeat requires a direct, decisive intervention to come *upon* them in the Consummation. In that hour, Satan and all his minions will experience the fury of our King, as described, for example, in Revelation 19:

> Then I saw Heaven open wide — and oh! a white horse and its Rider. The Rider, named Faithful and True, judges and makes war in pure righteousness. His eyes are a blaze of fire, on his head many crowns . . . *A sharp sword comes out of his mouth so he can subdue the nations, then rule them with a rod of iron* . . . I saw the Beast and, assembled with him, earth's kings and their armies, ready to make war against the One on the horse and his army. The Beast was taken, and with him, his puppet, the False Prophet, who used signs to dazzle and

deceive . . . *They were thrown alive, those two, into Lake Fire and Brimstone* (MSG, emphasis added).

- **Christ will permanently banish everything that is *incompatible* with his eternal kingdom purposes.** All that's good he will embrace. All that's evil he will destroy. Notice: In Revelation 19 at the siege of Armageddon (see text above) there is no clashing of armies. Rather the enemy is repudiated, routed, and ruined by Christ's command alone, pictured as Jesus wielding a sharp sword coming out of his mouth.

- **In the judgment at the climax of history, Christ personally engages with all humankind, taking us so seriously he will refuse to treat any one of us casually or with indifference**. Instead, he'll bring to closure all sin and rebellion against God, not only as expressed by the human race as a whole but also as exhibited by every member of that race, dealing each person one by one (Revelation 20). He will expose all of our deeds to the light of his truth, holiness, and righteousness. As the judge of all, he will honor our choices, either for or against God's will, taking those decisions seriously — including our choice to reject the gospel. Face-to-face with each one he will execute just verdicts with no hesitation, reservation, or condition.

- **When it comes to hell, the greatest tragedy of all is that *Jesus will not be there***. It will be populated by those who, because of their unbelief, have been excluded from the presence of Christ and his life-giving reign. Whatever other torments may be found there, the greatest of all will be the agony of knowing there is no further opportunity to experience the joy of the King's love or ever again see the glory of God in his dear Son.

By Final Redemption

- **But at the same time, in the Consummation our Lord Jesus will come *upon* the entire cosmos by a work of *final redemption*.** In that hour we will witness the fulfillment of creation's destiny through *simultaneous realizations* of all God's promises ratified in God's Son, for the sake of heaven and earth. Everything of Christ's current work in our lives will culminate in inexhaustible blessings throughout endless ages.

- **Everything in the universe that's dysfunctional or disordered or**

dislocated or diseased will be healed when Christ comes *upon* us in the Consummation. Peace with God will unite the saints by peace with one another, bringing about peace throughout the whole earth, all because the reign of the great Peacemaker has come ***upon*** us fully and totally and forever. Saturated with the grace and glory of Christ's supremacy the entire cosmos will prosper in peace — in *shalom* (Hebrew for wholeness, well-being, harmony, prosperity).

- **At the final hour, when God's people stand before their Savior, one of two conclusions will be evident for each believer.** Either the Consummation reveals how much of this life was spent, as Christians, in indifference to or even resistance towards the wide-ranging reign of Christ, or it provides convincing evidence that our commitment to Jesus was lived in willing response to, and in active pursuit of, his lordship in all things. As Paul cautions all of us:

> No one can lay any other foundation than what has already been laid. That foundation is Jesus Christ. A person may build on it using gold, silver, jewels, wood, hay or straw. But each person's work will be shown for what it is. On judgment day it will be brought to light. It will be put through fire. The fire will test how good each person's work is. If the building doesn't burn up, God will give the builder a reward for the work. If the building burns up, the builder will lose everything. The builder will be saved, but only like one escaping through the flames (1 Corinthians 3).

- **In view of our great hope, fixed on the consummation of all things in Christ, the spiritual dynamic evident in the early Thessalonian church sets a worthy standard for every church everywhere, at all times.**

> People come up and tell us how you received us with open arms, how you deserted the dead idols of your old life so that you could embrace and serve God, the true God. *They marvel at how expectantly you await the arrival of his Son, whom he raised from the dead — Jesus, who rescued us from certain doom* (1 Thessalonians 1, MSG, emphasis added).

- **We must never forget, however, that his grand work of redemption at what theologians refer to as the" Final Assize," was purchased at the price of the King's own life.** The cross remains the ultimate declaration, as well as the unqualified guarantee, that his final victory over Satan and sin and death is inevitable. No wonder heaven's choirs sing:

You are worthy because you were put to death. With your blood you bought people for God. They come from every tribe, people and nation, no matter what language they speak. You have made them members of a royal family. You have made them priests to serve our God. They will rule on the earth ... The Lamb, who was put to death, is worthy! He is worthy to receive power and wealth and wisdom and strength! He is worthy to receive honor and glory and praise! (Revelation 5).

A Trinitarian Consummation

- **When Jesus comes again, the whole Trinity will be involved in consummating the universal supremacy of Christ.** About the Trinity, Tim Keller writes:

  > Each of the divine persons centers upon the others . . . Each voluntarily circles the other two pouring love, delight, and adoration into them ... That creates a dynamic, pulsating dance of joy and love.

  Here's how Paul sets the stage to help us see this "dance" of the Trinity as displayed *at the Consummation*:

  > Then the end will come after Christ destroys all rule, authority, and power. Then he will hand over the kingdom to God the Father. Christ must rule until he has put all his enemies under his control. The last enemy that will be destroyed is death ... When he has done that, the Son also will be under God's rule. God put everything under the Son. In that way, God will be all in all (1 Corinthians 15).

- **In the magnificent drama of Revelation 5, the Consummation is unveiled as a collaboration of the triune God to bring about the fulfillment of all that Scripture has promised about the reign of Christ.**

In that great throne room scene, we witness the Father on the throne with the Lamb (Jesus) standing at the center of the throne. Like a lamb he is humble and yielded, exhibiting the permanent wounds from his sufferings for our salvation. However, he is portrayed simultaneously as the "Lion of Judah" — that is, our Lord remains the dominant focus of the throne.

This is what Scripture predicts in Philippians 2: Every knee will bow to Jesus and every tongue will proclaim him as Christ and Lord of all, which will become the paramount way to bring glory to God the Father.

Nothing in Scripture suggests that when Jesus submits himself to the Father he ceases to be supreme. No, all things *remain* under his feet; he is supreme in the universe forever, even as, at the same time, he designates all aspects of his reign to exist for the glory of the Father, so that (as 1 Corinthians 15 states) God, the three in one, might be "all in all" — in every way.

It's almost as if the Father were saying: "Son, I put the whole universe under your feet so that you have the supremacy in everything." Then, Jesus responds: "Father, in turn I bring back to you all that I have redeemed and conquered, all that comprises my kingdom, and surrender it over to you to bring you the greatest possible glory."

- **Within this eternal "dance of the Trinity" (as early church fathers phrased it), think of Jesus serving forever as the *prime minister* of the universe.** Literally, that official title used by democratic governments translates as "the supreme servant." Have you ever thought of Jesus as the *supreme servant* of the universe? An earthly prime minister should function as the supreme servant of his or her nation. Transcending all authorities, Jesus has become the supreme servant of the Father's purposes for all the nations.

- **But then, consider this: Since Jesus has become the *servant* of all does that not make him (based on his own teachings) the *greatest* of all?** Days before his death, he reminded his disciples:

> The most important person among you will be your servant. People who lift themselves up will be made humble. And people who make themselves humble will be lifted up (Matthew 23).

So at the Consummation who will be the greatest, the Father or the Son? The answer is that both are great and glorious, in distinctive ways. The Father is the final beneficiary of all things, glorified by all things placed in his hands. But the Son is the final ruler of all things, ensuring that everything under his scepter always resounds to the Father's praise.

But when Jesus has defeated all of his enemies, when everything in heaven and earth is laid at his feet, when he turns around to submit himself and everything under his reign to the Father, God will become "all in all" (1 Corinthians 15).

- **The Holy Spirit has an irreplaceable role he must fulfill in this "dance."** At the Consummation, the Holy Spirit will focus everything on Christ, just as he seeks to do today, as the Son transfers all he has redeemed to the honor of the Father.

As we asked in "Who Christ Is TO Us Today," when John is viewing this dazzling scene in Revelation 5, how was he able to see the action and the players before him, especially the Lord Jesus Christ himself in the thick of the worship? Answer: In God's throne room, John observed seven lampstands, which he is told represent the "sevenfold" Spirit of God (Revelation 4:5)—describing the Spirit in all his fullness as God.

Thus, we see again in the drama of Revelation 5 that the sovereign Third Person of the Trinity, "sent out into all the earth" (Revelation 5:6), provides the light source for the throne room, making all things visible.

- **Behold, then, the symphony of the Trinity as God fills eternity with his praise.** Though the Father dominates his glorious throne, the Son remains the central focus of angel choirs, while redeemed saints fall facedown at the Lamb's feet offering undiluted homage. As we've just noted, in Revelation 5 the Holy Spirit provides the massive cosmic floodlight the whole time, as it were, to illuminate the entire scene so all creation can become captivated and involved in the chorus of praise.

Selah

pause | think | pray

The Wrap

Prayer leaders from all over the United States were gathered in Washington, DC, one evening before America's National Day of Prayer in May. They represented diverse prayer movements and respected national prayer ministries; many had been involved in the work of prayer mobilization for decades.

The Chaplain of the United States Senate was invited to address them. A Christian leader loved all across the Body of Christ, Dr. Richard Halverson began by asking the audience a simple question, one few had ever been asked before: "How many of you pray on a consistent basis for the second coming of Jesus Christ? If you do, please raise your hands."

Not a single hand went up!

Many were thinking to themselves: "This is embarrassing. I thought I understood the power and purpose of prayer and yet I have failed to pray for the most important promise of Scripture, the one that will permanently settle the destiny of nations."

Then Dr. Halverson followed up with this astute observation:

> We cannot legitimately pray for revival if we do not, first of all, consistently pray for the second coming, because the one is simply a foretaste of the other. To be serious about one is to be serious about the other. To want the one is to want the other.

Most that evening will never forget his sobering rebuke.

Later, one member recalled how 2 Thessalonians backs up the chaplain's point with these words toward the end of chapter 1:

> This will happen when the Lord Jesus is revealed from heaven in blazing fire with his powerful angels. He will punish those who do not know God and do not obey the gospel of our Lord Jesus . . . *on the day he comes to be glorified in his holy people and to be marveled at among all of those who have believed*. This includes you, because you believed our testimony to you (NIV, emphasis added).

Next, carefully consider the subsequent verses, opening with the words "With this in mind":

> *With this in mind* [that is, the coming of Jesus, the judgment, the gathering of his people around him, the consummation of the age — this glorious hope of Christ coming upon the entire universe] *we constantly pray for you*, that our God may make you worthy of his calling, and that by his power he will bring to fruition your every desire for goodness and your every deed prompted by faith. We pray this [note that he is praying this for Christians right here and now] so that the name of our Lord Jesus Christ might be glorified in you, and you in him according to the grace of our God and the Lord Jesus Christ (NIV, emphasis added).

Notice the progression: Paul describes how Jesus will come **upon** us in his victorious return, and how he'll gather the Church to himself that he might be glorified in the midst of all whom he has redeemed. But then Paul goes further. In light of these glorious prospects — "with this in mind" — he prays that right now, in their own generation, God's people might experience a foretaste, *a substantial installment*, of that grand reunion by how their current relationship with Jesus focuses on his glory in ways similar to what we will share together at the consummation of everything.

Happily, this practical insight provides a nice segue into the second, but more *immediate*, expression of the spectacular supremacy of Christ **upon** us.

Who Christ Is UPON Us Today:
Through Approximations of the Consummation

More than once in our journey we have been reminded:

What Jesus will be lord of on *that* day he is
lord of on *this* day.

All the glory that he will display on *that* day is
the glory that belongs to him on *this* day.

All that will flow to the foot of his throne for final disposition
on *that* day already forms his inheritance
on *this* day.

All the promises of God he will fulfill on *that* day are
summed up in him on *this* day —
fully, with nothing left out.

That is why not only *at* the end but also unlimited times along the way *before* the end we should expect our Savior to come **upon** generations of his people with what I have chosen to call "approximations of the Consummation."

Approximations of the Consummation are those times when Jesus acts to deepen and intensify and accelerate all he is already accomplishing in our lives, our churches, and our mission to the world. These exceptional divine initiatives take their direction from the Consummation — and so become approximations of the foretaste of outcomes we'll experience in their full display at his final coming when he brings forth the most stunning miracle of all ages: his re-creation of new heavens and earth.

In one sense, we might retitle the end of time itself as God's "*Come-summation.*" In other words, the close of history will involve the Father *summing up* and fulfilling the purpose for all of Jesus' other "comings" **upon** his people and **upon** the nations as the gospel has spread its blessings throughout the centuries to the ends of the earth.

 Snapshots and Starter Thoughts

- **The Bible records how the Spirit comes *upon* God's people to usher us into encounters with Christ that are reflective of what it will be like when Christ comes *upon* the whole cosmos and we engage him face to face**. As we learned in previous chapters, fundamentally the Holy Spirit provides the world with the extension of Christ's ascension. In essence, the ministry of God the Spirit is the same as God the Son descending **upon** his people here and now in order to (repeating these key verbs one more time) invade, intensify, accelerate, deepen, sharpen, expand, multiply, magnify, and empower (*all* of this activity!) every way the Son is manifesting his reign in the life of the church today.

- **In Acts 2, Peter's Pentecost sermon put approximations of the Consummation front and center.** He declared:

  > God has raised this same Jesus back to life. We are all witnesses of this. Jesus has been given a place of honor at the right hand of God. He has received the Holy Spirit from the Father. This is what God had promised. It is Jesus who has poured out what you now see and hear.

  But before he said that, Peter quoted from Joel 2 to confirm that the outpouring of the Holy Spirit was a *preliminary* fulfillment of Israel's end times expectations:

  > In the last days God says, "I will pour out my Spirit upon all people. Your sons and daughters will prophesy. Your young men will see visions. Your old men will dream dreams."

Even though Joel actually referred to outcomes slated for the Consummation (see the entire context by reading Joel 3), Peter concluded that when the Holy Spirit came ***upon*** them in power at Pentecost, his mission was to transform the Church in ways dramatically similar to what all saints will experience when Jesus visibly returns to reign forever. Such amazing developments remain God's daily promise to believers in this age.

- **Right before he ascended, in fact, Jesus used "consummation language" when he promised that all of his followers would experience "power" when the Holy Spirit comes *upon* us.** "Power" in the original Greek is the root word of the English word "dynamite." Explosively, the Holy Spirit would propel God's people outward to proclaim Christ among all nations — a power amplified by what Scripture predicts when summing up another dimension of the Consummation with these words:

  > But the day of the Lord will come like a thief. The heavens will disappear with a roar. Fire will destroy everything in them . . . So everything will be destroyed in this way . . . On that day fire will destroy the heavens. Its heat will melt everything in them. But we are looking forward to a new heaven and a new earth (2 Peter 3).

- **In this age, Christians will never experience the *quantity* of the aftereffects of the Consummation; but often we will experience the *quality* of those promises because of Christ's reign now taking place in the midst of God's people by God's Spirit.** The Spirit provides us "interim" experiences of how Christ's lordship will prevail in the eternal state. Recall that the seven lampstands around the throne, which represent the sevenfold Spirit of God (Revelation 4-5), are duplicated by the seven lampstands among which Jesus walks, which represent seven churches in Asia Minor (Revelation 1-3). The point? Like flames on candles, the churches' very existence embodies a foretaste of the age to come as the "breath of life" keeps their fires burning — that is, as the Spirit continues his indwelling ministry to them for Jesus' sake.

- **Without a doubt, Christ Awakening-style breakthroughs, which we've frequently discussed in *Christ Is NOW!*, form some of the most vivid approximations of the Consummation one could ever hope to witness in this age.** Some scholars refer to a Christian revival as "a *visitation* of the Lord." Christians experience it as a welcome home party — as if someone has walked in to visit with us whom we've not hosted for a long time, someone we've missed, someone we've desperately needed to come back to take over.

Of course, Jesus never really leaves his Church; he remains steadily active with us and within us in one way or another. But the *sense* of his presence and the *reality* of the powerful working of his Spirit among us can *seem* to be faint, distant, even absent at times. A Christ Awakening becomes an approximation of the Consummation because in it Jesus by his Spirit "shows up" — he manifests the wonders of his presence and power in new ways; he reveals more of himself in a fashion that foreshadows the day when he will be revealed unavoidably in majestic splendor before the eyes of the whole world.

- **A Christ Awakening resembles the Second Coming because in true revival Christ becomes more openly proactive, a foretaste of how he will operate at the end.** He comes *upon* us to reconquer, restore, revitalize, and then redeploy us as individual Christians and local churches. Sometimes this awakening catches up an entire generation of Christians. When Jesus comes *upon* us like this, he does so to give us far more than *survival* — actually, far more than what many mean by *revival*. Every genuine Christ Awakening should be described as Christ's *arrival*, as he bursts in to reassert his lordship over us, before us, within us, and through us — in displays of his spectacular supremacy analogous to the impact of his second advent not long from now.

- **We might say, therefore, that Christ Awakenings come about when the Spirit pulls back the curtain before God's people to expose to us much more of the fullness of God's Son, the Head of the Church, who like an actor behind a closed curtain, has been present among us all along.** As a result, God's people are revitalized in their worship and fellowship and mission, sharing in preliminary but substantial foretastes of the full "drama" awaiting us when everything comes fully alive to the glory of Christ.

- **In the final revival (i.e., the Consummation), the *universe* will become fully alive to the supremacy of Christ. Even so, in every prior, preliminary revival (i.e., Christ Awakenings), the *Church* becomes more fully alive to the supremacy of Christ.** Biblically speaking, are there any *limits* to how extensively God might choose to transform the Body of Christ through a Christ Awakening? Potentially, could not any Christ Awakening bring us right up to the edge of the Consummation itself, where the next installment is the return of Jesus in victory?

  If not, then God's people must wrestle with this core question: How far are we *willing* for any contemporary revival to take us into an involvement with Christ today that mirrors what is waiting for us in the final revival?

  Following that, we also must ask: Are we willing to seek God for nothing less for the Church — for *our own* church — than to bring us into a God-given Christ Awakening that makes us more fully alive to the glory of Christ *even if* it results in the final conflagration between the kingdom of God and the powers of darkness, ushering all of creation into the climax of history?

  Are we ready to invite Jesus to come ***upon*** us to intensify and accelerate his reign in us and through us *that* much — even if it would lead to *that*?

- **Paul's recorded prayers show us he a was always looking for more of the fullness of Christ, for more of the reign of Christ — for more foretastes of eternity with Christ to come *upon* believers today.** The apostle's prayers confirm how the Father longs to give his people multiple experiences of the arrival of his Son ***upon*** us right now.

To take one example (and there are many), in Ephesians Paul writes out a prayer for a group of sincere and growing Christians shortly after he founded the church. His focus tells us that even though they had experienced a massive revival (laid out in Acts 19), still there remained much more of the Lord Jesus Christ for them to explore and experience.

> I pray to the God of our Lord Jesus Christ . . . I keep asking him to give you the wisdom and understanding that come from the Holy Spirit . . . Then you will know . . . God's great power. It can't be compared with anything else. His power works for us who believe . . . He showed this when he raised Christ from the dead. God seated him at his right hand in his heavenly kingdom . . . He appointed him to be ruler over everything for the church (Ephesians 1).

- **In a very real sense, *every* answer to any Christian's prayer that comes from the Father represents an approximation of the Consummation**. That's because ultimately, one way or another, *all* legitimate Christian prayers open doors wide to invite Jesus to come down, to come ***upon*** us, to manifest to us more of who he is by revealing more of his reigning presence among us and through us for the sake of his Church and the nations. In other words, every biblically-based prayer, rooted in God's promises and priorities, extends a hearty welcome to God's Son to sovereignly flood us with more of himself, doing so "far more than we could ever ask for or imagine . . . by his power that is working in us" (Ephesians 3).

- **Throughout the Church age, one special form of Christ's coming *upon* his people to give them approximations of the Consummation involves *miracles* and *signs* and *wonders*.** In this age, such extraordinary phenomena certify to the world Jesus' claim that one day he will come ***upon*** creation as the ultimate healer and deliverer of everything and every place and everyone that is broken.

Miracles are not *salutary* only, bringing wholeness and blessing; but also they are *revelatory*. When, for example, Jesus chooses to come ***upon*** a weakened body to restore a person to full health, this miracle serves to validate the good news of his saving power, temporarily displaying the authority waiting to be displayed permanently at the bodily resurrection of the saints.

- **In summary, all approximations offer us "sneak peeks" at the final denouement when all heaven and earth will be thoroughly transformed by the anointed Lamb.** Call them *"previews of coming attractions"* — extraordinary though provisional inbreakings of Christ's sovereign activity to remind us of an appointment just ahead when, through Jesus, God will:

  > ...shake the heavens and the earth once more...I will shake all the nations. Then what is desired by all nations will come to my temple. And I will fill the temple with glory (Haggai 2).

- **Approximations reaffirm for us as Christians that we must live by hope.** We dwell in a time of tension between redemption *inaugurated* (by our salvation, by our worship, by our mission as well as by miracles of all kinds) and redemption *consummated* (by the second advent of Jesus).

  All approximations, even the most widely celebrated healings, are partial and incomplete; they serve only to make us aware that we will not be completely satisfied until we finally enter into the depths of the riches of Christ that are waiting for us in the day of the Lord.

- **In the end, approximations are, at best, like "photos" of Christ — the Christ we will see, savor, and celebrate *in person* in his coming kingdom.** Christians must never forget that whatever we experience of Christ's glory and power today is always *less* than who he really is in his fullness, *less* than how we will soon behold him on the day he fills the universe with himself (Ephesians 1).

- **Augustine, the brilliant fourth-century North African church leader, who scholars note wrote more about Jesus than any other Christian author, spoke of his encounter with Christ in nearly apocalyptic terms:**

  > You called, you cried, you shattered my deafness. You sparkled, you burned, you drove away my blindness. You shed your fragrance and I drew in my breath and now I pant for you alone.

  Surely what Augustine expressed in his own experience is an unmistakable example of what an approximation of the Consummation looks like.

  That being said, imagine yourself using the very same words the hour you see Christ when he visibly comes ***upon*** the world followed by the armies of heaven as we read in Revelation 19. Can't you hear yourself saying something like this to him during that unprecedented encounter?

> Lord Jesus, the trumpet has sounded. I am arrested by your call and cry. You have shattered all my deafness, once and for all. I am marveling at how you sparkle and burn. You have driven away all of my blindness, once and for all. As you shed forth the fragrance of your everlasting redemption, I am drawing in my breath, and as I do I find myself savoring you alone and singing out for you alone as I have never done before!

Selah

pause | think | pray

The Wrap

As it will be at the culmination of God's eternal plan, even so in every Christ Awakening, God's people become newly saturated with very practical outworkings of the supremacy of Jesus.

In the generation following Jonathan Edwards, another Christ Awakening took place, global in scope. Identified by historians as the Second Great Awakening, it surfaced in the late 1700s and spilled over into the early decades of the 1800s. During that era, many streams in the Church came alive to the Savior in whole new ways, culminating in the modern missionary movement and much more.

There was a Christian leader who lived through that extraordinary work of the Spirit. He tasted the thrill of observing a Christ Awakening *firsthand.* During much of that time, Dr. Ebenezer Porter was the president of one of the leading seminaries in New England.

Around 1830, as their president emeritus, he was invited back to the school to present a series of lectures on revival based on what he had witnessed up close and personal as he ministered in the midst of it. Halfway through a subsequent publication of his lectures appears a single paragraph that sums up his personal observation of how any Christ Awakening embodies, as we've discussed here, an approximation of the Consummation. Dr. Porter wrote:

> *When the Redeemer comes in the triumphs of his grace to visit his churches*, then his true followers are seen waking from their apathy [note that even Jesus' true followers may need to be awakened to him in new ways], and going forth to welcome the King of Zion with an energy and an earnestness and ardor of affection *greatly surpassing their first love* (emphasis added).

His bottom line: In revival Christ comes **upon** his Church with a more direct, more intimate, more transformative impact, like the entrance of a conquering king. This revelation causes many believers to awake and rise to welcome him, to yield to him, to love him, and to follow him wherever he wants to take them.

This conclusion matches nicely with insights from another academician from the late 20th century. Dr. J. Edwin Orr held three earned doctorates in the study of the history of Christ Awakenings. An author of many well-researched works on the subject, Professor Orr clearly understood what a Christ Awakening entailed. With one paragraph he boiled down his years of teaching on the topic, writing that a Christ Awakening is:

> . . . a movement of the Holy Spirit bringing about a revival of New Testament Christianity in the church of Christ and in its related community. *The outpouring of Christ upon his people by his Spirit* affects the reviving of the church, the awakening of the masses, and the movement of instructed peoples toward the Christian faith; the revived church, by many or few, is moved to engage in evangelism, in teaching, and in social action (emphasis added).

The outpouring of Christ **upon** his people today, by his Spirit, provides a foreshowing of the final and fullest outpouring of Christ's glory and greatness

upon every square inch of the universe — that is, the all-encompassing revelation of the spectacular supremacy of God's Son, of which there will be no end.

Postscript

For anyone wanting a more detailed example of a Christ Awakening, here's a well-documented synopsis of one. It overtook New York City.

Ponder these actual headlines in the New York Times in 1857: "Biggest Church Packed Twice a Day for Prayer"; "Businesses Shut Down Daily for One Hour of Prayer"; "Political Leaders Get Down on Their Knees Before God"; "Revival Sweeps City."

That year in the Big Apple, what began as a prayer meeting of seven people mushroomed into tens of thousands gathered every day at noon to pray desperately for spiritual renewal, doing so in places of commerce during the day and filling all the city's church buildings with united prayer at night. Soon conversions to Christ started transpiring so rapidly and with such impact on the life of the city that the newspaper felt compelled to report each day the names of hundreds of New Yorkers who had committed their lives to Christ.

This is not a screenplay idea for a Christian movie. This was a genuine spiritual revolution — an overwhelming, overpowering phenomenon that resulted in what many historians call "the Third Great Awakening."

It was nothing less than an awakening to the glory of Christ that for a time not only spread across America from coast to coast but also to other lands.

Hundreds of new mission organizations sprang up in response, both domestic and international. It impacted the Civil War and the emancipation of slaves. The movement continued for decades.

Similar stories throughout Church history are countless. They all share one thing in common: They are approximations of the Consummation that the Father offers gladly to the Church in every generation. You may want to google "stories of spiritual awakenings and revival" to learn more about the history of these extraordinary awakenings to more of Christ and be inspired by the testimonies of those whose lives were transformed.

We always must remember whenever we read these exciting accounts, however, not to allow ourselves to be so taken with the result that we fail to keep our focus on Christ. The study of any church renewal must hone in specifically on how the movement revealed more of the person of God's Son. After all, it is a *Christ* Awakening above all.

We should ask: How did a specific revival season or movement evidence (in the words of our original definition of a "Christ Awakening") "God's Spirit using God's Word to reintroduce God's people to God's Son for ALL he is"?

Failure to fix our attention on that outcome as our main agenda in our studies of revivals renders all other characteristics essentially irrelevant because in the end revival is found in Christ alone. More than that, all true revival IS Christ!

Who Christ Is UPON Us Today:
As We Embrace a Lifestyle of Anticipation

The Church is summoned to gaze at the horizon, to persist in watching for the promised prevailing of Christ's kingdom purposes. After all, our whole destiny is tied up with Jesus' triumphant return.

Everything about the Christian walk, therefore, should be shaped by that expectation. In truth, we are urged to *rejoice because* of that hope — to rejoice in anticipation of seeing so much more of his glory revealed in his Son; to rejoice in the one expectation that will never leave us disappointed (Romans 5).

Once Christians are captured by a living hope in Christ — a hope based on prospects inherent in the Consummation as well as in more immediate approximations of the Consummation — quite naturally we want to embrace a *lifestyle* of anticipation. Looking for and seeking after more of the fullness of Christ and his kingdom agenda should be the hallmark of every believer's walk with him every day.

In his book *The Puritan Hope,* Reformed church historian Dr. Iain Murray describes how (what he calls) a *"theology of hope"* not only became the biblical underpinning of the First, Second, and Third Great Awakenings, but also the driving passion behind the incomparable spread of the gospel into all nations for the past 150 years. The fact is that an abounding hope in the reign of Christ, both his current and future kingdom, has *always* propelled the Church forward in a lifestyle focused on renewal, evangelism, church planting, and cultural transformation among earth's peoples.

A lifestyle of dynamic hope includes a lifestyle of active *preparation,* as we get ready for our future involvement in the new heaven and earth — so much so that we begin to *"act as if"* the Consummation was just around the corner. We deliberately build lifestyles compatible with how we expect to think and respond and act when Christ comes **upon** us to complete us — to "consummate" us, one could say — at the end.

The Christian life is less like a *dressing room,* where believers spend a lifetime trying to get themselves fixed up to inhabit their eternal home (like getting ready for a date). It is more like joining with a troop of actors in an exciting *dress rehearsal* where disciples practice together how to love and worship and serve and walk with Jesus — how to foster his kingdom concerns here and now — the way we expect to be involved for him and with him for unending days in the grand finale so close at hand.

When Jesus returns, don't you want to be so alive to him, abounding in him with firstfruits of the new creation, that you'll experience nothing of shame as you stand before him (1 John 2)? That your current responses to him will be vindicated, not repudiated? That you'll be able to transition freely, not fearfully, into the new Jerusalem when it appears (Revelation 21)? That with no regrets but with great joy you'll sit down at that grand marriage supper hosted by the Lamb of God for his bride, the Church (Revelation 19)?

Until then, we are called to embrace a walk with Christ permeated with God's promises in Christ (2 Corinthians 1). The fact is, there will always be *so much more of him* for us to discover and delight in, so much more from here to eternity — *so much more of the Son* the Father has designed for us, decreed for us, and desires for us. For example:

- **We read in Romans 5** that with Christ, where sin and all of its destructive poisons abound, God's gracious intentions and saving work in Christ abound far more, with transforming power that none of the disabling powers of darkness can match.

- **We're told in Romans 15** that out of our trust in Christ we should be overflowing with a hope unleashed in us by the ministry of the Holy Spirit — a hope regarding the power of Christ to bring salvation not only to his own people but to all the nations.

- **Colossians 1 assures us** that the greatest riches of the gospel of our redemption distill down to the person of Christ himself, who in the fullness of his supremacy dwells in the midst of his people in order to take us with him into the fulfillment of all the glorious things yet to come.

- **Paul urges Christians in Romans 13** to properly interpret their current situation in light of the Consummation, and then wake up to be ready for the culmination of the outworking of our salvation because it draws nearer with each passing day. The morning of the new day is almost here; the darkness is quickly fading. Therefore, be on guard for the final battle, wearing the armor of light. Remain so consumed with Christ that it's as if we're *wearing* Christ as our only apparel.

- **The apostle encourages us in 1 John 2-3** to maintain an abiding relationship with God's Son, so that when he appears we may be confident to stand before him in the Consummation just the way we've walked with him beforehand. Our motivation is to hold to the certainty that when he appears we will become like him on the day we meet him in his ascended, triumphant glory. Thriving with anticipation toward Christ, we will purify ourselves today the way he is pure. In other words, in anticipation of the Consummation we want to develop a lifestyle every day that's preparing us to be ready to live with Jesus for endless days to come.

- **In Philippians 4, Paul puts it simply**: We're to rejoice in the Lord and do so always. Why? We rejoice always because the Lord is near — which means he's forever ready to come ***upon*** us, to invade us, to conquer us. Therefore, we have *no* reason to be anxious about anything, and we have *every* reason to practice a lifestyle of hopefulness.

- **1 Peter 1 reminds us** that when we were born again, we were deposited into the lap of a hope that is jubilant and confident and resonant with the victory of the resurrection of Jesus Christ from the dead. Consequently, we celebrate him with an inexpressible gladness full of God's glory, as we look toward all that is yet to be revealed through the Savior whom we love even without actually seeing him — yet.

- **Our greatest expectation is found in this:** Our Savior is so wonder-filled we can expect his interventions always to be surprising, unprecedented, inexplicable, and amazing!

- **Our highest anticipation focuses on this:** Now and always, our Lord Jesus Christ is not only able, he's not only willing, but he's also *ready* to come **upon** us afresh again and again and again and again!

- **Our boldest confidence rests with this:** At any moment Christ may come **upon** us in new ways to do all that needs to be done in order to build and accelerate and intensify all he is already doing within us and through us, individually and together — to give us more of himself.

- **Our unceasing prayers arise from this:** As said earlier, essentially every authentic prayer consists of inviting Jesus to come down, to come **upon** us, to manifest more of his glory, authority, and sufficiency to us and to those for whom we pray. The promise of that creates in us hearts that seek God's face for nothing less.

- **That's why the fundamental issue for all Jesus followers comes back to this:**

First of all, how much do we *really* want Christ to come down **upon** us — at the end?

Then, how much do we *really* want him to come down **upon** us — right now?

How much do we *really* want him to minister to us and through us in ways that strongly prefigure how he will one day come **upon** and conquer the entire universe?

How willing are we *really* to seek God for nothing less than fresh revelations of all Christ is — to us and for us, over us and before us, within us and through us?

How prepared are we *really* to receive and participate in fresh approximations of the Consummation — as they touch and change our lives? our churches? our nation? the peoples of the earth?

pause | think | pray

The Wrap

The next time you catch a flight at the airport, get to the gate early enough to watch your plane approach for landing.

Notice how off on the distant horizon, for a brief time, the aircraft appears to be stalled, not moving at all, hanging in suspended animation. Of course, as you know, it's an optical illusion. In reality, every incoming flight is traveling around 200 miles an hour as it descends to the runway!

First it comes *toward* you. Then it comes *at* you. Then it feels as though it is coming down *on top* of you. Suddenly, what seemed far away, static and motionless, swoops over you to land safely on the runway right next to you.

Not once during the entire maneuver did the plane pull back on its descent to the airport. It just kept coming *upon* you, quite rapidly, even though it appeared to spectators as if nothing was happening, as if the flight was frozen in time.

It is like that today: Even while (and because) multitudes of Christians are praying for a nationwide Christ Awakening, answers are already on their way. In response to years of unified appeals to the Father for the spread of Christ's kingdom in our land, many of us believe that not long from now the Son will come **upon** the Church from sea to sea to effectively unleash more of his saving, transforming, spectacular supremacy.

Jesus is not stuck on the skyline. Our Lord is about to arrive, to come **upon** this generation to awaken us to what the Spirit has been doing in us and through us all along — and then he will accelerate, deepen, sharpen, inflame, expand, multiply, and empower all of it in renewed manifestations of his glorious salvation.

Look up! Do you hear him approaching? Can you feel him bearing down on top of us right now? Have you begun to sense him drawing near to overtake us with *himself*?

Who Christ Is UPON Us Today:
A Tribute

Paraphrasing and personalizing a wide selection of Scriptures

Father, we come to you to proclaim the name of your Son together — to spread his fame, embrace his reign, increase his gain, and honor his claim about who he is *upon* us. As we do, awaken us to him afresh for ALL that he is. May the praise we bring to him in these moments come forth alive in us by your Spirit and rise as a blessing to you forever. We use your Word to magnify your Son, without whom we are nothing and can do nothing. This tribute is all for Christ alone, our one and only hope of glory, and the hope of all the nations.

**Lord Jesus Christ, this is our tribute to you —
our tribute to who you are UPON us.**

Oh, that you would rend the heavens and come down. Come down to make your name known to your enemies. Come down to cause the nations to quake before you. For whenever you have done awesome things that we did not expect, you came down.

You said a day would dawn when the heavenly bodies will be shaken, and all will see the Son of Man coming in a cloud with power and great glory, causing our full redemption to draw near. You said that when you come in your glory with all the angels with you, you will sit on your throne in heavenly majesty and all the nations will be gathered before you. You said the Father has given you authority to judge because you are the Son of Man, and therefore a day is approaching when all who are in their graves will hear your voice and will rise to face your verdict as it comes *upon* all peoples with perfect justice.

Christ Is NOW!

Jude says you are coming with thousands and thousands of your holy ones, to judge everyone, and to convict all the ungodly of their ungodly acts. Truly, one day you will come *upon* the nations, even the whole creation, resulting in the heavens disappearing with a roar. On that day, when you come *upon* all nations, the earth and everything in it will be laid bare. O King of kings and Lord of lords, we tremble in anticipation of that hour when you will be revealed from heaven in blazing fire. We tremble because you will punish those who do not know God and do not obey the good news of who you really are as the Lord Jesus Christ.

Most of all, however, we tremble knowing that on that day you will come *upon* us too — as your people. You will descend to us to be glorified among your saints as you deserve, and to be marveled at among all who have believed. You will appear this second time, not to bear sin but to bring salvation to those who are waiting for you. And we are waiting for you!

As the righteous Judge, you will present a crown of righteousness to those who have longed for your appearing. And we long for your appearing! We do not fear your appearing. We look forward to that day when you will come *upon* a new heaven and new earth, bringing us forth to dwell in a habitation where righteousness forever will be our home.

Christ Is NOW!

But until that hour arrives, please come *upon* us now by the outpouring of your Spirit to awaken us, to revive us, to renew us, to empower us. Come *upon* us right now, by your Spirit, to fulfill every good purpose we have intended and every act of love prompted by our faith in you. Come *upon* us now, by your Spirit, so that your name, Lord Jesus, may be glorified in us and we may be victorious in you, more and more and more. Come *upon* us now, by your Spirit, that we might enjoy foretastes today of the powers of the age to come. Come *upon* us now with approximations of the Consummation, that we might be revitalized and redeployed by you alone. Wherever sin abounds, come *upon* your people now, abounding with grace far greater than our sin. Let your grace reign throughout your Church to bring forth the fruits of eternal life.

Christ Is NOW!

Behold, the night is nearly over; behold, the day is at hand. Therefore, you deserve to be the one with whom we clothe ourselves right now, losing ourselves in new ways in you and you alone. You deserve for us to awake from any form of deadly slumber that you might shine on us in new ways. Come *upon* the eyes of our hearts; heal our blindness, Lord! Dazzle us with the full extent of all we have in you.

Focus us afresh on the sure and victorious hope you have won for your people. Set our hearts on the riches in glory you have inherited for your people. Lift our eyes to behold the resurrection power you have unleashed in your people — the same power the Father exerted when he brought you out of the tomb, the same power which seated you at his right hand in the heavenly realms, far above all rule and authority and dominion, and every title that can be given, not only in the present age but also in the age to come.

Focus us afresh on our destiny in the plan of the Father who works everything according to his good pleasure. We celebrate the plan which he purposed in you, the plan to be put into effect when the times will have reached their fulfillment — his plan to bring all things in heaven and on earth together under you as the one and only Head. Yes, awaken us! Reintroduce us and reconvert us back to these awesome truths that proclaim the majesty of your everlasting supremacy *upon* us all.

Christ Is NOW!

Lord Jesus Christ, we worship you with reverence and awe. We worship you, the consuming fire you are. Even so, we invite you, as an act of devotion, to come like fire *upon* us right now so that we might live and labor in a way that hastens the day of the Lord. As Malachi envisioned, we invite you to suddenly come *upon* your temple. Come! Be a refiner's fire. Come! Purify your leaders! Refine them like gold so that all of your people might again bring you offerings in righteousness.

Great God and Savior, as we wait for the blessed hope of your glorious appearing, come ***upon*** us now to purify those you have already redeemed from all wickedness so that increasingly we become a people eager to do for you what is good. As we wait for that blessed hope, come ***upon*** us now in such a way that we might be confident and unashamed before you at your coming. As we wait for that blessed hope, help us *even now* to increasingly purify ourselves even as you are so pure, knowing that when you appear we shall be like you, because we shall see you as you really are.

Open the floodgates of heaven! Pour out ***upon*** us blessings that are so full of YOU, Lord Jesus, that it will feel to us as if there is not enough room for all that your visitation accomplishes. Pour out ***upon*** us your manifest presence so totally, that we, with all your saints, might have power to grasp how wide and long and high and deep is your unfathomable love, so that, in unexplored dimensions, we might be filled with the full measure of the fullness of God. Bring ***upon*** us immeasurably more than we ask or imagine by your power at work in us, so there might be even greater glory for the triune God, amplified in you and then in the people you have redeemed.

Christ Is NOW!

But we also stand in holy fear before you, for behold, your judgments have already begun with the household of God.

So in holy fear, we pray: Restore in us a supreme love for you, so that you will not need to come ***upon*** us to remove our lampstand.

In holy fear, we pray: Convict us of everything that offends you or denies you, so that you will not need to come ***upon*** us to fight us with the sword of your mouth.

In holy fear, we pray: Show us how to walk fully in the truth of *who* you are and *all* that you are, so that you, the One who searches hearts and minds with eyes like blazing fire, will not need to come ***upon*** us to discipline us for our spiritual adultery.

In holy fear, we pray: Wherever you find lukewarmness among us, come to the door of your Church. Speak! Knock! Be for us gold refined in the fire. Be for us clothes to cover our nakedness. Be for us salve to heal our blindness. Come *upon* us! Dine with us, then take us with you to sit with you on your Father's throne.

Christ Is NOW!

You are the Lion of the Tribe of Judah. You have triumphed! You are worthy to take the scroll and open its seals. Slain, you have purchased people from every tribe, language, and nation to make them a kingdom and priests to your God, and they shall reign with you on the earth. You are the Lamb at the center of the throne, destined to be our shepherd forever. You are the lamp of the new Jerusalem where the brilliance of your reign will invade the ends of the earth so that nations will walk in your light and kings in the brightness of your rising. From that day forward there will be no more night. Instead, your servants will see your face clearly, even as you inscribe your name of total ownership *upon* us.

Behold, on tiptoe we await the grand finale promised at your return. You said that your return is coming soon. So come! Come *upon* the redeemed of all the ages. Come! Come *upon* the entire cosmos. The Spirit and the bride say, "COME!" Even so, all of us here and now say to you, "COME! Come, Lord Jesus! Come!"

This tribute expresses only a small part of the inexhaustible riches of who you are UPON us and all peoples.

So, Father, here is how we celebrate your Son, our Lord Jesus Christ, in this hour. We exalt him. We exult in him. We do so because of all he is *upon* us — now. Therefore, everything we are and have, every breath we breathe, every step we take, every service we render, every prayer we pray, every praise we bring, is possible only by him and him alone. For without him — without all he is *upon* us — we are nothing, and we can do nothing. More and more, by the revealing work of your Spirit, awaken us to Christ alone — awaken your whole Church to Christ alone — so that increasingly he might become *upon* us our all in all.

AMEN!

Fervency for
His Supremacy

Fervency for His Supremacy

Consumed With Christ:
No Holding Back. No Turning Back.

As groups formed to pray publically around flagpoles at thousands of high schools, the annual See You at the Pole (SYATP) initiative celebrated its 15th anniversary with a theme that year comprised of a single word: *"Consumed!"*

Sponsored by a national network involving hundreds of youth ministries, SYATP asked participating young people a question in its promotional literature that most Christians have never had to answer:

> Do you want the fire of God to fall on your campus and in your community? Do you *really*? You must realize that when fire falls, it consumes *everything* that is unholy and ungodly. The fire of Christ purifies lives, melts hearts and devours sin. **How desperately do you want Jesus to become for you the fire of God?**

By the millions, students rallied to their Savior that September day. Gathered on campuses from coast to coast, they prayed for Jesus to become the all-consuming flame in their lives and to impassion their outreach to classmates and others. Many groups continued praying in organized weekly gatherings the rest of the year.

Consumed! Grasped so completely by the grandeur of Christ and the glorious hope we have in him that it is impossible to remain dispassionate toward him for long.

Consumed! Surrendered to, changed by, and totally occupied by Jesus —

the way logs are overcome by the blazing inferno of a bonfire.

Consumed! Aflame with — fully alive to — all Jesus is *to* us, *for* us, *over* us, *before* us, *within* us, *through* us, and *upon* us at this very moment.

Consumed! It's a relationship with Christ in which there is no turning back and no holding back.

Consumed! It's what a Christian's walk with God's Son should be!

In his sermon "The Weight of Glory," C. S. Lewis calls for nothing less:

> Indeed, if we consider the unblushing promises of reward and the staggering nature of the rewards promised in the Gospels, it would seem that **our Lord finds our desires, not too strong, but *too weak*** (emphasis added).

Eternity Itself Will Be Consumed With Christ

For Bible students, being "consumed" also speaks concerning the culmination of history, when everything arrives at the feet of King Jesus for final dispatch. We call that grand climax "*the Consummation.*" In that hour and ever after, all creation will be openly consumed with the person and presence and power of God's Son. In other words, we'll be consumed with Christ nonstop.

That long-anticipated hour might be correctly described, therefore, as an obsession with Christ *universalized* (as we find it to be in Revelation 4-5). In the meantime, however, before the time of the Consummation arrives, the goal of daily Christian discipleship might be properly understood as an obsession with Christ *personalized*.

Or to say it another way: As Jesus followers we are destined to become *fanatics* for him forever.

"Fanatic" comes from the Latin root word "fanum," and describes a Roman "temple dweller." In ancient times, an individual was considered "fanatical" if he was so devoted to his chosen deity that he refused to leave the idol's presence, remaining to worship and serve in its temple day and night. Consumed he was, but with a cold, hard, inanimate deity.

How much more fanatical should Christians become with Jesus — not by residing in some sacred structure but by abiding directly in him even as he abides in us (John 15)?

The Bible encourages a moment by moment, wholehearted engagement with our Lord today. We should exhibit an "undying love" for him (Ephesians 6:24, NIV), even unto our own death (John 21; Revelation 12) — a love that drives us to eliminate everything in our lives incompatible with making Jesus our one and only "magnificent obsession" (Philippians 3).

How Can We Not Be Passionate for Christ Right Now?

Consider, for example:

- God promises to usher Christians into eternal blessings in heavenly realms with Christ Jesus (Ephesians 1).

    Therefore, how can we not be passionate right now
        for the *exaltation* given to Christ alone?

- God promises to bring every facet of Christian existence under the redemptive control of Christ Jesus (Hebrews 1).

    Therefore, how can we not be passionate right now
        for the *reign* that rests with Christ alone?

- God promises to conform every believer to Christ's image, which means who he is now is who we're becoming day by day (Romans 8).

    Therefore, how can we not be passionate right now
        for the *character* we see in Christ alone?

- God promises to magnify his Son's saving ministry among the nations, using disciples like us to advance his global cause (Acts 1).

    Therefore, how can we not be passionate right now
        for the worldwide *mission* of Christ alone?

- God promises to take his people into immediate victories through Christ, which will culminate on the day he is revealed as our mighty Warrior (Philippians 1).

> Therefore, how can we not be passionate right now
> for the *triumphs* of Christ alone?

- Every eternal, God-given hope we hold is embodied in the message of Christ proclaimed among earth's peoples (Colossians 1).

> Therefore, how can we not be passionate right now
> for all the *promises* fulfilled in Christ alone?

Clearly, Christians can never think *too highly* of God's Son or put *too much* passion into advancing his kingdom agenda. An all-consuming devotion, an overt obsession, a fanatical focus, a supreme fervency — it all denotes the chief hallmark of every Jesus follower, in which there can be no turning back and no holding back from him.

Consumed: Discipleship as Jesus Means It to Be

None of this emphasis on passion should catch us by surprise, however. Have no doubt: From the beginning this is precisely why our Father redeemed us. He made us and remade us in order to give ourselves over to his Son with unqualified abandon. His perfect love for us can settle for no less.

The Master who marched out of a graveyard to ascend to the throne of the universe deserves radical commitment from us — as he spelled it out in the Scriptures (NIV, emphases added):

> Whoever wants to be my disciple must deny themselves and *take up their cross and follow me*. For whoever . . . *loses their life for me and for the gospel* will save it [a call to consuming passion!] (Mark 8).

> If anyone comes to me and does not hate father and mother, wife and children, brothers and sisters — yes, *even their own life* — such a person cannot be my disciple . . . those of you who do not *give up everything you have* cannot be my disciples [a call to consuming passion!] (Luke 14).

> Anyone who loves their father or mother more than me is not worthy of me; anyone who loves their son nor daughter more than me is not worthy of me . . . *whoever loses their life for my sake* [a call to consuming passion!] will find it (Matthew 10).

When Jesus beckoned his first disciples to "leave everything and follow me" this meant that from that point on there would be no return and no retreat. They became fully invested not only in what his mission was all about (no turning back) but also even more in the person for whose sake that mission existed (no holding back).

The New Testament community exhibited the same intense affection for Jesus, embodied in the apostle who pointed to himself as an example of how all disciples should respond to their Master:

> Yes, all the things I once thought were so important are gone from my life. Compared to the high privilege of knowing Christ Jesus as my Master, firsthand, everything I once thought I had going for me is insignificant — dog dung. *I've dumped it all in the trash so that I could embrace Christ and be embraced by him* . . .
>
> *I gave up all that inferior stuff so I could know Christ personally,* experience his resurrection power, be a partner in his suffering, and go all the way with him to death itself. If there was any way to get in on the resurrection from the dead, I wanted to do it.
>
> I'm not saying that I have this all together, that I have it made. *But I am well on my way, reaching out for Christ, who has so wondrously reached out for me* (Philippians 3, MSG, emphasis added).

These resolves show us what it is like to be as passionate for God's Son as the Father himself is, which merely reinforces Paul's main point in Colossians 1 when he writes that "in everything Christ is to have the supremacy." In other words, fervency for the supremacy of the Savior requires every born-again heart to be increasingly wrapped up in the totality of who Christ is right now. No turning back. No holding back. Not now. Not ever.

Remarkable!

Feeding On and Fascinated With Christ Now

Last Sunday nearly 400,000 sermons were delivered from pulpits across America, most of which were soon forgotten, most likely. Even so, out of the millions of words spoken how many would you guess made the wonder of Christ and the agenda for his current reign their primary focus? How many people left the worship service consciously feeding on and fascinated with who Christ is now?

How many ever witness anything like what a congregation in Northampton, Massachusetts, heard on a Sunday in 1742, when the popular New England theologian and pastor Jonathan Edwards preached what many scholars consider to be one of the greatest sermons in US history. The entire message, lasting close to two hours, was a call to fervency for Christ's supremacy. Edwards' opening premise boiled down to this:

> There is an admirable conjunction of diverse excellencies in Jesus Christ.

From there his message proceeded to lay out how justice and grace, glory and humility, majesty and meekness, obedience and dominion, resignation and sovereignty all converge in Christ to form an infinite display of his sovereignty.

Next, Edwards spoke candidly of his own zeal for such a magnificent Savior, urging his people to join him, saying:

> The excellency of Jesus Christ is suitable food of the rational soul. The soul that comes to Christ feeds upon this, and lives upon it . . . *It is impossible for those who have tasted of this fountain, and know the sweetness of it, ever to forsake it* (emphasis added).

Here was a pastor exhorting his people to be so thoroughly consumed with Christ that turning back or holding back from their Savior was unthinkable.

Again, in "The Weight of Glory," Lewis compares the experience of one's obsession with Christ to the experience of being transfixed by something of great beauty, like the splendor and brightness of the morning sun. He says:

> We do not want merely to see beauty, though, God knows, even that is bounty enough. We want something else which can hardly be put

into words — to be united with the beauty we see, to pass into it, to
receive it into ourselves, to bathe in it, to become part of it.

Similarly, Jesus' own do not seek merely to *see* the beauty of their Savior.
They yearn to be more deeply *united* with the Jesus they see — to know his
heart and his presence intimately, to remain in him as he remains in us
(John 15:4).

Consumed: to enter into more of Jesus as we grow to know him in the
fullness of his majesty. It's the pursuit of him that will occupy all saints for all
ages to come. It's the flame the Holy Spirit wants to ignite in *you* today.

So, "do not put out the Spirit's fire" (1 Thessalonians 5, ISV).

Practical Questions to Help You Uncover Your "Passion Quotient"

When it comes to your ongoing relationship with our reigning Lord Jesus
where does *your* **PQ** come out? In other words, what is your "*passion
quotient*"?

To get an answer, test-drive this set of questions — questions most
Christians have never tackled. You'll find them quite enlightening. Each one
probes where your obsession with Christ stands right now as well as where
it needs to burn stronger. Ask yourself:

1. On a daily basis what usually captures my affections? What do I get
   excited about? What issues regularly preoccupy my thoughts? More
   practically, how do I spend my time? Where do I spend my money?
   Generally, what am I most fervent about? How would people who
   observe me answer that question? Where does Jesus fit into my
   answers to these questions?

2. What challenges arouse my concerns? What causes inspire my
   commitments? Where do my true ambitions lie? In what ways does the
   cause of Christ inspire me and absorb me in conscious steps of
   involvement in it, both with him and for him? Are there *daily*
   expressions of this? What does that look like?

3. What would I define as the pinnacle of my life's purpose — the reason for which I was created and redeemed in the first place? Where does Jesus fit into this overarching narrative? Along the same line, in what sense has my Lord become for me in himself not only my identity but also my destiny? How intentional am I about living far more at the center of who he is, where he is headed, what he is doing, and how he gets blessed rather than seeking what I want him to do for me?

4. In what sense does my current vision of the greatness, goodness, and glory of God's Son instill in me a determination to live in such a way that all I do and say expresses fervency for his supremacy? As this vision of Christ increasingly motivates me, what will I do on a regular basis to enlarge and enrich and expand how I view Jesus and all the wonders found in him?

5. How has Christ's passion for me ennobled and shaped my passions and desires toward him? How frequently do I meditate specifically on the manifestations of his love for me as seen in his incarnation, crucifixion, resurrection, and ascension? Am I regularly aware that day by day I am living in his presence, under his reign, by his power, as the focus of his sovereign care? If so, in what ways am I responding to him each day by word and deed, to love him more fully the way he deserves?

6. How much do I think about the relationship of the Father to the Son — especially the depth of the Father's affection for and commitment to his Son from all eternity? In what ways has the Father's passion for his Son stirred up my desire to be much more passionate for Jesus? How often do I turn that passion into worship and praise toward the Triune God?

7. Do I ever fear being labeled as someone who is too fanatical toward the Lord Jesus? How often do I tone down for fellow believers, or even hide from them, that I have a growing passion for more of him? In any sense am I ashamed to openly express to other *Christians* (let alone non-Christians) a personal fervency for his supremacy?

8. In what ways do I intend to confront such fears as publically I declare, first of all to believers, how devoted I am to Jesus and his dominion? Am I willing to talk openly with fellow Christians about new wonders

I'm discovering every week about Christ? Am I willing to risk being misunderstood by my friends in my efforts to make much of Christ in every facet of my discipleship?

9. In practical ways, how do I intend to *increase* the evidence that my life is consumed with my Redeemer? How will my growing devotion to Jesus — by what I say about his glory and how my daily walk seeks to bring him glory — make a positive difference for other believers, inciting them to become more passionate for him themselves?

10. Am I prepared to pour out my life for the Christ Awakening movement that must come to the Church? Am I willing to foster Christ Awakenings within my own congregation by lovingly reintroducing fellow disciples to Christ for *all* he is — no matter what it may cost?

Be a Moth

Utterly the opposite of the deadly demise of a moth drawn to and then incinerated by the deceptive warmth and beauty of a candle flame, the closer Christians get to our Radiant Redeemer the greater our joys become in him, the more energized our labors become for him, the more enticing become our prospects in him — the more *alive* we become toward him.

Still, the example of the moth is worth considering. Like the irresistible attraction of moths to the flame, day by day we must allow ourselves — we must *dare* — to continue drawing closer to our Life-giving Flame, God's Son. As a way of life we must seek to "meet him again for the first time" — over and over. We must continue to explore and experience daily "Christ Awakenings" of our own.

So, be a moth.

In fact, for starters try this for just one day. Carry a 3 x 5 card with you wherever you go. Write on it any insights you gain during the day — every fresh revelation of the elevation of Jesus that the Holy Spirit gives you. In an early morning prayer time. While commuting to work. Out shopping. Sitting in class. During your lunch break. Using single words or phrases, jot down thoughts about what impresses you about our Savior and the reasons why Christians should be more passionate about him — why *you* should be more passionate about him!

For example, record reflections about:

- who Christ is as a person, alive and active and filling the universe — that is, some of the wonders of who he is TO us and FOR us.

- where Christ is headed as he leads us into the fulfillment of God's purposes — including some of the wonders of who he is OVER us and BEFORE us.

- what Christ is doing to unleash some of God's kingdom promises to you as well as for others around you and across the world — that is, some of the wonders of who he is WITHIN us, THROUGH us, and UPON us

- how Christ should get blessed by those who know him and love him and serve him — ways he deserves to be more fully exalted right where you live

Then at the close of the day, before turning in for the night, take five minutes to review what's on your card. Then translate each insight into a brief prayer.

Praise the Father for everything about King Jesus that the Holy Spirit has shared with you during the day. Tell him how much more your Savior means to you personally, in light of these reflections. Pray for the Father to give you greater manifestations of the glory of the supremacy of Christ. Pray for a larger work of God in the Church and among the nations that will help to magnify his name, spread his fame, extend his reign, increase his gain, and ratify his claim.

In other words, be a moth! By prayer draw as near to the Flame as you can get.

Then, fall asleep ready to wake up the next morning to spend another day consumed with Christ — another day in which you foster fervency for his supremacy in yourself and others, another day being a disciple fully alive to all of who Christ is right now.

No turning back. No holding back.

Fervency for His Supremacy
Seven Joyful Habits of Christians Who Are Hugely Passionate for Jesus

One glorious day not long from now, our Lord Jesus Christ will break in upon us, unmistakably and cosmically revealed for who he has been all along — the center and circumference of everything, for everyone, for all time.

But thankfully, our Savior has not postponed until the Consummation his intention to increase the flame of our love for him.

Indeed, throughout the Church by his Spirit, the Master of the universe persists at intensifying and deepening among his own a decisive devotion to his glorious person and his global purposes. According to Revelation 2:4, he aims to be no less than our "first love" (KJV). The Greek phrase used here for "first love" translates more accurately as "*supreme* love." In other words, Jesus is to be our all-consuming love.

Therefore, what we want to ask is this: What are the secrets for igniting and sustaining a fiery passion for his Royal Majesty *here and now* that is like what he will unquestionably and rightfully receive from us *there and then* when we stand before him face-to-face?

Thankfully, there's a clear answer because there is a well-worn path, navigated by saints across the ages, that has transformed a multitude of Christians into followers who are hugely passionate for their King.

In fact, I would suggest that every facet of godly devotion that the Bible talks about can be summed up by seven "secrets" — let's call them seven "*joyful habits*" — which can be easily incorporated into your daily walk with Jesus, helping you to become a disciple "filled with a glorious joy that can't be put into words" (1 Peter 1).

Here lies the hope that all of us can experience a life of "fervency for Christ's supremacy."

To make these core disciplines easier to grasp, I've assigned them seven easy-to-recall words that start with the letter "S." Together they capture everything the Bible teaches about how believers who supremely adore their Redeemer get that way and stay that way. Let's unpack them briefly, and provide one or two starter steps for each one.

Seven Joyful Habits

Robust affection for Christ can be cultivated as we: *See* him, *Seek* him, *Savor* him, *Speak* him, *Show* him, *Serve* him and *Share* him.

There's a logical sequence to these seven "joyful habits." As you faithfully practice one of them it prepares you to implement the next. Think of it like this:

1. **SEE** Jesus more fully for all he is by how you study about him throughout God's Word — w*hich leads you to . . .*

2. **SEEK** Jesus more fully for all he is by how you pursue and encounter him through prayer — *which leads you to . . .*

3. **SAVOR** Jesus more fully for all he is by how you exult in him through worship — *which leads you to . . .*

4. **SPEAK** of Jesus more fully for all he is by how you talk about him with believers — *which leads you to . . .*

5. **SHOW** Jesus more fully for all he is by how you imitate him in word and deed — *which leads you to . . .*

6. **SERVE** Jesus more fully for all he is by how you minister to others for his sake — *which leads you t0 . . .*

7. **SHARE** Jesus more fully for all he is by how you introduce unbelievers to him as Lord and Savior.

These seven "joyful habits" shape the lifestyle of Christians who become hugely passionate for Jesus. It's how they got that way and stay that way because one discipline quite naturally feeds into the next. Let's look at each one more thoroughly.

Joyful Habit #1
SEE HIM

First, we start by *seeing* clearly what the Bible teaches from cover to cover about Jesus' person and purposes right now, as he reigns at God's right hand. Study him. Survey him. Scrutinize him. Sit at his feet. Soak up everything he discloses.

One practical jump-start to do this: Take full advantage of the vast number of *free* resources at *www.ChristNow.com* (highlighted at the end of this book). Think of it as your one-stop hub for free Bible-based resources to help you explore and experience God's Son for all he is today.

For example: The ChristNow website offers you for free a *21-Day Journey* (which can accessed using our free smartphone app, Christ Now) or a *55-Day Journey* (brief, daily email videos viewed on your laptop) — two ways to transverse the nine hours of teaching presented by **The Christ Institutes Video Series**, which you can also complete online at your own pace.

Or sign up for the two-minute **Daily Devotions**, which are built around 365 titles for Jesus found in Scripture. Offering an optional audio version, these readings are sent automatically to your email inbox every day for an entire year.

Sample some of the **Teaching Videos**, which feature Christian leaders from many streams of the Church focusing on exciting facets of Christ's supremacy from God's Word.

You might try this approach that involves you more directly: Create your very own "**Regal Bible.**" There's nothing to it! Simply take a copy of the Bible and using a yellow highlighter pen, mark the mosaic of insights about Christ found throughout Scripture. Book by book, highlight every passage or verse or phrase that helps to reveal more of who Jesus is.

For example, you might highlight the dozens of Messianic prophecies found throughout Isaiah, the texts that *foreshadow* promised encounters with Jesus' kingly person and kingdom project.

Or, to make it easy on yourself: Throughout Colossians (a book bursting with truths about Jesus) mark texts that define how the glory of Christ and his kingdom purposes are being *fulfilled* in who Jesus is and what he's up to right now.

Once you've finished this exercise with just one book, go back through it to review your discoveries (all of which pop out in color!). Spend time reflecting on how the highlighted passages enable you to *see* God's Son more fully for all he is today.

As you move on from one book of Scripture to another, you'll be amazed at how much of God's Word turns *yellow*! Maybe we should identify them as the "supremacy Scriptures" — passages that are spectacular because they reveal the glory of our sovereign!

Joyful Habit #2
SEEK HIM

Those who *see* more of the greatness of Christ become motivated to *seek* more meaningful, more intimate engagement with the person of Christ. The greater our discoveries of his magnificent qualities, the greater will be our desire to draw closer to him and enter into the fullness of life we have in him.

Essentially this means we must continue nurturing an ongoing life of *prayer*, what Scripture calls "seeking God's face." But how do we do this well?

One practical suggestion: Return to some of the highlighted passages uncovered in your "Regal Bible." Then reformulate those verses so they are turned into prayers. For example, Ephesians 2:6-7 says:

> God raised us up with Christ. He has seated us with him in his heavenly kingdom. That's because we belong to Christ Jesus. He has done it to show the riches of his grace for all time to come.

As a focus for prayer that seeks more of Christ, use the emphasis of those verses to say this to the Father:

> Dear Father, thank you for raising us from the dead with your Son and then seating us in your kingdom to reign with him. Now convince the world of the revolutionary nature of the salvation found in Christ, by how you draw us nearer to him. Saturate your Church with visible demonstrations of his redeeming power that will flow from his throne for all time to come. Amen.

Based on what Scripture both teaches and models, your primary prayers as a Jesus follower should be for more intimate insights and revelations into specific truths about our Savior and his supremacy leading to a deepening of your relationship to him. Invite the Holy Spirit to teach you how to apply your ever-enlarging vision of Jesus in daily living. Ask for yourself and your fellow believers that the Father would wake you fully to the biblical realities about Jesus as Lord, opening up transforming encounters with him.

Seek the Father's help to deepen your devotion toward his Son, to make you as passionate for Jesus as he himself is — to be filled with a passion you express both in word and deed.

"[Help me to] grow in the grace and knowledge of our Lord and Savior Jesus Christ" (2 Peter 3) — *this* should be our heart's cry every moment we breathe. As we walk with him, we are called to pray for one another as Paul did in Ephesians 3:

> May his Holy Spirit give you his power deep down inside you. Then Christ will live in your hearts because you believe in him . . . May you have power together with all the Lord's holy people to understand Christ's love. May you know how wide and long and high and deep it is. *And may you know [Christ's] love, even though it can't be known completely. Then you will be filled with everything God has for you* (emphasis added).

Joyful Habit #3
SAVOR HIM

And so it follows: The more we *see* him and *seek* him, the more of himself and his global cause he reveals to us. Scripture guarantees it: "When you look for me with all your heart, you will find me. I will be found by you . . . " (Jeremiah 29).

In turn, "finding" him causes believers to *savor* him more than ever — that is, increasingly to worship him, exult in him, appreciate and enjoy him for all he is today — not only in our liturgies but also in our lifestyles.

One practical aid that has helped many Christians delight more fully in their reigning Lord is to revisit a traditional hymnbook. Study the words of some of the historic worship anthems of the Church that focus on the glory of Christ. Note the richness of the vocabulary believers used over the past three hundred years to reverence and esteem Jesus.

For example, in over one thousand of the hymns composed by Charles Wesley he unpacks what theologians term a "high Christology." These anthems praise Jesus not only for who he was and will be, but just as importantly, for who he is today exalted at God's right hand.

Reflect on how others have expressed what it meant for them to savor the wonders of Christ; then join their praises by whispering the words aloud, as an act of worship. You might even try to sing the hymn during your times of private devotions.

The free **Worship Videos** at *www.ChristNow.com* provide another effective resource to help you savor Christ. Representing a variety of worship styles and approaches, they are chosen expressly to incite believers to exult in God's Son.

As you begin a new day, you might incorporate one into your Bible study and prayer time. While you watch and listen, let its exaltation of Jesus fill your heart with new passion for praising Jesus. You even might even decide to sing along!

Then send the link to some Christian friends by email, Twitter, or Facebook so they can join you in savoring Christ in new ways.

If we heed the exhortation of Colossians 3 we can't go wrong:

> Let the message about Christ live among you like a rich treasure . . . *by singing psalms and hymns and songs from the Spirit* . . . Do everything you say or do in the name of the Lord Jesus (emphasis added).

Joyful Habit #4
SPEAK HIM

But there are more secrets to gaining "fervency for Christ's supremacy." As Christians *see, seek,* and *savor* the Ruler of all, we begin to discover a growing and unquenchable desire to *speak* about him to others and to do so frequently — starting off most naturally with the fellow believers we gather with every Sunday.

Speaking out about Christ to those who were *already* Christians defined the heart of Paul's two-year ministry in Ephesus, as he summarized it for the church's elders in Acts 20 (note words about verbal communication highlighted in italics):

> You know I have never shrunk from *telling* you anything that was for your good, nor from *teaching* you in public or in your own homes.

> On the contrary I have most emphatically *urged* upon both Jews and Greeks repentance towards God and faith in our Lord Jesus . . . [I want to] finish my course and complete the ministry which the Lord Jesus has given me in *declaring* the good news of the grace of God . . . as I *preached* the kingdom of God . . . I have never shrunk from *declaring* to you the complete will of God (PHILLIPS, emphasis added).

For Paul, speaking of Christ to God's people day in and day out was his priority mission, followed afterward by speaking of Christ to those who had never heard the gospel before (as he discusses in Romans 15). He states this succinctly in Colossians 1:

> God has given me the responsibility of serving his church by *proclaiming* his *entire message* to you . . . So we *tell others* about Christ, *warning* everyone and *teaching* everyone with all the wisdom God has given us. We want to *present* them to God, perfect in their relationship to Christ (NLT, emphasis added).

Then the apostle urges his readers to follow his example. As Paul states in Colossians 3, God's people must commit to nothing less than conversations about Christ whenever they come together. Here is his exhortation in three different translations:

> Let the message about Christ, in all its richness, fill your lives. *Teach and counsel each* other with all the wisdom he gives (NLT, emphasis added).

> Let the [spoken] word of Christ have its home within you [dwelling in your heart and mind — permeating every aspect of your being] *as you teach* [spiritual things] and *admonish and train one another* with all wisdom (AMP, emphasis added).

> Let the Word of Christ — the Message — have the run of the house. Give it plenty of room in your lives. *Instruct and direct one another* using good common sense (MSG, emphasis added).

In other words, regularly we need to focus on speaking openly of the glory of Christ in our conversations with other Christians. As we fellowship over coffee on a Sunday morning before the service, we should bring Jesus into our exchanges. Whatever the immediate topic during Sunday school discussions or in weekly Bible study groups we should give priority to exploring the truth about Jesus' supremacy as foreshadowed in Old

Testament passages and fulfilled in the New. During conversations among family members around the dinner table on any given night, at some point we should encourage a focus on something about the wonders of Christ.

In other words, make it your goal at every legitimate opportunity to speak into the life of a fellow disciple something exciting you've recently discovered about Christ — or include it in a PS in your next email, or post it on your Facebook page.

A seminary professor reported to me that one morning he tweeted to his nearly 2000 Twitter followers a fresh perspective on Christ's supremacy he'd gained from Scripture that day. In response it ended up being re-tweeted 10,000 times before the day was over! Through modern technology he "spoke" of Christ and thousands whom he will never meet "heard."

And as a result — and this is true about every time we share more of Christ with each other — the Holy Spirit had something to work with, with each follower, that the Spirit did not have before. And in light of his primary role to increase our vision of Christ exalted (see John 16) you can be sure he will fully exploit each opportunity!

That means whatever approach you take, great promise resides in speaking out to God's people about God's Son and his spectacular supremacy. Here's what Romans 10 promises you whenever you talk about the glories of God's Son with God's people (and unbelievers, as well):

> Faith comes from hearing the message and the message is heard through the word about Christ (NIV).
>
> So faith comes from hearing; that is, hearing the Good News about Christ (NLT).
>
> So faith\ *comes* from hearing [what is told], and what is heard *comes* by the [preaching of the] message concerning Christ (AMP, emphasis theirs).

As long as we keep pouring truths about the greatness of the Savior into those who belong to him, we challenge our fellow believers to keep growing in their own vision and faith and passion toward Christ for all he is today.

Finally, here's one more practical discipline for speaking Christ into his followers. I call it *"SEE something, SAY something."* There are two parts to this strategy:

1. **SEE something**: Commit to the Father that each week you will spend sufficient time in Scripture and prayer, however much is required, until you *SEE something* new about the wonders of Jesus' person and purposes that is fresh and alive to you. You want to discover an insight about him that excites you so much you know you would enjoy passing it along to another believer so that person too can experience a similar encounter with Christ in his fullness.

2. **SAY something**: The flip side of this strategy requires a second commitment. On the Sunday of that same week, you resolve to attend church on a mission — with the intention to pass along to a brother or sister your newly found truth about Jesus, taking a few moments to *say* to them what you *saw* a few days earlier.

   Consider this scenario, for example: Between Sunday school and church as everyone is mingling in the fellowship hall, you take thirty seconds to tactfully approach a friend with this request: "Bob (or Julie), I discovered something about God's Son this past week that's so exciting I simply have to pass it along to someone else! Could I take thirty seconds and tell you what I saw?" Of course, no Jesus follower will turn down such an offer!

   One additional step you might try: Once you've finished "saying" your new-found insight, conclude by praying with your friend about that truth, asking the Spirit to reveal to both of you the reality behind what you've talked about, thus increasing passion for God's Son in both of you as a result.

Joyful Habit # 5
SHOW HIM

Those of us who develop a lifestyle of *seeing, seeking, savoring,* and *speaking* Christ will over time experience a shift in how we *show* him as we increasingly imitate him. Why is that?

It has been rightly observed: "We end up looking *like* what we keep looking *at.*" In other words, the more we focus on Christ by practicing the other "joyful habits" and thus increasing our devotion to him, the more we will grow into the likeness of him. The one follows the other.

Often unconsciously — yet inevitably — we begin to incorporate and exhibit the qualities of his character, his strength, his compassion, his holiness. We enter into a fuller display of what Jesus' lordship looks like when his Spirit applies it in concrete ways.

Scripture points to this transformation in Romans 13: ". . . put on the Lord Jesus Christ as if he were your clothing. Don't think about how to satisfy sinful desires." Again, in 2 Corinthians 4: "We who are alive are always in danger of death because we are serving Jesus. *This happens so that his life can also be shown in our earthly bodies"* (emphasis added).

In Philippians 3, after Paul talked about his undiluted pursuit of more of Christ, he admonished the believers at Philippi: "Dear brothers and sisters, pattern your lives after mine, and learn from those who *follow our example* (Philippians 3, NLT, emphasis added). Likewise he wrote to the Corinthians: "You should imitate me, *just as I imitate Christ"* (1 Corinthians 11, NLT, emphasis added).

Again, based on the key principle, we end up looking most *like* the person we keep looking *at.*

Reflecting on the way Jesus will totally fill our vision on the day he returns in victory, John reminds us that this will conform us to his image as a result:

> Beloved, we are [even here and] now children of God, and it is not yet made clear what we will be [after His coming]. We know that when He comes *and* is revealed, *we will [as His*

*children] be like Him, because we will see Him just as He is [in all
His glory].* (1 John 3:2, AMP, emphasis added).

With the very next sentence, however, John calls his readers to put into
action *here and now,* on a daily basis, the same radical dynamic of "looking
like what we look *at*" — similar to what will happen at his glorious appearing:

> And everyone who has this hope [confidently placed] in Him
> purifies himself, just as He is pure (holy, undefiled, guiltless)
> (1 John 3:3, AMP).

Joyful Habit #6
SERVE HIM

Ministering to others' needs, especially those in the household of faith, is a
very tangible, hands-on approach to express a direct, undying love for our
King. As Jesus illustrated in Matthew 25:

> Then these righteous ones will reply, "Lord, when did we ever see you
> hungry and feed you? Or thirsty and give you something to drink?
> Or a stranger and show you hospitality? Or naked and give you
> clothing? When did we ever see you sick or in prison and visit you?"
> And the King will say, "I tell you the truth, when you did it to one of
> the least of these my brothers and sisters, *you were doing it to ME!*"
> (NLT, emphasis added).

Not long ago I wrote about this to dear friends who had spent weeks
ministering to a fellow Christian who was enduring unrelenting physical
suffering:

> Recall those encouraging words from the Lord Jesus that by serving
> the "least" of his followers we are serving HIM (Matt 25). This means,
> in one very real sense, though you are exhausted right now
> remember this: You've also actually expended yourselves in days of
> *worship* — that is, you've been loving and adoring and blessing the
> *Savior himself* as you gave yourselves so sacrificially to the precious
> saint who belongs to him. That's his promise in Matthew 25.

The fact is that when God's people see how much God's love for us is
displayed in his own passion for us — the passion of Christ exposed on the
cross — then loving his Son by loving each other with self-giving love

unleashes in us a similar passion back toward Christ as well. As Scripture urges:

> This is real love — not that we loved God, but that he loved us and sent his Son as a sacrifice to take away our sins. *Dear friends, since God loved us that much, we surely ought to love each other* . . . All who declare that Jesus is the Son of God have God living in them, and they live in God . . . God is love, and all who live in love live in God, and God lives in them (1 John 4, NLT, emphasis added).

Brother Lawrence, in his classic *Practicing the Presence of God,* relates that even while he was washing dirty dishes after the meals in the monastery he used the time to focus on worshipping God. Even so, when you serve God's people who are in union with God's Son, you are automatically doing so in "the presence of Christ," expressing your affections toward the person of Christ, ministering to him in the process.

So this is another way to express our fervency for his supremacy — by blessing those who live under the shadow of his reign.

Joyful Habit # 7
SHARE HIM

The more we practice these six joyful habits, the more we become intensely wrapped up with Jesus day by day. But the passion we are celebrating in our relationship with him is not for us alone. The Father intends for us to *share* him as our all in all with the world — the world at the end of our street and the world at the ends of the earth.

That means ultimately that wherever Christians go — to the marketplace, the schoolyard, the inner city, the rural poor, the government, or the unreached peoples around the globe — we should be stirred up to spread the good news of God's Son with unbelievers *because* we have become so zealous for his name and his reign ourselves.

We can begin this outreach to those around us in three basic ways: through our *prayer* for them and through our *care* for them, which prepares the way for us to *share* with them.

In the process of reaching out to unbelievers and the unreached, the unanticipated reward is how Jesus becomes even more precious to *us*, as a result.

It's like what often is observed when a bride-to-be eagerly reports to all her girlfriends what a wonderful man her future husband is to her. To her amazement, the very act of sharing him with others ends up deepening her *own* longings and passions for him as well.

Jesus taught that love for him results in obedience to him (John 14). And chief among his mandates is this from Matthew 28:

> All authority in heaven and on earth has been given to me. So you must go and make disciples of all nations. Baptize them in the name of the Father and of the Son and of the Holy Spirit. Teach them to obey everything I have commanded you. And you can be sure that I am always with you, to the very end.

Here's one crucial way fervency for Jesus' supremacy expresses itself: by our determination to *share* him and his gospel with those who are lost, doing so in such a way that we exalt his name to them, spread his fame around them, extend his reign among them, increase his gain from them, and ratify his claim before them.

Become Hugely Passionate for Jesus

These seven simple words beginning with "S" are visible in Christians who are developing a magnificent obsession with the King of glory, deepening in their love for him as they:

SEE him, **SEEK** him, **SAVOR** him,

SPEAK him, **SHOW** him, **SERVE** him, and **SHARE** him

for ALL he is today as our reigning Messiah and Lord.

When Paul declares of himself, "For me to live is Christ" (Philippians 1), these seven responses comprise what that way of life must have looked like to those who knew Paul. However, it was the pattern he expected every other believer to pursue.

Why not activate joyful habit #1 — SEE him — and work your way from there through all seven disciplines. Allow your practice of the first one to prepare you to step into the next, and so on. Finally, when all seven are actively a part of your life, they will ignite and sustain in you a hugely passionate heart for God's Son — amplifying the glory of Jesus through you wherever you go.

To get started right now, turn the page.

There you will learn more about the Christ-exalting website *www.ChristNow.com* that we spoke of earlier. It is filled with *free* resources from many streams of the Church to support you as you enrich your daily walk with the King of glory.

Log on to discover for yourself how ready it is to feed and fuel individual and corporate Christ Awakenings in this generation. It's there ready for *you*.

Appendix I
A Stream of Scripture
About His Gory Glory

The life of each creature is in its blood.

So I have given you the blood of animals to pay for your sin on the altar. Blood is life. That is why blood pays for your sin (Leviticus 17).

A lamb should be chosen for each family and home . . .

The whole community of Israel must kill them when the sun goes down. Take some of the blood. Put it on the sides and tops of the doorframes of the houses where you eat the lambs. That same night eat the meat cooked over a fire . . . It is the Lord's Passover . . . The blood on your houses will be a sign for you. When I see the blood, I will pass over you. No deadly plague will touch you . . . Tell them, "It's the Passover sacrifice to honor the Lord" (Exodus 12).

So when Christ came into the world, he said,
"You didn't want sacrifices and offerings.

Instead, you prepared a body for me. You weren't pleased with burnt offerings and sin offerings." Then I said, "Here I am. It is written about me in the book. I have come to do what you want, my God" . . . By that one sacrifice he has made perfect forever those who are being made holy (Hebrews 10).

"Look! The Lamb of God! He takes away the sin of the world!

This is the one I was talking about." I said, "A man who comes after me is more important than I am. That's because he existed before I was born" (John 1).

He did not enter by spilling the blood of goats and calves.

He entered the Most Holy Room by spilling his own blood. He did it once and for all time. He paid the price to set us free from sin forever ... The blood of goats and bulls is sprinkled on people ... to make them holy. That makes them clean on the outside. But Christ offered himself to God without any flaw. He did this through the power of the eternal Holy Spirit. So how much more will his blood wash from our minds our feelings of guilt for committing sin! (Hebrews 9).

That's why Christ is the go-between of a new covenant ...

He died to set them free from the sins they committed under the first covenant ... The law requires that nearly everything be made clean with blood. Without the spilling of blood, no one can be forgiven ... But Christ did not enter heaven to offer himself again and again ... Now he has appeared once and for all time. He has come at the end of the ages to do away with sin. He has done that by offering himself (Hebrews 9).

Long ago God planned that Jesus would be handed over to you.

With the help of evil people, you put Jesus to death. You nailed him to the cross (Acts 2).

All of them made plans against your holy servant Jesus. He is the one you anointed. They did what your power and purpose had already decided should happen (Acts 4).

Then the owner of the vineyard said,
"I know what I'll do: I'll send my beloved son.

They're bound to respect my son." But when the farmhands saw him coming, they quickly put their heads together. "This is our chance — this is the heir! Let's kill him and have it all to ourselves." They killed him and threw him over the fence ... [Jesus said], "Why, then, do you think this was written: 'That stone the masons threw out — it's now the cornerstone!?'" (Luke 20, MSG).

Jesus also suffered outside the city gate.

He suffered to make the people holy by spilling his own blood (Hebrews 13).

You have come to ... the city of the living God ... You have come to Jesus. He is the go-between of a new covenant. You have come to the sprinkled blood. It promises better things than the blood of Abel (Hebrews 12).

People treat me like a worm and not a man . . .

They are like roaring lions that tear to pieces what they kill. My strength is like water that is poured out on the ground. I feel as if my bones aren't connected. My heart has turned to wax. It has melted away inside me. My strength is dried up like a piece of broken pottery. My tongue sticks to the roof of my mouth . . . They have pierced my hands and my feet. I can see all of my bones right through my skin. People stare at me. They laugh when I suffer. Save the only life I have. Save me from the power of those dogs (Psalms 22).

. . . they shouted even louder, "Crucify him!"

Pilate . . . had Jesus whipped. Then he handed him over to be nailed to a cross. The governor's soldiers took Jesus into the palace . . . Then they twisted thorns together to make a crown. They placed it on his head . . . They spit on him. They hit him on the head with the stick again and again . . . Then they led him away to nail him to a cross . . . They came to a place called Golgotha. The word Golgotha means The Place of the Skull . . . When they had nailed him to the cross, they divided up his clothes by casting lots . . . Those who passed by shouted at Jesus and made fun of him . . . In the same way the robbers who were being crucified with Jesus also made fun of him . . . About three o'clock, Jesus cried out in a loud voice . . . "My God, my God, why have you deserted me?" . . . After Jesus cried out again in a loud voice, he died (Matthew 27).

. . . he said, "It is finished." Then he bowed his head and died . . . one of the soldiers stuck his spear into Jesus' side. Right away, blood and water flowed out (John 19).

Jesus Christ himself is the one who came by water and by blood — "

. . . not by the water only, but by the water and the blood . . . the blood of atonement . . . God has given men eternal life and this real life is to be found only in his Son (1 John 5, PHILLIPS).

You must eat the Son of Man's body and drink his blood.

If you don't, you have no life in you. Anyone who eats my body and drinks my blood has eternal life. I will raise him up on the last day. My body is real food. My blood is real drink. Anyone who eats my body and drinks my blood remains in me. And I remain in him (John 6).

This is my body. It is given for you.

Every time you eat it, do it in memory of me (1 Corinthians 11).

This cup is the new covenant in my blood.

Every time you drink it, do it in memory of me. When you eat the bread and drink the cup, you are announcing the Lord's death until he comes again (1 Corinthians 11).

It is true that Christ was nailed to the cross because he was weak.

But he lives by God's power (2 Corinthians 13).

Brothers and sisters, we are not afraid to enter the Most Holy Room.

We enter boldly because of the blood of Jesus.

His way is new because he lives. It has been opened for us through the curtain. I'm talking about his body . . . We have been made holy because Jesus Christ offered his body once and for all time (Hebrews 10).

The blood of Christ has made us right with God (Romans 5).

God gave him as a sacrifice to pay for sins. So he forgives the sins of those who have faith in his blood (Romans 3).

We have been set free because of what Christ has done. Through his blood our sins have been forgiven (Ephesians 1).

Jesus gave one sacrifice for the sins of the people. He gave it once and for all time. He did it by offering himself (Hebrews 7).

God made peace through Christ's blood, through his death on the cross . . .

God was pleased to bring all things back to himself because of what Christ has done. That includes all things on earth and in heaven . . . because Christ died, God has brought you back to himself. Christ's death has made you holy in God's sight (Colossians 1).

He spilled his blood for you. That has brought you near to God . . . At one time you were far away from God. But now you belong to Christ Jesus (Ephesians 2).

He bought [the church] with his own blood (Acts 20).

Christ loved the church. He gave himself up for her . . . He wants a church that is holy and without blame (Ephesians 5).

The blood of Christ set you free from an empty way of life.

That way of life was handed down to you by your own people long ago. You know that you were not bought with things that can pass away, like silver or gold. Instead, you were bought by the priceless blood of Christ. He is a perfect lamb. He doesn't have any flaws at all. He was chosen before God created the world. But he came into the world in these last days for you. Because of what Christ has done, you believe in God (1 Peter 1).

The blood of Jesus, his Son, makes us pure from all sin . . .

God is faithful and fair. If we admit that we have sinned, he will forgive us our sins (1 John 1).

[God] loved us and sent his Son as a sacrifice to clear away our sins and the damage they've done to our relationship with God (1 John 4, MSG).

We have one who speaks to the Father for us. He stands up for us. He is Jesus Christ, the Blameless One. He gave his life to pay for our sins. But he not only paid for our sins. He also paid for the sins of the whole world (1 John 2).

Give glory and power to the One who loves us!

He has set us free from our sins by pouring out his blood for us. He has made us members of his royal family. He has made us priests who serve his God and Father. Give him glory and power for ever and ever! Amen (Revelation 5).

I saw a Lamb that seemed to have been slaughtered . . .

There were myriads of myriads and thousands of thousands, crying in a great voice, "Worthy is the Lamb who was slain to receive power and riches and wisdom, and strength and honour and glory and blessing!" (Revelation 5, PHILLIPS).

. . . they have washed their robes
and made them white in the blood of the Lamb.

That is why they now have their place before the throne of God . . . for the Lamb who is in the center of the throne will be their shepherd and will lead them to springs of living water (Revelation 7, PHILLIPS).

I could see no Temple in the city . . . the splendor of God
fills it with light and its radiance is the Lamb.

The nations will walk by its light . . . only those whose names are written in the Lamb's book of life (Revelation 21, PHILLIPS)

The river of the water of life . . . flowed from the throne of God and of the Lamb . . . the throne of God and of the Lamb shall be within the city. His servants shall worship him; they shall see his face, and his name will be upon their foreheads (Revelation 22, PHILLIPS).

A Benediction

(based on the Lamb slain for the sins of the world)

May God, who puts all things together, makes all things whole,

Who made a lasting mark through the sacrifice of Jesus,

the sacrifice of blood that sealed the eternal covenant,

Who led Jesus, our Great Shepherd, up and alive from the dead,

now put you together, provide you with everything you need

to please him, make us into what gives him most pleasure,

by means of the sacrifice of Jesus, the Messiah.

All glory to Jesus forever and always!

Oh, yes, yes, yes.

(Hebrews 13, MSG)

Free Online Resources
for you
to Empower
Christ Awakenings
Everywhere

Free Online Resources

for You to Empower Christ Awakenings Everywhere

Visit us at:

www.ChristNow.com

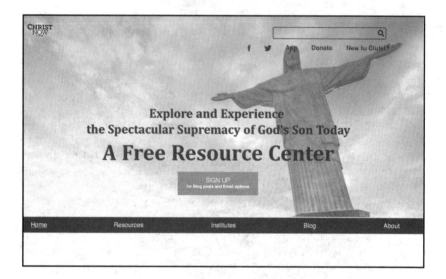

www.TheChristInstitutes.com

www.DavidBryantBooks.com

www.ProclaimHope.org

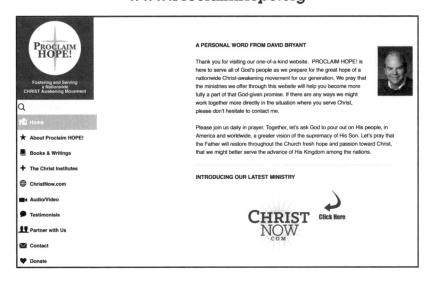

Also follow us at:

facebook.com/christnowonline

twitter.com/christnowonline

instagram.com/christnowonline

Acknowledgments

This book has been forty years in the making.

Therefore, expressing gratitude for others' invaluable input into what has emerged would require pages to list the names.

Take, for example, the myriad of strategic ministry alliances — national, international, academic, pastoral, missionary, denominational, collegiate and more — that I've enjoyed with Christian leaders from many streams of the Church. As we've labored together for the Kingdom, I've gained from them vital insights into the person of the King. Those key leaders would be on the list.

I am indebted to hundreds of Christian thinkers and theologians, down through the centuries, whose mining of Scripture coupled with their writings and teachings have enriched my Christology a thousandfold. They too would be on the list.

Beyond that, I could register the thousands from all walks of life and backgrounds with whom I've shared stimulating conversations around their vision and pursuit of the Lord Jesus for all he is. How much this has helped me view the majesty of our Savior in fresh ways is incalculable, and I am eternally grateful to them all.

So, instead of this long inventory, let me simply give recognition to four who have been directly involved in bringing this particular project to completion.

Thank you, *Beth Wolsey,* for bringing to bear on this book your God-given instincts, your clarity of biblical thinking, and your superb editorial craftsmanship. As a result, you have transformed the initial words of this author into a verbal portrait of Christ that is now a pleasure for all of us to read.

Thank you, *Bill Sahlman,* for taking your exceptional graphic skills and diligently using them to transform the book's presentation on the wonders of Christ into a visual feast. As a result, all along the way, you help us to explore and experience more of God's Son by very creative approaches.

Thank you, *Dick Griggs* (and through you I give thanks to the many who have served on the boards of our ministry over the decades) for your years of counsel and encouragement — not only as board chairman but, above all, as a co-laborer with me toward a Christ Awakening movement. Over and over you have kept this author going, despite significant challenges, so he could complete this volume.

But prior to these, thank you, *Robyne* — woman of God, servant of Christ, dearest wife and friend. From the beginning, as a way of life, you have plunged with me into intimacy with Christ in his supremacy. Declaring Romans 15:6 on our wedding day, we pledged to become one heart and one voice for the glory of the Father through the Son. And so we have. This book, therefore, represents your heart and your voice, as well as mine.

ABOVE ALL:

Thank you, *Father.* Because you have exalted your Son to the place of highest honor, you have given me truths of his supremacy that have formed the wondrously inexhaustible topic I've tried to write about.

Thank you, *Holy Spirit.* Because you've continued to magnify the greatness and glory of Jesus to me and all who belong to him, ultimately it is your vision of his supremacy today that I've sought to understand and record on these pages.

Thank you, *Son of God.* Because right now your supremacy remains so utterly spectacular, you embody the source and substance of everything I've attempted to describe here. However, I must declare that you truly are infinitely more priceless and precious than ten million books could ever contain.

David Bryant:

Meet the Man Behind the Message

For nearly 50 years, David Bryant has been defined by many as a "messenger of hope" and a "Christ proclaimer" to the Church throughout the world.

Formerly pastor of a university-focused congregation, minister-at-large for the *InterVarsity Christian Fellowship*, founder of *Concerts of Prayer International (COPI)* and chairman of *America's National Prayer Committee,* today David provides leadership to *Proclaim Hope!* whose mission is to "foster and serve a nationwide Christ-awakening movement."

For decades David played a widely visible role in the emergence of an unprecedented, worldwide prayer movement by employing citywide mass prayer rallies;

through national and international conferences; by training videos, seminars, and manuals; in the development of leadership coalitions; through the mentoring of younger leaders; and by media outreach (both TV and radio).

Among his many writings are five key books: *In the Gap: What It Means to Be a World Christian;* *With Concerts of Prayer: Christians United for Spiritual Awakening and World Evangelization;* *The Hope at Hand: National and World Revival for the 21st Century;* *Messengers of Hope: Becoming Agents of Revival for the 21st Century;* and *Christ Is ALL! A Joyful Manifesto on the Supremacy of God's Son* (with over 500,000 copies in the Mandarin version alone being used to train Chinese church leaders).

More recently, David has spearheaded an ambitious outreach to encourage Christ Awakening movements across America and beyond by creating *The Christ Institutes Video Series,* which has the stated goal of helping Christians *"to explore and experience together the spectacular supremacy of God's Son today."* His video teaching is complemented and expanded by his latest 600-page volume, *Christ Is NOW!*

Currently, David is the national facilitator for a one-of-a-kind website that serves as a hub for bringing together a vast variety of free resources from across the Church that focus on the glory of Jesus and his reign today. Go to *www.ChristNow.com* (also on Facebook and Instagram).

David and his wife Robyne were high school sweethearts in their hometown of Massillon, Ohio. They now call metropolitan New York City/New Jersey their home. Their three grown children, Adam, Bethany, and Benjamin, were adopted as infants from India.